**To All Those—Including Dario—
Who Have Inspired Me**

TABLE OF CONTENTS

- 9 Acknowledgements
- 11 Foreword by Luigi Cozzi
- 13 Preface
- 18 Chapter One: The Early Years
- 22 Chapter Two: Profession: Critic
- 25 Chapter Three: Once Upon a Time … The Screenwriter
- 46 Chapter Four: Screaming *Bird* and Flower in Bloom
- 62 Chapter Five: Jet-Set *Giallo*
- 74 Chapter Six: Bye-Bye, *Giallo*?
- 86 Chapter Seven: Changes of Pace
- 96 Chapter Eight: Dario + Daria = Aria and the *Giallo* to End All *Gialli*
- 112 Chapter Nine: Sighs and Sobs and Zombies in the 'Burgh
- 138 Chapter Ten: Darkness and Despair
- 152 Chapter Eleven: Brightness
- 166 Chapter Twelve: Bugs Gone Wild
- 182 Chapter Thirteen: Movie Theaters and High Rises; High Culture and Scandal
- 191 Chapter Fourteen: Flying High and Michele Rises
- 211 Chapter Fifteen: Coming to America
- 223 Chapter Sixteen: Personal and Professional Tragedy
- 234 Chapter Seventeen: A Cry from the Depths; *Ciao*, Lucio
- 250 Chapter Eighteen: Gothic Kitsch and Scarlet Divas
- 264 Chapter Nineteen: Sleepy in Turin
- 275 Chapter Twenty: Internet *Giallo*
- 283 Chapter Twenty-One: Back to TV
- 298 Chapter Twenty-Two: Tears
- 313 Chapter Twenty-Three: Hired Gun
- 332 Chapter Twenty-Four: Reflections in a *Giallo* Eye
- 340 Chapter Twenty-Five: Argento's Legacy—A Collection of Essays
- 372 Chapter Twenty-Six: The Interviews
- 394 Bibliography
- 396 Filmography
- 410 Videography: The Films
- 415 Discography: The Soundtracks
- 420 Index

Acknowledgments

Back in 2013, my publisher, Gary Svehla of Midnight Marquee, asked me if I'd be interested in writing a book on Dario Argento. I had already finished the updated edition of my book *The Haunted World of Mario Bava* and was intent on exploring the films of Lucio Fulci, but Argento seemed a little too "been there, done that" at the time and I said no. *Splintered Visions: Lucio Fulci and His Films* came out in 2015 and I had a feeling then that I would eventually change my tune about covering Argento's work in-depth. It looks like I was correct. I'm just grateful that Gary was still on-board with the idea by the time I finally got around to doing it. He and his wife/partner-in-crime Sue Svehla have my thanks, as always.

Every time I compose one of these acknowledgments sections for one of my books, I am reminded of how collaborative projects like this really are. I wish I could say I did it all by myself, but that wouldn't be true. I only hope that I don't leave anybody out!

I want to open with thanking my father, Gary Howarth, for his love and support. I'm fortunate indeed to have had such loving parents—they never chastised me for my love of the macabre and that enthusiasm continues to this day thanks largely to them, so take that as you will.

I'm also grateful to my friends Jon Kitley of *Kitley's Krypt*, Bryan Martinez of *The Giallo Room*, Brian Harris and Tony Strauss of WK Books, and Steve Fenton for their enthusiastic support and assistance in rounding up materials for this book. The images included herein were provided and in many instances painstakingly "cleaned up" by Tony and by Steve—and they have my sincere thanks. All images included herein are reproduced in the spirit of publicity for which they were originally created; neither the author nor the publisher claim the rights to any of these images. Bryan was also kind enough to put together a comprehensive videography of Argento's work which is included in this volume.

Filmmaker/DJ Jimmie Gonzalez has my thanks for helping me to put together a discography of soundtracks available from Argento's films.

When I first decided to do this book, I wasted no time in contacting Dario's long-time friend and colleague, Luigi Cozzi. Luigi had already contributed to a couple of my earlier books and I felt sure he could provide an appropriate foreword for the book. He did so with *molto* enthusiasm, as usual. Luigi also provided some valuable information regarding Argento's forays into episodic TV.

I also felt that a book like this called for something special where cover art was concerned. And who better to provide something special than master artist Mark Maddox, who created yet another masterpiece when called upon to do so; his work truly does this book proud. The final layout and design of the cover is the work of Tim Paxton, who has my thanks for ensuring that the cover looks like a million bucks.

Thanks to translator Patrick Lang and cineaste Paolo Tedoldi for their help in translating quotes from the, respectively, French and Italian editions of Argento's autobiography, *Paura*. Fortunately, Argento's autobiography has since been made available in English under the title of *Fear*, from FAB Press in the U.K. Readers who would like to learn more about the translating services offered by Patrick are directed to his social media page at: https://www.facebook.com/Patrick-Lang-Traducteur-Übersetzer-Translator-329831161166688/.

Thanks are also due to Alessio Di Rocco for his kind assistance in tracking down and providing me with a copy of the ultra-rare *Comandamenti per un gangster*, which Argento wrote early in his career.

I am, as always, deeply indebted to Jonathan Rigby and Kevin Lyons for their expert assistance with regards to shooting dates.

William Wilson was an invaluable help to me with regards to digging up news stories and box-office figures pertaining to Argento in the archives of *Variety* and *Box Office*; Roberto Curti, Francesco Massaccesi, and Peter Jilmstad were also kind enough to provide me with information pertaining to the Italian box-office performance of some of Argento's films.

Thank you to Mark Thompson Ashworth for kindly providing information about the original script for *The Card Player*. Mark's experience in the English dubbing side of the Italian film industry has given him a rare insight into the evolution of so many films, and he has my thanks for contributing to this book.

Vincent Pereira has my thanks for providing technical information regarding some of Dario's movies. Vincent is a long-time fan of Argento's films, and his expertise was of great help.

Thanks also to Ashley Cullen-Bandzuh, Joshua Kennedy, Andrew and James MacRae, and WT Solley for their kind assistance in the proofing and editing of the manuscript.

Thanks to Don May, Jr., of Synapse Films, for enabling me to contact Luciano Tovoli—and to *Signor* Tovoli for agreeing to answer my questions about his work with Argento.

Thanks to Henrik Möller for allowing me to print part of his podcast interview with T.E.D. Klein, and to Mr. Klein for his kindness in expanding on some of his

Claudio Simonetti and Dario Argento (photo courtesy Claudio Simonetti).

comments and allowing his comments about *Trauma* to be published in this context. Henrik also interviewed Italian screenwriter Dardano Sacchetti for his podcast, which yielded some helpful commentary from Sacchetti about his long-rumored involvement in the screenplay for *Inferno*. Thank you, Henrik, for allowing me access to using this material.

Many thanks to Fiore Argento, Sally Kirkland, Irene Miracle, and Claudio Simonetti for taking the time to talk about their work with Argento. Added thanks to Ms. Miracle for donating her personal behind-the-scenes images of her time on *Inferno*. Argento's long-time assistant Carla Alonzo was also of great help in facilitating the interviews.

Thanks are also due to my friend, the filmmaker Mark Savage, who set up the interview with Sally Kirkland.

I also want to acknowledge the work of Argento's biographer Alan Jones, whose book *Dario Argento: The Man, the Myths & the Magic* remains essential reading for all Argento fans. His book provided a lot of invaluable data with regards to shooting dates, budgets, and other behind-the-scenes factoids.

Maitland McDonagh also has my respect and esteem for publishing the first (and for my money, the best) serious analytical study of Argento's work in English. Her book *Broken Mirrors, Broken Minds: The Dark Dreams of Dario Argento* demonstrates that there is more to Argento than just flashy visuals.

In order to "mix things up" a bit, I elected to include some essays by other writers; I thought it would be helpful to get some alternative insight into the films, as inevitably others will pick up on certain elements, or have certain areas of expertise, which elude me. Jennifer Kellow-Fiorini, Randall D. Larson, Michael Mackenzie, and Rachael Nisbet have all brought something special to this project, and they all have my thanks for sharing their passion for Argento.

Of course, my eternal gratitude is also owed to Rob Ruston, who earned a special credit on this book (for what it's worth!) due to his kindness in interviewing so many people on my behalf during his visits to Rome. It was Rob's enthusiasm which rekindled my enthusiasm for this project, and his efforts have enriched this book tremendously.

I also want to extend my thanks to my good friends Douglas Bowers and Horace Cordier for their kind words of support and advice; it is deeply appreciated.

And last but most certainly not least: a very special thank you to Dario Argento—for making the films, of course, and also for very generously supporting this project and giving his time to discuss his life in the cinema. *Grazie, maestro!*

NEARLY 50 YEARS OF A PERSONAL AND PROFESSIONAL FRIENDSHIP:
Foreword by Luigi Cozzi

The first time I wrote an article about Italian movie director Dario Argento, I was very young, just 23, and he was 30. It happened in early 1970. Dario's first movie, *The Bird with the Crystal Plumage*, had just been released in Rome by a major Italian distributor and was doing so-so at the box office. But I had loved the film instantly, and fully understood its potential as a kind of a revolution in our static movie industry.

I immediately wanted to know its director and, since I was frequently meeting movie people like Mario Bava, Antonio ("Nini") Margheriti, and Riccardo Freda, I asked them about this new talent. Bava just said he was the son of an Italian producer and resented the fact, according to what he had been told by his own crew, that *The Bird with the Crystal Plumage* was a kind-of-reworking of his own 1963 thriller *The Girl Who Knew Too Much* (aka *Evil Eye*). Freda knew nothing about this newcomer, while Margheriti told me that Dario Argento was not *Bird*'s real director: there were rumors that it was actually helmed by his father, producer Salvatore Argento.

I then contacted the press office of *Bird*'s distributor, which gave me the address of Argento's production company. I called to their office in Rome, telling them that I wanted to meet Mr. Dario Argento for an interview, and the secretary immediately put me on the phone with Salvatore. He was very kind and most of all very excited, because, as I discovered later, I was the first member of the press to ask to meet his son for an interview after the film had been released.

In mid-March 1970 I met Dario Argento for the first time, in his small Roman house, after his then-wife had given birth to their daughter Fiore, who then was only 40 days old. We talked a lot and I discovered that I and Dario, as it were a sign of fate, shared the same birthdate, September 7 for both of us, with just a seven-year difference (1940 for Dario, 1947 for me)!

But, most important of all, almost immediately I also realized that all I had been told about Dario 'til then was just crap. He was a very, very competent man, who knew everything about classic thriller/horror movies and books and who had just come off a long working experience with great Italian director Sergio Leone, whom he really loved a lot to talk about.

This first meeting became the starting point of our 47-year friendship and working relationship that continues to this very day. And I'm proud to tell that I have had the honor and pleasure to be introduced to the world of professional moviemaking by Dario himself (and by his father, whom I will never forget), who wanted me as his own co-writer on his third film, *Four Flies on Grey Velvet*, and then also on his TV show *Door into Darkness* and on the political comedy *Le cinque giornate*.

Our personal and working relationship has continued all through the years. After I directed my

Old friends and business associates Luigi Cozzi and Dario Argento at the Fantafestival in 2016.

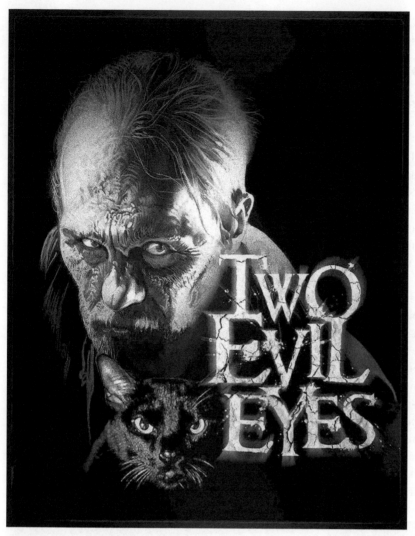

own *giallo*, *The Killer Must Kill Again/L'assassino è costretto ad uccidere ancora* in 1973, and several other genre movies like *Starcrash*, *Contamination*, and *Hercules/Ercole*, Dario wanted

me to take care of the special effects for his 1985 film *Phenomena*. Then I directed nine *Turno di notte* ("Night Shift") episodes for the Italian TV program *Giallo* hosted by Dario in 1987, and later I even followed him to Pittsburgh to work on *Two Evil Eyes*. Again, in 1995, I joined him as assistant and supervisor of the special effects for his film *The Stendhal Syndrome*, while in 2013 I wrote the scripts for his one-year-long Italian TV program *100 pallottole d'argento* ("One Hundred Silver Bullets").[1]

Meanwhile, Dario and I had joined forces again and opened "Profondo Rosso," a very unusual store in Rome, located at the Via dei Gracchi 260 (www.profondorossostore.com). It's a place where horror fans from all over the world can meet and buy books, DVDs, masks, action figures, costumes, posters, toys, T-shirts, and every other kind of memorabilia from the *giallo*, horror, fantasy, and science fiction movies they love. Underneath, in the dungeons beneath the store, we created "Dario Argento's Museum of Horrors," an exhibition of original props from some of Dario's most celebrated movies: *Deep Red*, *Opera*, *Phenomena*, *The Stendhal Syndrome*, *The Church*, *Demons*, *Two Evil Eyes*, and so on. It's unique, unlike anything else in the world. Thousands of visitors from all over the world have already come to visit this "Dario Argento's Museum of Horrors," including horror celebrities like Tim Burton, Rob Zombie, Alice Cooper, and Tom Savini.

Finally, in 2016, I decided to make my "comeback" as a director after more than 25 years with a weird mix of horror, science fiction, and *giallo* titled *Blood on Méliès' Moon*—and naturally, I invited Dario to take part in it as an actor, playing himself on the screen. He kindly accepted my offer, and so our work together continues!

Luigi Cozzi
June 15, 2017

Luigi Cozzi dons the mask of the killer in this creepy shot from *Four Flies on Grey Velvet*.

Notes:
1. *100 pallottole d'argento* was broadcast on RAI from the summer of 2012 until 2013 and it featured Argento introducing various thrillers and horror films; some of his own films were screened, as were films by Mario Bava, David Lynch, Alfred Hitchcock, George A. Romero, John Carpenter, Wes Craven, and others.

Preface

He's been called The Italian Hitchcock. But Dario Argento is considerably more than the "garlic flavored" alternative to the English-speaking cinema's Master of Suspense. The comparisons are inevitable: both men were bona fide celebrities—a bit of a rarity with directors—who made their reputations for scaring the hell out of viewers. As we shall see, however, Argento was, and is, very much his own man. He's synonymous with suspense and with horror and, along with Mario Bava and Lucio Fulci, remains one of the three masters of the Italian horror film.

As it happens, Argento's ascent to international popularity coincided with the rise of *Fangoria* magazine. It was there that I first read about the man, though I didn't make a concerted effort to seek out his work for many years. I can still remember being puzzled when I saw my first Argento film, *Creepers*—the butchered American edit of *Phenomena*. Argento wasn't even the name that drew me to the film—instead it was down to the presence of actor Donald Pleasence, who was already a firm favorite thanks to films like *Halloween* (1978) and *Dracula* (1979). Even in its original, far more coherent edit, *Phenomena* is a strange film—especially to viewers who aren't already fully indoctrinated into the weird and wonderful world of Italian horror. It was a little too much for me to cope with —bear in mind, please, I was less than 10 years old! I next remember seeing *Suspiria*, which at one time was the most requested title to be given a release on home video. Rather remarkably, for a film that was already a decade old, my local video store played it up with hanging posters in the shop, even taking the precaution of stocking several copies on their shelves; that certainly never happened with any other older catalogue title that I can remember. I freely admit I didn't get it at the time—not at all. The dubbing bugged me (though as shall be discussed, there's more live production audio than was the norm for an Italian film of the period), the story seemed to make no sense, and I couldn't comprehend why some of the weirder scenes (like the room full of wire) even happened. Happily, I was eventually freed from the more staid and conventional confines of my movie watching experience, and I underwent a full-blown "awakening" where Italian horror was concerned. It started with Mario Bava (as it truly must), then from there I savored the pleasures of Argento, Fulci, Riccardo Freda, Sergio Martino... you get the picture. I was an addict from that moment forward.

As fate would have it, my own interest in Argento peaked when his stock in the fan community began to decline. Following a problematic period in America, where it became evident he would never be able to function with the same creative and financial freedom he enjoyed in Italy, he returned to his native country and his work became more quirky and experimental. There was still much to savor in the 1990s, but as the 21st century got under way things became ... problematic. As an admirer of Argento, it pained me to see his name being dragged through the mud by so many fair-weather fans—yet I had to admit, I could see where they were

Ad for the U.S. VHS edition of *Creepers* from Media; artist unknown.

coming from. The purpose of this book, of course, is to celebrate the good—and there's a lot of it—while also talking frankly about the stumbles and the out-and-out failures; it simply wouldn't do to take the sycophant route and act like everything is on the same level as, say, *Deep Red* or *Suspiria*.

Argento's reputation as one of the masters of the modern horror film is secure, even if his more recent works have alienated many viewers. Unlike Bava or Fulci, both of whom were of older generations, Argento was part of that new generation of cineastes who became filmmakers. In the U.S., we saw an explosion of filmmakers who fit this criteria during the 1970s—George Lucas, Francis Ford Coppola, Paul Schrader, Brian De Palma, Martin Scorsese, Peter Bogdanovich, John Milius, Steven Spielberg, John Carpenter … these men, and others beside, grew up worshipping at the altar of the cinema; some of them—like Bogdanovich—even wrote extensively about their favorite films and filmmakers prior to making their own movies. Many of these directors attended film school, where film theory courses taught them all about subtext, while more practical production courses educated them on the nuts and bolts aspects of day-to-day film production. Prior to this new generation of talent in the late '60s and early '70s, however, there was a major renaissance in the European film scene—where the likes of Jean-Luc Godard and François Truffaut in France and Bernardo Bertolucci and Pier Paolo Pasolini in Italy brought their own enthusiasm for the medium to bear on their own cutting edge, often politically-incendiary works. Dario Argento was very much a part of that new movement. As we shall discuss, Argento started off writing about film for a very left-leaning (read: Communist) Roman paper. During that period, he had the good fortune to interview many of his idols and he happily devoured movie after movie, taking notes and writing about film with a lucid and sympathetic eye. Unlike many of his contemporaries, he valued genre cinema, and this would influence his later decision to focus on genre work himself. Argento never really set out to become a director, however; he was initially content to work as a screenwriter, as he preferred the solitude and peacefulness of working quietly behind the scenes as opposed to being in charge of the three-ring-circus atmosphere of a film set. And yet, he was a "natural," as they say, and in time he exploded onto the film scene in Rome, ultimately reaching the popularity level of a rock star.

While the Hitchcock comparison continues to this day, in many respects a more apt simile would be to Edgar Allan Poe. To look at Argento, especially in his younger years, is to see a man with a haunted look in his eyes; it was partly an affectation, no doubt, designed to play into his reputation as a master of the macabre. Yet, make no mistake, Argento's affection for Poe was a big part of his life since childhood—and the two men share a definite obsession for the horrific and the macabre. Like Poe, Argento also has the soul of a poet—it's not evident in his sometimes-clunky dialogue, it's true, but one can see it in the way in which he presents his imagery. Like Bava before him, Argento has always displayed a flair for finding the beauty in the horrific; images of violent death are common in his films, yet they often are presented as peculiarly beautiful. Argento's flair for visual poetry is in a league of its own and his artful approach to framing and choreographing scenes of violence inspired the title of this very book.

Inevitably, Argento's fascination with violence has led to his work being censored and misunderstood. Many critics insist on labeling him as a misogynist, though this label conveniently ignores the frequently strong and layered portrayal of women in his movies; yes, they're often subjected to vicious attacks by knife-wielding psychopaths, but they're also often the ones who possess the insight to unravel the puzzle and solve the mystery. Argento's cinema is not one of damsels in distress fainting at the first sight of trouble—if anything, the female characters are often more resourceful and intelligent than their male counterparts. They're also just as likely to be wielding the knife as they are to be being under attack by it. These mixed messages confuse the more facile critics who tend to think of horror and suspense films as being inherently misogynist, anyway. But a close reading of his films undermines such criticisms and reveals a psychology which is simultaneously fascinated by, attracted to, and occasionally frightened and even repelled by women. Similarly, his films may contain scenes of graphic gore and mayhem, but compared to the vicious excesses of contemporaries like Fulci or Ruggero Deodato, these scenes are traditionally presented with such aesthetic good taste that it's difficult to describe them as repulsive; only in more recent years has he gone off the deep end into sleazier imagery and scenes of *Grand Guignol* excess.

Yet, the cuts inflicted by censors and distributors have frequently obscured the virtues of Argento's movies. There's no doubt that we live in a period where it's far easier to access and appreciate the works of directors like Argento—but if you remember those dark days during the early period of the home video boom, the odds of seeing anything but a horribly panned-and-scanned and cut-down edit of *Deep Red* were very slim indeed. Now that it's easier to see these films as their creator originally intended, it's relatively simple to see that Argento's approach to narrative, though quirky, has its own internal logic. Argento has often spoken of being influenced by his dreams and that's easy enough to believe; there are indeed moments in his best films which feel as if they're unfolding like a sort of waking dream—or nightmare. That being said, the films tend to make a great deal more sense than they're often given credit for. His *giallo* films may go off into tangents of fantasy which can be jarring for some viewers, but the basic broad strokes of the narrative really do connect together and make sense, provided you're paying attention, of course. On the other hand, the supernatural films like *Suspiria* and *Inferno* are deceptively tricky. *Inferno*, for example, seems a lot more complex than it really is, since the waters are muddied by so many side vignettes and diversions; but when you break it all down, it really is a fairly simple and straightforward story. That's not to say that it "makes sense" in the conventional narrative manner, but don't forget, it's a supernatural horror movie. It's allowed to get a bit slippery on that level. Whether one finds the films to be engaging or even coherent on a narrative level, there's no doubt that the cuts inflicted by distributors for so many years did the films no favors; I can still remember watching the U.S. edit of *Opera* with a friend, not realizing that it was going to be missing some very important scenes present in the original edit, which I already knew and loved—at one point the heroine inexplicably escapes from a seemingly impossible situation and I had to explain that there was a scene missing which explained how that happened. Imagine seeing such an edited-down version without the "benefit" of somebody who knew what was missing at your side; no wonder that so many American critics were eager to dismiss Argento's films as all flash and no substance for so many years.

The notion of style over substance is a common theme in discussing Argento—as well as his colleagues in the field of Italian horror, including Bava and Fulci. For some critics, the emphasis on imagery and on set pieces indicates a lack of concern for narrative or logic. Sometimes this can be true—Fulci's horror films of the early 1980s deliberately eschew conventional narrative structure, for example. Yet, the underlining implication that it's impossible for a film to be both stylishly realized and also coherently plotted is a lot of nonsense. Argento's approach to his stories may not fit in with the classical

Dario directs Coralina Cataldi-Tassoni during her death scene in *Opera*.

tradition of English drawing room murder mysteries, but so what? Who says that's the only way a "proper" mystery should unfold? Given Argento's idiosyncratic approach, it's just as well that he passed on an offer from the great producer Dino De Laurentiis to do an Agatha Christie adaptation back when star-studded Christie thrillers were in vogue in the late '70s/early '80s! The clues are frequently hidden in plain sight—another Poe influence, for sure—but Argento isn't always interested in following the plodding path of linking together the clues and solving the puzzle; he likes to zig where others like to zag, and he will often take his characters down strange alleys which don't necessarily led to a resolution—but which offer their own pleasures, just the same. Like Bava and Fulci, Argento also understands the value of mood and atmosphere; and his best works display a feeling for timing and tempo which is truly exceptional.

As indicated above, this book is not intended to lavish praise on every film Argento has ever made. He's made great films. He's made good films. He's also made some very bad films. Given that the film industry as a whole is (un)fairly ageist by nature, it's not surprising when "elder statesmen" filmmakers come under attack for hanging in there for too long. One need only point to Quentin Tarantino's critique of Martin Scorsese after seeing the latter's flawed but brilliant historical epic, *Gangs of New York* (2002); Tarantino has long said that he plans to retire when he hits 60, though we'll see if he's true to his word. The notion that filmmaking is a young person's game therefore carries the implication that, once you hit a certain age, you lose your edge—you lose your mojo. It's true that many great directors have ended their careers making some terrible films—to choose but one example, while *Buddy Buddy* (1981) may have been a low spot for Billy Wilder, it wouldn't be fair to say that everything he made after he "went over the hill" age-wise was unworthy of his talents. In fact, the likes of Luis Buñuel, Samuel Fuller, Roman Polanski, Alfred Hitchcock, Akira Kurosawa, Howard Hawks, Stanley Kubrick, John Huston, Fritz Lang, Clint Eastwood, and many others have made wonderful, passionate films well past their 60th birthday. Tarantino may not have been impressed with *Gangs of New York*, but others (myself included!) would disagree with him; and Scorsese has continued to make films that are well worth seeing well into his 70s. William Friedkin, one of the top hotshot directors of the 1970s, underwent a notable decline and produced some very erratic work for many years, before proving he still has what it takes with the back-to-back double gut punch of *Bug* (2006) and *Killer Joe* (2011). Then there's Mario Bava, who continued making fine films past his 60th birthday, even if fate stopped him in his tracks at the relatively youthful age of 65. All this should be enough, hopefully, to invalidate the notion that directors should be put out to pasture before they get old and embarrass themselves. If there's been something amiss among Argento's more recent works—and make no mistake, there certainly has been—there's absolutely no reason to believe that he doesn't still have it in him to come back and make another worthy film, provided all the important elements (including a script he believes in and the right crew to support him) fall into place. At the time of writing this book, Argento is nearing 80 years of age, and he's teasing the possibility of returning to the director's chair for another thriller. Time will tell, of course.

Ultimately, the intention is to celebrate Argento's rich cinematic legacy with a clear head and an open heart; punches won't be pulled where they're deserved, but it is my contention that even the worst of Argento's films contain at least one sequence which demonstrates the sort of inspiration that typifies his best work. This is the first time I've written such a book about a filmmaker who is still alive and working, so I can only hope that it does the man the justice he deserves. In looking at the full scope of his work—including the early ones he contributed to as a screenwriter and his later work as a producer/creative influence—it is clear that he remains one of the most vital and significant figures in the modern horror and suspense genres; more than that, he remains a top level talent, regardless of genre.

One final note about titles. As this is a book for the English-speaking market, the films are referred to by their best-known English language titles. In some cases, Argento's films were retitled for U.S. consumption and sometimes these alternate titles denote a specific alternate edit (for example, *Creepers* is the drastically shortened version of *Phenomena*). The vast majority of Argento's films have been released in the U.S. market in one form or another. Since there has never been an official English-friendly release of *Le cinque giornate* under the title of "The Five Days," or any other title for that matter, I have elected to refer to that film by its Italian title. By the same token, the Argento TV series *Door into Darkness* may not exist with that actual *on-screen* title—but that is how it has been released to video in the American market, and that is almost certainly the way most English-speaking fans know and refer to it.

Nevertheless, some areas of confusion have arisen along the way: The full on-screen English title for *La terza madre* is actually *Mother of Tears: The Third Mother*; however, it is best known simply as *Mother of Tears*, so I have elected to stick with that title—it just flows better. Alternatively, his version of *Dracula* is usually referred to as *Dracula 3D*—but neither the Italian nor the English version bear that actual on-screen title; in order to differentiate between it and the Bram Stoker novel and the various other film versions, I have decided to go with the actual on-screen title on the U.S. print: *Dario Argento's Dracula*. But this begs the question: Is Dario Argento's name really intended to be *part* of the title, or is it a possessory credit along the lines of John Carpenter's films? An attempt at "branding" his name on the title of his American film *Trauma* comes to mind—but the Italian title was simply *Trauma* and that's how most fans refer to the film, and so I've decided to go with *Trauma* as the go-to title. Confused yet? Hopefully the use of titles will be clear enough while satisfying the pedants in the audience; in any event, all efforts have been made to be consistent.

Since the dates of production and release are covered in detail in the discussion of the films themselves, I have also elected not to place the release date in brackets beside the titles when referencing them throughout the text; thus, while I will refer to films and texts by others and make note of the relevant dates, I didn't see the need to do that in reference to Argento's own productions. Hopefully that, too, is clear enough.

Dario at a press conference.

The Unsane Cinema of Dario Argento

Chapter One: The Early Years

Our story begins in Rome on September 7 1940, where Salvatore Argento (born February 8, 1914; died April 19, 1987) and his wife Elda Luxardo (born 1915; died March 14, 2013) welcome the birth of their first child. Little Dario would soon be joined by a younger brother named Claudio (born September 15, 1943) and a little sister named Floriana (born in 1946). Theirs would be a comfortable upbringing as both Salvatore and Elda proved to be successful in their respective fields.

Tellingly, both Salvatore and Elda were connected to the then-burgeoning Italian film industry. Salvatore—the son of Domenico Argento and Laudomia Argento (*née* Mosca Moschini)—was involved in the public relations side of the industry through Unitalia, a government-funded organization that focused on the exporting of homegrown cinema product. Elda—the daughter of Alfredo Luxardo and Margherita Luxardo (*née* Perissinotto)—had been raised in Brazil, where her father, also a photographer, had relocated after failing to make a go of it in Italy. Specific biographical details about Elda and her background are difficult to come by and, in fact, even Dario himself is unsure about his mother's background, hinting at a distance which continued to exist between them through the years. "Nobody knew my mother's exact age. They guessed her age when she got a passport, which she used to come to Italy with her brother, Elio. She was born about 1920 and they didn't know much more. Even her birthplace was unknown. Some documents hint at Porto Alegre, in the south of Brazil, but it's not certain."[1] Dario places her date of birth at 1920 but most sources indicate that she was actually born sometime in 1915; evidently she was aged 97 years when she passed in March 2013, so that does make sense. In an interview with *La Republica*, conducted not long after Elda's death, Dario's youngest daughter and sometime collaborator, Asia Argento, would later observe: "Her age, like other things concerning her, is shrouded in mystery."[2] The family returned to Rome sometime between 1928 and 1932 (sources differ on the precise year), and Elda soon found herself eager to follow in her father's artistic footsteps. She would become one of the most renowned fashion photographers in Italy. Her specialty was glamor portraits of the top female movie stars of the period. Her portraits of classic screen icons like Gina Lollobrigida, Sophia Loren, Alida Valli,[3] and Claudia Cardinale still hang in the top galleries in Rome, for example. Her older brother, Elio (1908-1969) was also a major photographer in his own right; in fact, he had been selected by Benito Mussolini to be his official photographer during the black years of fascism in Italy. As for Salvatore, he would work his way up the ladder and establish a powerful presence in the Italian film industry; by the 1960s, he began to take an active role in film production, working for a time for Dino De Laurentiis. During Dario's first years, things were comparatively bumpy, thanks to the unsettled nature of the country as a whole, but when the big boom in cinema production hit in the 1950s, Salvatore was in a very good position indeed. By the end of the '60s, he was in just the right place to facilitate his first born son's ascent into screenwriting and ultimately directing.

By Argento's own reckoning, his childhood was a comfortable one. He and his siblings wanted for nothing and some of Dario's earliest memories include being in the presence of some of the superstars who came to sit for portraits taken by his mother. He attributes his flair for making the actresses in his own films look so glamorous to the time he spent observing his mother as she carefully lit and framed these women in her photography studio. It

was during this time, too, that he first felt the stirrings of the flesh. He recalls going home after school and being on the sidelines as various beautiful women changed in and out of costumes during their photographic sessions. "I just stayed there, in the background. They undressed in front of me. I would suddenly witness thighs, breasts … I felt the excitement rising, but to them I was barely more than a baby. We assume that kids don't understand the seduction game, but that's not true. They understand it better than adults."[4]

It seems as though Salvatore and Elda allowed their children a certain degree of freedom, which young Dario certainly appreciated. "Our apartment was huge […] we could make ourselves comfortable, Claudio, Floriana and myself. Each one of us had our own lives, it was like we were three single children."[5] That the Argento children took an interest in movies from an early age was understandable—in many respects, they grew up in the midst of the film industry as it bounced back from the devastation inflicted by the Second World War. Of the three children, two of them would go on to become actively involved in the cinema; only Floriana elected to avoid it altogether. Dario and his siblings spent many hours at local cinemas thrilling to domestic productions, as well as to American imports. One American import made a particularly vivid impression. In 1949, Universal's lavish *Phantom of the Opera* (1943) was re-released in Italy. When the Argento kids went to see it, none of them could have predicted what a major impact it would have on them—especially Dario. He would later recall seeing the film with his brother and sister, noting that they were so taken with it that they would play act their favorite scenes together.[6]

Argento has rarely touched upon his relationship with his mother, save for nostalgic reminiscences of spending time in her studio—and even those memories are geared more towards starry-eyed wonder and lip-smacking satisfaction at having been able to glimpse the naked bodies of so many beautiful starlets and models. Certainly, the image of "wicked mother" figures looms large in many of his films; it doesn't take a psychologist to work out that the director is exorcising some of his own personal demons on that level. Predictably, his memories of her are tinged with mixed emotions. Speaking about the impact that spending part of her childhood in South America made on her, he notes, "She was very attached to her origins. My siblings and myself, when we were kids, constantly wore the St. George medal she gave us. In Brazil, St. George is a highly respected saint. My father also always wore one. This talisman was an Argento tradition."[7] As the years wore on, Dario found himself growing closer and closer with his father, whereas relations would be strained

Daniele Luxardo, Antonella Lualdi and Dario Argento at a Luxardo Cinema Exhibition 2019.

where his mother was concerned. He would later claim that his issues with his mother caused him to have an eating disorder for many years.[8] He would insist upon adding anorexia into the plot of his American *Giallo Trauma*, despite the objections of his collaborators, while unbalanced, sometimes homicidal mother figures are a prominent presence in many of his films. Here, too, we can see Dario working out some of his personal demons and frustrations within the confines of his work.

His siblings would also remain an important presence in his life. Brother Claudio would follow in the footsteps of his older brother and their father by going into the film industry. He would join his brother's professional family on an official basis in 1973 when he served as a producer on the period comedy-drama *Le cinque giornate* and he would go on to co-produce a number of his brother's films up until the unfortunate *Giallo* in 2009. He also collaborated with Dario in co-producing *Dawn of the Dead* for American horror master George A. Romero. Claudio got his own start in the business in the publicity department at Paramount in Italy before joining forces with Dario and Salvatore. The Dario-Claudio dynamic would prove to be a bumpy one and the brothers would go through periods where they were not on speaking terms. Understandably, he was anxious to make his own mark in the world and didn't wish to be seen purely as "Dario Argento's kid brother." Dario's own quest for name recognition made it difficult for the younger man to establish his own identity, and temperamentally they were also polar opposites: Dario had a reputation for being moody and volatile in his younger years, while Claudio was known to be far more genial and easy-going. He finally broke free and went on

Dario confers with his brother Claudio (left), his father Salvatore (far right), and actor Adriano Celentano on the set of *Le cinque giornate* (1973).

Alejandro Jodorowsky's bizarre and brilliant *Santa sangre* (1989), which he also co-wrote. He would come back in and out of Dario's professional orbit intermittently, and on a personal level he and his wife Beatrice provided Dario with a niece, Claudia, and a nephew, Nilo; Claudia opted not to follow in the family business, while Nilo would go on to serve as a production secretary on *Do You Like Hitchcock?* (*Ti piace Hitchcock?*) before serving as production manager on *Mother of Tears* (*La terza madre*) and *Giallo*.

As for his sister Floriana, about whom the least has been written, she decided to follow a different path. By Argento's own admission, their age gap

to produce such films as Peter Del Monte's *Little Flames* (*Piccolo fuochi*, 1985) and, most impressively,

Dario's nephew Nilo worked as a production assistant on *Do You Like Hitchcock?*; the Portuguese DVD cover is more appealing than most.

created some distance, but he writes about her with warmth and affection in his memoirs. "Floriana traveled a lot and with her language skills, she worked for the Italian embassy in China. She then worked for the ENI (*Ente Nazionale Idrocarburi*)[9] and most recently she moved to New

Unlike her brothers, Floriana Argento did not go into a career in film.

York to become a real estate agent. I always admired her for her tenacity and her merits. Her longing for travel and her knowledge of the world made her go far, and I'm very proud of her."[10] To be the only daughter in a household dominated by strong male personalities could not have been easy for her, but it certainly didn't get in the way when it came to realizing her own dreams and ambitions. Floriana would go on to marry and give birth to a son, also named Dario, who never worked in the film industry.

In the midst of intermittent family drama, Dario's interest in and passion for the cinema continued to grow during his teenage years. He also took a typically rebellious teenage interest in politics. His views were not warmly received, especially by his mother. "One day we drove home from the sea with my parents. The whole family was in the car. The elections were coming up, and I was about to vote for the first time. My father asked me innocently, just for the sake of chatting: 'Who are you going to vote for, Dario?' 'You know, I am really ... a Communist.' The car skidded to the side of the road, as my father almost lost control of the wheel. 'What?' he demanded. 'A Communist! What does that mean?!' He was more of a liberal. He was a supporter of '*Giustizia e Liberta*' and really didn't like the word 'Communist.' I proudly explained my choice, but in the car there was dead silence. Even more so because my mother was a fascist. At home, we never discussed politics again."[11] Argento's connection to the Communist party was no mere teenage fad, however. He would continue on as a "sympathizer" for many years and to this day he regards himself as a proud Leftist. Discussing his feelings for the Communist party, he writes: "I was a supporter. I participated in all their demonstrations, even if I wasn't officially a member of the Party. Thus, I didn't participate in their reunions. That kept me safe from internal 'cleansings.'"[12]

It wasn't just Leftist politics that got the young man's blood racing, either. He'd already begun to take notice of the opposite sex as a young boy in his mother's studio, but as time wore on, his interest grew—as did his experience. On a trip to Paris in his teens, Dario made the acquaintance of a pair of "working girls" who took a liking to the young Italian; he was invited to stay with them and in the process received valuable lessons in the all-important matter of the birds and the bees. "When the one girl was asleep or not at home, the other girl gave me sex education. I was just a young boy and she seemed so mature, almost '*old*.' But I guess she really wasn't much older than 30. I have forgotten everything about the French girl, even her name—but not her eyes, nor the way she threw her head back when she laughed out loud, when she offered me her neck. She taught me everything I know about making love."[13]

Notes:
1. Argento, Dario, *Peur* (France: Rouge Profond, 2018), p. 49.
2. https://www.repubblica.it/spettacoli/people/2013/09/07/news/asia_argento-66047992/
3. Of course, Argento would end up directing Valli in two films: *Suspiria* and *Inferno*.
4. Argento, Dario, *Peur* (France: Rouge Profond, 2018), p. 14.
5. Ibid, p. 17.
6. Ibid.
7. Ibid, p. 345.
8. Jones, Alan, *Dario Argento: The Man, the Myths & the Magic* (Godalming: FAB Press, 2012), p. 216.
9. The ENI is a multi-national oil and gas company based in Rome.
10. Argento, Dario, *Peur* (France: Rouge Profond, 2018), p. 238.
11. Ibid, p. 48.
12. Ibid.
13. Ibid, p. 42-43.

Chapter Two: Profession: Critic

As he was entering into his late teens, Argento's interests in sex, politics, and the cinema (though not necessarily in that specific order!) were setx to shape his destiny. In 1957, at the age of 17, Argento decided that he wanted to pursue a career in journalism—specifically, he wanted to write about the cinema. It was his hope that he would further his cinematic education by being paid to watch and review movies, while at the same time having the opportunity to meet and interact with his idols by interviewing them. He wasn't interested in furthering his education at the university level; his education would take place in the movie theaters. His age posed a problem, however. As he later explained to his biographer, Alan Jones: "In those days it was illegal to work for a newspaper if you were under 21. So, I lied about my age."[1] He bluffed his way into getting a job with the newspaper *L'Araldo dello Spettacolo*, thanks in large measure to his father, who was friends with the publisher. Established in 1946, *L'Araldo dello Spettacolo* also employed other future filmmakers at various stages, notably Gillo Pontecorvo, Carlo Lizzani, and Marco Ferreri. Argento's job was basically that of an office boy, assigned to various tasks when the need arose. He made a good impression on the veterans in the office, which led to another golden opportunity. "I almost immediately made friends with one of the oldest colleagues, who found me particularly likeable. One day he told me that *Paese Sera* had asked him to curate a column about the most popular films. It was something completely new to Italian press, he told me; no other newspapers were doing that. He didn't have time to do it himself, so he thought I might be interested. I accepted without hesitation."[2] It was the start of a long and harmonious relationship between Argento and *Paese Sera*, which would serve as a valuable stepping-stone in his career. Given his Communist leanings, the "temperature" at *Paese Sera* was just right for him. "*Paese Sera* was closely linked to the Communist Party, and I worked there for a good part of the 1970s. I considered and still consider myself a left-wing person anyway: I keep whole years of *Lotta Continua*[3] in my library."[4] Argento's column originally focused on numbers and facts, but the young writer believed that if it expanded into film analysis and criticism, it might attract even more attention. "I was madly happy: sometimes I got to see six movies in a day. I could stay in the movie theater, watch movies for free *and* get paid for it: it was heaven."[5] As a critic, Argento did his best to approach films without prejudice; he treated genre films with the same deference he afforded to the latest *auteur* offering by Federico Fellini (1920-1993) or Luchino Visconti (1906-1976). By his own admission, this approach proved to be controversial—but that was good for readership, so nobody tried to put a cramp on his style. Trying to locate actual examples of his film criticism these days is next to impossible, but it has been said that he was one of the few critics in Italy who wrote favorably about "mere" genre artisans like Mario Bava (1914-1980) and Sergio Leone (1929-1989), for example. He also wrote effusively about Hollywood filmmakers during a time when the American studio system had fallen out of favor in Italy. "For me, 'bad films' didn't really exist. There was something to love in every picture—maybe even just five minutes, a single shot, a bit of sound design. Whenever I reviewed John Ford's movies with fervor—Ford was considered a huge fascist and nobody wanted to even hear his name—or I displayed passion for Alfred Hitchcock and suspense in American movies, I found a note from the editor-in-chief in my mailbox: American cinema is empty entertainment ..."[6] Argento would

Dario defied his parents by becoming a Communist and subscribing to papers like *Lotta Continua*.

In the March 17, 1966 issue of *Paese Sera*, Dario offered commentary on Marco Bellocchio's *Fists in the Pocket* (*I pugni in tasca*, 1966).

later recall that initially he was not permitted to sign his reviews with his full name; instead he simply signed them with his initials. But once the column started to really take off, the full name was in evidence. He had a very simple but lofty goal in mind: to become the most prominent and well-known film critic in Italy.[7]

During this time, Argento also felt the stirrings of first love. He was working for *Paese Sera*, where he was being paid to do what he regarded as a dream job. Life was good. And it looked even better when he made the acquaintance of a young woman who struck him as his ideal mate; he doesn't note her name in his memoirs, but it's clear that she made a vivid impression upon him. "We had the feeling we were soul mates; we considered ourselves to be very lucky to have met. She stayed at my place day and night and my family grew accustomed to always seeing her. I thought it would last forever."[8] It didn't. It proved to be the beginning of a long and rather tormented series of romantic relationships in Dario's life. On the one hand, he craved the company of women—not just for sex, but for companionship and for sharing ideas. And yet, he also would come to recognize that he was, in essence, something of a loner by nature. He'd continue to try to find that ultimate romantic relationship but, despite brief periods of intense happiness, it never really worked out for him. Rather perversely, he discovered the actual process of ending hopeless relationships to be a source of joy. "It may seem strange, but the best times of my life were when a doomed love affair would end. […] It was like this: The women I loved, or thought I loved, we simply broke up ... and I would feel strong euphoria, ready to face a new future."[9] But, of course, that realization was still many years off.

In the meantime, a significant presence entered Argento's life in a rather unusual way. It began with a public transportation strike which meant that Dario was inconvenienced with taking his sister, Floriana, to school. When Floriana asked him to make a special stop so they could pick up her friend along the way, he wasn't thrilled; he needed to get to work and get his own day started. His mood soon shifted. "The two girls chatted, and I soon realized that my sister's friend sounded more mature than her age. She studied foreign languages and the more I listened to her, the more she seemed to be my age. When we arrived at school, I almost regretted that I had to go to work. For the next days I constantly thought about the name she whispered when she got in the car: *Marisa*."[10] Unfortunately, virtually nothing is known about Marisa Casale and her background. By virtue of the fact that she is not part of the film industry, she has been reduced to something of a footnote in much of the writing about Argento. And yet, there is no doubt that her relationship with Argento was a significant one on many levels, even if it unfortunately did not end on happy terms. For now, however, young Dario was head-over-heels in love with the young student and he was determined to make a positive impression on her. He was impressed by her poise, her beauty, and her maturity—and he decided to try and impress her by boasting about his job as a film critic. The tactic worked and by his own admission, they became virtually inseparable—except when it was time for him to focus on his writing, which she had a tolerant attitude about.[11] Dario proposed to Marisa in 1965 and they remained engaged for the next three years.

That period saw a major transition in Argento's life as he became more and more important at *Paese Sera* and was entrusted with interviewing major figures in the world of cinema. In the spring of 1963, Fritz Lang

(1890-1976) was in Italy to film his scenes for Jean-Luc Godard's film *Contempt* (*Le mépris*, 1964). The once-mighty Lang hadn't directed a film since *The 1,000 Eyes of Dr. Mabuse* (*Die 1000 Augen des Dr. Mabuse*, 1960), but he still cut a fierce and intimidating presence. He also carried with him the legacy of being one of the world's most renowned filmmakers; and happened to be one of Dario Argento's idols. "I realized that I was getting bigger responsibilities when I got to interview Fritz Lang. This man was a myth to me. German Expressionism and the 'Doctor Mabuse' cycle completely changed my way of considering the cinematic narrative."[12] It's a shame that Argento's chat with Lang has evidently not been preserved for posterity; but Lang's influence remains writ large on Argento's own films as a director.

In May 1964, he was sent to the set of a horror film titled *The Castle of the Living Dead* (*Il castello dei morti viventi*), where he interviewed the film's star, Christopher Lee[13]; as luck would have it, their paths would cross again years later. In the course of their chat, Lee told Argento that he was gearing up for another Italian production, this one co-produced by American International Pictures (AIP)—an adaptation of H.P. Lovecraft's "The Dunwich Horror," to have been titled *Scarlet Friday*, which was to have been directed by Mario Bava and to have co-starred another major horror icon: Boris Karloff. That picture was delayed, and it eventually collapsed altogether, though art director-turned-director Daniel Haller would pick up the pieces and make a rather different adaptation, released by AIP January 1970 as *The Dunwich Horror*.

Another major opportunity presented itself in the latter part of 1964, when Argento got word that John Huston (1906-1987) was in Rome for the production of his epic, *The Bible: In the Beginning...* Through his father, who was old friends with the film's producer, Dino De Laurentiis, Argento discovered that the director was staying in his preferred suite at the Grand Hotel on the Via Veneto. Although nervous about dropping in unannounced on such a legendary figure, he decided to throw caution to the wind. The opportunity to speak to the man responsible for such classics as *The Maltese Falcon* (1941) and *The Treasure of the Sierra Madre* (1948) was simply too great to resist. "He was a bit drunk, thankfully; he had a scruffy beard and he was wearing a short robe. He looked slightly ridiculous. Without me saying anything, he looked at me for two seconds, then he grabbed me by the shoulder and dragged me into his room. And thus we began. He made me sit on a small sofa and asked me what I wanted to know. 'Everything,' I answered—and he gave me what I wanted."[14]

Notes:
1. Jones, Alan, *Dario Argento: The Man, the Myths & the Magic* (Godalming: FAB Press, 2012), p. 15.
2. Argento, Dario, *Paura* (Rome: Einaudi, 2014), p. 43.
3. *Lotta Continua* was a Communist newspaper which ran from 1969 until 1976.
4. Argento, Dario, *Paura* (Rome: Einaudi, 2014), p.44.
5. Ibid, p. 46.
6. Ibid, p. 51.
7. Argento, Dario, *Peur* (France: Rouge Profond, 2018), p. 56.
8. Ibid, p. 50.
9. Ibid, p. 53.
10. Ibid, p. 58-59.
11. Ibid, p. 59-60.
12. Ibid, p. 65.
13. Rigby, Jonathan, *Christopher Lee: The Authorised Screen History* (Richmond: Reynolds & Hearn, Ltd., 2007), p. 102.
14. Argento, Dario, *Paura* (Rome: Einaudi, 2014), p. 60.

Chapter Three: Once Upon a Time ... The Screenwriter

In 1965, right around the time he proposed to Marisa, Argento was looking to switch career paths. He enjoyed studying film and writing about it, but he was ready to make the transition to screenwriting. Using the contacts he had established interviewing filmmakers for *Paese Sera*, Argento secured an appointment from writer/director/star Alberto Sordi (1920-2003) to sit in on the writing of his new project, a comedy titled *Scusi, lei è favorevole o contrario?* (literally, "Excuse Me, Are You For or Against?"). The actual writing of the script was the province of Sergio Amidei (1904-1981). On Sordi's instruction, Amidei allowed the young wannabe screenwriter to sit in and observe the day-to-day writing of the script. As he recalls in his autobiography, "They had a funny method, which confused me. Amidei's partners would sit on a couch next to him, and they talked about many subjects (politics, family matters ...), but not about the movie they were supposed to discuss. [...] At one point, one of them would say: 'Let's talk about the movie, we lost quite some time.' They would concentrate, close their eyes. [...] Little by little, some interesting ideas for the movie would come up; when they both agreed, they wrote them down. Then they asked: 'Who is going to write this, you or me?' When they came to an agreement, they left. The day after, same process. It was a great training for me. When I became a screenwriter myself, I realized that this worked very well."[1] Because he sat in on these sessions, some have claimed that Argento collaborated on the script without credit; this is not true, however: he was simply there to observe.

The plot deals with the then-hot topic of divorce, which was still illegal in Italy at this time. A wealthy hypocrite, Tullio Conforti (played by Sordi), is very much opposed to divorce as a concept; this doesn't prevent him from being relentlessly unfaithful to his wife, as he tools around town having flings with a variety of desirable females. In addition to sitting in and observing—but not actively participating—in the screenplay phase, Argento was invited by Sordi to appear on screen in a

Italian lobby card for *Scusi, lei è favorevole o contrario?*.

The Unsane Cinema of Dario Argento

minor cameo role. Argento's distinctive looks—haunted eyes and painfully skinny frame—obviously made an impression on Sordi, who cast the young cineaste in the role of an altar boy; some references mistakenly credit him with playing a priest.

Scusi, lei è favorevole o contrario? made its theatrical debut in Italy just in time for Christmas of 1966—December 23, to be precise. By a remarkable coincidence, a very different film made its Roman theatrical debut that same day: Sergio Leone's *The Good, The Bad and The Ugly* (*Il buono, il brutto, il cattivo*, 1966). The timing was significant, as Leone—whom Argento already held in great esteem—would end up having a significant impact on Argento's development as an artist.

Prior to the all-important Christmas season of 1966, however, Argento had begun dabbling in writing screenplays and screen treatments. He had hoped to attract the attention of major directors and inevitably one of the ones he did his best to win over was Sergio Leone (1929-1989). Argento had been one of the few critics in Italy to write seriously about Leone's films and he was also friendly with Duccio Tessari (1926-1994), who collaborated with Leone on the screenplay for *Fistful of Dollars* (*Per un pugno di dollari*, 1964).[2] Through the good graces of Tessari, Argento submitted a screen treatment to Leone, hoping to interest the older man in bringing it to the screen. Nothing happened out of the meeting on an immediate practical level, but it marked the start of an important friendship in Argento's life. As he would later recall, "His honesty was disarming, but I felt comfortable around him. Sergio had straightforward ideas and always said what he had on his mind. [...] He told me about his projects, about how he worked; also,

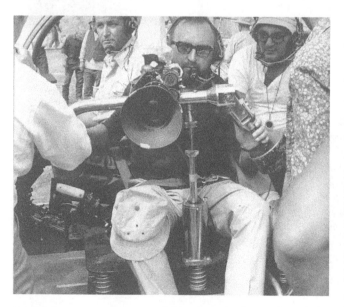

Sergio Leone on the set of *The Good, The Bad and the Ugly*.

very naturally, he talked about directing. [...] I was 26 years old and I was nobody. He was about 40 and he was already considered a *maestro*. For a reason I can't explain, we became friends."[3]

Now flash forward to December 23, and *The Good, The Bad and The Ugly* becomes Leone's biggest box-office hit to date. On one level, he's looking to leave the Western and try his hand at fresh fields; on the other, the success inspires him to think big and to try and outdo himself with his biggest, most ambitious Western. Sooner than rely upon his usual collaborators, he decided to look for a couple of younger, "hipper" writers to work on developing a fresh screen story. Bernardo Bertolucci (1941-2018), already well-regarded for having written and directed *The Grim Reaper* (*La commare secca*, 1962) and *Before the Revolution* (*Prima della rivoluzione*, 1964), was an odd choice on the face of it—but it pointed to Leone's art-house aspirations. Having proven his commercial muscle, Leone wanted to cement his reputation as a serious artist—and having a hot young director like Bertolucci on board to create the screen story was a step in the right direction. Sooner than rely exclusively upon Bertolucci, Leone decided to take a chance on Dario Argento and asked him to participate in the process as well. Argento's involvement in the film has sometimes been exaggerated in fan circles, but there's no denying that it was a seminal experience—and it undoubtedly opened many doors for him moving forward. "That day when he gave me an appointment, I was very emotional," writes Argento. "When I entered his office, there was another person I knew from sight; his name was Bernardo Bertolucci. Sergio asked us both generic questions, and we both would take turns answering, one after another. I knew right away that Bernardo was the most insolent, the most detached of us. He had already worked with Pasolini and had directed some of his own creations. […] I was intimidated by Sergio Leone, as it was obvious that he was putting me to the test. He suddenly asked if we'd like to write a movie for him. In fact, he wasn't asking. When we entered his office this morning it was like we were already hired. […] He could have the best screenwriters in the world, yet, to write the story for his next movie, he chose two young men, two up-and-coming hopefuls in the cinema, so to speak. It was incredible."[4] Bertolucci's recollection of his involvement in the project is somewhat more pragmatic—but don't forget, he was already an established filmmaker, so participating in a project like this wasn't as life-altering an experience. As he explained to Sir Christopher Frayling, "In the first place, I got involved because I didn't have any *lire*. Also, because, in the late 1960s, I liked the way some popular Italian films were going. I thought that Sergio Leone was brilliant—brilliant and vulgar at the same time. But I did not know him. On the first day *The Good, the Bad and the Ugly* was shown in Italy, I met Leone—in the projection booth. The day after, he called me and asked me to write the movie. I wrote a huge treatment—about 300 pages, full of 'quotes' from all the Westerns I love. Some of the 'quotes' even Leone did not recognize ... And I wanted to write the whole script, but I didn't, so I lost most of the money."[5] Interestingly, Bertolucci's recollection makes no mention at all of Dario—but Leone was clear on the point: the three of them wrote the story together.

How things progressed from there seems to depend on who you ask. It's generally agreed that the process relied largely upon Leone arranging screenings of every single Western he could get his hands upon for Argento and Bertolucci. He wanted them to take notes—to write down the best elements and then distill them into a virtual encyclopedia of Western cinema clichés and tropes. Argento and Bertolucci sat through everything from *Stagecoach* (1939) and *The Searchers* (1956) to *Red River* (1948) and *Johnny Guitar* (1954) and Leone would grill them afterwards, asking the young film buffs what they thought the most significant elements were. According to Argento, "Everyone worked on their own, then we met with Leone to submit our ideas. […] After six wonderful months, we had a first draft of 80 pages. We slowly shaped what was to become *Once Upon a Time in the West*, but it wasn't always easy."[6]

That's Argento's account. According to Leone, Bertolucci and Argento worked on the treatment for two months. Bertolucci claimed it was four months. As to the exact nature of the collaboration, Leone later remarked, "So we met, the three of us, and began to dream together. Very soon Dario Argento felt himself being overtaken. But Bernardo and I went further and further, always making reference to the American cinema we admired. Argento remained as a spectator, watching all the exchanges between us. He gave good advice and was, above all, good company."[7]

In any event, Argento's involvement in what became *Once Upon a Time in the West* (*C'era una volta il West*, 1968) drew to a close by the end of the first half of 1967; production was to have started in March 1968 but was delayed until April of that year, by which point Argento was long gone from the project. The actual shooting schedule, as outlined by Sir Christopher Frayling in *Once Upon a Time in the West: Shooting a Masterpiece*, stretched from April 1 through the May 10 in Italy, followed by a stint in Spain (bouncing back and forth between Almería, La Calahorra, and Guadix) which lasted from May 14 through July 29; the production wrapped in America,

Italian advertising for *Once Upon a Time in the West*.

with locations in and around Monument Valley in Arizona (revered by cinephiles as the favorite location of director John Ford), which lasted from August 2 until August 10.[8]

Once Leone had the treatment by Argento and Bertolucci in hand, he recruited his friend Sergio Donati (born 1933; he would go on to collaborate with Leone on his next picture, *Duck You Sucker/Giù, la testa*, 1971) to work with him in writing the finished filming script. Neither Argento nor Bertolucci had a hand in writing the actual script, though some of the more over-enthusiastic Argento buffs will insist upon arguing the contrary. That there are elements in the film which seem to be in line with Argento's own later works is undeniable. However, the chain of influence is often misinterpreted and misunderstood. Leone wasn't learning tricks from Argento; it was the other way around. Thus, for example, it is understandable that the touches of quirky humor—notably, gunslinger Jack Elam catching a fly in the barrel of his gun—may seem roughly analogous to the scene in *Four Flies on Grey Velvet*, where drummer Roberto Tobias (Michael Brandon) smashes a pestering insect between his cymbals. But while some fans will argue this as proof that this scene *had* to have originated with Argento, the more realistic explanation is that Argento recalled the scene from *Once Upon a Time in the West* and decided to include something like it in his own movie. None of this should undercut the significance of *Once Upon a Time in the West* in Argento's career, but it helps to keep things in perspective and not jump to the assumption that his role in the script was anything more than it really was. Indeed, Sergio Donati would later take exception to Argento playing up his involvement in interviews and he reportedly went so far as to threaten legal action if he continued to do so. In an interview with *L'Italo American* in 2015, Donati said, "Several years ago, a restored version of *Once Upon A Time in the West* was screened at the Rome Film Fest. In that occasion, Dario Argento introduced himself as co-screenwriter for the movie, rather than simply co-author with Bernardo Bertolucci of the initial story, from whom I and Leone developed the film."[9] Questions of authorship aside, the experience of working for Sergio Leone was of major importance to Argento—and with the experience under his wing, he was able to use it as a calling card to get further employment in the Italian film industry.

Over the next several years, Argento busied himself writing scripts in addition to performing a bit of cosmetic surgery on scripts penned by other authors. First up, he and Raimondo Del Balzo (1939-1995) were brought in to do a bit of work on Francesco Prosperi (1926-2004) and Giovanni Simonelli (1926-2007)'s script for *Every Man Is My Enemy* (*Qualcuno ha tradito*, 1967). Directed by Prosperi, it is a crime thriller and it features fading American star Robert Webber (1924-1989) as Tony, a safecracker who arrives in Marseille looking to pull off a major heist. Things become complicated when he runs into an old friend (Pierre Zimmer) who is now working as a police inspector.

As is with most of the scripts which followed, it's difficult to really pin down the precise nature of Argento's contribution to *Every Man Is My Enemy*; he isn't even credited on all versions of the film. He had nothing to do with the development of the actual screen story, which was the work of Prosperi and Simonelli, and likely he was brought in late in the game to help give the dialogue a polish. That aside, however, the film emerges as a surprisingly taut and enjoyable heist thriller. Prosperi's direction includes some flashy flourishes which wouldn't have been out of place in one of Argento's own films (framing a shot through the empty barrels in a gun, for example) and the anti-hero's subjective, sepia-tinted flashbacks to traumatic events also point the way to a recurring motif in Dario's later work. The almost fetishistic attention to detail in the preparation and execution of the robbery also adds considerable interest,

Spanish poster for *Every Man Is My Enemy*.

while there are some welcome touches of grim humor—as in the cut from a scene of violence to a close-up of a little boy devouring an ice cream cone. Webber adds the right touch of world-weary resignation to his role as the safe cracker, while the supporting cast includes a brief appearance by the character actor Umberto Raho (1922-2016), who would go on to make memorable appearances in Argento's first two films as a director.

1968 would prove to be a banner year for Argento. The script work continued to flow. *Once Upon a Time in the West* went into production in April and premiered in Rome in December (though it didn't go into general release in Italy until the following May). And, most significantly, he elected to take a very big step in his personal life. Dario and Marisa had gotten engaged in 1965 and they remained very much in love; they had their problems, as all couples do, but they both believed that they had found true love and that they would be together for the rest of their lives. They decided, like so many young people, that the key to life was to learn from the mistakes of their parents; where they had failed, they would succeed. It was a period of great optimism and they were determined to make the most of it. Perhaps seeking to ensure that their life as man and wife would remain as drama-free as possible, they made a bold move: they would marry in secret, savoring the moment on their own, without their parents getting in the way. "This is why, almost like a bad joke and without thinking too much about the consequences, we got married without inviting them. [...] I remember us being very calm and unaffected. We were young and, to us, it was a beautiful thing. We liked the idea of taking this big step behind their backs so to speak. The wedding day was for us alone."[10] Married life would be good for the young couple, though inevitably they hit a few roadblocks along the way. The nature of Argento's work necessitated a great deal of alone time, but fortunately for him, Marisa seemed to be of an understanding disposition. "Marisa left me lots of freedom. I went out whenever I wanted, and I often came home late. Sometimes I would lock myself away in my office a whole day to write in total solitude."[11] It's just as well, too, as things were beginning to take off for Dario on a professional level. Word was getting around about his involvement in *Once Upon a Time in the West*, and the anticipation building over that film signaled a change in attitude with regards to its director, Sergio Leone. He had initially been seen as a "mere" populist filmmaker, but as his films grew in size, it became apparent that he was no mere journeyman. *Once Upon a Time in the West* was, in a way, conceived as his attempt at wooing the art-house crowd; it would be a Western, yes, but a very special kind of a Western. Having come from a background writing about film for *Paese Sera*, Argento was coming into his own as a "player" in the field in his own right. Throughout 1967 and 1968, he continued to contribute to screenplays; sometimes writing them from scratch, sometimes coming in to polish the rough edges of other writers' work.

Following *Every Man Is My Enemy*, Argento spent the next several months working on a slew of different subjects in a variety of different genres. Now, Argento the director is known for specializing in a particular field—horror and suspense, specifically—but Argento the writer was able to adjust to working in a number of different styles. Had his personal situation been a little different, it's not inconceivable to imagine him working as a "jack of all genres" as a director, much in the same way as the other major Italian horror/suspense directors (Mario Bava, Lucio Fulci, and Riccardo Freda) had done before him. However, his situation was rather different from theirs, as shall be discussed. These early days of screenwriting were a different matter, however. By his own admission, he really wasn't at ease with every assignment he found himself working on. Naturally he was already comfortable working within the confines of the Western genre—he had pretty much started at the top, working for Leone, so it wasn't as if he was a novice in that field. Thus, he enjoyed the process of writing such films as *Today We Kill, Tomorrow We Die! (Oggi a me ... domani a te*, 1968) for Tonino Cervi and *The 5-Man Army (Un esercito di 5 uomini*, 1969) for the American director Don Taylor, but he was less at ease with his forays into war movies like *Commandos* (1968) and *Battle of the Commandos (La legione dei dannati*, 1969). "I never liked war movies. I only did them for the money."[12]

Today We Kill, Tomorrow We Die! became the first of the westerns co-written by Dario to be released to cinemas—though his involvement in it came well after *Once Upon a Time in the West* as well as his contested participation in Robert Hossein's *Cemetery Without Crosses* (more on that in a bit). This is easily explained by the fact that, unlike those other films, *Today We Kill* was a modest production—one of many low budget Italian Westerns being churned out to accommodate the public's interest in the genre. *Once Upon a Time in the West* was a major epic, of course, while the Hossein film also had a bit more scale and grandeur to it; by comparison, this offering from Tonino Cervi (1929-2002) is more in keeping with the general *filone* (streamlet) principle of the period, whereby cheap knock-offs sought to cash in on the popularity of the big hits at the box office.

American actor Brett Halsey (born 1933) was approached to play the lead; like Eastwood before him, he started at Universal in the 1950s and made his way to Rome during the great glut in Italian film production. Unlike Eastwood, he wasn't able to parlay his Roman holiday into international stardom, but he proved to be an agreeable, likable leading man and he brought a lot of charisma to his roles; when given a chance to do so, he also displayed genuine acting ability—though the quality of the scripts he was given to work with often did him no favors. One would think that the Argento/Cervi script stood out from the pack, but apparently that was not the case. By his own admission, Halsey wasn't keen on doing the film—he was feeling tired and he didn't believe in the script. When the production company agreed to allow him to use *a nom de plume*, he reluctantly signed on the dotted line.[13] It proved to be ironic on a couple of levels: for one, despite appearing under a phony name, the film actually preserves Halsey's speaking voice, though he ended up being dubbed by others in most of his Italian pictures; for another, the film was so successful at the Italian box office that Halsey was obliged to appear in his next westerns (*Wrath of God/L'ira di Dio* and *Kidnapping/Kidnapping! Pago o uccidiamo tuo figlio*, both 1969) under the same name: Montgomery Wood.

Argento and Cervi were clearly inspired by the John Sturges-directed Western *The Magnificent Seven* (1960), itself a thinly veiled remake of Kurosawa's *The Seven Samurai* (*Shichinin no samurai*, 1954). In fact, the model proved to be something of a favorite for Dario, who would also use it as the template for his next Western script, *The 5-Man Army*. The setup is relatively simple: Bill Kiowa (Halsey, aka Montgomery Ford) is released from prison following a five year sentence. When he gets out, he's determined to settle an old score with Elfego (Tatsuya Nakadai), a former friend who betrayed him and raped and murdered his wife. Kiowa rounds up a group of seasoned killers and sets out to get his revenge.

Today We Kill, Tomorrow We Die! may be lacking in originality, but it's realized with tremendous energy by Tonino Cervi, here making his debut as a director following a period as a producer and production manager. Plot is de-emphasized in favor of mood as the second half of the picture becomes one long game of cat and mouse between Kiowa and Elfego. There's a long, protracted sequence set in a spooky forest at night with various gunmen stalking each other and then killing each other off—all things considered, it plays a bit like the sort of thriller scenario that Argento would later relocate into the urban setting for his *gialli*. Cervi ticks all the boxes, including a nicely staged final duel between the two antagonists. One particularly inspired moment occurs when a character is killed and looks towards the heavens, trying to make sense of what has happened; Cervi includes a point of view shot of the bare branches of the trees bowing in the wind and it adds a nice touch of melancholy to the scene. Just as in *Every Man Is My Enemy*, there's even a sepia-tinted flashback detailing the betrayal of Kiowa by Elfego, the latter of whom emerges as a truly formidable villain. Halsey is nicely understated as the taciturn, psychologically wounded warrior, while the supporting cast includes such familiar Spaghetti Western veterans as Bud Spencer (real name Carlo Pedersoli, 1929-2016) and William Berger (1928-1993). Halsey and Spencer would both be reunited with Dario later on—Halsey went on to appear in one of the *Turno di notte* segments of the Argento-hosted *Giallo* TV series, while Spencer was memorably featured in *The 5-Man Army* and *Four Flies on Grey Velvet*.

The gangster film *Comandamenti per un gangster* (1968) is basically a Western in modern dress, and it was the first of Dario's projects to be produced by Salvatore Argento. Though set in Canada, it was actually filmed in Yugoslavia, with a largely Yugoslavian cast and crew. The director and co-writer, Alfio Caltabiano (1932-2007), was an experienced stuntman, choreographer, and master of arms who had been active in the Italian cinema scene since the mid-1950s. *Comandamenti* was his second crack at directing and he would only go on to direct a handful more pictures into the early 1970s; that's a pity, really, as he displays a kinetic sense of pacing here which is ideally suited to the genre.

The story deals with a retired gangster, Northon (Ljuba Tadic), who is anxious to avenge the death of his sister. He teams up with a Mexican gangster known as "Five Cents" (Caltabiano), and they follow a trail of clues which leads them to a sunken treasure which is somehow connected with the mob. They find a formidable foe in the form of rival gangster Alberto Torio (Rade Marcović), also known as "Santo," who proceeds to make life very difficult for the pair of them. They eventually find their way to the sunken treasure—but of course Torio is hot on their heels.

Comandamenti per un gangster is a surprisingly tense yet playful film, one which is undeserving of being so very obscure; sadly the film has yet to receive an English-friendly home video release so whatever virtues the dialogue may possess will be lost on many viewers. That said, Argento and Caltabiano's script is clear and loaded with action, and Caltabiano directs with a sure and steady hand which belies his comparative lack of experience behind the camera. Caltabiano also appears in the crucial role of the gangster known as "Five Cents"—precisely the sort of colorful but basically humane "bandito with a heart of gold" role which crops up in the form of Jason Robards' Cheyenne in *Once Upon a Time in the West*. The opening of the film is particularly riveting: we follow several men as they flee from an unseen aggressor. As Caltabiano cuts back and forth between the three men, they all appear to find refuge—only to then be shockingly dispatched by an off-screen assailant. It has something of the feel of a *giallo*, and the whodunit aspect remains in place until late in the film when the identity of the man responsible for killing the anti-hero's sister is finally revealed. Add in plenty of close-ups of hands clad in black leather gloves and an important clue being imparted by a chatty parrot and a lot of the tropes which would become so familiar in Argento's later films start to come into focus. The film also benefits from a colorful, baroque villain with a religion fetish and a propensity for dressing in an opera cloak and playing the organ at full tilt. The end result is briskly paced, unpretentious and frequently exciting, and the impact is aided immeasurably by a grand soundtrack from Ennio Morricone (1928-2020).

Morricone and Argento's paths would continue to cross over the next couple of years, culminating in the composer being invited to provide the scores for Argento's first three pictures as a director. A curious detail worth noting. The screenplay credit is afforded prominence above the cast list (which is a mess of "English-sounding" pseudonyms, such as "Sir John," which the present writer is unable to decipher; since so much of the cast is comprised of Yugoslavian talent, it's impossible to recognize most of the cast in relation to the

Italian *locandina* for *Comandamenti per un gangster*; artist unknown.

Italian film scene). Could this have been Salvatore's way of giving his son star billing of sorts? It's not common to see the screenplay credit moved up to such a prominent placement in the opening titles; the only other example that comes to mind is Mario Bava's blackly comic *giallo Twitch of the Death Nerve* (*Reazione a catena*, 1971).

Argento's next screenwriting credits would prove to be a lot less rewarding. First up was a war film called *Commandos* (1968), directed by Armando Crispino (1924-2003). Like Argento, Crispino would later go on to work in the *giallo*—albeit with far less commercial success. Even so, both *The Dead Are Alive* (*L'etrusco uccide ancora*, 1972)

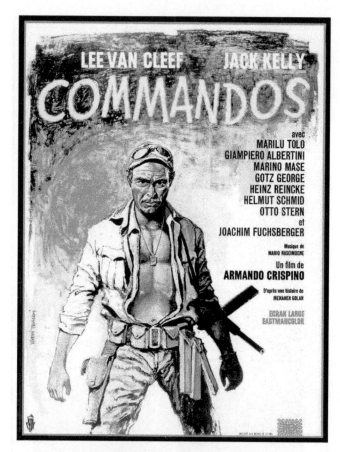

French poster art for *Commandos*; artwork by Vanni Teal.

and especially *Autopsy* (*Macchie solari*, 1975) are well worth seeing and stand well apart from the usual Argento cash-ins which flooded the Italian marketplace during that time. For Argento, the film was "a depressing, squalid experience. It was during this film I wondered about quitting the industry because there seemed to be nothing creative or artistic in the movie world."[14] Obviously his lack of affinity for the war genre worked against him, but he also found the film to be a chaotic experience requiring lots of on-the-spot rewriting; it was precisely the opposite of the more tranquil and serene way he preferred to work and it really took it out of him. Crispino would later recall their collaboration with ambivalence: "Personally, I don't feel I owe anything to Argento, who wrote the screenplay for my film *Commandos*; I think, instead, that Argento has taken things from me, except that I haven't been as good as him at selling myself and have not been as successful."[15] In truth, Crispino's words ring of sour grapes; if anything, it was Crispino who benefitted from the sudden interest in *gialli* triggered by Argento's films—and beyond the most superficial of factors, the work of the two men really couldn't have been much more different. There's no doubt that the tremendous success Dario enjoyed in a few years' time ruffled the feathers of a few people in the business, however, for reasons which will soon become apparent.

Sergeant Sullivan (Lee Van Cleef) is charged with assembling a group of Italian American soldiers for a top-secret mission in North Africa. The objective is to infiltrate an Italian camp and take control of the water supply for the Allies. Sullivan and his crew are joined by an ambitious Captain (Jack Kelly) who seems more concerned with his military record than he is with the safety of his men. As the Captain and Sullivan butt heads, they manage to take control of the Italian camp—but they soon find themselves rubbing shoulders with the enemy when a group of German soldiers make an unexpected visit.

Argento's name appears last in the screenplay credit—his name notably smaller than the ones which precede it. More than likely this was another case of his coming in late in the process to do some polishing and rewriting—and given his later recollections of having to perform script surgery as the filming unfolded, it's not surprising that he found it to be such an unpleasant experience. The film itself is well made, even suspenseful in places, but it is also much too long at about two hours (though it would be shortened substantially for U.S. consumption) and the pacing suffers accordingly. Once again there is an emphasis on a psychologically fragile protagonist—this time, the outwardly rugged and tough Sergeant Sullivan—who suffers from fragmented flashbacks which haunt him periodically throughout the picture.

Lee Van Cleef (1925-1989) is effortlessly convincing as the brash protagonist; nobody could sneer with greater authority, yet he is quite capable of conveying the character's more vulnerable characteristics, as well. Amid a solid supporting cast, it's particularly nice to see Marilù Tolo (born 1944) as a brutalized prostitute

Sergeant Sullivan (Lee Van Cleef) ponders the futility of war.

Sergeant Sullivan (Lee Van Cleef) and Corbi (Pier Paolo Capponi) mean business in *Commandos*.

and Pier Paolo Capponi (1938-2018) as one of the soldiers. Within a few years, Tolo would become a very important part of Dario's life, though evidently, they didn't actually meet during the filming of this picture, while Capponi would appear in a substantial role in *The Cat O'Nine Tails*. Much of the story is concerned with the war of wills between the Sergeant and his ambitious but inexperienced superior; that Sullivan himself comes off as such a disagreeable, even unbalanced sort rather undermines the dramatic potential of the conflict, however. In an interesting, seemingly intentional inversion of genre formula, the only character who appears truly sympathetic and likable is an avuncular German Lieutenant played by *krimi* star Joachim Fuchsberger (1927-2014).[16] Mario Nascimbene (1913-2002)'s solid if unspectacular soundtrack adds a touch of creepiness by quoting from the "Die Israe," while the widescreen images and impressive battle scenes ensure that the film appears appropriately "epic."

La rivoluzione sessuale did little to boost Argento's ego, either. "I revised an existing screenplay, a routine job. I can't say it belongs to me at all."[17] The film was based on the writings of the famed psychoanalyst Wilhelm Reich (1897-1957). Reich firmly believed that many of the ills affecting society were rooted in bourgeois morality and that by freeing oneself from these artificial rules of conduct and learning to embrace sex without being burdened with emotions such as love and jealousy, society would flourish. His writings included *The Sexual Revolution* (*Die Sexualität im Kulturkampf*), which was published in 1936. Like so many of his writings, it pushed the idea that people are burdened by social structure and that by repressing our natural sexual urges, we allow our baser instincts to take hold. His ideas were controversial, to say the least, and he ended up fleeing to America in the 1930s in order to escape the Nazi regime. He continued to write and even developed a machine known as an "orgone accumulator"—a large box which people could sit inside and was reputed to have the ability to harness positive energies connected to the libido; it was his contention that being exposed to these energies could have positive physical side effects, including the possibility to cure various ailments. When the Food and Drug Administration got wind of this, they slapped him with an injunction forbidding him to continue the sale of these untested publications and devices—but when he continued to do so anyway, he ended up being sentenced to jail in Lewisburg, Pennsylvania; he died of heart failure while he was serving his sentence.

Writer/director Riccardo Ghione (1922-2003) saw *The Sexual Revolution* as a good starting point for a "hip" sort of counter-culture movie, and he wrote the initial draft himself before enlisting Argento to help out with a bit of polishing. The story focuses on a Wilhelm substitute, Emilio Missiroli (Riccardo Cucciolla), who gathers several of his friends, students, and even his own wife and takes them to an off-season hotel by the sea. Since it's out of season, they have the full run of the place and Missiroli sets out to prove his thesis that social unrest is caused by stifled libidos. Using a "democratic," chance-based system, he draws names from two hats (one containing the names of the males, the other containing the names of the females, as his study doesn't appear to encompass bisexuality, homosexuality, and the

Cover art for the CD release of Teo Usuelli's soundtrack for *La rivoluzione sessuale* (*The Sexual Revolution*); artwork by "Aller"/Carlo Alessandrini.

Italian poster art for *La rivoluzione sessuale*; artwork by "Aller"/Carlo Alessandrini.

like) and each night the gathered disciples are paired off with a different lover. Unfortunately for Missiroli, the experiment proves to be a flop—love rears its head, as does its ugly twin: jealousy, and one of the participants is driven to commit suicide before the police come in and break the whole thing up.

La rivoluzione sessuale is an interesting curio. On the one hand, it manages to be playful and erotic; on the other, it feels half-baked and occasionally crashes under the burden of its own pomposity—nowhere is this more evident than in a painfully protracted sequence in which the characters don "far out" costumes and engage in a sort of "love-in." The cast is certainly game, and the likes of Laura Antonelli in the nude gives the film plenty of exploitation ammo, but it is easy to see why the film has drifted into obscurity. Given the tenuous nature of Argento's involvement in the enterprise, it's not really surprising that it doesn't appear to be among his favorite screenwriting experiences.

During this period, Dario's feelings about being a screenwriter were decidedly mixed. The money was good—which obviously was a major concern for him and Marisa—and he was working steadily, but it was seldom on projects he was particularly enthusiastic about. Nevertheless, the majority of these films were firmly in the "B" cinema category and must have felt like a comedown for Dario following the euphoria he experienced working with Sergio Leone and Bernardo Bertolucci; he would remain on friendly terms with both men, but they never collaborated officially ever again. Bertolucci would help Argento by suggesting a particularly significant literary property to him, but that's still a little further along in our story. Leone, of course, was destined to only direct two more features following *Once Upon a Time in the West*: *Duck You Sucker* (*Giù la testa*, 1971) and *Once Upon a Time in America* (1984). There would be at least one significant crossover between the latter title and Argento's own work, but that, too, is further along in the narrative. Bertolucci would follow the Leone experience by resuming his directing career, first with "challenging" works with virtually no mainstream appeal, such as *Partner* (1968), then with major crossover art-house hits like *The Conformist* (*Il conformista*, 1970) and, most infamously, *Last Tango in Paris* (*Ultimo tango a Parigi*, 1972). Bertolucci's work made him into one of the most respected filmmakers of his generation; Argento would find commercial success, but his choice of subject matter made him a trickier proposition for the *intelligentsia*. In the late '60s, however, he was still very much a film critic transitioning into making films—and while not every experience would prove to be equally pleasurable, they all provided important "on the job" training which would soon enable him to open yet another door.

Once Upon a Time in the West tells of Jill McBain (Claudia Cardinale), a former prostitute turned lady, who moves from New Orleans to the old West, where she is to join her new husband, Brett McBain (Frank Wolff). By the time she arrives, Brett and his entire family have been mercilessly killed by a gunman named Frank (Henry Fonda), who is in the employ of the railroad tycoon Mr. Mortimer (Gabriele Ferzetti). Mortimer is anxious to create a trans-Atlantic railroad and the McBain estate happens to fall right in the middle of the land he is looking to buy in order to realize his ambitious dream; McBain refused to sell and paid the ultimate price. Jill is no push-over, herself, and she also refuses to cooperate. She finds allies in the form of a bandit named Cheyenne (Jason Robards) and a mysterious stranger known as Harmonica (Charles Bronson), who has a score to settle with Frank.

From its opening, protracted credit sequence—depicting the fate of three gunmen (Al Mulock, Woody Strode, and Jack Elam) who attempt to get the jump on Harmonica at the train station—to its final, perversely satisfying reveal of the primal trauma which haunts

Harmonica, *Once Upon a Time in the West* is one of the most beautifully directed pictures ever made. Leone's control of the medium is in evidence throughout and he is ably complemented in his efforts by Carlo Simi (1924-2000)'s beautiful costume and production design work, the glorious widescreen vistas of cinematographer Tonino Delli Colli (1923-2005) and, best of all, the extraordinary music by Ennio Morricone. In some respects, it's a thin story for such a long film—nearly 3 hours in its original edit, though it would be cut down for U.S. theatrical consumption by Paramount to 2 hours and 25 minutes—but story isn't really what the film is all about. It's an elegiac meditation on the death of the Old West (symbolized by the emergence of the railroad), and it's also something of a compendium of elements cribbed from Leone's favorite Westerns. Leone allows scenes to unfold in a stately manner, which may prove off-putting for some viewers; those who are sympathetic to his aims, however, will find it a mesmerizing experience.

The director's mastery of cinematic technique was already in evidence in *For a Few Dollars More* and *The Good, the Bad and the Ugly* (his first features, including *Fistful of Dollars*, can't help but look a little crude by comparison), but this film allows him the scope to really show off his stuff, as it were. The higher-than-usual budget also allowed for a starry cast, all of whom rise to the occasion. Claudia Cardinale (born 1938) was an unusual choice for a subject such as this, but she lends equal measures of dignity and sensuality as the former "working girl" who stands up to the railroad tycoon and his hired goons. Charles Bronson (1921-2003) and Henry Fonda (1905-1982) had both famously rejected earlier overtures by Leone to appear in *Fistful of Dollars* and *For a Few Dollars More*—of the former, Bronson is reputed to have said that it was one of the worst scripts he'd ever read—but they ended up being perfectly cast in this film. Bronson's minimalist, stoic acting style is sometimes misconstrued as non-acting, but in fact he often displayed a remarkable ability to convey a wide range of emotions behind his stony facial expressions; his take on Harmonica as a traumatized warrior looking to confront the past and make peace with the present is beautifully rendered. As for Fonda, well known for portraying men of virtue in American Westerns, he provides the film with one of the most black-hearted villains in the genre's history. As the story goes, Fonda showed up in Rome with several days' worth of stubble and brown contact lenses obscuring his natural blue eyes, figuring this was the sort of look the character called for; Leone took one look at him and told him to shave and take out the contacts. Fonda finally caught on to Leone's intentions when the time came to film the scene where he massacres McBain and his children. "Very slowly the camera comes around and that's what Sergio was going for all the time. The main heavy. 'Jesus Christ, it's Henry Fonda!'"[18] As for Jason Robards (1922-2000), he may have been a curious choice to play a Mexican bandit, but he delivers a brilliant performance and it's he, rather than Cardinale, who really provides the film with its heart and soul; Cheyenne may be a cliché "bandito with a heart of gold" on the page, but with Robards' hang-dog expression and soulful eyes, he comes to represent the conflicting emotions of the Old West.

At the end of 1968, *Once Upon a Time in the West* premiered in Rome. Many were confused by the elegiac style; they were accustomed to the more raucous style of Leone's earlier Westerns, and this was clearly a very

Italian poster for *Once Upon a Time in the West*; artwork by Rodolfo Gaspari.

different proposition. It did excellent business in Italy, ultimately grossing $3.8 million compared to the $4.3 million netted by *The Good, The Bad and The Ugly*, and coming in at number 3 for the 1968-1969 box-office season in Italy.[19] In a way, it's easy to understand why it failed to surpass the box office of its predecessor. *The Good, The Bad and The Ugly* is a party film—it's lively, energetic and loaded with humor; *Once Upon a Time in the West* is deliberately slow and while it's not devoid of humor, it can't really be described as a rollicking good time. In a sense, it's the *Inferno* to Leone's *Suspiria*, if you'll pardon the comparison.

The film's salvation came in France, where it was enthusiastically received as a masterpiece and played in at least one local theater for two years.[20] The American reception was disastrous. Following some negative preview screenings in New York, Paramount arranged to have the film cut down; the thought was, remove some of the running time and you'll speed up the pace. Not so. It was still a slow movie—only now it was shorter, and far less coherent. Critics unimpressed by the film probably didn't look to the names of Argento and Bertolucci in the titles as a good omen; as luck would have it, of course, many of Argento's films would suffer a similar fate in the U.S. market, often being cut to the point of incomprehensibility by distributors who didn't care a damn about "art." Sadly, the same fate would befall Leone's next (and final) two works. Both *Duck You Sucker* (rechristened as *Fistful of Dynamite*, partly in the hopes of conjuring nostalgia for *Fistful of Dollars*, and partly because the title was nonsense, anyway; this despite Leone's insistence that "duck, you sucker" was a common American expression) and also, *Once Upon a Time in America* would suffer mightily due to cuts imposed by the American distributors. Leone took the wreckage of his long-gestating American epic very badly; some have suggested it directly contributed to his death from a heart attack in 1989 at the much-too-young age of 60. Time is the true test, however, and *Once Upon a Time in the West* would ultimately find the praise it so richly deserved. It is now regarded as the apex of the so-called "Spaghetti Western," which is perhaps underrating it ever-so-slightly, for it deserves to be known as one of the great films, period.

Cemetery Without Crosses (*Une corde, un colt...*, 1969) is a bit confusing where Argento's participation is concerned. His name is nowhere to be found on the French credits for the film; as the film is essentially a French production with some Italian co-financing, this is a point worth stressing. Added to that, director/star Robert Hossein (born 1927) has gone on record stating that Argento had nothing to do with the film.[21] It's certainly not uncommon for Italian films to contain phony credits for quota purposes—years later, Argento's *Mother of Tears* would add a couple of Italian names to the Italian advertising and print credits for that same reason—and in this instance it seems likely that this was the case where Argento's participation was involved. The film was an ambitious ode to the films of Sergio Leone; don't forget, in France, Leone was already lionized as a great director, while in Italy the critics were still a little unsure of his worth. Hossein and Leone were personal friends, and Leone was flattered when Hossein extended an invitation for him make a cameo appearance in the movie, which shot from January through March 1968; Leone was still a few months away from starting filming on *Once Upon a Time in the West*, so he accepted the offer. In fact, Leone returned the favor by casting Hossein in the role of the bartender in *Once Upon a Time in the West*, but that didn't pan out and American actor Lionel Stander (1908-1994) ended up playing the part instead. In an interview with Christopher Frayling, Carla Leone, the great director's widow, commented: "Sergio loved him a lot, because Hossein was completely crazy. *Simpatico*, a fascinating man. His father André used to write music for movie soundtracks ... Hossein asked him to be as bold as he liked with the role, although Sergio didn't participate in the making of the film."[22]

Contrary to Carla Leone's memory, Hossein later claimed that Leone did him a

Sergio Leone (in white hat, back to the camera) directs the shocking flashback reveal of *Once Upon a Time in the West*; this plot twist would have a major influence on Dario's own work as a director.

Italian poster art for *Cemetery Without Crosses*; artist unknown.

favor by directing the dinner scene during his visit to the production. In any event, Hossein theorized that Leone may well have shown Dario the script at some point, but he is insistent that he did not actually collaborate in any way in the writing of the film, which Hossein did with his usual writing partner, Claude Desailly (1922-2009). As for Argento, his main memory of Hossein is wryly amusing: "I loved Hossein because when we spoke about the script in his Rome house there were always semi-naked ladies popping in and out of the bedroom."[23] Other than that, Argento has never made any great claims for his participation in the film, so perhaps it was just a matter of batting a few ideas back and forth in between rounds of ogling half-naked ladies. Hossein and Argento would reunite many years later for the ill-fated Lucio Fulci "comeback" vehicle *Wax Mask* (*M.D.C.—Maschera di cera*, 1997).

The story deals with a woman, Maria Caine (Michèle Mercier), who witnesses the brutal lynching of her husband by the Rogers clan. Determined to have revenge on the men who were responsible, Maria reaches out to a loner named Manuel (Robert Hossein) for assistance. Manuel accepts her offer and worms his way into the Rogers household, where he begins to put Maria's plans into motion.

A dark, embittered take on the Western genre, *Cemetery Without Crosses* is more concerned with the psychology of its characters than it is with the usual genre tropes, including gunfights. There's plenty of violence, make no mistake, but the deliberately slow pacing and the generally introspective, even melancholy approach help to differentiate it from many of the other Euro westerns of the period.

Hossein's debt to Leone is definitely in evidence, and he even dedicated the film to the great director. Nevertheless, given the contested nature of Dario's participation in the writing of the script, it would be dangerous to try and ascribe any of its peculiar qualities to him; if indeed he did have some input into the script, it's a worthy addition to his early filmography—if he was merely credited for quota purposes on the Italian prints, as Hossein would have it, there were certainly far worse films he could have arbitrarily had his name affixed to.

Argento may have been disappointed by the quality of his screenwriting assignments post-Leone, but he continued to soldier on writing for *Paese Sera* while also working on various films as the opportunity arose. Along with *Once Upon a Time in the West*, the most prestigious of his early works as a writer—and the one which had the biggest impact on his transition to becoming a director in his own right—was *Metti, una sera a cena* (literally, "Suppose, One Night at Dinner," though when it played at the Juliet I & II in New York City in November 1971,

Italian advertising for *Metti, una sera a cena*.

Italian *locandina* for *Metti, una sera a cena*.

they advertised it as *One Night at Dinner*). The project was an adaptation of the hit stage play of the same name, written by writer/director Giuseppe Patroni Griffi. Griffi (1921-2005) was eager to bring the project to the screen, but he was having a difficult time convincing prospective backers of its cinematic potential. Argento's reputation for polishing "difficult" material put him in good stead with producers Marina Cicogna (born 1934) and Giovanni Bertolucci (1940-2005). The Bertolucci connection is significant, by the way; Giovanni was the cousin of Bernardo, and it's highly likely that he was also aware of Dario by virtue of his connection with *Once Upon a Time in the West*. In any event, Argento was tasked with translating a talky treatise on sexual politics into a workable and cinematic screenplay and he rose to the challenge. "[...] I was called in to make Griffi's dialogue less static. I actually ended up changing everything to make it better and that's what showed producers I could handle such an adaptation. Griffi was angry with me and hated what I did—until it became a massive hit in Italy and he told me, Oh, I always thought it was wonderful work."[24]

The story tells of a complex web of friendship and sex. Michele (Jean-Louis Trintignant) is an acclaimed writer who has "sold out" by writing screenplays for a fat paycheck. His wife Nina (Florinda Bolkan) is involved in a long-running affair with Michele's best friend, a vain actor named Max (Tony Musante). Max, looking to spice things up with Nina, brings in his sometime-lover, Ric (Lino Capolicchio), a would-be anarchist who isn't above selling himself to men and women for money. When Ric falls in love with Nina, things become complicated. Meanwhile, it turns out that Michele is carrying on with Giovanna (Annie Girardot) and that he is aware of the fact that Nina is anything but faithful.

In many respects, it's the stuff of soap operas—but in the hands of such a skillful ensemble (both in front of and behind the camera), *Metti, una sera a cena* emerges as a fascinating study of love, sex and friendship. It plays out a bit like an Italian variation on *Bob and Carol and Ted and Alice* (1969), though in fact Griffi's film (and the stage play which inspired it) came first. The characters play off of each other's weaknesses: Michele is the cynical intellectual who feels shame over his inability to feel jealousy; Nina craves affection but is not above playing head games in order to get what she wants; Max is vain, egotistical and prone to anger; Ric plays at being an anarchist but is essentially just a lazy day-dreamer; and Giovanna is a hypocrite who pretends to be virtuous even though she's engaged in the same behavior as everybody else. Individually they are all compromised in one way or another; as a group, they somehow complete one another and find a peculiar form of happiness.

The cast all perform their roles beautifully, notably the placid and casually sardonic Trintignant (born 1930); the French star was doing quite a few Italian films during this period, ranging from art-house offerings like Bertolucci's *The Conformist* (*Il conformista*, 1970) to lower-rent *gialli* like Umberto Lenzi's *So Sweet ... So Perverse* (*Cosi dolce ... cosi perversa*, 1969). He would even end up on the list of possible casting choices for Dario's third feature, *Four Flies on Grey Velvet*, though that never came to pass. Griffi directs with real cinematic flair and his efforts are ably complemented by the beautiful lighting by Tonino

Michele (Jean-Louis Trintignant) and Nina (Florinda Bolkan) bicker, while Max (Tony Musante) looks on.

Delli Colli, who also shot *Once Upon a Time in the West*. Argento's efforts to make the material more cinematic were undoubtedly given an enormous boost by the input of the great editor Franco Arcalli (1929-1978), who was another long-time collaborator of Bertolucci's. Arcalli's inventive editing allows for virtually invisible transitions between ever-shifting points of view while also taking the action back and forth in chronological order without ever tipping its hand; unlike so many films where flashbacks are codified through the use of artificial techniques, here the concept of time comes to be virtually meaningless. The unusual, highly experimental approach to structure keeps the action interesting throughout. Griffi's frank, adult approach to sex and sexuality is another point in the film's favor—the scene in which Max, Ric and Nina have their first *ménage-à-trois* is a breathtaking piece of filmmaking set to the track "Nina," which is one of Ennio Morricone's most powerful pieces of music. The end result is one of the finest films Argento was fortunate enough to be a part of in the first phase of his career.

Metti, una sera a cena became a box-office hit when it came out in Italy in April 1969—it came in at number 13 at the Italian box office for the 1968-1969 season[25], making it the second big box-office hit of the year to carry his name. They weren't just popular successes, either. Both films ended up being recognized come awards season, as well. *Once Upon a Time in the West* won Best Picture/*Migliore produzione* (tied with Mario Monicelli's *La ragazza con la pistola*, 1968) at the David di Donatello Awards, and it would also be nominated for Silver Ribbons for Gabriele Ferzetti (1925-2015, Best Supporting Actor/*Migliore attore non protagonista*) and Ennio Morricone (Best Score/*Migliore musica*) by the Italian National Syndicate of Film Journalists; it lost out to Nino Rota for *Romeo and Juliet* (1969) and Ettore Mattia for *La pecora nera* (1968), respectively. As for *Metti, una sera a cena*, Giuseppe Patroni Griffi was nominated for the *Palme d'Or* at the 1969 Cannes Film Festival, while Florinda Bolkan (born 1941) was awarded the Golden Plate as Best New Actress (*Migliore attrice esordiente*) at the David di Donatello Awards—and Ennio Morricone was awarded Best Score (*Migliore musica*) at the 1970 ceremony by the Italian National Syndicate of Film Journalists.

The acclaim for *Metti, una sera a cena* didn't translate to the American critics when the film made a belated—and very brief—appearance on November 16, 1971; its American tour was apparently limited to the Juliet I & II theaters in New York City, where it played with subtitles—it doesn't appear as if an English dub was ever prepared. In her review, Ann Guarino dismissed it as "erotic trash," adding: "The cast is much better than the material with which it is working."[26] John Crittenden was similarly unmoved: "*One Night at Dinner* is the kind of slow, boring, dreadfully decadent movie that used to give European films a bad name. […] Also quite early we start wondering how established performers like Trintignant and Miss Girardot got roped into making this film, trying to remember if Musante and Miss Bolkan have in their relatively short careers been in worse movies—they haven't—and if we'll ever have to see another movie with Capolicchio in it. The acting is that bad. And the story is worse."[27] Rex Reed was bitchier still: "Tony Musante is a very good American actor who for some unexplainable reason, keeps turning up in bad Italian movies (remember *The Anonymous Venetian*, or were you out of town that weekend?). The latest, called *One Night*

Young actor Tony Musante picks material gingerly

Wednesday January 12, 1972 — Hattiesburg American — Page 9

By NORMAN GOLDSTEIN
AP Newsfeatures Writer

NEW YORK (AP) — A film critic recently paid Tony Musante a left-handed compliment by wondering why the young, talented actor kept showing up in what he considered bad Italian films.

Many an actor would rest very comfortably on that laurel, implying personal performance exceeding the total project. But not so Tony Musante, a handsome, 35-year-old who has been acting professionally for more than 10 years.

"I choose my material very carefully," he says in defense of his role in the Italian-made "One Night at Dinner," a somewhat flawed effort at a fantasy-reality menage-a-quatre. "I personally feel the result is quite successful.... If I was 'caught' in a bad Italian film, I was 'caught' by a good script."

Musante recalled he was shooting another film in Spain a couple of years ago when the producer of "One Night at Dinner" came to him with the script.

"I read it in one night, from cover to cover," he said, and rushed off to Rome just hours after he finished the other film.

"I must have had the Spanish sand still on me....

"I said I would never go from one thing straight to another. But I thought that highly of the script."

Musante, Connecticut-born but now living in New York, played the musician in the Italian production, "The Anonymous Venetian," recently released here; a Mexican revolutionary in the made-in-Spain "The Mercenary," and a young American writer in "The Bird With the Crystal Plumage" — "the one picture I have been prominent in that grossed well in this country."

"I'm fascinated by the roles the story hangs on," Musante says in explaining his varied acting lures. "I'm not dramatic. I'm not comic. I have to 'shtik'. I'm the 'common man' in the audience going through the story."

In "One Night at Dinner," he plays opposite France's Jean-Louis Trintignant and Annie Girardot and Brazil's Florinda Bolkan—excellent acting company, but a babel of languages. Each acted in their native tongue, with the few problems worked out in rehearsals, Musante said. He added that the language problem may ironically result in stronger communication—"because you couldn't depend on the text, you had to watch the emotion."

As for filming in Italy, he appreciates the practicalities. "It's economically more feasible," he notes. "The government subsidizes film there.... Loans are easy to get.

"I like working in both countries. Just as I like working in both film and stage."

Musante just completed a role in the Off-Broadway production, "A Gun Play," and now is "ready to do anything that comes up; that is, anything I like, that seems right, that fits in."

He would like to do a film comedy next. "And I'd like to do television—but not a series. I've had offers to do a pilot film—but they want a five-year commitment! Right now, I won't do that."

The Unsane Cinema of Dario Argento

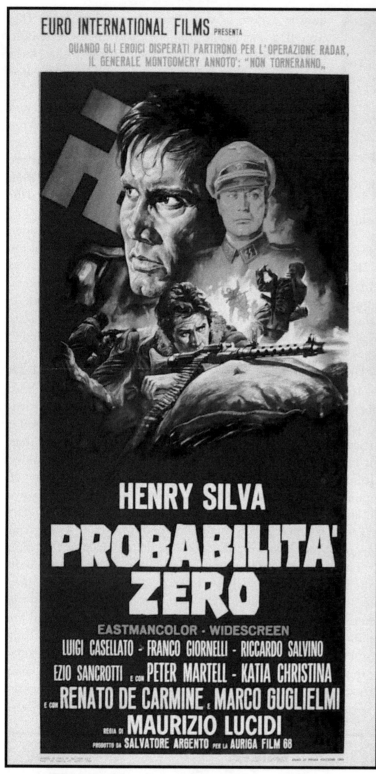

Italian *locandina* for *Probability Zero*; artist unknown.

[…] All told I'd say *One Night at Dinner* is one for the sanitation department."[28] Sheesh, tough crowd!

These early successes surely encouraged Argento, who was in the midst of mulling over further transitions in his personal life. Married life with Marisa remained good on the whole, and by the spring of 1969, they received some welcome news: Marisa was pregnant with their first child. The prospect of entering into parenthood was surely daunting in some respects, but they felt ready to take on their new responsibilities. Argento was earning good money with his script work and he was still doing his columns for *Paese Sera*, but could it be that the news of their upcoming "delivery" spurned him into yet another career change? Up until that time, Argento maintains he had absolutely no interest in directing. It wasn't something that appealed to him. He wasn't interested in the hustle and bustle of the film set; he preferred the quiet and solitude of his study, where he could write his scripts in peace. During this period of transition, however, he had a change of heart.

In the meantime, Salvatore produced his second film written by Dario: *Probability Zero* (*Probabilità zero*, 1969) was yet another war film, though this time he was more deeply involved in the development of the script—and he was even responsible for the original screen story, as well.

In it, an American officer known as "Duke" (Henry Silva) is tasked with a seemingly impossible mission. He needs to locate an underground Nazi stronghold and destroy an experimental new radar system before the Germans can decode it and start building their own variation on it. To do this, "Duke" assembles a team of misfits who are skilled in different areas; once they locate the place where the radar system has been stored away for study, they set out to complete their mission.

Like Dario's Western scripts, *Probability Zero* draws heavily on the formula established by Kurosawa in *The Seven Samurai* and later popularized by Sturges in *The Magnificent Seven*, as a group of disparate types come together to complete a difficult mission. The personality conflicts result in plenty of drama along the way, but ultimately the characters are able to unite in order to address their common goal; the suspense derives from not knowing whether or not they will succeed, as the deck is stacked high against them as they try to infiltrate Nazi terrain. As such, it plays out very much

at Dinner (at Juliet 2), is so terrible that when they get around to listing the all-time worst movies ever made, it's bound to be up there in the Top 10. […] When I saw the film on Tuesday, an elderly lady hit the usher over the head with a shopping bag full of heavy objects and two men in the projection booth had an argument so violent it was louder than the voices coming on the soundtrack.

like a Western in modern dress—and while director Maurizio Lucidi (1932-2005) isn't the most dynamic of filmmakers, it offers up some strong individual set pieces and passes muster as a competent time-killer; Lucidi would go on to direct the very interesting *The Designated Victim* (*La vittima designata*, 1971), which is one of many *gialli* inspired by the success of Dario's early box-office triumphs. The characters aren't particularly well delineated, unfortunately, which means it's difficult to become too emotionally invested in their plight. That said, stone-faced Henry Silva (born 1928) is ideally cast as the no-nonsense protagonist; he's been criticized in some quarters for being a wooden actor, but in fact he's extremely skilled at playing characters that don't wear their emotions on their sleeve. He may not be a flashy actor, prone to going over the top in big emotional scenes, but his deadpan approach is always enjoyable to watch. "Duke" isn't the most dynamic or interesting character he ever played, but his stoic interpretation is nicely judged, and he manages some nice touches of wry humor along the way. Perhaps the more appropriate point of comparison for the film would be Robert Aldrich's *The Dirty Dozen* (1967), though it certainly isn't in the same league as that lean and mean classic; taken on its own terms, however, it's a solid, unpretentious piece of work. Among the supporting players, it's nice to see the familiar-looking Fulvio Mingozzi (1925-2000) in a small, unspeaking role as a British Intelligence officer; Mingozzi would go on to become a recurring presence in Argento's films—appearing in small roles in every film Dario directed between 1969 and 1984.

Battle of the Commandos (*La legione dei dannati*, 1969) was yet another foray into the war genre; given Dario's dislike of such subject matter, he must have been growing very weary indeed of such assignments. This time he was tasked with helping to develop a hackneyed screen story by Stefano Rolla (1937-2003) and Romano Maschini into a workable screenplay. The director was the veteran Umberto Lenzi (1931-2017), who achieved success with a pre-*Bird with the Crystal Plumage giallo* titled *Orgasmo* that same year. *Orgasmo* was one of several Italian thrillers indebted to Henri Georges Clouzot's *Les Diaboliques* (1955), though some of Lenzi's later entries, including *Seven Blood-Stained Orchids* (*Sette orchidee macchiate di rosso*, 1972) would undeniably be indebted to Argento. With uncommon humility, the notoriously (but lovably) self-aggrandizing Lenzi would later admit that Argento didn't need to look to him for inspiration: "Dario Argento worked on the screenplay for my war movie *La legione dei dannati*, but I would be fooling myself if I thought I had taught him anything. [...] The screenplay was already complete by the time Argento took over. We just had a simple supervision job to do."[29] Argento

Italian *locandina* for *Battle of the Commandos*; artist unknown.

confirmed to Alan Jones that his contribution was indeed minimal—more of a general polishing job than anything substantial.[30]

The story tells of Colonel MacPherson (Jack Palance), a disillusioned soldier who is sent on a suicide mission to clear the path for the British army's planned D-Day invasion of the Normandy coast. He rounds up a group of disgraced soldiers, all in the brig on one charge or another, and sets out to prove their value by working with them to destroy a special artillery weapon which is capable of wiping out the opposition.

Once again, it's clear that *The Dirty Dozen* was on everybody's mind. as in that film, the "volunteers" are pressed into service with the promise of having their

Colonel MacPherson (Jack Palance) gets the drop on Pierre (Luis Induni) in *Battle of the Commandos*.

records expunged. Asked if they would participate in what promises to be a suicide mission. As with Dario's script for *The 5-Man Army*, there's a sense of ethnic diversity to the group, which is comprised of Scotsmen, Englishmen—even a horny American and a stoic Indian (played by Spaghetti Western veteran Aldo Sambrell, no less!). Unfortunately, there's virtually no time set aside for trivialities like characterization and it's easy to lose track of who is whom in the ensuing mayhem. Colonel MacPherson is haunted by flashbacks to a traumatic event, which gives way to a Western-style showdown at the end with a dignified German colonel; Dario was undoubtedly pleased to see Wolfgang Preiss (1910-2002) cast in the latter role, seeing as how he had played the last incarnation of Dr. Mabuse for one of his directing idols, Fritz Lang, in *The 1,000 Eyes of Dr. Mabuse* (*Die 1000 Augen des Dr. Mabuse*, 1960). Jack Palance (1919-2006) acts with vigor and commitment—but somebody really should have advised him that the Scottish accent isn't quite the same as the Irish variety. Once again, the German antagonist comes off as more level-headed and generally sympathetic, thanks in large measure to Preiss' understated performance. While the end result is more energetic than *Commandos*, it suffers from Lenzi's incredibly erratic direction, which is burdened with one clumsy crash zoom after another; the director was reportedly a major aficionado of world history, but *Battle of the Commandos* is anything but a sober insight into the complexities of the Second World War.

The 5-Man Army (*Un esercito di 5 uomini*, 1969) follows the exact same template. A gunman known as the Dutchman (Peter Graves) recruits four rogues with the intention of robbing a train which is carrying $500,000. The people he selects are Augustus (James Daly), an explosives expert; Mesito (Bud Spencer), who will serve as muscle; Luis (Nino Castelnuovo), an acrobat and killer; and Samurai (Tetsuro Tamba), who is recruited because of his skill with knife-play. It turns out that the Dutchman has altruistic reasons for staging the heist: he plans to use the money to help finance the poor Mexican farmers in their fight in the Revolution. The news doesn't go over well with his compatriots, who agreed to participate thinking that they would be splitting the fortune among themselves.

By all accounts, *The 5-Man Army* was a difficult shoot. American actor-turned-director Don Taylor (1920-1998), best remembered for playing Lieutenant Dunbar in Billy Wilder's *Stalag 17* (1953), was a curious choice to helm a Spaghetti Western. His name was suitable for the international marketplace, however, and producer Italo Zingarelli (1930-2000) knew him to be a solid, dependable journeyman of the old school. When Taylor arrived in Spain, where the location filming kicked off production in March 1969, he let it be known that he wasn't happy—not with the script, not with the budget, and not with the conditions in which the film was being made. Zingarelli tried to appease Taylor, but it was useless; accounts vary as to how long he was on-board as director, but it seems likely that Don Taylor was on a flight back to Los Angeles within a week of his arrival in Spain.

U.S. poster for *The 5-Man Army*; artist unknown.

The 5-Man Army strikes.

As reported by Kevin Grant, "What happened next is more contentious—one story has producer Zingarelli taking the helm, another that scriptwriter Dario Argento directed the remainder of the film, assisted by Enzo Castellari, and that none of the (minimal) footage shot by Taylor ended up in the finished picture. Actress Daniela Giordano (born 1947), who has a thankless role in the film as Tetsuro Tamba's love interest, has stated unequivocally in an interview that Taylor did indeed leave—after just one day—and that Zingarelli finished the film, not Argento."[31] Just how the rumor of Dario taking over got started is anybody's guess; it's not a story he has ever trotted out in interviews, and given his absolute and complete lack of experience as a director at the time, there's no reason to believe that he would have even entered Zingarelli's mind as a potential replacement. No doubt some over-enthusiastic fans were responsible for the story, hoping to add luster to the film by suggesting that it was a "secret" directing credit in Argento's filmography. The very notion of an untried director like Dario being asked to take command, with a far more experienced "assistant" in the form of Enzo G. Castellari (who had already directed some very fine Westerns of his own, including *Johnny Hamlet/Quella sporca storia nel west*, 1968) defies credibility. He would know what needed to be done in order to keep it on track—and besides, he had already gained experience taking over from directors in the past, as in the case of another Western he produced, Domenico Paolella's *Hate for Hate/Odio per odio* (1967). The fact of the matter is, Argento wasn't anywhere near the locations in Spain—he wasn't prone to going to the sets of the films he was working on as a writer unless it was absolutely necessary, and while the behind-the-scenes drama was playing out on *The 5-Man Army*, he was still several months away from making the transition from writer to director. As such, there's no reason to doubt Daniela Giordano's testimony: "Don Taylor started the film for the first two days. Then Italo Zingarelli continued the direction until the end of the film. Don't ask me why Don Taylor left. I have never found this out."[32] The Italian main titles sequence, which differs from the one in the American

Cover art for the expanded CD release of Ennio Morricone's score for *The 5-Man Army*.

print, lists the film as "un film di Don Taylor" (a film by Don Taylor), "prodotto e diretto da Italo Zingarelli" (produced and directed by Italo Zingarelli).

Argento is credited with writing the script with Marc Richards (1930-2006). Not much is known about Richards, but the odds of his having anything much to do with the writing beyond penning the English dialogue seem remarkably slim. Prior to *The 5-Man Army*, he had written for *The Soupy Sales Hour* and his later credits would be largely confined to family-oriented TV fare like *The Brady Kids*, *The New Adventures of Gilligan*, and *The Original Ghostbusters*. Given that the film (partly funded by MGM) was actually shot in English—with even the likes of Bud Spencer and Nino Castelnuovo (born 1936) doing their own looping for once—and was originally intended to be directed by an American with no real experience in the Italian film scene, it makes sense that a little more emphasis than usual would have been put on making the script suitable for the English-language market. In any event, it seems fair to conclude that the actual scenario was the work of Argento, while Richards tended to the dialogue; this is borne out by the fact that Argento is given full screenwriting credit on the Italian print, with Richards' name conspicuous in its absence.

Argento's script is a grab bag of elements familiar from other Westerns—on the face of it, it's an entry in the "Zapata Western" subgenre, sometimes also known as the "Tortilla Western," which focuses on the Mexican revolution, but it also works in plenty of elements familiar from his earlier Western scenarios, including the group of anti-heroes who assemble to defeat a greater evil. It provides a solid, colorful foundation, but unfortunately the film suffers from the lack of a truly visionary filmmaker at the helm—just imagine what somebody like Sergio Corbucci could have done with it, for example—and it has quite the wrong leading man in Peter Graves. Graves is the epitome of the solid, dependable character actor, but he lacks the charm and charisma needed to make the Dutchman come to life; somebody like Lee Van Cleef or Sterling Hayden or (if the budget had permitted) William Holden would have been far better suited to such a role. As such, the show is stolen by the supporting players, notably Spencer and Castelnuovo, both of whom are a good deal more at home in the Spaghetti Western milieu—indeed, Spencer was on his way to becoming one of the genre's biggest stars thanks to the success of the following year's *They Call Me Trinity* (*Lo chiamavano Trinità ...*, 1970).

Bearing in mind that it is virtually impossible to ascertain in what order Dario worked on these various screenplay assignments—even he isn't sure at this stage—the last of his pre-directing credits to appear theatrically was *La stagione dei sensi* (literally, "The Season of the Senses"), which went into release about a week after principal photography wrapped on *The Bird with the Crystal Plumage*. Actually, the Italian release of *The 5-Man Army* took place right around the time *Bird* wrapped (October 16, as opposed to the October 22 release date for *La stagione dei sensi*), so Dario's name was getting some good exposure that Halloween season. The story was the work of Amedeo Pagani (born 1940), who would later achieve some success as a producer (*Sailing Home/Tornando a casa*, 2001), though he also contributed to the scripts for such disparate projects as *The Night Porter* (*Il portiere di notte*, 1974) and *Pensione paura* (1978). The actual script was the work of Barbara Alberti (born 1943, who also worked on *Pensione paura*) and Franco Ferrari (1929-2000, who co-wrote Umberto Lenzi's excellent *poliziottesco Almost Human/Milano odio: la polizia non può sparare*, 1974); Peter Kintzel was credited, too, as he had been on Massimo Dallamano's *giallo A Black Veil for Lisa* (*La morte non ha sesso*, 1968)—in both cases simply to satisfy quota regulations with the German co-financiers. As for Dario, he later told Alan Jones that his input was minimal: "I did almost nothing on that either, just changed some dialogue bits."[33]

Notes:
1. Argento, Dario, *Peur* (France: Rouge Profond, 2018), p. 72-73.
2. Just to be pedantic about it: the English title is often given as *A Fistful of Dollars*, but the actual on-screen title on the English-language version is simply *Fistful of Dollars*.

3. Argento, Dario, *Peur* (France: Rouge Profond, 2018), p. 74.
4. Ibid, p. 75.
5. Frayling, Christopher, *Spaghetti Westerns: Cowboys and Europeans from Karl May to Sergio Leone* (London: I.B. Taurus, 1998), p. 195.
6. Argento, Dario, *Peur* (France: Rouge Profond, 2018), p. 77.
7. Frayling, Christopher, *Sergio Leone: Something to Do with Death* (London: Faber and Faber, 2000), p. 250.
8. Frayling, Christopher, *Once Upon a Time in the West: Shooting a Masterpiece* (London: Reel Art Press, 2019), p. 284-300.
9. https://italoamericano.org/story/2015-12-24/sergio-donati
10. Argento, Dario, *Peur* (France: Rouge Profond, 2018), p. 68-69.
11. Ibid, p. 70.
12. Jones, Alan, *Dario Argento: The Man, the Myths & the Magic* (Godalming: FAB Press, 2012), p. 16.
13. Murray, John B., *Brett Halsey: Art of Instinct in the Movies…* (Baltimore: Midnight Marquee Press, 2008), p. 190.
14. Jones, Alan, *Dario Argento: The Man, the Myths & the Magic* (Godalming: FAB Press, 2012), p. 16.
15. Palmerini, Luca M. and Gaetano Mistretta, *Spaghetti Nightmares* (Key West: Fantasma Books, 1997), p. 40.
16. The *krimi* films were thrillers based on the writings of Edgar Wallace; as it happens, there would be something of a crossover between Argento's *gialli* and the German *krimis*, as shall be discussed later.
17. Jones, Alan, *Dario Argento: The Man, the Myths & the Magic* (Godalming: FAB Press, 2012), p. 16.
18. Frayling, Christopher, *Sergio Leone: Something to Do with Death* (London: Faber and Faber, 2000), p. 271.
19. http://www.hitparadeitalia.it/bof/boi/boi1968-69.htm
20. Frayling, Christopher, *Sergio Leone: Something to Do With Death* (London: Faber and Faber, 2000), p. 296-297.
21. The comments from Robert Hossein are from his interview which is included on the Anolis/Buio Omega DVD release of the film.
22. Frayling, Christopher, *Sergio Leone: Something to Do with Death* (London: Faber and Faber, 2000), p. 268.
23. Jones, Alan, *Dario Argento: The Man, the Myths & the Magic* (Godalming: FAB Press, 2012), p. 16.
24. Ibid.
25. http://www.hitparadeitalia.it/bof/boi/boi1968-69.htm
26. Guarino, Ann, "Erotic Trash from Italy," *Daily News*, November 17 1971, p. 242.
27. Crittenden, John, "'Night at Dinner' Proves That Sex Can Be a Bore," *The Record*, November 17 1971, p. 65.
28. Reed, Rex, "You Can 'Ride a Rainbow' Past 'One Night at Dinner,'" *Daily News*, November 19 1971, p. 212.
29. Palmerini, Luca M. and Gaetano Mistretta, *Spaghetti Nightmares* (Key West: Fantasma Books, 1997), p. 67.

Italian *locandina* for *La stagione dei sensi*; artist unknown.

30. Jones, Alan, *Dario Argento: The Man, the Myths & the Magic* (Godalming: FAB Press, 2012), p. 16.
31. Grant, Kevin, *Any Gun Can Play: The Essential Guide to Euro-Westerns* (Godalming: FAB Press, 2011), p. 233.
32. https://www.spaghetti-western.net/index.php/Interview_with_Daniela_Giordano
33. Jones, Alan, *Dario Argento: The Man, the Myths & the Magic* (Godalming: FAB Press, 2012), p. 16.

Chapter Four:
Screaming *Bird* and Flower in Bloom

It all started when Bernardo Bertolucci presented Dario with a copy of the pulp thriller *The Screaming Mimi*, written by Fredric Brown (1906-1972) and first published in 1949. Bertolucci had read the book and liked it, he but didn't feel it was entirely suited to the sort of politically committed filmmaking he was doing at that time. He felt it might be up Argento's alley, so he decided to recommend it to him.

Argento devoured the book and immediately saw its potential as a film. Of course, it had already been filmed by Gerd Oswald (1919-1989) under the slightly abbreviated title of *Screaming Mimi* (1959), with sex siren Anita Ekberg (1931-2015, who gained immortality splashing in the Trevi Fountain in Fellini's *La dolce vita*, 1960). The Oswald film hadn't made much of a ripple, however, so Argento decided to take Brown's story and do his own adaptation. Now this is where things get a little bit … murky.

Argento's version of events is that, while on holiday in Tunisia, he was laying on the beach, feeling bloated and miserable following a big meal; in a state of semi-delirium, he came up with the idea of what would become *The Bird with the Crystal Plumage* (*L'uccello dalle piume di cristallo*, 1970). His initial accounts made absolutely no mention of Brown's novel, though he would begin to acknowledge its "influence" in later years.

Of course, in fairness to Argento, it's not a direct adaptation of Brown's book; it varies from the original story in many ways, though to be fair it probably should have at least acknowledged its debt to Brown's work with a proper screen credit. Muddying the waters even more are comments by one of Argento's contemporaries, the writer/director Aldo Lado (born 1934), who claims to have largely rewritten the script, only to be denied the promised screen credit.[1] Lado, incidentally, had served as the assistant director on *Probability Zero*, though whether the two men interacted much on that picture is unclear. Argento himself has never commented on Lado's claims. According to his version of events, the story gripped him like a fever, and he pounded out the first draft within the space of a week. It was his first crack at a genre with which he would become closely identified—the *giallo*—

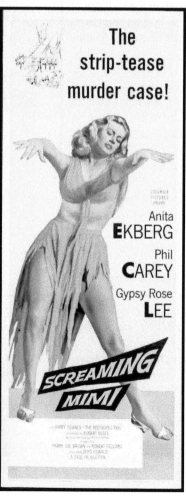

and he felt prouder than usual of the end result. Suddenly the young screenwriter, who abhorred the idea of taking command of a crew of actors and technicians, started to flirt with the idea of becoming a director.

The Bird with the Crystal Plumage was destined to become a very seminal picture. It belongs to the genre of films known as the *giallo*. The *giallo* is that most peculiarly Italian brand of thriller. It draws its name from a series of thrillers published in Italy by a publishing house known as Mondadori. These books—ranging from the classic drawing-room murder mysteries of Agatha Christie to the more hardboiled *noir* of Raymond Chandler—were massively popular with Italian readers, many of whom would collect every new volume, regardless of the author or the subject. These books were distinguished by their yellow (*giallo*) dust jackets, thus giving birth to the concept of the *giallo*. More often than not, they were also emblazoned with lurid cover art, the type of which would become all too familiar on the Italian advertising of their cinematic equivalent in later years. While there had been thrillers filmed in Italy well before Mario Bava came onto the scene, it's generally accepted that the cinematic *giallo* began with his tongue-in-cheek *The Girl Who Knew Too Much* (*La ragazza che sapeva troppo*, 1963). It's here that the lurid aspects of the genre come into focus—and with Bava's use of stark black-and-white imagery (which would eventually give way to eye-popping color) it set the precedence with regards to the highly stylized approach these films would take to suspense and to images of carnage and death. Numerous *gialli* were made throughout the 1960s, but very few of them made much of a ripple at the Italian box office; after *The Bird with the Crystal Plumage*, however, it became a prime money-maker for the Italian commercial film scene.

By his own admission, Argento wrote *Bird* for free; it wasn't commissioned by anybody, so there was a very good chance that it would simply sit in a drawer collecting dust.[2] Nevertheless, he believed in it and he took it to the producer/director Italo Zingarelli, with whom he had worked on *The 5-Man Army* and *La rivoluzione sessuale*. Zingarelli passed. Undeterred, Dario took it to Goffredo Lombardo (1920-2005), then the head of Titanus in Rome. Founded in 1904 by Goffredo's father, Gustavo (1885-1951), Titanus cranked out a lot of movies in varying genres—and they made a killing in the 1950s and '60s, often with films in the then-popular *pepla* (that is, sword-and-sandal) genre, as well as vehicles for popular comic actors like Totò and Franco Franchi and Ciccio Ingrassia. Lombardo was excited by the script and proposed hiring Duccio Tessari to direct. Tessari was a fine director in his own right, but Argento felt he wasn't the right man for the job, and he wasn't shy about saying so. Tessari *didn't* get the job, but he would end up making a very effective pair of thrillers for Titanus: *Death Occurred Last Night* (*La morte risale a ieri sera*, 1970) and *The Bloodstained Butterfly* (*Una farfalla con le ali insanguinate*, 1972).

As Lombardo mulled over who to approach next, Argento started to feel more and more inclined to do it himself. He was crestfallen when he received news that Lombardo had reached out to British director Terence Young (1915-1994), best known for directing the James Bond films *Doctor No* (1962), *From Russia with Love* (1963), and *Thunderball* (1965); more appropriately, given the nature of the material, he had also recently scored a major hit with *Wait Until Dark* (1967). Argento vented to his father that he was unhappy, and the older man

Italian *locandina* for *The Bird with the Crystal Plumage*; artwork by P. Franco.

put it on the line. Why don't you just direct it yourself, then? The proverbial light bulb went off, but it all hinged on whether or not Young elected to say yes. If he had accepted, Lombardo would surely have gone with him. Argento was thrilled when word got back to him that the British director decided to pass. "I could barely contain my joy. I had a movie project and I wouldn't let it go until

The Unsane Cinema of Dario Argento

I directed it myself. I understood something important, when the project was just about to slip through my fingers. It became clear to me that this project meant everything to me. I was on a delirious trip of possession; I wouldn't tolerate any interference from the outside. Now, in my deep self, I decided that it would belong to me alone."[3]

That was all well and good, but there was the little matter of persuading Lombardo to consider. The producer wasn't about to entrust a picture like this to a novice and he initially dug his heels in and said no. Argento and his father were relentless, however, and Lombardo eventually conceded defeat. There's no doubt that, were it not for Salvatore, Dario Argento would not have made the transition to directing—at least not at that time. And had he not made that transition at that particular moment in time, a large portion of Italian popular culture would have been forever altered. Salvatore was an old hand at selling and promoting, so it shouldn't come as a huge surprise that he exerted the sort of influence which enabled his oldest son to rise up the ladder so quickly; no doubt a number of people connected to the project were ready to expect the worst, since it was evidently a clear-cut case of nepotism, with an inexperienced film critic suddenly calling the shots on his very first film as a director—and at the age of 29, to boot. Nepotism it may have been, but crucially Dario had the talent to back it all up; he may not have envisioned himself as a director, but he proved to be ideally suited for the job.

Lombardo remained on board and committed to the project as the Italian distributor—but he was reluctant to actually put up the budget himself. Salvatore and Dario put their heads together and created a production company of their own—Seda Spettacoli—to produce the picture. As such, this would give Salvatore added leverage to act as a buffer between his son and the front office; this, too, would prove to be of vital importance to Dario on more than one occasion. Salvatore used his charm and salesmanship to raise the bulk of the money needed (approximately $500,000) and got the all-important final cash infusion—plus a guarantee of distribution in the German marketplace—from Artur Brauner (1918-2019) at Central Cinema Company Film (CCC). Brauner had produced the final German films of Dario's idol, Fritz Lang, and he also was responsible for the more down-market Lang-less sequels in the "Dr. Mabuse" franchise, as well as some knock-off titles in the Edgar Wallace (1875-1932) *krimi* film boom. The *krimi* connection is significant, as CCC would ultimately sell *Bird* in the German market as an adaptation of a Bryan Edgar Wallace (1904-1971) story under the title *Das Geheimnis der Schwarzen Handschuhe* ("The Secret of The Black Gloves"); Bryan was the son of Edgar Wallace, and he would subsequently be given a nonsensical credit on German prints of Dario's second feature, *The Cat O'Nine Tails*, as well. Brauner served as a sort of silent executive producer figure; given the popularity of the Wallace name in the German market, it virtually guaranteed him a return on his investment. With the money in place, the production was finally ready to proceed.

Dario Argento spent his first day as a director on the set of his first feature on August 25, 1969. By his own admission, he felt overwhelmed at times, inadequate to the task at hand at others; realistically, these "opening night" nerves are hardly unusual for anybody directing their first feature. He had a tremendous ally in the form of the cinematographer Vittorio Storaro (born 1940), who had been a part of Bertolucci's circle since *Before the Revolution*, on which he served as a camera operator. Storaro hadn't yet established himself as one of Italy's top cinematographers, but he was well on his way to doing so—within a few months of the release of *Bird*, he scored a major success with Bertolucci's *The Conformist*, and from there the accolades kept coming.

The German distributors sold *Bird* as an entry in their flagging series of Edgar Wallace thrillers.

Argento struggled with his uneasiness in dealing with the actors, but by and large the filming of *Bird* proceeded smoothly enough. All was not smooth behind the scenes, however. When Goffredo Lombardo sat down to look at the first week's rushes with Salvatore, he was livid. The style of the film was fresh, modern—in short, it wasn't anything close to resembling what he had in mind. He actively sought to have Dario fired, but Salvatore remained steadfast: he would not allow him to be removed from the film. Dario has good reason to regard Salvatore as his guardian angel figure. Were it not for him, who knows what would have happened. Dario—intense, moody and given to self-doubt at this stage in the game—was already under enough pressure on the set; thanks to Salvatore, he ensured that the young director had peace of mind when it came to keeping his job.

As the filming continued, Lombardo continued to decry the footage as inferior. He was convinced that he had agreed to distribute a turkey and he was growing testy and despondent. Salvatore weathered the storm and continued to shield Dario throughout what could have been a very trying experience. When the seven-week shoot drew to a close in October 1969, Argento worked with his editor, Franco Fraticelli, to put together the first rough cut. Fraticelli (1928-2012) was a highly experienced editor, well known for his work with Lina Wertmüller, and Dario was extraordinarily lucky to have him. He would remain a more-or-less constant presence in Argento's filmmaking family through the early 1990s; when he broke off from Argento and eventually retired, Argento's films suffered a major blow from which they never really recovered—but that's another story for later in our narrative. During this time, Argento also secured the services of another vital collaborator: the great composer Ennio Morricone. Morricone had already crossed paths with Argento on a professional level, of course. In addition to writing the iconic music for *Once Upon a Time in the West*, he also did the scores for several more of Dario's early screenwriting credits: *Comandamenti per un gangster*, *The 5-Man Army*, *La stagione dei sensi*, *Metti, una sera a cena*. The conflation of talent is pretty remarkable; a mixture of experienced veterans at the top of their game and young up-and-comers who were eager and ready to experiment.

Even so, Argento felt despondent. He knew that the executives at Titanus hated the film—and that, by implication, they hated him, too. To them he was a young upstart, the pampered son of a hotshot producer. Lombardo and company seemed to feel secure in the knowledge that Salvatore's faith in his son was misguided

Dario Argento on the set of *The Bird with the Crystal Plumage* (Photo by Francesco Alessi).

and that Dario's first crack at directing would likely remain his last. When the finished film was ready to be shown to Titanus, Argento elected to stay home; he didn't want to get upset by their wisecracks and ignorant comments. Salvatore went in his stead and it went as predicted, they hated the film and felt sure it would lay an egg at the box office.

If Argento had anything to take his mind off of the exasperation he was feeling, it was surely the knowledge that he and Marisa were due to welcome their first child into the world. The couple continued to have their trials and tribulations, but the good times still outnumbered the bad. Their relationship was based on mutual respect and a willingness to share ideas. They also shared a passion for the arts. "Our home was crammed with volumes about the history of cinema, screenplays, biographies, poetry books, art and music magazines, photobooks and many, many projects that were probably never going to see the light of day. We could literally stumble upon ideas and notes as they were written on the backside of bills and receipts, on notebooks and loose sheets scattered all over the place. Each room, even the bathroom, was there to attest the chaos going through my mind."[4] The

experience of writing, planning and actually making *Bird* took over Argento's life, but at this stage Marisa was willing to accept the fact that, when it came to work, Argento's focus was extremely narrow. When he wasn't on the set, he was thinking about being on the set; he brooded and fretted and was surely difficult to be around when he became preoccupied with some problem connected to the film. By the time *Bird* was finished filming, Marisa was already into her second trimester; and by the time it was edited, scored and ready for exhibition, Marisa was ready to give birth. The reality of their situation had fully come into focus. If Dario was to make it as a director, he could provide financial stability for his coming family; if not, they might have to scale back their ambitions accordingly. In any event, whether they were ready or not, Fiore Argento was born on January 3, 1970; the new decade started off with a bang, and things would continue to evolve in a big way.

The action kicks off with a credits sequence which serves as a template of sorts for so much of Argento's filmography. A mysterious figure dressed in black, complete with black leather gloves, sits in his or her inner sanctum, where preparations are under way for a fresh kill. Never mind the impracticality of typing detailed notes while wearing gloves: it's the attention to detail which counts, and it's a factor which will become a constant in Dario's work from here on out. There's a bit of knife fetishism, too, as the killer's black gloved hands fondle an assortment of weapons of violence in a very gentle and loving fashion. It's well known, of course, that Dario Argento got into the habit of standing in for the hands of his killers right off the bat—amateur psychoanalysts have long had a field day with this, but Argento initially did this for purely practical reasons:

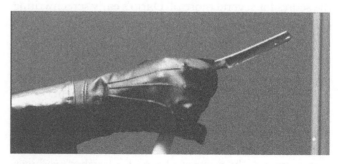

Argento's black gloved hand would become a recurring motif in his films.

it was simply easier for him to step in and do what he wanted, as opposed to having an extra try to realize the idea for him. After a certain point, however, it became a kind of signature flourish—Hitchcock had his cameo appearances, wherein his familiar rotund profile would crop up like a sort of cinematic game of "Where's Waldo?" and this is Argento's variation on the idea. The sequence ends with a pretty girl being stalked from afar by the killer, who takes various photos of her, apparently for the purposes of "studying" his or her prey. We don't actually see her subsequent murder—or the one which preceded it—but the creepy emphasis on the killer's ritualized approach to their work helps to get things started in a properly dynamic matter. It's not exactly comparable to the celebrated super-extended titles sequence of Leone's *Once Upon a Time in the West*, but it displays Argento's desire to grab the audience right off the bat.

Sam (Tony Musante) interviews the camp antique dealer (*krimi* regular Werner Peters).

Argento economically communicates to the audience that the girl from the opening of the film has been murdered—and that she's actually the third young woman to have been killed under similar circumstances—via a newspaper headline. Dario even works in a nod to his "other job" by having the headline featured on the front page of an issue of *Paese Sera*; an additional, almost subliminal touch has some *giallo* paperbacks on display at the newsstand. These are small directorial touches which have nothing to do with the plot per se; they're simply little signposts for people who are in on the joke. Those who don't "get it" will be none the wiser and the film can proceed without disruption.

At this point, we're also introduced to the protagonist, Sam Dalmas (Tony Musante, who previously played one of the leads in *Metti, una sera a cena*). He's the first of Argento's "fish out of water" protagonists—and like so many of the ones to follow, he's an artist. It's also implied that he's a bit of a failure—or at least a sell-out. Like Michele in *Metti, una sera a cena*, he's a writer whose early promise hasn't been fulfilled; in both cases, it's implied that they're suffering from writer's block where "serious" work is concerned. In Michele's case, he has elected to take the money and run by writing screenplays for frivolous movies; Sam, on the other hand, has been hired—at the behest of his friend Carlo (Renato Romano)—to write the text for a new book about rare birds. The irony is a delicious one, given how a rare bird comes to play a vital role in the drama he is soon to become a part of, but it also points to his lack of success. Argento doesn't hammer the point over the head, but he's able to communicate through the dialogue that Sam achieved success early on—and that since being lionized as a new literary genius, he's failed to fulfill that promise. Coming to Italy to write about rare birds is hardly what he had in mind for himself, but on the plus side, the money is good, the scenery is beautiful—and compared to the urban landscape of America, it's a place where "nothing ever happens." That's yet another irony, of course, as Sam comes to realize that violence is capable of erupting anywhere at any time; on the surface, Italy may be sunny and bucolic, but it is not immune to the social disorders of other cultures, either.

Tony Musante (1936-2003) gives a superb performance as Sam. Unlike many of the Argento protagonists which followed, he conveys a more rugged, macho sort of quality; by comparison, some of the later actors seem somewhat sexually ambiguous, which was undoubtedly a calculated move on Dario's part. Considering how natural and utterly charming he comes across in the film, it's amazing to know that Argento regarded him as a colossal pain in the ass. Bearing in mind that Dario had no real experience dealing with actors, he found himself in a difficult position when it came to dealing with Musante.

Argento offered him the role of Sam because he was a hot name at the time and because he had proved his acting chops in films like Larry Pierce's gritty thriller *The Incident* (1967). Musante was in the midst of a mini-career in Italy during that period—apart from *Metti, una sera a cena*, he had also appeared in Sergio Corbucci's *The Mercenary/Il mercenario*, 1968, and directly after this he would go on to appear in Enrico Maria Salerno's *The Anonymous Venetian/Anonimo veneziano*, 1970—so his casting made sense on a lot of different levels. Unfortunately, it did not prove to be a harmonious relationship—at least, not from Argento's point of view. He would rail in interviews later about how Musante showed up at his apartment in the middle of the night, after a long day's shooting, wanting to talk about character and motivation. Dario found him to be insufferable: vain, self-centered, egocentric … very much like the character of Max, which he had played in *Metti, una sera a cena*,

Lino Capolicchio, Tony Musante, and Florinda Bolkan explore the free-spirited sexuality of *Metti, una sera a cena.*

in fact. He would later say, "What began as a great friendship, a relationship of mutual affection, turned out to be … far less than good. We began arguing from the very first shot."[5] Musante, for his part, would later react with surprise when word got to him about how much Dario disliked working with him; from his point of view, it had been a pleasurable experience. In a Q&A session at the Anthology Film Archives in New York City in September 2012, Musante recalled: "Dario didn't speak much English. I didn't speak much Italian. The script was in English. […] Everybody was speaking English except for Enrico Maria Salerno; he's speaking Italian. But the picture was shot in English. […] So, Dario and I got along very well—because we didn't speak the same language! […] Dario would smile at me after a shot, and I would smile back at him—and Don Dunaway, who had done the English language translation, probably didn't translate some of the stuff that we had spoken to each other. So, we finished the film dear friends."[6] It just goes to show how two different people can react to the same exact set of circumstances. In any event, the experience of working with Musante soured Argento on actors—stars, more specifically—for many years. He would go on to have strained relationships with other actors, but Musante appears to have earned a special form of lasting contempt in his eyes.

Sam's idyll is disrupted when he is walking home late one night and he sees something unusual: through the glass doors of an art gallery, he spies a man and a woman struggling. As he draws nearer, he notices that a knife is involved. Remembering the recent string of killings, Sam is convinced he is seeing the killer at work trying to claim his newest victim. In fact, he's correct—but like so many Argento protagonists, he fails to correctly interpret what he is seeing. The struggle ends with the woman, later introduced as the art gallery's co-owner, Monica Ranieri (Eva Renzi), crumbled into a pitiful, crying mess on the floor—injured and unable to speak. Sam tries to gain access but is trapped between the two sets of glass doors when the apparent assailant manages to lock the outer set of doors behind Sam. It's a key sequence in

Sam is powerless to help as violence erupts.

Sam watches as Monica (Eva Renzi) suffers.

Argento's filmography—arguably *the* key set piece, really. For the remainder of his career, Dario would continue to explore the fallibility of perception as his characters consistently see important clues while failing to interpret them correctly until it is almost too late. Argento's clever use of *mise-en-scène* is a vital part of the process. By dressing Monica in white and the other character in black, it plays into the archetypes of good and evil, thus helping the audience to side with Sam in his perception of the event. The twist is withheld until the end, of course, and it's a good one. While Sam did indeed witness an attempted murder, the man in black was the intended victim while "poor helpless" Monica is revealed to be the psychopathic killer. The symbolism of Sam trapped between the glass doors is also interesting—on an obvious level, it makes him look like a fish trapped in an aquarium, but it also plays into the character's impotence. It's already been established that he's suffering from creative impotence and it will soon be implied that he's suffering from some temporary "performance issues," as well, and even in his big moment of would-be heroism, he's rendered totally helpless. This, too, would become a common trope in Argento's movies, where often the protagonists are crippled in one way or another and are haunted by the realization that they were unable to act when called upon to do so.

Monica doesn't die—but she sustained injuries in the struggle, and with Sam trapped in the foyer and unable to get out, he becomes a prime suspect when the police arrive on the scene. *Giallo* films are not noted for their sympathetic portrayal of the police: the inspectors and detectives who crop up in these films tend to be dull, plodding, unimaginative and even downright corrupt. Very often they're sidelined from the narrative altogether; as Hitchcock often remarked, the reason why the characters didn't call the police in his movies was because they're boring. The Italian filmmakers, beginning with Mario Bava in *The Girl Who Knew Too Much* (*La ragazza che sapeva troppo*, 1963) and *Blood and Black Lace* (*6 donne per l'assassino*, 1964) definitely followed on his example. Yet Dario goes against the grain here with the character of Inspector Morosini (Enrico Maria Salerno), who is depicted as an intelligent, compassionate sort of person; he's a good cop and there's no indication that he's the exception to the rule, either. As played by the veteran actor/director Enrico Maria Salerno (1926-1994), he's also warm and funny; not at all the kind of flatfoot viewers often would find in films such as this. Whatever problems Argento had with Musante were nicely counterbalanced by his working relationship with Salerno; and Salerno himself evidently didn't have any serious issues with Musante, as he hired him to play one of the lead roles in his film *The Anonymous Venetian*, which went into production in March 1970. Morosini realizes early on that Sam is innocent, but he's intelligent enough to recognize that he knows more than he's letting on. Sam isn't dishonest about that, either: by his own admission, he knows that he saw something important, but he simply can't bring it to the surface of his mind. Morosini is in a position to make life miserable for Sam— he initially withholds his passport, thus preventing him from fleeing the country—but he doesn't interact with him in a malicious way. Their relationship is notable for his good-natured humor and it definitely adds some real

The Unsane Cinema of Dario Argento

human interest to the police investigation scenes—which are frequently the weak spot in just about every other *giallo* film.

It soon becomes apparent that Sam is in deep trouble. While walking home from a long night of questioning at the police station, he's attacked by a stranger wielding a meat cleaver; only the intrusion of a passerby prevents him from being decapitated. Here, as elsewhere, Sam is reliant upon the help and assistance of others; he is a dynamic character, excitable and ready for action, yet much of his action doesn't really amount to very much—yet another hallmark of Argento's compromised hero figures. Even so, the message is clear: the killer knows he has seen too much and he needs to be removed from the equation.

Sam's relationship with his girlfriend, an English model named Julia (Suzy Kendall), proves to be less interesting. At this stage in his career, Argento hasn't quite figured out how to write really interesting female characters—well, at least interesting female characters who aren't bug-eyed psychopaths. Julia is the usual boring, doting girlfriend figure and while Suzy Kendall (born 1937) does her best with the material, there's really nothing interesting about her character; she remains pretty much fixed from beginning to end and her only real narrative function is to be placed in danger at the end of the picture. That said, some of the scenes between her and Sam come about as close to "normalcy" as Argento would ever get with regards to male/female relations on film. They tease each other and they even work together to try and unravel the mystery. Sam may be a swaggering sort, but he is affectionate and respectful towards Julia—that is until his fixation on solving the mystery causes him to inadvertently put her at risk. Even

Julia (Suzy Kendall) and Sam ponder the creepy painting which holds the key to the mystery.

Morosini picks up on this when he ultimately tries to convince Sam to take Julia with him and go back to the United States. Argento's later heroines would be drawn with considerably greater shading and texture, but in the case of Julia he lets the character down rather badly.

One of the most strangely haunting and enigmatic sequences occurs when Sam returns to Julia after his horrible night on the town. She thinks he's kidding when he tells her that he witnessed an attempted homicide and was nearly killed himself, which on the face of it is a fairly normal reaction. Looking to unwind after all the excitement, Sam takes Julia to bed—and, thanks to some very artful editing by Franco Fraticelli, their mood swings from giddy excitement to quiet contemplation. Nothing is explicitly stated, but the point is clear enough: now that his mind is fixated on trying to remember the all-important clue he has forgotten, Sam isn't able to function sexually. It's a brief scene, almost a throwaway, but it speaks volumes about the character's state of mind and it stands out because of it.

As the story unfolds, Sam continues to wrestle with the knowledge that there is an important piece of the puzzle locked away in his mind; Morosini, realizing that the American's life is in danger, gives him the

Suzy Kendall and Tony Musante helped provide the film with "name" value for the American market.

opportunity to leave. While Sam is in many respects a sympathetic and highly likable character, it's his obsessiveness which nearly proves to be his undoing—worse, it nearly ends up costing Julia her life, as well. In truth, he's not deliberately trying to hurt her or anybody else, for that matter. Yet he's also not really driven by a desire to help others. In essence, it's more of a challenge to himself. This sort of mentality is echoed in later Argento protagonists, including Franco Arnò in *The Cat O'Nine Tails* ("I like solving puzzles!") and Marcus Daly in *Deep Red* ("It's become a kind of a challenge ... to my memory."), though at least in the case of the former Franco is willing to let it all go when his beloved niece is put in danger. Undeterred by the violence, which is mounting around him, Sam continues to play the role of the amateur detective; clearly, he enjoys it and along the way he gets to encounter some colorful peripheral characters. Argento's flair for devising eccentric character parts was already in evidence in his early screenwriting works, but it really comes into its own here; he would continue to hone this skill in *The Cat O'Nine Tails*, *Four Flies on Grey Velvet* and *Deep Red*, though arguably he lost sight of it in many of his later films. Among the standouts are a camp antiques dealer (played by *krimi* veteran Werner Peters), a stuttering pimp known as "So Long" (Gildo Di Marco, born 1946, who would go on to appear in *Four Flies on Grey Velvet* and "The Tram" episode of the *Door into Darkness* series) since the phrase "so long" helps him to stop stammering, and a paranoid informer named Faiena (Pino Patti, 1926-1992, who would go on to appear in *The Cat O'Nine Tails*). The interesting thing about Sam's interaction with the antiques dealer is how non-judgmental Sam—and by extension, Dario—are about him. Yes, the character is a stereotypical "sissified" queer, but while he is a little excessive in his efforts to seduce Sam, he's not depicted as a negative character at all. Sam gets a little flustered when the character invades his personal space, which is entirely justified, but he's not at all disgusted or put off by the character's overtly "femme" demeanor. He even uses the man's obvious attraction to him as something of a bargaining chip in his quest for information. This denotes an open, tolerant attitude towards sexuality which is something of a running thread throughout Dario's films. He would continue to have gay characters appearing in both large (*Deep Red*) and small (*The Cat O'Nine Tails*) roles; in *Four Flies on Grey Velvet*, for example, the man who really uncovers the culprit responsible for the killings isn't the nominal hero, but the very effete private investigator. Argento may allow these characters to be seen as figures of fun on the one hand, but on the other he depicts them as genuine human beings with feelings of their own; sooner than put them down by having the "normal" characters mocking them, he allows them their dignity.

While Sam is off playing amateur detective, the killings continue to ramp up—and it is here, of course, that Argento really stakes out his terrain. In the course of his long career, Dario has specialized in images of violent death. His murder scenes aren't simply a means to an end—they're show stopping set pieces. His victims don't just get killed; they expire in an elaborately choreographed manner. This is a major contrast to Hitchcock, no matter how badly many critics want to insist upon calling Argento the "Italian Hitchcock." Hitchcock's murder scenes are generally built around suspense; the actual violence is typically muted by comparison. Obvious exceptions include the murder of Marion in *Psycho* (1960) or the brutally drawn-out, hyper-realistic execution of

Rosita Torosh provides a bit of teasing nudity before her run-in with the killer; the combination of the erotic and the horrific is a staple of the *giallo*.

the spy in *Torn Curtain* (1966). Argento's not after realism, however. His murder scenes are executed with an eye for macabre poetry. Like Mario Bava before him, Argento manages to find the beauty in the horror. The victims in *Bird* are all fairly interchangeable characters. We don't learn a thing about any of them, and we're not encouraged to identify with them too deeply. They're there to be sacrificed, and this Argento does in grand style. One of the women is seen preparing for bed before being attacked in her room; another makes her way up a creepy staircase in the dark, the killer having cut the power, only to be slashed to death when she apparently reaches a place of safety. As in the opening sequence with the killer in her lair, it's the attention to detail that's really striking. The use of elaborate camera movements (including alternating points of view, sometimes placing

The German financing resulted in some casting choices, including Werner Peters.

us in the shoes of the victim, sometimes in the mind of the assassin), the insistent, ever-building music score by Ennio Morricone, the precise editing by Fraticelli, and so on. Argento's emphasis on elaborately visualized scenes of death and violence tend to be off-putting for viewers who are accustomed to the old school approach to murder mysteries—where death is often fairly painless, and more often than not kept off-screen altogether—but it proved to be one of the "hooks" which attracted his defenders and helped to make his films so popular at the box office. As such, his work in the *giallo*—and that of his contemporaries—definitely laid the groundwork for the emergence of the slasher film. Yet, while the murder set pieces in the average *Friday the 13th* film are all about irony and excess, with Argento it's usually more in tune to a strange, off-kilter brand of poetry that simply isn't suited to all tastes.

The most significant clue uncovered by Sam in his investigation is a macabre painting which leads to an eccentric, anti-social artist in the countryside. The paining crudely depicts a brutal attack on a young woman in an open, snowy field; the image of the blood spilling from her wounds into the snow can't help but put one in mind of menstruation, which could arguably signal the victim's emergence from innocence into adulthood. Crude, child-like portraits such as this would also re-appear in *Deep Red*. The artist, Berto Consalvi (a wonderful cameo from Mario Adorf, born 1930), had walled himself into a house in the middle of nowhere. He explains to Sam, who makes his way into the place

Mario Adorf (left) makes a memorable cameo appearance as the cat-eating artist Berto Consalvi.

with some difficulty, that he's done painting "crap" like that. "I am going through a mystical period," he explains. "I only paint mystical scenes." "Why?" "Why, why? Because I feel *mystical*, if it's any of your damn business!" When it turns out that Consalvi has taken to capturing cats and cooking them up for dinner, Sam decides to cut their interview short. It's a very funny sequence—a bit of a digression, perhaps—yet the portrait itself remains of vital importance to the resolution of the narrative.

In addition to the stalk-and-kill sequences and the gallery attack on Monica, probably the best-remembered scenes in the film involve Sam and/or Julia being placed in jeopardy. In the first of these, a skull-faced assassin in a yellow (or *giallo*) jacket terrorizes Sam and Julia as they go out for a stroll, hoping to unwind. The assassin is played by Reggie Nalder (1907-1991), a Viennese character actor who is best remembered for playing the would-be killer who falls to his death at the Albert Hall in Hitchcock's *The Man Who Knew Too Much* (1956) and the

The crude painting that would provide Sam with a clue to an eccentric artist.

horrifying Mr. Barlow in Tobe Hooper's mini-series adaptation of Stephen King's *Salem's Lot* (1979). Truth be told, the material involving the assassin is pure filler: It doesn't add anything to the story beyond helping to stretch the movie out to a respectable running time. In a way it doesn't even make a lot of sense that the killer (or more likely, the killer's husband) would reach out to a third party and ask him to take care of Sam and Julia; but like so much in Argento's *oeuvre*, it's less about what makes logical sense and what "plays" on screen. And the scene of the assassin stalking Sam and Julia through a junk yard is brilliantly shot and edited, with the added bonus of some nerve-jangling musical accompaniment courtesy of Morricone. Sam and Julia manage to escape, and the episode is capped with a gag worthy of Hitchcock's *The 39 Steps* (1935). The hunter becomes the hunted as Sam follows him to a hotel, where one would think a man wearing such a distinctive jacket would be easy to pick out of a crowd; it turns out there's a convention of ex-prize fighters at the hotel and they're all dressed in similar jackets, so Sam is out of luck once more. Sam eventually finds the assassin in a squalid little domicile—the man is dead, obviously having been rendered "obsolete" for failing in his mission. The way in which the man's body is revealed to the audience sets up a visual flourish which Argento would revisit and perfect in *Tenebrae*. As Sam stoops down to look at something, the corpse is revealed to be stuffed in the rafters behind him. The next big "danger" scene occurs when Sam is stranded at the train station following his interview with Berto Consalvi; Julia is at home alone, packing her bags, when the killer suddenly appears in the stairwell. The ensuing game of cat and mouse as Julia desperately barricades herself in the apartment is a dress rehearsal of sorts for another similar sequence involving Stefania Casini's character in *Suspiria*. Here again, Argento's flair for arresting visuals is much in evidence, with the light streaming through a hole in the door illuminating Julia's wide-eyed terror and a fantastic use of reflective imagery as the shiny blade of Julia's knife hurtles towards the door from her point of view, as she tries to protect herself. Julia is only saved by Sam's timely appearance—a slightly disappointing and formulaic resolution which Argento would be careful to avoid in later films.

In addition to the painting, the other major clue is a sonic one. A recording of the killer calling to mock

Hitchcock veteran Reggie Nalder makes a vivid, unbilled cameo.

the police contains an unusual sound effect. Sam's friend, Carlo, happens to hear a recording of the call and suddenly he is bugged by the feeling that he knows what it is—but he can't put his finger on it. Eventually it hits him: it's the call of an unusual and very rare bird known as "*hornitus nevalis*," a bird with long feathers which look like glass—the bird with the crystal plumage, in fact. It transpires that there is only one in the whole of Italy at a local zoo. This enables Sam to tip off the police that the zoo happens to be located right next to the Ranieris' apartment building. The use of a sonic clue such as this would be trotted out again by Argento in films like *Suspiria*, *Tenebrae*, *Sleepless*, and *The Card Player*—but before anybody decides they want to go and see a real "*hornitus nevalis*" in captivity, don't bother. Dario invented the species specifically for the film—it certainly makes for an eye-catching title, and it proved to be massively influential, to boot. Apparently, the bird used in the movie is actually a gray crowned crane (*Balearica regulorum*), which is native to various African wetlands; it's the national bird of Uganda, in fact.

The finale of the picture offers a double climax: initially, it looks as if Monica Ranieri's husband, Alberto (Umberto Raho), is the guilty party and he is killed off following a stand-off with the police; when he falls to his death from his apartment, Argento and cinematographer Vittorio Storaro elected to include a subjective shot of his fatal fall—according to Argento, the camera was destroyed in the process. Stanley Kubrick would end up doing the same effect the following year in *A Clockwork Orange* (1971), though whether he was aware

The Unsane Cinema of Dario Argento

Monica (Eva Renzi) ponders what is to be done with the too-inquisitive Sam.

of Argento and his work is open to speculation. With Alberto out of the picture, it looks as if everything is back to normal—but Argento pulls the rug out from us by revealing the Alberto is just a red herring. In fact, the killer is Monica—and the thing which has been bugging Sam all along is his cloudy memory of noticing that the blade wasn't in the black clad figure's hand, but rather in Monica's when she was being "attacked." It's a clever and ingenious reveal and one which Argento would spend years attempting to top; arguably the only time he succeeded in doing so was in *Deep Red*.

It transpires that Monica was once brutally attacked and that her acquaintance, Berto Consalvi, immortalized the gruesome scene in one of his paintings; by chance, she happened to see the picture hanging at the antique shop and it triggered her homicidal rage, thus resulting in the string of killings. Alberto, loyal to his wife, attempted to intervene and she even attempted to kill him for doing so—thus explaining what Sam saw on his fateful late night stroll—and his final selfless gesture was to take the blame for the killings, hoping that Monica would stop and resume a life of normality. Sam and Julia find themselves in danger once more, and the scene of the totally unhinged Monica ranting and raving to Sam—again rendered impotent, this time by a piece of modern sculpture, which pins him to the ground and makes it impossible for him to fight back—is a template for the many Argento *gialli* to come, from *Four Flies on Grey Velvet* through *Trauma* and beyond. Come to think of it, the use of the sculpture also anticipates the ending of *Tenebrae*—though things turn out very differently in that film. Fortunately for Sam and Julia, Inspector Morosini is no fool and he makes it to the gallery in time to prevent them from being added to the roster of victims.

The ironically amusing coda sees Sam and Julia boarding a plane to America while an exhausted Morosini is grilled by TV interviewers about his role in the investigation. As Sam makes his way down the aisle to his seat on the plane, he flashes back to his earlier comments about how quiet and sedate everything is in Rome; he therefore returns to the U.S. a wiser man.

The Bird with the Crystal Plumage remains the ideal "primer" for Argento newbies, as well as a truly accomplished directorial debut. Though filmed on a lower budget than many of the films which followed, it never looks cut-rate. Vittorio Storaro's photography is stylish and Argento's use of the Techniscope format is consistently pleasing to the eye; unlike a lot of his contemporaries, who seemed to have difficulty filling the frame in interesting ways, Argento always manages to find a way to spread visual information throughout the entire frame. The film admittedly appears restrained, even sedate, compared to some of his later works—but the various themes and obsessions are all present and accounted for. The sly social commentary which is evident in so many of his works is here, too. Sam may be a successful writer, but he lives simply, and his apartment décor displays a sympathy with Leftist causes; he doesn't talk politics, but the visual signifiers seem to indicate an affinity for Communism which was shared by Dario himself. It's the wealthy, decidedly *bourgeois* Ranieris who prove to be unbalanced and homicidal, as is so often the case in these films. We never learn much about Monica's back story or how deeply her traumatic encounter with violence affected her, but by resorting to violence herself, she is no better than the man who attacked her so many years before. Argento's use of music as a sort of ironic counterpoint to the imagery is established here, as well. Morricone's lullaby-like themes may not be as aggressive as the prog rock of Goblin in *Deep Red* and *Suspiria* or the heavy metal themes of *Phenomena* and *Opera*, but the music still works because it's so seemingly at odds with the emotional tenor of what it is supporting. The end result is remarkably sure-footed and focused, belying the notion that Argento was tentative about transitioning from critic/screenwriter to director.

Titanus may have hated *Bird*, but that didn't mean they could just shelve the movie; Salvatore made sure of that. Advance publicity was skimpy, but they finally released the film in Rome on February 19, 1970. The initial response was lukewarm. Much like John Carpenter would experience with *Halloween* (1978), it wasn't destined to be an overnight hit; the critics weren't impressed, and audiences didn't exactly line up around the block. Dario had good reason to be worried, but things would take a turn for the better. As the film continued to play, it started to develop positive word of mouth—a number of younger cineastes saw it as a welcome change of pace from the stuffier, more formalized type of filmmaking to which they had become accustomed. Unlike a lot of his peers in the Italian horror-thriller scene, Dario was a young man—and youth was very much "in" during this period of social unrest and upheaval. His film reflected a "hip" sensibility—witness the touches in the art direction, for example, including a "black power" poster on the wall of Tony Musante's apartment; such a touch would have been unthinkable in a film by Riccardo Freda or Mario Bava, for example. It also helped to usher in a bold period of commercial filmmaking in Italy—the *giallo* became a force to be reckoned with and all of a sudden producers like Lombardo were falling over themselves to produce imitative thrillers with similarly baroque titles; Argento was flattered at first, but his flattery soured in time as he worried that people were being inundated with inferior product. In any event, *Bird* ultimately became a hit—first in Italy, where it ended up in the number 13 slot at the Italian box office for the 1970-1971 season[8], then in Germany and the U.S. when Constantin-Film and UMC Pictures, respectively, put it out in June 1970. By May 1971, *Variety* reported that the film had garnered over $2 million in the U.S. alone, ranking at number 43 for the 1970-1971 season, ahead of such titles as Hitchcock's *Topaz* (1969).[7] *Variety* even offered up some cute publicity gimmicks to help promote the movie: "Arrange for an exhibit of rare stuffed birds. Contact local zoos and local pet shops about having a display of live birds in cages."[9] One wonders if any

Positive word of mouth made *Bird* into a popular success.

The Unsane Cinema of Dario Argento

Argento, playing on the audiences' fear of the dark, shows Julia screaming for her life.

enterprising theater owners followed up on those ideas. The film reached Great Britain in March 1971, at which point it was retitled, somewhat less extravagantly as *The Gallery Murders*.

A lot of the mainstream reviewers were impressed; they picked up on its fresh approach, they liked the clever plot twists, and they recognized that Argento had a flair for composing vivid imagery. Roger Ebert awarded it three out of four stars and wrote:

> *The Bird with the Crystal Plumage* is billed as a thriller, and it's a pretty good one. But its scares are on a much more basic level than, say, a thriller by Hitchcock. It works mostly by exploiting our fear of the dark.[10]

Variety's critic was also impressed:

> There are some fascinating plot devices that have to be unraveled and an assortment of oddball characters to keep things moving, even though the action drags now and then. Dario Argento directed from his own screenplay and kept his eye open for bizarre touches at every opportunity.[11]

Even the notoriously waspish Vincent Canby found it praise-worthy, albeit with reservations:

> The dialogue is sappy; the post-synchronization dreadful; the blood too thin; the moods too thick—and yet *The Bird with the Crystal Plumage* has the energy to support its elaborateness and the decency to display its devices with style. Something from each of its better models has stuck, and it is pleasant to rediscover old horrors in such handsome new décor.[12]

That flair would continue to evolve, but paradoxically the reviewers tended to become more hostile; perhaps Argento was a victim of his own early success on some level. In any event, the success of the film ensured that he had a future as a film director—and he was resolved to make the best of that opportunity now that his case of "beginner's nerves" was beginning to wear off.

The film ended up being nominated for some awards, as well—something that wouldn't exactly become the norm for Argento's work moving forward. In 1970, the film was given the Best First Feature (*Migliore opera prima*) prize at the Italian Golden Globes. And that same year, the Italian Golden Goblet Awards handed Dario a prize as Best New Director (*Migliore regista esodriente*). In 1971,

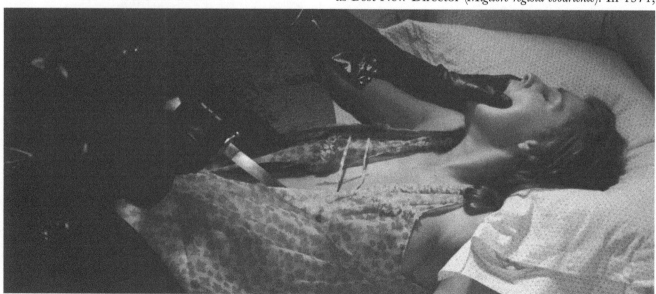

Rosita Torosh is attacked in *The Bird with the Crystal Plumage*'s most notorious sequence.

Argento's debut was nominated for the prestigious Edgar Award, named in honor of the great Edgar Allan Poe. Given Dario's obsession with all things Poe, he must have been over-the-moon about the nomination. 1971 was a pretty strong year and the competition was stiff: *The Private Life of Sherlock Holmes* (Billy Wilder), *Rider on the Rain/Le Passager de la pluie* (René Clément), *Borsalino* (Jacques Deray), and another, more high profile offering from Italy, *The Investigation of a Citizen Above Suspicion/Indagnine su un cittadino al di sopra di ogni sospetto* (Elio Petri); Petri's film, having already won the *Grand Prix* at Cannes, claimed the prize and would go on to win Best Foreign Film at the 1971 Academy Awards. Argento may have walked away empty-handed, but the experience of being nominated for such an award for his very first film as a director was still a heady experience.

U.S. lobby cards for *The Bird with the Crystal Plumage*.

Around this time, Argento also made the acquaintance of another significant collaborator. Luigi Cozzi, the Italian correspondent for Forrest J Ackerman's fanzine *Famous Monsters of Filmland*, was, like Argento, a major cineaste. While working for *Famous Monsters*, he even had occasion to meet with and interview some of his idols in the Italian film scene, including Mario Bava. Cozzi and Argento were among the few people writing about film in Italy who took directors like Bava seriously, and when he picked up on the word of mouth about *The Bird with the Crystal Plumage*, he knew it would be right up his alley. He was so impressed with it that he sought out a meeting with Argento. As luck would have it, they hit it off right away. They shared a sense of youthful enthusiasm for the movies and they discovered that they even shared a birthday—September 7, though Argento was his elder by seven years. With Dario on the ascent and Cozzi looking to hopefully make his own intro into the film industry—his own directing debut, *Il tunnel sotto il mondo* ("The Tunnel Under the World") had been filmed on a shoestring in 1969 and originated as a school project, but it never garnered much in the way of distribution—the meeting proved to be a fortuitous one. However, neither could have had any idea at the time that it would blossom into a lifelong friendship and ongoing business partnership.

Notes:
1. http://www.nocturno.it/l-uccello-dalle-piume-di-cristallo/
2. Jones, Alan, *Dario Argento: The Man, the Myths & the Magic* (Godalming: FAB Press, 2012), p. 20.
3. Argento, Dario, *Peur* (France: Rouge Profond, 2018), p. 87.
4. Argento, Dario, *Paura* (Rome: Einaudi, 2014), p. 67.
5. Quoted from the featurette "Crystal Nightmare," included on the Arrow Video Blu-ray of *The Bird with the Crystal Plumage*.
6. Quoted from the Q&A at Anthology Film Archives, New York City, September 20 2012.
7. http://www.hitparadeitalia.it/bof/boi/boi1969-70.htm
8. *Variety*, May 12 1971, p. 34.
9. *Variety*, August 3 1970, p. 124.
10. https://www.rogerebert.com/reviews/bird-with-crystal-plumage-1970
11. *Variety*, August 3 1970, p. 123.
12. Canby, Vincent, *The New York Times*, July 23 1970.

Chapter Five: Jet-Set *Giallo*

It has been said that making your second film is harder than making your first, and there's justification for this. When Argento made *Bird*, he was "a nobody"—and he could well have remained an obscure Italian filmmaker were it not for the success of his first film. Again, it's worth stressing: *Bird* was not an overnight hit. But when it finally did take off, it did so in a big way. 1970 saw a small spike in the production and release of *giallo* films—some, admittedly, were made before Argento's film helped to change the game. By 1971, however, production increased exponentially. No less than 23 *gialli* hit cinema screens in 1971, with another 33 following in 1972. Of those, two were directed by Dario Argento. Granted, Argento didn't create the genre himself, but it was the success of *Bird* which really opened the floodgates; a look at the titles removes all doubt as to what the producers were looking to cash in on, with examples like *The Case of the Scorpion's Tail/La coda dello scorpione*, *The Iguana with the Tongue of Fire/L'iguana dalla lingua di fuoco*, *The Bloodstained Butterfly/Una farfalla con le ali insanguinate*, *A Lizard in a Woman's Skin/Una lucertola con la pelle di donna*, and *Black Belly of the Tarantula/La tarantola dal ventre nero* standing out in the crowd. Argento became aware of the phenomenon early on, and he wasn't entirely happy about it. In fact, he was not obliged to follow up with another film in the same genre. The fact that he elected to do so, however, undoubtedly sealed his fate; for good or ill, he would become known as the grand master of the *giallo* and Italy's most famous (or infamous) purveyor of scares and shocks.

The origins of what became *The Cat O'Nine Tails* (*Il gatto a nove code*) can be traced back to the summer of 1969. Dardano Sacchetti (born 1944), a politically committed writer, was having a conversation with his friend Luigi Collo. Collo, about whom very little is known, was anxious to break into films as a screenwriter, whereas Sacchetti had no particular ambition in that direction. Collo told Sacchetti that he very much wanted to meet Dario, who was then in the throes of post-production on his directing debut. Sacchetti was able to get hold of Argento's number and the three men met—they hit it off and decided to collaborate on a screenplay. By Sacchetti's own account, they originally collaborated on a politically charged slice-of-life which was much indebted to the success of Dennis Hopper's epoch-making *Easy Rider* (1969). That film was all the rage at the time, and it seemed to make sense from a commercial standpoint to create a film in a similar vein. Argento and Sacchetti poured their youthful observations about the socio-political atmosphere of Italy into the script and it was more-or-less finished by the time *Bird* opened in February 1970; the script's title was *Montesa*, a reference to the Montesa Honda brand of motorcycles which were so popular in Europe. This was followed by a period of metaphorical wheel-spinning as the executives at Titanus gritted their teeth over the initially poor box-office receipts being generated by *Bird*; Lombardo and company felt vindicated and were hardly enthusiastic to back yet another bomb from Dario Argento. Thus, when he proposed *Montesa*, which called for plenty of location shooting in several different European countries, nobody was particularly excited, and the project was shelved. There was talk of getting Argento to direct a sequel to Pasquale Festa Campanile's box-office hit *When Women Had Tails* (*Quando le donne avevano la coda*, 1970), which Argento was evidently agreeable to doing—at the very least it would give him a chance to show a bit of range by doing something very different from his first film.

Then the unthinkable happened: *Bird* went on to become a big hit, especially in the United States, and word got back to Lombardo, who decided to re-release it on a wider scale. When the money started pouring

Argentine poster for *Bird*; artist unknown.

in, Lombardo changed his tune. *Why yes, of course* he would be eager to get on board with another Argento project. All talks of a sequel to *When Women Had Tails* were dropped at that point, though there would indeed be a sequel from Pasquale Festa Campanile himself (*When Women Lost Their Tails/Quando le donne persero la coda*, 1972) without any involvement from Argento. Lombardo made it clear, he wanted another *giallo*. Dario was a little disappointed to see *Montesa* shelved, but he knew he was on to something big and he readily agreed. According to Sacchetti, Argento first thought of doing a thriller inspired by Desmond Morris' book *The Naked Ape*. Published in 1967, *Ape* charts the evolution of humans and their behavior as influenced by the needs and demands of life in the primitive world. It was an ambitious concept, spanning a 60,000 year timeline, and it proved to be too difficult to develop into a workable script. Anxious to cut their losses and move on to something more realistic, Sacchetti, inspired by an article he had read in *Scientific American* about a theory which likened a rare chromosomal imbalance to violent behavior, suggested using that as the narrative hook. Dario responded with enthusiasm and the three men proceeded to develop the idea into a proper screen story.[1] Dario and Salvatore again set up the picture through their Seda Spettacoli imprint, but this time finding the money wasn't nearly so problematic. Additional financing was again secured from German investors—Terra Filmkunst this time—with some added cash supplied through Paris-based Labrador Film. They're not officially credited as producers, but Argento indicated that a deal was struck for American distribution through National General Film, and that they had some input with regards to the casting, as well as the admittedly nonsensical title. Labrador would remain a more-or-less unintrusive partner in the venture, but the head honchos at Terra Filmkunst weren't shy about voicing their views. They let it be known that they expected something very much like *The Bird with the Crystal Plumage*, which was doing robust business in the German market. Argento would later recall that they openly asked for a "jet set *giallo*."[2]

Still shy of his 30th birthday and with the added pressure of a wife and a baby to support, Argento elected to take the cautious route. Sooner than dig in his heels and insist upon finding backing for *Montesa*, he would deliver another *giallo*. However, he was just obstinate enough to do so on his own terms. The harder Titanus and Terra pushed for "*Bird* Redux," the harder he would pull the project in its own direction. The end result would be something of a compromise and for years, he would describe his sophomore effort as his worst film.

The finished script was credited only to Argento, with Dardano Sacchetti and Luigi Collo claiming

Italian *locandina* for *The Cat O'Nine Tails*; artwork by P. Franco.

credit for writing the original story along with Argento; some sources have mistakenly asserted that Collo was a pseudonym for Luigi Cozzi, but this is not true—as outlined above, it was he who initiated the collaborative process with Argento, with Sacchetti as a sort of interested party tagging along for the hell of it; unfortunately, Collo didn't have the same sort of luck as his writing partners and he remains an obscure figure. As Sacchetti would later recall in an interview included on the Arrow Blu-ray edition of *The Cat O'Nine Tails*, the issue of credit became a source of contention early on. Dario claimed that Lombardo didn't want to give Sacchetti and Collo credit. Thus, they initially settled for a quick pay day and the knowledge of a job well done. Subsequently, when Dario gave an interview in which he claimed to have developed

The Unsane Cinema of Dario Argento

the story on his own, Sacchetti went to the press and threatened to sue Argento and his father. Sacchetti and Collo secured proper screen credit in the process, and the ensuing press coverage resulted in Sacchetti being called on to collaborate with Mario Bava in the writing of his new *giallo*, *Twitch of the Death Nerve* (*Reazione a catena*, 1971), which in turn led to a very successful career as a full-time screenwriter. Sacchetti would continue to come in and out of Argento's professional life over the next 25-or-so years, but their relationship would remain one of grudging mutual admiration—and tension.

The budget was set at roughly double that of *Bird*: somewhere in the range of one million dollars. The increased budget allowed for a starrier cast, headlined by popular leading man James Franciscus (1932-1991) and Oscar winner Karl Malden (1912-2009), and it's definitely a slick, well-mounted production. Filming commenced at the beginning of September 1970 and would last for approximately eight weeks, stretching into October of that year. The title, *The Cat O'Nine Tails*, was a clear reference to Argento's first film, and if the director felt pressured to make the film to order to suit the Germans and the Americans, he stuck to his guns and insisted on making a film which was very different from his debut. It proved to be an experience of mixed emotions for Dario, who enjoyed working with Malden and even found a way to channel his newfound role as a father into the narrative, but who ultimately felt that the picture lost focus because of all the different directions he was being pulled in.

By the time production wrapped in October, things were beginning to fall apart where Dario and Marisa were concerned. The added pressure of raising a daughter, coupled with Dario's long hours at Cinecittà, started to take their toll. They would continue to work together to try and repair their relationship, but the writing was already on the wall so far as the fatalistic Dario was concerned. Squabbling with your significant other is one thing, but trying to juggle such huge emotions with a potentially major career is something else altogether; Dario knew he wasn't satisfied with *The Cat O'Nine Tails*, but he couldn't exactly tell that to the press—instead, he would have to wait it out and see how it did.

The film opens with a break-in at the Terzi Institute, a facility devoted to genetic research. While the break-in is in process, blind ex-reporter Franco Arnò (Karl Malden) is out taking a stroll with his young niece, Lori (Cinzia De Carolis). The theme of seeing—and more importantly, seeing and correctly interpreting—had already been a major motif in *The Bird with the Crystal Plumage*, and it's incorporated every bit as rigorously here, as well. Franco may not be able to see, but his other senses are all the sharper because of it; and unlike the many sighted characters he runs into, he's very clever with regards to interpreting the things he experiences. It can be said that the other characters are blinded by their sight, whereas he is unburdened by such distractions and is all the more competent because of it. Franco and Lori are established right away as plain-spoken, down-to-earth characters. He corrects her on a minor point of grammar ("So she says to her." "Said. Said to her.") and she tells him about how she called out a school friend for telling fibs, asking if she was right to do so. "Of course, you should have said it," he assures her. These brief dialogue exchanges help to humanize their characters; they will remain the most interesting characters in the film, in many respects, with Franco in particular emerging as one of Argento's most richly developed characterizations. As he and Lori walk past a parked car, he overhears an intense conversation taking place. He then uses Lori as his eyes and asks her to get a good look at the men in the car. Because of the lighting, she's only able to see one of them—but this will be enough to put her and Franco in a position to have some unique insight into the chain of events which are about to unfold.

Dario Argento discusses a scene with Catherine Spaak on location for *The Cat O'Nine Tails*.

The actual break-in sequence is depicted via subjective camerawork. The cinematography by Erico Menczer (1926-2012, who had recently shot the

Arnò (Karl Malden) and Giordani (James Franciscus) break into a crypt in this French lobby card.

historical drama *Beatrice Cenci*, 1969, for Lucio Fulci) is sleek and attractive; it's not quite as atmospheric as Vittorio Storaro's work on *Bird*, perhaps, but it suits the more "cosmopolitan" tone of the picture beautifully. As the camera roams about the hallways of the institute, Argento allows Ennio Morricone's nerve-jangling music to help ratchet up the suspense. Nobody is killed during the robbery, but it nevertheless sets off a chain of bloodshed.

The next morning, Franco goes back to the scene and finds a flurry of activity—the break-in has been reported and the press is starting to swarm the scene. It's here that he meets Carlo Giordani (James Franciscus), a brash reporter ... for *Paese Sera*. In a nice variation on the old "meet cute" shtick, Carlo bumps into Franco, causing the latter to drop his cane. Carlo chastises Franco for not watching what he's doing, which is nicely ironic on two levels. For one, it's actually Carlo who wasn't watching where he was going; and for another, since Franco can't see anything, he's obviously not at fault for not moving out of the young man's way in time. The cane and the dark glasses tell Carlo everything he needs to know; he's made an ass of himself and he knows it.

Their subsequent interplay is beautifully written and performed. Carlo apologizes, saying he was dumb. "I beg your pardon?" "I said I'm sorry, that was stupid." "That's what I thought you said." Thanks to his better-than-average hearing, Franco obviously heard him the first time—he just enjoys putting the arrogant reporter in his place by compelling him to apologize not once, but twice.

Franciscus brings ample charm to his role as Carlo Giordani; it's the sort of over-eager newsman character that Dario himself probably strongly identified with, and in the hands of a lesser actor he could have come across as obnoxious or even boring. Franciscus had recently finished filming *Beneath the Planet of the Apes* (1970), the first sequel to the 1968 box-office smash *The Planet of the Apes*, and in addition to being a handsome and charismatic screen presence, he was also a genuinely good actor; his take on Carlo humanizes the character and makes it easy for the audience to root for him throughout.

Malden, of course, was an even bigger casting coup. A distinguished veteran of stage and screen, he had won an Oscar as Best Supporting Actor for *A Streetcar Named Desire* (1951) and been nominated for the same

"We find that we need each other." Arnò (Karl Malden) and Lori (Cinzia De Carolis) provide some much-needed warmth in *The Cat O'Nine Tails*.

category for *On the Waterfront* (1954); just prior to going to Rome to work for Dario, he'd wrapped another acclaimed portrayal, that of General Omar N. Bradley, in the Oscar-winning *Patton* (1970). Sooner than play Franco as a pitiable handicapped cliché, Malden imbues the character with strength and courage. When he and Carlo team up, he reveals that he used to be a newspaper man, but he had lost his sight in an accident. When Carlo stammers some platitudes in response, Franco cuts him to the quick: "Wipe that expression of sympathy from your face. I can't see it, but I know it's there." Franco refuses to be defined by his disability; if anything, he's turned it into an advantage, and he uses his inability to see as a means of taking better notice of the things which unfold around him. Carlo is brash and ambitious but he's not always so quick on the uptake; it's Franco who recognizes some clues hiding out in the open, as it were, making them a very good team of amateur detectives.

The robbery is soon followed by a murder. Calabresi (Carlo Alighiero), one of the doctors at the Terzi Institute, is aware of who is responsible for the break-in—and he tries to use that knowledge as a bit of leverage for some blackmail. In fact, the whole affair runs a lot deeper than a mere case of robbery. There's some top-secret research being carried out at the Institute and the sensitive nature of the experiments happens to pertain to a closely guarded secret of one of the research team. Calabresi manages to work it out but his attempts at cashing in on it end poorly when he's pushed in front of a speeding train. The scene of his murder is staged with tremendous energy; it's different from the carefully orchestrated stalk-and-slash scenes of *The Bird with the Crystal Plumage*, but it still manages to serve up a real jolt when the would-be blackmailer falls, in slow-motion, to his demise. Argento experiments with slow-motion and various other techniques (subjective camerawork, elliptical editing rhythms, etc.) throughout the picture, setting the stage for the even more avant garde approach of *Four Flies on Grey Velvet*. In that sense, it's very much a transitional work—it finds him toying around with more and more of the tools at his disposal, thanks largely to the increased budget afforded by the success of his first feature.

The scenes between Franco and Lori are some of the warmest and most disarming to be found in Argento's filmography. While Dario struggled with the demands being imposed on him in his sophomore effort, he was still coming to the film from a happy place in his personal life. His marriage to Marisa was still going pretty strong and the arrival of Fiore in January 1970 was a major source of pride and happiness. It's possible to see the warmth, love, and affection he was feeling towards his first-born daughter in the scenes between Franco and Lori. It's revealed that they're not really related at all, though they identify themselves as uncle and niece. As Franco explains, "We find that we need each other." There's nothing unwholesome or off-kilter about their relationship; they feel genuine love and respect for one another, and this allows for some charming character interplay.

The various murder scenes are shot and edited with maximum effectiveness. Argento emphasizes tactile touches, including the gasping of the victims as they're garroted to death—an effect complemented by the weird, atonal vocals included in Ennio Morricone's soundtrack—and gruesome flourishes like the mucus which spills out of one character's mouth as she succumbs (which is later echoed when the killer, badly wounded in

Dr. Calabresi (Carlo Alighiero) comes to a messy end in *The Cat O'Nine Tails*.

a struggle, drools blood in the same manner). There's even some casual sadism thrown in, as when one victim, already dead and left staring aimlessly at the camera, has his cheeks slashed with a razor for good (?) measure. The manner in which these scenes are staged and executed differs wildly from *Bird*, however, suggesting that Argento was going out of his way to avoid repeating himself. In a way this isn't surprising, given the tumultuous nature of making the film—the more the producers encouraged him to recycle from the first film, the harder he fought by going in different directions. Thus, while the use of subjective camerawork is carried over from the first film (here it is used solely to represent the killer's point of view, however, whereas in *Bird* it would vary between stalker and victim), there are absolutely no shots of the killer's hands—making this a very rare movie in Argento's filmography where the director isn't afforded a chance to don a pair of black leather gloves. In an attempt to keep the killer's identity unknown to us, the shots are framed in such a way that we never see the assailant's hands. By doing so, Argento keeps us guessing as to whether the killer is a man or a woman. The actual killings have a brutal edge to them, but for the most part there really isn't a great deal of blood and gore; if *Bird* managed to straddle the line between thriller and horror, then this film is rooted more in classical suspense.

The humorous vignettes in *Bird* are repeated here, as well. Some of it works better than others. The oddball peripheral characters like Gigi the loser (Ugo Fangareggi), a safe-cracker with a knack for getting pinched by the police, and an angry barber (Pino Patti, who had played Faiena in *Bird*) ranting about the newspapers' suggestion that the killer could be a barber—not realizing that his current customer, Carlo, is the one who wrote the article in question—are very effective. The entire vignette with Gigi is particularly memorable. He's introduced in the midst of a very strange competition: a game to see who can come up with the longest streak of insults without stopping. Gigi emerges as the victor, but that's not exactly the norm for him. When Carlo proposes that they should break into Terzi's home and gain access to his safe, Gigi is reluctant. "Why do you think they call me Gigi the loser?" While their subsequent adventure in the Terzi house does yield some significant information, there's nevertheless the sense of Argento indulging the sequence because he's so fond of this strange peripheral character—which is definitely a point in the film's favor. The attention to detail in the scene with Gigi cracking open the professor's safe reveals a fetishistic love for technical detail which can't help but remind one of the safe cracking scenes in *Every Man is My Enemy*; Argento would continue to refine this in subsequent films, often treating viewers to glimpses of the inner workings of telephones (*Four Flies on Grey Velvets*), locks (*Opera*), and so forth. There's also some laughs to be had thanks to a corpulent policeman (Corrado Olmi), who is more concerned with talking about his wife's cooking than he is with doing his job. But on the other hand, the film gives us the one and only instance of a car chase in the Argento filmography—and it absolutely screams "filler," ultimately being played for laughs. Argento's complaints about being pressured into making a more overtly commercial thriller are borne out by scenes such as this, which simply aren't consistent with his way of telling stories.

As Carlo and Franco continue to investigate, the former begins a relationship with Anna (Catherine Spaak), the daughter of Professor Terzi (Tino Carraro),

Front cover for the U.S. press book for *The Cat O'Nine Tails*.

The Unsane Cinema of Dario Argento

the director of the institute. If the scenes between Lori and Franco radiate warmth, then the scenes between Carlo and Anna are precisely the opposite. It's not clear whether this is entirely intentional. Both Franciscus and Spaak (born 1945) are attractive performers, but they simply don't generate any chemistry. Of course, Carlo is basically using Anna for information, so some of that disconnect could well have been deliberate on Argento's part. And yet, when confronted with their love scene, which is staged very much like a showdown in a Spaghetti Western, it's difficult to reconcile what was really intended. It's a strange scene and it points to Argento's general awkwardness in dealing with sex in his

Anna (Catherine Spaak) succumbs to Giordani in the film's bizarre love scene.

films—indeed, there really isn't a lot of love making to be found in his films. The Sam/Julia relationship worked nicely in *Bird*—and the romance between Marcus and Gianna in *Deep Red* is utterly charming yet telling, we never see them making love. But the scenes with Carlo and Anna in this film, as well as the decidedly awkward romantic subplot between Roberto and Dalia in *Four Flies on Grey Velvet*, suggest that Argento did well to generally avoid such things in so many of his films. In any event, the film generally screeches to a halt whenever their courtship takes center stage. Anna is established early on as a coquettish brat who is accustomed to getting her way. She's headstrong and independent, which should theoretically make her more interesting than poor under-written Julia had been in *Bird*—but she's also spoiled, narcissistic and utterly devoid of personality.

Spaak's performance is remarkably wooden, but in fairness she fared much better for Damiano Damiani in his off-beat *giallo A Rather Complicated Girl* (*Una ragazza piuttosto complicata*, 1969), suggesting that she may have been undermined by the way the character was written.

Since we in the audience know that Carlo doesn't really care that much about her, it's difficult to become invested in them as a couple—thus making their scenes tough to warm to.

As accomplished as the film is—and it really is beautifully rendered in many respects—it also suffers from a lack of real forward momentum. *Bird* hit the ground running and relentlessly followed its protagonist as he follows a series of clues to the inevitable conclusion. *Cat*, on the other hand, seems a bit confused about where it's headed. This confusion is summed up by the title itself. While mulling over the various leads they have to work with, Carlo quips, "It's like a cat with nine tails." Franco finds the simile amusing and counters, "A cat *of* nine tails, like the old naval whip." That's all well and good, but what does it mean? At least the bird with the crystal plumage turned out to be a real bird—even if Dario had to invent it for the purposes of the plot. Here it's obvious that there was a need for there to be another eye-catching title, but it really doesn't mean much of anything. This extends to the plot. Argento would never again return to the theme of industrial espionage and for good reason. In the context of a *giallo*, this sort of motivation feels awfully out of place. The main thrust of the narrative—the investigation of the bland and rather colorless suspects who inhabit the Terzi Institute—is therefore a bit weak and flimsy. The film really comes to life when it digresses into sidebar incidents, nearly all of which don't really add anything to the main plot thread. Some of these digressions admittedly help to drag the film out to an overly-flabby one hour and 51-minute running time—a good 20 minutes or so could easily have been lost for the greater good. Yet the best of these sidebar sequences add immeasurably to the film's appeal. Consider, for example, the subplot with Gigi the loser, or the bravura set piece in which Franco and Carlo break into a graveyard to retrieve a clue from a dead woman's coffin. Granted, both of these scenes do advance the plot—in a way. Yet they play out like self-contained mini-movies and they can't help but stand out in relief from the more problematic central narrative.

Argento continues his exploration of "the other" here, as well. In most of his early works, he focuses in a lot on characters who are in some way or another disenfranchised or set apart from the mainstream of society. The upper crust characters, represented by the Terzis, are flat, boring and downright unsympathetic. The real color is to be found in the oddball characters like Gigi the loser, who tries every way he knows how to outwit the system—and invariably fails to do so. The fact that he keeps on fighting, even if it's with less-than-lofty goals in mind, makes him curiously appealing. Then there's the coded-as-underground gay scene, which

continues the dialogue on sexual diversity from *Bird*. In the earlier film, the gay antiques dealer was depicted as a limp-wristed sissy—but crucially he is not demeaned in any way, shape or form. Here, the character of Dr. Braun (Horst Frank), though far from sympathetic himself, is revealed to be a homosexual; he's not hiding that fact, either, even if he doesn't "advertise" it in the way that the antiques dealer in the earlier film had done. When Carlo goes to interview him, he finds him at the St. Peter's Club, a gay establishment; Argento depicts the club with a sympathetic eye. It's a place where people who don't fit in to the so-called "norms" of society can gather to unwind and have fun. There's nothing mocking about it and though Carlo is depicted as a conventional heterosexual male, he doesn't appear to be weirded out by the environment. When Braun comments that he has beautiful eyes, he seems genuinely flattered. "You really think so?" It's not done in a way that comes off as condescending or insincere, either. Braun may have his shortcomings as a character, but his sexuality is not one of them. Later on, Carlo is visited by an informer (Umberto Raho, who played Alberto Ranieri in *Bird*) who rats on Braun because the scientist has stolen his lover from him. The scene is unexpectedly bittersweet and moving, with the informer admitting that he's doing something "despicable," but because he feels he has nothing to live for now that his former lover has deserted him, he no longer cares. The scene ends with the man saying he plans to kill himself; Carlo looks on sympathetically but can't find the right words to fit the occasion. It's an irony, of course, since his profession revolves around finding the right words—but the scene, though brief, is yet another digression which adds texture to the bigger picture.

Carlo subsequently discovers that Anna is not actually the Professor's biological daughter. While rooting around in the professor's papers during his adventure with Gigi the loser, Carlo uncovers the older man's diary—it provides a glimpse into the man's dysfunctional mind. The notion of a seemingly respectable member of the upper strata of society hiding a terrible secret is something Argento returns to time and again, especially in his *gialli*. While Argento is not the most overtly political of filmmakers, there's an argument to be made that he uses genre tropes as a means of voicing his views on the various levels of Italian society. Put bluntly, it's evident that he's not in sympathy with the upper tier of society, whereas his sympathies extend more to working people like Carlo—and fringe figures like Gigi. The professor adopted Anna as a young child and as she grew into adulthood and became sexually mature, he found himself thinking less-than-fatherly thoughts about her. Anna, looking to capitalize on everything life has to offer, has willingly participated in these sexual escapades; the knowledge of this strains Carlo's already ambivalent attitude about her even further. Argento does not depict Anna as a victim: she's a willing participant, and as such she has knowingly entered into an arrangement which, if not technically incestuous, is far from healthy. In entering into a relationship with Carlo, she's finally opening herself up to a man who can't really do anything to further her socially or economically—Carlo is "beneath her" on that level, after all. She seems to have some affection for him but it's not necessarily reciprocated—and when he clumsily accuses her of being the killer, it appears to drive a lasting wedge between them.

Franco's role in the investigation becomes complicated when Lori is kidnapped; the killer promises to murder her if the two men don't drop their investigation. Franco displays a greater awareness of the danger he has subjected his loved ones to than most of Argento's protagonists—many of whom blithely endanger others without a care in the world, simply because they're so fixated on solving the riddle—but he is also insightful enough to realize that dropping the matter is no guarantee of her safe return. "When someone has committed four murders, he won't hesitate to commit the fifth!" Fortunately, by this stage he and Carlo have rounded up some useful information and they're both convinced that the drama will reach its climax where everything began, at the Terzi Institute.

With the aid of Carlo's friend, Police Superintendent Spimi (Pier Paolo Capponi, who had appeared in *Commandos*), they swarm the place and search it room by room. As the police conduct their search, Franco stands on the sidelines—silently hoping for Lori's safe return. The search doesn't turn anything up, but Carlo decides to keep looking on his own and he finally locates what he's looking for on the roof of the building. It turns out that the killer is Doctor Casoni (Aldo Reggiani), the youngest member of the research team. The random nature of the killer's identity has irked some viewers, but it seems perfectly consistent with Argento's world view—there's no telling who is a psychopath in his films, and frequently perfectly normal, benign-looking people are hiding awful secrets. Many of the characters are revealed to be deeply flawed, so while it may not seem like Dario is really "playing fair" here, he hasn't really cheated, either. In the subsequent very brutal hand-to-hand fight between Casoni and Carlo, the latter is seriously injured and left for dead.

Franco has also made his way to the scene, however, and he pins Casoni against the wall with the blade housed in his cane—even here, deceptively mundane objects prove to be hiding potentially lethal secrets. Casoni blurts out his motivation—while conducting research on a genetic defect whereby men with the XYY chromosome combination, as opposed to the standard XY, are revealed to be predisposed to violent behavior, he discovers that he, too, carries this genetic abnormality. In trying to keep it secret, he broke into the institute and removed the results of his tests from Calabresi's filing cabinet. Calabresi was already on to him, and thus the whole bloody series of events was set into motion. The XYY angle is actually derived from the British thriller *Twisted Nerve* (1968), directed by John and Roy Boulting, which drew controversy by drawing a link between "mongolism" (as down syndrome was then known) and psychotic behavior. As Maitland McDonagh argues in her book *Broken Mirrors/Broken Minds: The Dark Dreams of Dario Argento*, "rather than blaming Casoni's mania on his genes (as *Twisted Nerve* does), it suggests he's driven himself to acts of insane violence by brooding about the matter."[3] That's a point well worth considering as it suggests that Argento and his co-writers were actively trying to avoid the pitfall that plagued the Boultings; the end result manages to avoid being offensive and again displays a sensitivity on Argento's part with regards to how he interprets their behavior. Casoni is not genetically destined to become a killer, but he becomes one when he allows his obsession for perfection to take control of his life and his actions. Tellingly, Franco couldn't care less about his rationale. He just wants Lori back. When Casoni picks up on his distress, he decides to have some fun at his expense by boasting that he killed her—that he will never see her again. His choice of words is deliberately

Lori (Cinzia De Carolis) is abducted by the killer in this German lobby card.

The alternate ending of *The Cat O'Nine Tails* was scrapped prior to release, but that didn't stop the German distributor from using a still for one of their lobby cards.

insulting as he's never "seen" her to begin with, but in underestimating the capabilities of a "cripple" like Franco, whom he obviously deems to be an inferior, he sets himself up for a painful exit. While trying to escape from Franco, Casoni falls through the opening of an elevator shaft and plummets to his death—Argento adds an added touch of sadism by showing him grabbing hold of the elevator cables and getting one hell of a rope burn as he falls; it's a nasty touch, one which he would recycle later for one of his late period works, *Giallo*. The film ends on an ambiguous note, with Lori's voice calling out for Franco (or "Cookie," as she calls him); we're not told what has happened to Carlo and we're denied the closure of seeing Franco and Lori embracing for the camera. It wasn't always that way, however. Argento originally filmed a more conventional ending where Lori and Franco are reunited, followed by a brief, humorous coda showing Carlo recuperating in bed—with Anna at his side. According to Luigi Cozzi, when Argento showed him a rough cut of the film, he encouraged him to drop the happy business at the end, saying it felt too much like the ending of a Hollywood movie. Since Dario was already annoyed by the pressures placed on him by the moneymen to deliver a more conventional product, he took the advice—and it's a good thing he did. The ending, as it stands, is memorably vicious and breathlessly paced; its ambiguity adds to its appeal. To have ended on such a trite note would have undercut its effectiveness tremendously.

While Argento has long expressed disappointment with it, there is much to admire in *The Cat O'Nine Tails*. In addition to its warm and ingratiating performances from Karl Malden and James Franciscus, it shows Argento continuing to tinker with the medium in interesting ways. He and Franco Fraticelli indulge in some more overtly "arty" editing techniques here, with scenes often ending with odd "flash forward" cuts which take us from one set piece to the next; Argento would continue to refine this in *Four Flies on Grey Velvet* before basically abandoning the technique for good. The camerawork is slick and agile, and Morricone's music is extremely effective. If it suffers from a lack of focus and is in need of a bit of tightening for pacing purposes, it still emerges as a very entertaining piece of work. The best scenes—the swearing contest, the creepy cemetery sequence, the exciting finale—are as good as just about anything in Argento's work. True, the film loses its narrative momentum and the relationship between Carlo and Anna never convinces, but it's still a much stronger and more endearing work than it is often given credit for.

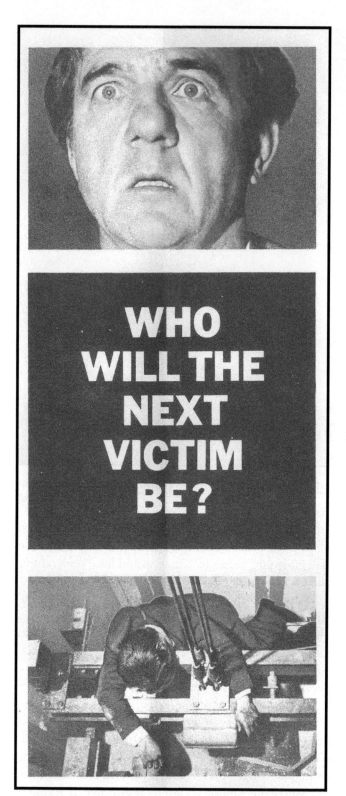

From the U.S. press book for *The Cat O'Nine Tails*.

The Cat O'Nine Tails opened in Italy on the February 11, 1971, just a week shy of the one-year anniversary of *Bird*. Titanus was pleased as it ended up doing outstanding business in Italy, coming in at number eight for the 1970-1971 box-office season.[4] As such, it did even better than *Bird* domestically, thus proving that Dario was no mere flash-in-the-pan. In a *Variety* report dated May 12, 1971, it was stated that the film was doing "smash trade" and that "*Cat* actually outscored *Dr. Zhivago* at the same house."[5] That same report also notes that Argento already had another project, *Four Flies on Gray* [sic] *Velvet*, lined up for a July start date.

Elsewhere, however, it was the exact opposite of *Bird*'s initial reception. The Italians may have embraced it, but nobody else was apparently ready to do so. National General put it out in the U.S. in May, with Constantin-Film and Warners following suit in Germany and France, respectively, in July and August. *Variety*'s "exploitips" for the film proposed an odd-sounding gimmick for the U.S. release: "Send a girl in hot pants around to distribute the nine *Cat* teaser ads and give special admittance to patrons collecting all nine."[6] The box office round-up in *Variety* in May 1972 noted that *Cat* ranked in the 148th slot for domestic U.S. releases[7], which was hardly a repetition of the brisk business *Bird* had done. National General, who had invested a lot of their resources in the picture, ended up losing out—and within a few years, they would go belly-up. Business may have been mediocre by comparison, but fortunately for Argento it made more than enough domestically to ensure that his ascent was unaffected.

As for the critics, they were generally cooler toward the film than they had been with *Bird*. A.H. Weiler, for example:

> Only blindly abject devotees of the whodunit should discover catnip in *The Cat O'Nine Tails*, which whipped into local theaters yesterday from Italy, complete with English dialogue, color and James Franciscus and Karl Malden to make this *Cat* hop sporadically. [...] Unfortunately, Dario and Salvatore Argento, the producer and director-writer, who previously were represented here by another sample of the genre, *The Bird with the Crystal Plumage*, have drawn mere surface portrayals from a scurrying cast, who only occasionally generate some tension. [...] You'd have to be dedicated to puzzles to love this *Cat*.[8]

Riccardo Menello also saw it as a step back from Dario's debut:

> Argento is still struggling with things like plausibility [...] In *The Bird with the Crystal Plumage*, story and script dictate the film's visual style, while in *The Cat O'Nine Tails* story and screenplay are in conflict with technique and it's often those scenes least tied to the plot that succeed most."[9]

And the respected critic Judith Crist pretty much loathed it, describing it as:

> "a sleazily sick and senseless murder mystery designed chiefly to provide close-ups of the death throes of several people who are garroted. [...] This vomitous offering comes from the Italian writer/director who made his debut with *The Bird with the Crystal Plumage*, an equally badly dubbed flashy-stylish murder mystery that had some popularity last summer among famished thriller nuts, ready to settle for cheap.[10]

The reviewer for *Variety* was more impressed:

> The father and son team specializing in Italian mystery thrillers continues to impress with an English-dubbed release from National General. [...] Again, the younger Argento takes a fairly routine murder mystery (screenplay by Dario Argento, from a story by him and Luigi Collo and Dardano Sacchetti) and embellishes it with a style that gives *Cat* a mystical quality, fascinating to behold. Subtlety is not one of the director's strong points and he tries for comedy at some odd moments, but overall, it's a good effort. Malden is greatly subdued and interesting to watch as a blind man who sees more than his sighted fellow investigators.[11]

Candice Tripp's eye-catching cover for the Arrow Films Blu-ray/DVD release of *The Cat O'Nine Tails*.

From the U.S. press book for *The Cat O'Nine Tails*.

Notes:
1. Sacchetti's version of events as recounted in the featurette "The Writer O'Many Tales," included on the Arrow Video Blu-ray release of *The Cat O'Nine Tails*.
2. Jones, Alan, *Dario Argento: The Man, the Myths & the Magic* (Godalming: FAB Press, 2012), p. 25.
3. McDonagh, Maitland, *Broken Mirrors/Broken Minds: The Dark Dreams of Dario Argento* (London, Sun Tavern Fields, 1991), p. 66.
4. https://boxofficebenful.blogspot.com/search?q=box+office+italia+1970-71
5. *Varietyy*, May 12 1971, p. 40.
6. *Variety*, June 21 1971, p. 102.
7. *Variety*, May 3 1972, p. 34.
8. Weiler, A.H., *The New York Times*, May 27, 1971.
9. Menello, Riccardo, "Dark Universe: The World of Dario Argento," *Photon*, #24, July 1975.
10. Crist, Judith, *New York*, June 7, 1971.
11. *Variety*, June 21, 1971, p. 101.

Chapter Six: Bye-Bye, *Giallo*

By the time he was set to make his third feature, Argento was in no doubt about the genre. It would, of course, be another *giallo*. In theory, however, it was to be his final foray into the genre. Every week seemed to bring another low-budget thriller clearly indebted to Argento's success and he was getting sick of it; crucially, he was also afraid that audiences would soon be overdosing on *gialli*. This time, there would be no German co-producers to impose their ideas on him; Salvatore and Argento had no difficulty raising the bulk of the budget themselves, while Universal Production France would pony up the rest.

To develop the story for his third feature, Argento reached out to Luigi Cozzi; Cozzi would have the added honor of serving as Dario's assistant, and he would even be drafted in to play a small but crucial role as the masked stranger who causes so much trouble for the protagonist. The story would offer a mélange of influences, many of them courtesy of Cozzi's literary tastes, with more ideas pilfered from *The Screaming Mimi* and a particularly effective sequence lifted from Cornell Woolrich (1903-1968)'s *The Black Alibi*. The Woolrich connection extended to Dario's original narrative "hook," in which the protagonist attends a séance run by a medium who senses the presence of a murderer in attendance; the medium is killed, thus setting off a chain of murders. Dario pulled the idea from Woolrich's *Night Has a Thousand Eyes*, which inspired a film *noir* of the same name in 1948, but he was very much opposed to the idea of making the medium into somebody with real supernatural powers; he felt it necessary to root the film in reality, and when neither he nor Cozzi could find a way to make the idea work without the medium having legitimate extrasensory powers, they decided to abandon the concept altogether. Of course, Argento would subsequently embrace the idea of making it a legitimate medium with real psychic powers for his *giallo* masterpiece *Deep Red*.

On a more personal level, the project also enabled Argento to wrestle with some his own inner demons. Ironically, while *The Cat O'Nine Tails* had been a tumultuous experience, the film itself displayed some real optimism, especially in the relationship between Franco Arnò and his adoring "niece," Lori. *Four Flies on Grey Velvet* (*4 mosche di velluto grigio*) would be a comparatively sedate and happy experience on the sound stage, but it arose out of a dark period in Dario's relationship with Marisa. Dario would later admit that he based the central couple, Roberto and Nina Tobias, on himself and Marisa. American actor Michael Brandon was slender and wore his dark hair long, as did Dario, while another American performer, Mimsy Farmer, would mirror the petite Marisa. The fact that the story hinges on the idea that Nina is secretly trying to murder Roberto, after first driving him insane, left no doubt as to the state of the Argentos' crumbling relationship. Even so, according to Cozzi, it was Mario Foglietti (1936-2016) who hit upon the idea of making the wife the murderer. Foglietti, a journalist friend of Dario's, had submitted a story outline to Argento hoping to catch his interest; Argento wasn't keen on the story, but he loved the revelation of the killer's identity and decided to make use of it—this is why Foglietti's name ended up on the story credit, even though he didn't play an active role in the writing, which was done in close collaboration between Argento and Cozzi.[1] No doubt the idea of making the wife into the killer appealed to Dario on a subconscious level because of the problems he was having with Marisa; his art would therefore allow him to work through his personal issues, even if the public at large had no idea about the autobiographical aspects.

Production on *Four Flies* commenced on July 12, 1971 and would last for nine weeks into the beginning of September. As a sign of his rising prominence in the film industry, Salvatore was able to ink a deal for his son's newest film with one of the major studios. Paramount Pictures would agree to handle the distribution in the United States, making it the first Paramount release to carry Argento's name since *Once Upon a Time in the West*; sadly, it would also prove to be the last. Paramount's French branch, Marianne Productions, was also actively involved in the production—thus necessitating the presence of a certain number of French names in the credits; more on that in a bit. By his own admission, Argento spent much of the filming concerned about what his early success had wrought on the Italian film

Nina (Mimsy Farmer) and Roberto (Michael Brandon) under stress in *Four Flies on Grey Velvet*; their relationship mirrored aspects of Dario's own failing marriage to Marisa during this period.

industry. With so many thrillers featuring baroque titles piling up on each other, he had good reason to worry that his own work might become lost in the shuffle. Factor in the problems he was having at home with Marisa and it seems that *Four Flies* arose out of a pretty dark place. Even so, Argento was determined to ramp up his technique as far as it could go—if this was to be his farewell to the *giallo*, then he was going to go out with a bang.

Remembering the advice he had received from Sergio Leone, who stressed the importance of grabbing the viewer in the very first scene, Argento kicks off *Four Flies* with a bang. The main titles sequence is something of a precursor to the modern music video, as it depicts rock drummer Roberto Tobias (Michael Brandon) rehearsing with his band. The scene is audacious as all get-out. Argento includes shots taken from inside of guitars, perched at odd angles focusing on the guitar player strumming the strings, even peering at Roberto through his cymbals. Intercut with the rehearsal are fragmented glimpses of Roberto going about his daily routine, gradually becoming aware that a mysterious man is following him. Every now and again, it cuts to a black screen where the various credits are superimposed—a black screen, that is, save for a pulsing and exposed human heart beating at the left side of the frame. When it cuts to these images, Morricone's music cuts out—establishing a "now you hear it/now you don't" editing rhythm which will come back later in the film. The titles climax with Roberto noticing that a fly which has been making a nuisance of itself while he's playing had landed on the cymbals—he bides his time then smashes the pesky insect between the two metal discs. It's a definite call-back of sorts to the opening of *Once Upon a Time in the West*, wherein sleepy gunfighter Jack Elam catches an annoying fly in the barrel of his gun, though Cozzi would later say that he pulled the idea from the opening of Raymond Chandler (1888-1959)'s *The Little Sister*.

From there, it plunges fairly rapidly into the action as Roberto leaves the venue where he's been practicing—only to notice the mysterious man lurking across the street. What follows is a classic case of the hunter becoming the hunted—or so it seems. On that level, it reminds one of the scene where Sam turns the tables on the assassin in yellow in *The Bird with the Crystal Plumage*, but we soon learn that it is a deception of sorts. Argento utilizes some striking camera set-ups in this scene, with a great split diopter shot which allows him to keep focus on a discarded cigarette in the foreground of the frame while also keeping focus on Roberto as he continues to chase his prey in the rear of the frame. There's also a nice use of "visual echoing" as Roberto has confetti thrown at him by a drunken passerby—in much the same way that the stranger had been by

a little kid during the opening titles montage. This use of repeated imagery would become a major motif in *Deep Red*. The scene climaxes, appropriately enough, in a theater. As Roberto enters, subjective shots show him as he pushes his way through heavy red draperies—a visual motif which Argento would utilize to great effect in later films like *Deep Red* and *Opera*. The stage is being set, literally and figuratively, for the first of the film's theatrical deceptions. Roberto confronts the man, Carlo Morosi (Calisto Calisti), demanding to know why he's been following him. There's a scuffle and it ends with Morosi being accidentally stabbed by Roberto, who is simply trying to defend himself. Left confused, frightened

U.K. poster art for *Four Flies on Grey Velvet*; artist unknown.

Bizarre English export ad for *Four Flies*, with a more literal translation of the title.

and holding a bloody knife in his hand, Roberto is none too pleased when somebody switches on a spotlight and begins taking photographs. The strange voyeur (played by an uncredited Luigi Cozzi) is hidden behind a creepy, doll-faced mask—and before Roberto can register what's going on, the spotlight goes out and the voyeur disappears. The entire sequence is staged with tremendous skill and visual élan by Argento; compared to the slick, sleek and rather modern look of *The Cat O'Nine Tails*, it finds him going back to the moodier, more atmospheric visual schematic of *Bird*. It's evident straight away that if *Cat* was a compromise, then *Four Flies* represents him aggressively pursuing his own vision without compromise.

Roberto is left badly shaken by the encounter at the theater, for good reason, but he does not find solace in the warmth of his home life. Unlike Sam or Carlo before him, Roberto is a man whose life is in turmoil even without the addition of the accidental murder.

Thus, he's the first of Argento's more "troubled" protagonists. On the surface he appears to have a lot going for him. His band is doing well, he's married to a beautiful woman, and they have a beautiful home in a swanky suburban neighborhood. All that glitters is not gold, however, and for all their material prosperity, there is a major hole at the center of his relationship. His wife, Nina (Mimsy Farmer), seems supportive and caring—but they display precious little in the way of chemistry. Unlike the awkward romance between Carlo and Anna in *The Cat O'Nine Tails*, this is a very deliberate move on Argento's part. Simply put, these two people do not belong together, and as the story unfolds it becomes apparent that their marriage is founded on a perversion of the ideal of love.

Michael Brandon was not the first choice to play Roberto, though he ended up getting along extremely well with Dario. According to Luigi Cozzi, there had been some talk of getting Tony Musante back to play the part—but he wanted too much money and that was the end of that. Having him back to play such a different character might have been interesting in a purely schematic sense, but it would have also encouraged more comparisons with *Bird*—and this is a very different film with very different aims. Dario liked the idea of casting the actor-musician James Taylor (born 1948); given that Roberto is a musician, the idea made sense—but nothing came of it. Paramount discussed using John Lennon (1940-1980) or Ringo Starr (born 1940), but the odds of that ever coming to fruition weren't very favorable. Jean-Louis Trintignant, the star of *Metti, una sera a cena*, was approached but had to pass owing to prior commitments; though a brilliant actor, it's difficult to envision him in the role of a rock and roll drummer. Terence Stamp (born 1938), who had already passed on the role of Harmonica

Roberto (Michael Brandon) thinks he's just killed a man.

"What have you got against mailmen, huh?" The mailman (Gildo Di Marco) pays the price for making a special delivery to Roberto.

in *Once Upon a Time in the West*, had reservations about the script—but another Englishman, Michael York (born 1942), was willing to do it. Argento was eager to make use of York, but then filming went over schedule on *Zeppelin* (1971) and Dario couldn't delay production to accommodate him.[2] It's interesting to consider how some of these actors might have fared, but ultimately Argento, remembering the film *Lovers and Other Strangers* (1970), decided to go for Michael Brandon, who accepted the part. Brandon's rather flat, unpleasant interpretation of the character seems to have been exactly what Dario had in mind. Roberto isn't really a hero; he's a deeply flawed character whose inability to understand what is going on around him nearly costs him his life. He doesn't even save the day or unravel the puzzle himself; that's left to other, more engaging characters to accomplish. It's a bold move for a thriller and one which can make the film difficult for some viewers to engage with, but there's no doubt it was an absolutely calculated move on Argento's part.

The fact that Roberto and Nina are so completely disconnected is central to the plot. It also allows for a bit of added "romance" in the form of Nina's cousin Dalia (Francine Racette), who comes to stay with them just as things are starting to get really awkward. Dalia is loyal to Nina but the same can't be said for Roberto; when they're left alone together, he seduces Dalia. Their bathtub love scene again demonstrates that Argento isn't particularly well-suited to depicting physical love on screen—and yet, here again it seems to be a deliberate decision, which underlines the notion that Roberto is far too self-absorbed and egotistical to properly engage with another human being. It's all about the thrill of the moment for him and it provides a brief moment of respite during what is admittedly a particularly unpleasant period for him.

The Tobias' maid, Amelia (Marisa Fabbri), is aware of what is going on and tries to indulge in a bit of blackmail; like Doctor Calabresi in *Cat*, she learns that playing games with psychopathic murderers is not a wise course of action. In one of the film's most audacious set pieces, she goes to a public park, where she is to meet with the person who is behind these strange events. The scene of her sitting in the sunshine, silently observing as young lovers make out and children play anticipates a similar scene in *Tenebrae*, wherein John Saxon finds himself in a similar situation. Having already started experimenting with jarring touches of "flash forward" editing techniques in *Cat*, Argento takes the technique further still in this scene. Time loses all meaning and the maid eventually realizes that she's lost all track of time as the park is suddenly dark and deserted, and she finds herself locked in for the night. She is not alone, however. The killer stalks her through the park and despite her best efforts to summon help from the other side of the wall enclosing the park, she ends up with a slit throat. It's a bravura piece of filmmaking, ranking up there with the gallery attack in *Bird* or the cemetery scene in *Cat*. It also inevitably recalls a very similar scene in Jacques Tourneur and Val Lewton's underrated horror/*noir The Leopard Man* (1943)—though both films were inspired by Cornell Woolrich's *The Black Alibi*.

As in *Bird* and *Cat*, Dario indulges his dark sense of humor by bringing in a variety of strange, quirky secondary characters: there's a paranoid mailman (Gildo Di Marco, the stuttering pimp from *Bird*) and a pornography-obsessed neighbor (Guerrino Crivello), both of whom are fairly minor in the plot. Far more

Roberto (Michael Brandon) finds "God" (Bud Spencer).

significant are the characters of a tramp named Godfrey, also known as "God," played by the mighty Bud Spencer—in his third and final collaboration with Dario following appearances in *Today We Kill, Tomorrow We Die!* and *The 5-Man Army*—and his sidekick, a Bible-quoting vagrant known as "The Professor" (Oreste Lionello). "God" is introduced when Roberto seeks him out, which is rife with all kinds of symbolism, and the point is underlined when Ennio Morricone pipes in a sardonic verse of "Hallelujah!" on the soundtrack. The character is actually another steal from Fredric Brown's *The Screaming Mimi*, though one would have to be awfully unforgiving to criticize Argento for dragging him into this story. Spencer's deadpan delivery (perfectly conveyed on the English soundtrack by dubbing veteran Edward Mannix) and hulking presence make him a very unusual "father confessor" sort, and the weasely "Professor" provides him with an ideal sparring partner. Best of all, however, is the character of the private investigator, Gianni Arosio (Jean-Pierre Marielle), to whom "God" sends Roberto for assistance. In a departure from his earlier *gialli*, Argento elects to keep the police pretty much out of the action in *Four Flies*; they appear only briefly and have no opportunity to really establish a meaningful presence. Arosio, however, is one of Argento's greatest character creations. When Roberto goes to see him, he expects an intimidating character in the tradition of Humphrey Bogart as Sam Spade or Philip Marlowe; what he gets, instead, is a very effete middle-aged man. Marielle's performance provides the film with its main source of warmth and humanity. Like the gay characters in *Bird* and *Cat*, he is undoubtedly camp—but also in common with them, Dario insists on seeing him as a human being, first and foremost. His open sexuality makes Roberto uneasy at first, but he is charming enough to disarm just about anybody. Arosio picks up on his ambivalence right away: "You're thinking this fairy is going to jump on a chair and scream bloody murder if he sees a mouse?" Roberto is embarrassed and agrees to employ him in trying to unravel the mystery. As it turns out, Arosio is a failure as an investigator. He cheerfully confesses this to Roberto when he says, "You see before you a fully-fledged, highly qualified private investigator with an extensive knowledge of modern science at his very fingertips. And in spite of this, in three years of honest practice … I haven't solved a single case!" According to Luigi Cozzi, the notion of the luckless private eye who feels sure that the odds are finally in his favor was influenced by a similar character in *Mindswap*, written by one of his favorite authors, Robert Sheckley (1928-2005). Arosio tries to console Roberto by assuring him that the odds are definitely in his favor—after an unbroken string of failures, he's bound to finally catch a break. It's a funny and genuinely disarming exchange—and it proves to be absolutely correct, though poor Arosio doesn't have the satisfaction of being able to actually enjoy his success. Jean-Pierre Marielle (1932-2019) steals the film with his charming performance; it may not be subtle, as such, but the character never loses his humanity nor does Marielle reduce him to an unbelievable stereotype.

Another character who adds to the warped sense of humor is Roberto's writer friend, Andrea (Stefano Satta Flores). He's a vaguely obnoxious sort of character: vain, self-important, and prone to expounding for the benefit of the entire room. When we first meet him, during one of the curiously joyless get-togethers at the Tobias house, he tells his own twisted variation on the *Frankenstein* story, which he calls "The Rape of Frankenstein, or: The Man-Made Molester"—in which the monster is possessed of an enormous ... libido. He also recounts the story of a famous French chef who had a very unusual funeral, with the fellow chefs sprinkling garlic and paprika on the corpse. The notion of laughing at death is echoed later on when Roberto, "God" and "The Professor" visit an exhibition of funerary arts—thus allowing Argento to really get chuckles out of the commercialization of death, as various funerary vultures try to con the public into buying gaudy, overpriced vessels for their final journey. In any event, the reference to *Frankenstein*—which smacks more of Cozzi's input than of Argento—is significant in that Dario would attempt to mount his own version of the Mary Shelley story not long after this picture. The party scene also allows Roberto's band mate, Mirko (Fabrizio Moroni), to tell of the gruesome details surrounding a public execution in the middle east; the guests (including future cult starlet Shirley Corrigan, in an unbilled bit as the blonde who asks about Mirko, "Who brought him here?!") aren't amused, but the story wedges its way into Roberto's mind. For the remainder of the film, Roberto is haunted by this account—and he has a recurring dream in which he sees the execution being played out. Every time the scene reappears, Argento allows it to last longer and longer—until the final version of it plays out and we see the executed man's head being severed and bouncing on the ground. This, too, provides a foreshadowing of what is in store for the end of the picture.

It eventually transpires that Carlo Morosi is still alive and well; not only that, but he is in cahoots with somebody who has it in for Roberto. Morosi plays along with the mastermind's head games up to a point, but when he learns of the murder of Amelia, he decides to ask for more money—a major mistake. Morosi meets his fate—his *real* fate—when the mastermind lunges at him and beats him senseless before strangling him with some wire. Argento utilizes subjective camerawork here, partly to obscure the identity of the killer, and partly to make the audience complicit in the mayhem as it unfolds; the subjective view of the man being bludgeoned to death is capped with a gruesome flourish as Morosi defiantly spits blood at the killer's face—that is, the camera lens. The use of "killers in cahoots" is nothing new, of course. In *giallo* terms, it recalls the twist ending of Mario Bava's ground-breaking *Blood and Black Lace* (*6 donne per l'assassino*, 1964), and it also points to later Argento films where the mayhem is divided among more than one psychopath. It's worth noting, by the way, that the murder scenes were originally filmed with a recurring visual motif in mind. As Luigi Cozzi later explained, the idea was inspired by the use of black gloves in *Bird* and the close-ups of the killer's staring eye in *Cat*. This time, he thought it might be a good, creepy idea to include close-ups of the killer's mouth contorted into a cruel, twisted smile during the murder scenes—it worked well on paper, but when the time came to edit the picture, Dario realized that showing the killer's mouth gave the game away, so the idea was scrapped. Cozzi's point of reference was Theodore Sturgeon's 1955 short story "When You're Smiling," which is precisely the sort of story that Argento would never have sought inspiration from; Cozzi was and remains an avowed fan of sci-fi, however, and he did his best to introduce allusions to his favorite authors in an otherwise reality-based (more-or-less!) *giallo* scenario.

Arosio continues his investigation and finally manages to get hold of some good leads. Just as he had predicted earlier in the picture, the law of averages is on his side. He manages to figure out who the murderer is. While shadowing his suspect, however, the killer gets wise to his presence and Arosio is killed. His death scene is one of the most profoundly upsetting in any of Argento's films—not because it's gory (it isn't, not at all) but because we're so emotionally invested in his character. Dario was

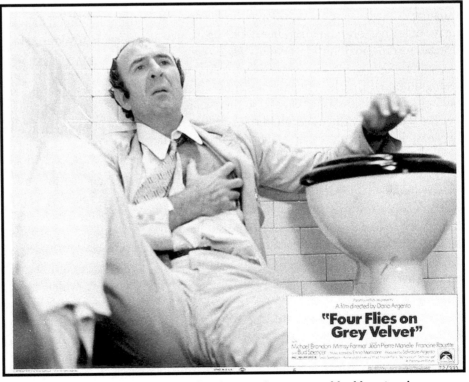

Jean-Pierre Marielle steals the show as the camp and luckless Arosio.

Dario questions whether Calisto Calisti really needs *parmigiana* for his pasta.

clearly aware of the need to tread carefully where killing off such a lovable character is concerned. Instead of a painful, protracted, elaborate death scene, he's merely conked over the head and then injected with poison; it's one thing to show the death throes of a vaguely defined character and quite another to watch somebody we really care about suffer. On that level, Argento is to be commended for his tact in this instance. As Arosio expires, he smiles to himself in satisfaction—he finally managed to break his losing streak.

Soon after Arosio's demise, poor Dalia is also targeted. Argento milks the suspense in this sequence for all its worth. When Dalia takes refuge in a cupboard, watching through a crack in the door as the killer searches the room for her, one can't help but notice the similarity to a later scene in John Carpenter's *Halloween* (1978). Carpenter (born 1948) is an avowed fan of Argento and openly admitted that he was influenced by his work in making that seminal slasher classic, so there's no doubt that the scene really did make an impact on him. When the coast is apparently clear, Dalia tries to make her escape—but of course it's just a trap, and she falls right into it. Argento utilizes some very stylish imagery here as her screaming visage is reflected in the blade of the knife as it advances towards her—he had done something similar in *The Bird with the Crystal Plumage*, but he refines the idea here and makes it even more visually dynamic. Dalia's death may seem an arbitrary one, but when one realizes that Nina is the killer, it makes sense: no doubt she became aware of the affair between her and Roberto and, feeling betrayed, she elected to get back at her, as well.

Dalia's death leads to the film's most bizarre conceit—the one which provides the film with its baroque title. Argento would later claim that the idea of the retinas of murder victims retaining an image of the last thing they saw was something he became aware of due to the research being conducted at the time by German scientists; maybe so, but as it happens it's an old idea—and one that has been thoroughly discredited in more recent years. As reported by Marissa Fessenden in *The Smithsonian*, research into this idea goes all the way back to 1876, when physiologist Franz Christian Boll "discovered a pigment hiding in the back of the eye that would bleach in the light and recover in the dark. He called this retinal pigment 'visual purple' and today we call it rhodopsin." The actual technique of attempting to photograph and develop the last images retained on dead retinas was known as optography. By 1877, attempts were under way to utilize optography in the field of criminal investigation; it was even suggested as a possible line of investigation in the Jack the Ripper killings. It was soon discovered that optography wasn't all it was cracked up to be—results could only be obtained in ideal circumstances, from "simple, high contrast surroundings"; moreover, it only had a chance of succeeding if the eye was removed from the body within a very short period of time of its death. Obviously, this was far from optimal. The only recorded instance of an optograph being (semi) successfully developed from a human eye occurred in 1880, when researcher Wilhelm Friedrich Kühne took the freshly decapitated head of a convicted murderer, sentenced to death at the guillotine, and developed an actual photographic image—the image was very vague and ill-defined, however, and much like a Rorschach test, it evidently looked like different things to everybody who got a look at it. Reports about these inconclusive studies fired the imagination of various people, including Jules Verne, who used optography as a plot point in his 1902 book *The Brothers Kip* (*Les Frères Kip*). Though it never really obtained credibility in the scientific community, it was accepted as fact in some circles—and it has been widely reported that gangsters often shot out the eyes of their victims, just in case there was anything to it. It also cropped up as a plot device in the Universal horror/sci-fi film *The Invisible Ray* (1936), starring Boris Karloff and Béla Lugosi as well as the cult favorite *Horror Express* (*Pánico en el Transiberiano*, 1972) starring Christopher Lee and Peter Cushing. All told it's precisely the sort of "weird science" which also informed the XYY chromosome plot device in *The Cat O'Nine Tails*—or which would later inspire the wacky plot of *Phenomena*.[3] Having established that, on a strictly realistic level, it's a load of nonsense—this being an Argento film, it doesn't really matter. As luck would have it, the police scientists are successful—they extract Dalia's eye and pull an image from it …

but much like the real optograph of 1880, it's vague, even impressionistic. "It looks like flies," the technician says. "Four flies." It doesn't appear to mean anything of substance with regards to identifying the killer, however, so for the time being Roberto is out of luck.

The finale finds Roberto holing up in his house, armed with a gun, as he waits for the killer to make his or her next move. When Nina turns up, he tries to send her away, arrogantly believing that it's for her own protection. In a rare moment of insight, he catches sight of her necklace and notices that, when it's swinging back and forth, it looks very much like the odd image contained in the optograph. Roberto flips out and attempts to brutalize an explanation out of her, but Nina gets the upper hand and takes control of the gun. Now that she is sufficiently "empowered," she proceeds to torment Roberto, shooting him in the shoulder (which Argento shows via an ultra-slow-motion image of the bullet entering his body), and ranting and raving about her horrible childhood; Mimsy Farmer's decision to underplay her early scenes pays off in dividends here, as the contrast between "nice, normal" Nina and the twitchy psychotic lurking beneath the surface comes into focus. It's a great performance piece for any actor and Farmer seizes the opportunity afforded to her with gusto. She explains that her father was an abusive bastard who beat (and implicitly molested) her because he wanted a son, not a daughter. The experience caused her to have a complete mental breakdown and she was institutionalized for years.

The above U.S. lobby cards show the finale of *Four Flies on Grey Velvet*.

Upon being discharged, she was crestfallen to find that her father, whom she had fantasized about murdering for years, had passed away. When she met Roberto, she says, "It was like a miracle ... you're just like him." Whether she's referring to his physical appearance or his personality or whether she just arbitrarily assigned these traits to him without justification is never made clear; all that matters is, in her mind, he is the embodiment of everything she loathed in her father. Their marriage is therefore built on a desire for revenge as she plotted it for years and finally set things into motion, hiring Carlo Morosi to harass him before staging a fake "death" to haunt Roberto's conscience. Like Monica in *Bird*, her bloodlust is so strong that she feels compelled to keep on killing. Before she can finish off Roberto, she is interrupted by the sudden appearance of "God"—a clever use of the *deus ex machina* device if ever there was one. Nina runs to her car and speeds off, only to meet her fate when she crashes into the back of a truck hauling trash. The crash is one of Argento's most technically audacious set pieces. To get the effect of the windshield shattering into millions of pieces and of the car slowly smashing

The Unsane Cinema of Dario Argento

Dario prepares Michael Brandon and Francine Racette for their bathtub love scene. (© Photographer: Alinari; Alinari Archives' agefogtostock).

into the back of the garbage truck, Argento used a special camera which allowed for ultra-slow-motion effects. The effect was tricky to pull off—an issue with the camera shutter results in a fracturing of the image which is still evident on screen—but it's so incredibly operatic, it hardly matters. Thanks to the melancholy effect of Ennio Morricone's lullaby-like theme "*Come un madrigale*," the use of slow-motion not only extends the moment as visual spectacle—it also underlines the tragedy of Nina's situation. In an inversion of the usual genre tropes, it's Nina, the murderer, who engages our sympathy and our compassion. While there's no denying that she has done some terrible things, it arises out of legitimate mental illness; in a sense, she's not really responsible for her actions—it's a side effect of the horrible abuse she suffered at the hands of her abusive father. Roberto remains, at best, an enigma; he's far from the most engaging of Argento's protagonists and given the sympathetic way he depicts his tormenter, there can be no doubt this was intentional.

With the production wrapped in September, Argento again turned to Ennio Morricone to write the soundtrack—just as he had done on *Bird* and *Cat*. Sadly, this time their collaboration proved to be a volatile one. The plot involved a drummer in a rock band and Morricone's attempts at rock music may have won over an older director like Mario Bava or Lucio Fulci, but it simply didn't impress a true dyed-in-the-wool rock fan like Argento. The two men had a major falling out over the soundtrack and Argento would later claim that he ended up taking over direction of the score himself.[4] Given that Morricone's usual conductor/arranger Bruno Nicolai also served in that capacity on this picture, however, Argento may well have been exaggerating the matter somewhat. Regardless, Argento certainly wasn't entirely satisfied with the score—which is admittedly uneven—and it would mark the end of their professional relationship until the mid-1990s. According to Luigi Cozzi, an attempt was made to secure the services of the English rock group Deep Purple to score the picture, but that fell by the wayside.

The problems didn't end there, however. Thanks to the co-production agreement with Universal Production, it was decreed that a certain percentage of the cast and crew had to be French. Argento was reluctant to give up his usual collaborators, but he agreed to allow the gifted Françoise Bonnot (1939-2018) to edit the picture. Bonnot was certainly no amateur—among her earlier credits were collaborations with Costa-Gavras and Jean-Pierre Melville, and she would go on to edit Roman Polanski's magnificent *The Tenant* (*Le locataire*, 1976)—but Argento's regular editor, Franco Fraticelli, took it as a betrayal. Argento would move heaven and earth to get Fraticelli back into his filmmaking family; he would sit out Argento's next project, but from *Le cinque giornate* through *The Sect* (*La setta*, 1991), he would have a hand in virtually everything Argento directed and/or produced.

When the film was finally assembled and ready to be seen, Salvatore arranged a special screening of *Four Flies* for the cast and crew. Argento invited Marisa along to the screening, which may or may not have been the best of ideas. "When the lights turned back on, I noticed that Marisa, sitting next to me, hadn't said a word since the beginning of the film. It was like she was frozen. 'Everybody is staring at me,' she said, almost crying. 'Do you even realize?' […] That very moment I realized that the public, especially the ones who knew us closely, could mistakenly assimilate Mimsy Farmer's character with my wife, and Michael Brandon with myself. I understood that what I thought was an innocent game of mirrors, was in fact a materialization of my unhappy feelings as a husband. It was as if I had told the story of my own life, *our* life, and that this story which was about to hit the world, would soon become unbearable to me."[5]

It was a bumpy ride, but *Four Flies on Grey Velvet* finally made its Italian theatrical premiere on December 17, 1971. This meant that, for the first and last time, Argento had two directorial credits playing in Italian theaters in the space of a single year; factor in the regional theaters which were still running *Bird*, and Argento's name was certainly beginning to get around! This time, it took longer for the film to reach other areas of the world; maybe the audience really was getting a little "*giallo*'d out," or perhaps there was just too much Argento in release already. In any event, Paramount didn't put the film out in the U.S. until August 1972, while the French premiere was delayed until the start of 1973. *Variety* suggested playing up Argento's name as a selling point for the U.S. release: "Display the name of Dario Argento

One-sheet poster for the Italian release of *Four Flies on Grey Velvet*; artist unknown.

The international lobby card set for *Four Flies on Grey Velvet*.

prominently, mentioning that he also made *The Bird with the Crystal Plumage* and *The Cat O'Nine Tails*."[6] As with *Cat*, it proved to be a big hit domestically—but the ever-escalating weirdness of his films seemed to make them a tougher sell abroad. That didn't prevent it from coming in at a very respectable number 12 in the 1971-1972 season at the Italian box office[7]; the big hit of the year at the Italian box office was *Trinity Is Still My Name/... continuavano a chiamarlo Trinità* (1971), but it still managed to eke ahead of Elio Petri's *The Working Class Goes to*

Heaven/La classe operaia va in paradiso (1971)—and its gross wasn't far removed from Leone's *Duck You Sucker* (*Giù la testa*, 1971), which had also been a much more expensive film to produce. All things considered, *Bird* was his only big international "audience pleaser" to date and with that in mind, Dario may well have been right to think it was time for a break from his usual subject matter.

The critical reception proved to be mixed—stronger, perhaps, than *Cat*, but not as favorable as *Bird*. Roger Ebert awarded it two-and-a-half out of four stars and said that the film:

> [H]as very little going for it except for Mimsy Farmer. [...] This is the kind of material that a disciplined director could get to hum right along. Instead, Dario Argento uses so many murky shadows, echoing footsteps and anonymous phone calls that we get confused right along with the hero. He also cheats in another way. He throws in absolutely no clues, so that we're just as surprised at the ending as the hero is. [...] [T]here are a couple of unbelievable characters—a bohemian artist and his scruffy friend—who wander into the plot by accident and clutter things up with distractingly mannered performances.[8]

Ebert's future reviewing sparring partner, Gene Siskel, was even less impressed; he awarded it only one out of a possible four stars and wrote:

> Argento's script contains more red herrings than the Cape Cod Room. Each time evidence overwhelmingly points to a possible threat to our bushy-haired hero that person is bumped off and the guessing games begin anew. I didn't find that rhythm the least bit entertaining.[9]

The reviewer for *Variety* felt it was a disappointment compared to Argento's first two films:

> After successes with a crystal plumaged-bird and a nine-tailed cat, the Italian filmmaker is less impressive with flies. The original story by Argento, Luigi Cozzi, and Mario Foglietti is not as far out as the previous efforts and relies far more on the suspense than the usual ingredients. One murder is patterned after a similar killing in *Psycho*, while the entire scene in the enclosed park is lifted almost intact from the cemetery sequence in the classic *The Leopard Man* (1943).[10]

Howard Thompson was a little more forgiving, at least:

> *Four Flies on Grey Velvet* is the third thriller from Italy's Dario Argento. It has striking, imaginative color photography and deep-freeze pacing and atmosphere. But they're simply not enough, even in such a classy, handsome production. The plot and denouement are not only old but far-fetched, and the dialogue is banal. The characters are generally a flabby lot, ranging from young urban jetsetters to scruffy bohemians. Nor are the performances of Michael Brandon, as the jittery, badgered hero, and Mimsy Farmer, as his wife, especially compelling, though Miss Farmer does handle one scene brilliantly. [...] In the guesswork department, Mr. Argento and his two writer colleagues simply aren't fair. All that circuitous teasing and those red herrings don't produce a shred of real evidence to nibble on.[11]

Notes:
1. Unless otherwise noted, all of Luigi Cozzi's recollections are derived from his interview included on the Koch Blu-ray release of *Four Flies on Grey Velvet*.
2. McDonagh, Maitland, *Broken Mirrors/Broken Minds: The Dark Dreams of Dario Argento* (London, Sun Tavern Fields, 1991), p. 78.
3. https://www.smithsonianmag.com/smart-news/how-forensic-scientists-once-tried-see-dead-persons-last-sight-180959157/
4. Jones, Alan, *Dario Argento: The Man, the Myths & the Magic* (Godalming: FAB Press, 2012), p. 40.
5. Argento, Dario, *Peur* (France: Rouge Profond, 2018), p. 148.
6. *Variety*, September 4, 1972, p. 134.
7. https://boxofficebenful.blogspot.com/search?q=box+office+italia+1971-72
8. https://www.rogerebert.com/reviews/four-flies-on-grey-velvet-1972
9. Siskel, Gene, *Chicago Tribune*, October 18, 1972.
10. *Variety*, September 4, 1972, p. 133.
11. Thompson, Howard, "'4 Flies on Grey Velvet,' Suspense Film," *The New York Times*, August 5, 1972.

Chapter Seven: Changes of Pace

The year 1972 would prove to be a time of transition. Argento's marriage to Marisa dissolved and they would split custody of little Fiore, who was only two years old. Argento was hardly finished with relationships, however; in short order, a new fling would be in the offing. (Marisa would also move on to enjoy a happy life, and she would later give birth to another daughter, Gioia, who would become a successful fashion photographer.) First things first, however. Though he was ready to switch things up and take his career in a different direction, Argento accepted an offer from RAI television to develop a series of short thrillers for TV. The idea was to trade on Argento's rising popularity by bringing him into people's homes, via their TV screen. Dario was canny enough to understand what an impact *Alfred Hitchcock Presents* had had on Hitchcock's level of fame, so he leapt at the chance with enthusiasm. To develop the series, he again turned to his friends Luigi Cozzi and Mario Foglietti. He also brought aboard his assistant director on his first three features, Roberto Pariante. The idea was for all four men to develop a segment of their own, with Argento serving as a sort of Master of Ceremonies and introducing them on a weekly basis. The scripts were written in haste and each of the four episodes were allotted a 12-day shooting schedule; a lot less than Argento was accustomed to on his films, but of course these pieces were also a lot smaller and less technically ambitious. Argento had concerns that directing for TV would be seen as a step back, so he elected to sign his one "official" episode, "The Tram" (*Il tram*) under the name of Sirio Bernadotte; it was the only time in his career that he would adopt a pseudonym, though he certainly had no reason to feel ashamed of the end product. "The Tram" kicked off the production schedule over the last week of August/first week of September 1972. Once Dario's episode was in the can, Luigi Cozzi stepped up to the plate for "The Neighbor" (*Il vicino di casa*) in the middle of September. This was followed by Roberto Pariante (1932-2009)'s directing debut, "Eyewitness" (*Testimone oculare*), which shot from the end of September through the beginning of October. The series came to an end in October, with Foglietti at the helm of "The Doll" (*La bambola*).

For the most part, the shooting went without incident. Argento's segment ran as smooth as silk, and Cozzi further endeared himself to his mentor by wrapping up "The Neighbor" three days ahead of schedule. However, Argento's faith in Pariante proved to be misplaced, as he was openly displeased with what his assistant had filmed; Pariante was removed from the segment before his work could be finished, and Argento took over directing it just to get the thing finished. When Foglietti went over schedule on "The Doll," a weary Argento asked Cozzi to come in and quickly shoot some second unit material, thus salvaging the budget in the 11th hour.

Door into Darkness (*La porta sul buio*), as the series was eventually released in September 1973, proved to be a significant experience for Dario on two levels. Firstly, its popular success cemented his reputation as "The Italian Hitchcock." In fact, the comparison between the two men is inherently problematic—Hitchcock's films are very cool and elegant and carefully planned, whereas Argento's are more overtly extravagant, operatic and prone to absurdity—but given their specialization in the field of suspense, it seems inevitable that they should be bracketed together in this way. The series obviously had no commercial appeal for audiences outside of Italy and besides, it wasn't the norm for Italian TV programs to be exported to other countries, anyway. But the Italian

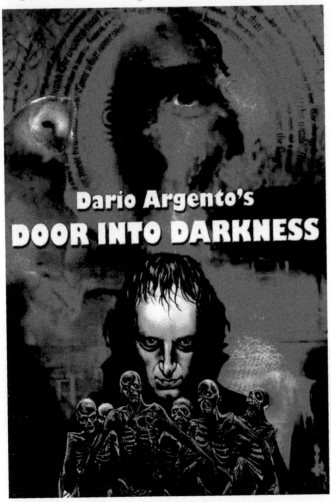

Export artwork for *Door into Darkness*, with a grotesque caricature of Dario; artist unknown.

Dario rehearses with Marilù Tolo on location for the "Eyewitness" episode of *Door into Darkness*. (© Photographer: Roberto Carnevali; Collection: Mondadori Portfoli: agefogtostock.)

audience ate it up and they really took to Dario's studied neurotic persona; he may have been on the cusp of switching things up, but the show and various other factors would ensure his lasting affiliation with the genres of horror and suspense.

On a more personal level, however, the series also introduced him to his next major love interest. In casting the "Eyewitness" segment, Dario met with the actress Marilù Tolo. In addition to being something of a staple in the Roman society columns, Tolo was also an accomplished actress—she made her debut in Lucio Fulci's musical *Urlatori alla sbarra* (literally, "Howlers of the Dock," 1960) and she had even appeared in Armando Crispino's *Commandos*, though evidently their paths did not cross at that time. She also had worked with everybody from Luchino Visconti (*The Witches/Le streghe*, 1967) to Mario Bava (*Roy Colt & Winchester Jack*, 1970) and just prior to auditioning for "Eyewitness," she had appeared in one of the many *gialli* flooding Roman cinema screens: Tonino Valerii's *My Dear Killer* (*Mio caro assassino*, 1972). There was no doubt she had the chops to play the part, and Argento was properly smitten. They did not fall into a romantic relationship straight away, but by the time *Door into Darkness* was broadcast by RAI,

they had become an item. Confusingly, some sources have indicated that they were even married, but Argento never refers to her as his wife in his memoirs. What's clear from reading about their relationship is that they were not meant to be together. It doesn't seem as if the sweetness and light which dominated the early years of the Dario-Marisa relationship was present for long in this context.

Nevertheless, they were drawn to each other and they became a strong presence in each other's lives. Still smarting over the divorce from Marisa, which undoubtedly carried some financial repercussions which Argento has elected not to discuss in print, he decided early on that their relationship would be unencumbered by any legal paperwork. The fact that their fiery tempers fed off each other so eagerly no doubt made that decision even easier to reach. "When I look back at my relationship with Marilù Tolo, what I remember are never-ending arguments, fights over nothing and everything. During the time we were together, we lived in a hotel apartment, which was the perfect place to work for me. She would have liked to settle down in a house of our own, but that was the exact opposite of what I wanted. The anonymous apartment in a casual

Dario goes over the script with Enzo Cerusico while the crew looks on during the filming of "The Tram."

hotel was a short-term solution and I felt secure there. I thought that if our tormented relationship would end someday, there would be no consequences, no arguments, no contract to break, no house to sell."[1]

As a series, *Door into Darkness* is inevitably uneven. Part of the problem stems from the need to conform to the censorship standards of the television market; but there's also something to be said for the greater canvas of the cinema screen versus the small screen. Argento's distinctive visual sensibility simply isn't as well-served by the small screen and the decision to shoot on 16mm, at a fairly breakneck pace, doesn't help matters in that regard, either. Despite its aesthetic shortcomings, the show certainly is not without interest.

Luigi Cozzi's segment, "The Neighbor," is a pleasant diversion. Cozzi indulges his inner film geek by having the protagonist fawn over a screening of *Abbott and Costello Meet Frankenstein* (1948), effectively contrasting the film's quaint horrors with the mundane terrors of the benign-looking elderly neighbor who has, in fact, just killed his wife in a bathtub. The killer is presented as a somewhat down-trodden, pathetic type; it would seem he was a henpecked husband pushed a little too far. Cozzi does not exactly encourage the audience to sympathize with him, but he certainly does not come off as the sadistic monster that one normally finds in these stories. Suspense is the key here rather than elaborate plot twists, as the murderer's identity is revealed at the very start, and the depiction of the killer's slow, deliberate shuffling anticipates later slasher icons like Michael Myers in the *Halloween* series.

Argento's first entry, "The Tram," is most definitely the series' highlight. Enzo Cerusico (1937-1991, who would go on to appear in *Le cinque giornate*) is in good form as the cocky but neurotic detective Franco Giordani who tries to outwit a killer who has had the audacity to strike aboard a crowded tram. Argento's penchant for elaborate murder set-pieces is not given full rein in the context of a television program, so he focuses instead on the inspector's dilemma as he tries desperately to make sense of the murder and how it was achieved without anybody noticing. There's a lot of attention afforded to his thought process, with his racing thoughts being visually aligned with the fast-moving tram as it prowls through the city streets. In a sense, it's Dario's opportunity to focus on pure detection, somewhat in the style of Sir Arthur Conan Doyle in the Sherlock Holmes stories. Argento has always been very fond of the Holmes canon, explicitly referencing it in *Tenebrae* for example; yet his own approach is typically far less ordered and conventionally logical, being driven instead by more visual and cinematic ideals. Thus, the episode is as close as he would come to a classical murder mystery during this phase in his career; later on, when he decided to focus more on the forensic aspects of police work in thrillers like *Sleepless* and *The Card Player*, he would revert to a similar format. Giordani, like so many Argento protagonists, is bugged by the feeling that he is missing a vital piece of the puzzle—so he decides to keep digging even after a viable suspect is found and convicted of the crime.

The story builds to a nail-biting finale as the murderer stalks the inspector and his girlfriend, Giulia (Paola Tedesco), as they begin to unravel the puzzle. Argento's penchant for striking imagery overcomes the rather flat TV lighting, as a close-up of Giulia's feet walking in the foreground gradually reveals the murderers' feet as they stalk in the background, or when the shiny surface of the tram reveals the killer's reflection as he stalks his prey. Argento's fondness for peppering his *gialli* with touches of comedy is evident in some of the secondary characters (including a baker with a bad cold played by Gildo Di Marco, previously seen as the stammering pimp in *The Bird with the Crystal Plumage* as well as the harassed mailman in *Four Flies on Grey Velvet*), while various character actors familiar from his other works—including "good luck charm" Fulvio Mingozzi as well as Tom Felleghy (born 1921) and Corrado Olmi (born 1926) both of whom were also in *The Cat O'Nine Tails* and *Four Flies on Grey Velvet*)—show up in supporting roles. Giorgio Gaslini's otherwise unremarkable lounge jazz score really takes flight in the finale, too, as it insistently builds and builds as Giulia is cornered and very nearly killed by the murderer. Giordani himself is sidelined from the action in the finale as the killer gets the drop on him and beats him up sufficiently badly that he ends up being told of the outcome of the case while recuperating in the hospital; it's hard not to think of the discarded ending of *The Cat O'Nine Tails*, where yet another character named Giordani was to have been shown reunited with a loved one while recuperating from the wounds he also sustained in battle. It ends with a pointed bit of commentary as Giordani's colleague, Morini (Olmi), assures Giulia that murderers are inherently stupid people because they take unnecessary risks. Giordani, emblematic of the hard-working street level police detective, counters that some criminals are very intelligent—they have villas, property, bank accounts ... and to the public at large, their hands appear to be clean. It's Argento's little jab at the upper echelons of society, carried over from his cinematic *gialli*, wherein the murderers invariably are revealed to be pampered upper class types with serious psychological issues.

Things take a major dip in quality with "The Doll." This sluggish and predictable entry from director Mario Foglietti tries to pull the wool over the eyes of the viewer by keeping the identity of the escaped lunatic a secret until the end, but the seasoned *giallo* fan should have no difficulty guessing the "surprise" finale. It is nice seeing genre veterans like Umberto Raho and Erika Blanc (born 1942) in supporting roles, but the handsome but terminally boring Robert Hoffmann (born 1939) proves to be an uninspiring lead. The segment is the same length as the other instalments, but it feels twice as long because the thin story is stretched out for far too long. Director/co-writer Mario Foglietti had contributed a key plot twist to the screenplay for *Four Flies on Grey Velvet*, but his career in the cinema never really took off. He would go on to direct another TV thriller with Hoffmann, titled *L'uomo dagli occhiali a specchio* (1975), but it was more of a straight crime thriller than a proper *giallo*.

The last segment is a marked improvement. "Eyewitness" endured the most behind-the-scenes difficulties of all the episodes, but happily this really isn't evident in the finished product. It's a tense and suspenseful piece starring Marilù Tolo as Roberta Leoni, a woman who stumbles across a murder scene and alerts the authorities; when the police come to investigate, the body and all traces of violence have disappeared. The scene of Roberta happening upon the body is nicely staged. There's a very effective montage of close-ups on Roberta taken from slightly different angles, really playing up her agitation and horror over the situation, and the close-up of the victim's mouth with a single drop of blood running down and staining the face is nicely done. Argento effectively plays with the audience, making them unsure if Tolo's character is crazy or if she is being subjected to a cruel game of cat-and-mouse. Things build to a very effective finale, with the woman boarding herself in her house as her husband, Guido (Riccardo Salvino), who is supposed to be away on a business trip, lays a trap to try and catch the killer. The scene wherein Roberta is communicating with Guido as he hides in the bushes, only to be answered at one point by a voice that is clearly not his own is positively spine-chilling. As noted earlier, the stricter censorship may have hemmed Dario in on certain levels, but this piece demonstrates that his talents extend beyond elaborate and gory murder scenes. There's plenty of suspense and a few genuine chills on display, making this a close "second" in terms of effectiveness in the series. The finale of the episode offers a reversal of the twist at the end of *Four Flies*, as it's revealed that Guido, anxious to get rid of Roberta and take control of her money, has engineered the whole thing to make his harried spouse appear crazy; the so-called victim (Altea De Nicola) is still very much alive and is in cahoots with Guido, as the two have been carrying on an affair. Only the vigilance of a sympathetic and efficient policeman (Glauco Onorato, 1936-2009, who would go on to join Tolo in *Le cinque giornate*) following Roberta's case saves her from being killed.

Roberta is a noteworthy character in the Argento canon since she's the first real female protagonist to be found in his films. It's perhaps fitting that the character be played by an actress who would become an important part of his life—indeed, the same could

Dario relaxes with Marilù Tolo between takes on "Eyewitness"; Tolo and Argento became an item during the making of *Door into Darkness*.

be said of his next fully realized *giallo* heroine, Gianna Brezzi, played so memorably by Daria Nicolodi in *Deep Red*. In Argento's earlier films, the female characters are alternately sketchy or severely compromised: Julia in *Bird* is something of a decorative cypher and much the same can be said of Anna in *Cat*—on the other hand, Nina in *Four Flies* is developed with a great deal more depth—she's a psychopath, albeit one who is depicted with some measure of compassion by Argento. In Roberta, he presents a strong-willed woman who refuses to give in to self-doubt. She knows what she saw and fights to assert herself, even as the male characters do their best to convince her that she's just being hysterical. Only the police inspector shows genuine compassion for her, and, of course, he provides her with some well-timed assistance at the end of the episode. Nina is the victim of a cruel game of cat and mouse engineered by her faithless husband—for whom the audience feels absolutely no empathy. Guido manipulates Roberta, making her look as bad as possible before killing her off. Their one scene of marital bliss, depicting a night on the town as they celebrate their anniversary (September 7—the birthdate of both Dario and his co-writer on the episode, Luigi Cozzi), neatly fools the audience into taking things at face value; when the mask comes off at the end, it's a truly effective twist. It would have been easy to depict Roberta as a shrinking violet or as a neurotic nut-job, but Argento and Tolo keep her firmly rooted in reality. The episode itself may be something of a sketch, building on themes and ideas introduced in the earlier, more fully fleshed-out feature films, but as a character Roberta bridges the gap between the problematic female characters of the Animal Trilogy and the more resourceful and empowered female characters of his subsequent works. On that level, at least, it is a seminal piece of work, deserving greater stature than is commonly afforded in the Argento canon.

As we've already discussed, Argento—like just about everybody else in Italy—was passionate about politics and, following the production of *Door into Darkness*, he embarked on the most ambitious and atypical production of his young career: his first openly "political film" to date. In fact, the resulting project had its origins with a film on which Dario had served as a sort of silent associate producer on, namely Sergio Corbucci's *Er più: storia d'amore e di coltello* (1971). In fact, the producer of that picture had been Salvatore Argento, though it was bankrolled at least partly through the Seda Spettacoli imprint, which father and son had established to produce *Bird* in 1969. The Corbucci film starred the popular singer/actor Adriano Celentano and it proved to be a success at the Italian box office, though it held little appeal outside of Italy and has never been given any sort of an English-language release. Even so, the idea of making a film with Celentano, who was still a major box-office draw in Italy, seemed like a no-brainer to Dario. He and Luigi Cozzi set about writing a screen treatment with the assistance of Vincenzo Ungari (1948-1985). The finished script was written in collaboration between Argento and Nanni Balestrini (born 1935), a poet and author who was a prominent member of the *Neovanguardia* ("New Vanguard") movement in Italy; the *Neovanguardia* writers were much inspired by English authors and adopted a Marxist mindset rejecting what they deemed to be a corrupt Italian past in favor of youth and vitality. As such, Balestrini was ideally suited to the subject matter at hand. Set amid the anti-Austrian

Italian *locandina* for *Er più: storia d'amore e di coltello* (1971).

revolt in 1848, it offered a bawdy mixture of political commentary and baggy pants farce—it couldn't have been more different from the sort of subject matter Dario was known for. To play the female lead, Argento turned to Marilù Tolo. "Her face, both provocative and angelic, was perfect for the part. At this time, we couldn't hide what was between us anymore. It became obvious to everybody."[2]

Dario may have been ready for a change, but he didn't feel comfortable taking charge of the new project as director. Instead, he reached out to Nanni Loy (1925-1995), the director of *The Four Days of Naples* (*Le quattro giornate di Napoli*, 1962), which had been nominated as Best Foreign Film at the 1963 Academy Awards. Loy was a prestigious name and he initially agreed to the offer, but by the time the film started filming on June 18m 1973, he was no longer on board. Argento had planned to produce the film but suddenly found himself needing to step in as the director. However, the cast was evidently agreeable to his taking charge and he dove in, albeit reluctantly. The schedule was luxurious—10 weeks, lasting through August—and the budget allowed for historically accurate set décor and costuming. For the very first time, Argento found himself at the helm of what could be termed "a costume picture," but in truth it's a venue in which he's never found much success—as witnessed by later forays like *The Phantom of the Opera* and *Dario Argento's Dracula*.

Le cinque giornate ("The Five Days")[3] was aimed pretty much exclusively at Italian audiences with no real hope of getting it exported abroad. *Variety* actually reported that it was due to go into production, but coverage of the picture outside of Italy would remain virtually non-existent.[4] The hope—indeed, the expectation—was that it would do well enough domestically to justify the monetary investment of Seda Spettacoli. Indeed, this was Argento's first "purely Italian" motion picture. The earlier *giallo* films had all received cash infusions from outside investors in Germany, Spain and/or France, but this time it was all down to what Seda Spettacoli could muster. It was an ambitious undertaking and it also marked the entrance of Dario's younger brother, Claudio, into his professional life. Claudio (then just a mere 19 years of age!) was entrusted with overseeing the production as executive producer, while Salvatore would act as the usual buffer/protection for Dario as the line producer. In an interview conducted for this book, Dario stated simply that he couldn't recall any difficulties during production; this is seemingly confirmed by his memoirs, in which he claims that Adriano Celentano (born 1938) was one of the brightest and most easy-going actors he had ever been lucky enough to work with. And yet, in conversation with his biographer Alan Jones,

Italian *locandina* for *Le cinque giornate*.

Argento sang a very different tune: "Celentano added even further costs to the production and he was the most difficult actor I've ever worked with. I contracted hepatitis during the shooting and became very ill. I blame that solely on the stress Celentano caused me."[5] Celentano certainly wasn't the only stressor: Dario's relationship with Marilù was also blazing ahead at full blast. "We repeated the same scenario over and over. We stayed together for a little while and we were seemingly in love and happy, until the day arrived when we would fight over some trivial detail. […] One day, when the fight was particularly violent, I stayed at Celentano's place in Milan for a week."[6]

Le cinque giornate opens with a Leone-esque titles sequence, with the titles superimposed over a profile view

Italian lobby card for *Le cinque giornate*: Cainazzo (Adriano Celentano) and Romolo (Enzo Cerusico) in danger.

of a cannon; when the time comes for Dario's directorial credit, the camera dollies around for a full-frontal view of the weapon, aimed directly at the viewer. We're then introduced to our protagonist, a petty thief named Cainazzo (Celentano), first seen sleeping in prison—indeed, he's often shown to be sleeping throughout the film, until he finally "wakes up" and becomes aware of what is really going on around him. The introductory shot of the interior of the large jail cell looks like something out of a Renaissance painting—Argento would utilize a similar aesthetic approach to his next period piece, a lavish remake of *The Phantom of the Opera*. As the camera trails through the cell, it finds Cainazzo snoring and blissfully unaware of anything outside of his dream world. A rat starts sniffing his hand, which causes him to awaken with a start—he smashes the rat on its head with his fist, and then hurls it across the cell, causing it to land in another inmate's open mouth. This type of lowbrow physical comedy is prevalent throughout *Le cinque giornate* and is definitely the film's most problematic aspect. Argento's taste for broad, grotesque comedy is actually reminiscent of Roman Polanski's forays into farce in films like *The Fearless Vampire Killers* (*Dance of the Vampires*, 1967) and *Pirates* (1986), which would prove to be somewhat annoying. The similarity to his later version of *Phantom* doesn't end with the aesthetics, either. That film also includes forays into grotesque physical comedy—some of it also involving rats.

Cainazzo is established early on as being utterly oblivious. He is disconnected from the growing political turmoil in his country; he doesn't even identify himself as being from Milan when he is asked. He's completely disinterested in politics and wants nothing more than to keep out of it while scrounging the countryside for any opportunity to make (or steal) a little money. Dario's intention in the film was to use the historical backdrop as a commentary of sorts on the social unrest which was so much a part of Italian life in the 1970s. The terrorist activities and various student rebellions made for a tense, volatile environment and while Dario identified himself very much with the left, his one foray into openly political cinema displays a disillusioned, even cynical sensibility. In many respects, the film it's most similar to is Sergio Leone's *Duck You Sucker* (*Giù la testa*). Like Argento, Leone specialized in "populist" cinema, and many of the politically committed critics in Italy tended to be dismissive of him because his films avoided overt political commentary. In making *Duck You Sucker*, Leone finally bowed to pressure to make a "political" movie—and perversely, he went against the grain by making a movie which suggests that the most sensible course of action is to keep out of politics; keep your head down, as the Italian title suggests. In *Duck You Sucker*, the protagonist is a Mexican bandit who finds himself swept up in a revolution he neither understands nor cares about; much the same can be said of Cainazzo in this film. In some respects, it seems as if this was Dario's bid for mainstream acceptance and respectability—yet his mixture of pathos, violence and farce made it a very tough sell for its intended market. Cainazzo is very much the cliché lovable rogue: he's not prone to being violent unless it's in self-defense, and his crimes seem petty in the big scheme of things, especially when so much of what he does is directed against an indolent and grotesque aristocracy.

Cainazzo finds himself freed from prison when cannon fire hits the prison's wall; he flees into the streets and thus begins a series of quirky adventures. One of the film's least successful components is actually its script, which is less a narrative than a loosely connected string of picaresque vignettes. Some of the vignettes are more interesting than others, but there's no sense of a coherent narrative "through line" to keep the audience interested; one could theoretically dip in and out of the movie, missing big chunks of it, and still come away with a basic understanding of what it's all about. As he escapes from prison, Cainazzo literally steps on top of an elderly prisoner as he makes his escape; it's clear early on that he's not a particularly altruistic sort and that he subscribes to the principle of "every man for himself," yet his character does undergo a significant arc.

One of the few truly successful comedy scenes occurs early on, when Cainazzo takes to the streets with a flag—the locals, caught up in the spirit of the revolution, think that he's making a political statement and follow in line behind him, showing solidarity. Of course, the reality is that Cainazzo couldn't care less about the revolution—and he is blissfully unaware, as usual, until he makes a quick stop to relieve himself in somebody's doorway. The notion of the bandit becoming an unwitting revolutionary figure is definitely indebted to Leone's film (as well as to earlier "Zapata westerns" like Sergio Sollima's *Faccia a faccia/Face to Face*, 1967), but Argento drops the idea, as Cainazzo goes back to his more self-absorbed existence. The comic effect is admittedly undermined by the use of fast motion photography—curiously, so many great filmmakers who've dabbled in farce have fallen back on this hopelessly dated technique (think of Polanski in *The Fearless Vampire Killers* or Sam Peckinpah in *The Ballad of Cable Hogue*, 1970, for example), and it certainly doesn't do anything to help the material. That said, the use of an electronic, synthesized version of Rossini's *La gazza ladra* ("The Thieving Magpie") on the soundtrack does suggest a definite Kubrick influence, recalling the use of music in *A Clockwork Orange* (1971).

While making his way through the chaos of the revolution, Cainazzo makes the acquaintance of a naïve baker, Romolo Marcelli (Enzo Cerusico); like Cainazzo, he is basically apolitical, but he is also a basically decent and law-abiding sort. Together they form a sort of Abbott and Costello or Laurel and Hardy type of team—really, perhaps the more apt comparison would be Trinity (Terence Hill) and Bambino (Bud Spencer) in the incredibly popular series of *Trinity* comedy-Westerns. Romolo's devotion to Cainazzo is rather touching and provides the movie with its dramatic core; initially the latter man regards him as a nuisance and does his best to shake him off, but he ends up developing an almost grudging affection for him.

As they do their best to keep their heads amid the violence unfolding around them, they encounter a series of colorful characters. For example, there's a beautiful Countess (Marilù Tolo) who uses her body to ensure her safety as the aristocracy falls out of favor. She has her servants haul all of her beautiful belongings into the street, using them to form a barricade between her home and the violent revolutionaries. One of the film's most striking and surreal moments occurs when her butler sets a table in the streets, amid the hustle and bustle of the fighting, and quietly serves his mistress her afternoon tea. The Countess pretends to be on the side of the revolutionaries and provides them with an added incentive when she offers herself to them for sexual gratification; the ensuing scene can only be described as a "gang bang" as she readily and eagerly services the various fighters. Like the other aristocratic figures depicted in the film, she is completely self-absorbed, corrupt and basically foolish; but she is able to spare herself from the harm being inflicted on so many of her peers by using her desirability to her advantage.

Cainazzo and Romolo move from one adventure to another—whether it be helping to deliver a baby for a woman who has been left completely on her own because of the insanity which has gripped the city, or currying the favors of a horny widow who takes a shine to Romolo in particular. If there is a narrative link to all of this, it chiefly comes in the form of Cainazzo's growing awareness and cynicism; by contrast, Romolo remains hopelessly naïve and sweet-natured: all he wants to do is get back to Rome, though he stands by Cainazzo, whom he regards as a brother. Cainazzo's final lesson in cynicism comes when he meets his old friend and colleague Zampino (Glauco Onorato, who played the sympathetic policeman in "Eyewitness"). Zampino has become a revolutionary, idolized and beloved by the poor people of Milan, who refer to him as "Liberty." Cainazzo discovers that Zampino is actually aligned with the Austrians and that he's been using the naïveté of the people to his own selfish ends. The Austrians provide him with a steady cash flow and his role as a revolutionary allows him to move among the people and gather the identities of "undesirables," who are promptly rounded up and executed. Zampino tries to recruit Cainazzo to join him, but he won't have

Cainazzo rallies the people in *Le cinque giornate*.

The Unsane Cinema of Dario Argento

Cainazzo becomes the unlikely revolutionary hero of *Le cinque giornate*.

it. Zampino scorns him, saying "You'll always be a poor thief." "Yes, but I won't let my own people be killed." It's taken a while, but Cainazzo has finally found his own moral compass—it's too late for him to do much to affect any kind of a positive change, but he refuses to allow himself to be bought. Zampino dismisses him and says he wants nothing more to do with him.

The surprisingly somber and affecting finale sees Romolo defending a poor woman (Ivana Monti) who is being raped by a revolutionary figurehead, Baron Tranzunto (Sergio Graziani). He accidentally kills the Baron when the latter falls down a flight of stairs and breaks his neck, causing him to be taken before the firing squad. The entire time he calls out for Cainazzo, who has been occupied elsewhere as he bickers with Zampino; Cainazzo arrives just in time to see Romolo being shot to death. He's unable to do anything to help his friend and when a passerby notices him crying, he pretends it's only because there's so much smoke in the air. The death of Romolo is far and away the most potent scene in the film, and Cainazzo's reaction to it is sincere and heart-felt; Argento avoids mawkish sentimentality while also milking the scene for everything it's worth. The film ends with Cainazzo stumbling into a public assembly: A group of revolutionaries are talking to the public about their acts of bravery, and Cainazzo takes the stage. He proceeds to tell the poor people that they've been duped—used by the aristocracy to do their dirty work. "It's all a lie," he screams. Far from glorifying the revolution and romanticizing the countless number of deaths it caused, Argento casts it in a very cynical light indeed.

Le cinque giornate is a curious film. At times it's highly effective, but the mixture of broad physical comedy along with its loose and rambling structure is not always successful. Adriano Celentano and Enzo Cerusico make for an appealing pair of protagonists, but many of the supporting performances (including that of Tolo) tend to be a little too broad. Luigi Kuveiller (1927-2013)'s cinematography is consistently pleasing to the eye and there are a number of interesting set-ups with plenty of roving camerawork—and yet there's a sense that Argento was overwhelmed with such a big canvas. The film doesn't have his highly distinctive, idiosyncratic style, though aspects of the plot do display a growing maturity with regards to characterization. Ultimately its combination of the sentimental and the cynical is an uneasy one, and it fails to settle on a consistent tone. Leone's *Duck You Sucker* was similarly cynical and prone to moments of baroque excess, but Leone was able to pull it off in grand style; Argento's efforts look a bit clumsy by comparison, even if it is interesting to see him making such a radical departure from his usual subject matter. It's a film that deserves more serious consideration than it often receives—it's truly more than just an odd footnote in his career as a director—but given its subject matter, it is inevitably a film of limited appeal to non-Italian audiences or non-completist fans of Argento.

Le cinque giornate wrapped in August 1973 and it hit theaters on December 20, 1973—roughly two years since his last feature for the big screen. The reviews were middling, and the box office was disappointing. Given the amount of money it took to mount such a complex period piece, it inevitably failed on a cost-to-

Dario, Adriano Celentano, and an unidentified woman on the set of *Le cinque giornate*.

Track listing for the Lucertola CD release of the score for *Le cinque giornate*.

profit ratio compared to the *giallo* films—and Salvatore, Claudio and Dario were forced to concede that maybe they shouldn't be so eager to turn their back on a good thing. When all was said and done, the film came in at number 48 in the Italian box-office rankings for the 1973-1974 season—well below the numbers generated by Argento's first three films.[7]

During this period, Argento mulled his options and gave careful thought about what his next project should be. He and Luigi Cozzi collaborated on a new version of Mary Shelley's *Frankenstein*, which would locate the action in 1930s Nazi-era Germany. Apparently eager to conquer fresh fields in more ways than one, Argento and Cozzi attempted to set the film up as a co-production with England's Hammer Film Productions in 1973. Argento's name didn't mean much to the producers at Hammer, however, and their own recent forays into Shelley's terrain with *The Horror of Frankenstein* (1970) and *Frankenstein the Monster from Hell* (filmed from late September through late October of 1972, but still sitting on the shelf at the time Argento made his proposal; it wasn't finally granted a release until 1974) had been less than successful commercially, so they elected to pass on the project. Interestingly, according to Luigi Cozzi, they actually had Timothy Dalton (born 1946) on-board and eager to play Dr. Frankenstein, but this was before his name meant much in the international market (his tenure as James Bond was still more than a decade into the future) and so the proposed Argento/Dalton/*Frankenstein* project was doomed to oblivion. News of the project didn't get around at the time, though a report in *Variety* did indicate that Seda Spettacoli was "bickering for an important novel and is shy about details until rights are secured, but producer Argento hopes it will be the second to roll for Seda Spettacoli this year."[8] Given the uneven results of Argento's own later forays into Gothic horror, it has to be said—it's probably just as well. The fascination with the evil of the Nazi party would continue to reappear sporadically in Argento's later films, however, as evidenced by the likes of *Suspiria*, *Demons*, and *The Sect*.

Notes:
1. Argento, Dario, *Peur* (France: Rouge Profond, 2018), p. 161.
2. Ibid, p. 159.
3. Many English sources list the film as *The Five Days of Milan*, but it never had an official English-language release and no prints actually carry that on-screen title.
4. *Variety*, May 3, 1973, p. 50.
5. Argento, Dario, *Peur* (France: Rouge Profond, 2018), p. 56.
6. Ibid, p. 161.
7. http://www.hitparadeitalia.it/bof/boi/boi1973-74.htm
8. *Variety*, May 9, 1973, p. 102.

Italian advertising for *Le cinque giornate*, highlighting Enzo Cerusico, Marilù Tolo, and Adriano Celentano.

Chapter Eight:
Dario + Daria = Aria
and the *Giallo* to End All *Gialli*

The year of 1974 would prove to be another time of transition for Dario. He decided that a return to the *giallo* was called for. But this would be no simple return to familiar terrain. To simply go back to the old familiar turf would surely be seen as a sign of defeat following the disappointment of *Le cinque giornate*. Instead, this would be a return on his terms. If *Four Flies* had been conceived as an elaborate farewell, then *La tigre dai denti a siabola* ("The Sabre-Toothed Tiger") would become the *giallo* to end all *gialli*. The title, of course, linked in with the "animal" theme present in the first three films—but it would soon be dropped, replaced by a shorter, punchier moniker which would end up becoming something of a signature for the director. The story would deal with a jazz pianist who witnesses a murder and is bugged by the feeling that he saw some all-important clue which he can no longer remember—an obvious nod to the plot structure of *Bird*, to be sure. To flesh the idea out into screenplay form, Argento elected to recruit the gifted screenwriter Bernardino Zapponi (1927-2000). It was a surprising move in so far as Argento, with his healthy ego, was insistent upon being seen as the author of his own material; he would utilize the input of associates like Cozzi and Sacchetti, but their names were never going to overshadow his own. With Zapponi, however, he was inviting a writer of real repute to share the credit. Zapponi was particularly well known for his collaborations with Federico Fellini, which yielded such gems as the "Toby Dammit" segment of *Spirits of the Dead* (*Histoires extraordinaires*, 1968) and *Satyricon* (1969). It proved to be an inspired collaboration and *Deep Red* (*Profondo Rosso*) would become one of the happiest experiences of Argento's professional career.

During the writing of *Deep Red*, the relationship with Marilù Tolo finally imploded for good. As Argento would later recall, it ended with a whimper rather than a bang:

> As we were driving to the restaurant, I noticed that Marilù was weird, she spoke slowly, closed her eyes a lot. I thought she was tired, and I just didn't care anymore. We had some wine with our dinner. In the middle of the meal, she started to tell me that she was feeling sick. I told her to go to the bathroom to refresh a little bit. When she stood up her eyes rolled back, and she fell on the floor; she had fainted. After the panic, a waiter called for an ambulance and a doctor. He gave her little slaps and tried to make her talk after giving her an injection. She slowly regained consciousness. We discovered that she took an excessive amount of sleeping pills; the combination of this and the wine made her pass out. We took her to the hospital to make some more tests. After the examinations, we went back to our apartment. While I was driving quietly, Marilù didn't lift her eyes. She was also very quiet. There was nothing left to be said. I understood that we had reached the end, and we broke up less than a month after. I was right to be against the idea of buying a house of our own.[1]

In fact, the timing of the demise of the relationship with Marilù would allow Dario to move on to a new relationship. In writing the script for *Deep Red* with Zapponi, Argento put a lot of himself into the character of the journalist, Gianna Brezzi, who helps to unravel the mystery. It was an important character and it called for a strong actress with plenty of charm and personality. It was Bernardino Zapponi who suggested a name which would loom large in the Argento story from then on: Daria Nicolodi. In fact, Argento was already familiar with her owing to her memorable role in Elio Petri's *Property is No Longer a Theft* (*La proprietà non è più un furto*, 1973). Nicolodi, born in Florence in 1950, was the granddaughter of the renowned Italian composer Alfredo Casella. She made her way to Rome and started in the cinema with a small role in Francesco Rossi's acclaimed *Many Wars Ago* (*Uomini contro*, 1970). She then crossed paths with Elio Petri, with whom she collaborated on stage as well as in the film *Property is No Longer a Theft*. Headstrong, independent, intelligent and outspoken, Nicolodi was just right for the role of Gianna Brezzi; to say Dario was impressed with her would be an understatement. "I don't remember if I fell in love before or after I hired her. The fact is, that day, Daria Nicolodi—her first name speaks for itself—came into my life."[2]

The arrival of Nicolodi in Argento's life signaled the beginning of a prosperous period for the director. Whether he realized it or not, he was about to reach the absolute peak of his popularity in Italy; the next several years would find him elevated to the level of a rock star in the Italian pop cultural scene. Admittedly, the success of his foray into TV had helped in that regard—just as it had with Hitchcock before him, it created a bond between Argento and the audience. Creatively, he was firing on all cylinders. It wasn't enough to make a good film—he wanted to make a film that would absolutely out-do everything he had done thus far. And on a professional level, the end of the increasingly stressful relationship with Tolo was about to give way to arguably the most significant personal and professional relationship of his life. The names of Argento and Nicolodi would become forever intertwined, whether they ultimately liked it or not; it's not common for directors to become associated with the society columns in the U.S., but in Italy, at least, the Dario-Daria romance had all the appeal of, say, Brad Pitt and Angelina Jolie.

Argento would later observe that it was the unpleasantness surrounding *Le cinque giornate* which helped to make *Deep Red* into such a positive experience. He no longer felt the need to prove himself by venturing outside of his chosen subject matter; if anything, he was resolved to return to it in grand style. That's not to say that *Deep Red* obliterates everything

Italian 2 *foglio* poster for *Deep Red*, in the style of Saul Bass; artwork by Sandro Symeoni.

Daria Nicolodi became Argento's lover and muse during *Deep Red*; it was far and away their happiest period together.

which came before it, of course; but in every respect, it would mark a quantum leap in his development as an artist. Once again Dario, Salvatore, and Claudio put the picture together through Seda Spettacoli. This time, however, sooner than entrust the Italian theatrical distribution to Titanus, a deal was reached with Rizzoli Film, who agreed to put it out through their Cineriz imprint; earlier releases through Cineriz had included the likes of Fellini's *8 ½* (1963) and *Juliet of the Spirits* (*Giulietta degli spiriti*, 1965) as well as Bertolucci's *The Grim Reaper* (*La commare secca*, 1962) and *Before the Revolution* (*Prima della rivoluzione*, 1964), meaning that Dario's super-*giallo* would be in very good company, indeed.

Production got under way on September 9, 1974— a mere two days following Argento's 34th birthday. While his earlier *gialli* had been filmed on relatively tight seven to eight-week schedules, this time Argento was allotted a very comfortable 16 weeks. While he undoubtedly felt a tremendous amount of pressure to deliver on the lofty goals he had set for himself, Argento nevertheless approached *Deep Red* with a spirit of great

The Unsane Cinema of Dario Argento

Bernardino Zapponi.

optimism. His collaboration with Bernardino Zapponi had been a happy one and it yielded an uncommonly rich screenplay, which served as the ideal foundation for his baroque vision. The cast and crew were very much to his liking and included a number of familiar faces, notably cinematographer Luigi Kuveiller, who had already photographed *Le cinque giornate*, and his trusted production manager Angelo Iacono (born 1937); Iacono had come into Argento's orbit on *The Cat O'Nine Tails* and he would remain a more-or-less constant presence through the making of *Phenomena* in 1984. Another holdover from *Le cinque giornate*, production designer/art director Giuseppe Bassan, would provide the film with backdrops which were as sumptuous looking as they were tasteful and imaginative; he, too, would become a recurring presence through *Tenebrae*. Add in the blossoming romance between Argento and his leading lady, and the atmosphere seemed positively serene, especially compared to the tense experience of making *Le cinque giornate*. Argento's perfectionism and desire to outdo himself didn't come cheap, however, which created some tensions between the director and his younger brother. Now that Claudio was overseeing things as executive producer, it fell to him to keep an eye on the cash flow at Seda Spettacoli. Like any good producer, he worried that Dario's extravagances were a little over the top and inevitably they would clash on occasion. He would later recall *Deep Red*—and the subsequent *Suspiria*—as being "extremely difficult to produce because Dario was attempting something entirely new and vivid."[3] This tension would ultimately boil over into a full-blown falling out that lasted for many years, but for the time being the overall atmosphere remained optimistic. Success has many fathers, while failures remain as orphans, but even so, the general consensus among those who participated in the filming is that they had a feeling the film was going to be something special.

As production continued and Argento pushed himself to the breaking point, things continued to evolve between him and Daria. They both decided to throw caution to the wind, and they gave themselves over completely to their new-found romance. "We moved in together during the production; by the ending of filming, she met my parents. When I met her parents, it was like finding a second family. We were happy and in love. We were aware that we were moving too fast, but we didn't care."[4] Inevitably, things wouldn't remain entirely harmonious for long. Both Argento and Nicolodi possessed strong, stubborn personalities; they were both opinionated and could be moody, to boot. They complemented each other beautifully when things were good; but when things got bad ... they got ugly. During that magical period of production on *Deep Red*, however, things remained positive; the script appealed to a serious, theater-trained actress like Nicolodi, and Argento continued to fire on all cylinders as he found increasingly interesting and innovative ways to frame and film his set pieces. When production finally wrapped around Christmas of 1974, the young couple was firmly established—and by the beginning of 1975, they took things even further, as shall be discussed.

It was the best of times for Daria and Dario.

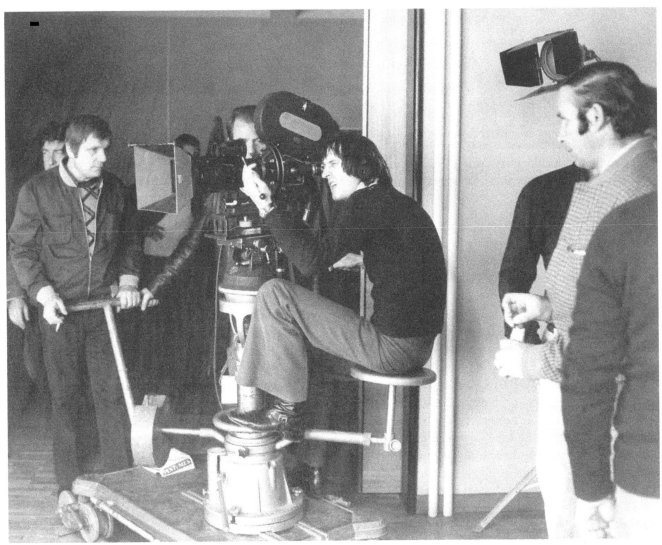

Dario Argento behind the camera on the set of *Deep Red*. (Photographer: Arnoldo Mondadori Editore; S.P. Collection: Mondadori Portfolio: agefogtostock).

It becomes evident right off the bat that this is no ordinary film thanks to the unusually structured titles sequence. Following the standard white lettering against a black background list of the principal players, the main theme by Goblin fades out and a child's lullaby takes its place—and the titles are suddenly interrupted by a strange, fragmented sequence depicting a scene of violence at Christmastime. The camera is at ground level and we see shadows struggling violently on the wall, close to a decorated Christmas tree. There's a scream. A knife is flung to the ground, its blade covered in blood. A child's feet enter the frame and stop right in front of the murder weapon. It fades to black and Goblin's music resumes, with the technical credits playing out. It's a striking opening, to say the least: it's almost as if Dario can't wait to get to the meat of the story and decides to tease the viewer with a glimpse of what is to come. Seeing the film for the first time, it's easy to become disoriented, which is obviously what Argento is hoping for. Unfortunately the novel structuring of the titles was compromised in the export edits of the film, which move the snippet of flashback action to before the titles, thus allowing the titles (the lettering in blockier, cruder lettering than the elegant art deco font of the Italian edition) to play out in a more conventional manner. This represents the first of many differences between the director's cut and the shorter export edit of the film; the American theatrical release is more compromised still, removing approximately 40 minutes from the original edit.

The differences between the Italian version and the English-language export version continue into the next scenes. The Italian version bridges the titles and the parapsychology conference sequence with a brief scene set in a music conservatory. The scene serves as our introduction to our protagonist, Marcus Daly (David Hemmings). He's not introduced by name, but we see him as he rehearses with his jazz ensemble on a new composition. It's kind of a throw-away scene, and it's easy to see why it was decided to drop it from the shorter

Cut from the English-language prints, this scene features Marcus (David Hemmings) rehearsing with some other musicians.

The parapsychology conference in *Deep Red*— Professor Giordani (Glauco Mauri), Bardi (Piero Mazzinghi) and German psychic Helga Ulmann (Macha Méril).

version; the edit also has the effect of delaying the introduction of Marcus, whom we first see interacting with his friend Carlo in the shorter version. Tellingly, it's the only scene which shows Marcus at work at the conservatory.

The parapsychology conference also includes numerous trims designed to tighten the pacing in the export edit. The scene commences with the camera barreling through the lobby into the theater, with the heavy red draperies pulled back as if introducing a scene on stage—which is precisely how the scene plays out. It's a deliberately stylized sequence in terms of staging and performance, setting the tone for much of the picture. The use of the draperies recalls the opening of *Four Flies on Grey Velvet*, when Roberto follows Carlo Morosi into the theater; and, of course, the scene itself is derived from the opening Dario originally envisioned for that film, with a medium sensing the presence of a murderer in the audience. It's worth stressing that Argento abandoned that idea because he and Luigi Cozzi simply couldn't think of a rational way of explaining how the medium could latch on to the presence of a murderer; the only way it would work would be if the medium really possessed extrasensory powers, and the more rational-minded Argento of that period simply couldn't cope with the idea of introducing supernatural elements into a *giallo*. It wouldn't have been the first time that the supernatural was utilized in this context, however. Mario Bava's *Hatchet for the Honeymoon* (*Il rosso segno della follia*, 1970) makes it pretty clear that its deranged protagonist really is being haunted by the ghost of his murdered wife. Bava wasn't very traditional where *giallo* plotting was concerned, however; after his early efforts in the 1960s, his *gialli* of the 1970s display a progressively unorthodox approach, one which has proved to be alienating for some fans of the genre. Argento, at least in the first part of his career, was more prone to relying on logic—at least up to a point—and in the writing of *Four Flies*, he couldn't reconcile the idea of introducing the supernatural into such a context. That he found himself willing to commit himself to the idea in the writing of

Deep Red is significant, as it helps to pave the way for the supernatural horror films which would follow. In any event, the entire scene at the parapsychology conference is a little tour-de-force in its own right, with Argento and Kuveiller maximizing the use of red in Giuseppe Bassan's eye-catching production design and focusing in on weird, quirky details. The use of the close-ups of the various spectators in the audience is very reminiscent of Sergio Leone. Some of these people are pointlessly, needlessly "odd," but that's precisely why they stick in the mind—just think of the priest seen theatrically lowering a cigarette from his mouth, for example. The conference is presided over by Professor Giordani (Glauco Mauri) and occult enthusiast Bardi (Piero Mazzinghi), and the guest of honor is a German psychic named Helga Ulmann (Macha Méril). As Helga explains her psychic processes, Argento cuts to a beautiful shot from behind the three characters on stage—the lights from the stage are aimed at them, so they are basically in silhouette and the camera tracks in gradually on the back of Helga's head. It's almost as if Argento is trying to take us inside her head to show us how her thought process works; by the time of *Opera*, he would do something very similar with the twisted mind of his murderer. After showing off some simple, basic psychic trickery, she is suddenly seized with horrible, invasive thoughts: she senses the presence of a maniac in the audience. "You … have killed. And you will kill again!" Bardi and Giordani offer her a glass of water to calm her nerves, but she is so excited by what is happening, she spills the water out of her mouth so she can continue speaking; Argento cuts in to a close-up of her mouth as this happens, recalling the emphasis on the saliva flowing from the mouths of the strangled victims in *The Cat O'Nine Tails*. Helga is badly shaken and because of the spotlights shining on to the stage, neither she nor her companions on stage are able to see what is taking place in the audience; a point of view shot shows somebody standing up and walking away. The scene ends with the camera retracing its steps, hurtling back up the aisle, with the curtains falling—like the end of a stage performance.

That night, Helga is alone in her apartment when she hears a children's song playing in the distance; Argento ensures that the audience and Helga are both aware of its significance. She has already heard the music during the scene at the theater, while we've already heard it during the mini-flashback scene that interrupted the main titles. Helga is aware of what is coming—a sort of variation on the old joke about the psychic who didn't see his own death coming—and sure enough the killer makes a violent entrance, striking her several times with a meat cleaver. The level of gore and brutality in this scene is beyond anything in Argento's first three films. It's edited for maximum impact and the use of Goblin's "Death Dies" theme gives it a savage impact. Argento had always placed a great deal of emphasis on "the trimmings" in his murder scenes, but this is the first one that plays out like a sort of proto-music video, as music and image combine to create a dizzying effect. It's horrific, but it's so elegantly presented that one can't help but admire the artistry. Not for nothing, Argento would later complain about viewers covering their eyes or turning away from the screen during such set pieces—he put a lot of care and energy into making sure they were as good as possible, so he expected the audience to sit back and drink it all in; this would culminate with the central conceit of *Opera*, where the protagonist has her eyes forced open with pins by the murderer, who wants her to see every horrific detail of the murders he commits as a form of "tribute" to her.

While Helga is being butchered, Argento cuts to the square below, where Marcus Daly catches sight of his friend, Carlo (Gabriele Lavia). The square is completely deserted, establishing a motif that occurs again and again in the film. The street scenes are unnaturally still and calm; there are very few extras milling around, and the few that are, are often seen posed in a very self-conscious and stylized manner. Argento's early interest in realism (of a kind!) has completely gone by the wayside; every single scene in *Deep Red* is very "composed" with an eye towards painterly compositions and generating an atmosphere that is subtly off-kilter and disturbing. Marcus and Carlo are shown to have much in common. They're both artists (pianists, specifically) and they're both somewhat neurotic in temperament.

Italian poster features Helga meeting a horrific fate at the hands of the mysterious murderer.

Marcus is the more successful and stable of the two, however. Carlo is basically what Marcus could have been if his circumstances had been less favorable. Carlo's in the midst of drinking himself into a state of extreme stupefaction while on a break from his gig playing music at the Blue Bar. Marcus feels sorry for Carlo and tries offering him advice, but it falls on deaf ears. "If you keep on the way you are, then you won't last very long." "Who says I want to last?" Marcus dislikes hearing such self-destructive talk, but there's no reaching Carlo—there's something in his past which is bugging him to such an extent that he no longer sees the value in his own life. Both men take solace from the harshness and drudgery of life through their music, but they have different attitudes. This is summed up by Carlo when he says, "You play for the sake of art; you enjoy it. I play for survival. That's not quite the same thing." Indeed, it's

The Unsane Cinema of Dario Argento

"I thought I saw a painting." Marcus (David Hemmings) comes to realize that the truth has been hiding in open sight. David Hemmings, star of Antonioni's *Blow-Up* (1967), provides Argento with one of his most memorable protagonists.

not. Marcus carries himself with a slightly pampered air; we get the sense that he's somebody who has had a lot of luck in his life. Carlo, on the other hand, is a pitiable mess. Argento's political commentary extends here, as Carlo describes himself as "the proletariat of the keyboard," whereas Marcus is the "bourgeois." Marcus is not an unsympathetic character, but he is a surprisingly complex one; in many respects, Carlo is the most tragic figure in the film—a man who seems to truly have had no say in what his life has become.

David Hemmings (1941-2003) gives as good a performance as anyone will find in Argento's filmography. He was not the first choice for the character, however, and the character was not originally envisioned as an Englishman. Dario originally planned to cast Lino Capolicchio (born 1943), one of the stars of *Metti, una sera a cena*, in the part. Using an American or English lead was better for the purposes of international distribution, however, and Argento hit on the idea of casting Hemmings, who had shot to stardom playing the cynical photographer Thomas in Michelangelo Antonioni's *Blow-Up* (1967). *Blow-Up* is one of Argento's favorite films and Antonioni is one of his cinematic heroes; indeed, in approaching *Deep Red* as an ambitious super production, he sought to elevate the *giallo* to something resembling an art-house piece in the style of Antonioni. Thus, the casting of Hemmings proved to be significant on a couple of levels. For one, he serves as a link to Antonioni; for another, in making the character an Englishman, the story becomes another "fish out of water" scenario. As such, it connects into the template established by *The Bird with the Crystal Plumage*, which is the film this most closely resembles. Marcus, like Sam, comes to Italy looking for artistic inspiration; his status as a foreigner also places him under suspicion by the police when he becomes involved in the series of murders. It wouldn't be accurate or indeed fair to describe *Deep Red* as a remake of *Bird*, but the similarities between the two films are striking; the "fish out of water" angle was abandoned in the other two parts of the Animal Trilogy, even if the casting of American leads seems to suggest otherwise—even so, they're meant to be full-blooded Italian characters, so it's a different proposition altogether. Hemmings loads his performance with interesting quirks and touches, some of which came naturally to him. Daria Nicolodi would later recall that he suffered from nervous tics and that he came to the film during a difficult period when he was divorcing from his wife, the actress Gayle Hunnicut (with whom he had appeared in the British thrillers *Fragment of Fear*, 1970 and *Voices*, 1973), and was drinking heavily. As if that wasn't bad enough, he was also subject to Dario's moody behavior. "Dario was quite tough with him," she would later recall. "He never understood why, as he was quite a timid guy. […] Dario was hard on him."[5] It could be that this was the reason why Hemmings evidently didn't hold any warm memories of the film—he dismisses it rather tersely in his memoirs—though it certainly didn't affect the quality of his acting in any kind of a negative way.

Carlo heads back to the Blue Bar to finish out his shift, leaving Marcus on his own in the square. He looks up at his apartment building and sees a horrible sight. Helga plastered against her window, screaming in pain; suddenly the hatchet comes down once more and her head smashes through the plate glass. Marcus runs to the apartment to offer aid, but by the time he gets there, it's too late; she's already dead and the murderer is nowhere to be seen. As he looks down on the square, he sees a figure in a brown leather raincoat walking away; he also sees Carlo staggering out of the Blue Bar. The latter point is significant as it removes any and all doubt as to his role in Helga's death; this will come into focus later on when the film is hurtling towards its breathless conclusion.

The police arrive to take Marcus' statement and gather evidence. Unlike Inspector Morosini in *The Bird with the Crystal Plumage* or Superintendent Spimi in *The Cat O'Nine Tails*, Superintendent Calcabrini (Eros Pagni) represents everything that is wrong with the Italian legal system. He's depicted as arrogant and unfeeling; he also comes off like a bit of a buffoon. While grilling Marcus, he asks what he does for a living. When Marcus replies that he's a pianist and that he teaches music at the conservatory, Calcabrini is condescending. "So, in that case, you don't have a job, eh?" Marcus is indignant and Calcabrini tries to smooth things over by saying he has a cousin who plays the violin. For plodding, by-the-book Calcabrini, Marcus is immediately suspect because he's an outsider; he's an artist—worse, he's also a foreigner. Sooner than work with Marcus, as Morosini had done with Sam Dalmas, he antagonizes him and belittles him every chance he gets. There's nothing remotely likable about Calacabrini, though there is some humor to be found at his expense (at least in the Italian edit) when we see him throwing a tantrum at police headquarters because the coffee machine took his money and didn't dispense his coffee. While Argento's first two films allowed the police a somewhat prominent position in the action, they had been almost totally omitted from *Four Flies*—and here they are depicted in mostly negative terms. Argento would introduce more sympathetic cops in *Tenebrae*—but then from *Phenomena* through *Trauma*, they're basically either omitted or depicted as cold, unfeeling sorts.

More significantly, the meeting between Marcus and Calcabrini also introduces the secondary lead: a brash journalist named Gianna Brezzi (Daria Nicolodi). She's well known by Calcabrini and his men and they obviously regard her as a pain in the ass; this can be accounted by the fact that she's an aggressive female in a society traditionally driven by machismo. Gianna proves to be every bit as tough as any man, however, and she takes an instant liking to Marcus, whom she recognizes as the eyewitness. Marcus insists that while he saw part of the killing, he's hardly privy to everything that has happened; and yet, like Sam before him, he is bugged by the feeling that he saw something important. He asks Calcabrini whether anything has been removed from the

Argento and Nicolodi on the set of *Deep Red*.

"Don't talk to me about all that woman's stuff!" David Hemmings and Daria Nicolodi make a winning team in *Deep Red*.

hallway of the apartment, but is assured that his men were careful not to touch a thing; Marcus tries to dismiss it as a mistake on his part, but secretly he is obsessed: he knows he saw something and that it could hold the key to figuring out the murderer's identity. In fact, he's absolutely correct—but just as in *Bird*, the mystery hinges on his ability to dredge up this bit of information from his memory.

Marcus and Gianna enter rather quickly into a romance—and while this aspect of the plot could have come across as a contrivance, it is conveyed with enormous charm and sincerity by Argento and his actors. Hemmings and Daria Nicolodi work well together, and she would later recall that they got along beautifully. Like Nicolodi, Hemmings was a serious actor with a theater background, so they had much in common. Argento may have been tough on his leading man, but things were different with his leading lady, as they quickly fell in love—thus mirroring the relationship she was enacting with Hemmings on screen. Gianna is one of Argento's most beautifully realized characters. Unlike the mostly decorative characters played by Suzy Kendall in *Bird* and Catherine Spaak in *Cat*, or the psychotic one essayed by Mimsy Farmer in *Four Flies*, Gianna is a completely positive presence. Her closest antecedent is undoubtedly the character played by Marilù Tolo in the "Eyewitness" segment of *Door into Darkness*; her character, Roberta Leoni, is something of a neurotic, however, who is ultimately saved only by the intervention of a male authority figure. Gianna is tougher than any of her male counterparts and in fact she's the one who ends up pulling Marcus out of the fire—literally—at one point in the narrative. The scenes between her and Marcus were savagely cut for the export edition, but in the original Italian edit, the relationship is detailed with sweetness and humor.

They also have some very interesting discussions about gender politics, which was something of a novelty in a genre piece such as this. "I think a woman's got to be independent," she says, before Marcus cuts her off. "Don't start with me about that woman stuff. It's a fundamental fact: men are different from women. Women are weaker. Well ... they're gentler." Gianna promptly disabuses Marcus of this notion by challenging him to a match of arm-wrestling; she wins, but Marcus, his masculine pride on the line, insists that she cheated and quickly discounts the match. As the story unfolds, Marcus finds himself interacting with strong women—and at the end of the story, there's little doubt that his outdated chauvinistic attitudes have been changed for the better.

Argento obviously funneled aspects of himself into both of these characters: Marcus embodies some of his nervous habits and his "artistic temperament," while Gianna evokes his early persona as an ambitious writer for *Paese Sera*. That the romantic subplot works is down to the sincerity of its presentation, as well as the obvious talent and chemistry of its actors. Nicolodi, of course, would become the most significant female presence in Argento's life—both personally and professionally—but this is the one and only film where their relationship was completely positive, thus adding to the film's unexpectedly charming and disarming romantic subplot.

Marcus and Carlo discuss the vagaries of memory and perception in yet another scene that was truncated in the export edit. It's another overtly "artificial" scene in terms of staging, as they go back and forth in the same square as before—only this time, an imposing piece of sculpture is used as a sort of centerpiece in the frame. Marcus insists that he saw something that is no longer in the apartment. "I thought I saw a painting. And then, a few minutes later, it was gone." Carlo, violently hung-over and ready for bed, says, "Maybe the painting was made to disappear because it represented something important." There are some delicious ironies in this scene which only become evident once one has seen the film the whole way through and knows the final outcome. Carlo has no way of knowing it yet, but the murderer is somebody deeply connected to his life; in fact, it's somebody who is responsible for his life being the chaotic mess that it is. He's inadvertently helping to steer Marcus in the right direction, not realizing how it will come to impact him later on. Marcus is convinced something has been changed or removed, and he's also absolutely correct. He did see something that isn't there, but it's not a piece of décor. Marcus insists that he's telling the truth, and Carlo tells him, "You think you're telling the truth, but in fact you're only telling your version of the truth. It happens to me all the time."

The point is clear: objective truth is not always easily accessible. Individual bias and prejudice enter into how human beings assess the data they are presented with; some people are also a lot more observant than others. Marcus, like Sam in *The Bird with the Crystal Plumage*, is unable to summon the all-important clue to mind because he's interpreting what he's seen incorrectly. It's only after the mystery is apparently solved that he's able to relax sufficiently to finally come to that important realization—and it very nearly costs him his life.

While Marcus and Gianna continue to vie to see who will solve the mystery first, Marcus meets a couple of significant people in Carlo's life. First, he meets Carlo's mother, Marta (Clara Calamai), a Norma Desmond type who is evidently in the grips of the early stages of some sweet, deluded form of dementia. There's ample humor in their interplay as she repeatedly asks him what he does for a living and he keeps having to tell her that he's a pianist. The only glimpses we get into the family home suggests a shrine to the past. This definitely ties into the overall theme of the primal trauma which motivates the action. Marta talks wistfully of her past as an actress and excitedly tells Marcus that the pictures on the wall are from her old movies; he is sweet with her and says he wishes he could have seen some of the films. In fact, Clara Calamai (1909-1998) was a major star in her time. One of her best-known films was Luchino Visconti's *Ossessione* (1943), an uncredited variation on James M. Cain's *The Postman Always Rings Twice*, which caused a scandal; it is one of many films that can be seen as a precursor to the *giallo* genre. Significantly, too, she was among the many starlets photographed by Dario's mother, Elda Luxardo, in her studio. With this in mind, it's hard not to wonder whether one or more of the images we see of her as a glamorous younger woman had been taken by Elda herself. Marta presents as benign and utterly harmless—the very embodiment of a doddering old lady. Marcus' assumptions about her prove to be way off-base, however.

He also discovers something about Carlo that he evidently never suspected. He tracks him down to an apartment, where he finds him in the company of an androgynous young man, Massimo Ricci—Carlo is once again in his cups and mockingly says, "Good old Carlo; he's not only a drunk, but a faggot as well." Marcus is obviously flustered by what he's learned, but he doesn't necessarily come off as a homophobe. If anything, Massimo seems to make him a little uncomfortable, though he remains polite and sympathetic in his disposition. The ambiguity of the Massimo character can be explained by the fact that Dario cast an actress named Geraldine Hooper (best known for her prominent role in Corrado Farina's offbeat vampire allegory, *They Have Changed Their Faces/Hanno cambiato faccia*, 1971) in the role. It's not a unique piece of casting in that sense—just think of James Whale's use of elderly actress Elspeth Dudgeon as the ancient family patriarch in *The Old Dark House* (1932)—but it points to a surprisingly sophisticated take on gender politics which runs through so many of his films. Many of his films revolve around strong females—both as heroines and as villains—and he would later cast a transsexual performer as a fetish presence in *Tenebrae*, for example. In the case of both *Deep Red* and *Tenebrae*, however, it's not something that is underlined or made into a big deal; if you're in on it, it adds an extra layer of ambiguity to the proceedings—if not, it won't affect your ability to enjoy and process the plots in the least. The knowledge of Carlo's sexuality does not affect Marcus' attitude towards his friend; and Argento doesn't use it as an excuse to mock or vilify his character, either. Argento's open attitude towards "fringe figures" therefore gives his work a more compassionate disposition than may be initially apparent.

Another bravura set piece occurs when Marcus is alone in his apartment practicing a new composition on the piano. Like Helga before him, he suddenly hears the nursery rhyme theme echoing in the distance. Unlike Helga, he doesn't possess the knowledge to realize this means the murderer is present; but it rattles him sufficiently to place himself on guard. As he continues to play the piano, he realizes somebody has broken into the apartment. Sooner than give away his suspicions, he continues to play the piano with one hand while grabbing a heavy object to defend himself with his other hand. As the shadow of the intruder looms into the room, he's able to rush towards the partition door

Marcus (David Hemmings) realizes he is not alone.

and secure himself on the other side. It's a beautifully staged sequence, capped with a chilling moment when the killer whispers hoarsely through the door, "This time you're safe." The cat and mouse aspect between the killer and the amateur sleuth is another recurring motif in Argento's *gialli* and it's undoubtedly one of the genre's greatest pleasures in general.

The nursery rhyme inspires Marcus to investigate a different avenue. In talking with Bardi and Professor Giordani, who becomes a major ally in his quest, he discovers a local legend about a house in the country that was once the site of a violent crime; ever since, it's said that a child's singing can be heard there in the depths of the night. Marcus finds a book devoted to local legends and sets out to interview its writer, Amanda Righetti (Giuliana Calandra), in the hopes of finding some more information. Unfortunately for Marcus, the killer is one step ahead of him. In another of the film's elaborately extended, fetishistically-detailed murder scenes, Amanda meets her fate. It starts with the inevitable stalking and psychological tormenting of the victim, as the murderer gains access to her cottage in the country and sets the stage for the kill. Amanda keeps myna birds, and their squawking adds an additional creepy factor to the scene; it also serves as a call-back of sorts to Dario's debut feature. The killer cuts the power and as Amanda gropes about the darkened house looking for the intruder, there's a fantastic shot of the killer's eye staring wildly out of the darkness—it's definitely reminiscent of a similar shot in Mario Bava's *Hatchet for the Honeymoon*, and it anticipates hair-raising moments in *Suspiria* and *Inferno*, as well. Amanda is ultimately scalded to death in a tub full of hot water; John Carpenter and Debra Hill would reprise this later in their screenplay for *Halloween II* (1981). The scene ends with Amanda, in the final painful throes of her life, writing something on the mirrored tile of her bathroom wall; when the window blows open, letting in the cold air, it vanishes from view.

Marcus' interview with Amanda obviously doesn't pan out, but he isolates another clue in the image of the house included in the late author's book. An exotic-looking plant at the front of the house proves to be an unusual sight in Italy—much like the bird in *The Bird with the Crystal Plumage*, or indeed like Marcus himself, it's not native to the region, so consulting with some local horticulturists allows him to track down the house in question. It's currently uninhabited—not surprising, given that it's reportedly haunted—but Marcus secures access by pretending to be interested in renting it from the caretaker (Furio Meniconi); it proves to be yet another fortunate meeting, as the caretaker's daughter (Nicoletta Elmi, born 1964, who would go on to appear in Argento's production of *Demons*) ultimately proves to have an important piece of the puzzle, too. For the time being, however, Marcus searches the house looking for a possible lead. It's another "music video"-style sequence, with Goblin's pulsing, insistent music taking control of the soundtrack; it's pure cinema, entirely reliant on visuals and music, with absolutely no dialogue to get in the way. Argento's staging of the scene is fantastic. Lots of odd angles and cubist compositions as Marcus makes his way through the creepy villa, trying to uncover its secrets. He finally finds a mural in the one room; it's been plastered over, but there's just enough bleeding through to compel him to scratch away the plaster, uncovering a macabre image underneath. It depicts a Christmas scene: a tree decorated in a living room, with a man being stabbed by a child holding a knife. The mural was the work of Francesco Bartoli and Enrico Colombatto Rosso, who also did the other pieces of macabre artwork glimpsed throughout the movie. Inevitably, this reminds the viewer of the flashback scene at the beginning of the picture; the pieces of the puzzle are starting to fall into place. Marcus is excited by his discovery and leaves, not realizing that there's yet more visual information that he hasn't uncovered; as he leaves the house, the camera tracks in on the mural as another chunk of plaster falls, revealing the presence of another character in the scene.

Meanwhile, Professor Giordani has made his way to Amanda's house, where he discovers something unusual. The police tape outline of Amanda's body indicates that she was pointing to the wall when she expired. He realizes that the shiny surface of the tile functions like

Italian lobby card for *Deep Red*, highlighting the painful death of Amanda Righetti (Giuliana Calandra).

glass, so he runs the hot water in the tub, generating the steam needed to cause the tile to fog up; it's then that he discovers the last message she wrote to help identify her murderer. Giordani's mistake is in waiting to consult with Marcus before going to the police; but given how unpleasant and downright unhelpful the police come across as in the film, one can hardly blame him. The killer follows Giordani back to his apartment, where the film's most memorably vicious and frightening murder scene plays out. The killer taunts Giordani by whispering his name before unleashing a mechanical wind-up doll on him—Giordani, armed with an ornate letter opener, strikes at the doll, bisecting its head. The image of the doll flailing on the ground, its face cut in two, is one of the most disturbing things Argento has ever captured on celluloid; but the lead-in, with the doll gliding across the room, is equally striking. It's not clear how the doll was able to move across the room, but it doesn't really matter. It's the creepy imagery which counts. A lesser filmmaker may have abandoned the idea as being too fanciful, but Argento, finally embracing the fantastic, utilizes it for all it's worth. The incident with the doll causes Giordani to become distracted, allowing the killer to strike him from behind with a fireplace poker; the killer then forces Giordani's face against the sharp edges of a fireplace mantle and a desk, shattering his teeth in the process. Giordani is put out of his misery when the killer uses the letter opener to pin his neck to the desk. The image of the teeth being broken is incredibly disturbing, and in many respects Argento has never topped it for sheer cruelty; it helps, too, that we actually like Giordani as a character and hate to see him being dispatched. In an example of the "rhyming" or "twinning" motif which runs throughout the film, it refers back to an earlier comment of Marcus. When asked by Gianna why he plays the piano, he says, "My psychiatrist would say it's because I hated my father. Because when I'm banging the keys, I'm really bashing his teeth in." There are numerous other examples of this, as well, ranging from the hot water which scalds Marcus in one scene at a little café, echoed when Amanda is murdered, to the seemingly unmotivated shot of a sanitation truck which is echoed later when Carlo meets his fate. Even Marcus and Carlo can be seen in purely symbolic terms as twins.

Marcus, still unaware of what Giordani was so eager to tell him (or indeed of his grisly fate), notices something amiss in the photograph of the house—so he sneaks back in the middle of the night. His suspicions are confirmed. The picture displays a window which is no longer visible in the façade of the house itself. He scales the wall and starts chipping away at it with a pick-axe; sure enough, there is a walled-in room. He finds the dusty remnants of the scene depicted in the mural: a room decorated

Spanish lobby card for *Deep Red*: Marcus (David Hemmings) uncovers a clue in the old dark house.

for Christmas, complete with the rotting remains of a corpse propped up in a chair. He's struck from behind and awakens outside, where he's being tended to by Gianna. Marcus, the chauvinist who believes that men are stronger than women, is something of an overgrown child—it's Gianna who proves to be his protector. The house is going up in flames and the evidence Marcus uncovered is going up with it. Marcus and Gianna go to the caretaker's house to report what has happened and Marcus notices something extraordinary: hanging in the room of the man's daughter is a picture which looks almost identical to the mural in the house. The child claims to have drawn it herself, and the father validates this by saying she has a macabre imagination, but Marcus persists. She admits to have copied it from a drawing she found in the archives at her primary school. Marcus and Gianna head to the school, thus allowing for another extended suspense scene as they break in and sift through the hundreds of drawings on file in the archives; Marcus finds the drawing in question, but Gianna is surprised by an intruder and is stabbed. Marcus thinks he's figured it out and his suspicions are apparently confirmed when Carlo reveals himself. Marcus is torn between pity for his tormented friend and anger over the attack on Gianna, but he is unable to act since Carlo has a gun trained on him. It's worth stressing that, throughout the movie, Marcus has proved to be a remarkably passive protagonist. He tries to assert himself but always ends up coming up short. It's not clear whether it was Argento's idea or if it was a touch introduced by David Hemmings, but this is evident even in the character's attempts at smoking cigarettes; he's often seen fiddling with cigarettes, but he never has a lighter and nobody else seems to be carrying one, either. It's almost as if Argento is suggesting that Marcus is stymied even in simple tasks such as this, so

This Spanish lobby card shows the rotting skeleton Marcus finds in the old dark house.

how can he possibly be up to the task he has set for himself to solve the murders? Don't forget, it's Giordani who uncovers the clue in Amanda's bathroom; and it's Gianna who saves him from being burned alive when the villa goes up in flames. Marcus stumbles and gropes his way throughout the narrative, but he accomplishes remarkably little; his main character arc is to come to the understanding that things are not as they always appear to be and that his ideas about the frailty of womankind are a load of nonsense. Carlo also proves to be incapable of decisive action as he's stabbed Gianna, but not fatally, and he can't bring himself to kill his friend; he flees when the police show up and he ends up getting his leg caught on some metal hooks hanging from the rear of a garbage truck. There's dark comedy inherent in the images of the poor man being dragged through the streets, while the driver and his passenger are blissfully unaware and merrily crack jokes back and forth to each other, but the scene is legitimately painful. It builds on the nasty rope burn at the end of *The Cat O'Nine Tails* by having Carlo shredded as he's dragged through the streets. When the driver realizes what is going on, he stops the truck—just in time for a speeding car to come along and squash Carlo's head like a melon; one can't help but be reminded of the touch of dark humor in *The Bird with the Crystal Plumage*, where the vegetable vendor smashes one of his peppers to illustrate what happened to Alberto Ranieri when he fell to his death.

With Carlo dead and Gianna recuperating in the hospital, the case appears to be successfully resolved. But as Marcus makes his way home and stops in the same square where he had met with Carlo on the night of the murder, the proverbial light bulb goes off. It's simply not possible that Carlo was the murderer. He remembers being with him the night Helga was murdered; don't forget, too, Argento went to the trouble of showing Carlo as being in the same shot at the same time as the raincoat-clad killer made their escape from the scene. Marcus sneaks back into Helga's apartment, hoping that something will click into place, and it does. While looking at the strange, macabre artwork lining the dead woman's hallway, he sees a mirror. "What an idiot," he says, "that's what I saw: a mirror." It's Argento's most audacious visual clue and repeat viewings confirm it. He doesn't cheat. Just slow down the film when Marcus rushes down the hallway and you'll see it in plain view, the killer's face framed among the artwork and reflected in the mirror. His self-satisfaction is short-lived. Marta, Carlo's mother, shows up, ready to avenge her son's death. It transpires that Marta killed her husband on Christmas Eve because he had signed committal papers for her to be admitted to an asylum. Carlo bore witness to the death of his father at the hands of his mother, and it has profoundly affected his life. It would be regressive psychology to suggest it impacted his sexuality, but it does account for his self-loathing and alcoholism; and despite the ambivalent feelings he has for his mother (which were often echoed by Argento himself), he attempts to kill Gianna and Marcus because he feels the need to protect her from being found out. Marcus makes a run for it but trips—as usual, he's utterly ineffective when called upon to act. Marta hacks at his shoulder with the cleaver but when her heavy necklace gets caught in the grating of the elevator outside of the apartment, Marcus thinks fast and pushes the button; the elevator pulls at her necklace, causing it to slice through her skin, decapitating her. The film ends with Marcus, dazed and traumatized by what he has been through, staring at his reflection in a pool of blood. This is the first of Argento's *gialli* to utilize this kind of an ending. *Bird* ended happily, with Sam and Julia boarding a flight back to America; *Cat* was more ambiguous, though it is at least suggested that Franco and Lori will be reunited; *Four Flies* evokes sympathy for its killer's demise, but there's nothing to suggest that superficial Roberto will be adversely affected by what he has been through. *Deep Red*, on the other hand, leaves Marcus in a state of abject despair; he has survived, but what will become of him? We never find out. Similar endings would continue through many of Argento's subsequent films, notably *Suspiria*, *Inferno*, *Tenebrae*, *Opera*, and *The Stendhal Syndrome*.

Different viewers hold differing views, of course, but for many—this writer included—*Deep Red* emerges as Dario Argento's masterpiece. It's certainly the first of his films where everything clicks perfectly into place; it works as a suspense thriller, but it also has aspirations which elevate it into something that's more significant than a "mere" *giallo*. Everything he had learned about cinematic technique is put into play here and as he was fortunate enough to have found the right collaborators to help realize his vision, the end result is immaculately rendered. The film looks gorgeous and the choice of music is incredibly innovative; it also benefits from an outstanding cast, all of whom deliver fine performances. The chemistry between Hemmings and Nicolodi is a major asset and the latter's importance in Dario's evolution as an artist certainly should not be underestimated. Nicolodi would later state that Dario's focus was narrowly limited to the cinema when they first met; but as their relationship blossomed, she introduced him more to painting, architecture and other aspects of the visual arts. That's evident in the film, with its very pointed references to the importance of art (a holdover from *Bird*, arguably, but given additional weight here) and even down to the recreation of works like Edward Hopper's famed 1942 painting "Nighthawks"—which is virtually recreated in some of the shots of the Blue Bar where Carlo is employed. Their professional and personal relationship resulted in Argento's greatest period of popularity and success. Individual viewers may differ on which film they like the best, but most fans tend to agree that their favorite was one of the half dozen titles they collaborated on (to one extent or another) until 1987.

Once again, Argento entrusted the material with the gifted Franco Fraticelli. It became evident early on that the "bigger" approach extended to the running time. When all was said and done, the final running time ran two hours and seven minutes—a good deal longer than any of Argento's earlier *gialli*. Such a running time didn't pose a problem in the Italian market, where a new Argento film would be seen as an event of sorts, but Salvatore and Claudio realized that this could pose problems for the all-important export market. Fraticelli wasn't interested in creating an alternate export edit and given the problems they had already had over *Four Flies on Grey Velvet*, Dario knew better than to press the issue; instead, Fraticelli's assistant, Piero Bozza, would be responsible for whittling down a shorter version for the non-Italian markets. Sadly, despite such precautions, the film would still endure further "cosmetic surgery" in certain markets. In fact, the initial export edit is a very respectable presentation of the movie; while it's a shame to lose some of the material, Bozza's edits are respectful to the overall structure and don't negatively impact the movie. Some viewers actually prefer this version, whereas nobody seems to be on board with the truly "gutted" version released to U.S. theaters.

At this time, fences were still not mended between Argento and Ennio Morricone, and in the interim he had formed a good professional relationship with the composer Giorgio Gaslini (1929-2014). Gaslini did the music for *Door into Darkness* and *Le cinque giornate*, so he seemed an ideal choice to compose the music for *Deep Red*. Gaslini's specialty was jazz—and since the protagonist was himself a jazz musician, it seemed likely that Gaslini would fit the project like a black leather glove. Unfortunately, when he delivered his music to Argento, the director was less-than-enthusiastic. He knew he had created something new and modern and it called for a more dynamic sound than Gaslini was able to muster; Nicolodi was in agreement and encouraged him to follow his instincts and commission something stronger and more modern. This would inevitably mark the end of the collaboration between Dario and Gaslini. Argento tried to interest Pink Floyd in coming on board, but they had no interest in writing the music for an Italian horror-thriller; with the deadline looming, Argento started to make inquiries around Rome and he eventually found a group performing under the name of Cherry Five. In fact, the group had been formed in 1972 under the name of Oliver, and it was comprised of Claudio Simonetti (born 1952) on keyboards, Massimo Morante on guitar, Fabio Pignatelli (born 1953) on bass guitar, and Walter Martino (born 1953) on drums. Martino dropped out fairly early on and was replaced for a period by Carlo Bordini. After signing with the Italian label Cinevox, they added a singer named Tony Tartarini, and the label elected to rename them as Cherry Five; during this transitional period, Bordini was dropped and Martino was briefly back in the picture. By the time the *Deep Red* recording sessions were under way, however, Martino was out once again and a new drummer, Agostino Marangolo (born 1953), took his place. Argento was impressed by their sound—progressive rock—and he approached them with an offer: he needed a lot of new music to supplement the music he had elected to hold on to from Gaslini. The catch? It needed to be recorded quickly. Simonetti and

Marta (Clara Calamai) hacks at Marcus' shoulder during the finale of *Deep Red*.

Marta is killed by her necklace in the surprise finale.

company were up to the challenge, however, and since the score didn't need the services of their vocal artist, Tony Tartarini, it was decided that they should create a new moniker for the project—thus, Goblin was born. As such, *Deep Red* represented the coming together point of so many of Argento's most valuable collaborators; it also marked the beginning of a remarkable string of films, not all of them created in such perfect harmony as *Deep Red*, but collectively representing the pinnacle of Argento's career as a filmmaker.

With Argento focused on creating the perfect sound for his masterpiece, it came as a welcome surprise when, in January of 1975, Daria made an announcement: she was pregnant. It was to be the second child for both of them, as Nicolodi had already given birth to a daughter, Anna, on June 9th 1972, during the course of her relationship with the sculptor Mario Ceroli (born 1938). It seemed like the ideal start to the perfect relationship. There would be talk of marriage, but Dario remained gun-shy following his divorce from Marisa and he wasn't prepared to rethink his cynical attitude on the topic of matrimony. For her part, Nicolodi was evidently content; they shared their life just as fully as any married couple, and the two of them had plenty on the plate on a professional level, as well.

By March, *Deep Red* was finally complete and ready for exhibition. Cineriz launched an imaginative, eye-catching ad campaign and the trailers stressed that it was Dario Argento's long-awaited return to the thriller genre. All the chest-thumping paid off in dividends when the film opened in Rome and Milan on the March 7, 1975. The reviews was enthusiastic and the box office was fantastic. *Deep Red* ended up ranking 9th at the Italian box office for the 1974-1975 box-office season— well ahead of Sidney Lumet's star-studded *Murder on the Orient Express* (which came in at number 17) but behind the popular box-office champ, Luciano Salce's *Fantozzi*.[6] Just in case there was any doubt, the public and critical feedback sealed the deal: Argento was an acknowledged master of the genre and while he would continue to experiment and test new waters, for all intents and purposes he would remain devoted to the macabre for the remainder of his career. The shorter "export edit" (running approximately 105 minutes) prepared by Piero Bozza was put to good use for the foreign markets: it would open in Spain in October 1975, in France in August 1977, and so forth. The American release would be cut down even further, however, without the participation or blessing of Argento himself— for its June 1976 release through Directors-Mahler Films, it was cut down to an incomprehensible 98 minutes; and by January 1980, when Directors-Mahler reissued it, they added insult to injury by replacing the evocative original title with the tackier moniker of *The Hatchet Murders*. *Variety*'s "exploitips" again offered up some eccentric ideas for ballyhoo purposes: "Obtain the fright masks which more sensitive patrons can wear during the bloodier scenes. Tie-ins with red-colored products are naturals."[7] That the American critics were unimpressed is hardly surprising, given that the carefully layered plotting had been ruined through all the blunt editing; no wonder Vincent Canby was sufficiently annoyed by the end result to declare Dario "a director of incomparable incompetence."[8] *Variety*'s reviewer was able to muster a little more enthusiasm, writing:

> Argento has a reputation here for offbeat horror and suspense thrillers with a touch of class—*The Cat of* [sic] *Nine Tails, Bird with the Crystal Plumage, Four Flies on Grey Velvet*— and he uses some interesting techniques. [...] For once, the clues are valid and sharp observers will notice the killer's face at the very beginning as Hemmings rushes in to find Macha Méril's body. Story and screen treatment don't define the characters' relationships too closely and the viewer may get lost occasionally: the victim of a grisly tub-scalding is seemingly brought in just to be murdered. There are a few brief scenes which strain for comedy.[9]

Even so, it made good money and it also made a vivid impression on a young director named John Carpenter.

The Italian National Syndicate of Film Journalists ended up nominating Giorgio Gaslini for best score—though for whatever reason the nomination didn't include Goblin. No doubt the band took solace in the knowledge that their soundtrack was a massive hit with the public. And in October 1976, Argento claimed "Best Director" at the ninth edition of the Sitges Film Festival; among the judges who voted were Terence Fisher, director of *The Curse of Frankenstein* (1957) and *Horror of Dracula* (1958), and Luis Buñuel, the legendary surrealist responsible for *Belle de Jour* (1967), *The Discreet Charm of the Bourgeoisie* (*Le charme discret de la bourgeoisie*, 1972), and many more classics. *Deep Red* was beaten out as "best film," however, by William Fruet's sleazy exploitation gem *Death Weekend* (1976), which also won an award for Fruet's screenplay and for Brenda Vaccaro as "best actress." Peter Cushing nabbed "best actor" for *The Ghoul* (1975). It would remain Dario's only prize at Sitges until 1999, when he was given the special Time-Machine Honorary Award for his contributions to the fantasy/horror genre.

As an ironic postscript, the film resulted in a bit of added tension between Argento and his former paramour, Marilù Tolo. While casting the film, production manager Angelo Iacono put forth his girlfriend to play a small role; her photo was submitted to Argento, who elected not to cast her. He did, however, make use of the photo for the scene in which Daria's character throws the picture of Marcus' old girlfriend into the trash; the girl in the picture bore a resemblance to Tolo and an Italian journalist started the rumor going that it was actually Tolo's picture, and that this was Dario's final vindictive gesture towards his old flame. Tolo got wind of this and sent Argento a very heated letter; he elected not to reply.

The year 1975 would become the happiest personal/professional year for Argento since 1970. *Deep Red* continued to do well at the box office, he and Daria were both much in demand, and most importantly—the new couple welcomed their first daughter together, Aria, on September 20, 1975; she would later change her name to Asia, with her father's blessing. September was clearly a banner month for the Argento family: Dario, Claudio and Aria/Asia were all born that month, albeit not all on the same day. For the time being, at least, the stars were aligned and everything was going well. Dario and Daria remained committed to each other and though their strong personalities and wicked tempers would occasionally lead to showdowns, they possessed the strong sense of mutual respect and admiration which marks the best relationships. "I felt something I hadn't felt in a long, long time: I was happy. My greatest joys, personal and professional, were often linked."[10]

Deep Red helped to establish Dario Argento as a major commercial force to be reckoned with—and it also cemented his reputation as an honest-to-goodness *auteur*. Clearly he wasn't a mere journeyman scurrying from genre to genre, depending on the whims of the public. If anything, he was a legitimate trendsetter; leave it to the other peons of the commercial film scene to latch on to his coat tails and drain his ideas dry. Amazingly, the success of *Deep Red* didn't lead to a flood of more *gialli*; the genre really peaked in the early '70s, from 1971 to 1973; by the time of *Deep Red*, the films were starting to file out a lot more gradually. Indeed, as the decade wore on, the genre became more and more desperate—even resulting in a small subsection of literal "porno *giallo*" films, like *Play Motel* (1979) and *Giallo a Venezia* (1980), which added in touches of hardcore sex to the usual form of "penetration" found in these movies. Argento wasn't about to go down that road, of course, and he was eager, once more, to prove that he was no one-trick pony. The success of *Deep Red* allowed him the chance to carefully plot his next move—and he would insist on confounding expectations, even if Salvatore and Claudio were more inclined to stick to the familiar terrain. The relative failure of *Le cinque giornate* wasn't far off in the distance, after all, so any misgivings they may have had were perfectly understandable with that in mind. Undaunted, Argento set his eyes on a new type of subject matter.

Notes:
1. Argento, Dario, *Peur* (France: Rouge Profond, 2018), p. 163-164.
2. Ibid, p. 173.
3. Jones, Alan, *Dario Argento: The Man, the Myths & the Magic* (Godalming: FAB Press, 2012), p. 60.
4. Argento, Dario, *Peur* (France: Rouge Profond, 2018), p. 188.
5. Unless otherwise specified, Daria Nicolodi's comments are quoted from the featurette "Lady in Red" included on the Arrow Video Blu-ray of *Deep Red*.
6. https://boxofficebenful.blogspot.com/search?q=box+office+italia+1974-75
7. *Variety*, July 5 1976, p. 84.
8. Canby, Vincent, "Deep Red is a Bucket of Ax-Murder Cliches," *The New York Times*, June 10 1976.
9. *Variety*, July 5 1976, p. 83.
10. Argento, Dario, *Peur* (France: Rouge Profond, 2018), p. 189.

Chapter Nine:
Sighs and Sobs and Zombies in the 'Burgh

Suspiria (and its eventual follow-up, *Inferno*) were as much the products of Dario's relationship with Daria as little Asia had been. Were it not for the influence and collaboration of Daria, there's little doubt that these films wouldn't exist. Inevitably, who first came up with the idea of exploring witchcraft and the occult varies on whomever is telling the story. According to Nicolodi, "He [Argento] had reached a point where, after the thriller period, he didn't know which path to take and I suggested the field of fantasy."[1] As Nicolodi has repeatedly stressed, there is a bit of her family history in the story of *Suspiria*, as her grandmother, the pianist Yvonne Müller Loeb Casella, used to tell her of her unusual experiences studying piano at a music academy:

> When she was 14, she went to study in an Academy to improve her piano playing and discovered instead that black magic was being taught there, so she ran away. Afterwards, I learned that the same Academy had burned down and been rebuilt in cement, so I went there with Dario without revealing our names, but they wouldn't let us in. But Dario was determined to watch a dancing lesson, so he made friends with a Pakistani girl and thanks to her, we were able to see with our own eyes that everything my grandmother had told us was true.[2]

Nicolodi is also insistent that it was she, rather than Argento, who had a familiarity with the works of the writer Thomas De Quincey (1785-1859); De Quincey's *Suspiria de Profundis* (the title means "Sighs from the Depths") had outlined an elaborate fantasy scenario involving Levana, the Roman goddess of childbirth, and her three sinister familiars: Mater Lachrymarum (the mother of tears), Mater Tenebrarum (the mother of darkness) and Mater Suspiriorum (the mother of sighs). *Suspiria de Profundis* (first published in 1845) is more of a collection of fantastic essays than a narrative novel, but it provided the inspiration for what would become Argento's greatest commercial triumph. Conflating De Quincey's "three mothers" with the strange story involving Nicolodi's grandmother seemed an ideal starting point for a new and radically different film—but, naturally, Argento differs in his recollection of how the project came into being.

"I became convinced that it would be interesting to make a film about witches, and one day I told Daria about it. I remember we were in our bedroom, on the big mattress on the ground—no bedframe, which was a fashionable thing at the time. Behind us, hanging on the wall, there was a huge wooden red star: my father would have disapproved, but he wasn't the only one. An American producer, who came to dinner once, joked that he'd have ripped our contract to shreds if he had known about the red star before. 'Witches?' said Daria, looking into my eyes, serious. I confirmed: 'Witches.'"[3] Argento's version of events is properly dramatic, of course, but it seems likely that the truth rests somewhere between the two opposing narratives. In any event, the overall point remains the same: Without Nicolodi, *Suspiria* as we know it simply would not exist.

Argento and Nicolodi set to work on their first collaborative venture as screenwriters together, their imaginations fired up by their discussions about witchcraft and the occult. Nicolodi brought a special insight to the project, which would revolve around female characters—a first in Argento's filmography. Typically, the women in his previous films were stronger and more resilient than their male counterparts, yet films like *The Bird with the Crystal Plumage* and *Deep Red* were carried by male leading men. This would not be the case with *Suspiria*. Their narrative focused almost exclusively on female characters, with the few male characters being relegated to minor narrative importance—a creepy servant, a well-meaning but ineffectual psychologist, an aged expert on the occult, and so forth. Argento and Nicolodi let their imaginations run wild—and if Dario seemed to feel obliged to allow some *giallo* elements to creep in, the film would nevertheless go in a very different and much more hallucinatory direction than his earlier pictures.

The image of the young couple collaborating on a project designed to shock and terrify while tending to their infant

Dario clowns around with Giuseppe Bassan on the set of *Suspiria*.

daughter is irresistible to consider. During this period, from late 1975 through the first half of 1976, things were going well between Dario and Daria. They respected each other's talents and they fed off of their mutual energy and imagination; for all intents and purposes, it was a match made in heaven. The writing of *Suspiria* proceeded without incident and Argento was determined he wasn't going to approach anything by halves; if *Deep Red* had been his "super *giallo*," then this would become his biggest, most insanely ambitious project to date. Salvatore and Claudio had good reason to be fearful of the young *auteur*'s go-for-broke mentality—after all, if his first foray into supernatural horror didn't connect with audiences, the fate of Seda Spettacoli would be well and truly sealed. There was no deterring Dario from his fevered dream, however, and it soon became evident that the project would pose many technological challenges.

Dario decided early on that he wanted the film to evoke the vivid Technicolor films of his childhood; he had always been a major fan of Walt Disney's *Snow White and the Seven Dwarfs* (1937), and of course memories of the candy colored delights of *Phantom of the Opera* (1943) were never far from his mind, either. Getting such a particular visual style on film called for careful and precise planning and the collaboration of a sympathetic cinematographer. Luigi Kuveiller, the gifted D.P. responsible for *Le cinque giornate* and *Deep Red*, opted out early on; in his stead, Luciano Tovoli (born 1936) proved to be the ideal choice. He, too, was determined to push the envelope and together they would create one of the most visually stunning films in modern Italian cinema. Argento again turned to trusted collaborators—notably the brilliant Giuseppe Bassan, who outdid his impressive work on *Deep Red* thanks to increased resources and an overwhelming desire to "go big or go home" on Dario's part. The extraordinary artistry evident in the sets, the costumes and the cinematography would make *Suspiria* into an eye-dazzling experience; even the critics who weren't taken with the story would be forced to concede that it was an amazing visual showcase.

Though credited solely to Seda Spettacoli, *Suspiria* would be produced in association with a major American studio: 20th Century Fox. The success of *Deep Red* made Argento into a viable commercial property and while Fox wasn't necessarily inclined to over-extend their involvement in an off-beat Italian horror movie, they provided Argento with the assurance of wide theatrical exposure. Even that aspect of their involvement, however, would become muddied for reasons which will be discussed in short order.

and simple. That was relatively easy, but it opened up a new can of worms. Nicolodi found herself wanting to play the role of Susy; no doubt she thought it would be something of a *fait accompli*, given her relationship with Dario and her popularity in the Italian marketplace. Unfortunately for her, however, Argento had other ideas. Having been impressed by Brian De Palma's rock musical *The Phantom of the Paradise* (1974), he sought that film's leading lady, Jessica Harper. Her name was more than suitable from the point of view of the suits at Fox and the actress was impressed by Argento's fervor and creativity. To say that Daria took the news badly would be an understatement.

"Our first huge dispute was during the preparation of *Suspiria*. There was a misunderstanding because I didn't make myself clear; she was sure that I was going to give her the main part. She, with whom I had shaped the character of Susy."[4] Whether it was the money men at Fox or Argento himself didn't much matter to Nicolodi; she inevitably saw the casting of Jessica Harper as a personal betrayal. The Dario-Daria dynamic, which so far had been so positive, nurturing, and productive, hit its first major point of crisis; in many respects, the damage inflicted as a result of this would never really heal—they would fight, make up … fight, make up … rinse and repeat. Dario took Daria with him to Germany for some location scouting and things became more heated. "Every situation was good for an argument. […] Daria was agitated, and she was angry with me. It was now set in stone that Jessica Harper was going to play the lead in my upcoming movie. As a form of reparation, I offered Daria the role of Sarah. It was only a supporting part. Daria refused immediately."[5]

Despite the growing tensions and the ever-increasing arguments, Argento resorted to his tried-and-true methodology. He threw himself into pre-production with absolute abandon. The work was therapeutic on the one hand, and it enabled him to take some welcome breaks from the drama brewing at home. Through it all, he was confident that it would all work out okay in the end. Could it be that he fell back on the old way of thinking, that if it wasn't meant to be, it was just as well that it should end quickly? It's difficult to say for sure, but this would not be such a clean and easy break as it had been with Marilù Tolo, for example. Daria was the mother of his second-born child, after all, and while things were heated and occasionally nasty, their connection was a deep and profound one.

The first snag was hit early on when Argento was told in no uncertain terms that the script needed to be altered. In the original draft, the characters were meant to be about 12 years old; little Susy's descent into the maelstrom of the Tanz Akademie would therefore become a symbolic journey towards maturity. The idea of having an intense horror film being carried by kids was certainly a novel one—but neither Salvatore nor the executives at Fox could see their way clear to allowing that to happen. Argento and Nicolodi had no choice. They had to adjust the script to make the characters a bit older—they needed to become young adults, pure

Suspiria commenced its 16-week shoot on July 26 1976. The first weeks were devoted to location filming in Germany—indeed, the very first day would be spent filming outside of the remarkable-looking BMW Building in Munich. Argento had Daria along with him for the German shoot, no doubt hoping that they could continue to work on mending fences during the downtime in production. All the optimism in the world didn't help and one evening Argento made an unwelcome discovery.

> One night, when I returned to our hotel room after an entire evening filming with the crew, I found it completely empty. She was gone with all her luggage. No note, nothing; she had gone back to Rome. Daria and I remained separated throughout the entire period of principal production; we didn't even talk to each other. Asia wasn't even a year old and I felt so far from her, too. I felt so much pain. I felt hopeless. But the production of the film was in full swing and I couldn't stop it.[6]

Quite a contrast from the bucolic experience of making *Deep Red*! And yet, despite whatever pain he was feeling, Argento managed to rise to the occasion—his vision remained crystal clear and he and his collaborators were determined to make *Suspiria* into a film that nobody would ever forget. He would later admit, however, that he felt sufficiently low at one point that he contemplated committing suicide. In a conversation with friend and colleague William Friedkin (the Oscar-winning director of *The French Connection*, 1971, and *The Exorcist*, 1973, who has referred to Dario as one of his favorite Italian directors[7]), Argento said:

> When I was making *Suspiria*—I tried to take my life. I don't know why; I had lots of lovers, I had a successful film. […] I was staying in a hotel on the sixth floor with a big window overlooking Via Veneto. A doctor friend of mine told me suicide can happen in an instant. So, I called the porter and asked if he would move all of my hotel furniture against the window—that way if I wanted to jump, it would take more than a few seconds to move everything.[8]

Fortunately the black mood passed.

The opening titles recall the opening of *Deep Red*: that film featured a brief flashback vignette which interrupted the titles; here, Goblin's "assault on the senses" soundtrack is briefly disrupted by a bit of voice over narration—it's the only instance of narration in the film, and it helps to establish a sort of fairy tale vibe: "Suzy Banyon decided to perfect her ballet studies in the most famous school of dance in Europe. She chose the celebrated academy of Freiburg. One day, at nine in the morning, she left Kennedy Airport, New York, and arrived in Germany at 10:40 PM, local time." The narration is spoken on the English soundtrack by the familiar voice of dubbing actor William Kiehl—but on the Italian soundtrack, it is actually spoken by Dario himself. It's a shame that his voice isn't on the English track but knowing this helps to underline the notion of the director as a storyteller, gathering the audience around him as he tells them a macabre fairy tale. And that's precisely what *Suspiria* is; the "realism" of the Animal Trilogy had already given way to more baroque

Dario hams it up with the stuntman playing the mysterious, hairy-armed murderer.

excess in *Deep Red*, but with this film Argento completely breaks free from any kind of verisimilitude; nothing that happens in the film can be understood in purely rational, logical terms—one must accept its dreamy, nightmare-based aesthetic or be completely incapable of getting into the intended mood of the piece. That said, it's curious that Argento is so careful to establish a sense of time, place and even geography. We know precisely where the heroine is coming from, where she is arriving at, and even what time it is. This is the only real concession to "the real world," and it allows the story to take root in a kind of reality before blossoming into something completely artificial and stylized.

From there, the action commences at the Munich-Riem Airport, where Suzy arrives following her long flight from America. It has been said that Daria Nicolodi

The Unsane Cinema of Dario Argento

makes a cameo in this opening scene, but that isn't true; she was still smarting over the loss of playing the role of Suzy, and she does not actually appear anywhere in the film. Though the action is set in Freiburg—a popular tourist site in the Black Forest region of the south-west of Germany, whose name literally means "Free City," owing to the fact that it was established as a free trading zone—but the German location filming actually took place in Munich, located over 250 miles from the actual city of Freiburg. Argento's decision to film in Munich was part of a deliberate scheme to instill a sense of unease in the viewer by utilizing locations connected with the real-life horrors of the Nazi party. As the story unfolds, the film alternates between stylized, artificial interiors and actual locations which are filmed in such a way as to look artificial themselves. As luck would have it, cinematographer Luciano Tovoli had already filmed at the Munich-Riem Airport on Michelangelo Antonioni's *The Passenger* (*Professione: reporter*, 1975), but it was selected for the sake of convenience as opposed to any attempt to deliberately reference that film.

Suspiria is Argento's first female-driven film. The male characters are few and far between, and none of them affect much change within the narrative. We've already seen how Argento started to develop more interesting and complex female characters in his earlier films, culminating with Daria Nicolodi's winning characterization as Gianna Brezzi in *Deep Red*, but this takes things to the next level. This time it's a young woman who controls the narrative and fruitless attempts at securing assistance from male authority figures compel her to assert herself and unravel the mystery on her own. It's easy to see why Daria was so keen on playing the role of Suzy herself, but it's basically impossible to picture anybody but Jessica Harper (born 1949) in the part. Harper is actually older than Nicolodi, but she conveys a doe-eyed innocence which Nicolodi may have had a harder time putting across. It pays to remember that Argento originally intended the story to revolve around young children, in the 12-13 years of age bracket; as such, the story can be read as a metaphor for the transition from childhood into young adulthood. We know virtually nothing of Suzy's background. All that matters is, she's from America, she's an aspiring dancer, and she's a fish out of water. The theme of outsiders undergoing a radical change in a strange land is nothing new in Argento's films, but in the case of Suzy it can be argued that everything she goes through merely serves to make her stronger; she stands up to the dark forces and comes out on the other side. Harper's performance perfectly captures the outward naïveté and frailty of the character, while conveying the backbone and strength which transforms her from prospective victim to strong-willed heroine.

Suzy is greeted in Freiburg by a colossal storm. The rain is coming down in sheets and there's lightning and thunder aplenty. It has been said that Argento attempted to film this impressive opening in the middle of a real storm, but it simply didn't register well on film; he finally conceded defeat and brought in fire trucks to create the illusion of a torrential downpour. She hails a cab (driven by the ubiquitous Fulvio Mingozzi) and has a difficult time communicating with him; the theme of the breakdown in communication is established here and reoccurs at other key points in the narrative. The driver finally catches on to where she's heading and takes her 7to the Tanz Akademie. The entire opening is a major tour-de-force in its own right. The combination of the storm, the elaborate use of deliberately unrealistic color effects (with the characters often bathed in red, green, or blue light, with no realistic reason provided), and, above all, the presence of Goblin's throbbing soundtrack takes the film from fairy tale into the realm of a nightmare. Suzy arrives at the school—the exterior of which was based on *Haus zum Walfisch* ("The Whale House") in Freiburg. As the plaque on the front of the building

Italian 2 *foglio* poster for *Suspiria*, Dario Argento's biggest box-office success; artwork by Mario de Bernardinis.

Production designer Giuseppe Bassan built this façade, based on the exterior of the *Haus zum Walfisch* in Germany, on the soundstages of De Paolis Studios in Rome.

attests, it was once the home of the Dutch Renaissance-era humanist and philosopher Erasmus of Rotterdam. Argento was so taken with the look of the place that he had his production designer, the great Giuseppe Bassan, create a huge façade at De Paolis Studios. Because of the location filming in Germany, some have mistakenly concluded that the crew grabbed exterior shots of the actual building, but this is not so; the replica took up an entire soundstage, thus allowing Argento to have greater control over the elements for these "exterior" scenes. As Suzy arrives, she sees another student, Pat Hingle (Eva Axén), making a hasty and very dramatic exit from the building; she has a hard time hearing over the downpour and the thunder, but a couple of words stand out: "secret" and "iris." These words will haunt Suzy for the bulk of the narrative, establishing a link to the "half-remembered clue" motif which runs throughout Argento's *giallo* films. She doesn't know it yet, but these words will be vital in helping her to survive the horrors to which she is about to become subjected. Suzy tries to gain entry but is unable to do so; she's forced to spend the night at a nearby hotel instead.

Meanwhile, Pat runs through the forest and seeks shelter at her friend Sonia's (Susanna Javicoli) apartment. The exterior of the building is a real place, a very distinctive office building in Munich which fits perfectly into the film's art deco architectural design; the interior, however, is one of Bassan's most remarkable designs: all sharp angles, elaborate stained glass, bold colors, and a dazzling tile floor done in red, black, and white. Pat tells Sonia that she had to get away, that there's something horrible afoot at the school. Sonia tries to placate her, but soon all hell breaks loose—while drying herself in the bathroom, she notices yellow, cat-like eyes staring back at her, from outside the window; the problem is, it's well removed from ground level, so there is no logical explanation for how this could possibly be. (The image of the eyes is very reminiscent of a similar effect achieved by Mario Bava in *Baron Blood/Gli orrori del castello di Norimberga*, 1972; some sources indicate that Argento included a special thanks to Bava in the credits, but this is an error.) Suddenly a hand crashes through the window and grabs Pat by the throat, pushing her face up

U.K. quad for *Suspiria*; artist unknown.

The Unsane Cinema of Dario Argento

Above: Pat (Eva Axén) meets a grisly fate early in the film. Right: Italian 2 *foglio* shows Sonia (Susanna Javicoli) being killed by Pat's falling corpse.

against the glass and ultimately forcing her head through the window as well. Pat fights back but the mysterious intruder draws a knife and stabs her repeatedly—Argento even includes a gruesome image of the knife penetrating her exposed, beating heart—before using a clothesline to form a noose around her neck; the stained glass skylight in the floor gives way and she crashes through, hanging like a pathetic rag doll, and the glass and metal structure of the skylight falls on Sonia, killing her as well. The scene climaxed with a dazzling overhead view of Sonia dead on the tiled floor, her face bisected by a piece of glass. If ever a scene summed up Argento's aesthetic approach to images of violent death, this is the one. It's rightly celebrated as the most horrifying opening scene in horror film history, which is an incredibly audacious move on Argento's part. By opening the film with a set piece that would normally end most films of this type, he sets himself for an impossible task; after all, how *does* one follow up on such a showstopper? It can be argued that nothing which follows equals its savage impact, but the incredibly focused and detailed approach to the language of the medium ensures that *Suspiria* doesn't really let up; Argento never loses sight of his goal to overwhelm the viewers while frightening the hell out of them.

Following that horrific opening, Argento varies the visual and emotional palette by cutting to a peaceful, bucolic exterior of the school—it's the next morning, and Suzy is finally able to gain access to the building. Upon her arrival, she's greeted by the intimidating Miss Tanner (Alida Valli), one of the teachers, and her boss, Madame Blanc (Joan Bennett), who runs the school in association with a mysterious unnamed directress whom nobody but the teachers has evidently ever seen. Miss Tanner is one of the most striking and intimidating figures to be found in an Argento film; the brilliant Alida Valli (1921-2006) is perfectly cast in the part and responds with a pitch-perfect performance. If anybody succeeds in stealing *Suspiria* from Jessica Harper, it's undoubtedly Valli. Of course, she was one of the many starlets whom Argento had met as a child at his mother's photographic studio, so her casting had particular significance for him; she was a great beauty in her youth and she remains a striking and charismatic presence here, with Valli playing up the character's more "masculine" traits as a means of contrasting with the delicate and waif-like students.

Joan Bennett (1910-1990) is a formidable presence, as well, though she inevitably fades into the background somewhat compared to Valli; Argento remembered her from some of the films *noir* of the great Fritz Lang, including *The Woman in the Window* (1944) and *Scarlet*

Miss Tanner (Alida Valli), Madame Blanc (Joan Bennett), and one of Blanc's minions (actress unknown) give Suzy a frosty greeting.

Street (1945), though she hadn't been seen on the big screen for several years by the time she accepted this role—in her later years, she was best known for playing Elizabeth Collins Stoddard on the popular Gothic TV soap opera *Dark Shadows* (1966-1971). Miss Tanner is a martinet with predatory undertones; Madame Blanc is a condescending snob. Suzy discovers early on that life is going to be a lot different at the academy, and she doesn't find much solace from her fellow students. Madame Blanc and some of the other students put a lot of emphasis on money, which overwhelms Suzy; unlike some of her peers, she doesn't come across as if she were born with a silver spoon in her mouth. The students appear to be a catty, bitchy bunch—notably Olga (Barbara Magnolfi), a *femme fatale* type who carries herself with slinky, seductive sexuality—and most of the staff don't seem any better. There's a creepy handyman with false teeth named Pavlos (Giuseppe Transocchi), an even creepier little boy named Albert (Jacopo Mariani, born 1965, who played the young version of Carlo in the flashback scene in *Deep Red*), who is Madame Blanc's nephew, and a ferocious-looking cook (Franca Scagnetti), among others.

The one person Suzy finds to befriend is Sara (Stefania Casini), who is another outcast of sorts. She's not popular among the other students and she seems to have grown accustomed to leading a fairly solitary sort of existence; with Suzy, she opens up and they become fast friends. Stefania Casini (born 1948) is very good in the role; she works well with Harper and she gives the character a sense of curiosity and determination, even if she is ultimately not as strong and resourceful as Suzy; she had already played Neve, the epileptic woman who has a ménage-à-trois with Robert De Niro and Gérard Depardieu, in Bertolucci's *1900* (1976), as well as one of the not-so-virtuous Di Fiore sisters in Paul Morrissey's *Blood for Dracula* (1974)—which starred Udo Kier, who also appears briefly in this film. Sara and Suzy provide some calm amid the storm of the various eccentrics and egocentrics who dominate the academy and their friendship is the only source of warmth to be found in the film.

Olga is another fascinating character—less because of the depth of her character (which is remarkably shallow) than because of how she is presented. Actress Barbara Magnolfi (born 1955) perfectly conveys the

The Unsane Cinema of Dario Argento

The sexy and vamp-like Olga (Barbara Magnolfi) pressures Suzy.

character's self-serving nature; she thinks she is better than everybody else and she isn't afraid to say so, either. Working in tandem with Argento and the hair, makeup and costume departments, she makes Olga into a vain, self-centered clotheshorse who wouldn't hesitate to sell her own mother down the river if it benefitted her in some way. The character's porcelain-like skin is contrasted against her jet-black hair; indeed, this is reflected in the art direction of her impossibly lavish private apartment—unlike the other students, she lives away from the academy, and it's suggested that she may well be in league with the teachers and their awful plot. It's probably a coincidence, but her monochromatic appearance (save for bright red lipstick and nail polish) anticipates the appearance of Isabelle Adjani in Werner Herzog's *Nosferatu the Vampyre* (*Nosferatu: Phantom der Nacht*, 1979).

Once Suzy settles in, she begins attending dance classes—and it's here that the cruelty of Miss Tanner starts to become more obvious. In a way, she seems to admire Suzy: at one point, the younger girl stands up to Madame Blanc, and Tanner responds by giving her a pat on the back; it's not just anyone who would think to answer back at Madame Blanc, so Miss Tanner picks up on her strong-willed determination. Possibly she sees something of herself in that aspect of Suzy's character, but in other respects they are very different. Suzy is light, while Miss Tanner is dark. She controls her dance classes like a petty dictator, barking orders at the students and pushing them past their breaking point. It's hard not to be reminded of Boris (Anton Walbrook), the brutal impresario who also strives for perfection in Michael Powell and Emeric Pressburger's *The Red Shoes* (1948); the use of color in the Powell and Pressburger film definitely anticipates the vivid hues of *Suspiria*, so it's entirely likely that either Argento or Nicolodi were thinking of the film when preparing their screenplay. Suzy, already stricken ill by a sudden, inexplicable ailment, tries to oblige Miss Tanner's whims—but she ends up collapsing in the middle of class. She's tended to by yet another idiosyncratic and creepy peripheral character, a doctor known as Professor Werdegast (Renato Scarpa); the character name is almost certainly a reference to Edgar G. Ulmer's perverse horror classic *The Black Cat* (1934), in which Béla Lugosi played one Dr. Vitus Werdegast—given Argento's love of Poe and his familiarity with classic horror cinema, it seems a deliberate move on his part. In any event, Werdegast, like most of the male characters, appears only briefly and then he's out of the narrative for good; his main function is to prescribe Suzy the glass of wine with every meal, which we later discover is laced with a drug—as in Roman Polanski's film of *Rosemary's Baby* (1968), one of Argento's favorite movies, the so-called cure turns out to be part of the diabolical plot against the heroine.

One of the film's most celebrated scenes occurs when Suzy is getting ready for bed; as she combs her hair, the audience may notice that something … odd is going on. She catches sight of something disgusting: There are maggots trapped in the teeth of her comb. That's bad enough, but then she notices more dropping onto the immaculate surface of her bureau—looking up, she sees maggots crawling on the ceiling. This sets off a hysterically pitched sequence in which the entire student dormitory is revealed to be infested with maggots. Miss Tanner makes her way to the attic, where it's revealed that a consignment of food for the school has spoiled. The scene doesn't really make any logical sense, but that's consistent with Argento and Nicolodi's *modus operandi*: all that matters is the effect. The image of the maggots falling from the ceiling, writhing on the floor or trying to break free from the teeth of the comb are truly creepy, especially if one is not predisposed to being fond of insects and the like. Just why anybody would store cases of meat in an attic is open to speculation; since heat rises, it is usually standard practice to store such things in refrigeration units in the basement, for example. We don't get a particularly good look inside the case containing the food—suggesting the possibility that there could be something truly awful stored in the attic that's started to spoil.

That night, with the dormitory area sectioned off for fumigation, the students and teachers bunk down in the gymnasium area. In order to keep the male and female students separate, sheets are hung up as a barrier; when the lights go out, Argento and Luciano Tovoli ratchet up the theatrical lighting effects: the scene is bathed in an eerie, unnatural shade of red, and the backlighting with the sheets create a wheezing sound of snoring coming from behind them; the framing of the shot recalls the scene in *Deep Red*, where Carlo and Marcus discuss the nature of memory in the deserted square; this time, the two girls are at the peripheries of the frame, while the shadowy form of the character behind the sheet occupies the center of the frame. Sara believes it's the mysterious director of the academy—the one whom nobody but the teachers appear to have ever seen. It's worth noting that while Dario's first five films were all shot in the cut-rate Techniscope format—a system utilizing a two perforation 35mm frame instead of the usual four perf, creating a widescreen 'Scope image at half the cost—*Suspiria* was actually shot in true anamorphic Technovision, resulting in a much more lush, finely-grained image than what Techniscope could offer. Only one more of Argento's films would utilize actual anamorphic photography: *Trauma*. Other than that, his later 'Scope films *Opera* and *Mother of Tears* were shot in the Super-35 process, where a full 1.33:1 35mm frame is exposed but the image is "composed" for a 2.35:1 image by matting the top and bottom of the image, while *Dario Argento's Dracula* was shot digitally.[9]

The next day, things go from bad to worse: Daniel (Flavio Bucci), the most prominent male figure in the film, runs afoul of Miss Tanner. It's significant that, in such a female-centered narrative, the only major male character is blind; this marks him as an outsider and it also enables the authoritarian Miss Tanner to view him as an inferior. When Daniel's seeing-eye dog—which has been a peaceful, loving animal—suddenly attacks Madame Blanc's nephew, Albert, Miss Tanner verbally attacks Daniel and humiliates him in front of the class.

Her response is one of utter hysteria. She shrieks and gets in his face, challenging him by threatening to kill the dog if she ever sees it again. Daniel asserts himself and elects to leave his job sooner than put up with her bullying; he even enjoys a blackly humorous joke at her expense when he replies that she needn't shriek at him: "I'm blind, not deaf! Not deaf, you understand?!" Unfortunately for him, the confrontation marks him for death. The subsequent scenes of Daniel trying to unwind at a German beer hall before walking home with his beloved canine companion are set in locations hand-picked by Argento: the beer hall is the *Hofbräuhaus*, while the square where Daniel meets his demise is *Königsplatz*; both are located in Munich, of course. *Hofbräuhaus* is significant as the location where Adolf Hitler held the first meeting of the National Socialist Party in 1920; *Königsplatz*, modeled on the Acropolis in Athens, was used as the location for many Nazi rallies—though nowadays it houses the State Museum of Classical Art and Antiquities. Argento felt that the use of locations such as this would have a subliminal effect on the viewer, as if the horrible events which took place in them would add to the disorienting quality of the picture. Much like the other references and quirky pieces of casting in his filmography, touches like this add something special for those who understand it; those who don't pick up on it can still understand what is going on in the narrative.

Daniel senses the presence of something or someone, and his dog also picks up on it—Argento conveys the idea of a supernatural presence as a stone gargoyle apparently comes to life and swoops down from above; the point of view shot swooping down on Daniel was achieved by attaching the camera to a pulley stretched from one side of the square to the other. It's a startling moment, and the overall effect is again complemented by the shrieking music of Goblin, which Argento plays

Daniel (Flavio Bucci) and his faithful seeing-eye dog are stalked by evil.

The Unsane Cinema of Dario Argento

at full blast. Just as things seem to be settling down, the dog, possessed by the evil spirit, turns on Daniel and tears out his throat. There's an irony in the sense that Daniel defended the dog against the accusations of Miss Tanner, but of course the animal is not behaving instinctively: it's being manipulated by some force of evil, and poor Daniel suffers for it. It's a rather tragic end for the character, who is destroyed by the only other living creature he appears to have a real emotional connection with. This entire episode, and Daniel's character in general, was negatively impacted by the cutting imposed by Fox (or International Classics) for the American theatrical release version. For whatever reason, they elected to remove the entire scene involving Miss Tanner and Daniel, making his subsequent murder appear utterly random and nonsensical; and the gorier close-ups of the dog tearing at his throat were also sacrificed to secure an R rating. The notion of a loyal seeing-eye dog turning on its master was later recycled in Lucio Fulci's *The Beyond* (*L'alidà*, 1981).

In the midst of this, Suzy continues to struggle with the feeling that she overheard something vital when she arrived at the academy in the middle of the storm. Her inability to recall precisely what she overheard mirrors similar dilemmas faced by Sam in *The Bird with the Crystal Plumage* and Marcus in *Deep Red*, as well as many other protagonists in later Argento films. It's the same basic conceit and it plays into Argento's obsessive exploration of the fickle nature of memory and his characters' seeming inability to properly process what they see and hear. It's true of people in general: so many of us go through life oblivious to our surroundings. When accidents suddenly take place in the real world, it's not unusual to have witnesses giving radically different, even contradictory, accounts of what took place. Like Carlo told Marcus in *Deep Red*, it's "your version of the truth"—that is, a highly selective and biased version of events which may or may not sync up with objective reality. It's the same principle which drove Akira Kurosawa's *Rashomon* (*Rashomōn*, 1950), the popularity of which infiltrated the public consciousness with what is known as "the Rashomon effect": that is, an event with multiple witnesses, all of whom have their own differing interpretation of the key event. The difference in Argento is, it's not a matter of various witnesses contradicting one another. It's all down to one character who sees (or hears) it all, but is unable to process it correctly until it's nearly too late. Marcus, as previously noted, is a remarkably ineffective protagonist—virtually impotent, in fact. That's not the case with Suzy, who emerges as one of Argento's strongest and most resilient characters. For the time being, however, she remains stymied; her big mistake is in telling Madame Blanc what she overheard—in so doing, she almost certainly signs her death warrant.

The use of sound in *Suspiria* is actually quite sophisticated. Argento didn't just obsess over the look of the picture; he was also very particular with regards to the soundtrack. While Goblin had been hired late in the day to rescue the soundtrack of *Deep Red*, they were involved from the very beginning with this film. Argento instructed them to create music which would assault the viewer. Even in benign scenes, it would be intended

Original Italian soundtrack for *Suspiria*.

to remind the audience that the powers of evil are still afoot. In order to really show off the music, Argento decided to utilize the four-track stereo system as opposed to the then-new Dolby system, which rose to prominence with the release of George Lucas' *Star Wars* (1977)— which went into release at the end of May, placing it in between the Italian and American theatrical release dates of Argento's movie. In an interview with Martin Coxhead, Dario said: "I studied using Dolby and then decided that four-track is better, the sound is much more powerful. More expensive but the sound is worth it."[10] The four-track system had actually been in use since the 1950s, when it was often used on the big Cinemascope productions like *The Robe* (1953); such sophisticated sound recording was not really the norm in the Italian film industry, however, making its application here all the more unusual. In utilizing the four-track sound system, Argento also made the relatively unusual decision to utilize a fair amount of live production audio in the English-language mix. It's something of a misnomer that Italian films are shot "silent," that is without any

Suzy (Jessica Harper) and Sara (Stefania Casini) figure out where the teachers go every night.

live audio being recorded; to do so would be highly impractical. That said, most Italian films—especially prior to the 1990s—tended to use rough guide tracks as opposed to the pristine live production audio, which is the norm for American and British films, for example. There are many reasons for this—it can be traced back to the devastation wrought by World War II, which resulted in many of the soundstages being destroyed; without sound proofed environments, Italian filmmakers got into the habit of simply dubbing the films in post-production—but it was very much the norm and Argento's early films were all hewed to the same example. Argento's friend and colleague Bernardo Bertolucci went to the trouble of using live sound recording on *Partner* (1968), noting that Italian films do not have a "spoken tradition," so much as a visual one—so, on that level at least, the move was by no means without precedence. Dario has always been interested in embracing new technology, however, and in deciding to make use of the possibilities of stereo, he (or possibly executives at Fox) decided it would be best to utilize live production audio as much as possible.

Thus, while some of the actors did end up being revoiced (notably Stefania Casini, though her English in the earlier *Blood for Dracula* was certainly more than adequate), many of the actors' own voices can be heard on the English track, and with the live on-set sound used in several scenes. Great care was also taken with the overall design of the soundtrack, with subtle use of sound effects complementing the music; the full possibilities offered by the multi-channel system are also very much in evidence, with dialogue and sound effects emanating from all directions, thus really enveloping the viewer in the film's sonic landscape. When the time came for *Inferno*, however, Argento would utilize the Dolby stereo format—and in the case of that film, the English language soundtrack was completely dubbed, as well.

The main casualty in this is poor Sara, who has become Suzy's only real friend and ally at the academy. Sara is also a clever and resourceful character, as it's she who figures out that the footsteps heard every night, seemingly signaling the exit of the teachers from the academy, are moving in the wrong direction; instead of leading to the main exit, they seem to be heading somewhere inside the building. Sara is anxious to put her theory to the test but finds herself terrorized when Suzy is drugged, leaving her to fend for herself. Suzy

Sara realizes her life is in danger.

is capable of fighting back; Sara is not. In another fantastically choreographed set piece, she is terrorized by an unseen assailant and tries desperately to save herself. Here again, the use of color is deliriously unnatural. In evoking the visual aesthetic of films like *Snow White and the Seven Dwarfs* and *The Red Shoes*—both filmed in three-strip Technicolor—Argento not only eschews the "look" of his earlier works (especially the pre-*Deep Red* titles), he also creates one of the most consistently dazzling looking films ever made. The colors are so dynamic, in

Sara is murdered in a nightmarish room full of wire.

fact, that many have mistakenly asserted that Argento and Tovoli filmed the movie in three-strip Technicolor. Argento let it be known early on that he wanted unusually bold, vivid primary colors, and Tovoli came up with the idea of utilizing the standard Eastmancolor film stock—and then manipulating the colors during post-production by processing the film with the last three-strip Technicolor printer still in operation in Italy. The results are quite extraordinary: there isn't a frame that doesn't look gorgeous and the effect frequently takes on a hallucinatory, almost three-dimensional effect. That's certainly the case during Sara's stalking and her eventual murder. After making her escape from one room, she ends up in a room full of metal wire; just why there's a room full of wire is never explained—nor does it need to be. Argento's use of dream (more precisely, nightmare) imagery is justification in itself. We've all experienced the classic dream where we find ourselves trapped and unable to move while something horrible moves towards us, and that's exactly how Sara's death plays out: she struggles mightily but is unable to wrench herself free. A black gloved hand enters the frame and slashes her throat; the final zoom-in on her staring, uncomprehending eye carries emotional resonance, since the viewer is encouraged to identify with and feel empathy for her character.

The film definitely includes what can be termed "*giallo* imagery." The half-remembered clue, the black gloves, the elaborate murder scene, the riddle which the narrative revolves around … these are all elements we tend to associate with the *giallo*. As such, it's not entirely surprising that some viewers insist on bracketing *Suspiria* in with the *giallo* genre. It's a point worth considering. It can certainly be argued that it has *giallo* tropes, and it most definitely does, but it's ultimately a full-blown supernatural horror movie—not a mystery-thriller. Bearing in mind that the definition of the genre is a little slippery, it nevertheless is pretty constant that *giallo* films—irrational as they may be—are rooted in reality. *Suspiria* is not. Neither is its "sister film," *Inferno*, which is also sometimes classed as a *giallo*. Given Argento's reputation as the master of the genre, it seems to be a knee-jerk reaction more than anything else to classify these films in this manner. While Argento would later introduce paranormal elements into *Phenomena* and had already toyed with supernatural elements in *Deep Red* (something Bava had done before him, in *Hatchet for the Honeymoon*), these films are far more concerned with evoking the notion of violent crimes in a (semi) realistic setting. *Suspiria* is anything but realistic; it's a phantasmagoria wherein any plot obstacle can be overcome by flights of fancy. No doubt the debate will continue to rage as time

Frank (Udo Kier) listens as Suzy (Jessica Harper) talks about the strange goings-on at the Akademie.

Milius (Rudolf Schündler) tells Suzy that "magic is everywhere."

goes on, but ultimately *Suspiria* is no more a *giallo* than *The Bird with the Crystal Plumage* is a Gothic horror movie.

Suzy does not become aware of Sara's murder until the end of the picture; in the meantime, she arranges to meet with Sara's friend, a psychiatrist named Frank Mandel (Udo Kier). This allows Argento a chance to show off one last Munich landmark, as they meet outside of the ultra-modern BMW Building. Designed by Karl Shwanzer, it was built between 1968 and 1972, and it was designed to evoke the cylinders of a car engine, appropriately enough. While the building itself is not specifically linked to the horrors of the Nazi party, film theorist Marcus Stiglegger points out in his visual essay "Suzy in Nazi Germany," included on the Synapse Blu-ray edition of *Suspiria*, the BMW corporation has a connection with the theme, as the BMW company provided planes and vehicles to the Nazis during World War II. Could this have been a happy accident? Possibly. It seems more likely that Argento was keen to use the building for its eye-catching architectural possibilities, and he certainly shows it off from virtually every conceivable angle, adding visual interest to what could have been a relatively inert dialogue scene. Suzy tells Mandel about her concerns about the school and they both are dismissive toward the idea of the supernatural, which is certainly understandable; even in the context of a fairy tale, it seems fair to have a healthy dose of skepticism where the characters and their reactions are concerned. "Bad luck isn't brought by broken mirrors," he tells Suzy, "but by broken minds." Mandel's colleague, Professor Milius (Rudolf Schündler), is far more in tune with the world of magic and the esoteric. He assures Suzy that magic is everywhere and that witches are real; that they are concerned with amassing personal wealth while doing damage to others. The casting of Schündler (1906-1988) is interesting in that, in his younger years, he had appeared in a small role in Fritz Lang's *The Testament of Dr. Mabuse* (*Das Testament des Dr. Mabuse*, 1933)—the last film Lang made in Germany before he fled to France and then to Hollywood to escape from the rising Nazi party. He had also appeared in some of the Edgar Wallace *krimi* films of the 1960s (don't forget, Argento's first two *gialli* were sold as *krimi* films in the German market) and had appeared as the Swiss butler, Karl, in William Friedkin's blockbuster, *The Exorcist* (1973).

Armed with knowledge about witchcraft and the occult, Suzy returns to the academy only to find that the students have all gone to the ballet; thinking she's more-or-less alone, she uses Sara's notes to try and figure out where the teachers go every night. She ends up in an elaborate room, dominated by a beautiful mural, and something catches her eye: a blue iris. Suddenly what she heard upon her arrival comes into focus and makes sense: "There are three irises ... turn the blue one!" Suzy places her hands on the blue iris in the mural and finds that it is an optical illusion of sorts. It's not a one-dimensional part of the artwork, but a triggering mechanism which, when turned, opens the door to a secret chamber. She makes her way down the darkened hallway, the walls of which are done up in gold leaf lettering of various Latin phrases, only to find the teachers in congress. Madame Blanc drinks a strange liquid and exclaims, "We must get rid of that bitch of an American girl! Make her disappear! Understand?!" Miss Tanner and the other teachers are also present, and they appear to be summoning some awful force through their sheer strength of will. Suzy is again struck with a strange sick feeling, but she snaps

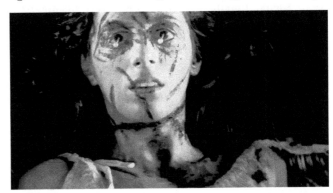

Suzy makes a horrific discovery when she finds Sara's mutilated body.

The Unsane Cinema of Dario Argento

Italian *fotobusta* features Suzy (Jessica Harper) as she discovers Mater Suspiriorum.

out of it when she discovers Sara's mutilated body—her eyes have pins through them, and her pale night dress is stained with blood. Suzy stumbles into another chamber, where she hears the awful, labored breathing she and Sara had heard in the gymnasium. It turns out that the mysterious director is Helena Markos, a legendary witch who acquired the name of Mater Suspiriorum—the mother of sighs. She's a purely spectral, supernatural presence; she can be heard, but not seen. Suzy arms herself with an unusual weapon: an ornate pin which she pulls from a crystal bird statue—its crystal plumage, so to speak, making this the most overt instance of "self-referencing" in Argento's canon to date. A flash of lightning illuminates the witch's outline and Suzy, seizing her opportunity, plunges the sharp blade into the woman's rotting flesh; as she expires, the building starts to catch fire and generally collapse into chaos, while the other witches, including Miss Tanner and Madame Blanc, are destroyed by the powers they have been exploiting for their own gain. Suzy flees from the academy as it

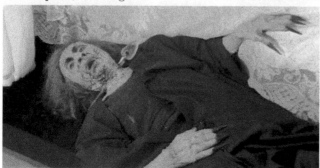

Helena Markos (Lela Svasta), aka Mater Suspiriorum, underestimated Suzy's resourcefulness.

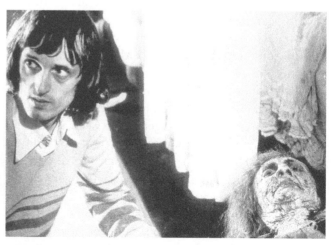

Dario prepares for Mater Suspiriorum's death scene.

Posed publicity still for *Suspiria*. From left to right: Giuseppe Transocchi, Joan Bennett, Flavio Bucci, Jacopo Mariani, Alida Valli, Stefania Casini, Miguel Bosé, Jessica Harper, and Barbara Magnolfi.

burns; the final image of her walking past the camera shows her smiling and laughing, in shock perhaps, but also relieved to have come through the adventure in one piece. The trauma of violence which is vividly reflected in the final shot of *Deep Red* is nowhere to be seen here; this represents Argento's first triumphant ending, really, since *The Bird with the Crystal Plumage*. Evil has been defeated, at least temporarily, and the fairy tale has a happy ending, even if many innocent people lost their lives along the way. Even more significantly, the ending marks Suzy's symbolic transition into womanhood; she finds her inner strength and fights back against the forces of darkness—and while she doesn't escape completely unscathed, it's implied that she will be leaving Freiburg as a stronger, more resourceful and independent woman than she was when she first arrived.

Suspiria vies with *Deep Red* as Argento's most popular film; if his name is known among cineastes of a certain disposition, it's almost certainly because of one or both of these titles. Along with his earlier "super *giallo*," it represents the climax of his artistic collaboration with Daria Nicolodi. There's a tendency to sometimes undervalue what Nicolodi brought to these films—and indeed the ones which followed. True, the story of *Suspiria* is less interesting than how it is realized on a purely technical level, but it seems likely that, without Nicolodi to inspire and collaborate with him, Dario would have had a difficult time making the transition from the world of the *giallo* to the super-stylized milieu of supernatural horror and the occult. Some fans have criticized the film for its simplistic depiction of witches as forces of evil, and this is something Argento would address later in the belated third part of the Three Mothers series, *Mother of Tears*; that film includes white witches as well as black witches. As the name suggests, the white witches represent all that is good and positive about the occult; it's the black witches who pervert these things into acts of pure evil. As Professor Milius points out in his talk with Suzy, the witches in this film are concerned only with personal gain—the glittering world of the Tanz Akademie comes at an awful price as the corrupt elders who run the establishment do so by sacrificing innocent souls in exchange for more and more wealth. Ultimately, these ideas bubble beneath the surface of the film; it's not a heavy-handed treatise but can best be experienced and appreciated as a macabre fairy tale. The film finds Dario continuing to push the envelope by utilizing every technical trick at his disposal, delivering ample suspense

The Unsane Cinema of Dario Argento

Full-page *Variety* ad, dated Wednesday May 11, 1977, for *Suspiria*, before 20th Century Fox got cold feet about putting their own imprint on the movie.

as well as plenty of shock horror. Like *Deep Red*, it shows him applying the same basic principles he had learned from Sergio Leone. When making films, hire the best of the best to help realize the final vision; remove Luciano Tovoli's exceptional cinematography, Giuseppe Bassan's breathtaking production design or Goblin's extraordinary music score, for example, and the end result would surely suffer. Whether or not it represents the pinnacle of Argento's career may be debatable, but the film's lasting impact and influence is beyond question.

By the time principal photography wrapped, Dario was on his way to making a reconciliation of sorts with Daria. All was hardly forgiven and forgotten, but at least they were on speaking terms once more and some semblance of normality was restored for the time being. 1977 therefore started on a positive note, though there were many changes still in the offing. "Daria came back into my life one morning in January. She rang me up and wanted to see me. It wasn't right that I never got to see Asia, it wasn't right that we were separated; everything that happened wasn't right. Without saying it out loud, I felt the same. I must admit, if she hadn't made that first step, who knows how much longer we would've stayed separated. [...] When *Suspiria* was released, we shared the applause, the congratulations, the success of a story we wrote together."[11] For her part, Nicolodi was convinced that Dario, still smarting over the problems they had endured, might take it out on her by depriving her of a screen credit; she would later state that "up until a few days before the premiere, I didn't know if I would see my name in the film credits,"[12] though ultimately Argento did the right thing and gave her credit for co-writing the screenplay.

Post-production proceeded smoothly, with Franco Fraticelli assembling the footage with his customary care and precision. Argento knew that the film's vivid visuals called for something equally vivid in terms of music. There had never been any doubt about getting Goblin back in to score the film—not only was *Deep Red* a hit, but the soundtrack album had sold remarkably well, to boot. Goblin was therefore enjoying a rare sort of popularity for a group primarily identified with scoring movies, and Argento wasn't about to let them slip through his fingers. In fact, he had engaged them very early in the process—remembering how Sergio Leone had encouraged Ennio Morricone to write and record themes for *Once Upon a Time in the West* before any footage had been shot, so that he could play the music on set to inspire his actors, Argento decided to do the same thing with Goblin. In fact, Argento's predecessor in the field of Italian horror, Mario Bava, had done something similar on the set of his pet project *Lisa and the Devil* (*Lisa e il diavolo*, 1973), where he played the Paul Mauriat rendition of *Concerto d'Aranjuez* on set in order to create the right mood. Like Morricone, Goblin was working in the dark without the benefit of any images to inspire them, but they came up with some music, which Argento reportedly cranked up and played on set to create the right sort of frenzied reactions. As Claudio Simonetti explains elsewhere in this book, however, the music played by Argento on set was not the same music which ultimately made its way into the movie; once the band was able to see the extraordinary images Argento had managed to capture, they rethought the music and recorded it all over again. It was worth the effort as the music for *Suspiria* became even more popular than their score for *Deep Red*; if anything, it remains one of the key film soundtracks of its vintage.

Suspiria made its Italian theatrical debut in Italy on the 1st of February 1977. It was a smash at the box office and ultimately it ranked as number 7 in the Italian box-office chart for 1976-1977.[13] It wasn't only a hit in Italy, either—it would go on to achieve a great deal of success throughout Europe and especially in Japan, where Argento's stock continued to rise as a filmmaker of considerable audience appeal; the success of the film prompted the Japanese distributor to import *Deep Red*—and to affix the cheeky alternate title of *Suspiria Part 2!* The involvement of Fox ensured that it would receive good theatrical exposure in the U.S., but evidently the top brass was a little concerned over the oddball Italian horror movie they had an interest in. Sooner than risk "embarrassing" themselves by affixing the Fox moniker to such a picture, they put it out through a phony subsidiary label, International Classics, Ltd. The American print was cut by approximately six minutes and included a new "breathing letters" title card in place of the original, more elegant title card; when it came out in July 1977, it attracted plenty of attention—in essence, it would become Argento's signature film in the American marketplace as well as the film which established him as a true "master of horror" in the international film scene. Compared to some of the ideas *Variety* proposed to exploit Argento's earlier films, their "exploitips" for *Suspiria* seemed surprisingly banal. "Mention the score by The Goblins [sic] and some of the actors in the cast. Refer to Argento's other horror pix. Use the beating heart motif as a gimmick."[14]

Critics were a bit perplexed by the film; on the one hand, even the more squeamish were forced to concede the film's aesthetic merits, but many stubbornly fixated on perceived narrative deficiencies. Gene Siskel's take on the film was unenthusiastic—and at times, downright nonsensical. He praised Argento's "stylish" visuals but felt it paled in comparison to *The Bird with the Crystal Plumage* and played like "a weak imitation of *The Exorcist* (1973)."[15] Bruce McCabe of *The Boston Globe* wrote:

> *Suspiria* is a giddy, hysterical, fitfully entertaining imitation of *The Exorcist*, *The Sentinel*, *The Omen* and almost any fantasy you can connect about the occult.[16] [...] It's got more ups and downs than a rollercoaster and it's much harder to characterize. The music, by a group called The Goblins, is frequently effective and carries the film over some of its duller parts. But it remains a fitful, uneven piece of work too often more uncontrolled than the hysteria it's trying to create.[17]

Janet Maslin, of *The New York Times*, expressed mixed emotions:

> Writer-director Dario Argento has an unusually horrific slant on life, to say the very least, and his film's most powerful

Films feature formula car chases and gore

By RICHARD DOBBINS

As is often the case with movies released at the end of summer, "Grand Theft Auto" and "Suspiria" are both thrill-geared films, crude and singularly lacking in redeeming qualities. Those who have an affection for crudeness, however, might find these flicks to be a fitting way to end their summer vacations.

"Grand Theft Auto" is the severest charge levied at Ron Howard in his filmaking debut, but he is also guilty of such misdemeanors as impersonating a movie director, contributing to the delinquency of an audience and driving under the influence of Roger Corman.

Nonetheless, he does manage to get a sort of enjoyable mindless comic momentum going in this story of a youth whose request to marry Nancy Morgan is refused by her rich father. So the two young lovers take off for Las Vegas in the old man's Rolls-Royce.

When a huge reward is offered for the car, every road-rat in West takes after this modern-day Romeo and Juliet, in the grand tradition of such movies as "Eat My Dust!, "Big Bad Mama" and "Gone in 60 Seconds."

movie review

But it's all par for the course of the releasing company, Roger Corman's New World Pictures. Corman is the only mogul who gives untried writers and directors a chance to practice their trade, and his past proteges have included Peter Bogdanovich, Martin Scorcese and Francis Ford Coppola. Since they did not turn out products akin to "The Last Picture Show," "New York, New York" or "The Godfather" during their respective apprenticeships, it seems safe to give 23-year-old Ron Howard the benefit of the doubt regarding his talents as a director, co-screenwriter and leading man.

"Suspiria," however, deserves no such consideration. It is being released by 20th Century Fox through a "straw man" distribution company called International Classics Inc., probably because of the excessive violence.

An executive from the Los Angeles office of Fox (as well as International Classics) said that this was a "routine procedure" and that "the decision to do so was made high in the corporate ranks."

The last time Fox used this company was in 1964 when it originally released the Greek director Michael Cacoyannis' film "Zorba the Greek." However, when the controversial film won acclaim, it was released under the Fox logo.

The executive further said that Fox was releasing "Suspiria" under the subsidiary because it was a foreign film, like "Zorba." "Suspiria" was made in Italy by native director/writer Dario Argento, with America's Jessica Harper (best known for her work in "Inserts" and "Phantom of the Paradise") playing the lead.

Fox has also released less-controversial foreign films such as the French "Lucien, Lacombe," in 1974 and Italy's "Scent of a Woman" in 1975. Both films, although rated "R", stricly avoid-sensationalism, unlike the new Argento film.

The film tells of a series of gruesome murders at a girl's school, that occur under a shroud of santanism and witchcraft. It is on a similar plane with Argento's "Dripping Deep Red" which opened here a few months ago. It would be inconsiderate to reveal the ending of the current movie, but "Deep Red" ended with a man getting decapitated when his necklace got caught in an elevator. Which should offer some idea of where Argento's head is at.

"Grand Theft Auto" is rated PG, and is showing at the Santa Anita cinemas, and "Suspiria" is rated "R," and showing in Pasadena at the State.

Review from *Star News*, Pasadena, CA, 1977.

moments have a way of making one think about open-heart surgery. But *Suspiria*, which opened yesterday at the Criterion Theater, does have its slender charms, though they will most assuredly be lost on viewers who are squeamish. [...] *Suspiria* is really quite funny, during those isolated interludes where nobody is bleeding.[18]

The unnamed reviewer for the *Colorado Springs Gazette-Telegraph* seemed to get it, however:

> More than a movie to see, *Suspiria* is a film to experience and for lovers of cinematic suspense and shock, *Suspiria* may prove the most harrowing shocker ever filmed.[19]

Variety's critic wasn't entirely keen, either:

> The horror touches are not for weak stomachs, but the overall result is disappointing when matched up against earlier efforts. [...] Most impressive elements are the carefully planned color camera setups and the interiors of a ballet academy and hotel, vividly photographed in Eastman Color (Technicolor is also credited) and Technovision by Luciano Tovoli. The acting leaves something to be desired, although an amount of suspense is generated.[20]

It's like they say, though, critics don't pay for movie tickets; so far as the general public was concerned, logic be damned: *Suspiria* was a major box-office hit.

Despite the success of *Suspiria*, Argento was faced with more personal problems. His relationship with Daria continued to deteriorate and they would perpetuate a cycle of breaking up and getting back together again. Tellingly, Dario and Daria seemed determined to at least try and make a go of it; by contrast, the split with Marisa had been fairly straightforward, with custody of Fiore being split between the two of them, while the break with Marilù, though unpleasant, was a definitive one. By Dario's own admission, he was often eager to move on when he felt like the bloom was off the rose of his relationships; but with Daria, things were different. It wasn't just due to Asia, though that certainly did play a role in it. There was also a definite love and mutual admiration between the two of them, and severing those kinds of ties is never an easy process. The triumph of *Suspiria* should have been cause for celebration, but it didn't help. Daria remained angry over what she deemed to be Dario's betrayal over his casting of Jessica Harper, and she continued to fume as the adoring critics lavished praise on Dario while appearing to ignore her vital contribution to the screenplay altogether. All told, it was too deep and profound a bond for it to ever be completely severed, but the romance was pretty much in ashes by the time *Suspiria* was conquering the box office. "My relationship with Daria had deteriorated anew. We both had a hard time admitting it, but we had reached a point of no return. [...] Our girls were the main reason we continued to stay together. Anna and Fiore were inseparable, and they looked after Asia with such care, that to separate them would have been extremely cruel. That being said, I often slammed the door to leave. I'd become so edgy, every move Daria made seemed inappropriate, as if it was being directed against me. So, I packed and went to the hotel or at my parents for brief periods. When I was calm again, I went back and we made peace."[21]

The truces were merely that, however. Inevitably the relationship dissolved altogether and though they would remain bound together, in a sense, by their visibility in the Italian movie scene and by virtue of their shared responsibilities as parents, the period of bliss and harmony which greeted the start of their relationship would never return. As it happens, the dissolution of

Dario and Daria in happier times.

Claudio Argento produced *L'albero dalle foglie rosa* for Seda Spettacoli.

to produce, something which didn't always sit well with the older and more conservative Salvatore. Dario loved horror; Salvatore did not. Sooner than remain under his father's thumb, he decided it was time to dissolve the company. Younger brother Claudio was content with the move as he was also eager to find his own way without feeling beholden to his father and his older brother. "Our father was very sad to see us part ways. Cinema unites, but cinema also divides."[22] This didn't mark the end of Dario's professional relationship with his father and his brother, of course; they would continue to be a part of his films for years to come. But the end of the relationship with Daria coupled with the closure of Seda Spettacoli marked significant signposts as the '70s started to draw to a close.

In May 1977, *Variety* made an intriguing report: "From a property acquired by Seda Spettacoli, Folco Quilici is preparing the next Argento project for filming in South America while Dario Argento seems decided to shoot his next one in the Soviet Union."[23] The South American project was *The Guyana Massacre*, which was to be based on the then-current Jonestown tragedy which came to a tragic end on November 18 1978; Claudio was originally involved in producing a film version, but he ultimately decided to drop out of it—whether this ultimately mutated into René Cardona, Jr.'s notoriously tacky *Guyana: Cult of the Damned* (1979) is not clear, however. As far as Dario's Soviet Union project is concerned, he later told Alan Jones that, around the time he finished *Suspiria*, he contemplated making a version of *The Phantom of the Opera*, which he decided to set against the backdrop of the Russian Revolution. When it became apparent that the project was going to be a little too costly and ambitious, he decided to shelve it[24]; 20 years later, however, he found himself in Hungary making a very offbeat version of *The Phantom of the Opera*.

Later in 1977, Argento received word that American master of horror George A. Romero (1940-2017) was interested in making a sequel to his landmark classic *Night of the Living Dead* (1968). For the better part of a decade, Romero resisted the urge to make a sequel; he even tried to escape being typecast as a horror director by following *Night* up with a counter-culture comedy titled *There's Always Vanilla* (1971). But *Vanilla* was a flop and his subsequent features were generally poorly distributed and unenthusiastically received. In 1974, following the release of *The Crazies* (1973), Romero hit upon a possible idea for a sequel, inspired by a visit to the Monroeville Mall, which had been in operation in Monroeville, just outside of Pittsburgh, since 1969. Partly driven by the practical reality that his recent films weren't doing much for his career, he seized on the idea of survivors of the "zombie apocalypse" holing up in the

their relationship coincided with another major change. Salvatore had started Seda Spettacoli with Dario (the name, incidentally, is a reference to [S]alvatore and ['e' in Italian] [D]ario [A]rgento) as a means of giving his son a foothold in the industry; together they had collaborated in the production of all of Dario's films. Salvatore had also made time for a few other projects not involving Dario including *Er più: storia d'amore e di coltello* (1971, Sergio Corbucci), *Antoine et Sébastien* (1974, Jean-Marie Périer), *L'albero dalle foglie rosa* (1974, Armando Nannuzzi), and *Carioca tigre* (1976, Giuliano Carnimeo). The company was in good financial condition, but in a sense, Dario viewed it as a symbol of his past—whereas he had his eyes fixed firmly on his future. He was looking to branch out into producing the sort of films he wanted

The Unsane Cinema of Dario Argento

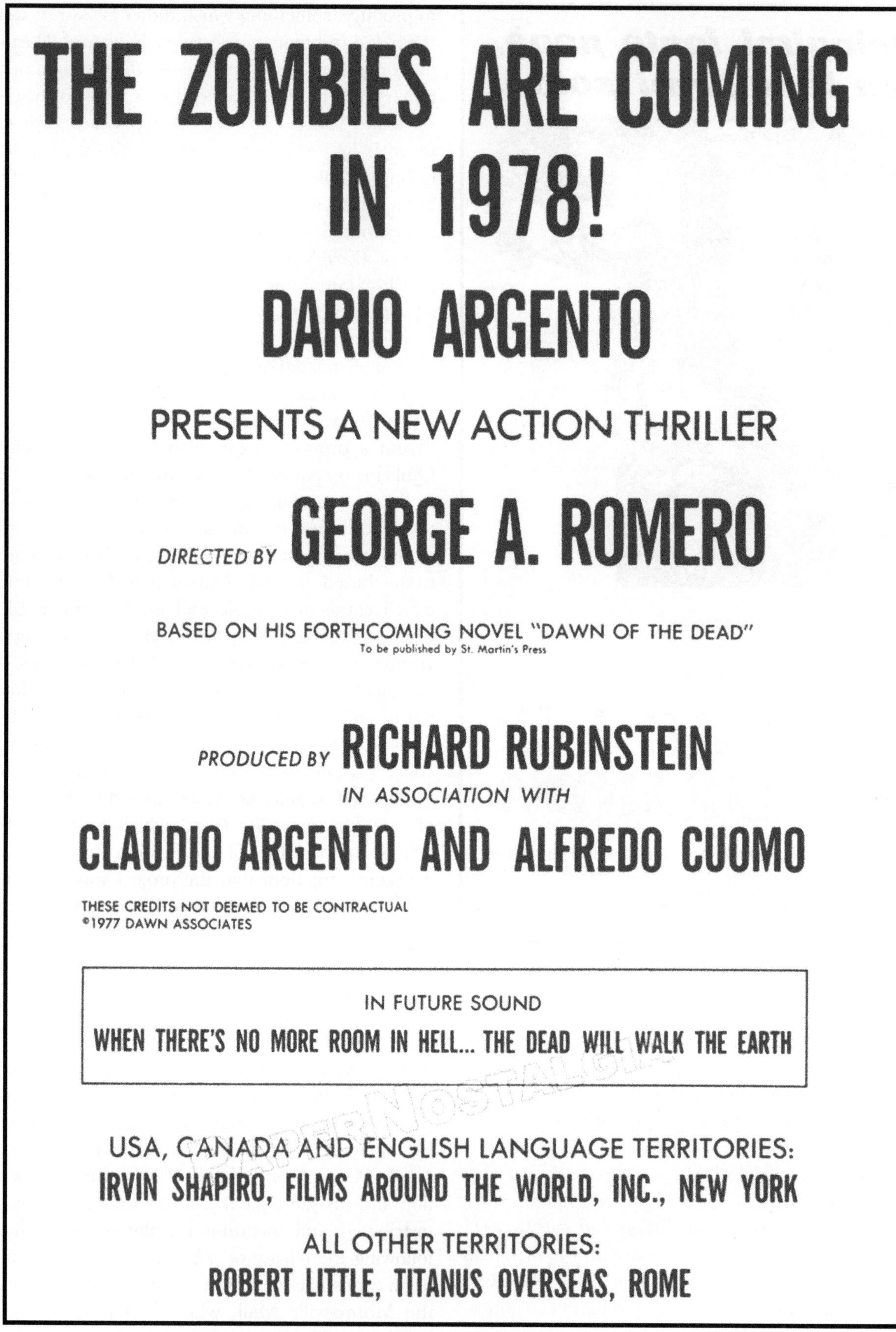

THE ZOMBIES ARE COMING IN 1978!

DARIO ARGENTO

PRESENTS A NEW ACTION THRILLER

DIRECTED BY **GEORGE A. ROMERO**

BASED ON HIS FORTHCOMING NOVEL "DAWN OF THE DEAD"
To be published by St. Martin's Press

PRODUCED BY **RICHARD RUBINSTEIN**

IN ASSOCIATION WITH

CLAUDIO ARGENTO AND ALFREDO CUOMO

THESE CREDITS NOT DEEMED TO BE CONTRACTUAL
©1977 DAWN ASSOCIATES

IN FUTURE SOUND

WHEN THERE'S NO MORE ROOM IN HELL... THE DEAD WILL WALK THE EARTH

USA, CANADA AND ENGLISH LANGUAGE TERRITORIES:
IRVIN SHAPIRO, FILMS AROUND THE WORLD, INC., NEW YORK

ALL OTHER TERRITORIES:
ROBERT LITTLE, TITANUS OVERSEAS, ROME

Full-page ad for *Dawn of the Dead* in *Variety*, dated Wednesday, January 4, 1978, formally announcing the collaboration between the Argentos, Alfredo Cuomo, George A. Romero, and Richard Rubinstein. Note the reference to "Future Sound," whatever that's supposed to be.

mall and making use of its seemingly endless supply of food and amenities. He was thinking big, however, and he knew that the scope of his vision would not be met by the money he and his collaborators in Pittsburgh were going to be able to raise on their own.

That's when Dario and his brother Claudio entered into the picture. Their mutual business associate, Alfredo Cuomo (a veteran of Spaghetti Westerns like *Tepepa*, 1969, and *Una ragione per vivere e una per morire/A Reason to Live, A Reason to Die*, 1972), had access to Romero's proposed screen treatment and Dario eagerly read it over; he saw the potential in the project right away and reached out to Romero. It was Dario who proposed to Romero that he should come to Rome and work on the script there, with the natural beauty of the eternal city serving as inspiration. Romero eagerly accepted the offer. "That was an experience let me tell you. When I look back on that period now all I can remember is going out to dinner with Dario every night, sitting at tables with 20 multi-lingual people and ordering pasta and Caprese salads."[25]

The filming of *Dawn of the Dead* got under way on November 13, 1977 and lasted through the end of February 1978. The production was ambitious and complex, and Romero pushed himself and his collaborators to their limit; filmmaker Roy Frumkes was invited to cover the production, and the wear and tear visible on Romero by the time the film was ready for release versus his bubbly enthusiasm at the start of the shoot is plain to see. Argento visited the location at the Monroeville Mall (where Romero was allowed to film at night after closing until the mall opened again the next morning) only once and their deal was a straightforward one: he, Claudio and Alfredo Cuomo[26] would pony up half the budget and provide European distribution, in exchange for which Argento was permitted the right of final cut over the non-English-language edits of the film;

Behind the scenes glimpse of filming at the Monroeville Mall outside of Pittsburgh, PA.

Scott H. Reiniger, David Emge, and Gaylen Ross in *Dawn of the Dead*.

in the English-speaking market, the final cut would go to Romero. It proved to be a harmonious collaboration and it marked the start of a long-running friendship between the two filmmakers, which lasted until Romero's death from cancer on July 16, 2017.

The action picks up a few weeks after the events of *Night*, as society is on the brink of total collapse due to the zombie epidemic. Fran (Gaylen Ross), an employee at a Philadelphia area news station, is joined by her fiancée, helicopter pilot Stephen (David Emge), and they decide to make a run for it before things get worse. Stephen commandeers the station's traffic chopper and they are all set to leave when they're joined by Roger (Scott H. Reiniger) and Peter (Ken Foree), two SWAT team members who've also decided it's time to cut their losses. They head off for an unknown destination, hoping to find some place where they can hole up until things settle down. They end up at a shopping mall in Monroeville, where they are able to rest and load up on supplies. Peter decides that they shouldn't be in a rush to evacuate the mall, as he figures they can barricade the doors and make indefinite use of the seemingly boundless supplies stores throughout the facility. Their temporary idyll is disrupted when a roving gang of bikers who've been moving from town to town and looting every step of the way sets their eyes on the mall and tries to take it for themselves.

Like *Night of the Living Dead*, *Dawn* offers up a heady mixture of social criticism and graphic gore. Yet while *Night* was stark and fairly serious in tone, *Dawn* is far more extravagant and light-hearted. Romero decided early on that he was going to push the envelope where the violence was concerned; by filming in color (as opposed to the cost-efficient black-and-white of the earlier film), he was aware that it would make the film an even tougher sell where the ratings board was concerned. Sooner than fret over that, he and his collaborators decided to go for broke, cramming in plenty of elaborate special make-up

The French lobby cards for *Dawn of the Dead* were much more exploitive than the U.S. advertising.

effects courtesy of Tom Savini. Savini, another native of the Pittsburgh scene, had actually attempted to join the production of *Night*—but he was called up for duty in Vietnam and had to miss out on it. His experiences in Vietnam as a combat photographer provided him with plenty of insight into the inner workings of the human body, something he put to great use in the many elaborate gore effects he created as a special make-up effects artist. Savini had already worked with Romero on *Martin* (1978) but *Dawn* tested his abilities. Romero's ambitious script contained a lot of gory "gags" and he knew full well that he would have to deliver or the film would suffer accordingly. There's been some criticism of the film's blue-faced zombies and unnaturally red blood effects, but apparently this was a calculated move on the part of Romero, who figured that going for more unrealistic effects might take the curse off some of the more violent imagery. Even so, *Dawn* proved to be as much of a watershed moment in the evolution of "splatter" cinema as *Night* had been; if it's not as relentlessly grim as the earlier film, it doesn't come at the expense of the shock value or the feeling of claustrophobia. Romero's finely-etched characterizations also provide ample human interest, making it easy to become emotionally involved in the action.

Comparing Romero's edit with that of Argento's, it's evident that they approached the material with different goals in mind. Argento decided that the abundance of comedy would work against the shock effects, so a lot of the humor is pruned from his version of the film. The basic structure is more-or-less the same—Argento and editor Piero Bozza worked from Romero's own early rough-cut assembly—but the two films diverge in

other areas. Some material jettisoned by Romero from his own version is present in the Argento cut, while the Argento is cut in a way that emphasizes action and incident over characterization. The two filmmakers also use music quite differently. Romero was always fond of using existing "library" tracks, sometimes in an ironic fashion, while Argento was all about creating a new and aggressive sound for the picture. Argento's respect for the music composed by Goblin is particularly evident in the scene where the SWAT team break down a wooden barricade in the old tenement building—in the Romero edit, it is followed quickly by the emergence of outstretched zombie arms shooting through the wooden slats on the doorway; in the Argento edit, the editing is dictated by the music. Argento and Bozza extend the shots of the SWAT team members staring into the room, thus accommodating the crescendo in the music, which is timed to coincide with the zombie arms thrusting out of the doorway. Romero's approach is preferable as it captures the urgency of the situation; while it's easy to see what Argento was going for in his edit, it simply doesn't make any sense for the men to stare aimlessly at what is surely an approaching army of the living dead. This is

Lenny Lies gets a head full of metal in *Dawn of the Dead*.

but one example in the two different approaches adopted by Romero and Argento in their respective edits of the film. Romero's more varied soundtrack is also preferable. His judicious use of library cues is always on-point, and the Goblin music becomes much less overly familiar because he varies the soundtrack so much; Argento's use of Goblin's music in *Deep Red* and *Suspiria* was inspired, but here it sometimes feels like it's being slathered on too liberally, thus diluting its impact. Ultimately the European edit is an interesting variant edition, and fans would definitely do well to give it a try just to see how it varies, but Romero's version offers up the more complete experience—one which hits all of the various different emotions from pathos to humor to extreme shock horror. The difference in running time isn't substantial (Romero's theatrical edit runs only approximately eight minutes longer than Argento's version), yet the Italian edit comes off a bit like the "Cliff's Notes" version by comparison.

In any variant, *Dawn* remains one of Romero's most beloved films; its combination of social commentary and splatter remains as audacious as ever, and time has done little to dilute its impact. Romero would return to the living dead realm with *Day of the Dead* (1985)—but it proved to be a commercial disappointment, though many fans have since embraced it as the best of his zombie epics. Romero and Argento would remain friends and they would collaborate once more on the Edgar Allan Poe omnibus *Two Evil Eyes*, which marked the beginning of Dario's ill-fated attempt to infiltrate the American film market. Over time, all three of

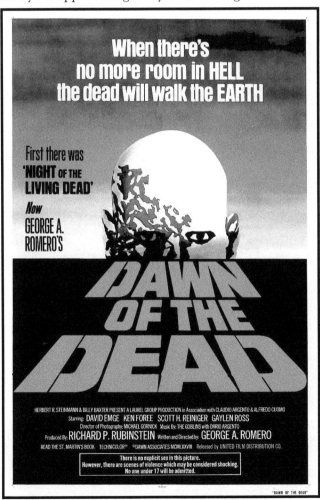

U.S. poster art for George A. Romero's *Dawn of the Dead*; artist unknown.

Dario and George A. Romero were all smiles during the filming of *Dawn of the Dead*.

music himself), with the balance of the soundtrack being sourced from the stock music library; Argento's shorter, less humorously-inclined edit is scored with wall-to-wall Goblin, however. As he would later recall, "Dario made it clear right away, he said, 'Look, I won't touch your version; you make the film you want to make. But I need to be able to change it for non-English-language European audiences.'"[28] Argento's instincts proved to be on the money and *Dawn of the Dead* opened in Italy under the title *Zombi* (literally, "Zombies") in September 1978—a full seven months before the film made its proper theatrical bow in the U.S. in April 1979.[29] Having shot a considerable amount of footage, Romero was faced with the unenviable task of quickly assembling an edit in time for the 1978 Cannes Film Festival, which was held in the second half of May; he managed to do so, but rightly reckoned that considerable tightening was needed for the film's proper American theatrical release. Argento used Romero's initial work print as his starting point, however, thus enabling him to get the film into Italian theaters well ahead of its American release; this also helps to account for the presence of some footage not included in either the Cannes edit or the American theatrical release version.

Romero's original zombie films would be remade with varying results: first there was Tom Savini's interesting but uneven take on *Night of the Living Dead* (1990), then Zack Snyder made a respectable go at *Dawn of the Dead* (2004), and finally *Day of the Dead* was remade not once, but twice, with poor results both times, with *Day of the Dead* (2008) and *Day of the Dead: Bloodline* (2018); as for Romero, he ended up finishing his career trapped in "living dead purgatory," desperate to make other types of films but only finding financing for *Land of the Dead* (2005), *Diary of the Dead* (2007) and *Survival of the Dead* (2008) prior to his death in 2017; *Survival* proved to be a disappointing swansong, but there is much to admire in *Land* and *Diary*—the former of which features Dario's daughter Asia in a major role.

Romero was an accomplished editor in his own right, and he assembled a rough-cut which was then shipped off to Rome for Argento to tinker with as he saw fit. One of the ideas Argento had early on was to recruit Goblin to compose the soundtrack; given the success of *Deep Red* and *Suspiria*, it was something of a no-brainer, really. Goblin responded with a terrific soundtrack, but Romero was reluctant to make too much use of it, as he preferred to make use of existing library tracks, as he had done on so many of his previous films. Thus the American version would feature some music by Goblin (resulting in the bizarre screen credit "Music by The Goblins in association with Dario Argento,"[27] as if Argento had anything to do with the composing of the

French poster for *Dawn of the Dead*.

The Italian release was a major success, prompting a renaissance of Italian gore epics, including Lucio Fulci's *Zombie* (*Zombi 2*, 1979). Argento had already been annoyed with Fulci in the past due to the older filmmaker appearing to "horn in" on his *giallo* turf with imitatively-titled movies like *A Lizard in Woman's Skin* (*Una lucertola con la pelle di donna*, 1971) and *Don't Torture a Duckling* (*Non si sevizia un paperino*, 1972), so the emergence—and subsequent popularity—of *Zombi 2* did little to repair the friction which already existed between them; Argento and his partners even tried to sue the production company responsible for Fulci's film, but a judge decreed that the term "zombie" did not originate with them and that they had no legal control over it. *Zombi* came in at number 24 at the Italian box office for the 1978-1979 box-office season[30]; by contrast, Fulci's film came in at 57 for the 1979-1980 season.[31] In any event, Argento's participation was really played up for the European release, while his name figured far less prominently in the American advertising; *Suspiria* may have been a success, but he was still something of an odd man out where the U.S. market was concerned, and with Romero capitalizing on his iconic hit from 1968, there was no need to play up the participation of yet another horror *auteur*.

German lobby card for *Dawn of the Dead*.

Notes:
1. Palmerini, Luca M. and Gaetano Mistretta, *Spaghetti Nightmares* (Key West: Fantasma Books, 1997), p. 114.
2. Ibid.
3. Argento, Dario, *Paura* (Rome: Einaudi, 2014), p. 196.
4. Argento, Dario, *Peur* (France: Rouge Profond, 2018), p. 208.
5. Ibid, p. 210.
6. Ibid, p. 211.
7. "His work is so unique. The color, the settings, the music, the strange angles: he's an impressionist painter like Goya or Caravaggio. He has the ability to let his imagination go on set. Who else can make fear and death entertaining?" (Quoted by Tiffany Pritchard in her *Screendaily* article "Rome: Dario Argento and William Friedkin deliver candid retrospective," October 22, 2015)
8. https://www.screendaily.com/rome/rome-dario-argento-and-william-friedkin-deliver-candid-retrospective/5095816.article
9. Thanks to Vincent Pereira for the technical information.
10. Coxhead, Martin, *Fangoria* #35, April 1984, p. 17.
11. Argento, Dario, *Peur* (France: Rouge Profond, 2018), p. 223.
12. Palmerini, Luca M. and Gaetano Mistretta, *Spaghetti Nightmares* (Key West: Fantasma Books, 1997), p. 114.
13. https://boxofficebenful.blogspot.com/search?q=box+office+italia+1976-77
14. *Variety*, August 22, 1977.
15. Siskel, Gene, "Fox Covers Its Prints on Its Part in *Suspiria*," *Chicago Tribune*, August 8, 1977.
16. While Goblin's music for *Deep Red* bore some similarity to the "Tubular Bells" theme in *The Exorcist*, there is literally nothing else to justify this arbitrary connection to *The Exorcist*. *The Sentinel* opened on February 11, 1977, 10 days *after* Argento's film debuted in Italy, making it impossible that it was any kind of an influence. And while *The Omen* (filmed from October 6 to mid-December 1975) was already taking the box office by storm by the time *Suspiria* went into production, there is nothing to suggest that Dario was in any way inspired by the film.
17. McCabe, Bruce, "'Suspiria' is Fitful," *The Boston Globe*, August 25, 1977.
18. Maslin, Janet, "'Suspiria,' a Specialty Movie, Drips with Gore," *The New York Times*, August 13, 1977.
19. Unsigned, "'Suspiria' horror sensation, *Colorado Springs Gazette-Telegraph*, August 27, 1977.
20. *Variety*, August 22, 1977.
21. Argento, Dario, *Peur* (France: Rouge Profond, 2018), p. 247-248.
22. Ibid, p. 248.
23. *Variety*, May 11, 1977, p. 234.
24. Jones, Alan, *Dario Argento: The Man, the Myths & the Magic* (Godalming: FAB Press, 2012), p. 249.
25. Ibid, p. 102.
26. In a *Variety* report dated May 9, 1979, it was reported that: "For a time, Claudio Argento was associated with Alfredo Cuomo in *The Guyana Massacre*, but exited when the project was absorbed by Alessandro Fracassi's Racing Pictures." (p. 308).
27. In fact, *Suspiria* bore exactly the same credit, with Goblin misspelled as Goblins on the U.S. print.
28. https://www.bfi.org.uk/news-opinion/sight-sound-magazine/interviews/george-romero-sight-sound-interview
29. There had been a preview screening in Los Angeles in February 1979, however.
30. http://www.hitparadeitalia.it/bof/boi/boi1978-79.htm
31. http://www.hitparadeitalia.it/bof/boi/boi1979-80.htm

Chapter Ten: Darkness and Despair

According to Dario, while Romero was busy assembling his initial edit of *Dawn*, he decided to take a trip to New York—it coincided with a long and bitter winter, and he ended up feeling poorly and being confined to his hotel near Central Park. During this rather miserable period, he started to work on the script for his first follow-up to *Suspiria*. The first film had established a potential trilogy, each one based around one of the so-called "Three Mothers." *Suspiria* had focused on Mater Suspiriorum, the mother of sighs, and for the second installment he elected to focus on Mater Tenebrarum, the mother of darkness. Once again, there is some controversy over the precise authorship of the screenplay. The film itself credits Argento as the sole screenwriter, but according to Daria Nicolodi, this is not the case. She has steadfastly maintained that she collaborated once more with him on the writing, but following the heartache and drama surrounding *Suspiria*, she decided to kick up less of a fuss this time. "I didn't want to live through that experience again, so I said, 'Do as you please, in any case, the story will talk for me because I wrote it. [...] [A]ll the ideas on alchemy and occultism in general belong to my knowledge of fantasy as does much of the romanticism present in the film."[1] The waters have also been muddied by some reports that Dardano Sacchetti—the co-author of *The Cat O'Nine Tails*, who was then enjoying a fertile collaboration with Lucio Fulci—had a hand in the writing, also without credit. Sacchetti, for his part, repudiates these stories. "I was contacted by [Argento's] father and his brother to help Dario, who a few days before the start of filming had a moment of hesitation. I spent a week with him, we talked about a scene to be rewritten; and then it was not. [...] It's true that the film had a point of contact with a story I had read Dario—but the script is his stuff."[2]

To produce *Inferno*, Argento again turned to his family. Salvatore would serve as the executive producer, while Claudio used the film to inaugurate his own production company, Produzioni Intersound.[3] Given the success of *Suspiria* in the States, Fox was interested in actively taking part in the production, as well. The involvement of a major studio seemed like a major coup, as it enabled Argento the financial freedom to realize some ambitious flights of fancy, but it came at a terrible cost. *Inferno* became the most traumatic film for Argento to create to date, and it would remain the most unpleasant experience of his professional career until *Opera* in 1987. The problems may or may not be evident on screen, depending on your point of view. For years, Argento would remain dismissive of the finished

One of Mario Bava's amazing matte paintings for *Inferno*, creating the illusion of the NYC skyline.

film, saying it stirred nothing but unpleasant memories; its relative failure at the box office also did him no favors, though he would be able to weather the storm in the long run.

Production got under way on May 21, 1979 and lasted through the end of August. The May start date was preceded, however, by a week's worth of location work in New York City—Manhattan and Central Park, specifically—in April of that year.[4] Argento was present to direct the location work and the production's needs were facilitated by New York-based director William Lustig (born 1955), who leapt at the chance of working side-by-side with the director of *Deep Red* and *Suspiria*; not long after working on *Inferno*, Lustig made his mark with the gritty and disturbing *Maniac* (1980), which was originally to have co-starred Daria Nicolodi—and which makes use of some helicopter footage of the Big Apple which Argento scrapped as unusable for his picture; waste not, want not! As it happens, Lustig would later be instrumental in presenting deluxe special edition DVD and Blu-ray releases of many of Dario's films through his video label Blue Underground.

To create the illusion that a number of scenes were filmed on location, Argento turned to an old master—Mario Bava (1914-1980). Bava's son, Lamberto (born 1944), had been hired to assist Argento on the film and it marked the start of a long and fruitful collaboration between the two men. Argento knew of the elder Bava's flair for problem-solving using simple and economical methods, and he asked Lamberto to talk him into joining the production. "I knew we were going to have big problems on *Inferno* because, at that time, it was before the digital age, so we would need glass shots, mattes, and so forth to recreate New York. It would be difficult, very complicated—and I thought Mario would be good to have around, because he was the father of this. He was tired and not working. So I asked Lamberto if he might help us, and he asked him."[5] Bava's mastery of matte paintings and miniatures were put to excellent use and that so many people who see the film believe that a good deal of it was actually filmed on location speaks volumes about his skill and resourcefulness. Mario elected to take no credit on the film, as he was concerned that working in a technical capacity might be seen as a step backwards for an experienced director such as himself. Bava would end up doing quite a few impressive effects for the film and it has also been rumored that he directed some sequences when Argento was sidelined with illness; Argento denies this out-right in the interview included in this book, but actress Irene Miracle, who is also interviewed, remembers him being present for a good portion of the filming. In any event, this would become the final film Mario Bava worked on—he was preparing to return to the director's chair for a new science fiction

Lamberto Bava, Salvatore Argento and Dario on the set.

movie when he died of a heart attack on April 27, 1980; he was only 65 years old. As for Lamberto, he would continue to be a presence in Argento's "professional family" through the 1980s.

Argento has often bristled at being compared with Bava, though such comparisons are almost inevitable. It was Bava who really established the horror genre in Italy—and he also laid the groundwork for the *giallo*, which proved to be Argento's most fertile terrain. True, their films are different and deserve to be assessed on their own merits, but some of Argento's comments about Bava and his influence come off as slightly disinguous. From Argento's point of view, however, "We were always very close, because we liked the same things, the same authors, the same movies. But he obviously went into a totally different direction. I always thought his movies were way too ironic and fantasy inspired."[6] And yet, he would later tell Tim Lucas, "I particularly liked *La maschera del demonio* and *6 donne per l'assassino*. I don't remember reviewing them, but I wrote in some magazines about them. I think some of the irony of Bava influenced me."[7]

Inferno would see Argento pushing the notion of "dream logic" to its extreme; in many respects, it would be the most esoteric and "art-house" of his films. As such, it's a film that inspires strong reactions: People either seem to love it or hate it. As luck would have it, he picked the wrong time to become "artsy fartsy." As he would later recall, things became incredibly strained between him and the executives at 20th Century Fox. They were horrified by the footage they were seeing—and not in the desired way. Salvatore and Claudio again did their best to shield him from the front office drama, but there was only so much they could do; they fired off memos to him while he was hard at work and they even created problems where the casting was concerned.

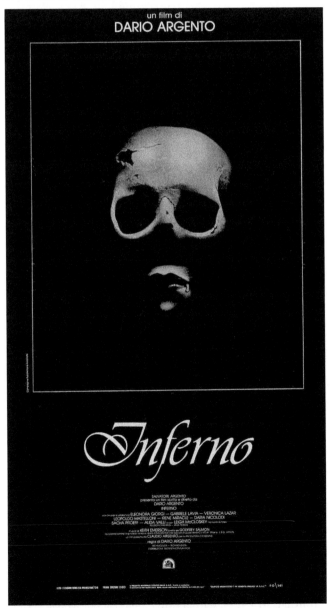

French poster for *Inferno*, using the same art as the Italian; artist unknown.

Rose (Irene Miracle) explores the creepy attic of her apartment building.

With some measure of hyperbole, he would later recall that "the whole shooting of *Inferno* was like being in a Russian prison camp!"[8]

Rose Elliot (Irene Miracle) is a poet who lives in an old apartment building in New York. She discovers a strange old book called *The Three Mothers*, written by an alchemist named Emilio Varelli. Varelli's voice dominates the opening titles sequence, as his voice solemnly intones the opening passages from his book; the "director as author" angle is surprisingly absent here, as Dario does *not* read these lines aloud on the Italian soundtrack—however, since Varelli is an actual character in the film, it made better sense to use the voice of the actor in question. As she pores over the book trying to decipher its secrets, she discovers more questions than answers. The book indicates that Varelli was responsible for designing and constructing three buildings for the powerful witches known as the Three Mothers—one of the buildings is in Rome, one is in Freiburg, Germany, and the third is in New York. "I failed to discover, until it was too late, that from those three locations, the mothers rule the world with sorrow, tears, and darkness." Mater Tenebrarum, the youngest and cruelest of the sisters, holds sway in New York. Rose is convinced that her own apartment building is the location in question and tries to find the key to discovering her secret hiding place. The opening reflects the opening titles of *Deep Red* and *Suspiria*, as Varelli's voice over narration is interrupted by the sudden swelling-up of Keith Emerson's main title theme when the title envelops the screen; once the title leaves the screen, the music quiets back down and the narration continues. Even so, it's evident early on that *Inferno* is being presented in a very different key from *Suspiria*. The look of the film is still deliberately artificial and stylized, but it is quieter and more low-key; this is reflected in Emerson's piano-based soundtrack, which doesn't strive for the same sort of sonic insanity as Goblin's music for the earlier film. In fact, Emerson was not Argento's first choice to score the film. According to Fabio Treversari, the assistant to special effects artist Germano Natali, he first offered the scoring duties to Rick Wakeman (born 1949), the keyboardist for Yes; when Wakeman passed owing to other commitments, Dario then reached out to Mike Oldfield (born 1953), the renowned composer of "Tubular Bells." They couldn't come to an agreement, so then Argento tried Emerson, who agreed to do the picture[9]; it led to a small side career in scoring Italian genre films, which would also include Argento's production of *The Church*.

The emphasis on the book suggests a link to the writings of the French author and alchemist Fulcanelli, about whom virtually nothing is known. Fulcanelli—the name itself is enigmatic and may or may not have been a pseudonym—wrote two books: *The Mystery of the Cathedrals* (*Le Mystère des Cathédrales*, published in 1926) and *Dwellings of the Philosophers* (*Les Demeures Philosophales*, published in 1929), with a third, *Finis Gloriae Mundi* ("End of the World's Glory"), teased but never completed.

Together, the three books sought to offer insight into the secrets of alchemy and the occult, but since the third volume—which would have offered the "key" to fully interpreting and comprehending the other two—never came to fruition, it remains enigmatic. As filmmaker and Argento devotee Richard Stanley explained in an interview with Henrik Möller on the podcast *Udda Ting* (which also featured input from the author), trying to get hold of Fulcanelli's writings in English-friendly editions is a frustrating experience, but the first volume did eventually emerge in an English translation in the 1990s; even so, the esoteric langue and use of deeply coded symbols makes fully grasping what Fulcanelli was trying to convey virtually impossible. Fulcanelli is not cited explicitly in the film, but the emphasis on the three mothers and the three keys and the use of architecture suggests that Argento (or possibly Nicolodi) was definitely inspired by him in the writing of the film. Interestingly, Fulcanelli and *The Mysteries of the Cathedrals* would be explicitly name checked in Argento's later production of *The Church*, which definitely evokes something of the mystique of this film.

Rose attempts to seek some answers from Kazanian (Sacha Pitoëff), who runs a bookstore next to the apartment building. Kazanian is a surly sort—crippled and embittered—and he snidely insinuates that women are more susceptible to fairy tales like *The Three Mothers* because, "They want very much to believe." Rose tries pointing out the similarities between what is described in the book and the strange ambience of the neighborhood, including a strange "sickly sweet smell" which hovers in the air, but Kazanian rationalizes that by saying, "They say it comes from the cake factory. It's been here as long as I have. You'll stop noticing it." Their conversation ends with Kazanian stating the film's signature line, "The only true mystery is that our very lives are governed by dead people." It's a beautiful line and it suggests that Kazanian is not the cynic he pretends to be; if anything, he's simply not interested in interacting with Rose on anything other than a business level.

Rose is established early on as our point of identification—she is one of the few truly engaging people to be found in the film. Irene Miracle (born 1954)'s performance suggests a quiet dignity and inner strength which sets her up as another Suzy-like figure, but Argento elects to shift points of view pretty regularly, especially in the first half of the picture, thus denying us the comfort of a single point of identification. The film has been criticized for its sketchy characterizations, but there's no doubt this was a deliberate and calculated move on Argento's part. While *Suspiria* focuses on strong female characters—both positive and negative—here the emphasis is more random and varied, and few of the characters emerge as either positive or remotely engaging. Kazanian is a memorably twisted character, thanks largely to Sacha Pitoëff (1920-1990), who imbues the role with a Lugosi-like aura of mystery. He's a complete loner, a misanthrope who has elected to isolate himself from everybody around him. Pitoëff was best known for playing one of the leads in Alain Resnais' art-house classic *Last Year at Marienbad* (*L'Année dernière à Marienbad*, 1961), and while he delivers a scene-stealing performance, he was reportedly not one of Dario's favorite actors to work with; he was at the end of his career by this stage and he followed *Inferno* with an appearance in Mario Landi's ultra-sleazy *Patrick Still Lives* (*Patrick vive ancora*, 1980) before retiring in 1981.

Rose decides to continue her quest without the help of Kazanian and starts poking around in the building's basement. She notices a leaking pipe and follows the trail of water—which has been leaking long enough to have eroded part of the cement floor—to a puddle in the middle of the room. While looking down into the puddle, she accidentally drops her keys into the water. What follows is one of Argento's most spectacular set pieces, one which has sometimes been mistakenly attributed to the great Mario Bava—more on that later. Against all odds, the puddle proves to be very deep indeed—in fact, it is the opening to an underground room which has been flooded with water. Rose needs to retrieve her keys, so she dives in after them. The scene is symbolic of delving into the murky waters of the

Dario directs Sacha Pitoëff as the embittered Kazanian in *Inferno*.

The Unsane Cinema of Dario Argento

Rose (Irene Miracle) explores the submerged ballroom in this German lobby card.

subconscious, as Rose obsesses over trying to unravel the ancient building's secrets. It's all completely illogical on a rational level, of course, but much like *Suspiria*, this is a film where conventional, plodding logic simply does not apply. As Rose swims around the submerged room, Argento artfully details her point of view as we see what appears to be a lavishly-appointed ballroom which has been lost to the dusts of time; there's even a glimpse of the word Tenebrarum written on the wall, much like the use of the Latin phrases on the halls of the hidden chamber of the Tanz Akademie in *Suspiria*. It's a poetic, beautiful sequence and it's capped with a shock effect as a rotting corpse floats into view and frightens Rose, who makes a hasty retreat. According to Luigi Cozzi, Argento took the submerged room idea from a treatment submitted by writer Vincenzo Ungari, Argento and Cozzi's collaborator on the screenplay for *Le cinque giornate*. According to Cozzi, Ungari gave Argento a couple of treatments for the *Door into Darkness* TV series. "The most interesting one was a *giallo* about a house with a completely flooded room. And the main character had to dive in to find an object that is the key to the crime." The story was too ambitious and expensive to realize in *Door into Darkness*, but Argento liked the idea of the flooded room and trotted it out for *Inferno*.[10] After Rose flees from the cellar, we see a black gloved hand entering the frame and stealing her lighter, which she accidentally has left behind. Here again, the use of *giallo* imagery has made some conclude that the film is a part of that subgenre, but in many respects *Inferno* is a film which utterly defies classical categorization.

The point of view shifts twice in rapid succession as the action transfers to Rome, where we are introduced to Rose's brother, Mark (Leigh McCloskey), who is studying music. Mark receives a letter from Rose in which she explains that there have been some strange things going on in her apartment building; his reading is interrupted during class when he notices a beautiful student (Ania Pieroni) staring at him from across the room; she's not one of the usual students and she's holding a cat, suggesting some strange, witchy vibe. It's not spelled out, but it's strongly suggested that she's Mater Lachrymarum. The experience leaves Mark a bit rattled and he leaves the class, accidentally leaving behind Rose's letter. The point of view shifts once again, as Mark's friend, Sara (Eleonora Giorgi), takes the note, intending to pass it on to him. As Sara makes her way home in the middle of a storm—in a sequence highly reminiscent of the opening of *Suspiria*, right down to the presence of Fulvio Mingozzi as the taxi driver—she decides to take a look at the letter. Its contents fire her imagination and she asks the driver to drop her off at the library—a magnificent Gothic construction which is comprised of two separate locations, both located in Rome. The exteriors are the Piazza Mincio, while the interiors are the Biblioteca Angelica, which is about four miles away. Location hunters will also want to take note that scenes for Richard Donner's *The Omen* (1976) were also filmed at Piazza Mincio, while the Biblioteca Angelica was used as a stand-in for the Vatican's library in *Angels & Demons* (2009). Giuseppe Bassan's art direction and production design is every bit as eye-catching as it had been in *Suspiria*, and the use of such striking locations adds to the film's baroque visual aesthetic.

The library sequence is loaded with eye-catching details, ranging from the image of Sara pricking her finger on a sharp pin protruding from the door of the taxicab to the sight of a young woman looking up from her book as Sara passes by, smiling up at her for no apparent reason. Her entry into the library is preceded by a tracking shot through a set of heavy red curtains—

Carlo (Gabriele Lavia) gets a major pain in the neck in this Italian lobby card.

recalling similar images in *Four Flies on Grey Velvet*, *Deep Red*, and others. Sara stops and asks an elderly patron for assistance in finding *The Three Mothers*, only to be told it's on the shelf right behind her; this is consistent with the film's dream logic, whereby things are always within reach while seeming utterly unobtainable. Sara soon realizes that she is being watched and she tries to escape the building through the basement; while the basement of the apartment building revealed a hidden, submerged ballroom, the basement of the library yields an alchemist's lair. Amid the bubbling cauldrons and exposed flames, she finds a mysterious figure with his back to her—when he notices that she's carrying the book, he attacks, revealing that his hands are rotting and talon-like. Sara manages to escape back to her apartment building—and her entrance recalls the shot of Pat entering Sonia's apartment building, with the camera panning up to admire the building's architecture. Just as in the earlier film, this serves as a prelude to a vicious double murder. Sara, badly rattled by her encounter in the library, seeks out another tenant, a sportswriter named Carlo (Gabriele Lavia), for company. The casting of Lavia (born 1942) is significant, as his presence and the character name recalls his role in *Deep Red*; one might think that he's being set up as a significant character,

but much like Sara, his appearance will ultimately be a fleeting one. Sara tries to unwind by putting on some Verdi (*Va, pensiero* from the opera *Nabucco*, the same piece played during the scene in the music class when Mark caught sight of Mater Lachrymarum) and Argento foreshadows what is to come by cutting to some strange images. A pair of hands, wearing black gloves, holds a string of paper dolls and begins cutting the heads off of the figures; when the first head is cut off, it cuts to a woman committing suicide in her apartment; when the second is cut off, we see a lizard eating a helpless moth; and when the third and fourth are cut off, we see Carlo and Sara sitting in the apartment, blissfully unaware of what is about to happen to them. The power cuts in and out, allowing Argento and cinematographer Romano Albani to play havoc with the lighting and color scheme; the action culminates with Carlo getting a knife plunged into his throat (the image of him drooling blood on Sara echoes earlier death throes in *The Cat O'Nine Tails* and *Deep Red*), and Sara being viciously knifed in the back. Sara's shocking, sudden exit from the narrative is troublesome because she's established as a possible heroine; this will not be the last time the film undermines audience expectations by suddenly removing a seemingly important character from the

Dario preps Sacha Pitoëff for his death scene.

Below: Eleonora Giorgi as Sara makes her exit.

action. This sort of narrative structure irks some viewers, but it is absolutely consistent with the film's nightmarish atmosphere, wherein nothing is as it seems and nobody is safe from the powers of darkness.

Mark arrives at the apartment hoping to retrieve his sister's letter, only to find that it has been torn to pieces; the only pieces he is able to recover carry an ambiguous message: "The third key is under the soles of your shoes." This offers a variation on the "half-remembered clue" motif which runs through so many Argento films. Mark has the information recorded on paper, but he is unable to decipher its meaning. The film relies heavily on the idea of esoteric texts and information and the inability of its characters to comprehend what it's all about; given the influence of Fulcanelli on the script, this is entirely appropriate. It eventually becomes clear that the "meaning" is reflected in the architecture of the apartment building in New York—this, too, is consistent with Fulcanelli's conviction that Gothic architecture was a kind of secret language containing clues and insights into the magic of alchemy; those with the knowledge and insight can decipher these messages, while others would never give it a second thought. Mark is certainly in no position to have much insight into any of this, but in time, with the fragments of information retained from what his sister passes on to him, he will come to a deeper understanding. Argento caps the scene with another deliciously irrational image. Sara's mutilated body falls through some fabric which has been stretched across one of the doorways; how or why such a thing could/would have been orchestrated is beside the point—it's precisely the kind of strange, inexplicable image that can occur in the random landscape of dreams.

Argento has often claimed his images and scenarios have derived from his dreams. On more than one occasion he has claimed to have written numerous films based on scribbling down things he remembered from nightmares. It's a romanticized idea, of course, and there's no doubt he has exaggerated it to play up his image as a sort of haunted poet of the cinema. In the case of *Inferno*, however, one could readily believe this. *Suspiria* was an aggressive, fast-paced cinematic assault; *Inferno*, by contrast, is druggy, hazy and very deliberately paced. In a way, it plays out like the anti-*Suspiria*; it was a bold move on Dario's part, and arguably it worked against the film's popular reception, though in time it would be rightly embraced as one of his finest works. It's not a film where the characters run in terror; they tend to react as if they're staggering in the midst of some sort of a collective delirium. This is definitely clear in the scene detailing Rose's fate: she gets hold of Mark by phone and begs him to join her in New York, but the phone lines go down before she can tell him everything she has learned. Like Sara before her, she realizes that somebody is stalking her and she proceeds to work her way through the labyrinth-like apartment building—the structure of which seems to defy all rational geography. Rose meets her fate when a pair of talon-like hands reach through an open window (shades of Sonia's demise in *Suspiria*) and pulls her head back through the opening; the sharp edge of the colored glass is used to slice her throat. The film isn't even halfway over and we've already lost two major figures of identification in the narrative; it's a bit like Hitchcock's shocking dismissal of Marion Crane (Janet Leigh) from the action in *Psycho* (1960). Both Rose and Sara come across as resourceful and empowered figures; could killing them off in such a fashion be a reflection of Argento's state of mind due to his increasingly negative and hostile relationship with Daria? That question seems to answer itself when Nicolodi makes an appearance later in the film—only to be similarly dispatched after a handful of scenes.

Mark arrives in New York and finds that Rose is nowhere to be seen; as it happens, he never does

Rose comes to an untimely end in this Italian *fotobusta*.

discover what has happened to her. He's never granted closure on that level. He picks up where Rose left off and becomes our protagonist—and what a very strange sort of protagonist he is, too. Originally there had been talk of casting James Woods in the role, but that fell through; Woods is a brilliant actor, but arguably he is too distinctive and idiosyncratic to have functioned in the way that Argento envisioned Mark. John Amplas, in his audio commentary for the Anchor Bay DVD release of George A. Romero's *Martin* (1978), claims to have flown to Rome at Dario's request to audition; his sensitive performance as the disconnected, psychologically unstable young man who may or may not be a vampire suggests that he could have done very well by Mark—but the executives at Fox favored Leigh McCloskey (born 1955), who was gaining momentum at that time due to his appearances in some popular TV movies and series, including *Rich Man, Poor Man* (1976), *Executive Suite* (1976-1977), and *Alexander: The Other Side of Dawn* (1977). He's an odd choice for the role, no question, yet he and Dario were very much on the same wavelength; in a later interview, McCloskey confirmed that Argento instructed him to play Mark as if he were in a daze.[11] McCloskey was also genuinely interested in the occult and alchemy and he was fascinated to see the sort of richly-detailed symbolic imagery Argento and his collaborators were bringing to the picture. While he's undeniably flat and not very engaging in the part, that's exactly what Argento asked of him; as such, his performance is sometimes unfairly criticized—one could knock Argento for electing to detail Mark in such a manner, but McCloskey was merely doing as his director requested.

A nice detail incorporated into the art direction of the façade of the apartment building is a plaque, which notes that G.I. Gurdjieff resided there in the year 1924; it's reminiscent of the plaque on the Tanz Akademie which notes that Erasmus of Rotterdam had once lived there. Gurdjieff (1877-1949) was a Russian-born mystic and philosopher who traveled the world in search of spiritual enlightenment; he came to believe that human beings, as a species, spent their life in a state of collective sleep—but that individual consciousness could be awakened by what he termed "the Fourth Way," a spiritual conceit which encourages people to be constantly mindful and alert, thus allowing people to maximize their inner potential. As it happens, Mark is about to embark on his own "Fourth Way," though whether he will ultimately benefit from becoming "woke" is open to debate.

Mark finds a possible ally in the form of a sickly resident, Elise De Longvalle Adler (Daria Nicolodi),

Elise (Daria Nicolodi) is in danger in this German lobby card.

who was one of Rose's few friends; the surname seems to be a reference to Irene Adler, known as "*the* woman" among Sherlock Holmes fans—Argento is a fan of Sir Arthur Conan Doyle's immortal sleuth and would work an explicit reference to the Holmes canon into his next *giallo*, *Tenebrae*. Elise is an aristocrat—a Countess—and in depicting her as so weak and frail, Argento is suggesting the feeble nature of the ruling classes. Even so, Elise is depicted sympathetically. She is the only person in the building who seems to have had a real connection with Rose and she's anxious to try and help Mark to unravel the mystery of her disappearance. Unfortunately for her, she's about to face her own "proletariat uprising" when her butler (Leopoldo Mastelloni) joins forces with the building's unscrupulous manager, Carol (Alida Valli), and they conspire to kill her for her money. Nicolodi's screen time is brief, but she manages to make a powerful impression; compared to her strong, confident characterization in *Deep Red*, this shows her in a much more demure and insecure light. She manages to generate empathy, however, which is more than can be said for her assassins. After her terrifying performance as Miss Tanner in *Suspiria*, it's a bit disappointing to see Valli in a relatively minor and colorless part; she doesn't even get to retain her voice on the English track this time, as she's dubbed by the familiar voice of Carolyn De Fonseca (who also dubbed Daria in *Deep Red* and *Phenomena*). Elise exits the narrative when she's lured into a deserted part of the building and is set upon by a group of flesh-hungry cats; Argento has carefully set the stage for this sequence earlier in the picture by showing somebody (presumably Carol) taking meat to some hungry cats who are being kept in the attic.

The presence of the cats is a source of irritation for Kazanian, who complains to Carol that unless she does something about them, he will take matters into his own hands. This gives way to one of the film's big set pieces when Kazanian gathers several sacks worth of cats and takes them to a lake in Central Park, where he proceeds to drown them. The character's petty sadism is confirmed by his smug self-satisfaction when the cats stop breathing; he gets his just desserts when he falls into the shallow end of the water and, due to his physical limitations, is unable to get back up. A hoard of rats descend upon him and begin to tear at his flesh; it's a delicious irony when one realizes that the cats may have been able to fend off those rats if only Kazanian hadn't sadistically murdered them. All of this unfolds against a lunar eclipse, which is one of several seamless visual effects which were engineered by Mario Bava. Kazanian screams for help and a local food vendor runs to his aid—or so it seems. The man proceeds to use a butcher knife to stifle Kazanian's cries for good. This is one of those scenes that really irk the more logically inclined viewers in the audience: Why does the man kill Kazanian? Is he under the control of Mater Tenebrarum? Is he affected by the lunar eclipse? Is he just flat-out crazy? We never find out, and that level of ambiguity is simply unacceptable for some viewers; those who can get on board with the film's dreamy sensibility just go with the flow and accept it without question.

Mater Lachrymarum (Ania Pieroni) makes a surprise appearance during a lecture on Verdi.

Mark continues to mull over Rose's ambiguous clue about the key being "under the soles of your shoes," and he suddenly is seized with an inspiration. He rationalizes that it may be a fairly literal clue and he digs a hole in the apartment floor; it doesn't give way to the apartment below, but rather to a secret crawlspace which allows him access to a secret series of rooms. He works his way through the crawlspace—to the accompaniment of Emerson's rock-opera fusion "Mater Tenebrarum," one of the few pieces of music in the movie which evokes the hysteria of Goblin's work on *Suspiria*—and finds a couple of characters he had previously met in passing: the elderly Professor Arnold (Feodor Chaliapin, Jr.) and his nurse (Veronica Lazar). When they met earlier, the

Mark (Leigh McCloskey) discovers that "the key is under the soles of your shoes."

scene was pitched for the sort of comedy which typified Marcus' interactions with Carlos' mother in *Deep Red*—that is, until Marcus realized she was the murderer. Much the same happens here, as these two apparently benign, comic figures turn out to be anything but. The professor has lost the ability to speak, but he has rigged up an elaborate voice box which allows him to speak through stereo speakers—and he explains to Mark that he is actually Emilio Varelli. "I built the houses for the three mothers," he explains, "houses which became their eyes and ears. This building has become my body. Its bricks, my cells; its passageways, my veins. And its horror, my very heart." It seems highly appropriate that the stern-looking Chaliapin (1905-1992) would later go on to play a key role in Argento's other Fulcanelli-inspired film, *The Church*. Mark doesn't entirely comprehend what it's all about and all he cares about is finding out what has happened to his sister. Varelli tries to dupe Mark, but he thinks quicker than usual and evades danger. The nurse then reveals her true nature when she tells Mark that she's the culprit he has been searching for. The pretty façade drops and she transforms into a Grim Reaper-like wraith; Mark makes a run for it and the building, already engulfed in flames due to an accident involving Carol, burns around them. The film ends with Mark looking dazed and confused, while Mater Tenebrarum shrieks as the building is destroyed. It's an open ending, even more so than *Suspiria*: in the earlier film, there's a sense that Suzy leaves the Tanz Akademie a stronger, more resourceful person—she's solved the mystery and lived to tell of her experiences. We don't get that vibe from the ending of *Inferno*: Mark, fairly passive and blank throughout, looks utterly shattered and confused; he's uncovered the truth, yet he lacks the insight to comprehend what he's been through. The earlier film also showed Suzy killing off Mater Suspiriorum, whereas Mater Tenebrarum's fate is less clear. We last see her shrieking in despair as the building burns around her—but has she truly been vanquished or is this just a temporary setback until she can arrange to have a new domicile built? We don't know for sure.

Inferno may not aim for the kind of aggressive shocks and scares as *Suspiria*, but in many respects it emerges as the more insidiously creepy film. It's easy to see why it might prove to be disappointing to those who prefer the fast-paced, in-your-face approach of the earlier film, but it demonstrates Argento refining his technique in the supernatural horror genre while finding a fresh way of approaching the subject. *Suspiria* is the rollercoaster

The architect Varelli (Feodor Chaliapin, Jr.) is unmasked in this Italian *fotobusta*.

The Unsane Cinema of Dario Argento   *147*

Japanese one-sheet poster for *Inferno*.

to favor red, yellow, pink and deep blue—sometimes combining to create purple effects—as opposed to the red/green/blue aesthetic of the earlier film. Albani later said that Argento told him right away that he didn't want him copying Tovoli's work. "He asked me to look at—and I still have it here—a book about the pre-Raphaelite Brotherhood, like Dante Gabriel Rossetti and so on. And the colors are very similar, very chromatic, very precise. There's an interior sequence with lateral lights—very precise, very chromatic, almost geometrical. So we agreed about that as well."[12]

Argento certainly didn't make things easy for himself where winning the audience was concerned, but to his credit he stayed true to his vision and didn't compromise; the executives at Fox were totally baffled by the movie and many of the critics reacted in a likewise manner. Time and reflection help to put things into perspective, however, and it's easier now to appreciate the film's ambitious exploration of the more esoteric aspects of alchemy without getting hung up on the fact that it isn't a continuation of the same themes as its predecessor. True to form, Argento would willfully, almost perversely, defy expectations with the long-gestating third part of the series, *Mother of Tears*, even though it emerges as the least accomplished of the three films by far.

When the production finally wrapped in the sweltering summer of 1979, Argento and his regular editor Franco Fraticelli set about making sense of what they had shot. Argento continued his love/hate relationship with the material and started to think about who would be appropriate to score the picture. Goblin was almost certainly considered, but following *Dawn of the Dead* the group started to have serious internal difficulties; as members came and went, as if entering a revolving door, they would be credited with writing such scores as *Patrick* (1979)[13] and *Beyond the Darkness* (*Buio omega*, 1979), though core member Claudio Simonetti had left in 1978 and was not involved during this stage. Argento decided to try instead for the gifted Keith Emerson (1944-2016) of Emerson, Lake & Palmer—one of Argento's favorite groups. Emerson was looking to expand his horizons and go into film scoring, so the offer came at the opportune time. He provided *Inferno* with a score that was as distinctively different from Goblin's work as the film itself was separate and distinct from *Suspiria*.

Inferno proved to be a risky venture and it didn't entirely pay off. The Italian release came on February 7, 1980—three full years following the release of *Suspiria*,

ride, while *Inferno* is the moody, contemplative, and enigmatic fusion of genre and art-house sensibilities. The look of the film definitely is in the same hyper-stylish key as *Suspiria*, but this time Argento elected to film in the standard 1.85:1 aspect ratio; the smaller canvas seems appropriate for the film, which feels somewhat claustrophobic and insular by comparison. There had been talk of getting Luciano Tovoli back to photograph the film, but he was otherwise engaged; he suggested his former operator Romano Albani (1945-2014), who proved to be an ideal substitute. Albani had served as Tovoli's operator from 1971 through 1975, though by the time Tovoli lit *Suspiria*, he had become a full-fledged director of photography in his own right, leaving Idelmo Simonelli to serve as operator on that film instead. Argento liked working with Albani and would collaborate with him again on *Phenomena*. His use of color is every bit as bold as Tovoli's had been, though his palette tends

Keith Emerson and Argento.

and a few months shy of Dario's 40th birthday. Anticipation for the film was keen, at least so far as the Italian audience were concerned, and it was warmly received by the Italian public—even if it didn't come close to matching the success of its predecessor. Argento had elected to go against the grain by making a film that was superficially similar to it, but which displayed a very different temperament and sensibility; audiences who embraced the theatrics of *Suspiria* felt a bit perplexed by *Inferno*, and it simply didn't stand much of a chance with regards to recapturing the earlier film's box-office success. It ended up coming in at number 15 for the 1979-1980 season at the Italian box office; the big hit had been *Kramer vs. Kramer* (1979), which couldn't have been more different in every respect.[14] Complicating matters, once more, were the executives at Fox. They gave the film a release in France in April 1980 and in Germany in September 1980, but the all-important American playdate never materialized; they elected to shelve the movie and it would sit gathering dust until given a belated release on home video in 1985; a token theatrical release followed in 1986, but all in all, the film simply never had the sort of exposure it really deserved. Between the problems behind the scenes, the bouts of hepatitis which kept him bed ridden at times, and the eventual poor performance at the box office, Argento had good reason to believe that *Inferno* may well have been cursed; he wouldn't embrace the film for many years and it seems likely that the traumatic emotions associated with it put him off the idea of completing the trilogy in a timely fashion.

Since the film didn't secure much in the way of theatrical exposure in the U.S., contemporary reviews are almost impossible to find. *Variety*'s "Yung" wrote that the film was:

> [A] lavish, no-holds-barred with story whose lack of both logic and technical skill are submerged in the sheer energy of the telling. [...] Argento's unmistakable technical style has a kind of cheap vulgarity that borrows heavily from Hollyw-ood classics like Hitchcock, maximizing the viewers' emotions through identification and point-of-view shots and directing every minute of screen time to getting an 'effect.' [...] It is also full of clumsy shots that cannot be edited together.[15]

Nina Darnton was also unimpressed:

> The movie's distinguishing feature is not the number or variety of horrible murders, but the length of time it takes for the victims to die. This is a technique that may have been borrowed from Italian opera, but without the music, it loses some of its panache. The film, which opens today at the Thalia, is shot in vivid colors, at some striking angles, and the background music is Verdi rather than heavy metal. But the script and acting are largely routine.[16]

Given the state of his relations with Nicolodi by this stage, there was also good reason for Argento to want to disassociate himself from the world of witches and the occult. He and Daria created *Suspiria* in an atmosphere of harmony which collapsed when he elected to cast an American star in the role Daria had created for herself. Their loving relationship, which encompassed everything from parenthood to creative partnership, fell into disarray and they grew completely distant from each other; they'd continue to work together, because the audience expected it to be so, but the joy and optimism was gone and had been replaced with tension and venom. Whatever one may think of Nicolodi's claims that she had a heavy hand in the writing of *Inferno*, there's no doubt that the film is very

Turkish one-sheet poster for *Inferno*.

The Unsane Cinema of Dario Argento

different from anything Argento made before or after it; it's so different from *Suspiria*, in fact, that one can't help but assume that the nature of their collaboration simply had to have been on a different keel. If one accepts her narrative as fact—and I would argue that one should do just that—then the absence of a co-writing credit must be interpreted as a major slap to her face. With that in mind, the odds of them getting together to write the story of Mater Lachrymarum, the mother of tears, was less than realistic. The obvious solution, then, was for Argento to turn to his tried-and-true formula: the *giallo*.

The 1980s were off to a mixed start for Argento. His first new film of the decade hadn't done as well as anticipated, and it proved to be a deeply unpleasant experience to make, as well. He was also dealing with the on-again, off-again drama surrounding his shattered relationship with Daria. Again, they weren't in a position to be able to just move on and forget—they had formed a family together, so for better or worse, they were obliged to remain a part of each other's lives. On a professional level, too, they remained linked—they were very much an "it" couple in Italy and, as such, there was the expectation that they would continue to be involved in their professional lives, as well. As time wore on, things got uglier and uglier; as many have commented, it's possible to chart the decline and utter ruination of their relationship by watching the films they made together. Dario would continue to have flings, of course, but he would never find another woman who would become as deeply entrenched in his life as Daria had done. By his own admission, he would enjoy himself when the opportunity allowed: "In Germany, I had an affair with an actress from *Suspiria*; in the U.S.A., I had some wild nights with a make-up artist, then with another collaborator; I had a longer affair with an ex-model from the cast of *Opera*[17], which was intense and beautiful; and another affair with a famous Italian photographer."[18]

While still recuperating from the traumatic experience of *Inferno*, Dario finally accepted an offer from his father's old friend, producer Dino De Laurentiis (1919-2010), to make a film for him; the famed mogul

Daria Nicolodi, Dario, and Keith Emerson are all smiles at a screening of *Inferno*.

Argento, still passionate about politics, attended the Congress of Christian Democracy 1980, r to l: Argento, Carlo Vanzina, Enrico Vanzina, Steno, Enrico Lucherini. (© Photographer Angelo Palma; Marka Collection, agefotostock).

had originally tried to entice Argento to direct an Agatha Christie adaptation in the '70s, but at that time Dario wasn't keen on adapting the work of others for the screen. Argento conceived of a scenario involving cannibalism among the homeless population of New York City—a reflection, no doubt, of some of the less "tourist-friendly" sights he had seen while writing *Inferno* in the Big Apple. Titled *Oltre la morte* ("After Death" or "Beyond Death")[19], the scenario proved a little too violent for De Laurentiis. After spending some time developing a detailed plot outline, the project eventually disappeared into the ether when the producer decided not to back the picture. Argento may have felt frustrated by the time wasted on developing the project, but he did not remain idle for long.

Dario's "rock star" celebrity status in Italy gave him access to the best that life had to offer—but it also carried the double edge which is so typical of fame. On a trip to Los Angeles in 1980, he was menaced by a psychologically unstable fan who kept pestering him with phone calls and letters; over time, the letters and calls became more intense, even threatening. Nothing ultimately happened out of it, but the experience made an impression and inspired him in the writing of his return to the *giallo*.

Notes:
1. Palmerini, Luca M. and Gaetano Mistretta, *Spaghetti Nightmares* (Key West: Fantasma Books, 1997), p. 114.
2. Email interview with Henrik Möller.
3. Produzioni Intersound would go on to produce such films as *Piccoli fuochi* (1985) and *Santa Sangre* (1989).
4. *Variety* reported on May 9, 1979 that part of the film would be shot in London. (p. 308)
5. Lucas, Tim, *Mario Bava: All the Colors of the Dark* (Cincinnati: Video Watchdog Press, 2007), p. 1011.
6. https://www.vice.com/en_us/article/7b74x9/inter-view-dario-argento
7. Lucas, Tim, *Mario Bava: All the Colors of the Dark* (Cincinnati: Video Watchdog Press, 2007), p. 810.
8. Jones, Alan, *Dario Argento: The Man, the Myths & the Magic* (Godalming: FAB Press, 2012), p. 108.
9. Quoted from the documentary "Of Fire and Darkness," included on the Koch Blu-ray of *Inferno*.
10. Ibid.
11. Quoted from the "Art & Alchemy" featurette included on the Blue Underground Blu-ray release of *Inferno*.
12. Quoted from the documentary "Of Fire and Darkness," included on the Koch Blu-ray of *Inferno*.
13. An Australian production, *Patrick* was originally scored by Brian May; Goblin did the music for the Italian version only.
14. https://boxofficebenful.blogspot.com/search?q=box+office+italia+1979-80
15. Yung, "Inferno," *Variety*, April 2, 1980.
16. Darnton, Nina, "Film: 'Inferno,' Mythic Horror Tale," *The New York Times*, August 15, 1986.
17. Antonella Vitale, who plays the role of Marco (Ian Charleson)'s girlfriend.
18. Argento, Dario, *Peur* (France: Rouge Profond, 2018), p. 282-283.
19. Not to be confused with the 1989 Claudio Fragasso film of the same name, known in English as *Zombie 4: After Death*.

Chapter Eleven: Brightness

Originally conceived as *Sotto gli occhi dell'assassino* ("In the Eyes of a Killer"), Argento's newest thriller scenario would prove to be his most self-reflexive to date. While Argento had occasionally included nods to his past successes—for example, the use of a crystal bird ornament as a weapon in *Suspiria*—this new project would mark a transition to a more "knowing" and self-referential phase in his cinema. The story deals with a writer of thrillers who goes to Rome to promote his latest novel; while he's there, a series of killings seemingly patterned after the killings depicted in the book put him in an awkward position. Argento uses the story as an opportunity to assail his critics while also, somewhat perversely, twisting things on their head and suggesting a potential link between an artist gone bad and the real-world repercussions that his art can yield. In a sense, it was the logical progression from the "super giallo" approach of *Deep Red*—sooner than try to outdo it in terms of its scope and ambition, he would take it in a completely "meta" direction which was unlike his previous works.

On the personal front, the project would not be free of discomfort. Salvatore, now nearing 70, was beginning to suffer from health woes. Dario had enjoyed a particularly close and special bond with his father and was surely terrified by the reality that age and physical infirmity was beginning to take its toll. Up until this stage in Dario's career, Salvatore had been his primary cheerleader—and his first line of defense where the production executives were concerned. As production was about to get under way on *Sotto gli occhi dell'assassino*, however, Salvatore found himself preoccupied with his worsening heart problems; sooner than risk exacerbating his already-precarious condition, he elected to remain on the sidelines for the first time and he would not play an active role in the production. Argento decided to entrust the heavy lifting to his brother, Claudio, though things were starting to become a bit frayed around the edges where their relationship was concerned: Claudio was still chomping at the bit to get out and establish his own identity, whereas Dario regarded himself as the man of the hour and he expected his younger brother to remain in a more subservient position. There were also the on-going issues with Daria to consider. Though their personal relationship was more-or-less in ruins by this stage, they were mutually agreeable to continuing their professional partnership—at least up to a point. Initially Daria favored playing the role of the protagonist's embittered ex—a suitably autobiographical flourish which definitely fit in to the reflexive bent of the material. Unfortunately, there was a shake-up and the casting had to be adjusted.

> I like all characters with a double personality, you don't know whether they're good or bad; moreover, I'm an expert at creating the ambiguity you need in parts like that ... then, at the last minute, the actress who should have played the role of [Anthony] Franciosa's partner withdrew, so Dario asked me to replace her and, although I was reluctant, I accepted. So, I acted a little out of character, without identifying much with the role, but I still had fun in my unending final scream. I gave vent to my anger at not having had the part I wanted![1]

Once filming got under way, the old resentments started to simmer once more and the tension occasionally spilled over into what was generally a fairly agreeable ambience on the set.

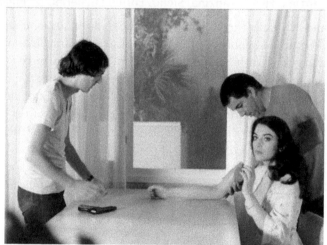

Dario helps prepare for Veronica Lario's death scene; Lario was married to former Italian Prime Minister Silvio Berlusconi from 1990 to 2014, and she also dated Dario's *Bird with the Crystal Plumage* star Enrico Maria Salerno in the late 1970s.

Production got under way on May 3, 1982 and would last until the middle of July. Perversely, Argento decided to change the title to the shorter, more evocative *Tenebrae* (*Tenebre*, in Italian), which translates as "Shadows"; it's a good title, no doubt, but it carries a strange double meaning. In short, it seems to promise a couple of things that the film has no intention of delivering. On the one hand, it suggests a potential finale to the Three Mothers trilogy, while on the other it

Argento chose to use bright lights even in dark scenes, such as Maria (Lara Wendel) picking the wrong house to escape from danger.

indicates the sort of moody, shadowy imagery which had been so prominent in Argento's *giallo* films of the 1970s. In the former category, the film really couldn't be any further removed from the world of the supernatural—if anything, Argento was looking to totally distance himself from the Three Mothers mythology, as the experience of making *Inferno* coupled with its subsequent disappointing performance at the box office had proved to be virtually unbearable. With regards to the latter point, this newest *giallo* boldly sets itself apart from the '70s films not only by virtue of its reflexive nature, but also by adopting a very different kind of aesthetic sensibility. The film is set very deliberately in bright light—even the night scenes are deliberately bright and over-exposed. This was no accident, either. In working again with Luciano Tovoli, his cinematographer on *Suspiria*, Argento decided to stray away from the *noir*-infused look of his earlier thrillers by making something more in the stylistic vein of Andrzej Żuławski's austere and disturbing *Possession* (1980). The end result is designed within an inch of its life, yet it works beautifully and evokes a vaguely unreal sort of atmosphere; he would even comment in interviews that the film is meant to be taking place a few years into the future, at a time when some strange illness has wiped out a lot of the population, thus leaving the comparatively sterile and unpopulated cityscapes which dominate so much of the picture. It's not something that figures at all into the plot, of course, but it denotes a self-conscious desire to create a universe out of whole cloth; *Tenebrae* would therefore become the ultimate *giallo* of the slick, cocaine-infused '80s, where yuppies rose to prominence and Gordon Gekko (played by Michael Douglas in Oliver Stone's *Wall Street*, 1987) would preach: "Greed is good."

The shoot finished, not entirely without drama, in mid-July of 1982 and post-production duties once again involved the trusted Franco Fraticelli working his magic in the editing room. Argento was eager to get Goblin back into the fray, but there were continuous problems on that front and a compromise was reached whereby former members Claudio Simonetti, Fabio Pignatelli and Massimo Morante would come on-board to write and perform a decidedly disco-influenced soundtrack. Their score proved to be another hit on its own terms, surely helping to make the film itself more popular than *Inferno* had been—even if some of the fans felt that moving back to the thriller without finishing off the Three Mothers trilogy was a step in the wrong direction.

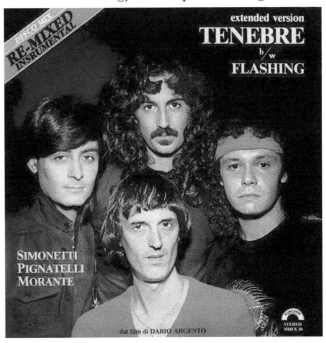

The film opens, like *Inferno*, with a character reading from a book. While the character in the earlier film was a nominal heroine, here it is the killer—relaxing by a roaring fire, reading from his favorite *giallo* … his fingers stroking the very words through black leather gloves. It's a preposterous image in many respects and yet: it works. The book in question is *Tenebrae*, and it's the latest work of acclaimed novelist Peter Neal (Anthony Franciosa). In a repetition of the "authorial voice" motif from *Suspiria*, it's Dario who reads aloud from the book on the Italian soundtrack; once again, this touch is absent from the English version. The passage from the book is significant: "The impulse had become irresistible … and so he committed his first act of murder." In *Tenebrae*'s

The Unsane Cinema of Dario Argento

Anne (Daria Nicolodi), Peter (Anthony Franciosa), and Gianni (Christian Borromeo) put their heads together to unmask a murderer in this Spanish lobby card.

twisted psychosexual landscape, murder is something of a rite of passage.

The introduction to Peter Neal establishes him as a sort of yuppie. He's stylish and elegant—a middle-aged man, but still in good shape, who even goes so far as to bicycle to the airport in New York; how Argento was able to grab those shots of Peter cycling down the expressway during the day is almost a magic trick in itself! Peter comes off as affable and very professional; he's "all business" when needed, but he also has a playful, witty side which comes out in his interactions with the other characters. There's a touch of smug condescension in some of his reactions, but he emerges as one of Argento's most thoroughly engaging protagonists—in short, he's the exact opposite of Mark in *Inferno*. Dario would later indicate that he first offered the part to Christopher Walken (born 1943), who passed on the project. He eventually settled on the veteran actor Anthony Franciosa (1928-2006); as Argento relates in the interview included in this book, they did not hit it off. Along with Tony Musante, Franciosa proved to be the most "difficult" actor Argento had worked with up until this point. Daria Nicolodi, on the other hand, saw him as a total professional: "He was a true gentleman, with lots of experience. During breaks in filming, he was as professional as he was during the scenes. But sadly he and Dario argued quite often."² Argento had long acquired the reputation of being a moody taskmaster with his actors, and as Nicolodi recalled in regards to David Hemmings, he could sometimes be nasty even when the actor in question was laid back and agreeable; with Franciosa, Argento met his match—he, too, had a reputation for having a volatile temper and the two men butted heads throughout the shoot. That said, none of this is evident on screen. Franciosa proves to be the ideal casting as Peter Neal—as opposed to Walken, whose inherent oddness would have likely tipped the audience off much too early about a major plot twist—and he delivers a performance that is rife with thoughtful details.

While Peter is on his way to Italy from New York, Argento introduces us to the film's vaguely futuristic version of Rome. He avoids the usual touristy sights and sets much of the action in slick, ultra-modern locations located in the city's EUR district; this was the place Benito Mussolini had selected for the 1942 World's Fair, where he intended to celebrate the 20th anniversary of Fascist rule in Italy. Those plans fell through thanks to the Second World War, and much of the architecture which had been left half-finished while the country was at war suffered severe damage from bombings and the like. Following the war, through the 1950s and '60s, the project was finally completed—though by that point, fortunately the Fascist regime was just an unpleasant memory for most Italians. The architecture in the EUR district was informed by rationalism—that is, the notion that architecture can be comprehended rationally; the buildings avoid the baroque and favor clean lines and simple geometric forms. In simple terms, it's also the wealthy section of town. *Tenebrae* therefore unfolds in a world of affluence and rationalism and clean, simple, minimalist spaces—a far cry from the baroque world of *Deep Red*, *Suspiria*, and *Inferno*. That said, the emphasis on the psychological underpinnings of architecture does form a link of sorts to *Inferno*, wherein the "key" comes from an understanding of the principles of alchemy. *Tenebrae*'s emphasis on the rational, which is echoed in the quotations from Sherlock Holmes that occur at several key points in the narrative, marks a break from the world of the magical—and yet, in a fitting irony, *Tenebrae* also emerges as Argento's most irrational *giallo* to date.

Sleazy agent Bullmer (John Saxon) in a very different version of Rome.

The atmosphere may be clear and perpetually sunny, but the characters are often affected by darkness. Elsa Manni (Ania Pieroni), an attractive young woman, is seen perusing the copies of *Tenebrae* sitting on the shelves of a chic department store; she slips a copy into her purse and tries to walk out, but is stopped by the store detective (Ennio Girolami, the older brother of director Enzo G. Castellari). The detective threatens to call the cops, but Elsa uses her sexuality to manipulate him. "Come on, you're not gay, are you?" The detective falls for it and arranges to meet with her to settle accounts at a later time. Corruption and "deviant sexuality" are recurring themes in the film—people are often shown to be selling themselves in one way or another, and it's not uncommon to see figures of authority disregarding the rules in order to get something they want. When she returns home, she's attacked on the street by a homeless man; it's the only sign we see of poverty in the film's ultra-slick milieu. She fights him off and manages to get back to her apartment, where she is surprised by an unwelcome intruder. The killer, who happened to see what took place at the store, has followed her home and makes her pay for her indiscretions. He stuffs pages from her stolen copy of the book into her mouth, while hissing, "Pervert! Dirty little thief!" Then he slices her throat with his straight razor, before taking some pictures of the carnage as a sort of twisted memento. The casting of Ania Pieroni (born 1957) as Elsa is significant. She had previously played the mysterious woman who bewitches Mark in *Inferno*; she's never identified as such, but even Dario has confirmed that she's Mater Lachrymarum. On a symbolic level, by killing her off in such a fashion, Argento is underlining his break from the world of witchcraft and the occult; the experience of making *Inferno* had been too difficult, and now it's time to return to more comfortable environs.

When Peter lands in Rome, he's greeted by his agent, Bullmer (John Saxon). Like Franciosa, John Saxon (1935-2020) is a member of the Italian American community in Hollywood and they have tremendous chemistry together on screen; Argento may have loathed Franciosa, but he liked Saxon well enough to invite him back later on to appear in his *Masters of Horror* episode *Pelts*. Bullmer is a stereotypical agent—fast-talking, slick, always concerned about closing deals—and Saxon plays him with humor and charm. When Peter notices that Bullmer has taken to wearing a hat, he asks him whether it ever tends to "drop off"; Bullmer replies by shaking his head back and forth and demonstrating how snugly it stays in place. It's an amusing scene, well performed by the two actors, but it also foreshadows something significant which happens later in the film. Bullmer whisks Peter off to a press conference where he's able to hold court with the Italian press. One of the reporters present is Tilde (Mirella D'Angelo), who is an old friend of Peter's. He's therefore taken aback when she tears into him: "*Tenebrae* is a sexist novel. Why do you despise women

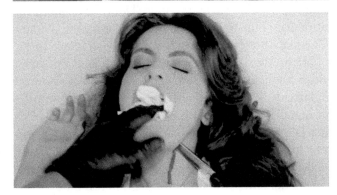

Ania Pieroni learns it's not wise to shop lift.

so much?" Peter defends himself, pointing out that he supported the equal rights movement, but Tilda won't be put off. "Do you write to a fixed pattern, or do your publishers tell you that this kind of sexism sells copies?" It's precisely the kind of back-and-forth Argento had long been engaging in with his critics; because his films often depict images of violence against women, Dario has long faced charges of misogyny. Yet these claims are often of a knee-jerk and highly superficial variety, as his films are also loaded with strong, resilient female characters; in *Deep Red*, for example, it's Gianna rather than Marcus who proves to be the stronger character, while *Suspiria* is absolutely dependent upon the actions of its female characters. It's an old debate, one which will rage long after Argento is gone, but a close study of his work reveals that he is often very sympathetic and progressive in his attitudes towards women and other minority figures. Argento would continue this sort of self-referential dialogue in his later *giallo Opera*, wherein the character of the director is an obvious stand-in of sorts. In both cases, however, Argento rather perversely toys with the audience by making these characters into complex, morally ambivalent figures; Peter may seem to be a positive character early on, but that changes as the story unfolds—and while the director in *Opera* is not a bad guy, per se, he has a mean streak that can make him off-putting for some viewers.

Daria Nicolodi, unlike Dario, got along very well with Anthony Franciosa.

Once the meeting with the press is over, Peter is reunited with his secretary, Anne (Daria Nicolodi), who introduces him to his new personal assistant, Gianni (Christian Borromeo). There's a lot of warmth to be found in the scenes between these three characters, which is a major contrast to the film's generally artificial and decidedly "chilly" approach. Unfortunately, Anne is an underdeveloped character and it represents Daria's first faltering performance in an Argento film. She let it be known that she hated the part and that she didn't really want to play it, but she gave in to pressure and one can see her struggling with it throughout. In the absence of anything interesting to say or do, Nicolodi tends to fall back on overly extravagant, highly theatrical actor's "tricks," that is bits of business designed to suggest an inner life that simply isn't present on the page; it comes off as hammy, especially compared to the relaxed and naturalistic performances by Franciosa and Saxon. On the other hand, young Christian Borromeo (born 1957) is thoroughly winning as Gianni; the hero worship the character feels for Peter is evident throughout, but one can sense early on that his naïveté will make him a likely casualty in the film's web of violence and betrayal.

The film starts to incorporate elements familiar from *The Bird with the Crystal Plumage*: the killer begins taunting Peter, first with letters, then with phone calls; yet while the contact between Sam and the killer in *Bird* was designed to frighten Sam into dropping his investigation, here the killer is letting it be known that he admires Peter and is trying to emulate the "lessons" set forth in his novel, *Tenebrae*. The relationship between Peter and Captain Germani (Giuliano Gemma) also recalls the one between Sam and Inspector Morosini in *Bird*. Like Morosini, Germani is a sympathetic and likable character; he's also a truly intelligent and efficient policeman, unlike the plodding and prejudiced cops presented in *Deep Red*, for example. Spaghetti Western star Giuliano Gemma (1938-2013) is perfect casting in the role. He echoes the slick, preppy look of Franciosa, playing into the film's use of rhyming imagery and doubling effects, and the two characters feed off each other in interesting ways. Germani echoes the killer by expressing admiration for Peter's books; he's currently engrossed in *Tenebrae*, and he realizes early on that it contains plot elements which may prove useful in his investigation. Peter is confused as to why the police are asking him about the death of a woman he never even met and Germani explains that pages from his book were found stuffed in her mouth. "When somebody is shot with a Smith and Wesson revolver, do you go and interview the president of Smith and Wesson?" Germani is good-humored enough to acknowledge the validity of the comparison, and this links into one of the film's major themes—the relationship between the artist and their public. It's a long-running debate, of course, but the notion of "responsibility" in the arts continues to rage to this day. When teenagers snap and commit acts of murder, it's not unusual for the press to latch on to the fact that they loved horror movies or rap music or violent video games, thus setting off the usual cries of outraged indignation from the public. Argento recognizes that art has no moral obligation—unless one counts Billy Wilder's "commandment" that "thou shalt not bore." Argento's films deal in violence but they do not advocate for violence; just because they depict acts of violence against women, for example, doesn't mean that the director is suggesting that women are "asking for it." Argento doesn't get too heavy-handed about it, but plot elements such as this help to make *Tenebrae* into his first truly "meta" work—that is, a film which explicitly comments on its relationship to the genre it is a part of. It also sees Dario becoming more self-conscious about his role as a celebrity; don't forget, the plot was inspired by his own run in with a deranged fan, but it also allows him to acknowledge and embrace his role as a master of the *giallo*. Like Peter Neal, his efforts in this field are met with popular success and critical backlash; and like his protagonist, he often finds himself under suspicion of harboring some awful psychological defect because of the violent nature of his art.

Argento also introduces strange, fragmented flashbacks—always preceded by Expressionist imagery of shadows on the wall, suggesting a man writhing in pain. It's more than likely the killer, but there's a surprise or two where this is concerned, as it is ultimately revealed to be Peter's "primal trauma." Argento shows a bright sunny beach scene, as a group of shirtless males are gathered around a sexy woman wearing red high heel shoes. One of the boys becomes upset and slaps her, causing her lip to bleed; the others chase him and hold him down while she stands over him, spits blood in his face, and then rams her heel into his screaming mouth. The scene essentially is one of rape. The boy isn't "penetrated" in the conventional way, but the symbolism of the phallic heel being forced into his mouth is obvious enough. While there had been brief flashes of nudity in the Animal Trilogy as well as a more raucous approach to sexuality in *Le cinque giornate* (just think of the horny Contessa whose breasts are always ready to fall out of her tight-fighting corset), this is certainly the most explicitly "sexy" and fetishistic scene in Argento's films to date. There's a touch of Tennessee Williams about the overheated sexuality and the scene gets an added kinky twist when one realizes that the sexy woman in the red heels was played by Eva Robin's—a transsexual performer who had been born under the name of Roberto Coatti. Born in 1958, Robin's (that's how it is supposed to be spelled, though the credits simplify it as Robins) came to prominence as one of the few openly transsexual performers in the Italian film scene, along with Ajita Wilson. Together with Wilson, she appeared in *Eva Man* (1980) and *El regreso de Eva Man* (1982), both of which capitalized on her notoriety. Argento's decision to cast Robin's in this small but important role adds all kinds of interesting psycho-sexual subtext to the film, though those viewers who aren't clued on her background can also enjoy the film well enough. Assuming that Argento was hoping that viewers would be in on it, however, one can't help but wonder whether Peter's suppressed sexual fantasies have generated his psychotic break; certainly this would be consistent with the regressive attitude towards sexuality voiced later in the film when he is interviewed by a conservative critic. Argento doesn't buy into that himself, of course, but it's there to tease the viewers and make them wonder.

These flashbacks continue to recur at key points in the narrative, always building on each other until we're fed a complete picture of their basic significance. Later on, we see another flashback where the girl is attending a swanky poolside party, while somebody watches her from behind the bushes; this gives way later still to another flashback, where the voyeur knifes her to death—before stealing her red high heel shoes. The use of the shoes could well be a reference to Michael Powell and Emeric Pressburger's *The Red Shoes* (1948), which also served as an inspiration on *Suspiria*, but it underlines the killer's twisted psycho-sexual hangups as well; the shoes have already been shown to be a symbol of phallic aggression, but in his mind they also serve as a keepsake, in much the

Spanish lobby card for *Tenebrae*: Peter Neal's primal flashback, with Eva Robin's on full display.

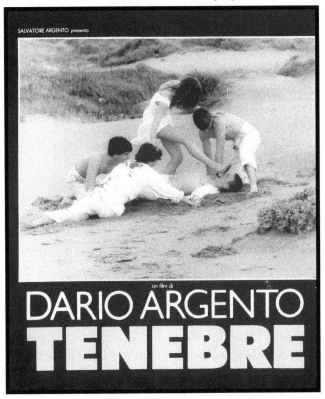

Italian lobby card: The teenaged Peter Neal undergoes a fetishistic form of violation.

The Unsane Cinema of Dario Argento

same way as the photos and other mementos gathered from the crime scene. They're also a fetish object and a reminder of the trauma which unleashes his incipient murderous rage.

The dialogue about so-called "aberrant behavior" comes to a head when Peter is interviewed by Cristiano Berti (John Steiner), a talk show host who presents himself as a big fan of Peter's books. Berti describes *Tenebrae* as being about "human perversion and its effects on society." Peter bristles at the suggestion and states that that isn't really what he was trying to convey. Berti counters that "two of your victims were deviants," and Peter quickly contradicts him—one of the victims may have been gay, but so what? To Peter, the sex and sexuality of the victims in the plot are of no importance; these details are merely there to humanize the characters and reflect what is going on in the real world. Here again, one can't help but think of the way in which Dario's own work was often misinterpreted, much to his own chagrin. Berti explains that he was raised a strict Catholic and asks if Peter was, as well; he gives a non-committal "Yes, I guess so." Berti explains that while he's a strict Catholic, he believes in things like abortion and divorce—thus making him a deviant from the point of view of some of his fellow Catholics. It's an interesting and fairly loaded conversation, again playing into the film's playful examination of art versus reality. It's worth considering in the sense that the killer feels that he is helping to wipe out anything which he deems to be perverse or deviant; as such, he feels that he is doing society a service. Could it be that Peter, outraged by the traumatic event which happened to him on the beach when he was a teenager, is also falling back on his perverted take on Catholicism by justifying his own violence on purely righteous grounds?

Tilde, the critic who previously gave Peter such a hard time at the press conference, ends up on the killer's list for two reasons: for one, it's implied that he is doing it to "protect" Peter from such invasive and "inappropriate" criticism; for another, he discovers that she is openly lesbian and is living with another woman. The scene of Tilde fighting with her girlfriend, Marion (Mirella Banti), is delightfully overheated, bordering on camp. Argento doesn't depict them unfavorably because of their sexuality, though his killer deems them to be deserving of punishment for not conforming to societal norms. Tilde is an intelligent, dignified and capable character; Marion, by contrast, is depicted as "slutty" and trashy. Their subsequent murders led into the film's most celebrated sequence: an elaborate Louma crane shot which runs for a staggering two-and-a-half minutes of screen time. In a way, it's the ultimate Argento set piece—that is, extravagant technique for the sheer hell of it. The lack of narrative "purpose" in the scene inevitably troubles some viewers, yet it can be argued that the film's reason for being boils down to this one seemingly gratuitous directorial flourish. Argento has always tried to remain on the cutting edge of technology and his awareness of the acrobatic camera movements afforded by this special piece of equipment—previously used by Roman Polanski in his psychological horror movie *The Tenant* (*Le locataire*, 1976), as well as by Antonioni and Luciano Tovoli on *The Passenger*—made it something he was very eager to make use of. The shot in question begins as Tilde hears a noise and looks outside—the camera proceeds to crane up from her looking through the window to the ceiling of her stylish Roman townhouse; the camera glides over the tiles of the roof and climbs over the entire exterior of the building, ultimately craning down the other side of the building, where it's revealed that the killer is at work breaking into the place. The shot is scored with the pulsing, disco-influenced main title theme composed

Argento used an elaborate crane shot to set up the killing of Tilde and Marion.

Tilde (Mirella D'Angelo) gets an eyeful of the killer. Below: Dario supervises the "eye through the hole in the shirt" gag.

by Claudio Simonetti, Fabio Pignatelli, and Massimo Morante and it's another example of Argento creating proto-music videos for inclusion in his movies. The shot doesn't tell us anything on a narrative level—a simple cut-away to the killer breaking into the house would have accomplished that in a fraction of the time—but that's the essence of Argento's cinema. It's not so much about the needs of the plot as it is the way in which the director manages to find interesting ways of framing and presenting scenes. To gripe over the indulgence of it would be to miss the point; it's impossible to picture *Tenebrae* without the shot, and it's justly celebrated as one of Argento's most spectacular visual inventions. Once the killer gains access to the house, he proceeds to murder Tilde and Marion in rapid succession; here again, the use of camerawork and editing gives the attacks a savage impact, and the emphasis on "staging" makes the aftermath look even more like a macabre fashion shoot than usual. That point is emphasized by the fact that the killer—like the protagonist of Michael Powell's classic *Peeping Tom* (1960)—is in the habit of taking very slick and professional-looking photographs of his handiwork. In fact, the killer's inner sanctum is yet another callback to *The Bird with the Crystal Plumage*—but that aspect is ramped up considerably here, as the killer keeps very detailed files and obviously goes to great pains to capture the most beautiful images of violent death. The similarity to Dario and his own emphasis on staging and imagery is yet another of the film's "meta" flourishes and it adds a macabre irony to the film.

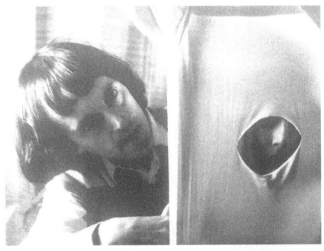

The next major murder set piece happens more-or-less by chance—or by a cruel twist of fate, as the case may be. Maria (Lara Wendel), the daughter of the porter at Peter's hotel, has a fight with her boyfriend (Michele Soavi in one of two uncredited acting appearances, the second being during one of the flashback sequences; he was also one of Dario's assistants on the film, along with Lamberto Bava) and she walks home alone in the middle of the night. A ferocious dog frightens her, and she reacts by kicking at its enclosure—this is a big mistake, as the animal escapes and chases her down the deserted streets until she stumbles into a very well-appointed villa with a beautiful swimming pool. She tries to find somebody to help her but notices some strange snap shots on a table in the basement. Sure enough, it's the killer's domicile. She's unable to run back outside because of the dog, so she

The Unsane Cinema of Dario Argento

Italian lobby card for *Tenebrae*: Maria (Lara Wendel) fends off the guard dog. Below: Dario and Luciano Tovoli (right) stage Maria's death scene.

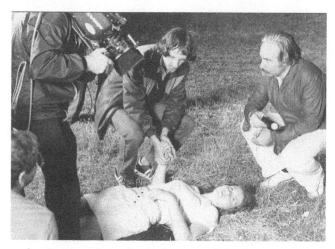

makes her way into the main part of the house—a truly dazzling location secured thanks to Argento's friendship with the house's owner, architect Sandro Petti—where the killer sees her and mistakes her for a spy. She flees for her life but is ultimately dispatched in an open field, with the killer repeatedly chopping at her with an axe. Maria's death scene is one of the most affecting in the film precisely because she's an innocent; she has done nothing to deserve what has happened to her and as such she's collateral damage in a world driven by violence and corruption. The look of the nighttime chase scene is particularly striking. Luciano Tovoli elected to bring a very different visual aesthetic to the film compared to his earlier work on *Suspiria*; here the color scheme leans towards cool blues and shimmering whites—it's all shades of pastels, really, apart from the occasional splash of vivid red blood. Argento and Tovoli give the film a vaguely futuristic look, which Dario would later say was an attempt at suggesting that the film takes place in some undetermined future where there are less people around, and those who remain are generally part of the upper class. Apart from the scene with the homeless man who harasses Elsa Manni, virtually everybody in the film looks chic and stylishly dressed. The look of the film isn't just pastel—it's also very bright, which is an obvious irony when one considers that the title alludes to darkness and shadows. To get the desired effect, Tovoli shot the film on special Kodak film stock, deliberately overexposing the images to ensure that they were as clear and pristine as possible.[3] This results in a very different "look" from Argento's previous *gialli*, notably *Deep Red*, which embraced a darker, richer visual aesthetic. It proved to be an inspired move: having already mastered the dark, moody style in *Deep Red*, the brighter, crisper and more pastel-oriented look of this film allows him to master something different.

Peter isn't compelled to be the amateur detective in quite the same way that Sam Dalmas and Marcus Daly had been, but there is good reason for this. Using his own flair for mystery plotting as a guide, he's able to work out that Cristiano Berti, the creepy TV interviewer, is the most likely suspect. He doesn't confide his suspicions to Captain Germani, either; while Germani has been sympathetic towards him, he has his own reasons for wanting to verify this independently. He ropes Gianni into going with him to Berti's house—and sure enough, it's the same impossibly lavish home that poor Maria had stumbled into by mistake; obviously Berti must be independently wealthy, as the odds of his being paid enough by the TV network to afford a place like this are slim to nil. This makes Berti into yet another corrupt member of the upper strata of society. While Peter and Gianni watch over the house looking for clues, Gianni sees something horrible. Cristiano is surprised in his living room by an intruder, who ends up splitting the interviewer's head with an axe; presumably it's the same weapon he had used to murder Maria. Gianni runs in a panic and finds Peter in the garden, his head bloody; he, too, claims to have been surprised and attacked from behind.

The mystery is apparently resolved, but Gianni is bugged by the feeling that something isn't right. Peter agrees and when he talks to Captain Germani, he says, "I just have this hunch that something is missing, some piece of the jigsaw. Somebody who should be dead is alive—or somebody who should be alive is already

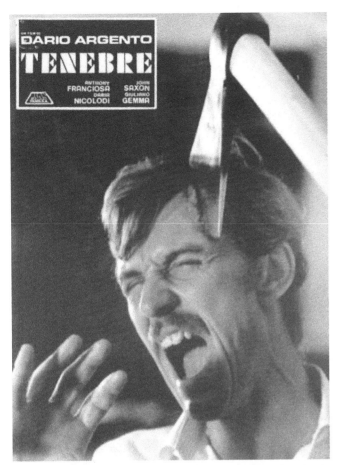

Berti's (John Steiner) reporting days are over when he is axed by the killer in this Spanish lobby card.

somebody killed him—and that, too, will require a solution. Peter is several steps ahead of Germani because he has an unfair advantage: after all, he's the one who is responsible for Berti's murder. Germani isn't such a fool, however: he already has some suspicions about Peter, though he hopes those gut instincts will prove to be incorrect. Peter claims to have had enough of sunny Italy and since he is free to do so, he catches a plane to Paris.

Gianni, meanwhile, is haunted by what he saw at Berti's villa. He returns to the scene of the crime and keeps flashing back to what he saw. In yet another variation on the "half-remembered clue" motif, Gianni focuses in on what he heard Berti saying just before he was killed: "I killed them! I killed them all!" Before Gianni can work it all out, however, he is strangled by Peter, whose departure from Rome proves to be yet another red herring.

The last act offers up a rapid succession of bloody murders. It's revealed that Bullmer and Peter's neurotic ex-wife, Jane (Veronica Lario, the future wife of media tycoon and future Italian prime minister Silvio Berlusconi), have been carrying on an affair; Peter is aware of this and, seized with rage, he takes on the mantle of murderer in order to get revenge on both of them. Bullmer meets his end in a square in the EUR

dead." Germani doesn't understand what he means, and Peter quotes from Sir Arthur Conan Doyle: "Whenever you have eliminated the impossible, whatever remains, however improbable, must be the truth." In fact, Peter is initiating a sophisticated game of cat and mouse with Germani. Both men are stylish, affable and intelligent; they also have a subtly antagonistic relationship which is nevertheless rooted in mutual admiration. Berti may well have been responsible for the murders, but obviously

Bullmer (John Saxon) meets his end in this French lobby card.

district, which is loaded with people going about their day-to-day lives without paying much attention to what is happening around them. It's a variation of sorts on the death scene of the maid in *Four Flies on Grey Velvet*, but it's even more impressive. As the sun shines down and Bullmer derives amusement and even a touch of sympathy from the various vignettes unfolding around him—ranging from a couple of testosterone-fueled men getting into a fight to a woman sobbing as her boyfriend breaks up with her—there's little indication of what is about to happen to him. Suddenly he's approached by

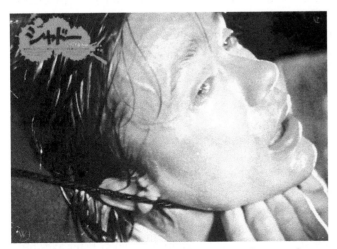

Gianni (Christian Borromeo) figures out the puzzle too late in this Japanese lobby card.

The Unsane Cinema of Dario Argento

Jane (Veronica Lario) is horrifically attacked by Peter.

somebody from behind and when Bullmer sees it's Peter, his smile of recognition changes to shock and horror as he stabs him in the stomach three times; Bullmer is left to bleed to death and nobody takes notice of who his attacker was. It's another classic set piece, perfectly visualized, and capped with a touch of dark humor as Bullmer's beloved hat flies off his head when he is attacked by his number one client.

Jane, the primary target of Peter's rage, is subjected to the film's most elaborately choreographed piece of "designer gore." As she sits in her pristine, white apartment, a storm rages outside; she's aware that she's in danger and is armed with a gun, but Peter surprises her by swinging the axe through her plate glass window—the axe severs her arm, unleashing a cascading fountain of blood, literally painting the walls red in the process. In many respects it's Argento's most overt commentary on the "designer" aspects of his death scenes; the wall is left looking like a piece of modern art, and the contrast between the clean white canvas and the crimson color of the blood is truly startling. Peter's rage compels him to keep chopping at Jane's body and the image of her lifeless body staring back at him is as pitiful as it is unsettling.

Anne and Germani arrive on the scene only to find Peter completely disconnected from reality; his desire for revenge has unhinged him completely, and the façade of amiability and elegance that he has carried throughout the film reveals a real monster lurking beneath the surface. It's a great opportunity for Franciosa to go deliciously over the top, which he does without resorting to insincere ham acting. Peter commits suicide, cutting his throat with a razor much like the murder weapon

Argento and Veronica Lario work on the axe scene.

described in his book. Germani accepts this at face value and takes Anne out to his car, where he explains that he started to have suspicions about Peter when he learned that a young woman he knew had been killed many years before. Peter had been accused by some of his friends of being the murderer; he managed to get off without being charged (no doubt his posh family connections had something to do with that), but the memory of the act continued to play havoc on his mind. Germani is a good cop—clever and resourceful—however, he makes a major mistake in underestimating Peter. When he returns to Jane's apartment to look some things over, he finds that Peter's body is gone; he takes a closer look at the razor and finds it's a joke shop model, complete with a button which allows fake blood to be discharged from the dull blade. It's a great commentary on cinematic trickery and illusion, and it's particularly apt in a film such as this, where facades and surface appearance play such a vital role. Germani pays for his mistake when Peter axes him to death. Anne, hearing the commotion, comes back to

He's not dead yet.

the apartment—Peter prepares to kill her, too, but a piece of modern metal sculpture, lodged against the door of the apartment during his struggle with Germani, comes loose; the sharp edge of the artwork impales Peter against the wall. Argento maximizes the nasty effectiveness of this final scene by having Peter struggling to wrestle free from the sculpture, his bloody hands proving incapable of getting a solid grip on the shiny surface; he finally expires. Throughout his death throes and beyond, Anne's horrified screams continue to echo on the soundtrack. The ending is incredibly satisfying and effective, largely because it's so clever in its usage of visual tricks, but also because there's something inherently satisfying about the idea of an artist being destroyed by a work of art. As Argento would later explore in *The Stendhal Syndrome*, we revere art for its ability to elevate the human spirit; but in the wrong hands, it can also be deadly and destructive. As such, the film doesn't allow him a clear-cut and easy riposte to his critics. While the point that violence in the arts does not necessarily led to violence in the real world is made loud and clear, he doesn't allow his own artistic alter ego to escape unscathed. Peter's psychosis compels him to cross the line from fantasy into reality, and in so doing he sets the stage for his own spectacular demise.

Tenebrae represents further evidence of Argento's mastery of cinematic technique. In revisiting his beloved *giallo* tropes, he finally initiates a dialogue with the viewer where he begins to acknowledge his role in the genre that brought him fame. By this stage in the game, he's not just one of the directors known for their work in the field—he's the acknowledged master. The film's playful exploration of the relationship between art and reality makes it one of the most sophisticated and infinitely rewarding examples of the genre; it's not coincidental that the release of this film (along with Lucio Fulci's ultra-gory *giallo*-slasher *The New York Ripper/Lo squartatore di New York*, 1982) signaled a kind of climax within the genre; Argento would continue to revisit it for years to come, of course, but essentially the genre had evolved about as far as was possible, and the non-Argento *gialli* which followed into the remainder of the '80s and beyond tended to look very weak by comparison. In many respects it remains Argento's most self-consciously stylized film. Every set (or location), every piece of costuming, every camera movement ... it all seems to have been thought through with tremendous attention to detail, with absolutely nothing left to chance. In a way, it seems to play like something of a response to the American *giallo*-style thrillers by Brian De Palma (born 1940), notably *Dressed to Kill* (1981). Like De Palma's films, it completely eschews naturalism in favor of studied stylization, and the mixture of violent bloodshed and kinky eroticism sets it apart from Dario's earlier, more sexually neutral works. If *Deep Red* had been the *giallo* to end all *gialli*, then *Tenebrae* hardly represents an artistic backslide; it adopts a different aesthetic and sensibility and emerges as the ultimate commentary on the genre as a whole. Thanks to Luciano Tovoli's expert cinematography and another hypnotic soundtrack (essentially by Goblin, though the absence of a drummer prevented it from being credited as such), it looks and sounds terrific—and with Franciosa's fantastic performance at its core to help root it in some semblance of reality, it builds to a climax that still retains its frenzied power.

Dario and John Saxon work out Bullmer's death scene.

Rare British quad for *Tenebrae:* note the cheeky addition of a red bow around the victim's neck, to spare the queasy British public from an ugly knife wound. Artwork by Renato Casaro.

When *Tenebrae* went into general release in Italy on October 28, 1982, it proved to be a popular success, ranking number 12 at the Italian box office for the 1982-1983 season—the big hit was Steven Spielberg's *E.T.: The Extra-Terrestrial*, of course, but to even be within striking distance of that behemoth was no small accomplishment.[4] This helped Argento regain the footing he had lost at the Italian box office thanks to *Inferno* and it would embolden him to strike out on his own once his brother Claudio let it be known that the time had come for them to go their separate ways. The U.K. theatrical release came in May 1983, though it would be shorn of some "sexualized violence" by the British Board of Film Censors. *Time Out*'s reviewer, "FL," wrote:

> A hybrid of horror, both thriller and slasher, not to mention chopper and shocker, this confirms what *Suspiria* and *Inferno* led one to suspect. When it comes to plotting, Argento is one hell of a basket weaver. With holes in his story big enough to sink credibility, he cheats and double-crosses like mad to conceal the killer's identity. [...] It does confirm Argento's dedication to the technicalities of construction images—*Grand Guignol* for *L'Uomo Vogue*, perhaps—but you'll still end up feeling you've left some vital digestive organs back in the seat.[5]

It was the censored version which initially made its way to British home video, but in 1984 the film landed on the infamous "video nasties" list as part of the Video Recordings Act 1984. *Tenebrae* would remain on the "nasties" list until 1999, when it was finally issued to video in the U.K. with only some minor trims; in 2003, it would

Italian lobby card for *Tenebrae*: Mirella D'Angelo bleeds; Daria Nicolodi screams.

A not-very-enthusiastic write-up for *Tenebrae* in the *Tallahassee Democrat*, Friday, July 13, 1984.

> **Unsane** — Not only unsafe and unpretty, but also ungrammatical! This "descent into madness" co-stars John Saxon, veteran of such monster classics as "Blood Beast from Outer Space" and "Queen of Blood," and Tony Franciosa, who once was married to Shelley Winters. Opens today at Capitol Cinemas, daily at 3:30, 5:30, 7:30 and 9:30 p.m. Rated R.

be reissued fully uncut. By way of a bit of background: 72 films were included on the official "nasties" list, and they were divided into two sections: section two titles carried a stiff penalty and anybody distributing such films were liable for heavy fines and even potential jail time; the section three titles were films which had been unsuccessfully prosecuted, meaning they were declared to be "less obscene." Films that were classed as section three could nevertheless still be removed from any video store if a cop deemed it necessary for the sake of public safety and decency, though fines and jail time could be avoided in that context. Of the 39 titles deemed obscene, *Tenebrae* was the only one to carry the Argento imprint; by contrast, Lucio Fulci's *Zombie* and *The House by the Cemetery* (*Quella villa accanto al cimitero*, 1981) were both on the list—while *The New York Ripper* was banned outright. Another Argento title, *Inferno*, landed on the section three list, due no doubt to the images of a cat chewing on a real mouse.

The U.S. release proved to be even less auspicious—it took years[6] for it to finally reach American theaters, at which point it was released by Bedford Entertainment in a re-titled version known as *Unsane*; this version was also cut by about 10 minutes, removing most of the more violent images, and a song by Kim Wilde was imposed over the ending titles. *Unsane* failed to make much of a ripple, though by that point a lot of dramatic developments had already unfolded both in Argento's personal life—and in his professional one.

Notes:
1. Palmerini, Luca M. and Gaetano Mistretta, *Spaghetti Nightmares* (Key West: Fantasma Books, 1997), p. 116.
2. Quoted from the featurette "Daria Nicolodi Remembers *Tenebrae*," from the Arrow Video Blu-ray release of *Tenebrae*.
3. As per Thomas Rostock's audio commentary for the Arrow Video Blu-ray release of *Tenebrae*.
4. *Variety*, May 4, 1983, p. 292.
5. https://www.timeout.com/london/film/tenebrae
6. Some sources indicate it played American theatres in February 1984, while Alan Jones lists a February 1987 release date. A brief article in the *Tallahassee Democrat*, dated July 13, 1984, confirms that the film opened there on that date; special thanks to William Wilson.

Trade ad promo for *Tenebrae* from 1982.

Chapter Twelve: Bugs Gone Wild

Having already disbanded Seda Spettacoli, Argento finally decided to take the plunge and begin his own company. DACFILM (or, alternately, ADC Films, as it would later be known) would be responsible for the balance of Argento's films as a director and/or producer through the early 1990s. In May 1984, *Variety* reported on the creation of the new company, noting that Dario's split from Salvatore and Claudio had been an "amicable" one.[1] The DACFILM years would encompass a period of financial prosperity for Dario, though admittedly it was not without its share of bumps and heartache along the way. Following the release of *Tenebrae*, Argento started to give some serious thought about what his next picture would be. Having already climbed about as high as he could possibly hope to climb within the *giallo*—first with the ambitious and fairly definitive *Deep Red*, then with the most self-reflexive and "meta" thriller of them all in *Tenebrae*—he knew it was necessary to find some different approaches in order to keep things fresh.

In 1983, he started working on a new script—with a new writing partner in tow. Franco Ferrini (born in 1944) had a similar background to Dario. He, too, was a major cineaste and his early professional years were spent organizing tributes to his favorite films and writing books on some of his favorite directors, including Sergio Leone. Ferrini started working his way into the Roman film scene in the mid-'70s and had his first brush with the *giallo* when he contributed to the screenplay of the troubled *Rings of Fear* (*Enigma rosso*, 1978), which was originally conceived as a vehicle for Massimo Dallamano. Dallamano, the gifted cinematographer who shot Leone's *Fistful of Dollars* (*Per un pugno di dollari*, 1964) and *For a Few Dollars More* (*Per qualche dollaro in più*, 1965), had turned to directing in the mid-'60s and he made a major mark in the *giallo* with his "schoolgirls in peril" movies *What Have You Done to Solange?* (*Cosa avete fatto a Solange*, 1972) and *What Have They Done to Your Daughters?* (*La polizia chiede aiuto*, 1974). *Rings of Fear* was originally intended to cap off a trilogy of sorts, but Dallamano died in a tragic car accident in 1976, leaving the script only partway finished. It went through a number of different hands, including Ferrini's, before finally getting produced; as it happens, the cash-strapped production ran out of funds and the picture was never properly finished, but the producers managed to put together a semi-coherent edit and released it, anyway. From there, Ferrini went on to work with such directors as Sergio Corbucci, Alberto Lattuada—and even Leone himself, when he contributed to the script of what became Leone's final film, *Once Upon a Time in America* (1984). Leone's final masterwork ended up having some unexpected crossovers and even influence on Dario's latest project. In fact, by Ferrini's own account, his involvement in Leone's gangster epic was initially fairly minimal—a bit like Dario's participation in *Once Upon a Time in the West*. "He [Leone] was very obliging, but progress on the film was very slow, and so, in the meantime, I moved to Rome and tried to do something as a scriptwriter. [...] Then between 1977 and 1978, I wrote *Enigma rosso* and *La cicala* [...] and the first versions of *Once Upon a Time in America*, for which I was simply an onlooker at the beginning, but became one of its authors over the years."[2] Ferrini entered Argento's circle in the summer of 1983 when he sent him a script for a thriller he had written, titled *Minaccia d'amore*; Argento liked the script, but preferred writing his own material, so he elected to pass on it—it would later be filmed by Ruggero Deodato (born 1939) in 1988, though it is better known in the English market as *Dial: Help*. In any event, Ferrini found himself welcomed into Argento's circle and it was during this time that he was invited to help develop the screenplay for what would become *Phenomena*. "We wrote *Phenomena* together at my home; he wrote the action-filled scenes, such as the whole last part, and I made general alterations to the whole thing and constructed the minor scenes that linked the main parts of the story."[3] Somewhat incredibly, given how bizarre the finished film would turn out to be, the story had its origins in reality. "Dario had heard on the French radio that insects could be of help to the police in criminal investigations, and the news made a vivid impression on him. So he asked his friend and entomologist, Leclercq[4], to send him a book on the subject, which he began to study, discovering strange things such as the story of the Italian pilots shot down during the last war in the Libyan Sahara desert; their corpses were later discovered to have larvae inside them or to have been eaten by larvae;

the strange thing being that flies do not live in that zone, which means that they must have been driven there by some sort of mediumistic instinct."[5]

According to Dario, he first heard about this exciting idea when he was on vacation on the island of Giannutri, where his mother's family had some property by the Tyrrhenian Sea. Though he had long had a difficult relationship with his mother, he still made a point of spending some time with her, enabling him to bask in the memories of his seminal experiences in her photography studio. By this stage, however, she had given up photography. "No one knew why she stopped, not even my father. She was still very young. Maybe, unlike myself who embraced change, she felt uncomfortable with these new sophisticated devices. They sort of drained the poetry out of her work. For her,

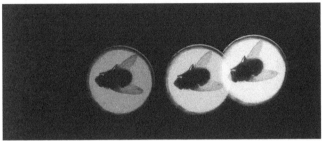

"It looks like flies... four flies." Well, three flies in this image, to be precise—from *Four Flies on Grey Velvet*.

photography was a master stroke: she only did one take, sometimes after hours of preparation, but it was always the right take."[6]

Argento would later tell Alan Jones that he spent over a year and a half studying this strange insect phenomenon—which, even allowing for Argento's tendency to exaggerate a bit in these matters, indicates that the writing of the script was longer and more torturous than usual. Argento's fascination with the world of insects was already evident in films like *Four Flies on Grey Velvet* and *Suspiria*, of course, but this would take things to a different level—calling for a production which couldn't help but be technologically challenging. Argento also took inspiration from Nicolas Roeg's *Don't Look Now* (1973), specifically the idea of the hideous dwarf-like killer, but he admitted to having major problems in getting the ideas to come together into a cohesive whole. Sometime in 1983, however, he decided to change his lifestyle—he had long had issues with regards to eating (this would inform his later *giallo*, *Trauma*, as well) and he decided to pursue the healthier option of living as a vegetarian; he checked into a clinic in Zurich in order to acclimatise himself to this new and potentially improved style of living, but by his own admission it was no walk in the park. "It was like being in school again—escaping through windows for midnight feasts—and I returned to Rome feeling like a child."[7] The feeling of childhood inspired him to set the film in a school for girls—thus recalling *Suspiria*, inevitably. The script would also include plenty of personal connections to Dario, making it a peculiarly autobiographical piece in some respects: the character of the protagonist would be modeled on Dario's own daughter, Fiore, while her status as a vegetarian with a fascination for insects could hardly have gone unnoticed by those close to Dario during that period[8]. By Ferrini's account, work on the script finished in February or March 1984, at which point Dario decided to put it formally into production as the debut project of his new company.

Sooner than worry about endangering his financial stability, Argento put together a fairly lavish budget for *Phenomena*. He knew the film would call for plenty of elaborate visual effects and he decided to go for broke—if it didn't pan out and the film failed, his company would surely be in ruins, but if it succeeded … All told the budget was in the range of $4 million—and the no-expense-spared attitude extended to hiring Giorgio Armani to work on the costumes. He naturally turned to a number of tried-and-true collaborators—production designer Maurizio Garrone, editor Franco Fraticelli, cinematographer Romano Albani, assistant

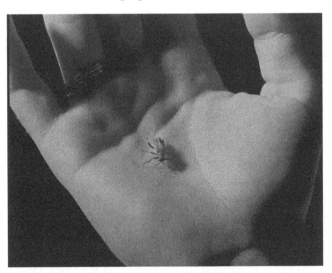

Phenomena explores the psychic link between human beings and insects.

director Michele Soavi—and he welcomed a new face to provide the all-important special make-up effects. Sergio Stivaletti (born in 1957) had been working in the field of make-up effects for some time—one of his first credits was Riccardo Freda's swansong, *Murder Obsession* (1981)—but his association with Argento would propel him to the front ranks of his profession in Italy. *Phenomena* would be an unusually effects-heavy film for Argento, so Stivaletti had his work cut out for him—but he threw himself into the assignment with enthusiasm and

Dario films Jennifer Connelly on the set of *Phenomena*.

delivered some memorably gruesome images. Owing to the complexity of the project, Argento decided to create a second unit, which he entrusted to his old friend Luigi Cozzi. Cozzi's crew set to work filming in April 1984 while Dario was still preoccupied with casting the picture; the second unit would focus on the insect material, which freed Argento up to focus his attentions on the actors and so forth. *Variety* reported in May 1984 that Argento was actively pursuing Lynn [sic] Ullmann (the daughter of the legendary Liv Ullmann) as well as "thesps from *The Big Chill* and *Footloose*" to appear in the picture.[9] The article doesn't specify which role Linn Ullmann was being sought for, though it's likely Dario had her in mind for the central role of Jennifer—which ultimately went to Jennifer Connelly, whom Argento first learned about thanks to Sergio Leone, who cast her in a small but crucial role in *Once Upon a Time in America* (1984). According to Alan Jones, Argento also had his eye on Liv Ullmann to play the role of the school's headmistress, though she ultimately passed owing to the level of violence in the script.[10]

Filming on the primary material finally got under way in August 1984 and production would last through the end of October. As anticipated, it proved to be a difficult shoot—not only did Argento have insects to worry about, but there was also a trained chimpanzee named Tanga to contend with. Tanga proved to be a fairly remarkable performer in many respects, though she sometimes could be unpredictable. Daria Nicolodi became more and more convinced as time wore on that Dario was deliberately putting her in positions where she could be injured or even killed. The wild and wooly climax sees the chimpanzee exacting gory revenge on her character with a straight razor—an endearingly absurd image if ever there was one. Filming it was no walk in the park, however. "The hand that attacked my face really did belong to the monkey and the iron razor, even though it wasn't sharp, still cut me. Immediately after shooting that sequence, the monkey, which had become quite ferocious, turned on Jennifer Connelly and bit the top off her finger!"[11]

In a radical departure from his previous films, Argento decided to assemble a "greatest hits" soundtrack. He enlisted Claudio Simonetti and Fabio Pignatelli, both estranged from Goblin during that period, to compose some new material—and he likewise reached out to a variety of composers, including Bill Wyman (of The Rolling Stones), Terry Taylor (of Tucky Buzzard), Brian and Roger Eno, and Simon Boswell to bring their own unique talents to the picture. To supplement their

Cover art for the 1987 vinyl release of the *Phenomena* soundtrack from Cinevox. Artwork by Enzo Sciotti.

efforts, he decided to include hit songs by popular heavy metal groups of the period, notably Iron Maiden and Motörhead. The "mix and match" approach would become the norm for Argento throughout the rest of the '80s, both on the films he directed as well as on the pictures he produced. On a commercial level, it certainly made sense, even if it added more upfront in terms of costs for hiring and licensing; even so, adding names like Iron Maiden to the advertising helped to curry the favor of the youth market, which Argento seemed to be more interested in appealing to than ever. To capitalize on the film's aggressive use of music, Argento even footed the bill for a pair of music videos—the one, "Jennifer," using Claudio Simonetti's main theme for the film, was directed by Argento himself; the other, "Valley," based around the exceptional piece Bill Wyman and Terry Taylor wrote for the film, was entrusted to Michele Soavi.

The action kicks off with a tour bus making a stop in the Swiss countryside; when it pulls out and continues on its journey, we see a young girl running and trying to catch the attention of the driver. The girl is Vera Brandt (Fiore Argento), a Dutch tourist, and she finds herself alone and stranded in the middle of nowhere. The eerie atmosphere is perfectly complemented by the use of the theme "Valley" by Bill Wyman and Terry Taylor; the piece is used several times in the film, in fact, and it's easy to see why Dario was so taken with it. As Vera weighs her options, Argento cuts to an impressive craning shot, which rises through the trees and shows the wide-open countryside which stretches for as far as the eye can see.

In a way, it's a bit of a repeat of the famous Louma crane shot in *Tenebrae*; and there will be plenty more instances of self-referencing throughout the picture, as well. Once the credits are finished, Vera starts walking through the landscape and notices a house in the distance—she thinks she's in luck, but she has no idea what she's setting herself up for. As the music continues to build and intensify, Vera arrives at the house and says the one thing stranded tourists should never, ever say in a horror movie: "I'm a foreigner, and I'm lost!" Argento cuts to chains straining against a bracket in the wall—clearly something or someone is attempting to break free. The chains eventually do break and when Vera makes her way into the house looking for somebody to help her, she is greeted instead by chains wrapping around her neck, as somebody off-screen tries to strangle her. She breaks free but not for long: the maniac chases her outside and stabs her to death prior to decapitating her. Argento's use of ultra-slow-motion effects when Vera's head smashes against a window, causing it to shatter and splinter into thousands of pieces, recalls the ending of *Four Flies on Grey Velvet*. Like the opening of *Suspiria*, this is intended to be a big "audience grabber." It's definitely effective, though some of the tin-eared dialogue given to Fiore is squirm-inducing in the worst sense of the term. It wasn't the first time Dario filmed in English with live production audio—as previously noted, there's a great deal of production audio in evidence in *Suspiria*—but a number of the actors (including Fiore) ended up being revoiced in post-production; while Argento's earlier films weren't always revered for their sparkling dialogue, they tended to at least be acceptable on that level. In *Phenomena*, however, there's more clunky dialogue than usual, indicating a shakiness to the film as a whole which definitely marks a regression from the extraordinary run of titles lasting from *Deep Red* through *Tenebrae*. As for

Vera (Fiore Argento) finds herself stranded in "the Swiss Transylvania."

The Unsane Cinema of Dario Argento

Dario prepares a scene with Jennifer Connelly; Fiore Argento and Michele Soavi are at the right.

Fiore, she doesn't have a lot to do here. She's required to act scared before being brutally killed. Unlike her younger half-sister, Asia, she didn't end up becoming a constant presence in the cinema scene; for the time being, however, she was at the start of a brief acting career which would continue with another role for Dario (as producer) and Lamberto Bava (as director) in *Demons*.

From there, the action shifts to the home of the renowned entomologist John MacGregor (Donald Pleasence). Obviously modeled on Marcel Leclerq, the entomologist whose studies of insect behavior inspired the film, MacGregor emerges as the film's most interesting and engaging character. Much of this is down to the warm and sympathetic portrayal of Donald Pleasence (1919-1995). Dario has never really been in the habit of casting actors with recognizable genre cachet in his films, but Pleasence is a welcome exception; in fact, according to Alan Jones, he originally tried to entice Peter Ustinov (1921-2004), but he passed on the project. In the feature-length documentary about the film included on the Arrow Video Blu-ray release of *Phenomena*, Argento and production manager Angelo Iacono recall another early front-runner for the part: Orson Welles (1915-1985).

Welles, of course, was in the habit of accepting acting jobs in order to finance his own directing projects, so he agreed to the terms and was all set to travel to Rome to do the picture; not long before he was due to arrive, however, he had to break his contract owing to health woes. Argento and Iacono were disappointed, to say the least, but they finally were able to reach an agreement with Donald Pleasence. Pleasence proved to be the ideal man for the role and he responds with a performance which is mercifully free of the ham which he brought to so many of his later low budget horror movie roles. A gifted stage and screen actor, Pleasence found himself inextricably linked to horror movies after the surprise success of John Carpenter's *Halloween* (1978); Pleasence accepted his fate and could always be relied upon to behave in a professional manner, but he found himself saddled with some terrible scripts and on many occasions he simply resorted to over the top theatrics and mugging for the camera to get through the day. None of that is visible here, however; Argento enjoyed working with him and Pleasence provides him with an utterly winning and believable performance. MacGregor (Pleasence's Scots accent has taken heat in some circles, though it sounds

Italian lobby card for *Phenomena*: The killer strikes; Donald Pleasence with Michele Soavi.

perfectly acceptable to this writer) is a brilliant mind who has suffered a life-altering accident; like Franco Arnò in *The Cat O'Nine Tails*, his life has been forever altered and he is forced to live as an "outsider" figure by virtue of his disability. Franco lost his sight, while MacGregor is confined to a wheelchair. His mind is unaltered, however, and he is still of valuable assistance to his friends on the Swiss police force.

Inspector Geiger (Patrick Bauchau) brings MacGregor an unusual piece of forensic evidence: a rotting, decapitated head which is covered in maggots. Using his knowledge of the life cycle of insects, and their particular relationship with dead bodies, MacGregor is able to deduce that the victim has been dead for about eight months—by Geiger's calculations, this ties in with the disappearance of Vera Brandt. It turns out that Vera was the first in a string of disappearances, all of them involving young girls. MacGregor has an emotional stake in this as his friend Greta is among the girls who have gone missing. Isolated and prone to fits of melancholy, MacGregor takes solace in his work—but he has difficulties acclimating himself to his life of enforced solitude. In addition to his research, his other joy in life is his helper chimpanzee, Inga—a highly intelligent and sensitive creature who ends up playing a surprising role in the narrative.

At this point, Jennifer Corvino (Jennifer Connelly) arrives from America. She has been enrolled by her father, a well-known movie star named Paul Corvino, at the prestigious Richard Wagner Academy for Girls. She's greeted at the airport by Frau Brückner (Daria Nicolodi), who is one of the head teachers. On their ride to the school, Brückner learns something important about Jennifer: she has a peculiar affection and affinity for insects; a bee that makes its way into the car and nearly causes the driver (an uncredited Fulvio Mingozzi in the first of two uncredited bit appearances in the film, the second being a brief appearance on a TV screen, playing the father of one of the missing girls; this would be his final film for Dario) to crash behaves with uncommon serenity when Jennifer takes it into her hands. She tells Brückner that she loves insects; as the story unfolds, we learn her relationship with them is unusual, to say the least.

When they arrive at the school, there's a bit of dreamy, out-of-left field narration—just as in *Suspiria*, it helps to set the movie up as a fairy tale of sorts. It's the only time the device is employed in the film; Argento again provides the voice over in the Italian version, but it is spoken by another voice over actor on the English soundtrack. The similarities to *Suspiria* don't end there. The staff, presided over by a severe headmistress (Dalila Di Lazzaro), react as coldly to Jennifer as they had to Suzy in the earlier film; and Jennifer also finds herself feeling cut off and disconnected from the bulk of the students, most of whom are shown to be catty and downright bitchy. The exception is her roommate, Sophie (Federica Mastroianni, the niece of the great Marcello Mastroianni), which allows for a dynamic which is similar to the Suzy-Sara friendship in the earlier film. There's nothing inherently wrong with Argento reaching through his back catalogue and culling elements for *Phenomena*; the problem stems from the fact that so much of it feels arbitrary and half-baked, making it his weakest film up until that point in time.

While Argento later said that he based Jennifer on Fiore, there's also a good bit of his own autobiography

Italian lobby card for *Phenomena*: Donald Pleasence with Tanga the chimp; Jennifer Connelly cracks a smile.

The Unsane Cinema of Dario Argento

Jennifer (Jennifer Connelly) and MacGregor (Donald Pleasence) team up to catch a killer.

to be found in the character. Jennifer is a vegetarian, which is a lifestyle Argento was dabbling in during that time, though he would give it up after several years. She also comes from a background connected to the cinema, which is of course true of both himself and Fiore. When Sophie, a huge fan of Paul Corvino, tells Jennifer about all the stories she's read about him and his family in the various film magazines, Jennifer tells her a story that isn't so well known. When she was seven years old, on Christmas day, her mother packed up and left her father for another man. According to Dario, the story was based around his breakup with Daria—and by making Jennifer seven years of age when it happened, it ties in with the initial big split with Nicolodi which occured after the release of *Suspiria*, when Fiore was also seven years of age. The scene allows Jennifer Connelly (born 1970) an opportunity to bring the audience close to her character, and she does a capable enough job; on the whole, however, her performance ranges from convincing to rather stiff. Admittedly she had her work cut out for her given the wonky nature of the script and the sometimes-ludicrous dialogue she's expected to spout, but even so, Jennifer Corvino doesn't emerge as one of Dario's more compelling protagonists.

That night, Jennifer experiences bad dreams and she ends up sleepwalking—she later reveals that she used to sleepwalk when she was younger, but that it hadn't been an issue for many years. Clearly there's a negative energy surrounding the school which triggers it into happening again, thus giving the other students yet another reason to regard her with suspicion and disdain. In the midst of her fitful first night of "rest" at the school, Argento shows another killing in the offing. A screaming student runs through the school grounds chased by a lunatic wielding an unusual elongated pole with a very sharp-looking blade affixed to the end. The hysterical atmosphere of the scene is set by the use of Iron Maiden's "Flash of the Blade" on the soundtrack; it's Argento's first usage of heavy metal music in his films, something which would become fairly prominent over his next several projects, both as a director and as a writer/producer. The use of metal music in *Phenomena* is uneven, much like the film itself; when it works (as it does in this sequence), it's because it works in harmony with the imagery it is accompanying. Jennifer, still sleepwalking, stumbles onto the scene just in time to see the girl being finished off by the murderer; still asleep and not comprehending what she has seen, she ends up wandering into town, where

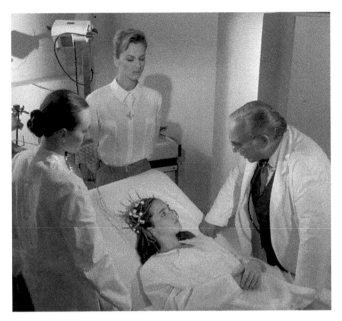

In the film's most ill-advised scene, a doctor (Antonio Maimone) tries to administer an EEG to a defiant Jennifer, as the nurse (Francesca Ottaviani, left) and the headmistress (Dalila Di Lazzaro) look on.

she's nearly run over by the passing traffic. She finds an unlikely savior in the form of Inga, who shepherds her to MacGregor's house.

Connelly is better in her scenes with Pleasence than she is in much of the film, suggesting that she benefitted from the veteran actor's advice and guidance; there's also a great deal of live production audio in their scenes together, which definitely adds to the more natural flow of their interaction. Jennifer and MacGregor form a fairly instantaneous bond. She reminds him of Greta, and he hopes that she will start coming by to visit and break the monotony of his lonely existence. Owing to his work with insects, she is particularly attracted to him. She tells him of her peculiar link to insects—she almost seems to have a psychic connection to them. MacGregor is fascinated and hopes to learn more from her about this strange phenomenon.

The fact that Jennifer wandered off the school grounds while sleepwalking has the teaching staff concerned, so she is subjected to an EEG to see if they can figure out if there is something seriously amiss with her. This entire episode was deleted from the U.S. theatrical release, known as *Creepers*, and for once the cutting did the movie a favor. It adds nothing to the film, and it is capped with one of Argento's (and Connelly's) more embarrassing moments, when Jennifer haughtily assures the doctor and teachers that, "I am not crazy, schizophrenic, epileptic, or stoned!" Perhaps it sounds better in Italian? Scenes like this demonstrate that there's something seriously amiss in *Phenomena*; though not without its pleasures (and there are many, without doubt), it simply isn't up to the same standard of the Argento films which came before it. Even *Le cinque giornate*, uneven as it is, didn't stumble as badly as the worst parts of this film.

Another cringe-inducing scene soon follows, as Jennifer and Sophie talk about the night before in the middle of a poetry lesson being given by the headmistress. The teacher notices that they are not paying attention and calls on Sophie to interpret a piece of poetry, hoping to embarrass her. Jennifer saves her friend by whispering the right information, which has to do with the dangers of turning one's back on the past. When the headmistress asks whether Sophie agrees with that thesis, Jennifer mutters "screw the past"—and Sophie parrots it without thinking. The headmistress is offended, of course, but the other students rally to her defense. It's just a flat-out badly written scene, the sort of sequence that could only be written by a member of a different generation who is trying to show some sort of kinship with the youth of today. "What about Richard Wagner?" protests the headmistress, to which one of the students exclaims, "Richard *Gere*!" It's clumsy and awkward and certainly doesn't do the film any favors.

That night, Sophie is lured outside by her boyfriend—when he leaves and she starts to head inside, she realizes that somebody is stalking her. Jennifer is still inside, in the grips of yet another dream; remembering MacGregor's advice, she snaps herself out of it by telling herself she's sleepwalking and that she needs to wake up. She awakens just in time to hear Sophie's final scream. When she goes outside to investigate, a firefly appears and leads her to an important clue: a glove accidentally left behind by the killer which contains some maggots. Jennifer's special connection to the insect world allows her to glean from the maggots that Sophie is now dead, as well. The image of the firefly leading Jennifer to the glove is lovably bizarre, even surreal, and the impact

A firefly leads Jennifer to an important clue.

of the scene is greatly aided by Claudio Simonetti's fantastic "Phenomena" theme; it's still one of his best compositions.

Jennifer takes the glove to MacGregor, who wants to run some tests on the bugs before forming a conclusion. When Jennifer tells him about the firefly, he accepts what she tells him without question; she's relieved, as this sort of reaction is not what adults and authority figures tend to do in such situations. MacGregor recognizes her sincerity and he knows that she possesses some unusual gift. He also realizes that they're both outsiders, seen by the world at large as being "different." As he explains, he has lost an important part of his independence because he's trapped in a wheelchair—but Jennifer has access to a special power which can be of great use, not only to herself but to society as a whole.

Things continue to get more and more unpleasant for Jennifer at school. The other students dislike her, and the headmistress is definitely on their side. Sooner than encourage the other girls to be more accepting, she feeds into their petty paranoia and even stoops to snooping around in her room, looking for something that will be worth punishing the poor girl for. One gets the impression that Dario is working through some long-lasting issue of his own with regards to the world of academia; neither this film nor *Suspiria* paint a particularly warm and friendly image of school life. When the students gang up on Jennifer, she subconsciously calls upon the insect world for help. A swarm of flies descends upon the school (the effect of the flies swarming on the exterior of the building was achieved in the same way as the swarm of locusts engineered by Mario Bava for the mini-series *Moses the Lawgiver/Mosè*, 1974: by dumping coffee grounds into a clear pool of water, then superimposing the image over a still shot of the school—simple, yet highly effective). No harm befalls anybody, but the experience convinces the witchy headmistress that Jennifer is "diabolical," and she initiates a plan to have her hospitalized in a mental institution. She manages to escape before that can happen.

Jennifer makes her way back to the only adult who seems to really understand her. MacGregor chuckles when she tells him that the headmistress said that she is diabolical. He is also able to tell her what he discovered about the maggots found on the glove: they belong to a very special strain known as "the great sarcophagus," a type of fly which feeds on rotting flesh. MacGregor feels sure that Jennifer has the ability to discover the lair of the murderer; he would gladly go himself, but his physical infirmity makes that impossible. He proposes that she be his legs, so to speak. He can't go and investigate the murders himself, but she, with the aid of her insect friends, can. He provides her with a fully grown specimen of "the great sarcophagus," explaining that once it smells the presence of a dead body, it will go crazy and led her to where the body has been hidden; by his reckoning, the killer's lair must be on a local bus route, as Vera Brandt had disappeared while on a bus trip. Jennifer, eager to avenge Sophie's death, agrees. The relationship between Jennifer and MacGregor admittedly harkens back to the one between Franco and Lori in *The Cat O'Nine Tails*; they're both misfits in a cruel and unforgiving world, and they provide each other with a sense of feeling connected. It's a completely platonic relationship, free of any seedy or dark undertones. Unfortunately, it is not destined to turn out as well for them as it had for Franco and Lori in the earlier picture.

The long sequence of Jennifer riding the bus and finding the creepy house in the woods is nicely done, but in truth—it adds absolutely nothing to the film. It doesn't answer any questions for Jennifer and it merely restates to the audience what we already know. Not surprisingly, it was one of many scenes which were shortened for the U.S. release; and here again, truth be told, the "less is more" approach actually works in favor of the *Creepers* edit. Her journey proves to be for naught. The inhabitants of the house vacated several months before, and Jennifer is left without any more insight into the murderer's identity than she had when she set out on her trip. The main narrative function this digression serves is to ensure that she and MacGregor are separated, thus allowing the killer the opportunity to kill the old man. MacGregor's death—and Inga's pained reaction to it—is far and away the most affecting incident in *Phenomena*; he's a lovable character, extremely well-played by Pleasence, and his death snuffs out the only real source of warmth to be found in the entire film. Unfortunately, Argento demonstrates a tin ear for music

MacGregor pays the price for playing amateur sleuth.

Inga (Tanga) reacts to the death of her master.

in the scene where Jennifer sees his body being wheeled out on a gurney; such a sad scene called for something very different from "Locomotive" by Motörhead. No doubt the intention was to play against the grain of the scene, but it doesn't work; worse still, it undercuts what should be a truly moving scene, as Jennifer bids farewell to her friend and fellow amateur detective.

With MacGregor's death, Jennifer decides that it's time to make a hasty exit from Switzerland; that's a rare moment of self-preservation in Argento's world. Often times the protagonists in his films are so preoccupied with solving the mystery that they willfully endanger themselves—and their loved ones, as well. But because Jennifer is a minor and doesn't have access to money or credit cards, she doesn't have an easy time getting out of the country. She dickers with her father's attorney, Morris (Mario Donatone), who is supposedly in the process of wiring funds for a plane ticket to a local bank. In the meantime, Frau Brückner finds Jennifer waiting at the bank and assures her that the school will pay her way home; the problem is, there are no more flights until tomorrow, so she will need to stay with her for the night. Jennifer agrees, failing to realize that she's being set up. When they get to Brückner's house, the teacher's demeanor becomes stranger and stranger. Jennifer notices that the mirrors are all kept covered and Frau Brückner explains this by saying that she has a deformed son; keeping the mirrors covered is for his benefit. When Frau Brückner tries to get Jennifer to take a sedative, Jennifer is understandably reluctant. Like Suzy in *Suspiria*, she demonstrates a backbone and doesn't simply obey orders "like a good little girl." She finally decides to placate the increasingly agitated teacher and swallows one of the pills—but she becomes violently ill and forces herself to throw up in an unpleasantly realistic-looking sequence. Jennifer tries to make another escape, but Frau Brückner prevents her from doing so. When Inspector Geiger unexpectedly shows up looking to talk with Frau Brückner, the teacher clubs Jennifer over the head and locks her into one of the bedrooms.

Inspector Geiger doesn't play a major role in the narrative. Unlike the charming and highly competent policemen in films like *The Bird with the Crystal Plumage* and *Tenebrae*, he barely registers. Every now and again he shows up, as if to remind us that the police really are doing their job, but as a character he is completely flat and lacking in personality. Patrick Bauchau (born 1938), who plays the character, is a good actor—but he makes virtually no impression here. Indeed, he comes across as very wooden. It seems likely that this approach was encouraged by Dario, who elected to keep the character fairly cold and remote from the viewer. In any event, he has stumbled upon some information which appears to link Frau Brückner to the killings—but before he is able to act on it, she chains him to a wall in a dungeon-like inner sanctum beneath the house. While this is going on,

The Unsane Cinema of Dario Argento

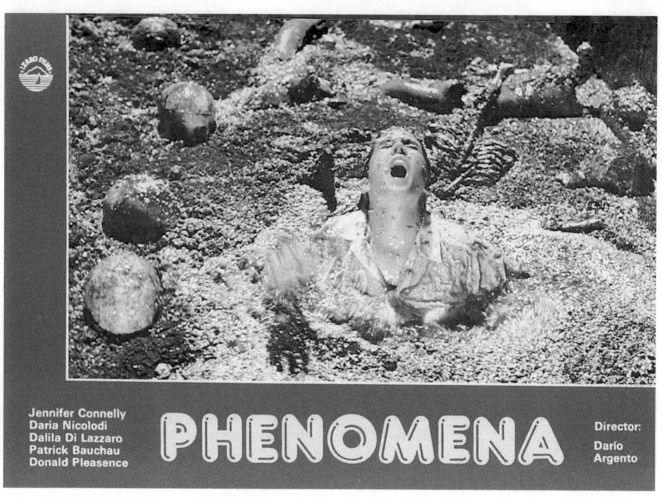

PHENOMENA

Jennifer Connelly
Daria Nicolodi
Dalila Di Lazzaro
Patrick Bauchau
Donald Pleasence

Director: Darío Argento

Dario tips into full-blown *Grand Guignol*, as Jennifer ends up in a pool full of maggots and body parts.

Jennifer attempts to summon help by calling the police, but the phone drops through a hole in the floor; she follows the cord (which is unusually, almost comically, longer than usual) and basically goes down the rabbit hole, much like *Alice in Wonderland*. The irrational fairy tale aspects of the plot confirm that Argento doesn't intend for this to play out in any kind of a realistic fashion; *Phenomena* is therefore a combination of the horror tropes of *Suspiria* and *Inferno* and the thriller aspects of his *giallo* films. The supernatural (or more precisely, paranormal) aspects may seem to disqualify it as a proper *giallo*, but it still manages to function as one. Whether it succeeds in convincingly combining the two different approaches into a cohesive and coherent whole is quite another matter.

Jennifer finally gets hold of the phone, at which point Inspector Geiger pulls her from a hole in the wall; he's trying to help her, but she doesn't know that, and she pulls away from him, falling backwards into a pool of body parts, maggots, and God-knows-what-else. *Phenomena* is the first of Argento's films to really go for the disgusting. His earlier works all included images of violent death and bloodshed, but they were rendered with such a meticulous and painterly eye that one couldn't help but admire their beauty. That's not the case here, as Jennifer flails about among severed limbs and maggots in a sludgy mixture of water and rotting flesh. The entire climax is pitched towards the hysterical and the grotesque; it's *Grand Guignol* times 10, as things go from bad to worse for the characters. Argento wouldn't manage to top this protracted finale in terms of sheer "*what the fuck*" excess until *Mother of Tears*.

As Jennifer tries to stay afloat amid the flotsam and jetsam in the pool, Frau Brückner arrives to cackle at her misfortune. Geiger shows a pulse for the first time in the film as he rails at the teacher, calling her a "fucking bitch" and trying desperately to free himself from his chains. He finally succeeds in doing so—by smashing his own thumb and slipping the one manacle from his hand. It's a genuinely painful moment and it is soon followed by even more over-the-top gore and mayhem as he grabs hold of Frau Brückner and proceeds to beat the living hell out of her. Jennifer pulls herself out of the pit and runs off, and the audience is left believing that Geiger has killed Brückner.

While making her way out of the house, Jennifer comes face to face with Frau Brückner's little boy (played by little person actor Davide Marotta), in a repetition of

Argento watches as Jennifer is lowered into the gross pit.

the shock reveal ending of Nicolas Roeg's *Don't Look Now* (1973), Argento has the sobbing child turn into close-up, revealing a monstrous countenance—and a personality to match. The child is afflicted by some horrible disease, caused by the violent nature of his inception (as discovered by Geiger, Brückner was raped by an inmate at the mental hospital at which she used to be employed), and it has also rotted his mind, compelling him to run amok and commit murder. Brückner's main "crime" has been to be a fierce protector of her child—though in doing so, she has succumbed to the same insanity, leading her to kill MacGregor because she fears he is on his way to uncovering the truth. Jennifer flees from the boy, but they end up confronting one another outside. She calls upon the insects to help her, and a terrific swarm of "great sarcophagus" flies come down to feast on him.

Argento lulls the viewer into a state of false security—much as Brian De Palma had done in *Carrie* (1976) or as Sean S. Cunningham had done in *Friday the 13th* (1980)—before revealing that Frau Brückner isn't dead yet; she's killed Geiger, and now she threatens to decapitate Jennifer as revenge for the death of her son. As Brückner rants and raves, ideally there should be some sense of compassion and empathy for her—don't forget, she is the victim of a violent sexual assault, and her primary motive has been to keep her son safe. It's not even the child's fault that he is the way he is; he was brought into the world by violence, and violence is the

Frau Brückner (Daria Nicolodi) is about to get some rough treatment at the hands of Inspector Geiger (Patrick Bauchau) in *Phenomena*'s deranged finale.

The Unsane Cinema of Dario Argento

The deterioration of the Argento/Nicolodi relationship is painfully apparent in the finale of *Phenomena*.

only thing he knows. It's clear by this stage, however, that Argento's once-adoring view of Daria Nicolodi has deteriorated—badly. The character is presented as a one-dimensional psychopath and he seems to have instructed the make-up and costume people to make her look as frumpy and unattractive as possible. True, the character isn't a vamp and doesn't need to be presented as such, but even Nicolodi would later comment on how she was convinced that Dario was getting revenge on her for their relationship problems by making her look so awful. She responds with a performance that's as hammy as her turn in *Tenebrae* had been awkward; following on her outstanding work in *Deep Red* and *Inferno*, it's difficult to reconcile these two characterizations. The truth of the matter is, she was a reluctant participant in *Tenebrae* and while she liked her role in *Phenomena*, she is frequently made to look ridiculous in the part. In an interview in the documentary on the film included in the Arrow Video Blu-ray release, she said, "There was a difference in his attitude towards me. In *Deep Red* and *Inferno*, he looked at me in a loving way. In *Phenomena*, his look meant that he would have killed me, if he could have." She does manage to make a vivid impression as she rants and screams at Jennifer during this final scene, but she soon finds herself on the receiving end of a particularly nasty death scene. In a delightfully strange twist, Inga turns up and stabs Frau Brückner to death; the close-ups of the razor being run across her face and throat have a really sadistic edge, again suggesting that Argento may have been milking the scene as a way of giving voice to his anger and frustration with his former life partner. With Brückner dead, the film closes on a tender image of Jennifer and Inga holding each other; the connection with the natural world, symbolized by the chimpanzee, suggests that Jennifer has finally come into her own, much like Suzy had done in *Suspiria*. It's difficult to characterize any ending which is so full of blood and gore as being a positive one, but at least where Jennifer is concerned, it is exactly that.

Phenomena is a curious film, to say the least. At its best, it demonstrates Argento's mastery of the medium. There are some truly effective set pieces as well as some unforgettable imagery to savor. Yet too much of it feels like a half-baked and self-indulgent exercise in self-celebration, as the director trots out reference after reference to his earlier works. Self-quotation is nothing new in Argento's films, and it's not necessarily a bad thing in itself, but here one gets the impression that his inspiration was running a little low. That being said, it's also the most downright bizarre story he would ever concoct; the mixture of the *giallo* and the supernatural/paranormal may recall *Deep Red* (don't forget that film, too, included a reference to insects having telepathic powers), but it's developed in a way that feels unhinged and unfocused. Perhaps if Argento had elected to film the movie in the same dreamy, ultra-stylized manner as one of his flat-out supernatural horror movies, the mixture would have come across more persuasively. As it stands, the visual aesthetic seems to have been informed by *Tenebrae*, with lots of pastels and bright lighting. For arguably the first time, one gets the impression that Argento didn't really have a clear-cut vision for this film; too much of the action seems to be devoted to killing time, and the inability to give his characters anything remotely interesting or even credible to say works against its effectiveness, as well. And yet, it would be a mistake to suggest that it's a failure. It may not come together as effectually as the films which preceded it, yet *Phenomena* still manages to offer up some dazzling filmmaking, and the batshit crazy finale earns added points for sheer audacity; Argento wouldn't return to that sort of grotesque excess (arguably of a bad taste variety) until the tail end of the 1990s, so in a sense the film at least offers a brief taste of things to come.

Phenomena went into general theatrical release on the January 31, 1985. It was a smash hit, signaling very good things for DACFILM and for Argento in general. The film's box-office takings were hurt somewhat owing to the Gaumont cinemas in Italy going on strike; as reported in *Variety* on March 6, 1985, "Gaumont cinema strike in Rome and a few others hurt *He's Worse Than Me* [*Lui è peggio a me*, which starred Dario's old *Le cinque giornate* collaborator, Adriano Celentano] in Rome, but

Phenomena 2 *foglio* poster; artwork by "Jano."

the New Line edit was overseen by director Jack Sholder (born 1945)—who had just finished directing New Line's production of *A Nightmare on Elm Street 2: Freddy's Revenge.* Sholder's edit deprives the film of most of its suspense and atmosphere; it's edited with an emphasis on action at the expense of plot, thus undermining the film's already wonky narrative structure even further. While Argento's original edit is problematic in itself and in dire need of tightening, the New Line version takes things much too far; thus, the "international" edit emerges as the preferable option, even if some of the deletions in the *Creepers* edit are for the greater good.

New Line put it out on August 30, 1985, and it did good business. Argento had no way of knowing it at the time, but it would remain the last of his directorial efforts to receive a really respectable American box-office release. The U.K. release, through Palace Pictures, made use of the same highly abbreviated edit—though it was cut even further to appease the squeamish British Board of Film Censors. No matter how ruinous the editing proved to be, it didn't stop *Phenomena* (or *Creepers*) from becoming a box-office hit. For the time being, at least, Argento was still very much at the top of the heap.

reduced fast-starting *Phenomena* to last place in the top 10."[12] Strike or no strike, the film did fantastic business in Italy and it came in at number 11 for the 1984-1985 box-office season; the big champ was *Nothing Left to Do But Cry* (*Non ci rest che piangere*, 1984) by Roberto Benigni and Massimo Troisi, but *Phenomena* held its own against the likes of Ivan Reitman's *Ghostbusters* (1984) and Steven Spielberg's *Indiana Jones and the Temple of Doom* (1984), which ranked at numbers 2 and 3, respectively.[13] Given that the original Italian edit was a little top-heavy at 116 minutes, Piero Bozza was again called upon to create a tighter edit for export—running 110 minutes, the shorter edit helped to tighten things and drop a few of the more excessive *longeurs*. None of the edits affect the continuity or the story in any way and it emerges as the more satisfying version. It was not enough to appease the English market, however, and *Phenomena* would undergo some serious surgery when it was acquired for release by New Line Cinema in the U.S.A. All told, the American version—rechristened as *Creepers*—was reduced to 83 minutes, thus making its already shaky narrative downright incomprehensible at times. As explained in the liner notes for the Synapse Blu-ray edition of *Phenomena*,

New Line original one-sheet; artist unknown.

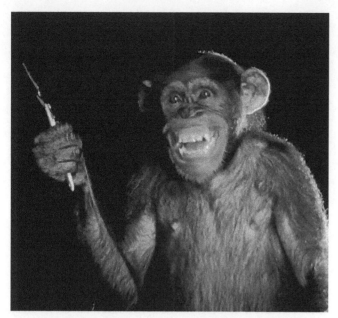

Tanga the chimp pretty much steals the show.

The good news continued into the film's "second life" on home video, with *Variety* reporting that *Creepers* "is one of the hits of the U.S. home video season, racking up sales of around 50,000 units for Media Home."[14]

Predictably, the reviews weren't entirely enthusiastic. Reviewing for *The Village Voice*, David Edelstein wrote:

> Dario Argento is the rock Toscanini of the hack-em-up; people are carved up to the accompaniment of synthesized guitars … maggots do the twist on severed limbs; and for the grand finale, heads burst through windows in slo-mo.[15]

Kim Newman blasted the "astonishingly awful performances" and felt that Argento was going for "sickness after the manner of Lucio Fulci."[16] Derek Malcolm also felt the movie was a significant comedown for the maker of *The Bird with the Crystal Plumage* and *Suspiria*, but felt "Donald Pleasence does his best with the script, Jennifer Connelly doesn't even bother to do battle."[17] Jon Pareles echoed those sentiments, writing:

> The gore starts spattering in earnest too late to save *Creepers*, a dim-witted horror movie that opened yesterday at the RKO Warner and other theaters. It creaks along for its first hour or so, failing to work up any chills as a killer terrorizes a Swiss girls' school that has cuckoo clocks in every salon. Jennifer Connelly, as the teen-age heroine, was apparently chosen because she can hold a fly on her hand without flinching. […] The best acting is by an expressive, resourceful chimpanzee—definitely the year's Best Supporting Primate.[18]

The reviewer for *The Boston Globe* was also unimpressed:

> The dialogue, which the actors seem to be reading off Teleprompters, is ludicrous. […] Director Dario Argento makes movies with a logic seemingly improvised by Dr. Irwin Corey and can't even keep his storyline straight. Characters appear and disappear without rhyme or reason, the result being nonsense instead of plot. But *Creepers* is, above all, boring.[19]

The Catholic Conference was pretty much disgusted by the film and advised its followers to steer clear:

> Because of the profusion of blood and gore, it has been classified 0—morally offensive—by the U.S. Catholic Conference.[20]

In the summer of 1985, Dario, Lamberto Bava and Pupi Avati were all feted at the Fantafestival, where they were given the special "FantaItaly" prize for their contributions to the horror film. Then, in 1986, *Phenomena* joined the likes of Tom Holland's *Fright Night*, Lars von Trier's *The Element of Crime/Forbrydelsens element*, Andrzej Żuławski's *L'amour Braque*, and others (including his own production of *Demons*) when it was nominated for Best Picture at the Fantasporto festival in Portugal; when the festival held its awards in February 1986, however, it lost out to José Ángel Rebolledo's *Eternal Fire/Fuego eternal*.

On the personal front, there were some dark times on the horizon. Salvatore, already sidelined with heart issues, suffered his first stroke in 1985. The sight of his father's declining health rattled Argento, who did his best to focus on staying productive as a means of dealing with the stress. Salvatore would rally for the time being, but his days in the film industry were over; he would not have anything to do with any more film productions. Salvatore, of course, had been a profound influence on Dario—his business acumen can be traced back to his father's influence, and the older man was directly responsible for facilitating Dario's entry into the film industry as a director. To say that they were close would be an understatement; theirs was the parental bond that truly mattered in Dario's life, though his involvement in his own children's life tended to be tempered somewhat by his fixation on his career. Fiore, who found acting for her father in *Phenomena* to be an experience of mixed emotions (by her own admission, she had no particular

Dario Argento receiving the FantaItaly prize at Fantafestival for his contributions to the horror film.

drive with regards to becoming an actress), continues to recall her relationship with Daria and her mother, Marisa, with warmth and affection; on the other hand, Asia (already nearing 10 years of age by the time *Phenomena* came out), has often expressed ambivalence with regards to her relationship with both of her parents. Within a couple of years, she would begin acting—first in films produced by her father, then in a series of movies directed by him. "I acted to gain my father's attention," she told Travis Crawford. "It took him a long time to notice me—I started when I was nine, and he only cast me when I was 16."[21] A lot of high emotions and family drama were still in store for the Argento family, and the financial success achieved early on by DACFILM would soon give way to frustration and scandal.

Notes:
1. *Variety*, May 9, 1984, p. 312.
2. Palmerini, Luca M. and Gaetano Mistretta, *Spaghetti Nightmares* (Key West: Fantasma Books, 1997), p. 49.
3. Ibid, p. 49-50.
4. Dr. Marcel Leclerq (1924-2008), a well-regarded pioneer in the field of forensic entomology; he worked on at least 132 cases involving dead bodies, and his expertise in insects proved to be of invaluable help to the police in their investigation into these deaths.
5. Palmerini, Luca M. and Gaetano Mistretta, *Spaghetti Nightmares* (Key West: Fantasma Books, 1997), p. 50.
6. Argento, Dario, *Peur* (France: Rouge Profond, 2018), p. 247.
7. Jones, Alan, *Dario Argento: The Man, the Myths & the Magic* (Godalming: FAB Press, 2012), p. 127.
8. Fiore also plays a small role in the film, as the ill-fated tourist who is killed in the opening scene.
9. *Variety*, May 9, 1984, p. 312.
10. Jones, Alan, *Dario Argento: The Man, the Myths & the Magic* (Godalming: FAB Press, 2012), p. 129.
11. Palmerini, Luca M. and Gaetano Mistretta, *Spaghetti Nightmares* (Key West: Fantasma Books, 1997), p. 116.
12. *Variety*, March 6, 1985, p. 346.
13. https://boxofficebenful.blogspot.com/search?q=box+office+italia+1984-85
14. *Variety*, May 7, 1986, p. 452.
15. Edelstein, "On a Wing and a Prayer," *The Village Voice*, September 17, 1985.
16. Newman, Kim, "*Phenomena (Creepers)*," *Monthly Film Bulletin*, Vol. 53, #624, 1986.
17. Malcolm, Derek, "A Fistful of Blood and Goo," The Guardian, April 17, 1986.
18. Pareles, Jon, "The Screen: Horror Tale, '*Creepers*,'" *The New York Times*, August 31, 1985.
19. Unsigned, "Without Rhyme or Reason," *Boston Globe*, October 26, 1985, p. 9.
20. *The Catholic Advance*, September 12, 1985, p. 9.
21. https://filmmakermagazine.com/105305-everything-in-this-film-is-autobiographical-but-then-again-everything-is-not-asia-argento-on-her-debut-feature-scarlet-diva/#.XBQuX_ZFyUk

Chapter Thirteen:
Movie Theaters and High Rises;
High Culture and Scandal

Next up on the slate was an original treatment prepared by Argento's old collaborator, Dardano Sacchetti. By 1984, Sacchetti's fruitful association with Argento's so-called "rival," Lucio Fulci, had come to a sad end; the writer and the filmmaker fell out when Fulci started telling interviewers that Sacchetti had stolen an original idea of his and repackaged it as his own. The fertile creative period which yielded everything from *The Psychic* (*Sette notte in nero*, 1977) to *The New York Ripper* (*Lo squartatore di New York*, 1982) had been capped off by the less-than-exciting *Manhattan Baby* (1982) and the intriguing but fatally under-funded *Rome, 2072 AD: The New Gladiators* (*I guerrieri dell'anno 2072*, 1983) and Sacchetti was looking for fresh people to collaborate with. According to Lamberto Bava, he and Sacchetti came up with the idea of a possible series of horror films and brought their proposal to producer Luciano Martino. Martino, the older brother of director Sergio Martino, had recently produced several pictures for Bava, including *Blastfighter* (1984). Martino wasn't overly keen on their proposed horror project, but serendipity struck when Bava received a call from Dario Argento, who was looking to break into producing. Bava told Dario that he had a project he was looking to get funding for and sent him the treatment. Argento was impressed with Sacchetti's treatment, though he felt it needed a good deal of work. Even so, he agreed to fund the film through DACFILM, provided the kinks in the script could be worked out.[1] Thus, *Demons* (*Dèmoni*) would become his first "official" credit as a producer; he had been credited with script and music collaboration and with "presenting" on *Dawn of the Dead*, but this would be a chance for him to play up his name value by actively controlling a film from behind the scenes, while allowing another person to take charge on set.

Sacchetti would later explain that his original concept was somewhat different from the finished picture. "After a whole series of situations, the youths go down into the underground passages of the cinema-studio, where there are stacks of old backdrops, costumes and gadgets. Suddenly these things come to life and the protagonists have to live through innumerable horror film clips in order to get back to the outside world. It was an amusing idea, but in the end, Dario opted for simplicity and decided to have just one monster, changing the whole film substantially in order to do something more along the lines of Romero's *Dawn of the Dead*."[2] The comparison to *Dawn* is telling. There's no doubt that Argento felt confident in the basic structure of that film (that is, a group of people trapped inside of a claustrophobic location while evil forces try to claim them) and recognized its commercial potential; simply put—it was a sure-fire set-up for a good scary movie, and his instincts during this period were certainly in tune with the youth market, so he had good reason to believe that Sacchetti's treatment, while promising, needed some heavy duty reworking. Sacchetti delivered his own take on the material and Argento elected to go to work on it himself. He again called upon Franco Ferrini to assist in the writing chores. "I only got involved after the first

Italian 2 *foglio* poster for *Demons*, produced by Dario Argento and directed by Lamberto Bava; artwork by Enzo Sciotti.

draft had been completed. Dario asked me to make some changes, because Sacchetti's script simply didn't hold together, so I had to work quickly to bring some order back to the story. I remember working on it, even though I was ill in bed! My main contributions were delating the arrival of the demons, who appeared immediately in the first version, and creating that claustrophobic environment in the cinema, which I believe is the best part of the film."[3]

Dario's personal and professional relationship with Lamberto Bava extended back a number of years. Lamberto had served as Argento's assistant on *Inferno* and was initially engaged to do the same on *Tenebrae*, but he ended up leaving the production part-way through because he had an opportunity to direct a film of his own, a *giallo* titled *A Blade in the Dark* (*La casa con la scala nel buio*, 1983). Bava had just finished back-to-back assignments for producer Luciano Martino—*Blastfighter* and *Devilfish* (*Shark: Rosso nell'oceano*, 1984)—both of which had been filmed largely on location in the U.S., and both of which had been co-written by Dardano Sacchetti; in fact, *Blastfighter* evolved out of a project Sacchetti was writing with Lucio Fulci which had fallen apart after Fulci quarreled with the producers—they had guaranteed their American distributors a movie titled *Blastfighter*, so they commissioned Sacchetti to write something else to suit the title, since the Fulci project was now dead in the water. Bava, who learned his craft on the sets of his father's films, was a more diplomatic and serene presence on set than Fulci—and he proved to be ideally suited to *Demons*. By his own admission, however, much of the project was really guided by Argento, though Bava certainly had ample input into the writing of the script, as well. In fact, it was Bava who came up with the film's title—Argento tasked him with coming up with a punchy title that would grab viewers; while he was mulling it over, Lamberto glanced over to his bookshelf, where he noticed his father's old copy of Fyodor Dostoyevsky's *Demons* (*Bésy*, 1871-1872). When he suggested the idea to Argento, Dario knew it was the perfect title.[4] Bava was no novice as a director and had already proved himself to be a strong and authoritative presence on set when he assisted on *Inferno* and *Tenebrae*, but Argento made his presence felt, and while he did his best to allow Bava to realize the picture in his own way, he wasn't about to sit idly by and allow anything with which he was not personally in agreement. It pays to remember, too, that Dario had a heavy hand in the writing of the script, and that he would also influence one of the film's most popular features: its heavy metal-driven soundtrack.

Because the script was geared more toward elaborate make-up effects and transformations, there wasn't much

Full-page teaser ad for *Demons* in *Variety*, Wednesday May 1, 1985; artist unknown. At the time of this ad, location filming was still planned for London.

effort made to secure big-name actors. Lamberto Bava later claimed that the role of the blind man, ultimately played by Alex Serra, had once been intended for horror icon Vincent Price (1911-1993). "If Price had done it, the part would have been more substantial. As it was, we cut it back."[5] In May 1985, *Variety* announced that filming was due to start in April and that the cast included Gaspare Capparoni, Andrea Bianchi, Laura Franci and Patrick Bouchan[6]—none of whom ended up in the film. In fact, most of these people don't seem to actually *exist*; it could be that the reporter got the names or the spellings mixed up, but of the actors announced, the only familiar names are Andrea Bianchi (1925-2003), a veteran screenwriter and director who had never dabbled in acting, and Gaspare Capparoni (born 1964), who had just played a small role as Sophie's boyfriend in *Phenomena*.

While work continued on pre-production on *Demons*, Argento's attentions were divided between the film and an exciting offer he received from an unlikely source. Earlier in 1985, he had been approached by the management of the Sferisterio di Macareta, an open-air theater in central Italy, with the idea of having him

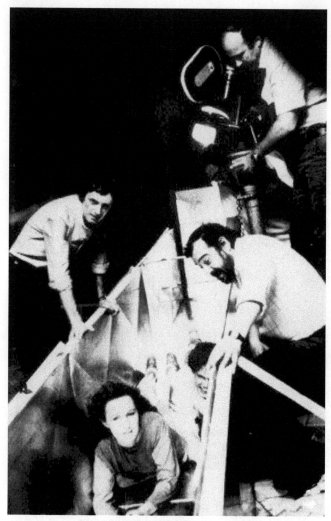

Fiore Argento goes down the chute while Dario and Lamberto Bava look on.

direct their production of Giuseppe Verdi's opera, *Rigoletto*. First performed in 1851, it was based on Victor Hugo's play *Le roi s'amuse* (literally, "The King Amuses Himself") and it tells the story of the Duke of Mantua, who seduces the daughter of a humble courtier; this is actively encouraged by the Duke's hunchbacked jester, Rigoletto. When the father finds out what has happened, he places a curse on the Duke and on Rigoletto. The curse comes to fruition when Rigoletto's daughter falls for the Duke and succumbs to his advances; a furious Rigoletto hires an assassin to kill the Duke, but the daughter is killed instead.

Admittedly, Dario wasn't the first choice to direct—they had already approached Peter Ustinov and Martin Scorsese, neither of whom were interested. Argento, on the other hand, was excited by the possibilities and welcomed the challenge of staging a radical new version. Pre-production began in earnest in the early months of 1985 and Argento enlisted some top-flight people to help realize his vision, including the celebrated costume designer and fashion icon Karl Lagerfeld (1933-2019).

Romano Albani, the cinematographer responsible for *Inferno* and *Phenomena*, was tapped by Argento to orchestrate the elaborate lighting schemes he had in mind. Argento eagerly started planning the production, which was due to go live on July 20.

In his version, the Duke would be a vampire—and Argento let it be known that his take would include plenty in the way of blood and gore. "I was very dedicated. I hid myself in a hotel in Capri, where I invented my own version of Verdi's opera. I imagined a story set during the time of the Vikings, where the Duke of Mantua was really a vampire and he would transform in the middle of the show. I also wanted to include a ballet in the style of Busby Berkeley; in short, I wanted all hell to break loose. I wanted to give genuine chills to the audience, not only with lots of blood, but I also wanted to put electric wires on the seats—so that, during the thunderstorm, they would receive tiny shocks."[7]

The management of Sferisterio di Macareta, still smarting over Ken Russell's similarly outrageous take on *La Bohème* (staged in the summer of 1984), decided to go with a more traditional staging—and Argento formally announced that he was parting ways with the theater in April.[8] The distinguished director Mauro Bolognini (*Il bell'Antonio*, 1969) was drafted very late in the game and delivered a more conservative take on the material.

Disappointed by his fruitless brush with "high culture," Argento had no idea that things were about to get even trickier. The production of *Demons* got under way in June 1985, with location work in Berlin. The actual filming was generally smooth and free of excessive drama, but Argento found himself immersed in a rather different nightmare of his own. On June 19, he received a letter from a mysterious person who enclosed a few grams of heroin as a gift; Dario was no stranger to recreational drugs and would often imbibe where marijuana was concerned, but by his own account he never tried his luck with something as strong as heroin. He was on his way to the airport and absent-mindedly put the envelope in his pocket—and unluckily for him, the letter and its illegal contents were found by airport security, who summoned the police. Dario was taken to jail, where he spent three long days fretting over what was going to happen to him. He details the experience of being in prison in his autobiography, but by and large it appears to have been an uneventful annoyance more than anything else; the food wasn't suited to his new-found vegetarian lifestyle, the other inmates bickered and fought, and he did his best to remain invisible while awaiting his sentencing. Fortunately for him, the overworked judge assigned to the case decided that there were bigger issues to deal with than a first-time offender with a minor amount of heroin in his possession, and

Kathy (Paola Cozzo), Cheryl (Natasha Hovey), George (Urbano Barberini), and Ken (Karl Zinny) "meet cute" in *Demons*.

Dario was finally set free. The newspapers and the scandal columns ate it up, of course, but Argento was too preoccupied with keeping tabs on *Demons* to allow it to get him down too badly.

The set-up of the film is fairly simple. A group of strangers are invited to a sneak preview of a new horror film. The screening is at the ultra-modern Metropol cinema. The attendees include George (Urbano Barberini, who went on to co-star in Argento's *Opera*) and his friend Ken (Karl Zinny), Cheryl (Natasha Hovey) and her friend Kathy (Paola Cozzo), and Hannah (Fiore Argento) and her boyfriend Tommy (Guido Baldi). The film they go to see deals with a group of teenagers who disrupt the final resting place of Nostradamus; they discover a grim prophecy involving the arrival of demons who are destined to take control of the world. As this plays out on screen, some of the patrons become infected by a strange virus which turns them into demons. As the patrons try to survive, the contagion spreads to the outside world and all hell breaks loose.

In many respects, *Demons* emerges as *the* perfect '80s horror film. It's short on plot and long on elaborate shock effects. The emphasis on youthful characters, splashy make-up effects and a heavy metal-driven soundtrack was perfectly in tune with the MTV and *Fangoria* crowds, ensuring that the film would connect favorably with the targeted youth audience. Argento had already tapped into this market with *Phenomena*, but whereas that film boasted an almost absurdly convoluted narrative, here the emphasis is squarely placed on shock horror. There's very little preamble and the blood starts to flow early on as Rosemary (Geretta Geretta) scratches her face with a replica of the demon mask hanging in the foyer and goes to the bathroom, knowing something isn't right with the seemingly minor nick on her face. The wound starts to pulse and finally explodes in a welter of green goo; Sergio Stivaletti and Rosario Prestopino's use of bladder effects was much influenced by the work of Rick Baker on *An American Werewolf in London* (1981) and Rob Bottin on *The Howling* (1981) and *The Thing* (1982), and they manage to come up with images which are simultaneously fascinating and repulsive.

The characters are as disposable as they are interchangeable. In a way it's surprising that Bava and company even bothered to give them names; they're all

Tragedy strikes when Cheryl realizes that Ken has been infected by the demons.

Rosemary (Geretta Geretta) begins to really regret putting that mask on her face.

basic stereotypes and function as such. If the film has a significant weakness, it is that it's difficult to really care about what happens to any of these people—they're so thinly drawn and generally indifferently acted that they virtually fade into the background, thus allowing Stivaletti and Prestopino to walk away with the show. And yet, this is precisely the sort of thing that was so popular in the '80s—this was the period where makeup whizzes like Tom Savini and Dick Smith were being idolized in the pages of *Fangoria*; the emphasis on star actors like Christopher Lee and Vincent Price gave way to a new period where directors and special effects artists became the major draw. Thus, *Demons* played quite cannily right into this new demographic, especially with Bava's ascending reputation being bolstered by the presence of the already-established Dario as co-writer and producer.

As in his earlier films, Argento's use of a German setting had specific connotations. The location filming took place in Berlin, in the west side of Germany (this was the period when the wall was still in existence), but the Metropol is supposed to be set in the Eastern side of the country. Thus, the demons themselves are emblematic of fascism and oppression—specters of the past who force their way back into the present and seek to take control of the world. The film ends with a small group of survivors heading towards the west, where they hope to find safety. Given the film's fast pacing and emphasis on incident over dialogue, this aspect isn't hammered home too forcefully—but it is there for those who are open to seeing it.

Demons is 99% surface, however, and one's enjoyment depends largely on the willingness to go with the flow and enjoy it as a sort of cinematic funhouse experience. It's not a particularly suspenseful film, but it's executed with such ferocious energy that it flies by at a rapid clip; it's also genuinely effective where its big shock set pieces are concerned. The effects are appropriately repulsive—lots of emphasis on boil-like protrusions oozing with pus, and lots of blood, bile and spittle drooling from the creatures' mouths—and the scene where one infected character's back opens up, allowing a fully formed creature to emerge, is

Demons by way of *The Manitou*, as a fully-formed creature emerges from one unfortunate patron's back.

186   **MURDER BY DESIGN**

reminiscent of Graham Masterton's book *The Manitou*, which had been filmed by William Girdler in 1976. Bava also works in references not only to his father's work (the demon mask is an obvious reference to *Black Sunday/La maschera del demonio*, 1960) but to Dario's back catalogue, as well—note the presence of a poster for *Four Flies on Grey Velvet* in the theater lobby.

Once principal photography on *Demons* wrapped in July 1985, the vital post-production shooting was entrusted to the capable hands of Sergio Stivaletti. Stivaletti had proved to be a great addition to the Argento filmmaking family on *Phenomena*, but even though that film was more effects heavy than Argento's previous films, it was positively skimpy on the effects front compared to *Demons*. Stivaletti had his work cut out for him and he delivered in grand style, helping to make *Demons* into one of the wildest and goriest Italian horror films of its vintage. It remains his most consistently impressive showcase, demonstrating a mastery of practical and mechanical effects which sadly would not extend to his later forays into the realm of digital effects.

As he had done on *Phenomena*, Argento elected to score *Demons* with a mixture of fresh material by Claudio Simonetti and a heaping helping of popular rock and heavy metal hits. Simonetti contributed some catchy new material—notably the groovy main theme—while the likes of Rick Springfield, Billy Idol, Mötley Crüe and others helped to ensure the film's acceptance among the rebellious young horror buffs who comprised such a large part of Argento's fan base. The film made its Italian theatrical debut on October 4 1985—and it proved to be another box-office hit, ranking at number 42 for the 1985-1986 Italian box-office season.[9] DACFILM was therefore in very good shape, indeed, thanks to two major box office hits in the space of a single year. The film was so successful, in fact, that Argento and Bava soon started to give serious though to a sequel—something Argento had never really done in the past. It wouldn't be quite proper to call *Inferno* a sequel to *Suspiria*, for example, as they formed the first two-thirds of a proposed trilogy; *Demons*, on the other hand, was conceived as a stand-alone venture, so any attempt to continue the story would necessitate thinking fast while the iron was still hot.

According to Lamberto Bava, talks of a sequel started in earnest when the box-office receipts started to tally up; this was before the film even went abroad, by the way. Argento had started to develop a major cult following in Japan following the success of *Suspiria*, and *Demons* proved to be a major hit there in April 1986. An outfit named Ascot Entertainment Group acquired the film for U.S. consumption and released it in May 1986, with the French and U.K. releases following in October 1986 and January 1987, respectively. As reported by *Variety*, "Price paid for all U.S. rights to Lamberto Bava's *Demons*; it was the highest for any Italian film this season, except for *Macaroni*, according to Intra Film topper Paola Corvino and sales exec Ronald De Neef."[10] Though subjected to cuts in various markets owing to Stivaletti's gruesome and imaginative effects work, it drew big crowds—it was certainly the most successful film Lamberto Bava had directed, even if his participation was somewhat unfairly played down compared to that of Argento. Ascot even went to the trouble of tinkering with the English soundtrack for the film's American release; Nick Alexander, who oversaw the dubbing of many of Argento's films, prepared an English dub in Rome—but Ascot elected to make some changes to it. At least two characters were completely revoiced—gang member "Baby Pig," played by Peter Pitsch, and Frank, played by Stelio Candelli—and they tinkered with some of the music as well. Nick Alexander dubbed Candelli himself in the original English version, but apparently the executives at Ascot felt that his thick English accent posed a problem. Like the majority of Argento's films, English was the spoken language on set, though the

Japanese poster for *Demons*.

majority of the actors ended up being revoiced for the English track; a notable exception is Geretta Geretta (aka Geretta Giancarlo), who plays the role of Rosemary. Many minor tweaks were made to the music, including a different cue for the opening introductory title cards, as well as adding in some additional music "sting" effects to underline some of the shock effects (notably when Rosemary strangles Liz and her lover). The Ascot sound mix is actually a good deal punchier than the English dub prepared by Alexander, making it the preferable option. It was time and money well spent. The film did excellent business, thus making it clear that a sequel was inevitable. By February 1986, *Variety* reported that Argento was in Los Angeles to discuss *Demons II* (as it was then being called) as well as his own untitled project, which he was at that point hoping to get on its feet by the end of the year; according to the same article, Argento was considering filming the *Demons* sequel at least partly in the U.S., though this ultimately fell through.[11] It was Argento who devised the basic concept this time—a high rise would become overrun with demons who emerge out of various television screens, infecting the inhabitants and causing mass hysteria. It was clearly informed by Argento's admiration for the Canadian *auteur* David Cronenberg (born 1943). The high rise setting, and the spread of the infection recalls *Shivers* (*They Came from Within*, 1975), while the TV aspect can't help but remind one of *Videodrome* (1983).

Production on *Demons 2* (*Dèmoni 2 … L'inubo riotrna*) proceeded with almost indecent haste in late May of 1986—a mere seven months following the release of the first film, which was still unspooling in various parts of the globe. Argento was correct in assuming that it was best to strike while the film was still on people's minds, but it feels as if the production was skimped on—there's a cheapness to the film and even to some of its effects which make it feel like a third-rate knock-off instead of a worthy, well-thought-out sequel. All told, Argento allotted the film a quick four-week schedule, and the principal photography was in the can by late June. In many respects, its most interesting feature is the presence of Asia Argento, making her first appearance in a film for her father—though she had already made her debut on the small screen in 1985 with an appearance in the mini-series *Sogni e bisogni*, directed by Sergio Citti.

A swanky high rise named "The Tower" serves as the portal for the return of the demons. A spoiled brat named Sally (Coralina Cataldi-Tassoni) has some friends over for a birthday party, but she throws a fit and isolates herself in her room. A program about the demons catches her eye, and sure enough history repeats itself when a demon bursts through her TV and infects her. As the contagion spreads throughout the building, various other characters are drawn into the drama, including expectant parents George (David Knight) and Hannah (Nancy Brilli), fitness instructor Hank (Bobby Rhodes), and little Ingrid Haller (Asia Argento) and her family.

Demons 2 proved to be as light as *Demons* had been dark. There's still plenty of violence and carnage, but the overall tone is more tongue-in-cheek. Bava and his son Roy (aka Fabrizio, born 1967, who served as the assistant director on the film) confirm this in their audio commentary recorded for the Roan Group laser disc, noting that the film was meant to be more "ironic" than the first one. The shift in tone is evidenced by the soundtrack, which is largely the work of Simon Boswell (born 1956), with selections worked in from groups like The Smiths, The Cult, and Art of Noise. The film itself is maddeningly uneven. On the one hand, there are moments that are as poetic and beautiful as anything Lamberto Bava has ever directed—the shots of the infected Sally making her way towards the birthday cake, for example—while other parts come across as almost indecently slapdash. There's some location footage that

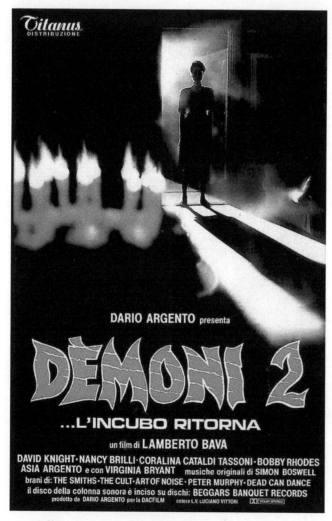

Italian poster art for *Demons 2*; artist unknown.

Mr. Haller (Antonio Cantafora) is overpowered by the demons.

was compromised by a defect in the camera, resulting in some very jittery and unstable images; one is hard-pressed to believe that Dario would ever have permitted such material to have made the final cut in one of his own movies, though here it was obviously determined that it wasn't worth the time and expense to go back and take the scenes over again.

There are some nice directorial touches, including the opening shot: the camera pans along a large knife, and what appears to be blood drips down on the glistening blade; it turns out the "blood" is jam from an overturned jar on a shelf in the kitchen. Like the first film, however, there's so much emphasis on action and mayhem that it's difficult to really connect with the characters; even the presence of a mawkishly sympathetic (and impossibly photogenic) couple expecting their first baby fails to elicit much interest. Most of the characters are either obnoxious or downright unsympathetic, notably prima donna Sally; Coralina Cataldi-Tassoni (born 1971) would go on to become a semi-recurring presence for Argento, cropping up alongside him in his drugged-out host segments in the *Giallo* TV series, as well as playing roles large and small in *Opera*, *The Phantom of the Opera*, and *Mother of Tears*; she also was Dario's girlfriend for a brief period during this time frame. Asia Argento manages to make a good impression in her rather small supporting role, and her on-screen father is played by Antonio Cantafora (born 1944)—who worked earlier with Bava, father and son, on *Baron Blood* (*Gli orrori del castello di Norimberga*, 1972) and would go on to appear for Argento in *The Card Player*.

Bava again manages to work in references to his father's back catalogue, ranging from the blood drops on the tomb reviving the demon (*Black Sunday/La maschera del demonio*, 1960) to the little kid with the ball (*Operazione paura/Kill, Baby ... Kill!*, 1966), while the demons' acidic blood melting through the floors can't help but remind one of Ridley Scott's *Alien* (1979). Sergio Stivaletti's effects work is considerably more varied and uneven this time, though part of the problem could be the way in which they are filmed; with greater care, they may have come off a little more convincingly. Ultimately the film seems rushed because it was. The first film, for all its flaws, had the benefit of time and care being expended on the production, whereas here the incentive was obviously to follow up as quickly as possible. The end result is undoubtedly the *sloppiest* film to carry Argento's name to date, though it's certainly not without its pleasures.

The film marked the beginning of the end of Argento's professional association with Lamberto Bava, who would never achieve the same level of international success—but who would, in time, become one of the highest paid directors in Italian TV thanks to his immensely popular fantasy mini-series *Fantaghirò* (*The Cave of the Golden Rose*, 1991). He would later admit that, while there was talk of their collaborating on further projects, he wasn't very keen on the idea. "I didn't want to work with him again. He's important to Italy of course, and the few times he came on the *Demons* and *Demons 2* sets he galvanized the acting troupe. But he's not always an honest person in the sense that not everyone gets due credit on the films he produces."[12] Bava would stick around for Argento's next project, but after that they ended up parting ways professionally for good, though they have maintained a friendship down through the years. As for *Demons 2*, it made its Italian theatrical debut on the 9th of October 1986—almost precisely one year after the release of the original film. It actually did comparable business to the original, ranking number 48 at the Italian box office for the 1986-1987 season[13], but it struggled to find acceptance in the international marketplace; when Argento struck a deal with Vittorio and Mario Cecchi Gori to produce several pictures, one of the projects on the plate was *Return to the Land of the Demons*—but that mutated into a very different picture, as will be discussed in short order.

In between the two *Demons* films, Argento became involved in a rather unusual project. He was approached by fashion impresario Nicola Trussardi, who proposed hiring him to direct the Autumn/Winter 1986-87 fashion show for their Trussardi Action line. Always ready to try new things and expand his horizons, Argento eagerly seized on the assignment and worked with Trussardi on developing a show which would really take the fashion world by storm. Unlike the stuffy traditionalists who cancelled his version of *Rigoletto*, Trussardi was excited to combine Argento's flair for expressive, vivid imagery with his fashion house's latest creations and the project unfolded with remarkable ease. The show was put on at the Piazza del Cannone in Milan on March 9, 1986—and it proved to be controversial. Argento mixed fashion with mayhem as the show included set pieces in which the models were slashed to death and carted off stage in see through body bags. It was all set to Pino Donaggio's score for Brian De Palma's *Body Double* (1984) and the finale even managed to recreate the iconic opening of *Suspiria*, complete with rain and theatrical lighting effects. Trussardi was pleased with Argento's efforts and a video of the show, titled *Fenomeni di Moda Trussardi Action*, played in Trussardi's shops, where the violent, fetishistic imagery couldn't help but make an impression.[14]

Notes:
1. As related by Lamberto Bava in the featurette "Carnage at the Cinema: Lamberto Bava and His Splatter Masterpiece," included on the Synapse Blu-ray of *Demons*.
2. Palmerini, Luca M. and Gaetano Mistretta, *Spaghetti Nightmares* (Key West: Fantasma Books, 1997), p. 126.
3. Ibid, p. 50.
4. As related by Lamberto Bava in the featurette "Carnage at the Cinema: Lamberto Bava and His Splatter Masterpiece," included on the Synapse Blu-ray of *Demons*.
5. Jones, Alan, *Dario Argento: The Man, the Myths & the Magic* (Godalming: FAB Press, 2012), p. 149.
6. *Variety*, May 1, 1985, p. 312.
7. Argento, Dario, *Peur* (France: Rouge Profond, 2018), p. 266.
8. https://ricerca.repubblica.it/repubblica/archivio/repubblica/1985/04/24/niente-rigoletto-per-dario-argento.html
9. http://www.hitparadeitalia.it/bof/boi/boi1985-86.htm
10. *Variety*, May 7, 1986, p. 280.
11. *Variety*, February 19, 1986, p. 212 & 362.
12. Jones, Alan, *Dario Argento: The Man, the Myths & the Magic* (Godalming: FAB Press, 2012), p. 150.
13. http://www.hitparadeitalia.it/bof/boi/boi1986-87.htm
14. For more information on the show, check out Rachael Nisbet's blog: http://hypnoticcrescendos.blogspot.com/2016/12/trussardi-action-x-dario-argento.html

Nicola Trussardi invited Dario to stage an unorthodox fashion show in March of 1986.

Chapter Fourteen:
Flying High and Michele Rises

April 19, 1987 marked a sad and life-changing date for Dario: Salvatore died at the age of 73. His health had been in decline since the early 1980s and he spent his final days in a clinic in Rome. Dario and Claudio watched helplessly as their beloved father gradually slipped away, and his death would affect them both deeply. Dario's relationship with his mother, Elda, had long been complicated—they didn't see eye to eye on many things, though he has always conceded that she had a profound influence on his aesthetic sensibility and his appreciation for glamor and photography. With Salvatore's passing, Dario found himself yearning for a better relationship with his mother. "After my father's passing, my relations to my mother became more intimate, more intense."[1]

As was so often the case, Dario dealt with the grief by throwing himself into more projects; all the better to take his mind off the pain. He and Franco Ferrini were already at work on another *giallo* scenario—this one very much indebted to the film which had made such a profound impact on him as a child: *Phantom of the Opera* (1943). The project would also contain more autobiographical and self-reflexive flourishes, keeping with the approach of *Tenebrae* and *Phenomena*. Unlike *Demons 2*, however, it was not a project that could be tossed off in haphazard fashion; if anything, it called for a more lavish budget than anything he had worked with in the past. As such, there was no way for him to produce the film completely independently through DACFILM—he needed to find additional financing, which he initially sought through Titanus, his old collaborators from the days of *The Bird with the Crystal Plumage* and *The Cat O'Nine Tails*. That proposal didn't shake out, so he ended up striking a deal with Mario and Vittorio Cecchi Gori, whose media empire encompassed both the big and the small screen.

Opera would become Argento's biggest, most ambitious production up until that time. As the title indicates, it was inspired not only by his love of *Phantom of the Opera*, but also by the frustration he had experienced with regards to *Rigoletto*. He and Ferrini put their heads together and developed the story, but they had differing views on how best to approach the subject matter. Ferrini was more prone to indulging in flights of fancy, but Argento worried that going too far off into the realm of fantasy would prove alienating to viewers. The story essentially rehashes the basic set-up of *Phantom*, as an ambitious young soprano gets her chance at the big time when the diva playing the lead in avant garde production of Verdi's *Macbeth* is sidelined by an accident; it seems as if an unbalanced admirer is orchestrating things to help her ascent to stardom. In place of the romanticism of *Phantom*, however, Argento brought the violence of the *giallo* together with a deliberately icy emotional tenor which was inspired, according to him, by the fear over the then-rising AIDS epidemic.

The film had ample scope and ambition and it would find Argento experimenting with every technological tool at his disposal; it would also prove to be the most profoundly unpleasant experience of his professional career since *Inferno*. Dario was still rattled over his father's death when the project finally got off the ground on May 25, 1987 and he faced difficulties in just about every possible facet of the production. One of the few bright spots for him was his collaboration with the cinematographer Ronnie Taylor (1924-2018). In fact, Argento first had Luciano Tovoli, the cinematographer

Mr. Argento goes to the opera.

on *Suspiria* and *Tenebrae*, in mind—but Tovoli was unavailable and Argento was keen to find a director of photography with a flair for theatrical pieces. The two men actually first collaborated late in 1986 when Argento was asked to go to Australia to direct a commercial for Fiat. The commercial, which makes use of smooth gliding camerawork, provided Dario with a chance to experiment with some new camera equipment and "limber up" before getting back into the director's chair. Argento and Taylor hit it off and since he had recently lit *A Chorus Line* (1985) for Richard Attenborough, he struck Argento as the ideal man to photograph a film set in the opera world. Together they created some of the most fluid and remarkable images to be found in any of Argento's films, though unfortunately the script would suffer as it became necessary to condense and compress certain incidents in order to avoid over-swelling the already lavish budget and generous shooting schedule.

The film also marked another tense collaboration with Daria, who by this stage was absolutely convinced that Dario was harboring malicious intentions towards her. The role he offered her was that of the protagonist's friend and mentor, but it offered her few opportunities to really shine. She later admitted that she disliked the part and felt that the script was a mess, but was pleasantly surprised when Argento gave her the option to rewrite her dialogue and make the character more to her liking.[2] She would even hint to Alan Jones that Dario used Asia as a pawn to compel her to accept the part, though she stopped short of explaining precisely how he had managed to engineer such a stunt.[3] Nevertheless, when the time came for her big death scene, which involved putting an explosive squib at the back of her head to complete the illusion that she had been shot point-blank in the eye, she had genuine concern that he was trying to engineer her demise for real. Fortunately, the stunt went off without a hitch, but that would mark the end of their professional relationship—their personal one having already collapsed into bickering and mutual nastiness years earlier. In fact, they would reteam after an extended break, but by then the magic was gone; the special chemistry between them simply could not be recreated.

Production on *Opera* drew to a close after a long and exhausting 15 weeks of filming. The cash infusion provided by the Cecchi Goris resulted in lavish production values and plenty of bravura (and experimental) filmmaking, but Argento fell into a deep depression; he was convinced that he had made a terrible film and the normally harmonious process of working with Franco Fraticelli to assemble the final cut in the editing room did little to dissuade him from this notion. It wasn't really true, of course—in fact, *Opera* would prove to be one of his finest films—but the combination of his father's death, the heated confrontations with Daria, the difficulties he encountered with leading lady Cristina Marsillach, and a general grocery list of technical and production woes gave him good reason to believe that the film was cursed; that the plot involved the staging of the opera of *Macbeth*, itself rumored to be a project tainted with bad luck in the theatrical community, seemed only too fitting in that respect. Even so, Argento forced himself to soldier on to the best of his ability and post-production at least proceeded with comparatively little in the way of drama. The use of classical music in the soundtrack was already a given, of course, but Dario would again indulge his love of heavy metal by utilizing loud and aggressive metal music during the film's vicious murder sequences; elsewhere, he again assembled a patchwork of cues composed by some of his favorite musical collaborators, including Claudio Simonetti and Bill Wyman & Terry Taylor. The contrast between the classical and the modern proved to be inspired, even if some reviewers chastised the use of metal for being ham-fisted and out of place.

The film begins, appropriately enough, with a gigantic close-up of an eye—the film is all about seeing and voyeurism and spectacle, really, so such an image is especially apt. The eye is not human, however, but that of a raven. The juxtaposition between the close-ups of the squawking creature and the notion of "high culture," as an operatic rehearsal carries out in the background is striking, and Argento even treats the viewer to a view of the action reflected in the bird's retina. *Opera* shows Argento busting out every visual trick and flourish at his disposal; the larger-than-usual budget allowed him to really cut loose and experiment and this is evident in the film's visual style and its use of a constantly roving camera.

The squawking of the raven upsets the opera's star, grand diva Mara Czekova, and she responds by throwing one of her shoes at the bird. It's established immediately that she's not in sympathy with the show's director, Marco (Ian Charleson), and that his attempts to bring a more extravagant visual finesse to

Mira (Daria Nicolodi) is about to meet her fate; Daria was terrified during the filming of this sequence, as she worried that Dario might be trying to kill her for real.

Italian lobby card featuring a staged shot of the killer with a feathered friend, and a very glamorous view of Daria Nicolodi at the right; note that Ian Charleson's first name is misspelled as John in the Italian advertising.

the world of opera is deeply upsetting to her and the other traditionalists. "What is this, an opera or an amusement park!" Marco does his best to remain cool and impassive, but Mara decides to storm off in a huff. Mara is a classic diva figure. It's easy to see her as a stereotype, but as Argento discovered during his forays into the world of opera, these stereotypes have their basis in reality. In fact, the original plan was to cast the distinguished Vanessa Redgrave in the role of Mara, but there was a disagreement over her salary and she walked; if she had remained on board, this would have marked another conscious echo of Antonioni's *Blow-Up* (1967), as her co-star in the classic, David Hemmings, had already top-lined *Deep Red*. There was evidently some discussion of allowing Daria Nicolodi to take over the part, but Dario elected to express his frustration with movie stars and their temperaments by keeping the character (almost) completely off-screen; in essence, the role is "played" by Dario's preferred star: the camera. The use of subjective camerawork is, of course, nothing new in Argento's cinema—but this was the first time a major character was substituted in its entirety by subjective camerawork. Granted, we do get some glimpses of Mara later in the film—notably a shot of her leg in a cast—but ultimately, Argento gets the last laugh, as his diva character is left for the viewer to imagine and envision as they see fit.

The extravagant use of subjective camera sets the film off on an appropriately artificial note. *Opera* is very much about opulence—it's designed within an inch of its life, in every sense of the term—and the melodrama and theatricality associated with its milieu gives Argento freedom to cut loose and go for broke with his approach to the visuals. The subjective shot of Mara storming out of the theater is deliberately unnatural—she seems to be running backward as she shouts abuse at Marco and ignores pleas from the opera's managing director (Antonio Iuorio) to be reasonable and continue with the rehearsals. The sense of hysteria crescendos when Mara is stuck down outside by a passing car, causing the managing director to announce, with ample melodrama, that their star has been cut down in her prime; Mara survives, but she's reduced to a sideline presence, spitting abuse at the TV later on when her understudy, Betty (Cristina Marsillach), scores a major success in the role she gave up in the midst of a tantrum.

The Unsane Cinema of Dario Argento

Top: Betty (Cristina Marsillach) triumphs on stage as Lady Macbeth.
Below: Dario gives direction during the filming of the opera.

Betty is introduced in a scene which highlights how isolated she is from the outside world. She lives in a very well-appointed apartment which is loaded with high tech audio equipment; Argento shows these devices in a sensual, almost fetishistic manner as the camera pans along, looking on at them with admiration. Just how a poor understudy is able to afford such a lavish apartment and trappings is never made clear; possibly she comes from a well-to-do background. In classic "rags-to-riches showbiz" fashion, Betty is suddenly thrust into the limelight because of Mara's accident. She first gets some inkling of what's coming when she receives a call from a mysterious stranger—the first of several such calls she'll receive in the film—and then when her friend and agent, Mira (Daria Nicolodi), arrives to give her the news in person. Betty is a strange character. She seems slightly disconnected from everything and everyone around her. In that sense, she's more reminiscent of a character like Mark in *Inferno* than she is of, say, Suzy in *Suspiria*. Like Suzy, however, she undergoes a major transformation as the story unfolds and the horrible things she is subjected to force her to become stronger and more assertive. Her relationship with Mira is one of the few sources of warmth to be found in a deliberately "chilly" film.

Cristina Marsillach (born 1963)'s performance as Betty has been somewhat underappreciated by many Argento fans. It's well known that Dario took a severe dislike to her—thus allowing her to join the ranks of actors he has absolutely nothing positive to say about, along with Tony Musante and Anthony Franciosa. (In a fitting irony, Marsillach co-starred with Musante in Giuseppe Patroni Griffi's *The Trap/La gabbia*, 1985, which was based on a script by Dario's old "rival," Lucio Fulci.) Marsillach evidently wasn't particularly well-liked by the crew in general and if the rumors are true, she tended to carry on like a bit of a Mara-like diva herself. All that to one side, however, she gives a thoughtful performance as Betty. She captures the character's insecurity and awkwardness very well, and it never comes across as if she is merely going through the motions. It's easy to dismiss her as wooden, but it pays to remember that her awkwardness is very much a part of the character's DNA; as the story unfolds and we learn more about her, we come to realize that she has good reason to be this way.

Adding to the awkwardness on set was the presence of Daria Nicolodi as Betty's surrogate mother figure, Mira. Nicolodi was openly critical of the role, saying it gave her nothing to sink her teeth into, yet she comes across much better here than she had in *Tenebrae* or *Phenomena*; it helps, too, that she was actually able to dub her own performance into English—a first for her where Argento's films were concerned. She and Marsillach work well together and Nicolodi adds a great deal of interest and backbone to what could have been a dull and functional supporting part.

Betty is delighted by her good luck, but she's also fearful. Not only is it a major role, but the opera is *Macbeth*—and the story itself is reputed to be cursed. This is not an embellishment on Argento's part. For many years, *Macbeth* has had a reputation for being unlucky in its various permutations (the play, the various film versions, and Giuseppe Verdi's opera version), and given the problems surrounding the production of the film, he had good reason to believe there was some basis in reality for this; that said, it didn't stop him from staging the opera nearly 30 years later.

Marco, the director, picks up on Betty's nervousness and advises her to seize the opportunity with both hands; he dismisses the stories about Macbeth as superstitious nonsense and reminds Betty that such good luck "normally only happens to people in the movies." There's a thread running through the film which toys with the whole concept of illusion versus reality, and this extends to the world of art (be it film or theater) and the real world at large. In much the same way as *Tenebrae* allowed Argento to explore the link between *giallo* literature and real-life violence, *Opera* gives Dario the chance to explore his own relationship with the world of "high culture," while also commenting on his role as a filmmaker. On this level, Marco emerges as the film's most interesting character. He's written as a bit of a bastard, quite frankly, but Ian Charleson (1949-1990)'s performance manages to bring out some charm and humor which makes him likable, anyway. Argento would later claim that he wasn't looking to make the character a stand-in for himself, but this simply doesn't ring true. The character is known for making horror movies, and he's just had an ill-fated run-in with a staging of *Rigoletto*. The autobiographical aspects are underlined by Charleson's decision to mimic some of Dario's hand movements, while the casting of Antonella Vitale as his girlfriend couldn't have gone over the heads of those inside of Argento's circle; she would go on to play a recurring role in the *Turno di notte* segments of the *Giallo* TV series as well as a supporting part in his production of *The Church*, and they were involved in a hot-and-heavy romance at this time. It's another perverse joke of sorts, really, with Dario inserting himself into the narrative in the form of a character who can be seen as callous, cold, and downright sexist. It's not a "confessional," really, but it allows for a continuation of the dialogue between Argento and the audience from *Tenebrae*—as in that film, he's "represented" on screen through a character who is far from ideal, but that's all part of the fun. Charleson's performance is relaxed and winning and loaded with sly, sardonic humor. Whether

Ian Charleson modeled some of his movements on Dario.

he truly cares about anybody but himself is open to interpretation, but Charleson makes him into somebody worthy of our affection. Sadly, the gifted Scottish actor was already suffering from HIV by the time he signed on to do the film—and when he got into an accident during a break in the production, he was terrified that the news of his illness would be spread to the British press; Dario, looking to minimize any possible insurance woes, and not wanting to be put in the position of having to start the film over with another actor taking his place, agreed to keep the news under wraps and Charleson was able to finish his role (including the dubbing) before his tragic death at the age of 40.

Betty's debut performance goes beautifully, though the evening is marred by violence when a stagehand is murdered in one of the opera boxes. Argento and Franco Fraticelli make excellent use of cross-cutting as they shift perspective from the opera performance to more prowling subjective camerawork as the killer makes his way into the stalls to get a better look at Betty's performance. Intercut with this are some elliptical views of the killer's warped memories—Argento even allows for some views of the killer's brain as it pulses with sheer rage and bloodlust; it's an audacious touch, to be sure. Argento has often allowed audiences to get a glimpse into the inner workings of his killers' deranged psyches, but the shots of the brain take this notion to an altogether heightened level of "reality." The murder of the stagehand is presented as fairly quick and brutal—but the glimpse into the killer's past, as he remembers random images of a naked woman in bed, a knife, and the binding together of hands with rope, climaxing with implicit bloodshed, are considerably more haunting and unsettling.

Betty's triumphant debut is therefore marked by violence, something which will continue to dog her and her professional ascent as the story unfolds. We learn that she has a lover, a stagehand named Stefano (William McNamara), and that her love life is a bit of a mess. Stefano is depicted as a sweet, almost naïve character. He desires Betty and wants to make her happy, but she is too caught up in her own neuroses to be available for a deep, meaningful relationship. His attempt to make love to her is thwarted by "performance anxiety," and she tells him that she is "a disaster in bed, I don't know why." Argento has stated repeatedly that the specter of AIDS loomed over the film; while this may seem to be a bit of a stretch at first glance, it takes on more weight as one reflects on the film. The characters all appear to be emotionally disconnected. Stefano craves a normal, healthy relationship, but Betty is not open to this. Marco has a girlfriend, but whether there's anything to their relationship beyond sex is open to interpretation. Sex and love are therefore isolated from one another; the characters are too wrapped up in their own inner-conflicts and professional aspirations to be really open to the possibility of a loving, intimate relationship. It isn't even just a question of their being too selfish and self-absorbed to allow for intimacy; on a subtextual level, there is this notion of fear of intimacy which unites the majority of the characters. The party atmosphere of the '70s and early '80s gives way to the paranoia and isolation inflicted by the AIDS epidemic, which made people all over the globe afraid of catching the illness; some right-wing fundamentalist types even saw this as "punishment" for too many years of unfettered sensuality and excess. On a symbolic level, this is represented even in the killer's black gloves—in order to keep them from being stained with blood, he wears condom-like plastic gloves over them. Argento had no way of knowing just how deep the connection would run when he cast Ian Charleson, of course, as he only discovered the actor's illness later on, but there's something inherently sad about this which adds an additional air of melancholy to the finished film.

Betty's would-be romantic interlude with Stefano is interrupted when he steps out to get something from the kitchen and the killer surprises Betty, tying her to a pillar, gagging her and taping needles underneath her eyes, thus forcing her to keep her eyes open. This is Argento's most audacious concept to date, though it definitely has its origins in the "Ludovico Treatment," first described by Anthony Burgess in his novel *A Clockwork Orange* and then visualized on film in Stanley Kubrick's 1971 film adaptation. In truth, it's also another one of Argento's little jokes on the audience: it arose out of his frustration over seeing audiences turning their heads or covering their eyes during his elaborately designed and choreographed murder scenes. Argento put time and a

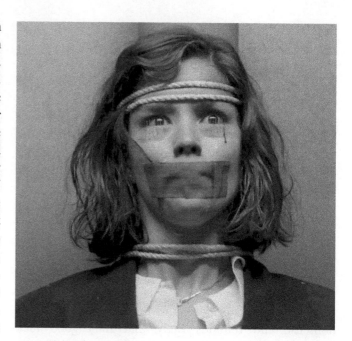

Betty is bound and forced to watch as the murderer strikes again.

lot of thought into these scenes and hated to see people turning away from them, even if this reaction obviously underlined just how successful he was in his goal to shock and terrify the viewer. That Betty is rendered mute during the attack is also of significance—by stifling her voice, the killer is obliterating the one thing that really empowers her. This ties into an idea that Argento and Franco Ferrini toyed with including in the script. As Ferrini later explained, "We'd wanted to give *Opera* the form of a fable in which Betty had a sort of super-power over the murderer, in that she was able to keep him at bay by singing. It was a tempting idea and I was quite taken with it; she would have managed to get outside and escape by singing and it would have been like taking opera into the streets ... into the underground ... but Dario thought it a bit far-fetched and decided against

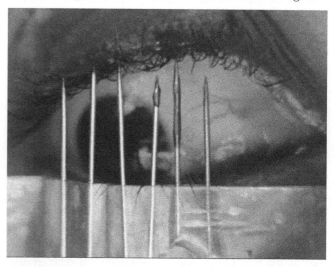

One of Argento's cruelest and most iconic images.

Stefano (William McNamara) is savagely murdered.

it."[4] It's an interesting idea, but perhaps after the wonky excesses of *Phenomena*, Argento felt it preferable to at least pay lip service to a greater sort of realism—even if *Opera* can hardly be described as a realistic film.

Stefano is attacked by the killer when he returns. His death is the most brutal and vicious in the film, and it's hard not to interpret this as a commentary of sorts on his sweet and innocent personality; these are traits which have no place in the hard, cruel world in which the film takes place. In casting such a "pretty boy" type as McNamara (an American actor, born 1965, though his dubbing with a thick British accent on the English soundtrack is a little jarring), Argento has yet another opportunity to present the ruination of beauty, as the killer savagely stabs and slashes at Stefano's hands and face. It's a brutal and deeply disturbing scene, partly because Stefano comes across as such a basically decent character, and partly because the imagery itself is so vivid and gruesome. Argento underlines the savagery of the murder by blasting heavy metal music on the soundtrack; he'd been using such music since *Phenomena*, of course, but here it feels particularly effective as it serves as a stark contrast to the austere setting and the use of classical themes.

When Betty escapes from Stefano's apartment, she finds herself in the middle of a torrential downpour—but unlike the storm in *Suspiria*, this comes across as a "cleansing" experience. The difference in mood is highlighted by the use of Claudio Simonetti's achingly beautiful "Opera Theme" on the soundtrack. Betty is rattled by her experience, but she copes with it surprisingly well; she doesn't seem to be unduly affected by the loss of Stefano, though she is disturbed by the memories the murder stirs in her. She remembers a recurring childhood dream involving a man in a black face mask who looks very much like the killer. Could it be a premonition, or a memory of suppressed trauma? It turns out to be the latter, though the film doesn't reveal its secrets until much later.

Betty runs into Marco, who is on his way to collect the late edition of the papers so he can see how the critics have reacted to *Macbeth*. The reviews are blistering— "Advice to the director: go back to horror films, forget opera."—except where Betty is concerned. Here again, her joy is severely undercut by violence, but even so— the performance has made her into a star. Marco, who is normally fairly chilly and flippant, appears to have a special interest in Betty and her welfare. Part of it is down to the fact that she's his star, but Marco's girlfriend senses a more selfish, even predatory motivation. Betty explains what she's seen and tells Marco that she's already reported it anonymously to the police; Marco figures they will take care of investigating it and that it's best for her to keep out of it, so he advises her to lock herself

Giulia (Coralina Cataldi-Tassoni) finds an important clue.

into her apartment for the night. The unwillingness of Betty and Marco to "get involved" in the situation again speaks of the cold, callous nature of the characters and their absolute focus on their respective careers. Sooner than risk having their success tainted by the murder of a mere underling—note how he's often referred to as the "stage manager," as opposed to by his name—it's better to stick their heads in the sand and feign ignorance.

The police, represented by Inspector Santini (Urbano Barberini, the star of *Demons*), show up at the theater the following day to question the troupe. Santini is familiar with Marco's movies and their dialogue reveals a kinship of sorts to the relationship between Peter Neal and Detective Germani in *Tenebrae*. Yet, while the interplay and banter between those characters had warmth and humor, here their interplay is much more chilly and reserved—befitting the overall tone of the movie. Santini tells Marco that he's seen a few of his films and that he seems to be an expert where murder is concerned. Marco's reply is terse but significant: "I think it's unwise to use movies as a guide for reality, don't you, Inspector?" One can't help but be reminded of Peter Neal's quip about interviewing the president of Smith and Wesson when somebody is killed with one of their handguns. By virtue of his profession, Marco is an even more overt "stand-in" for Dario than Peter Neal had been. He's not just a director: He's a director who specializes in images of violent death. Any protestations by Dario that this is simply a coincidence simply don't hold water; clearly, on some level, he was looking to use Marco as a means of commenting on his image as a purveyor of cinematic shock and horror. Marco may not be an entirely positive character, but he has humor and intellect; Santini, on the other hand, comes off as plodding, unimaginative and completely lacking in feeling. His interplay with Betty is limited but curiously off-kilter. When he introduces himself as a fan, she's flattered; when she finds out he's a cop, she turns icy and says, "So you're a policeman, not a fan?" His retort, "Can't a policeman be a fan?" is more than reasonable. And yet, there's something obviously a little bit "off" about Santini; unlike Germani or Inspector Morosini in *The Bird with the Crystal Plumage*, he seems mechanical and aloof—not at all the sort of character one would turn to for comfort and guidance.

The next big set piece occurs when Betty goes to see the wardrobe mistress, Giulia (Coralina Cataldi-Tassoni), about her wardrobe, which has been damaged when the killer decided to slash up the costumes. There's a lot of quirky humor in the Giulia character, thanks in large measure to the endearingly theatrical portrayal of Cataldi-Tassoni (born 1971). Born in New York, Cataldi-Tassoni is the daughter of parents deeply connected to the world of opera—her father is a renowned opera director, while her mother is an accomplished singer in her own right—and so this film proved to be right up her alley. She first entered Argento's orbit when she was cast as bitchy birthday girl Sally in *Demons 2*, then after *Opera* she would go on to appear opposite Dario in his spacey intros to the *Gli incubi di Dario Argento* segments of the *Giallo* TV series. Giulia obviously affords her a better opportunity to display her acting chops and she responds with a quirky and engaging performance. She has some nice witty banter with Betty and seems poised to become a surrogate sister figure, but in *Opera*'s cruel milieu, anybody who gets close to Betty is destined to be killed. Giulia discovers a personalized cufflink among the destroyed dresses, but before she can figure out its significance she is distracted by the arrival of the killer. Betty is again bound, gagged and forced to watch as the killer turns his violent aggression on Giulia. To her credit, Giulia proves to be a strong and resourceful victim—she fights back and manages to outwit the killer, knocking him out cold. However, her insatiable desire to discover the killer's identity proves to be her undoing. Sooner than run and get help when the killer is knocked cold, she removes his mask and gasps in horror; before she can share the information with Betty (whose view is obscured by the scenery in the costume department), the killer awakens and stabs her to death with a pair of costume shears. As Giulia flails about during her death spasms, the cufflink falls from her hand into her open mouth and lodges in her throat; the killer tries to retrieve it with his hand but is unable to do so. In one of Argento's more nauseating—but tactfully conveyed—scenes, the killer uses the shears to cut into the dead woman's throat; in so doing, he's able to retrieve the cufflink, lest it give away his identity. Argento resists the urge to show too much, but the implication is horrible enough; and in focusing on Giulia's eyes as they stare blankly while her body spasms and shakes as the killer tears into her flesh, he conveys something truly horrible without really showing anything at all. Apparently a more elaborately gruesome sequence was filmed, but Dario was obliged to cut it down in order to appease the censors. Here again, the concept of seeing is very important. Betty is forced to watch as the killer turns murder into a kind of performance art, while the framing of the action prevents Betty and the audience from discovering the killer's identity. The killer, professing a perverse love and admiration for Betty, lets her go free; and yet, Betty is painfully aware that she is still subject to his whims.

Betty reports what has happened to Inspector Santini, who advises her to take refuge in her apartment. There she is joined by Mira, who serves as a mother-protector figure for the emotionally frail younger woman. In one of the film's most impressive sequences, Betty and Mira find themselves being terrorized by the killer. A police inspector named Daniele Soave (a nice cameo/in-joke appearance by second unit director Michele Soavi) is already inside the apartment, but because Betty failed to get a good look at him when he entered (she had just put drops in her eyes to sooth them after her run-in with the killer), neither she nor Mira can be sure that he is who he claims to be. The inspector is called downstairs, so Betty and Mira lock the door and try to defend themselves as the killer cuts the power. Cinematographer Ronnie Taylor utilizes some magnificent pulsing lighting effects in this scene, as light from a neon sign flashing somewhere outside of the apartment building adds a touch of atmosphere and

Italian lobby card for *Opera*: Betty makes a lucky escape thanks to the help of Alma (Francesca Cassola); Stefano (William McNamara) incurs the killer's displeasure.

mystery to the scene; it's similar to the lighting effects utilized by Mario Bava in the "Drop of Water" segment of *Black Sabbath* (*I tre volti della paura*, 1963) and *Blood and Black Lace* (*6 donne per l'assassino*, 1964). Mira is a strong presence and she does everything she can to shield Betty from harm; however, when the killer appears at the door, brandishing a badge and a gun in an attempt to get them to open the door, he uses the gun to kill her, as she has her eye pressed against the peephole. The effect of the bullet entering the peephole, entering Mira's eye and exiting through the back of her skull, before smashing a telephone in the background of the shot is one of the most impressive and visually dazzling things Argento has ever done. Daria's exit from the film is therefore appropriately explosive—and it would mark her final collaboration with Dario as a director for two decades, until she agreed to return for a small cameo appearance in *Mother of Tears*.

The death of Mira unhinges Betty, but sooner than collapse under pressure, she continues fighting back. She does not rescue herself from the situation, however. Her guardian angel emerges in the unlikely form of an abused child named Alma (Francesca Cassola) who helps her to escape from the apartment through the building's extensive air conditioning duct. Argento has carefully prepared for this by showing something lurking about in the ductwork at different points in the film; when it turns out to be a frightened and lonely child, it goes against expectation—and it certainly provides Betty with the most fortuitous *deus ex machina* since the appearance of "God" at the end of *Four Flies on Grey Velvet*. In any event, Betty and Alma seem to share similarly fractured psyches. They're both loners and they both find escape and indeed retribution through the power of art and music.

Tellingly, Betty escapes by returning to the only world she really feels comfortable in: the opera. Marco proposes an eccentric idea for trapping the murderer and she agrees without question. It's interesting that it apparently doesn't even occur to her to try and make a run for it; the opera is her only real passion, her reason for being, and she's not about to turn her back on it in order to save her life. In Marco, she finds a collaborator whose flair for the theatrical is second to none; their relationship never quite crosses over into one of romance, but there's ample suggestion that Marco is interested in her, even if she doesn't necessarily reciprocate. The interplay between Marsillach and Charleson adds a touch of humanity to the film. Their characters may be dysfunctional, but they have their sympathetic attributes and the two actors manage to convey this while also remaining true to Dario's hard-edged vision for the film.

The following night, during a performance of *Macbeth*, Marco puts his plan into action. He arranges for the ravens that are part of the stylized imagery in the performance to be set loose in the audience. Earlier in the film, the killer had killed several of the ravens when they started disturbing him as he slashed up the costumes; the film's most daring narrative conceit suggests that the birds are vindictive and vengeance-minded enough to remember their assailant, thus allowing them to unmask the murderer. In a sense, it's a continuation of the themes of *Phenomena*, wherein the insect world can be utilized to track down the murderer. As the ravens fly about the auditorium, Argento shows their point of view in a dazzling overhead craning shot—if anything manages to top the classic Louma crane shot in *Tenebrae*, then this is arguably it. As the camera sweeps the audience, moving progressively closer to the spectators as they recoil in fear, the shot becomes the cinematic equivalent of a roller-coaster. Seen projected on the big screen, it's one of the most visually dynamic shots ever executed. Dario's friend and sometime-collaborator George A. Romero would later cite the "raven point of view" shot as his favorite shot in any film, and it's easy to see why; it sums up the audacity of Argento's approach to visual storytelling beautifully. The shot was accomplished with an elaborate crane system and cinematographer Ronnie Taylor had to secure permission from the directors of the Teatro Regio (where the stage and auditorium scenes in the film were shot) to remove the massive antique chandelier in order to set up the appropriate rigging for the camera; the mechanism would then spin in a circular fashion, as the crane allowed the camera to be lowered gradually from up high, thus creating the illusion of the ravens zeroing in on their intended target. The revelation of the killer seems obvious in hindsight: it's Inspector Santini. Santini is more than a little odd and off-kilter in his earlier scenes, yet Urbano Barberini (born 1961) plays him in such a deliberately flat and bland manner that it's understandable when he fails to register as a likely suspect. Like Inspector Geiger in *Phenomena*, he just seems to be a plodding plot device as opposed to a fully-realized character—but now that the mask is off and his true nature is revealed, he obviously gains considerably in interest. The image of the ravens pecking away his eye is not only gruesome—with Rosario Prestopino really excelling in the make-up department—but it also plays into the film's focus on vision and seeing. Betty is rendered blind at various points in the film—with a blindfold or with her eye drops—while at other times she is forced to keep her eyes open as the killer performs a sick, twisted mating ritual by killing in her honor. Of course, by now it's almost a running "gag" in Argento's films, but the concept of seeing is also linked in with the inability of the characters to properly process visual information. This is underlined when Santini kidnaps Betty and takes her to a neglected room in the theater; there, he reveals that his mind was warped because of his kinky sexual relationship with Betty's mother. Like Betty, she was also a singer; but whereas Betty is seemingly "frigid" or at least disinterested in sex, the mother possessed a cruel and twisted psychopathology which fixated on the link between sex and violence. Santini ties her to a chair and blindfolds her, supposedly to keep her from looking at the scars inflicted by the ravens. According to Santini, she used him in her sex games, compelling him to tie her up and force her to watch while he killed for her; in this way, he comes to associate sex with death—making his bizarre overtures to Betty into a strange mating ritual of sorts. Santini forces Betty to use his gun on herself, in an apparent suicide, but the room—which he's doused with kerosene—catches fire, threatening to consume Betty as well. She's rescued when Marco comes to her

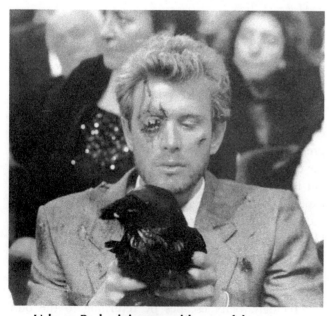

Urbano Barberini poses with one of the ravens.

Italian lobby card for *Opera*, with some heavy-duty spoilers.

aid. It's telling that, up until this point, Betty has proven incapable of rescuing herself from danger. She's had to rely on others, including Marco, Mira, Alma, and Giulia, to do that for her. On this level, at least, she has yet to make that final jump into adulthood; she still needs "looking after."

The coda is *Opera*'s most hotly debated facet. Most fans will agree that the bulk of the film represents Argento at the peak of his powers, but when the action switches to Switzerland for its final minutes, it alienates many viewers. Even Daria Nicolodi has referred to this section as "pointless and wrong."[5] It offers up further Argento/Marco parallels by showing the character tinkering with photographing flies for an upcoming film project; anybody familiar with Argento would immediately think of *Phenomena* in this context. The setting is sunny, bucolic, and inviting—but the danger is not vanquished yet. A news report reveals that the charred remains found in the opera were not human, but those of a theatrical mannequin; Argento includes a brief flash-cut to a shot of Santini hurling a dummy outfitted in a suit identical to his own into the fire as he makes his escape. Putting it mildly, it's a preposterous revelation. The idea that a charred mannequin could pass muster as human remains to the police for such an extended period of time—as a period of at least a week seems to have passed since the fire—defies credulity and threatens to undo the film in its final minutes. According to Franco Ferrini, this improbable, borderline-insulting plot twist was the result of Dario trying to get an unwieldy screenplay into workable condition: "The screenplay was cut a good deal because it was too long, around two and a half hours. At the beginning of the second half, there was a long and complicated sequence in which Betty moves into a luxurious apartment created inside the police station, and the commissioner asks her to sing just for him. Then while she is drinking a coffee alone, with the commissioner out of the room dealing with a prisoner who has tried to commit suicide, the girl is seized, bundled into an ambulance and taken to a secret place where she is tortured and raped. […] In the screenplay, a scene was envisioned in which the killer took a corpse and brought it to the theater as if hinting at what would happen. There were two things he could do with this body: it could have been either the 'masked' character that had fallen from the stalls and been distressed, like in *The Phantom of the Opera*; or a tramp who'd been killed and then thrown onto the fire, but in both cases the film would have gone on too long, so Dario opted for the dummy."⁶ While it's easy to understand the need to simplify the narrative, it's hard to reconcile this with Argento's decision to go with such a hackneyed and utterly unbelievable plot development; it's the sort of thing that could pass muster in a 1930s serial, but here it seems a very big lapse in judgement. Fortunately the plot point is passed over fairly quickly and everything which follows happens with such force and conviction that it doesn't succeed in completely undermining the rest of the film.

Marco warns Betty that the killer is still alive and tells her to run; she does so, with Santini, emerging from the idyllic scenery, fast on her trail. Marco tries to intervene and is brutally stabbed to death for his troubles. Betty decides to use her knowledge of Santini's perverse obsession to her advantage and tells him that she's just like her mother and that she wants to go off with him in order to continue their twisted games of sex and violence. When she notices the police in the distance, scouring the countryside, she gets the advantage on Santini and clubs him over the head with a rock. The police arrive to cart him off in handcuffs, and she taunts him by screaming that she's "nothing like my mother ... *nothing at all!*"

The scene which follows is another controversial one, as Betty wanders off from the mayhem and starts crawling on the ground, where she catches sight of a lizard trapped under a branch; she lets the lizard free while musing on the soundtrack about her connection with nature. It's an ambiguous finale, to say the least: it's possible to read it as Betty losing her already-tenuous grasp on reality and succumbing to madness, but it's also possible to see it as a positive ending, with Betty finally asserting herself and finding her place—in the natural world, as opposed to the social one, in which she has struggled to find acceptance. In this sense, it ties in with the finale of *Phenomena*, where Jennifer's connection with the natural world proves to be her salvation. Some critics have lambasted it as a pretentious digression on Argento's part, but there's no doubt that it is consistent with his thematic concerns. That said, he didn't always have such an ending in mind for the film. As indicated

Betty (Cristina Marsillach) becomes one with nature... or simply goes insane; it's all in the eye of the beholder.

earlier, Argento and Ferrini toyed with the idea of using Betty's singing voice as a sort of "super power" which would allow her to assert dominance over her would-be assassin. With this in mind, they originally conceived a much darker and more despairing finale: "The ending would have been the key to the story if we'd kept the idea of Betty's super-power: the killer would reappear and assault her, she would start singing to block him, but her voice would be drowned out by the noise of the Shaffhausen falls, the biggest in the world, and so she would have met her death."⁷ That would have provided *Opera* with a very different finale, no question about it, but arguably there's something perversely satisfying about Betty's final "commune with nature." Whether one reads it in a positive or negative light, it is consistent with the film's offbeat tone and it provides Argento with yet another opportunity to stress his role as author—it's his voice which recites the final bit of voice over on the Italian soundtrack, whereas the lines are spoken in English by Marsillach on the English dub.

Opera is a marked improvement on *Phenomena*. Whereas the earlier film feels like a half-baked hodgepodge, with too much of an emphasis on self-quotation, this film sees Argento expanding on the concerns of his earlier *gialli* while stepping up his game even further as a prime visual stylist. The increased budget and production resources are obvious. The film looks positively massive and imposing throughout, and the extensive use of Steadicam results in some of his most fluid and energetic imagery to date. The deliberately cold and flinty tone can be off-putting for some viewers, yet the film is not completely devoid of humanity. For all their faults, Betty and Marco, for example, turn out to be characters worth rooting for. The florid, theatrical nature of some of the performances is perfectly in tune with the film's setting, while the bold use of music—ranging from original compositions by Simonetti and Bill Wyman & Terry Taylor to previously recorded heavy metal music and classical/operatic compositions—is judicious and sophisticated throughout. Argento would begin to shy away from using aggressive metal music in his subsequent pictures, but here the contrast between the elegantly austere world of opera and the in-your-face sensibility of modern metal is key to the film's impact. While the script has its problems, especially in the last act, the film shows off Argento's mastery of the medium and remains one of his richest, most technically polished and sophisticated achievements.

Opera went into release in Italy on the 19th of December 1987. The Italian public reacted favorably, even if the reviews were more mixed than usual. It ended up coming in 12th at the Italian box office for the 1987-1988 season—Dario's old friend Bernardo

Italian *2 foglio* for *Opera*; artwork by Renato Casaro.

Bertolucci was the champion for the season thanks to his Oscar-winning *The Last Emperor* (*L'ultimo imperatore*), but the film still managed to come in ahead of *Dirty Dancing*, for example.[8] Given the unusually large budget, there was a lot riding on the film's box-office performance—but fortunately for Dario and the Cecchi Goris, it proved to be money well spent. The Cecchi Gori connection facilitated a sale to Orion Pictures in the U.S., but their proposed American theatrical release was scuttled by their growing financial difficulties; it ended up sitting on the shelf for several years before finally being acquired by South Gate Entertainment, who gave it a limited run in 1991, under the title of *Terror at the Opera*. Orion had actually prepared their own edit of the film, whittling it down from 107 minutes to a 95-minute running time; among other trims, they cut the scene with Mara Czekova reacting with anger to Betty's debut, the scene with Betty and Stefano reacting to and disposing of the foul-smelling perfume gifted to Betty by Mara, the scene in which Alma explains that she has been watching Betty and that she comes from an abusive household, and the final "crawl in the grass" as Betty affirms her connection with nature. The edits to the Alma scene are particularly vexing as it makes nonsense out of her relationship with Betty. Fortunately, the South Gate release didn't follow this example, though an alternate R-rated edit did trim the gorier bits; an unrated VHS edition was also made available, however. The film also made its way to Japan in February 1989, but for whatever reason it proved to be a tough sell elsewhere in the world; it didn't receive any kind of a theatrical release in the U.K. and sadly it ended up going straight to video in most markets. It wasn't exactly a repeat of what had happened with *Inferno*, of course, but the film's spotty distribution and exposure proved to be an ill omen of sorts for Argento, as his films would begin to face greater difficulties in finding their place in the international marketplace. As it happens, he was one of the relatively few filmmakers in Italy whose films were getting any kind of regular theatrical exposure—many of his contemporaries were spending more and more time working in television, where the limited scope and more stringent censorship standards effectively neutered their efforts. Dario's old rival, Lucio Fulci, was about to dive into TV production, for example, while Lamberto Bava would find steady employment making horror and fantasy movies for the small screen. Work is work, of course, and many of these directors were just glad to have some money coming in—

Dario attends a function with his daughters Asia and Fiore in 1987. (1987 © Arnoldo Mondadore Editore; S.P; Mondadori Portfoli: agefogtostock.)

but Dario wasn't ready to give up his place in the food chain just yet, and his deal with Cecchi Gori seemed to promise him further opportunities to make his presence felt in the international film market.

Like *Phenomena* before it, *Opera* ended up being nominated for Best Picture at the Fantasporto festival; this didn't happen until 1990, however, which provides further proof of the film's sluggish exposure in the international market. This time the nominees ranged from the sublime (Peter Greenaway's *The Cook, the Thief, His Wife & Her Lover*) to the ridiculous (Joe Johnston's *Honey, I Shrunk the Kids*) and Argento lost out to Mike Hodges' *Black Rainbow*.

Drained but by no means broken following the experience of making *Opera*, Dario decided to make his return to the small screen for the first time since *Door into Darkness* in 1973. *Giallo: la tua impronta del venerdì* ("*Giallo*: Your Friday Imprint")—the subtitle appears on-screen, though most people refer to the series simply as *Giallo*—was the brainchild of Italian television mogul Enzo Tortora (1928-1988). According to Luigi Cozzi, Tortora devised the series following a major personal scandal where he was accused of being a drug dealer and sent to prison; the accusations were eventually proven to be false, however, and he was released after serving only part of his sentence.[9] The RAI network took advantage of the scandal and offered the TV veteran a chance at redeeming his ruined career by coming up with a new program to fill an open Friday night slot. Tortora devised the idea of a *giallo*-themed series and wasted no time in securing the services of Dario Argento. The format of the series, which ran from October 1987 until January 1988, was somewhat convoluted. The first part of the show was hosted by Tortora and focused on the *giallo* in literature and in the cinema, sometimes with an emphasis on real-life mysteries as well; the next part of the show, titled *Gli incubi di Dario Argento* ("Dario Argento's Nightmares"), allowed the director to come on and discuss a thriller scenario, which he would dramatize in the form of a three-minute short film he directed himself; this would segue into a segment wherein Argento would interview pop culture personalities about their art (the guests would include genre-related actors such as Anthony Perkins and musicians who interested the director, such as members of the group Pink Floyd) while providing some behind-the-scenes glimpses into the making of his own films; after that, Tortora would come back and introduce a short thriller featurette, which would pause before the final revelation of the killer's identity, thus enabling Tortora to invite members of a studio audience to take a crack at guessing the ending—those who succeeded could win a cash prize. As Cozzi explained, "these mini-movies were all supervised by Dario and given the title *Turno di notte* ("Night Shift"). [...] We shot them in two days prior to airing and it was an enormous undertaking. The show failed because it was considered too talky although most people did watch the first part because of Dario's involvement and then switched to another channel when Tortora's section took over."[10]

As Cozzi indicates, the show was assembled in a very chaotic fashion. As it was a live broadcast interspersed with filmed segments by Dario and others, it required everybody involved to work at lightning speed. The show ran on Friday nights, commencing at the end of September 1987, and it would run through the first week of January 1988. "Inside this live two-hour program, there were 15 *Turno di notte* episodes shot on 35mm; six of them were directed by Lamberto Bava and nine by me. Each of them had to finish shooting only two days before they were aired, which meant that everything had to be made with enormous speed, because in these remaining two days before airing, each episode had to be edited, dubbed, mixed; the negative then had to be printed on a 35mm positive, which finally needed to be transferred to tape for airing from the studio, live in Milan. All this work was being done in Rome, while the live studio and the airing machine were in Milan; this meant that about eight additional hours were needed to bring every finished *Turno di notte* tape from Rome to Milan."[11] It was grueling work but Argento and his collaborators managed to deliver the goods every week; by the time the series was finished in January 1988, everybody involved was pretty much drained—and that the series wasn't renewed for another season probably came as a bit of a relief.

The show has since slid into obscurity and there have been no official DVD releases. One can only imagine that Argento is only too happy for this as the series does not show his talents off to their fullest. Apart from participating in the gameshow segment supervised by Tortora, he also was responsible for writing and directing nine brief segments (more like sketches, really) for the "nightmares" segment; these segments weren't present in every single episode. Unfortunately, the majority of Argento's "nightmares" are lame beyond belief; in fairness, given the hectic speed with which they were made, this is hardly surprising. Hosted by a haunted-looking Argento (perhaps a sleep-deprived Argento would be more appropriate?), with actress Coralina Cataldi-Tassoni lurking around in the background, staring like a mad woman, they traded on the notion of the director as a celebrity; this was why Tortora reached out to him in the first place, as his participation would likely draw viewers who might otherwise not be inclined to explore Tortora's interest in crime stories, itself doubtlessly rooted in the scandal which ruined his name for a period of time. The stories range from the pointless to the absurd, but one vignette does stand out from the rest of the pack: "*Il vermen*" ("The Worm"), which deals with a young woman who realizes that she has been infected by a deadly parasite. The segment has nothing to do with the *giallo*, but it builds to a memorably gruesome finale and lingers in the mind in a way that the other vignettes he directed decidedly do not. The other segments include "*La finestra sul cortile*" ("The Courtyard Window"), "*Riti notturni*" ("Nocturnal Rites), "*Nostalgia punk*," "*Amare e morire*" ("Love and Death"), "*Le Strega*" ("The Witch"), "*Addormentarsi*" ("Falling Asleep"), "*Sammy*," and "*L'incubo di chi voleva interpretare l'incubo di Dario Argento*" ("The Nightmare of the One Who Tried to Interpret Dario Argento's Nightmares").

Coralina Cataldi-Tassoni with Dario in one of their strange intros to the *"Gli inclibi di Dario Argento"* segment of the *Giallo* TV series.

Argento supervised the production of the *Turno di notte* segments, but he didn't actually write or direct any of them himself. Predictably they're a rather uneven lot, and only the real diehards will feel compelled to stick with them to the bitter end. Lamberto Bava provides a sure and steady hand in guiding the first six segments, while Luigi Cozzi brings a different, more film buff-oriented sensibility to the remaining nine installments. In "*È di moda la morte*" ("Death is Fashionable") a model jumps to her death and another is stabbed to death before driver "Rosso 27" (the drivers are nicknamed based on the names of their respective cabs) is able to uncover the culprit; David Brandon guest stars. "Heavy Metal" begins with "Calypso 9" picking up a punk rocker and nearly ending up mincemeat when the youth leads her into a murder plot; Bava makes good use of moody lighting in this segment, while the use of metal standbys like Iron Maiden's "Flash of the Blade" and Saxon's

The Unsane Cinema of Dario Argento

"Fast as a Shark" recalls its usage in other Argento projects like *Phenomena* and *Demons*. "*Buona fine e miglior principio*" ("Good End and Best Principle") deals with a murder committed at a crowded New Year's party; *giallo* veteran Maurice Poli (who appeared in Mario Bava's *Five Dolls for an August Moon/5 bambole per la luna d'agosto*, 1970) is among the red herrings and the music quotes from Goblin's score for *Deep Red*. "*Giubbetto rosso*" ("Red Jacket") begins with "Rosso 27" being flagged down by a hysterical woman who claims to have escaped from the clutches of the so-called "Red Jacket Killer," who has been terrorizing the region. He takes the girl back to the scene of the crime, where he makes a surprising discovery. "*Il bambino rapito*" gives some decent screen-time to the otherwise ill-used "Tango 28," who gets mixed-up in a kidnapping scenario and helps the police in discovering the identity of the culprit. Bava's final installment, "*Babbo Natale*" ("Santa Claus"), deals with "Rosso 27" trying to keep the Christmas spirit while investigating the murder of a man in a Santa Claus outfit. Cozzi's contributions kick off with "*L'impronta dell'assassino*" ("Footprint of a Murderer"), which tells of a murder that takes place in the gym that "Calypso 9" uses to work out; Brett Halsey (the star of *Today We Kill, Tomorrow We Die!*) and Mirella D'Angelo (who appeared as the ill-fated journalist in *Tenebrae*) are among the suspects. "*Ciak si muore*" ("Clap, You're Dead") borrows its name from an obscure 1974 *giallo* and tells the more-clever-than-usual story of "Calypso 9" picking up celebrity fare Corinne Cléry and taking her to film a thriller at Cinecittà. The star-struck cabbie sticks around to observe and is on hand when Cléry is unexpectedly butchered during a take. Cozzi's film buff leanings are evident as he seems to relish the behind-the-scenes atmosphere of the famous Roman film studio and the soundtrack is awash with (presumably unlicensed) cues by John Williams from *Star Wars* (1977) and *Raiders of the Lost Ark* (1981). "*Sposarsi è un po' morire*" ("Marriage is to Die For") begins with "Rosso 27" picking up a bride-to-be who is running away from the altar; as he carts her to her uncertain destination, she is shot and killed in the back seat … it is up to Rosso to figure out who could have done it. Cozzi again lays on the library music, this time with an over-generous helping of Bernard Herrmann's iconic score for *Psycho* (1960). "*Delitto in Rock*" ("Murder in Rock") features "Calypso 9" as she helps a friend in locating a tape the woman had left behind in the cab which contains a rare, unpublished song by Jim Morrison; the problem is, the person who has it is not ready to give it up and somebody is ready to commit murder in order to covet it. "Calypso 9" is back for "*L'evasa*" ("The Escape"), in which she is forced at gunpoint to take an escaped convict on the run; the soft-hearted cabbie believes the woman when she says that she is innocent and that she is trying to catch the person who is really guilty of the crime of which she is accused; some of Ennio Morricone's music for *The Cat O'Nine Tails* is on display in this segment. "*La casa dello Stradivari*" ("The Stradivari House") puts the luckless "Rosso 27" in danger when his cab is stolen and he goes to a secluded villa for assistance; while waiting for "Calypso 9" to come to the rescue, he bears witness to a crime. "*Giallo Natale*" ("Christmas *Giallo*") has a cast and a set-up to die for (at least for the initiated): Daria Nicolodi plays a woman who swears to kill her ex-husband, while her real-life daughter Asia is on hand to play her little girl, who tries to avert tragedy; one can only imagine the atmosphere on set with Argento supervising the production. Another *giallo* veteran, Renato Rossini (aka Howard Ross), is also on hand, and the segment is enjoyable in a silly sort of way, though it does not quite live up to expectations. "*Via delle streghe*" ("Witch Street") is the most stylish of Cozzi's contributions, and it deals with a costume party in which everybody is done up as a recognizable horror or sci-fi icon: The Invisible Man, the Creature from the Black Lagoon, etc. Goblin's iconic score for *Suspiria* is

The *Turno di Notte* segment of the *Giallo* TV series is more substantive than the surrounding material.

included, as are some snatches from Ennio Morricone's score for John Carpenter's *The Thing* (1982). The series limps to a very uninspiring ending with "*Il taxi fantasma*" ("The Ghost Taxi"), which seeks to wrap-up a running reference to a mysterious "Ghost Taxi" which "Rosso 27" is particularly fixated on. That the series wraps up with a half-hearted foray into the supernatural and the paranormal suggests that everybody involved had grown tired of the *giallo* format.

Early in 1988, following the release of *Opera*, Argento and the Cecchi Goris started to give serious consideration to a third *Demons* film—they originally announced the project as *Return to the Land of the Demons*, then the title changed to *Demon Cathedral*. In May 1988, *Variety* indicated that the project was to be called *Return from Demon Country*—with Lamberto Bava listed as director.[12] As the title indicates, the isolated setting this time would be a church. By this stage, Lamberto Bava was working pretty consistently for the small screen and by his own admission, he wasn't keen to collaborate with Argento on any other projects. According to Argento, however, the Cecchi Goris let it be known early on that they didn't want Bava to direct the picture. Bava was particularly annoyed when he saw that his name was not included in the screenplay credits, as he claimed to have had a heavy hand in the writing of it. Wherever the truth of the matter rests, it seems likely that Bava at least deserved some credit for helping to develop the original story. When it was decided that a new director was needed, Argento turned to his former assistant, Michele Soavi (born 1957), who had just done such a splendid job of directing the second unit material in *Opera*. Soavi's rise from his early days as an actor and frequently uncredited production assistant for everybody from Lucio Fulci to Aristide Massaccesi had been fairly meteoric. After assisting Dario on *Tenebrae* and *Phenomena* and participating in *Demons* as an actor (he's the masked man who hands out the free movie passes to the characters), Soavi made his debut as a feature director with the stylish *giallo*-slasher *StageFright* (*Deliria*, 1987), which was filmed in 1986. His first directing credits were relatively minor assignments connected to Argento: Dario entrusted him with directing the "Valley" music video for *Phenomena*, and then Soavi assembled the celebratory documentary *Dario Argento's World of Horror*, which was made specifically for the Japanese TV market in 1985. He was not idle in between *Opera* and this new project for Argento, however. As it happens, *StageFright* had a fan in the form of director Terry Gilliam, who sought Soavi out to be his second unit director on his Italian-made fantasy-comedy *The Adventures of Baron Munchausen* (1988). The shoot was long and problematic, but Soavi performed his duties with flying colors—so much so that

Dario clowns around with Michele Soavi, although their collaborations were not free of drama.

Gilliam would seek him out again to direct second unit for *The Brothers Grimm* (2005). Soavi was actually hopeful that Dario would back him to direct his first feature, but for whatever reason Argento was reluctant to do so. Instead, *StageFright* was put together on the cheap by his old friend Aristide Massaccesi (aka Joe D'Amato, 1936-1999). The budget was low, and the schedule was short, but on the upside, Massaccesi trusted Soavi and gave him freedom to make the film as he saw fit. The freedom he enjoyed working on *StageFright* would not be recreated when the time came to work for Argento, however. "Dario being my producer was like a tax I had to pay. Aristide had left me to my own devices on [*StageFright*] so to have Dario breathing down my neck all the time was annoying and off-putting. I kept strong throughout because I kept reminding myself that I already had directed one film and I didn't have to prove anything to anybody. Had *The Church* been my debut then I don't know how I would have responded to the unnecessary pressure."[13]

Soavi made it clear from the outset that he wasn't interested in directing a sequel to *Demons*. He took the script prepared by Ferrini and Argento and reworked it to suit his own tastes; in the process, he removed all the references to the earlier films and made it into something unique which could stand or fall on its own merits. As Soavi notes, he and Dario frequently clashed—whether it was simply Dario throwing his weight around or challenging his young protégé in order to bring out the best in him and the project is open to interpretation. But despite the difficulties, he proved to be the ideal director for the project and his distinctive artistic sensibility made it into a far more sumptuous and imaginative picture than either of the Bava films.

The Church went into production in early September of 1988 and it shot over a period of 11 weeks, lasting until the middle of November. The shoot encompassed several weeks of filming on location in Budapest and

Italian *locandina* for *The Church*.

have liked. Argento, of course, had the right of final cut as the producer and the end result would be something of a compromise between his vision and that of Soavi. The young director was disappointed but even in its compromised state, it clearly was the work of a gifted and highly imaginative filmmaker. Despite it all, Argento was impressed and was ready and willing to back future projects directed by Soavi.

The story starts off in the Middle Ages, with the Teutonic Knights hard at work persecuting suspected witches. They find a settlement of witches and massacre them, burying the bodies in a mass grave; a church is erected over the grave. Hundreds of years later, in contemporary Germany, art historians Evan (Tomas Arana) and Lisa (Barbara Cupisti) are hired to do some restoration to the church, which is falling into disrepair. Lisa uncovers an ancient scroll which reveals some hidden evil about the church and, in so doing, she opens a portal allowing the demonic entities to break free and wreak havoc.

The Church is a much more ambitious and elaborate production than either of the *Demons* films. While it definitely bears some resemblance to its predecessors—and to Dario's own *Inferno*, thanks to explicit references to the alchemist Fulcanelli—it stands on its own as a separate and distinctive piece of work. Michele Soavi's visual sensibility is considerably more imaginative and poetic than that of Lamberto Bava. While Bava tended to emphasize action and shock effects, Soavi is much more concerned with building mood and atmosphere.

The first half of the film, including its earthy medieval prologue, is the most accomplished. Here we can see Soavi finding his voice as a cinematic poet, using sensual camera movements and constantly roving camerawork to generate a sense of unease; the church itself, with its imposing Gothic architecture, becomes a character in its own right and one can easily buy into the notion that something horrible is trapped within its very foundations.

The performances certainly help: Tomas Arana (born 1955, who would go on to appear in the next Argento/Soavi collaboration, *The Sect/La setta*) has an electric, edgy quality which makes Evan into a likably eccentric leading man, while Barbara Cupisti (born 1962, who had previously starred in *StageFright* and had played a minor role for Argento in *Opera*) adds inner-strength to the character of Lisa. Hugh Quarshie (born 1954) registers strongly as the righteous Father Gus, who is one of the few characters to remain unaffected by the church's evil powers, Feodor Chaliapin, Jr. (previously seen as Varelli in *Inferno*) is a fearsome presence as the ancient Bishop, and Asia Argento excels in a much more

Hamburg; the Budapest locale was selected because none of the churches in Italy would allow such "blasphemous" material to be filmed on its grounds. Sections of the church would be recreated at De Paolis Studios, Argento's familiar stomping ground, thus allowing some of the more risqué sequences to be filmed without concerning the clergy. By Soavi's admission, Argento tried not to make himself too much of a presence on the set—but when the time came to assemble the picture, the squabbles began. Soavi hadn't indulged in as much gore as Argento had been hoping for and his emphasis on mood and atmosphere made the film longer and more slowly paced than Argento would

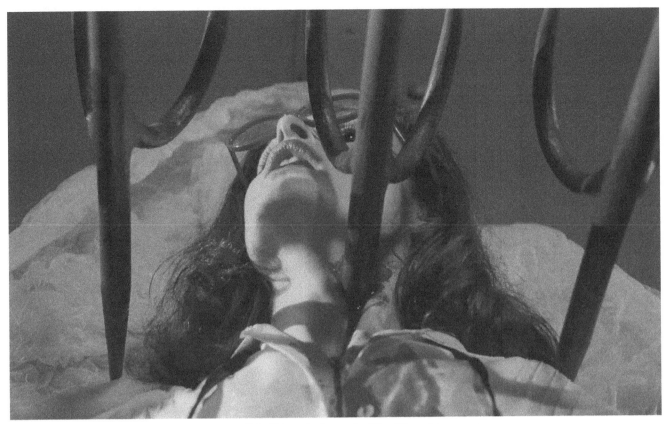

All hell breaks loose in *The Church*.

sizable and intriguing role than she had been given in *Demons 2*.

Working in tandem with cinematographer Renato Tafuri (another *StageFright* vet, who also collaborated with Soavi on the second unit work for *Opera*), Soavi creates some of the most beautiful and haunting imagery in the Argento canon. The scene where Evan discovers that something strange is trapped beneath the huge stone crucifix in the church basement is particularly striking, as the stone cross appears to give way and collapse into the blackness; Soavi also maximizes the off-kilter weirdness with odd cut-aways to people behaving strangely when the film settles into its more conventional second half—a group of characters are trapped inside the church while the contagion spreads by cuts from the infected, à la *Demons*. The images of the bridal model's (Antonella Vitale, in her final film for Dario—their relationship ended not long after the film wrapped) elaborately billowing white dress catching in the church's heavy metal doors, trapping her until she can be cut free, are eerily beautiful. There are a few shock effects—notably a character eviscerating himself with a power drill—but they tend to be glossed over in a perfunctory manner, suggesting that the director was less interested in gore than in mood and visual design.

Soavi also recreates the dream sequence from Roman Polanski's *Rosemary's Baby* (1968), with the "Possessione" theme by Goblin also echoing Krzysztof Komeda's iconic music for that film, as well as the classic Boris Vallejo portrait "Vampire's Kiss," which depicts the embrace of a naked woman by a dragon-like vampire figure. There isn't a scene that doesn't contain some sort of interesting visual flourish, though the progression of the narrative is sometimes compromised by Argento's decision to chop the movie down to accommodate a more reasonable running time; just how much material was trimmed is not known, but the pacing does feel "off" at times and the second half doesn't quite live up to the promise of the first. Even when it enters the more familiar *Demons*-style territory, however, it asserts a very different personality from the Bava films. While *Demons* and *Demons 2* went for fast and furious shocks once all hell breaks loose, with lots of deafening metal taking over the soundtrack, Soavi elects for something much dreamier and trippier—and the score is generally more low-key, with quotations from Philip Glass in addition to new themes from Keith Emerson and Goblin. The end result is imperfect but frequently beautiful and confirmed that the promise shown by *StageFright* was no fluke; Soavi seemed poised to become the new major voice in Italian horror.

Unfortunately, like *Opera* before it, *The Church* became the victim of spotty distribution. The Cecchi Goris gave it a very good run in Italy, where it did good business, ranking number 37 for the 1988-1989 box-office season[14]—but the rest of the world wasn't so lucky.

The exterior of "Profondo Rosso" in Rome.

The Italian release took place on March 10, 1989, while it played in Japan—where Argento was still a major draw—in August 1990. In most markets, however, it ended up going straight to video—a sad commentary on the declining state of the Italian genre cinema scene, and a tragic fate for an ambitious, visually sumptuous production such as this one. Soavi was also disappointed by the ad campaign, which Argento had signed off on. "I can't tell you how annoying it was to see *The Church* poster and needing a magnifying glass to read my name in the small print. I wanted the poster to read 'Dario Argento presents a Michele Soavi film' like Dario had done with Bava on *Demons*. Yet it didn't and that was the first real crack in our relationship."[15]

1989 also saw the opening of the "Profondo Rosso" shop, located at Via dei Gracchi 260 in Rome. Named for Dario's 1975 *giallo* masterpiece, the store was the brainchild of Luigi Cozzi, who saw it as a great opportunity to promote the fantasy and horror genres in general and Argento's work in particular. Dario recognized its potential to help keep his name alive in the mind of the Italian public and jumped at the idea. As reported by Alan Jones, Dario had actually rented the Via dei Gracchi location for Antonella Vitale, who had ambitions of opening an *haute couture* salon; when Vitale suddenly left him for another man, he decided to use the place for other purposes.[16] In addition to selling books, movies and sundry other items pertaining to the genre, it also includes a special exhibition known as "Dario Argento's Museum of Horrors," which includes props from some of his most popular productions, including *Phenomena* and *Demons*. Cozzi actually attends to the day-to-day running of the shop himself, and fans are given an opportunity every Halloween to stop by and meet Dario and get his autograph. It's proved to be a successful venture, one which helped to cushion Argento's bank account during a period when his commercial viability in the international marketplace was beginning to falter noticeably. Argento tried to replicate its success with another shop in Milan, but it didn't work, and it was quickly shut down. Still looking to diversify, Dario also tried lending his name to a proposed restaurant based on his cinematic legacy; the project was developed in association with Umberto Ferri, who devised a chain of Hard Rock Café–style restaurants/pubs in Italy called "Transilvania Horror Rock Kafé."[17] The Argento-themed restaurant never came to fruition—oh well, you can't win them all.

While the combination of the Italian box office and foreign video sales were enough to ensure that Argento's company—now known as ADC Films—was financially healthy enough to stay afloat, Dario had concerns that his filmmaking was becoming a little too limited in its appeal. Gone were the days of his films playing across the globe, so he had good reason to believe that a radical change was in order. He announced a project to be titled *Undici* ("Eleven") which was supposed to involve "fish in the Caribbean," but not much was ever said about the project; presumably it called for a greater budget than Dario was comfortable spending during this rocky period, and it was ultimately shelved. He could not afford to rest on his laurels for long, however.

Notes:
1. Argento, Dario, *Peur* (France: Rouge Profond, 2018), p. 346.
2. Jones, Alan, *Dario Argento: The Man, the Myths & the Magic* (Godalming: FAB Press, 2012), p. 75.
3. Ibid, p. 75.
4. Palmerini, Luca M. and Gaetano Mistretta, *Spaghetti Nightmares* (Key West: Fantasma Books, 1997), p. 50.
5. Ibid, p. 116.
6. Ibid, p. 50-51.
7. Ibid, p. 51.
8. https://boxofficebenful.blogspot.com/search?q=box+office+italia+1987-88
9. Jones, Alan, *Dario Argento: The Man, the Myths & the Magic* (Godalming: FAB Press, 2012), p. 50.
10. Ibid.
11. Email correspondence with the author.
12. Jones, Alan, *Dario Argento: The Man, the Myths & the Magic* (Godalming: FAB Press, 2012), p. 184.
13. *Variety*, May 4 1988, p. 314.
14. http://www.hitparadeitalia.it/bof/boi/boi1988-89.htm
15. Jones, Alan, *Dario Argento: The Man, the Myths & the Magic* (Godalming: FAB Press, 2012), p. 184-185.
16. Ibid, p. 51.
17. http://members.tripod.com/HORROR_guide/italy.html

Chapter Fifteen: Coming to America

After a period of animosity, Dario and his brother Claudio finally mended fences. While Dario was working as his own producer, Claudio had gone on to produce some interesting films, notably Alejandro Jodorowsky's *Santa Sangre* (1989), which filmed in Mexico in the latter part of 1988. The two brothers sensibly realized that their relationship meant more than any business disagreements, and they decided to collaborate once more on a new project. Dario's life-long obsession with Edgar Allan Poe (1809-1849) prompted him to come up with something new and, for him, radically different. He had refused offers in the past to direct adaptations of works by the likes of Agatha Christie and Stephen King on the grounds that he wanted to write his own material—but for his new film he would adapt Poe … and that was just the tip of the iceberg. The Poe project was originally conceived as a TV series. "I had the idea in mind for a TV series for some time. Different international directors would direct a series of episodes based on the stories of Edgar Allan Poe. I already started making preparations, but sadly it never materialized. I then thought that I could make a documentary about his life […] With a little crew of just two people, I filmed everything that had a relation to him: his home, the street where he fell and was run over by a carriage, the room at the hospital where he spoke his last words, 'Lord, help my poor soul!' Sadly, that project was also dropped."[1]

With the TV series and documentary projects dead in the water, Argento decided on a new approach. It would be a portmanteau picture, with each segment being directed by a major figure in the horror genre. The original plan was to get George A. Romero, John Carpenter, and either Clive Barker (born 1952) or Stephen King (born 1947) on board to write and direct segments; King was actually considering doing an adaptation of "The Tell-Tale Heart," but his unpleasant experience in making *Maximum Overdrive* (1986) dissuaded him from taking part in the picture. Carpenter was tempted, but he was already developing a sci-fi movie called *Victory Out of Time*, which ultimately fell by the wayside; not long after, he was signed by Warner Bros. to direct the high-tech comedy-suspense film *Memoirs of an Invisible Man*, which filmed in early 1991 following an extensive pre-production schedule. One wonders if he had participated whether he would have ended up scoring the entire picture himself. Romero, already an honorary part of the Argento filmmaking family thanks to *Dawn of the Dead*, remained attached—but Argento thought of getting Wes Craven on board and turning it into a film in three parts. It soon became apparent that trying to negotiate and schedule three different directors to make three segments was more trouble than it was worth, so Dario and Claudio settled on making the film in two parts.

For his segment, Dario initially planned to do a politicized take on "The Pit and the Pendulum" before he finally settled on "The Black Cat." From his point of view, the story had never been properly translated to the screen—but one can't help but wonder whether this was his subtle way of throwing shade at Lucio Fulci, who made his own version (*Gatto nero/The Black Cat*) in 1980. Whatever his motives, Argento enlisted Franco Ferrini to help him with writing the script, which would be fairly awash in references to Poe's entire body of work. Romero, meanwhile, was keen on adapting "The Masque of the Red Death." Neither Dario nor Claudio were happy with his choice and it seems there were some communication issues early on which made things a bit tricky for Romero. As time went on and more and more concerns were voiced about his potentially costly treatment for "Masque," Romero relented and settled on the more obscure "The Facts in the Case of Mr.

Advance publicity for what would become *Two Evil Eyes*, back when it was still called *Poe*, in *Variety*.

Valdemar," which had nevertheless already been filmed in 1961 as part of Roger Corman's *Tales of Terror*. As luck would have it, it was Poe's only story to deal with the living dead—and the fact that Romero, master of the zombie film, was now translating it for the screen delighted Dario. The project was formally announced as *Edgar Allan Poe*, with Argento and Romero's names prominently displayed to hook potential theatrical distributors; it finally changed to the more evocative *Two Evil Eyes* (*Due occhi diabolici*). Romero had been looking forward to going to Rome to make his first Italian film, but Argento had other ideas: he wanted to use *Edgar Allan Poe* as his way of breaking into the American film scene. Commercially, it made sense—his recent films hadn't been securing American exposure, except for home video, and if it panned out as he had hoped, it could have helped him to expand his business empire. Pittsburgh became the agreed-upon location: it had been Romero's base of operations for many years, and he had access to a full crew of technicians and artisans who would be ideally suited to working on the movie.

The crew would be a mixture of Italian and American (and quite a few Italian American!) talents. Romero's chosen director of photography was Peter Reniers, while Argento favored using Giuseppe ('Beppe') Maccari, the long-time camera operator for the great Giuseppe Rotunno (*The Leopard/Il gattopardo*, 1963, etc). Much of the remaining crew would be culled from Romero's regular list of collaborators, notably make-up effects master Tom Savini (born 1946), who had risen to prominence as a celebrity in his own right thanks to his work on Romero's *Dawn of the Dead*, as well as such popular slasher fare as *Friday the 13th* (1980) and *The Burning* (1981). As it happens, Savini was already a big fan of Dario's work, so the opportunity to collaborate with him was something of a dream come true. In order to maximize the efficiency of making his segment, Dario brought along Michele Soavi to take charge of the second unit; sadly, Soavi was having health issues at the time, so he dropped out early on and Luigi Cozzi came to the rescue. To minimize the difficulties with regards to the language barrier, Argento hired local Pittsburgh Playhouse director Ken Gargaro to act as a go-between with the actors; he also helped them to better adapt their lines into English, which allowed Dario to focus on his preferred interest in the visuals.

Production on Romero's segment got under way on the July 10, 1989. There were some technical difficulties early on, but Romero persevered and managed to keep to the agreed-upon schedule of 22 shooting days, at which point he took his material and worked with his old friend Pasquale Buba (1946-2018) in assembling a rough cut. While Romero was at work in the editing room, Argento started his 32-day shoot and finished on September 12—a mere five days after his 49th birthday. There had been talk early on of hiring Donald Sutherland to play Poe as a sort of linking device, but the idea was soon dropped; Argento was able to make use of some of the footage he grabbed for his aborted Poe documentary, however, by using some snippets as a sort of prologue. With Romero's initial edit already in place, Argento and Buba worked together on assembling "The

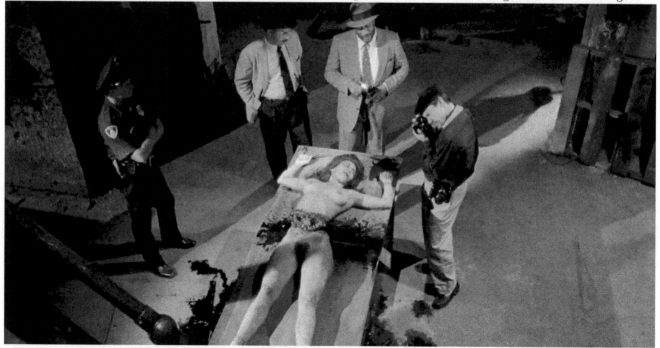

Detective Legrand (John Amos, at the head of the table) ruminates on violence as Rod (Harvey Keitel) takes photos of a murder victim; the body of the victim was cast by Tom Savini from a local stripper.

Black Cat"—it would be his first time putting together a feature without Franco Fraticelli since *Four Flies on Grey Velvet*, and as fate would have it, Fraticelli would not edit any more of the films directed by Dario Argento.

"The Facts in the Case of M. Valdemar" was first published in December 1845 in two separate publications: the *Broadway Journal* and *American Review: A Whig Journal*. The story is related by an unnamed narrator who tells of his friend Ernest Valdemar, who is dying from tuberculosis. The narrator is experimenting with hypnosis and asks Valdemar if he would consent to be hypnotized at the moment of death in order to see what might happen. Valdemar consents and within a short period, his time of death is at hand. The hypnotist puts him under a hypnotic spell, leaving him in a state of suspended animation for a matter of months. The narrator and the attending physicians continue to monitor Valdemar as his body remains inanimate and icy cold, though his spirit remains active and reports on what he is able to see in the great beyond. Valdemar begs to be put out of his misery and the narrator complies; as soon as the trance is ended, Valdemar's body finally succumbs to the several months of delayed decay.

Romero's adaptation depicts Valdemar (Bingo O'Malley) as a ruthless business tycoon with a trophy wife named Jessica (Adrienne Barbeau). Jessica conspires with her lover, Dr. Hoffmann (Ramy Zada), to keep Valdemar in a state of suspended animation in order for them to get their hands on his vast fortune.

Unfortunately, Romero's half of *Two Evil Eyes* is its Achilles heel. It starts the film off on a sour note, though in fairness, even switching the order of the stories would be problematic. It's not that it's a bad piece; it's just awfully bland. It plays out like a soap opera with some macabre elements—*Dark Shadows* for the more permissive '90s, perhaps—and while Romero works in some of his usual commentary on greed and consumerism (notably when the policeman played by Tom Atkins ([born 1935] quips, "Rich people. The sick stuff always turns out to be rich people."), it doesn't do much to overcome the overall air of déjà vu. Romero's take on the material is simply too predictable, and the finale doesn't pack nearly the same *Grand Guignol* punch as the one in Roger Corman's earlier adaptation. Barbeau (born 1945) adds some shading to her role, ensuring that she's more than just a scheming bitch, at least in the early scenes, but Zada (born 1958) is hopelessly wooden as her paramour. Overall it emerges as slick, impersonal, and blandly inoffensive—precisely the opposite of Romero's best work.

Romero would later complain that he was displeased with the final sound mix, which was completed without his direct input in Rome, while Dario would accuse him of not giving the film his full passion and enthusiasm. "I

George A. Romero and Dario Argento, reunited from the old days of *Dawn of the Dead*; *Two Evil Eyes* would prove to be an uneasy collaboration.

criticized him for not being as committed as he should have been. We attended the first screening of *Two Evil Eyes* together but then lost touch with each other for some time after that."[2] Their friendship would survive these bumps in the road, but they would never collaborate on any more projects.

No such accusations can be leveled against Dario's half of the film. The truth of the matter is, Romero simply didn't feel the same sort of passion for the project that Argento had; perhaps if he had been able to indulge

French lobby card for *Two Evil Eyes*: Detective Legrand (John Amos) orders some lunch while his colleague is about to lose hers.

The Unsane Cinema of Dario Argento

his dream to go to Italy to film, it might have inspired him more—or if his "AIDS parable" take on "The Masque of the Red Death" hadn't been shot down as too expensive. But the difference in approach between the two filmmakers is obvious from the very first images of "The Black Cat." Photographer Rod Usher (Harvey Keitel) specializes in "still life" photography—of a violent nature. He's called to a crime scene where a woman has been severed in two by a pendulum. Argento uses the same kind of fluid, prowling camerawork he had perfected in *Opera*, as the camera crawls along at floor level, observing Usher and the police as they dispassionately survey the gory crime scene. Always looking for an arresting image, Usher sets off the pendulum to get some "action shots," and naturally Argento can't resist the opportunity to strap the camera to the pendulum, providing the audience with a dizzying point of view shot of the action. The link between Usher and Dario is obvious. They're both visual stylists in their own ways, and they both focus on the macabre. It's interesting that Argento manages to consistently find unappealing—or at least deeply flawed—surrogate figures in his films. From Peter Neal in *Tenebrae* through Marco in *Opera* and Usher in "The Black Cat," the people who bear the closest resemblance to Argento as a filmmaker/artist can hardly be said to be idealized portraits of their creator.

The difference between the Argento and Romero segments isn't just down to visual flash, however. Romero's segment plays out like a workmanlike update of a respected literary property. It hits all the major points while working in some personal observations, but it generally comes off exactly as what it was, a gun-for-hire assignment. On the other hand, Argento, who had long avoided doing adaptations of other people's work (well, officially, anyway), throws himself into the task of bringing Poe to the screen with gleeful abandon. His segment is literally loaded with references to Poe's canon of work—some of the references are more obvious than others, but those who aren't in tune to the references can still enjoy the piece as a stand alone work in its own right. Those who are familiar with Poe and his output will definitely enjoy spotting all the various references, which demonstrate an obsessive, almost encyclopedic knowledge of the great writer. For Dario, "The Black Cat" isn't just a simple adaptation, it's an opportunity for him to express the love, admiration, and gratitude he had felt for so many years for his favorite author.

The story's protagonist—unnamed in the 1843 original—is named in honor of the hyper-sensitive anti-hero of "The Fall of the House of Usher." In other respects, however, Argento let it be known that the character was based on Ascher Fellig (1899-1968), who is better known as Weegee. Born in the former Austro-Hungarian Galicia, he immigrated with his family to New York in the early 1900s—at which point his name was Anglicized as either Arthur—or Usher. He became famous for his vivid, artistic portraits of crime scenes—and his distinctive voice actually inspired the voice used by Peter Sellers when he played the title role in Stanley Kubrick's *Dr. Strangelove, or: How I Learned to Stop Worrying and Love the Bomb* (1964). Though updated and embroidered-upon to suit the purposes of his own adaptation, Usher is depicted with much the same character arc as the protagonist of the original short story. His relationship with his paramour, Annabel (Madeleine Potter), initially seems positive and loving. This changes, however, when she introduces a new member to their household: a black cat. Usher tries to befriend the cat, but it is hostile in return. He develops an irrational paranoia and even objects to having it sleeping with them in the same room. "What if it decides to jump up here in the middle of the night and claw my eyes out?" It's not far removed from the old wives' tale about cats stealing the breath from people as they sleep, and it denotes a latent paranoia in Usher that starts to spiral out of control as his drinking starts to escalate.

Usher and Annabel are an awkward couple. They're both artists, but temperamentally they are polar opposites. Annabel is arty and ethereal, while

"The Black Cat" allowed Tom Savini to go wild with his special effects.

Usher comes off more like a blue-collar "manly man." It's not clear how long they've been together—long enough, apparently, for the neighbors to come to the conclusion that they're married, though Usher is quick to point out that they are not—but evidently their best years are in the rearview mirror by the time the story picks up. Usher almost seems to harbor a sick resentment towards Annabel. His dislike of the cat is less about the cat itself than what it comes to represent. Annabel treats it as if it were her child and Usher can't seem to tolerate the idea of her finding solace and joy in its presence. In one of the film's most interesting segments, he follows the cat around the house, using his fingers to simulate the framing and action of a camera, eventually cornering the terrorized creature and taking pleasure in the knowledge that he's able to intimidate it. Usher is an alcoholic and a bully, and while he is still in love with the idea of keeping Annabel at his side, the truth is he is a toxic personality and Annabel is ready to be done with him.

Sally Kirkland poses with the cat at the left, while at the right the resurrected Valdemar (Bingo O'Malley) looks for revenge.

Harvey Keitel (born 1939) is perfectly cast as Usher. His intense screen presence and ability to disappear into the skin of the characters he portrays provides Argento with one of the most perfectly realized characterizations in any of his movies. Argento and Keitel weren't necessarily a match made in heaven—Keitel is a serious "method" actor, while Argento tends to regard actors as a necessary evil—but they appear to have worked mostly harmoniously on the picture. Keitel was actually no stranger to offbeat Italian genre films—he had just recently pinch-hit for a mutinous Klaus Kinski in *Grandi Cacciatori* (shot prior to *Two Evil Eyes*, but released after it, later in 1990), taking over as the lead for part of the movie when the infamous *enfant terrible* walked out on the production—but in this instance he was on more familiar terrain, while Argento was at the disadvantage where the communication factor was concerned. Keitel's tendency to ad lib in the moment reportedly did irk Dario at times, but no matter: His performance is electrifying and galvanizes the whole piece. Without him, it's unlikely that "The Black Cat" would carry so much weight in the Argento filmography.

As Usher continues to drown himself in self-pity and copious amounts of alcohol, he progresses from childish cruelty to out-and-out sadism. Upset that his proposed book project, devoted to his crime scene photography, has been rejected, he decides to add some particularly nasty images in order to increase its appeal. One day, with Annabel out of the house, he takes a series of photographs of the cat as he tortures and eventually strangles the life out of it. Annabel is crestfallen because the cat has gone "missing," and Usher denies all knowledge. Their confrontation in the kitchen is an extraordinary piece of back and forth acting, unlike anything in any of Dario's earlier films. Usher's insolent, indignant anger boils over when Annabel accuses him of killing the cat. He feigns ignorance and trivializes her grief: "It's a fucking cat! Meow! Meow! A *cat*!" When he lashes out and slaps Annabel, she runs to her room and locks the door; Usher is forced to spend the night on the couch, where he experiences a vivid nightmare. In her book on Argento, Maitland McDonagh was cool toward "The Black Cat" as a whole, but she lavished praise on the dream sequence, arguing it was the one scene that showed off Argento's visual poetry. With all due respect, I would have to differ. The entire episode is realized with tremendous visual élan, and the dream sequence, while interesting, seems the most forced episode in the piece; it feels unduly drawn out, as if Argento was eager to expand the segment to an hour at all costs. As Usher staggers from the apartment and ends up in a field, where medieval pageantry is in full swing, the whole sequence screams, "It's a dream" in a way that feels phony and artificial. In the dream, Annabel is represented as a witch—making her connection with the cat more symbolic of the occult than might have first

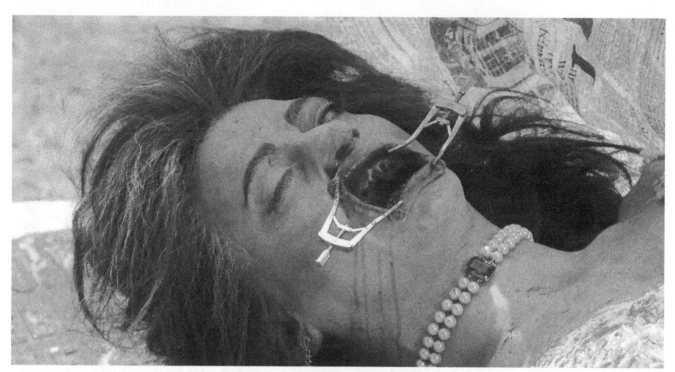

Dario's reference to Poe's "Berenice."

been apparent. She points out the strange design on the cat's chest, but Usher, like so many Argento protagonists, is unable to properly interpret the meaning of this until it is too late for him. The dream ends with him being hoisted above a stake, then dropped on top of it—the image of the stake emerging from his mouth provides Tom Savini with a chance to work his magic.

The following day, Usher is called to another crime scene. This time, a corpse has been disinterred and its teeth extracted from its mouth; the culprit is the dead woman's cousin, who is obsessed with unrequited love (a nice acting cameo for Savini, who even does his best to look like Poe). The episode is based on one of Poe's lesser known but most disturbing and poetic works, "Berenice," which was first published in 1835. The story is told from the point of view of a man, Egaeus, who is due to marry his cousin, Berenice; he becomes fixated on her teeth and when she dies unexpectedly, he digs her up and steals the teeth—though he has no memory of doing so. Unlike some of the more often-adapted works, this is a comparatively obscure story—Argento's determination to incorporate this reference into his tapestry of Poe quotations speaks volumes about his desire to do justice not just to "The Black Cat," but to the Poe canon in general.

Meanwhile, Annabel is out running errands when she passes by a bookstore advertising Usher's new book, titled "Metropolitan Horrors." The book shows off his grisly crime scene photos, as well as some startling images of her cat being tortured. Usher has finally crossed the line from depicting horrific images to staging them himself; Annabel is disgusted and frightened for her safety and decides it's time to make a clean break. Madeleine Potter (born 1958)'s performance as Annabel tends to be underrated by critics. She conveys the character's innocence while also demonstrating a strong, determined quality. Annabel is willing to put up with Usher's moodiness and his excessive drinking, but when he finally crosses the line and alienates her, she decides it's time to stop being his victim. Unfortunately for her, she has waited too long and will pay the ultimate price.

While Annabel is at home getting her things together, Usher stops at the "South of Heaven" bar, where a sexy, witch-like bartender (Sally Kirkland) engages him in some banter. He notices that she has a cat much like the one he's already killed; convinced that it's the same cat come back to devil him, he arranges to take it with him. When Usher returns home, he looks at the cat's chest—it has the same white spot, and for the first time he notices that it forms the design of a noose. Sooner than accept the sign as a foreshadowing of his own demise, he tries to outwit fate by strangling the cat with a cord; Annabel hears the commotion and intervenes, only to end up being killed herself. Annabel's death carries real weight in the film—partly because of the gruesome effects engineered by Savini (the image of her hand sliced open by a meat cleaver as Usher takes out his frustrations on her is particularly nasty), but largely because her character is established as such a sweet and positive presence. She is everything that Usher is not; as such, he can't abide the idea of her leaving and enjoying a happy, serene existence away from him. Sooner than allow her to flourish on her own, Usher would much rather snuff her out for good. It's his selfishness and his willful desire for self-destruction which propels the narrative, whereas she is collateral damage.

The noise of the music Usher has blaring on his stereo to cover up his activities arouses the ire of his elderly neighbor, Mr. Pym (Martin Balsam), who comes over to complain. Pym, of course, is a reference to *The Narrative of Arthur Gordon Pym of Nantucket* (1838), which remains Poe's only completed novel. However, it's the casting of Balsam (1919-1996) which is most significant in this context. He is best remembered to many viewers for playing the role of the ill-fated private investigator, Arbogast, in Hitchcock's *Psycho* (1960); his death on the staircase is one of the film's most celebrated set pieces. Argento plays on this cinematic association by having Pym mount a similar-looking set of stairs when he comes in to Usher's house to see what's going on; in a reversal of expectations, Argento allows the old man to live when Usher is able to make his excuses and get him to leave without incident. It's a minor sequence in the big scheme of things, but it's notable for Argento's playful use of cinematic references and in-jokes.

In order to cover up what has taken place, Usher takes a page out of Poe and walls up Annabel's body; this inevitably recalls the walled-up body in *Deep Red*, as well, though of course Argento was also thinking of Poe when he wrote that particular incident. With Annabel's body safely interred, he stages an elaborate ruse to fool the neighbors. He rigs up a dummy with a photo portrait of Annabel's face and drives by the neighbors, making it look as if they're going on a vacation. The use of the dummy and the photograph is a clever commentary on the illusory nature of the cinematic medium—a practice with which Argento was already well familiar by this time. When Usher returns from their "trip," he tells everybody that Annabel has accepted an offer to go on tour (she's a violinist) and that she may be gone for some time.

Unburdened by matters of conscience, Usher continues to go about his daily life, but some friends of Annabel get suspicious and the police are summoned. Detective Legrand (John Amos) is already familiar with Usher from the crime scenes they've covered together, but beneath their exterior of friendly banter, there's a certain degree of nervous tension—much like the banter between Peter Neal and Germani in *Tenebrae*, in fact. Legrand is depicted as a cynical sort, always ready to make crude jokes about the horrible crimes he is covering, but he proves to be a capable and intelligent investigator. Usher apparently satisfies him that everything is normal and above board, but as Legrand leaves, he can't resist a bit of grand standing: "What did you expect to find between these solidly put-together walls?" It's exactly

Italian lobby card: Madeleine Potter at the left, while the army of the dead in Romero's segment is given too-close scrutiny at the right.

the same mocking comment spoken by the character in Poe's story, and of course it proves to be his undoing; Legrand realizes that Usher is bluffing and hangs around long enough to hear an awful noise coming from upstairs. Legrand's junior officer locates where the noise is coming from and tears down the wall erected by Usher—uncovering Annabel's rotting corpse, and the mutated kittens birthed by the black cat, which was also accidentally walled up with her. Legrand manages to get a handcuff on Usher, who suddenly turns violent and tries to escape; he kills Legrand and his assistant, but he's unable to get free from the cuffs. The neighbors, roused by the commotion, start pounding on the front door and Usher makes a feeble attempt at fleeing before accidentally hanging himself—the symbol on the cat's chest therefore proves to be a self-fulfilling prophecy of sorts.

"The Black Cat" is one of Argento's finest pieces of work, but for whatever reason it seldom gets the respect it deserves. It could be that the film's anthology format is to blame. Romero's opening story gets the film off

Spanish lobby card: Rod (Harvey Keitel) attempts to dispose of Detective Legrand.

The Unsane Cinema of Dario Argento

Rod (Harvey Keitel) plots his next move.

on the wrong foot, and by the time Argento's segment rolls around a lot of viewers have already checked out mentally. This is indeed a great pity, as it shows him at the peak of his game. The story is a fascinating study in self-destruction as a selfish and paranoid sociopath succumbs to his baser instincts and destroys almost everything he touches. His opening comment in the voice over narration is telling: "Perversity is one of the prime impulses of the heart." Usher doesn't go down the rabbit hole of violence and murder in order to save himself; instead, he's motivated by a perverse desire to destroy himself—and rather than just commit suicide, he'd sooner prolong the agony and take everybody else along with him. Keitel's expert performance anchors the film in psychological reality, while the supporting performances are also nicely judged. The use of camerawork is almost as audacious as it had been in *Opera*, making nonsense of the notion that Argento had his artistic wings clipped by the mechanics of the American movie-making system.

Interestingly, while Pittsburgh native Romero elects to set his segment in an anonymous cityscape, Argento uses the Gothic architecture and signposts of the city to make it clear that his story is set in Pittsburgh. The images are frequently arresting and the effect is nicely underlined by Pino Donaggio's (born 1941) insistent soundtrack; Donaggio had become Brian De Palma's composer of choice after the death of Bernard Herrmann in 1975, and he would return to score *The Sect*, *Trauma*, and *Do You Like Hitchcock?* for Argento, as well. The presence of a more conventional soundtrack marks a break from the "mix and match" approach used to score *Phenomena*, *Opera*, the *Demons* films, and *The Church*, but Donaggio's music is by no means lacking in imagination; his themes are alternately seductive and nerve-jangling, evoking the approach of Ennio Morricone in Argento's first three films.

Thus, "The Black Cat" isn't quite as in-your-face or aggressive as the Argento films which preceded it, but this hardly means that it is a step back for him, artistically. If anything, it shows him telling a far more controlled and coherent narrative than had been the norm over his past couple of films, and it also works very well as a psychological character study. Coming in at around an hour in length, it is generally smoothly paced and only the slightly overbaked dream sequence threatens to throw off its momentum. If only the first half had been realized with greater vigor, chances are *Two Evil Eyes* would be far better regarded by the fans; as it is, it's often viewed—erroneously—as a major miscalculation on Argento's part. In truth, from a commercial perspective, it *was* a miscalculation of sorts; but now that the dust has settled, it should hopefully be easier to reflect on "The Black Cat" and recognize and celebrate its many virtues.

Two Evil Eyes received its Italian theatrical release on January 25, 1990. The early numbers were promising—in early February it was still in the top 10 at the Italian box office, holding its own against the likes of *When Harry Met Sally* and *Sea of Love* (both 1989)[3]—but it ended up sinking like a stone. It was Argento's first bona fide flop at the Italian box office since *Le cinque giornate*, ranking at number 49 for the 1989-1990 box-office season; that was just enough to put it ever-so-slightly ahead of Eddie Murphy's flop *Harlem Nights* (1989), which came in at 50, but it was a very poor showing indeed compared to the likes of Steven Spielberg's *Indiana Jones and the Last Crusade* (1989) and *Dead Poets Society* (1989), which claimed the number one and number two slots, respectively.[4] In the U.S., a small outfit named Taurus Entertainment put it out on a limited run in October of that year, but it barely made a ripple; Argento's plan to conquer the American market was not off to a good start. On the plus side, the picture was not massively expensive—the budget was in the $9 million range—so it certainly recouped its investment, but it wasn't the sort of major box-office hit Dario and Claudio had been hoping for, either. It would eventually make its

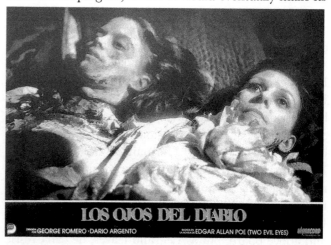

Spanish lobby card, showing some carnage that didn't make its way into the finished film.

way to France in 1992, but in most markets, once more, it was consigned to direct-to-video status.

Richard Harrington reviewed the film for *The Washington Post*, and he summed up the major problem with the film quite nicely:

> The movie's called *Two Evil Eyes*, but one *Evil Eye* is clearly better than the other. […] 'The Black Cat' has more visual shocks in its first minute than Romero's entire segment. […] But where Romero goes for the cheap, linear approach, Argento's storytelling is painfully poetic, with ever-shifting points of view and asides. […] There's a madness in Argento's approach and it's always appropriate.[5]

The unnamed reviewer for *TV Guide* was less impressed, awarding the film two out of four stars:

> [T]hough technically impressive, *Two Evil Eyes* amounts to less than the sum of its parts. Each director wrote his own screenplay (Argento with Franco Ferrini), but both had problems fleshing out the source material […] Argento's trademark visual flamboyance is nowhere in evidence. While far from the worst adaptation of Poe's work (there are so many candidates for that dubious honor it's hard to know where to start) *Two Evil Eyes* breaks no new ground.[6]

While *Two Evil Eyes* proved to be a disappointment in some respects, it didn't appear to slow Argento's momentum significantly. Back in 1988, he had received a script from the writer Gianni Romoli (born 1949), which dealt with a fanatical religious sect. The script landed on his desk thanks to Romoli's relationship with the Cecchi Goris, but Argento disliked it and elected to pass on it. Then in 1989, following the release of *The Church*, and during the protracted pre-production on *Two Evil Eyes*, he started having second thoughts. He contacted Romoli and told him that he thought the script had potential, though it also needed a great deal of work. It wasn't a project he was particularly interested in directing himself, but he was keen to give Michele Soavi another picture as a reward for how well *The Church* had turned out. While Soavi had been drafted in fairly late in the game on *The Church*, this time he would be involved early on—and he let it be known to Dario that if he was going to direct, he expected to be given a freer hand than he had been on *The Church*. Dario no longer had any uncertainties as to his abilities, so he readily agreed. The script for *The Sect* (*La setta*) would be a proper collaboration between

Italian *locandina* for *Two Evil Eyes*; artwork by Enzo Sciotti.

all three men, all of whom brought different things to the project. Argento introduced the 1970s prologue and the concept of the motorcycle gang that was somehow connected with the sect, while Romoli and Soavi worked in tandem to provide the rest of the story. The final result was a very strange and decidedly arty witches brew, a sort of nasty amalgamation of a fairy tale world crossed with *Rosemary's Baby* (1968) and *The Wicker Man* (1973), though the finished film is very much its own thing.

Production on *The Sect* got under way on September 20, 1990, almost exactly one year after Dario wrapped "The Black Cat" in Pittsburgh. Unlike *Two Evil Eyes*, *The Sect* was very much a European affair, with location

Italian poster for *The Sect*; artist unknown.

filming in Frankfurt followed by location work in the Marino Hills and studio work at De Paolis. By all accounts, filming proceeded smoothly enough and while Argento was still prone to looking over Soavi's shoulder, the young director felt a good deal more confident this time around. "I no longer give a shit if Dario lurks around on the set. I'm not paranoid anymore about him creating tension, putting the crew on edge because he's the *maestro* or offering me advice that I might not take."[7]

The Sect marked a period of transition for Argento. It would be the last of his productions to be edited by Franco Fraticelli. Fraticelli had been a part of Argento's filmmaking family since *The Bird with the Crystal Plumage*, and his expert insight into pacing and cutting would have a major impact on Argento's style as a filmmaker. Sadly, as is so often the case, his contributions have not been fully appreciated bya great deal of fans, many of whom tend to discount or at the very least undervalue the work of behind the scenes technicians such as editors. Argento would go on to work with several different editors in the following years, but none of them were as vital a part of his filmmaking as Fraticelli had been; he would continue to remain active (notably serving as editor on Michele Soavi's hit *Dellamorte Dellamore/Cemetery Man*, 1993) until retiring in the early 2000s—he died in 2012 at the age of 83. Speaking of Michele Soavi, he, too, would move on from the Argento camp following this picture. He found the experience of directing *The Sect* to be a lot less stressful and frustrating than *The Church* had been, but like Lamberto Bava before him, he felt that his contributions weren't always properly credited and appreciated—and he decided it was best to make a clean break than have his personal relationship with Dario suffer as a result. Argento would never find another assistant with the same flair and eagerness to experiment, and arguably his work would begin to suffer because of it. For the time being, however, he still had reason to be optimistic that there was new ground to explore and conquer.

California, 1970: a hippie commune is decimated by a motorcycle gang led by a man named Damon (Tomas Arana). Germany, 1991: a schoolteacher named Miriam (Kelly Curtis) nearly runs over a mysterious old man, Moebius Kelly (Herbert Lom). She takes him back to her place so that he can rest. That night, the old man ventures into the basement, where he opens a strange portal. It turns out that he's connected with a strange religious sect which has been claiming victims all over Europe. Unbeknown to Miriam, she has a special connection to the old man, and she finds herself immersed in some strange goings on as various people connected to her start dying. The sect is determined to use Miriam to help bring forth the living Anti-Christ. Damon and his gang arrive to help Moebius Kelly and his followers to accomplish their goal, but Miriam fights back and does not make it easy for them.

The great Herbert Lom relishes his last really meaty big screen role as Moebius.

Miriam (Kelly Curtis) under attack.

From the opening panning shot following insects as they dance over a stream, accompanied by the sounds of "A Horse with No Name" on the soundtrack, Soavi again demonstrates a keen understanding of visual poetry. *The Sect* is a longer, more rambling and occasionally more frustrating film than *The Church*—but it is also absolutely unique and filled to the brim with imagination and audacious ideas. It seems clear that the director's taste for quirky detail—including a fetishistic fascination with the inner-workings of devices, something he surely learned from Dario—got the better of him this time around, as the somewhat muddled script is stretched well beyond its breaking point. That said, it would be unfair to sum it up as a disappointment. While it definitely overstays its welcome, it is realized with such a poetic sensibility that it manages to succeed in spite of its excesses.

The theme of rebirth and fertility is ever-present as Soavi uses the floating seeds of the May blossom as a recurring visual motif—and it is also evident in the more esoteric Celtic visual symbolism of the blue ribbons which crop up with unexplained regularity. The atmosphere is deliberately dreamy and eerie, and despite a few moments of gore (such as the opening attack on the hippie commune, or the murder of a woman who has her heart ripped out by her assassin), Soavi again demonstrates an interest in mood and atmosphere as opposed to engineering cheap shock effects. Kelly Curtis (born 1956), the older sister of Jamie Lee Curtis, makes for a quirky and likable heroine, while the imposing Herbert Lom (1917-2012) shines in his last really good role for the big screen. Pino Donaggio contributes another powerful soundtrack and the cinematography by Raffaele Mertes (born 1959) evidently impressed Dario, as he would hire him to photograph his next picture as a director, *Trauma*. The best word to describe the film is "oneiric," and in many respects it sets the stage for Soavi's finest genre work, *Dellamorte Dellamore*, as the two films share a similar preoccupation with lonely, isolated characters and a mounting sense of surrealistic, almost existential dread.

Unfortunately, the film almost collapses under the weight of its ambitions. At nearly two hours, it goes on for a good 20 minutes too long, and the subplots involving Miriam's luckless friends often feel like filler material. While Soavi and Argento had clashed on the editing of *The Church*, it seems as if there were no such stand-offs during the making of this picture; it might have been better if there had been. Despite its sometimes-clunky narrative, *The Sect* offers further proof of Soavi's superior aesthetic sensibility as well as his playful sense of humor. A sequence in which Miriam's pet rabbit watches TV, using its paws to switch the channels from an old monster movie to a cheesy TV magician (played by Soavi himself) pulling a rabbit out of his top hat, is one of the quirkiest and most disarmingly charming digressions to be found in an Italian genre film. Nevertheless, it manages to deliver the goods where needed. Lom's patriarch figure is truly creepy and the scenes of the sect tearing

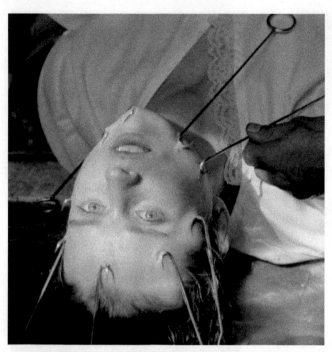

The cult practices horrific rituals in *The Sect*.

the face from one poor victim and using the flesh in their ceremony is skin-crawling stuff. It's not all doom and gloom, however, as Miriam proves to be another character like Suzy in *Suspiria* or Jennifer in *Phenomena*. Her transition from implicitly virginal naïf to resourceful woman of action is handled nicely by Curtis and Soavi, and evil does not prove to be triumphant in the end.

The Sect opened in Italy on March 1, 1991, where it proved to be a box-office disappointment. It ultimately came in 88th in the 1990-1991 box-office season in Italy, outgrossing the likes of Wes Craven's *Shocker* (1989) and Joe Dante's *Gremlins 2: The New Batch* (1990), but comparing very poorly with Kevin Costner's Oscar-winning *Dances with Wolves* (1990), which came in at number one.[8] There were some compensations to be had with regards to foreign TV and video sales, but once again the film ended up being denied theatrical exhibition in most areas—it played at a few festivals and drew intrigued, if sometimes baffled notices, but it was becoming painfully obvious that Argento's commercial cachet was no longer what it had been. Chances are, if he had decided to return to Italy and continue his association with the Cecchi Goris, he might have been doing himself a favor—but he still had the misguided notion of forging ahead in America. There would be talk of further co-productions between them in the future, but the Cecchi Gori empire collapsed amid scandal and bankruptcy—and for a period of time, the fate of the films they co-produced with Argento seemed unclear, as the rights to them remained a tangled mess for some time before they were finally ironed out and *Opera*, *The Church*, and *The Sect* found new life on home video in remastered Blu-ray editions.

But we are getting ahead of our story. For the time being, Argento was still sold on the idea that he needed to find an "in" to winning over the all-important American film market. The problems with this idea were many and varied; Luigi Cozzi put it best when he said that in Italy, Argento's name carries real weight and inspires reverence, whereas in the States he was seen as just another oddball genre director. John Carpenter, Argento's friend and colleague in the American horror scene, has repeatedly commented on the snobby attitude towards genre cinema in this country; as he has said on more than one occasion, in the eyes of most American critics, horror is just a small step above pornography. Argento wasn't really working entirely in the horror genre, per se, of course—many of his films were thrillers, after all. And yet they're thrillers with a macabre sensibility; by default, they come off as horror films. As a commercial artist, Dario had enjoyed a long and prosperous run in Italy—he was continuing to make movies, too, that were still being played on theater screens… they weren't getting meaningful distribution outside of Italy, perhaps, but that was still a lot more than most of Argento's contemporaries were managing during this tumultuous period. Sooner than sit back and count his blessings, Argento elected to take another chance by making a proper *giallo* on American soil. Granted, other *gialli* had been partially filmed in the U.S., including Argento's own *Tenebrae*, which had some location material in New York. And there were certainly plenty of American films which seemed to be directly inspired by the example set by directors like Argento and Mario Bava—from Carpenter's *Halloween* (1978) and Sean S. Cunningham's *Friday the 13th* (1980) to any number of stylish psycho-sexual thrillers from Brian De Palma. Argento's next project, however, would be the first true-blue (or yellow, if you prefer) *giallo* to be made entirely in America.

Notes:
1. Argento, Dario, *Peur* (France: Rouge Profond, 2018), p. 289.
2. Argento, Dario, *Fear* (Godalming: FAB Press, 2019), p. 236.
3. *Variety*, February 21 1990, p. 19.
4. http://www.hitparadeitalia.it/bof/boi/boi1989-90.htm
5. Harrington, Richard, "Two Evil Eyes," *The Washington Post*, December 9 1991.
6. https://www.tvguide.com/movies/two-evil-eyes/review/128146/
7. Jones, Alan, *Dario Argento: The Man, the Myths & the Magic* (Godalming: FAB Press, 2012), p. 205.
8. http://www.hitparadeitalia.it/bof/boi/boi1990-91.htm

Chapter Sixteen:
Personal and Professional Tragedy

Soon after the release of *The Sect*, Argento approached Franco Ferrini and Gianni Romoli with a nebulous idea. He wanted to make a thriller with a character who suffered from anorexia. Dario had some personal experience with eating disorders, which he traced to his complex relationship with his mother, so the plot point definitely had a special resonance for him. It was also a problem for Dario's stepdaughter, Anna—the product of Daria's first marriage—and he was keen to try and bring more attention to and shed some light on the condition, even if it was in the context of a thriller narrative. The initial heavy lifting was done by Ferrini and Romoli, who struggled to find a suitable narrative. It finally clicked into place when they decided to look back to Argento's past success *Deep Red* for inspiration; their story borrowed from the earlier masterpiece and offered up a similar blend of offbeat romance and gory thrills, at which point Argento decided it would be best to work with an American writer to develop the final screenplay. Romoli was particularly incensed by this perceived slight, but he took solace in a fruitful and financially rewarding a string of collaborations with Lamberto Bava (for whom he penned the enormously successful *Fantaghirò* films for the Italian TV market), as well as a repeat engagement with Michele Soavi on *Dellamorte Dellamore*.

To help adapt the script for the American market, Argento turned to the accomplished author T.E.D. Klein (born 1947). Klein was not a prolific author—at the time of working with Argento, he had only published one novel and a collection of short stories—but his work was outstanding, and he was also well-regarded due to his work as editor on the *Twilight Zone* magazine from 1981 until 1985. Even so, he was an odd choice in that he had never written a screenplay before; he was also only somewhat familiar with Argento's work as a director. As Klein explains in comments reproduced elsewhere in this book, his agent was approached by Argento, who provided the writer with a screen treatment. At this stage, the project's title was *Aura's Enigma*—and in its original version, it was extremely gory indeed. Klein didn't particularly care for the over-the-top violence, and since Argento was actively trying to curry favor in the American market, Dario decided to cut back on that aspect; as time went on, he found himself being pressured to cut it back further and further, much to his dismay.

Klein even went so far as to accompany Dario to Pittsburgh in the early part of 1992, where he was considering filming once again. While in Pittsburgh, he paid a visit to Tom Savini, his make-up effects wizard on *Two Evil Eyes*, and persuaded him to work on the picture; at this stage, there was still a lot more in the way of elaborate gore and make-up effects planned for the picture, so Savini enthusiastically signed on. As it happens, Savini was at work on John Landis' vampire movie *Innocent Blood* at the time, and when Landis got word that Argento was in town, he asked Savini to get Dario to come down to visit them on location. When he arrived, Landis asked him if he'd like to a do a brief cameo appearance in the movie, and Argento immediately said yes; he ended up playing a creepy-looking paramedic who attends to an ailing Don Rickles in one scene.

Dario makes a comical cameo appearance as an EMT in John Landis' *Innocent Blood.*

Pittsburgh was soon mooted in favor of New Orleans, but for budgetary reasons the location was changed once more to Minneapolis, Minnesota. Klein was crestfallen by the change, describing it as "one of the least atmospheric cities in America," and he was further dispirited when the budget started to shrink, and the more elaborate sequences started to fall by the wayside. Argento had already dealt with script changes dictated by budgetary concerns on *Opera*, of course, but that was still a big and elaborate production; *Aura's Enigma*, however, would look positively diminutive by comparison. To produce the movie, Dario sought assistance from other production companies. ADC took care of a third of the budget, with Italian distributor Penta putting up another third in exchange for the Italian theatrical rights; the American-based Overseas Group took care of the balance and the production was finally up and ready to go in the summer of 1992. In a repeat of his experience making an ad for

Fiat back in 1987, Dario decided to "limber up" for the assignment by accepting a job directing a commercial for the Johnson Wax company in Italy; the gig gave him a chance to try out a new piece of equipment which would enable him to simulate a butterfly's point of view in his new thriller. Unlike the Fiat ad, however, this one is not so easy for the Argento completest to track down and it doesn't appear to be in circulation any longer.

Trauma (as the project came to be known) started filming on August 3, 1992, and the production would continue to be beset with budgetary woes and script changes. The most significant aspect of the filming proved to be the casting of Dario's youngest daughter, Asia, in the central role. Asia had a tumultuous childhood, thanks to the fighting and drama that went on between Dario and Daria, and she ended up living in Daria's home—but with Daria preoccupied with her film and theater engagements, she often felt as if she had been cast aside by her parents. Unlike her older half-sister Fiore, who has always spoken with love and reverence for her father, Asia would go on record stating that she felt like she was unwanted; in her mind, Dario favored Fiore, while Daria favored Anna, leaving Asia pretty much out in the cold. This instilled a deeply anti-authoritarian mentality in

Full page ad for Overseas Filmgroup in *Variety*, May 4, 1992—with a reference to their upcoming release of *Trauma*.

Asia from an early age and she proved to be a handful—she was as stubborn and outspoken as her parents, and she was also incredibly headstrong and determined. She had already appeared in two films produced by her father, *Demons 2* and *The Church*, but *Trauma* would be her first time being directed by Dario. It was an intimidating and frightening experience—yet by her own reckoning, it was the first time she felt a genuine connection with her famous father. "I can't remember too much about my father until I was eight. Up until that point he used to tell me that all kids smelt of shit and so he couldn't be bothered with them. [...] It was only when I started working with my father that a strong bond formed between us. That's when I really got to know him. But my unusual childhood did make me a strong character so I'm not complaining."[1] Despite the distance she felt in her personal relationship with Dario, Asia admired him as an artist and was desperate to work with him. "The day he offered me *Trauma* was one of the happiest days of my life," she later told Alan Jones.[2]

As far as Dario was concerned, it was an exciting collaboration; he saw star potential in his daughter, and he knew she had the talent to pull off the difficult character that she was expected to play. This was no small supporting role, either. If her performance didn't work, it would effectively sink the movie. All things considered, for as frustrating and financially devastating as the movie ultimately proved to be, it marked the beginning of an exciting new chapter for Dario and Asia—both as father and daughter and as director and muse. The excitement they felt wasn't lost on the crew, either. Tom Savini would later recall, "It was great to see Dario and Asia's relationship blossom on *Trauma*. It was the perfect artistic relationship between father and daughter that I could see."[3]

Despite the warmth and excitement generated by the collaboration between Dario and Asia, *Trauma* proved to be an overall disappointing experience. Argento's original plan had been to make his goriest *giallo* to date—but in an effort to satisfy the American co-producers, he agreed to tone the violence down—way down, in fact. This was disappointing in turn for Tom Savini, who was eagerly anticipating filming certain scenes which ended up being dropped. T.E.D. Klein was concerned by all the cuts to the script and suggested an elaborate opening which would hopefully make better sense of the mystery; Argento loved his idea (which Klein outlines in his interview later in this book) but there was no way to make it financially feasible. *Trauma* was Argento's first film in many years to really suffer from a cash-flow problem, and he also found himself in the vulnerable position of working with a lot of unfamiliar faces in an unfamiliar land. The respect he had earned among his Italian colleagues was notably absent, and he found himself having to justify including things that he'd never had to squabble over in the past. Even with regards to casting the film, he faced opposition due to the violence and mayhem—he would later recall being told that American actresses wouldn't participate in the sort of scenes he was dreaming up, which left him more than a bit flummoxed.

The filming finally wrapped on September 26, 1992, at which point Argento found himself working with a new editor, an American named Bennett Goldberg. The Italian version, which runs approximately five minutes longer, is credited to Goldberg and to Argento himself—it was the only time in Dario's career that he took such a credit. The differences between the two edits boil down to a few extra dialogue scenes; obviously the American producers regarded them as extraneous, while Dario elected to include them in his cut, for example an added phone call between characters David and Aura, Aura running into Dr. Judd at the Farmer's Market, and David trying to outwit the clerk at the hotel where one of the victims-to-be is in hiding. To score the picture, Argento selected Pino Donaggio—who had also composed the scores for *Two Evil Eyes* and *The Sect*. Donaggio provided a playful score full of riffs on Bernard Herrmann's classic scores for Alfred Hitchcock, but the fans who thrilled to Argento's use of prog rock and heavy metal found his more traditional approach somewhat lacking in color and imagination. It soon became apparent that the film was in serious trouble. It was simply too weird to work for a mainstream American audience, yet it was also a little too sedate and restrained to really appeal to the hardcore Argento audience. Co-producer Robbie Little (1945-2018) got on Dario's nerves by pressuring him to lay off the gore, then by complaining that the film could have used a bit more of the red stuff. Argento was furious and felt as if he had been misled. "It's true what they say about the American movie business—no one knows anything!"[4]

Following the opening credits, there's a brief, enigmatic scene featuring the French Revolution—in the form of a child's toy diorama. A rebel is sentenced to death and is summarily decapitated. The way Argento gets his camera into the action recalls the fetishistic views of childhood objects in *Deep Red*—and as it happens, the film contains many other echoes of that film as well. From there, the action cuts to a city street in the midst of a violent storm. Georgia Jackson (Isabell Monk), a chiropractor, is visited by a new client. She asks the client whether they've ever met before, but the client doesn't answer. The use of subjective camerawork is enough to tip the audience that the client is not what he appears to be—and in not trusting

Behind the scenes glimpse of Asia Argento during the filming of the scene where she witnesses her parents' murder. Courtesy Carla Alonzo.

her gut instincts, Georgia is quickly dispatched. The killer uses a hammer to stun her, then produces a small "electric guillotine" device which is used to decapitate the victim. The killing emphasizes the character's confusion and pain as opposed to welters of blood and gore; this will remain the case for the bulk of the film, which generally eschews graphic violence. While Dario had said early on that he intended to go for broke with the blood, he would later change his tune and say that he decided that the shock effects would clash with the more human story he was looking to tell. Of course, the reality is that the American producers kept a close watch on the violent content and Argento simply wasn't in a position to go for broke as he had originally intended. This is one of the aspects which has made many fans deem *Trauma* to be a failure, but this is hardly fair to the film or indeed to Argento himself. There's more to his films than blood and gore and in de-emphasizing the blood, he doesn't present a film that's lacking in other departments as well. In many respects it's as fluid and cinematic as its direct predecessors, but to hear many of the fans tell it, the film could have been directed by anybody; it's an absurd position, of course, one which is not supported by the movie itself. Georgia's death is capped by a strange, poetic coda. As opera music blares

The Unsane Cinema of Dario Argento

Aura's mother Adriana Petrescu (Piper Laurie) holds a séance in *Trauma*.

on the soundtrack, the killer frees a lizard which is kept in a cage in the chiropractor's office; the symbolism of the beast being freed from its captivity is in keeping with the ending of *Opera*, where the natural world is emblematic of peace and tranquility, while man-made cages represent the worst aspects of society.

From there, the action shifts to a young man, David Parsons (Christopher Rydell), who notices a teen runaway perched on a bridge, apparently ready to kill herself. David intervenes and talks the girl into coming with him for something to eat. David learns that she is Aura Petrescu (Asia Argento), the daughter of Hungarian immigrants, and that she has escaped from the Faraday Clinic—which specializes in the treatment of eating disorders. David sees some needle marks on her arm and assumes that she is a drug addict; he is a recovering addict himself, so he offers to try and help her. Aura, who demonstrates a headstrong and fiercely independent spirit, assures him that he has the wrong idea. As is so often the case in Argento's films, the characters are at cross-purposes, as visual information is observed but interpreted incorrectly. The needle marks in her arms don't denote drug use. They're the scars of the horrific treatment she has been undergoing at the clinic. Aura isn't interested in being "saved," so she breaks free from David—only to end up in the arms of Child Protective Services.

Aura's return to her home marks the film's most overtly theatrical and eccentric stretch of running time. The house itself is a looming Gothic structure and Donaggio's music hammers home the Hitchcock connections for all its worth. And then there are her parents, professional mediums Stefan (Dominque Serrand) and Adriana Petrescu (Piper Laurie). Though introduced as Hungarian immigrants, they basically behave like stereotypically flamboyant Italians; it's hard to believe that Argento wasn't aware of this himself, or that by casting Asia in the role of Aura, he wasn't trying to depict his own dysfunctional family life on screen. Aura is convinced that the doctors at the clinic are trying to kill her, and her relationship with her parents is strained. Her father is more loving, whereas her mother is too involved in her own personal drama to give her much notice. That night, they are hosting a big séance, and Adriana can't be bothered to give any time to Aura and her problems, so she has Stefan lock the girl into her room.

The séance is probably the film's big standout sequence. The various eccentrics—a strange young man hoping to connect with his late mother, a neurotic young woman, a doddering old lady who can barely walk, etc.—make for a very strange audience, and stranger still is the medium herself. Adriana presides over the proceedings with an arch, imperious quality. She is completely disconnected from the feelings and desires of her clientele and she runs the entire proceedings as if it were some kind of theatrical performance—which, in many respects, it really is. The *Deep Red* connection is obvious, and it becomes more so as the scene unfolds. Argento's use of restless camerawork manifests itself in the various sharp camera moves, and as he isolates various weird details in stylized close-ups; as the séance unfolds and the "spirits" take hold, he even presents what can only be described as a "spirit's eye view," as the camera weaves and makes its way in to a close-up of Adriana as she holds court. She perceives an unclean presence, just as Helga Ulmann had done in *Deep Red*: "I'm the only one who knows ... the killer is ... *present!*" In classic horror movie style, just as Adriana makes this theatrical statement, the lights go out and all hell breaks loose. She runs out into the storm that is raging outside and Stefan follows after her; Aura, observing this from her room, climbs down from the bedroom window and runs after them. She makes a horrific discovery when she finds their bodies in the field—and when she looks up,

Tom Savini's severed head props of Piper Laurie and Dominique Serrand. Courtesy of Carla Alonzo.

Asia Argento as Aura Petrescu, recreating her mom Daria Nicolodi's iconic screaming in the rain scene from *Tenebrae*, in *Trauma*.

she observes a mysterious figure holding their severed heads in front of his face. Aura is only able to catch a brief glimpse of this, illuminated by a lightning flash, and she will continue to struggle with this image as she tries desperately to figure out the killer's identity. This entire stretch of film is realized with tremendous vigor and visual imagination; the criticism that the film lacks Argento's signature style is simply not supported by the film itself.

Aura is taken in for questioning by the police, but she manages to break free and seek out David, hoping that he might still be interested in helping her. Aura and David are arguably the most appealing pair of protagonists in an Argento film since Marcus and Gianna in *Deep Red*. This film, too, turns into a love story—but it's a very different type of a love story, to be sure. For one thing, Aura is only 16 years old; we're never told David's age, but we can conclude that he's probably in his mid-20s. This reveals a very European mentality with regards to sex and sexuality, as their growing romance is not depicted in a leering or lascivious way by Argento. They're both psychologically scarred—the result, it is implied, of their fractured childhood. David is a recovering drug addict, while Aura is wrestling with anorexia. David is also another in a long line of Argento protagonists who is an emotionally vulnerable artist. He works as a graphic designer for a local news station.

He and Aura are both basically alone in the world and they turn to each other for solace and warmth. David's ongoing relationship with a local news anchor, Grace Harrington (Laura Johnson), is depicted as cold and cynical; she uses him for sex but is far too narcissistic to be available to him on a truly emotional level. David

Anne (Daria Nicolodi) screams her head off in the rain in *Tenebrae*'s final, unforgettable image.

yearns for that feeling of being connected and he ultimately finds it in Aura. Aura, whose young life has been marked by emotional abuse and horrible violence, ultimately learns to trust people again thanks to David's selfless attempts to help save her from self-destruction. While Usher in "The Black Cat" is determined to destroy himself, Aura's suicidal leanings are an outgrowth of her miserable home life; once she finds love and compassion in David, these tendencies disappear, and she becomes a happier and more stable person. Thus, *Trauma* emerges as Argento's most "positive" *giallo* by far. It tells a dark story, but it centers on a very positive character arc as David and Aura essentially save themselves from oblivion through their love. Unlike the "battle of the

Asia Argento and Christopher Rydell prepare for a scene while Dario appears lost in thought.

sexes" which fuels the Marcus/Gianna dynamic in *Deep Red*, there is mutual respect between Aura and David. They collaborate as equals and together they manage to unravel the mystery. The performances of Asia and Christopher Rydell (born 1963) are absolutely central to the film's effectiveness. For one thing, they work very well together, and this is essential to preserving the sweetness of their relationship; if this hadn't come off more convincingly, the whole idea of a partnership such as this could have appeared either ludicrous or sleazy or even both. Rydell's film career never really seemed to take off, which is a shame; he's absolutely convincing and utterly winning as David. As for Asia, this was her first starring role for her father—though not her first leading role altogether, as she had already top-lined *Close Friends/ Le amiche del cuore* (1989) for Michele Placido—and it presented her with some major challenges. In addition to the character's darker elements, it also required her to act in English—with a Hungarian accent. She even speaks Hungarian a few times in moments of stress. She responds with a performance that is every bit as good as that of Rydell; Aura is a tricky character in some respects, but Asia makes her somebody worth rooting for, and she never stumbles. Some critics have expressed concern over the scene in which she bares her breasts for the camera, but it pays to remember that, on the set, Dario and Asia are director and actress—not father and daughter. The scene itself is not gratuitous as it underlines both the character's self-loathing with regards to her burgeoning sexuality as well as David's growing attraction to her; it's not presented in a way that seems sleazy, though inevitably it does make some viewers feel a little uncomfortable.

The quirkiest facet of the film is a seemingly disconnected subplot involving a precocious little boy, Gabriel Pickering (Cory Garvin), who lives next door to the murderer. His scenes are played for sly comedy, a tone reinforced by Donaggio's whimsical music. At various points we see him watching the house, spying on its mysterious resident in much the same way a James Stewart in Hitchcock's *Rear Window* (1954). The character's name, Pickering, is an H.P. Lovecraft reference; Professor Pickering, in the series of sonnets collectively known as "Fungi from Yuggoth" (1929-1930), is also an observer, though his specialty is outer space.

The scenes with Cory appear to be a strange, pointless digression for much of the film, but that character ends up playing a surprising role in the film's finale. The child is fascinated with the natural world, insects in particular, and Argento even indulges in a bit of "butterfly point of view" action, recalling the celebrated raven point of view scene in *Opera*. He also plays into the film's running theme with regards to the disconnect between parents and their children; Cory is often left alone while his mother is busy at work and in being left unsupervised for long stretches, he is placed in danger. The bland suburban neighborhood is the perfect front for the killer, as it's precisely the sort of neighborhood where bad things couldn't possibly take place.

David continues to wrestle with concern over Aura's anorexia; like so many people, he has no idea how common the condition really is. As noted previously, the anorexia angle had a particular meaning for Dario, as he had hoped that talking about the condition might be helpful to his stepdaughter, Anna Lou. David turns to his friend Arnie (Ira Belgrade) for advice. It's Arnie who warns him that many anorexics end up committing suicide and that the problem is often connected to a troubled relationship with an unbalanced parent figure. Despite the girl's young age, Arnie makes some tacky comments about "getting into [Aura's] play clothes," which offends David—at least partly because he realizes he is deeply attracted to her on a physical level, as well. Arnie tells David that "anorexics are afraid of sex. They want to go back to childhood, before all the scary stuff started." It's pure armchair Freud, of course, but it does have some basis in reality. Aura is indeed stuck in between a miserable childhood and a potentially hopeless young adulthood, and she has a difficult time coming to grips with the idea that she is blossoming into a young woman. David's interest in her is not purely selfish; his feelings are sincere, and working together with Aura, they are able to help each other to find the sort of deep emotional connection which has been lacking in both of their lives.

Things become complicated when Aura is located by Dr. Judd (Frederic Forrest), her psychiatrist at the Faraday Clinic. Judd is one of the film's most bizarre characters, and veteran character actor Frederic Forrest (born 1936) responds with a performance that can best be described as eccentric; he apparently didn't take the film terribly seriously, so he elected to go for tongue-in-cheek excess, though it just about manages to work almost in spite of the negative attitude behind it. Judd is convinced that "each human being's head contains the soul… the one remaining riddle in the universe." He uses unorthodox methods in order to test his theories, and Aura is his favorite guinea pig. When he gets her back to the clinic, he proceeds to grill her about what she saw on the night of the murder. She insists that she can't remember anything more than what she already told the police, but he believes that she is suppressing a key piece of information. He uses a rare psychotropic berry and forces her to drink the juice from it, leading to the film's most baroque sequence, wherein she "trips" while the effects of the berry take hold. The scene is utterly ridiculous in many respects, yet it's executed with such flair for expressive imagery that it hardly matters. Unfortunately for Judd, the experiment fails: Aura merely repeats what she's been saying all along, that the murderer's face was obscured from view by the severed heads of her parents. Judd's motivations remain obscure, though it's ultimately revealed that he has a particular vested interest in Aura, as he was having an affair with her mother; as such, he functions as a symbolic wicked step-father figure of sorts, locking her into a psych ward and continuing to experiment on her in order to satisfy his own morbid curiosity.

When David realizes what has happened, he gains access to the clinic and tries to find Aura. At the same time, the killer has also made his way to the clinic, where another murder is about to take place. The nurse (Sharon Barr) who is "treating" Aura is added to the roster of victims when the killer uses the same methodology on her as had been used on the chiropractor at the start of the film. The murder itself is hinted at rather than shown in graphic detail, but it takes on a queasy tone by virtue of the fact that it is carried out in front of a horrified patient who is unable to speak—as he looks on while the killer goes about removing her head, the man's reactions convey the horror without needing to show much of anything.

Italian lobby card: Dr. Judd (Frederic Forrest) attempts to abduct Aura (Asia Argento); at the right, Aura screams in the rain.

The Unsane Cinema of Dario Argento

David manages to get Aura away from the clinic, and they find a clue which leads them to a storage locker; there, they find an old photograph which yields an important clue. Three of the people in the picture have already been killed, and the other two may well be in danger of joining them. They manage to track down one of the people in the photograph, a nurse named Linda Quirk (Hope Alexander-Willis), but she is already on the run; frightened by the news that her friends have all met horrible deaths, she goes into hiding. David and Aura track her down to a local hotel, but they are too late. The killer arrives and decapitates her, too. The killer's *modus operandi* is unusual. Apparently, he can only strike in the rain. Why this is, is not revealed until the end of the picture—but in the case of Linda Quirk, it's a bright and sunny day, so the killer engineers "rain" by setting off the hotel's sprinkler system. When David arrives and sees her decapitated head on the floor, Argento uses one of his beloved "weird science" flourishes by allowing her to mouth one last ambiguous clue—a man's name: Lloyd. The "talking head" bit is inspired by a centuries-old myth about severed heads continuing to live on for a few seconds after the death of the body. Given the French Revolution angle, Argento is specifically alluding to the decapitation of Jean-Paul Marat's assassin, Charlotte Corday, who reportedly looked in disgust at her executioner when he held up her severed head for the crowd to see. Scientists differ on whether these stories have any weight at all. It's generally agreed that the head would cease to function as soon as it becomes severed from the body, but some studies involving lab rats indicate that some brain activity continues to register for a few moments following decapitation. That said, the notion of a severed head speaking is pure fantasy—but in the context of a Dario Argento *giallo*, it doesn't seem so utterly incredible.

The name "Lloyd" turns out to be a reference to disgraced surgeon Dr. Lloyd (Brad Dourif), who has been disbarred and has slumped into drug addiction. David traces him to a seedy section of town—where he notices him selling drugs to David's estranged ex, Grace—but his attempt to enlist the doctor's aid falls on deaf ears. Brad Dourif (born 1950)'s cameo appearance is brief, but he makes a vivid impression as a man fallen on hard times. Unlike some of the other veteran performers, he appears to have taken his duties very seriously; when he freaks out on David when the young man tries pumping him for information, he's genuinely frightening. Dourif was in the midst of establishing himself as a sort of genre icon at the time, thanks to his vocal performance of homicidal killer Charles Lee Ray in the *Child's Play* franchise, but his vivid interpretation proves the old adage that there are no small roles, only small actors. Perhaps appropriately, he is given the film's most elaborate and protracted death scene, as the killer tracks him to his rundown apartment building and toys with him in much the same way as the killer taunted Professor Giordani in *Deep Red*; there's even a doll used in the scene, though here it has a double meaning as the use of such dolls was also a tactic employed by anti-abortion protestors during this time frame—and while Lloyd is not an abortionist, per se, his role in the narrative emanates from a tragic

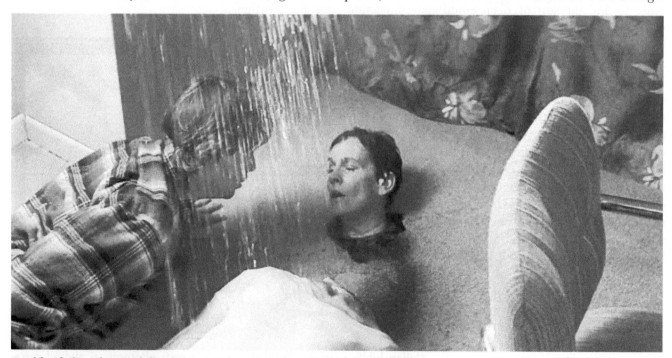

David (Christopher Rydell) gets a clue from the still-talking decapitated head of Linda (Hope Alexander-Willis) in one of *Trauma's* more eccentric scenes.

accident which resulted in an abortion. The killer has difficulty with his favorite electric guillotine device, so Lloyd is ultimately decapitated with the aid of the building's old fashioned elevator system—another call back to *Deep Red*, here given a cartoonish punchline when Lloyd's severed head screams as it falls into the abyss of the elevator shaft. It has to be admitted that Tom Savini's severed head effects are not among his finer efforts; whether this was down to his being given too much to do without the benefit of enough money or if it's the result of the heads not being lit properly, it's hard to say. Savini's real life experience with carnage on the battlefield of Vietnam did compel him to give each of the heads a different look. Each face is frozen with a different sort of an expression, ranging from horror to surprise. It's a nice touch, but the end results are seldom very convincing; his work on "The Black Cat" was much more persuasive, but there he was working in his familiar environs in the Pittsburgh area, whereas here he was on location with the crew in Minneapolis.

Following Dr. Lloyd's demise, Dr. Judd again tries to lure Aura away from David; this time, the young man gets into a fight with the doctor, and when the police arrive, Judd tries to make a getaway. He crashes and is killed by the impact; the police discover the severed heads of the victims in his trunk, so the case is evidently closed. Aura, evidently pushed beyond the brink by all that has happened, leaves David a note stating that she's gone to rejoin her mother; he takes this as a suicide note and plunges into despair, which prompts him to fall off the wagon and start using again.

This kind of emotional reaction to violence is something new in Argento's films; previously his characters manage to compartmentalize their feelings, often because they are not directly impacted by the violence as such. Here, David is so invested in Aura that losing her causes him to back slide into depression and drug abuse. In many respects, it displays a deeper sensitivity to the emotions of the characters than usual; perhaps this, too, seemed out of character in a bad way to the critics who slammed the film on its initial release, but in fact it gives the film an emotional weight and resonance that is very interesting.

David hits rock bottom only to see something unexpected. He notices a woman walking down the street wearing the same distinctive bracelet Aura had always worn. He follows the woman to her home—and Argento shows young Cory standing outside, lurking and watching as usual. David breaks into the house and finds a strange room—a shrine of sorts to somebody named Nicholas. It's a fantastic and very dreamy scene, as David makes his way through the room, which is decorated with billowing sheer curtains, all featuring

Tom Savini's crew prepares for Piper Laurie's decapitation. Courtesy of Carla Alonzo.

the name "Nicholas" embroidered into the fabric. At the center of the room, he finds a grim sight. A baby's crib with the rotting, decapitated remains of a child. Adriana Petrescu emerges, still very much alive, and hits him over the head; he awakens in a makeshift prison in the basement, where he is being cradled by Aura. David had misread Aura's note. In rejoining her mother, she wasn't committing suicide, but rather she was following a lead given to her by Dr. Judd. The irony is, in seeking out her mother, she really is committing suicide—the mother figure in this instance is not kind and nurturing, but rather is a force of evil and violence.

Adriana is another in a long line of Argento "wicked mother" figures. She's extravagantly played by Piper Laurie (born 1932), whose casting is a deliberate reference to her Oscar-nominated turn in Brian De Palma's film *Carrie* (1976). Laurie slices the ham thick, but she's still a memorably baroque and theatrical monster figure. Her motivation is sympathetic enough. As she explains, she was in the midst of giving birth to a child—a boy, whom she was going to name Nicholas—when a storm raging outside caused the power to go out; in the ensuing confusion, Dr. Lloyd accidentally decapitated the child. Encouraged by his nurses to do what was necessary to keep the accident quiet, they all—including Adriana's

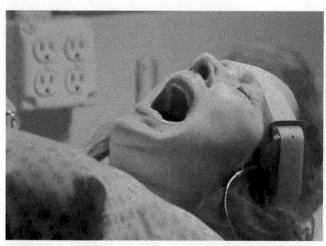

Electroshock therapy did little to erase the memory of Adriana (Piper Laurie)'s botched delivery.

shell-shocked husband—conspired to keep word from getting out about what had happened. Shock treatment was used to erase Adriana's memory, but after years of keeping it suppressed, it finally came back to the surface and inspired her to commit the string of murders.

The trigger for the string of murders is the plot's weak point; as explained by T.E.D. Klein in an interview included later in this text, a prologue was envisioned in which a freak accident involving the decapitation of a window cleaner (which was to have been played by Tom Savini) was to have been witnessed by Adriana, thus triggering her memory of the traumatic event. This scene was nixed due to budgetary concerns and so Adriana's descent into murder and madness comes off as arbitrary. Laurie's performance is strictly superficial—she's the ultimate mother from hell—and she doesn't manage to evoke the sympathy which ideally should be a part of her make up; that she elects to kill the people responsible for the botched delivery of her child and the subsequent attempts to erase her memory of it is understandable, and it could have had a tragic dimension, but it's rendered obscure between Laurie's histrionic acting and the muddled motivations of the script.

The finale is yet another variation on the ending of *The Bird with the Crystal Plumage*, as Aura realizes that she incorrectly interpreted what she saw on the night of the murder. While the killer was indeed holding her father's severed head up for her to see, Adriana fooled the young girl by using her hand to look as if they were also holding her head up as well—in fact, she saw the killer's face as plain as day, but she couldn't bring herself to interpret the horrible reality correctly.

As Adriana rants and raves, little Gabriel makes his way into the house and finds the electric guillotine; having already been terrorized by Adriana earlier in the film, he knows what she is capable of, so he uses the guillotine on her before she's able to dispatch David and Aura. Here again, Argento goes for dramatic effect by having her severed head repeat "Nicholas … Nicholas …" as it rolls across the floor. The film ends on a positive, uplifting note as David and Aura are reunited, and he promises to stay with her forever. Argento then includes a very strange flourish as the camera roves down the street towards the sound of a reggae band playing in the distance; the end titles play over the band jamming while a pretty—possibly anorexic—girl dances along to the music.

Trauma is an imperfect film, but it is most definitely a more worthy piece of work than most of the fans and critics tend to give it credit for. The script definitely has its problems, but Argento manages to make the bland mid-western settings look atmospheric and striking through the use of foggy, sometimes hazy interiors. Raffaele Mertes (born 1959), who did such a splendid job on *The Sect*, provides some painterly images. This was Argento's second film to be shot in authentic anamorphic widescreen, following *Suspiria*, and it could be that the film's reputation suffered for years due to the lack of a nice widescreen video transfer. Fans were disappointed by the lack of gore, but the film really doesn't suffer because of that. The violence still has a nasty edge to it and the plot is far from conventional. In telling a very unorthodox love story, Argento gives the film a sense of depth and urgency; David and Aura are sympathetic figures, and the audience is with them every step of the way as they fight through their personal demons and solve the mystery.

Despite a few clunky performances—notably James Russo (born 1953), a very good actor who simply can't make anything out of the robotic police captain character he is saddled with—and a few narrative hiccups, *Trauma* is realized with tremendous visual imagination. The criticism that the film lacks the flair of Argento's Italian films is simply not supported by the film itself. Argento uses plenty of agile, nervous camerawork, often honing on strange details, adding an off-kilter vibe to even ordinary sequences. While the mid-western setting may seem bland, this is part of the film's thesis, wherein madness, despair and violence can be found lurking under even the most banal of exteriors. To argue that the film loses points by virtue of the American setting is pure snobbery; on the contrary, it's fascinating to see these very American settings through the eyes of his distinctive and very European artistic sensibility. The action is generally well paced and the "hidden in plain view" clue is an ingenious one. Perhaps more than any Argento film which preceded it, *Trauma* is in dire need of proper reassessment; it may not be one of his major works, but it is a stylish and very enjoyable film just the same.

The release of *Trauma* signaled the start of a long, dark, and despairing period for Dario. The Italian release took place on March 12, 1993, and it didn't go over well at all; it ranked at number 48 for the 1992-1993 Italian box-office season—making it his third dud in a row, following *Two Evil Eyes* and *The Sect*.[5] The Italian audience evidently felt as if their *maestro* had turned his back on them by going to America, and the watered-down end result alienated fans, many of whom regarded it as his first out-and-out terrible movie. Worse, Overseas Film Group failed to secure any kind of an American theatrical release—thus, the whole point of the entire frustrating exercise had been rendered null and truly void. The film was a box-office bomb and Argento found himself in the midst of a financial crisis. According to Dario, his business manager started behaving strangely toward him—then one day Dario decided to send a lawyer friend to the business offices to look over the books. "They stayed until late at night. The verdict was terrible: I was in deep financial trouble. My manager had been spending double on the budgets of what the production companies allowed us. He said he had always believed we would get it back when the movies did well. But it didn't go as planned. The lawyer told me that I had to declare bankruptcy, but with this huge debt, my real estate assets would also be seized. My house in Coppedè, the flat I had rented for Fiore and Asia… […]"[6] ADC Films was shut down as Argento and his business partners scrambled about trying to figure out what to do, and it would never get off the ground again; Argento would ultimately start up a new production company with his brother Claudio a few years later, Opera Films, but by that stage the glory days were definitely in the rearview mirror. It became apparent that Argento needed a hit—badly. He mulled over a variety of options, including an offer to remake *The Bird with the Crystal Plumage*, but he decided to follow his gut instinct and develop a new *giallo* instead. The development of the new project proved to be a difficult process, encumbered, no doubt, by the drama surrounding his terrible financial woes. Argento called in favors and managed to pull off a small miracle. "When I managed to sort my financial issues and reimburse my debts, my one daughter was staying with her mother, while the other was living with a boyfriend; I had been staying in a hotel. I discovered that my house in Coppedè hadn't been sold yet, so I was able to buy it back."[7]

After that, another disaster struck. Dario's stepdaughter, Anna Lou Ceroli, died in a motorcycle accident on September 29 1994. The entire family took the loss badly. Asia had formed a particularly strong bond with her, as they were so close in age (Anna was born on June 9, 1972, while Asia was born on September 20,

Teaser ad for *Trauma*—which almost certainly didn't come to a theater near you.

1975). Anna, of course, was a source of inspiration for Dario in the writing of *Trauma*, something which Daria Nicolodi resented. As Asia told Alan Jones, "It was weird when we all attended the *Trauma* premiere because Anna was still alive at that time. Daria freaked out completely saying it was a scandal we had used her illness as a plot device, but Anna just smiled. She was still suffering from anorexia at the time and I hoped the film might make her wake up to the dangers."[8] Anna was only 22 years old; Asia would later name her own first-born daughter Anna Lou as a tribute to her late half-sister.

Notes:
1. Jones, Alan, *Dario Argento: The Man, the Myths & the Magic* (Godalming: FAB Press, 2012), p. 266.
2. Ibid, p. 271.
3. Ibid, p. 202.
4. Ibid, p. 221.
5. http://www.hitparadeitalia.it/bof/boi/boi1992-93.htm
6. Argento, Dario, *Peur* (France: Rouge Profond, 2018), p. 306.
7. Ibid, p. 307.
8. Jones, Alan, *Dario Argento: The Man, the Myths & the Magic* (Godalming: FAB Press, 2012), p. 274.

Chapter Seventeen:
A Cry from the Depths; *Ciao*, Lucio

Despite the failure of *Trauma*, Argento gave serious thought to making his next film in the U.S. Working with Franco Ferrini, he developed an unusual thriller scenario which used another psychological condition as its narrative hook: the Stendhal Syndrome, a psychosomatic condition which affects people who are negatively affected by their exposure to works of art. The original plan was to film in Phoenix, Arizona—perhaps Argento had been influenced by Donald Cammell's brilliant *giallo*-esque thriller *White of the Eye* (1987) when he selected that location—and he entered into talks with Bridget Fonda (born 1964) to play the lead character. Fonda was keen to work with Argento and had originally been considered to play a key role in *Trauma*, but that fell through; fortunately, or unfortunately, depending on one's point of view, history repeated itself and Fonda passed on the film. Jennifer Jason Leigh (born 1962) and Darryl Hannah (born 1960) were reportedly considered for a hot minute, but Dario decided that he had had enough of the headaches and hassles of working in America and he decided it would be in his best interests to return to Italy.

The script was heavily revised to accommodate the change in locale and Dario decided to strengthen his bond with Asia by offering her the leading role, which she readily accepted. The project was darker than usual—a side effect, no doubt, of all the darkness and drama which had entered into his life during this period. It would become his first film to really deal with the psychological scars of violence and it's difficult not to see it as being a meditation of sorts on his feelings over the loss of Anna and his growing realization that he had often placed his career before the needs of his family. The return to Italy also permitted him to cut loose and not worry about the violence, but the bloodbath he hinted at in the interviews leading up to the film's release wasn't quite what fans had in mind. *The Stendhal Syndrome* (*La sindome di Stendhal*) would prove to be an uncommonly unpleasant movie. If his earlier *gialli* played a fun game of cat-and-mouse with the viewer and offered fetishistic views of acts of violence, this film marked a new-found maturity. There's nothing pretty about the violence in this film; if anything, it proved to be a little off-putting for some of the fan base precisely because it adopts a greater realism in its aesthetics as well as its approach to violence.

The Stendhal Syndrome therefore marked Argento's triumphant return to Italy following a period of scrambling around for greater audience exposure and approval in America. The Italian cineastes were excited by the prospect of a new, homegrown Argento movie, and the production was covered with greater-than-usual enthusiasm in the Italian press. *Trauma* had been beset by budgetary woes, but the deal Argento struck with the Medusa company in Italy allowed him access to a top-notch crew of technicians. As cinematographer, Argento selected the great Giuseppe Rotunno (born 1923), who was well known for his collaborations with masters like Fellini and Visconti; his exquisite cinematography on films like *The Leopard* (*Il gattopardo*, 1963) and *Fellini's Casanova* (1976) is among the finest in cinema history, so Dario was appropriately thrilled to have him in his corner. And for the first time in over 20 years, Argento would reach out to Ennio Morricone to compose the score; the two men patched over their differences and Morricone responded with his all-time best score for the director. The script called for some ambitious visual effects and Sergio Stivaletti (back on board following

Beautifully stylized artwork for *The Stendhal Syndrome* by Malleus.

Argento's back-to-back collaborations with Tom Savini in the U.S.) would be called upon to create some of the first digital special effects ever created for an Italian picture. The production was a high profile one, and it was very much a make-or-break proposition where Argento was concerned; on paper, at least, the elements looked promising and suggested a major "return to form" for the director following his period in America.

Argento commenced filming on *The Stendhal Syndrome* on July 17, 1995; filming would wrap on September 15, a week after Dario's 55th birthday—and a few days shy of Asia's 20th. The shoot proved to be an intense one. Part of it was down to the subject matter. Dario's decision to go for broke with regards to the violence was partly a reaction to the censorship he had been subjected to during his period in America, yet the approach to the violence was decidedly different from his earlier films. The emphasis on sexual violence was a new wrinkle, too; while *Tenebrae* had dabbled in fetishistic eroticism (the girl in the red high heel shoes), it didn't go in for scenes of rape. Making things even tougher was the fact that it was Dario's youngest daughter who was on the receiving end of all the brutality. Crew members had already found it odd that Dario had his daughter baring her naked breasts in *Trauma* (she turned 17 towards the end of the shoot), but here the scenes of her being brutally raped were particularly unpleasant to film. Dario reportedly found it difficult, but he tried to separate his emotions by telling himself that, on the set, Asia was an actress—and as such, undeserving of special treatment. Asia endured the psychological head games like a champ, but she still found herself suffering mightily during the tougher scenes in the shoot. On the plus side, her older sister Fiore was on board as the assistant production manager—and she spent part of her time on set consoling Asia and helping her to sort through her emotions while Dario focused his energies on the project at hand. Dario found himself getting frustrated with the slow (read: expensive) methods of his great cinematographer, but he was justifiably proud when he secured permission from the directors of the famous Uffizi Gallery in Florence to film a key sequence there; *The Stendhal Syndrome* became the first film to be granted such an honor, which spoke volumes about Argento's cachet in the Italian market, especially compared to the quizzical looks his name elicited in America. Luigi Cozzi also brought a supportive, familiar presence to the shoot as the second unit director.

Having severed ties with Franco Fraticelli, Dario found himself working with a new editor in the post-production phase. Angelo Nicolini had been editing films since the early 1980s, but he was very much an untested property where Argento was concerned. Looking at the end result, he displayed a feeling for tempo and rhythm

Italian *locandina* for *The Stendhal Syndrome*; the film was Argento's long-awaited return to Italian filmmaking; artwork by Immagine e Strategia.

which wasn't far removed from that of Fraticelli—but sadly, this would remain his one and only collaboration with Argento. Ennio Morricone's long-awaited return to the fold proved to be worth the wait. He provided the film with an exceptional score, alternately lyrical and chilling. *The Stendhal Syndrome* appeared to have all the makings of a winner.

The action kicks off with an extraordinary set piece—arguably the best opening scene in any of Argento's films since *Suspiria*. The comparison is not

Anna Mani (Asia Argento) experiences *The Stendhal Syndrome* in the world-famous Uffizi Art Gallery.

arbitrary. At the time of the film's release, Argento made a point of stating that he wanted to recapture that kind of hallucinatory intensity, and he certainly succeeds in his goal. We see a young woman, subsequently introduced as Anna Manni (Asia Argento), making her way through the multitude of tourists lining the streets of Florence. As she walks through the streets, the ancient statues and sculptures loom down on her, establishing the theme of the dominance of art in our lives. Argento plunges us into the action with absolutely no explanation or contextualization. The effect is extremely disorientating, which is absolutely deliberate. Anna makes her way into the famed Uffizi Gallery; as noted above, Argento was the first filmmaker granted access to filming in the museum, though others would eventually follow suit, including Franco Zeffirelli (*Tea with Mussolini/Un tè con Mussolini*, 1999), Ridley Scott (*Hannibal*, 2001), and Marco Tullio Giordana (*The Best of Youth/La meglio gioventù*, 2003). As the scene unfolds, Anna moves through the various rooms of the gallery—and the works of art appear to exude a powerful effect on her. It's clear that she's in search of *something* or *someone*, but Argento provides no explanation—the goal is to make the audience identify with her confused mental state. Things come to a head when she sees Caravaggio's *Medusa* (1597) and Pieter Bruegel's *Landscape with the Fall of Icarus* (circa 1560s). The paintings exude a strange, hypnotic effect, causing her to pass out—cracking her lip on a table in the process—and hallucinate that she's entered into the water depicted in the Bruegel piece. She sees herself sinking into the water and she catches sight of a strange fish with a human-like face—looking rather like a caricature of Edward G. Robinson, funnily enough. She kisses the fish, then rises to the surface; this coincides with her snapping out of her little trance, though she has now lost her memory. This entire sequence is a *tour de force* of pure cinema. There's no dialogue for these first seven-and-a-half minutes, only the insistent building of Ennio Morricone's main theme on the soundtrack; it was Morricone's first score for Argento since the *Four Flies on Grey Velvet* debacle, and it's arguably the best of all the scores he composed for the director.

Anna manages to compose herself and she leaves the gallery; outside she is approached by a young man who introduces himself as Alfredo Grossi (Thomas Kretschmann). Alfredo seems genuinely concerned for her well-being, but Anna is still in the grips of the feverish delirium which struck her down inside the gallery. She

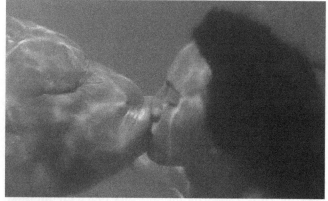

While in an altered state, Anna imagines kissing a fish with a human-like face.

finds a key to a hotel room in her purse, which enables her to hail down a cab and give the driver a destination. While in her hotel room, she desperately tries to remember her name or what she's doing in Florence. A pill bottle containing a sedative provides her with her name, but beyond that everything is still a blur. When she takes a couple of pills, Argento indulges in one of his trademark visual flourishes, as the camera follows the pills as they go down her throat and into her stomach; it's a shot Dario originally envisioned for *Phenomena*, but at that time there wasn't a way to realize the idea effectively—here Sergio Stivaletti utilizes CGI (a first in an Italian production) and while the result is artificial-looking, it works on the level of sheer stylized audacity. While Anna tries to relax and collect her senses, she notices the print of Rembrandt's *The Night Watch* (1642) hanging on the wall; in a repeat of what happened at the gallery, she appears to enter into the painting—but this time it transports her to Rome, where she learns that she is a police woman with the anti-rape squad, and that she's been assigned by her boss, Inspector Manetti (Luigi Diberti), to investigate a series of rapes which have escalated into homicides. Manetti has reason to believe that the culprit is in Florence, so he sends Anna there to see what she can discover. As her vision ends, she notices the reflection of Alfredo Grossi joining her own reflection in the glass covering the Rembrandt print; at first, we are led to believe it may be part of her hallucination—but then Alfredo grabs Anna and throws her into bed, where he proceeds to terrorize her. Alfredo is the rapist/murderer Anna has been seeking and he is aware that she has been following him; her current psychological breakdown allows him to get the upper hand, and the hunted becomes the hunter, with Anna as his latest prey. Alfredo tells Anna that the sight of the blood on her lips at the gallery, caused when she cracked her lip on the table, was a major turn-on—he produces a razor blade and uses it to inflict an ugly gash on her lip, then licks the blood away from her mouth. Alfredo rapes Anna at gunpoint, and she eventually passes out from the trauma. Violence is nothing new in Argento's films, of course, but the rape scenes in *The Stendhal Syndrome* are a very different thing from his usual stock-in-trade. This is grim and disturbing stuff and Argento does not sugar coat it in the least. It seems as though there was a little extra nudity originally filmed (with a body double standing in for Asia), some of which is visible in the Italian theatrical trailer, but Argento elected to keep things more suggestive in the final cut, which is honestly for the best. There's nothing sexualized about these scenes; they are rough, they are brutal, and they are unpleasant, but they are never titillating nor do they ever tip into bad taste eroticism.

Sonia Topazio is given an ultra-slow-motion death scene in *The Stendhal Syndrome*.

Argento lulls the viewer into expecting a respite when the rape fades to black—but a shock cut takes us to the backseat of Alfredo's car, where Anna awakens to see her attacker raping another young woman (Sonia Topazio). Tellingly, she also notices a "keepsake" stolen by Alfredo from her hotel room: a tacky tourist shop water globe containing a reproduction of Michelangelo's *David* (1501-1504). Images of art are literally inescapable in *The Stendhal Syndrome*, whether in the Uffizi Gallery or in the reproductions and prints which loom over the scenery in virtually every location. As Anna tries to focus and get a sense of where she is, Alfredo continues to viciously rape the unidentified woman; at the point of his orgasm, he pulls out a gun and uses it to shoot the woman in the head. Argento includes a dazzling slow-motion shot of the bullet discharging from the gun and entering the woman's face, but this sort of gimmicky imagery is actually in short supply in *Stendhal*; for the most part, he shows restraint, especially where the violence is concerned. That's not to say that the use of flashy imagery here is in poor taste, but the overall approach is far more austere than usual, and the emphasis is on the brutal and deeply unpleasant reality of the violence as opposed to going for more expressive or poetic techniques. Anna manages to break free from

Thomas Kretschmann is one of Argento's most horrifying monsters in *The Stendhal Syndrome*.

Asia Argento gives a heartbreaking performance as the psychologically scarred and brutalized heroine.

her captor and runs down the street, where she finds assistance from the local police.

While these opening 20-odd minutes aren't as aggressively stylized and overtly "scary" as the opening of *Suspiria*, they nevertheless stand out as some of Argento's best sustained pieces of filmmaking. The decision to plunge the viewer into the action without the benefit of clarification can be alienating, but the more patient viewers are rewarded as information is gradually revealed as the action unfolds. It's revealed that Anna is suffering from the Stendhal Syndrome, so-called because the writer Marie-Henri Beyle (aka Stendhal, 1783-1842) was the first to make a record of the condition in one of his diaries; he described the condition thus: "I was in a sort of ecstasy ... absorbed in the contemplation of sublime beauty ... I reached the point where one encounters celestial sensations. Everything spoke so vividly to my soul. Ah, if only I could forget. I had palpitations of the heart ... life was drained from me ... I walked with a fear of falling." In addition to the initial reactions of feeling faint and increased anxiety and agitation, the condition can also result in short-term memory loss and personality changes. Argento and Franco Ferrini—who collaborated on the screen story, though Dario ultimately wrote the script on his own—would both claim to have been affected by the syndrome at different points in their life. The renowned Italian psychiatrist Graziella Magherini published her book *La sindrome di Stendhal* in 1989 and it was based on her experiences treating people struck with the illness during her tenure at the Santa Maria Nuova Hospital in Florence. The reason why so many people, especially foreign tourists, have been affected during visits to Florence is the higher-than-usual array of great works of art clustered in the city; great art is literally all around one and it can be overwhelming to those who are not accustomed to it and are of a particularly sensitive disposition. Argento's script is not based on Magherini's book, per se, as that is more of a psychological tract examining various different real-life cases—but he did call upon Magherini to serve as a special consultant on the picture.

Anna begins to show radical changes in her personality. When first introduced at the beginning of the film, she is more stereotypically feminine, with long hair and a taste for conservative but conventionally "feminine" attire befitting her role as a police detective; after the combined shock of the Stendhal Syndrome and the rape by Alfredo, she becomes more "masculine," as she cuts her hair and starts wearing button-down shirts and jeans. She also displays uncharacteristic personality changes (for example, eating chocolates, something she never used to do) and her attitude towards her boyfriend, fellow policeman Marco (Marco Leonardi), also changes. Marco is depicted as a rather sweet and well-intended sort, but he is admittedly tone deaf with regards to his reactions to

Anna's trauma. He tries to comfort her and make her feel "safe," but in trying to play the role of protector he comes off as inadvertently clumsy and thoughtless. He shows up at her apartment, for example, bringing frozen pizzas and roses, hoping for a bit of intimacy; the fact that Anna has just been brutally raped is known to him, but he is more concerned with his own needs, whining that it's been so long since they last made love.

Marco doesn't mean to be so callous, but understandably it upsets Anna, who reacts by turning the tables on him, mimicking male-on-male rape and humiliating him in the process. The shifts in Anna's personality are beautifully conveyed by Asia, who gives arguably the performance of her career. Anna is a complex character—and a challenging one. The nature of the script made the film difficult for her to cope with at times, but Dario proved to be generally sensitive to her needs and provided her with the freedom and emotional support needed to make the character come to life. Not surprisingly, she remains proud of the end result, even if it proved to be an emotionally draining experience: "I remember that after shooting some of those scenes I went home quite shaken. [...] This is my favorite movie among all the movies I did with my father. [...] I felt that more than the others it was very personal."[1]

As part of her recovery process, Anna is mandated to see a police psychologist, Dr. Cavana (Paolo Bonacelli). Cavana offers a sympathetic ear and proves to be insightful, but ultimately, he is mostly ineffectual. Argento's ambivalent attitude towards psychiatry comes through in this context. Many critics insist on applying Freudian theory to his films—not surprising given the abundance of phallic symbols and beautiful women-in-distress—but Dario has said many times that he is more interested in the theories of Carl Jung; given the emphasis on dreams and visions in his films, this certainly makes sense. Cavana is not depicted as a corrupt or unsympathetic figure, far from it, but apart from diagnosing Anna with the Stendhal Syndrome and encouraging her to find productive avenues in which to channel her emotions, he doesn't succeed in accomplishing much. Nevertheless, it's Cavana who suggests that Anna return to her hometown of Viterbo for a bit of rest and relaxation. Anna expresses concerns with this but agrees to do so; when she arrives home, it's easy to see why she was ambivalent. Her father (John Quentin) is an imposing block of ice; when he meets Anna at the door, she moves in to hug him, but he reacts in a stiff and stolid fashion. Her brothers (Leonardo Ferrantini and Sandro Giordano) aren't much better: They show absolutely no empathy for what she's been through and they mockingly tell her that her new, short hairdo makes her "look like a boy."

Anna's time in Viterbo demonstrates that she has changed, whereas the town itself has not; typical of most small communities, it remains fixed in time and the petty, small-minded mentality suggests that they have no sense of the world outside of their small part of it. The scenes with Anna and her father are brief, but they have great emotional resonance. We see them sitting in silence at dinner, unable to communicate with one another, and when Anna reveals that she's seeing a psychologist, he reacts with disdain: "Is that really necessary?" The implication is that, in his mind, seeing a mental health specialist is a sign of weakness; better to "tough it out" than let everybody know you're "crazy" by seeing a shrink. Anna stands her ground and makes it clear that she's determined to play an active role in her recovery process; she refuses to be reduced to the role of victim.

As part of Anna's therapy, she starts painting pictures of her own; Asia actually painted the pieces of art in question herself, and they provide a glimpse into the character's tormented soul. Images of faces contorted in pain, crying tears of blood, or of a child cowering in fear. In one scene she even covers herself in paint from head to toe and rolls around on a canvas. The character's determination to overcome the Stendhal Syndrome and the self-loathing inflicted by her brutalization at the hands of Alfredo marks her as one of the strongest characters in the Argento canon; she may be suffering, but she refuses to give up without one hell of a fight. She also takes time out to prime her body by boxing—another pasttime of Asia's which Dario worked into the script. All of this material has nothing to do with the plot, as such; it's more a matter of taking the time to delve into the character's fractured emotional state as she tries to get her life back in to order. This approach would have

Anna (Asia Argento) continues to struggle with *The Stendhal Syndrome*.

Alfredo (Thomas Kretschmann) strikes a Christ-like pose after killing again.

been unthinkable in one of Argento's earlier *gialli*, which tended to favor incident over characterization; here the pace is slower, the tone darker and the overall effect far more introspective.

As Anna continues to grapple with her precarious psychological state, Alfredo continues his horrific crimes. He takes notice of a girl working in a shop (Lucia Stara) and seduces her, before violently raping her and killing her. Alfredo is undoubtedly the most frightening monster to be found in any of Argento's films. As played by Thomas Kretschmann (born 1962), he is handsome, sophisticated, charming, and utterly innocuous. His crimes have nothing to do with frustrated sexuality—he is good-looking and outgoing enough to attract the attention of any woman who strikes his fancy—but are rather rooted in deep-seated sadism. He's a complete sociopath, a narcissist who uses his attractive exterior to take advantage of his intended victims. His crimes are all the more disturbing because they are so utterly pointless; he's cruel for the sheer love of being cruel. He's not motivated by a desire for revenge or to acquire wealth; he just gets off on tormenting random people before killing them. Kretschmann's performance is outstanding, adding touches of grim dark humor while making absolutely no apologies for the character's cruelty; he would later return to play the lead in Argento's *Dario Argento's Dracula*. This kind of random, irrational violence has its roots in *Tenebrae*, but it cuts even deeper here; perhaps it is the predatory nature of the violence that makes it so, but *The Stendhal Syndrome* emerges as the darkest and most disturbing film of Argento's career.

Anna's progress is undone when Alfredo tracks her down and kidnaps her from her father's house. He takes her to a secluded, abandoned factory where he ties her down to a filthy mattress, and proceeds to rape and brutalize her once more. At one point, he leaves her alone while he goes home to collect some items; the graffiti on the wall, including a demon with a monstrously oversized penis, appears to come to life as Anna succumbs to utter

Anna is tied to a bed and repeatedly raped by Alfredo.

Anna (Asia Argento) gets some well-deserved revenge on Alfredo (Thomas Kretschmann).

hysteria. When Alfredo returns, she surprises him by wrenching springs from the mattress and using them to puncture his neck; as they fight on the floor, she uses her fingernail to gouge out one of his eyes. Still determined to show his superiority, Alfredo tries using a gun to intimidate her, but Anna gets the weapon away from him and uses it to shoot him in the chest before using the butt of the gun to snap his neck. She drags his body outside and after some well-earned ranting and raving, kicks his body into the canal below. Anna's revenge is brutal and difficult to watch, but given everything Alfredo has subjected her to, it's difficult not to derive satisfaction from it. There is nothing remotely sympathetic about Alfredo. There is no underlining trauma to rationalize his violence or cause the viewer to feel some measure of compassion for him; he is purely and simply evil. He even mocks Anna's status as a policewoman, smugly reminding her that she can't attack him because her job dictates that she has to arrest him and put him on trial; Anna circumvents the legal machinery and serves as judge, jury, and executioner. There's no doubt that she has ample justification for reacting as she does, but there is nothing triumphant about the scene; if anything, it reinforces the cyclical nature of violence, as the victim resorts to much the same tactics utilized by her attacker. In a way, Alfredo has come to "possess" Anna—and this idea will continue to play itself out in the second half of the film.

Most critics and fans tend to feel that the first half of the film works well, whereas the second half sputters and stalls before reaching a non-ending. This criticism more-or-less misses the overall point of the film entirely, which is less concerned with elaborate plot twists than in exploring the mental deterioration of its protagonist. Most Argento *giallo* films deal with violence in a fairly superficial manner, but that is not the case here; Anna is irrevocably scarred by her encounter with Alfredo and getting rid of him is not as easy as it first appears. She undergoes another transformation, going from "masculine" to much more conventionally feminine; she even dons a blonde Veronica Lake-style wig in order to cover up the facial scars inflicted by Alfredo. Her symptoms associated with the Stendhal Syndrome appear to dissipate, but the fact remains the combination of the syndrome with Alfredo's brutality has left a lingering impact on her psyche. She continues to check in with Dr. Cavana, who obviously has concerns for her safety and well-being, but for the time being he can do nothing but observe; here again, his intentions may be good, but he is basically powerless to avert the inevitable tragedy.

While browsing some art prints at a local shop, Anna meets an art student named Marie Beyle (Julien Lambroschini); the name is a reference to Stendhal's birth name, and it plays into the film's dialogue on

Marco (Marco Leonardi) discovers Anna's secret; the wall splashed with blood echoes a celebrated scene in *Tenebrae*.

sexuality and gender, as characters consistently mistake the character as a female because of the name, though as he explains, in French the gender is not so specific. They begin seeing each other and quickly fall in love. The relationship between Anna and Marie is the only real source of warmth to be found in the film, and it appears to signal a positive transition in Anna's life. Marie treats her with respect, and they enjoy spending as much time together as possible.

Meanwhile, Marco continues to pine for Anna; it's hard not to feel some sympathy for him, despite his sometimes-insensitive reactions to Anna, he really does love her, and he never sets out to deliberately cause her pain. When he discovers that Anna has found love in the arms of another man, he's obviously hurt—but he stops short of causing a scene over it. To his credit, he allows her the room to grow and he accepts the reality that their relationship has finally come to an end. The scene where Anna and Marie meet in a beautiful, sunlit park and make love behind some bushes is one of the most tender and lyrical episodes in any of Argento's films. Giuseppe Rotunno's lighting for the film is consistently pleasing to the eye, but this episode is particularly lovely; reportedly Rotunno's exacting methods caused some conflict with Argento, but the end result proves he was correct to take his time. This would remain his only collaboration with Argento, which is a shame; the Fellini veteran provides the film with top class lighting, and many of Argento's subsequent films would surely have benefitted from a cinematographer with his level of good taste and experience.

Now that Anna's life finally seems to be getting back on track, more cracks begin to appear; she starts receiving threatening phone calls, and she is convinced that Alfredo is still alive. Everybody assures Anna that this is not true, but she is sure of it; she describes him as a cancer that continues to grow inside of her—and in many respects, she's correct in her assertion. Tragedy strikes when Marie is killed in his studio; the images of his canvases and statues streaked with blood inevitably recall the death of Jane in *Tenebrae*, while the use of close-ups of the killer's eye recalls *The Cat O'Nine Tails*. Dr. Cavana is set up as a possible suspect when he shows up at Anna's house to talk to her about everything that has been happening. Their confrontation is beautifully played by Asia and Paolo Bonacelli (born 1937), who conveys just the right mixture of mounting suspicion and dread as the well-meaning but ill-prepared psychiatrist. As Anna continues to cling to her assertion that Alfredo is still alive, Dr. Cavana does his best to get her to see reason; in pushing her to confront the truth, he effectively bullies her into a classic "fight or flight" scenario—which ends up going very poorly for him indeed.

In the meantime, Alfredo's body is found and fished out of the canal—it having been lost in a tangled mess of tributaries before the police have been able to locate it. This removes all doubt. Alfredo is indeed dead. And yet, he does live on—as Anna correctly asserts, he has infected her like a disease or a virus, and in the process, his madness has been transmitted to her. When Marco goes to tell her about the discovery, he arrives just in time to see the aftermath of Dr. Cavana's "intervention."

In a repeat of the "violence as art" imagery from earlier in the film, the wall is stained with blood, and Marco finds the doctor dead on the floor, his throat having been cut. Anna is completely beyond all reason by this point and Marco makes the mistake of thinking he can outwit her by playing into her delusions; she leads him to the garage, supposedly to give him her gun, which she has stored in her car. Instead she kills Marco by viciously and repeatedly slamming the lid of her trunk down on his neck. The revelation that Anna is the murderer has been criticized as being predictable—and maybe it is. However, this is only an issue if one believes that the film is intended to astonish and surprise with this revelation. *The Stendhal Syndrome* is far less concerned with whodunit plot mechanics than it is with exploring the lingering effects of violence on Anna's psyche; on that level, it seems *inevitable* that she should also become a murderer. Yet, through it all, Asia's sensitive performance ensures that we remain emotionally invested in Anna's plight. She does not deserve what has happened to her and while this hardly excuses the murders of Marie, Marco and Dr. Cavana, Argento encourages us to remember that she is a victim, as well. In killing Alfredo, Anna may believe that she will be rid of the violence he has inflicted upon her, but the scars run too deep. Despite her best efforts to return to some semblance of "normality," he continues to torment her while inspiring her to do awful things.

The film ends with Inspector Manetti and his men cornering Anna, as she tries to flee from the scene. As they swarm in on her, Argento incorporates shots from Anna's point of view. She again feels victimized, as if she is about to be subjected to another sexual assault. The symbolism is clear, and the viewer is encouraged to sympathize with her. Manetti and his men show tremendous compassion, however, and the final view of them cradling her as she sobs is a very apt reference to the image of the *Pietà*—with Anna as a sacrificial Christ figure. It's by far the most emotionally draining and bleak finale to any of Argento's films, though the tenderness demonstrated by Anna's fellow police officers leaves room for hope that she may receive the care and support she needs in order to hopefully recuperate. On the whole, however, the ending is a chilling portrayal of Anna's final descent into the depths of insanity and despair. There's nothing to suggest that she will ever be able to rebound from what she has been through; indeed, the knowledge of the violence she has inflicted upon the men who tried so hard to help her will surely haunt Anna for the rest of her life, regardless of her capacity to reconnect with reality. Anna is not a villain, of course—but in many respects she is the most tragic victim in any of Argento's films. She survives in a physical sense, but her mind will forever be altered by the violence inflicted by Alfredo. And that is the ultimate tragedy. Many Argento films stop short of showing the lingering after-shocks caused by violence,

The devastating final image of *The Stendhal Syndrome*, as Inspector Manetti (Luigi Diberti, second from the left) and his men attend to a completely shattered Anna.

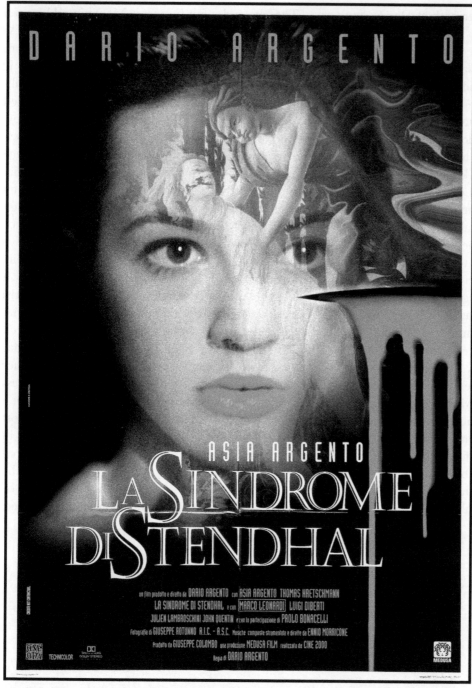

Italian poster art for *The Stendhal Syndrome*; artwork by Immagine e Strategia.

but *The Stendhal Syndrome* offers a prolonged look into the abyss—and it isn't pleasant.

The Stendhal Syndrome baffled fans in 1996 and in many respects it's easy to understand why. It's a relentlessly dark and grim film. No doubt part of that is down to the frustration he felt over his ill-fated sojourn into making films in America. Irked by the censorship and compromise inflicted upon him during the course of making *Trauma*, he returned to Italy determined to make a film with absolutely no compromise. But the depth of pain and suffering visible in the film also suggests that Argento was trying to work through the pain following the death of his stepdaughter Anna; that he elected to call Asia's character Anna is surely not a coincidence on that level. The film is darker and more mean-spirited than any of his earlier films. Even Franco Ferrini picked up on this, as he tried to encourage Dario to include a coda, hoping to soften the film's grim ending. He proposed that the film should end with Anna in a cell with a pastoral landscape hanging on the wall—the Stendhal Syndrome allows her to enter the painting and take solace in its bucolic landscape, thus freeing her spiritually.[2] It definitely would have altered the overall effect of the film, but Argento is to be commended for having the courage to stick with his conception of the picture. The fans and critics who complained that *Trauma* was too "soft" wouldn't be able to say the same over this film—but it's so unrelentingly grim and downbeat that they rejected it for going too far in the opposite direction.

On the face of it, the film seemed to indicate a new direction in Dario Argento's work—sadly the controversial reception, and perhaps his own reluctance to keep going down such a dark path, seemed to put that idea to rest. Consciously or not, Argento would begin to adopt a more arch and tongue-in-cheek approach in his subsequent films; nothing which follows would match the film's gut-wrenching impact. *The Stendhal Syndrome* remains Argento's last truly great film to date. Everything clicks. The script—though admittedly fanciful where police protocol is concerned—is tight, focused, and gripping, the performances are consistently convincing, and the filmmaking displays genuine maturity. Argento's use of camerawork is as inspired as ever and while the film is presented in a more "realistic" manner than his earlier works, he is still able to utilize some inspired touches of visual flashiness, whether it be the ultra-slow-motion bullet effect, a disorientating 360 degree revolving view of Anna as she consults with Dr. Cavana, or the subtle craning shots which allow us to adopt a "God's eye" view of Anna in her surroundings. The opening 20 minutes are remarkable, of course, but contrary to what some of the critics have suggested, the rest of the film does not pale in comparison. Fortunately the negative reception of the film has given way to a more positive reassessment in more recent years; now that one can better appreciate it for what it is instead of being put off by what it isn't, it's easier to value the film for its many subtle—and some not so subtle!—virtues.

The Italian theatrical release came on January 26, 1996—and business was solid ... but unspectacular. The early buzz over Argento's return to Italy generated a strong opening—*Variety* reported in March 1996 that, four weeks into the film's theatrical run, it was holding strong in the number 6 slot at the Italian box office, placing it well behind Michael Mann's *Heat* (1995) but ahead of the family comedy *Babe* (1995), for example[3]—but the word of mouth wasn't very positive; the reviews were largely hostile and the fan base didn't quite know what to make of the new approach Argento had adopted for the picture. Compared to the baroque, stylized aesthetics of the earlier films, *The Stendhal Syndrome* appeared a bit staid—even stuffy. It was a deliberate, calculated move on Argento's part, one which seemed to indicate a transition into a new style of filmmaking, but the fan base wasn't impressed. Ultimately the film ranked number 44 in the 1995-1996 Italian box-office season[4], which was a marked improvement over *Two Evil Eyes*, *The Sect*, and *Trauma*, but still a major comedown compared to the popular success of his earlier films.

There were talks early on of a deal through Miramax Pictures in the U.S. that would provide wide theatrical exposure—but that deal fell through. Given the scandal that would break years later with regards to Asia and Miramax head Harvey Weinstein, one can't help but wonder what that was all about. Prior to securing an official American distributor, the film made its debut on July 19, 1996 at the American Cinematheque in Hollywood.[5] For reasons best known to Dario, he elected to accept an offer from Lloyd Kaufman at Troma—the company responsible for direct-to-video schlock epics like *The Toxic Avenger* (1984). To say that Argento's stately, stylish psychological *giallo* looked out of place in the Troma stable would be an understatement, but evidently Kaufman convinced him that they would be able to provide the film with the American release it really deserved. A deal was formally announced in March 1998.[6] However, when Kaufmann succeeded in giving the picture only a very limited run in 1999—mostly in the Los Angeles/San Francisco area, with some scattered screenings in Austin, Texas, and at the Huntington Cinema Arts Center in New York—Dario was livid. Obviously Argento had some reason to believe that Kaufman would make good on his word and give the film a really wide release and an appropriately eye-catching ad campaign—but in hindsight it was a foolish move that doomed the movie to a notably shabby fate in the American marketplace. Troma would eventually dump the movie on video in a muddy, murky transfer which did Rotunno's golden-hued images no favors; no wonder so many American fans looked at it as a major disappointment, if not a complete and utter fall from grace. The Troma release also made use of the inferior English dub, which pretty much ruined Asia's exquisite performance. The film didn't fare that much better in the world market, garnering a Japanese release in June of that year, followed by a Spanish one in March 1998, but by and large *The Stendhal Syndrome* ended up going straight to video in most markets. It was hardly the triumphant return to form Dario had been hoping for.

Maitland McDonagh, a vocal supporter of Argento's films through the '80s, regarded *Stendhal* as another misstep. Awarding it only two out of five stars, she wrote that the film was "harrowing and occasionally macabre," but was left wondering what compelled Dario to cast his daughter in "such a sexually brutal film."[7] As it happens, she wasn't the only one left wondering that. Steve Biodrowski was similarly underwhelmed, writing:

"You have to arrest me!" Alfredo (Thomas Kretschmann) taunts Anna.

The Unsane Cinema of Dario Argento

Anna (Asia Argento) tries to reinvent herself with a Veronica Lake-style wig; Dario would later complain that Asia insisted on wearing the wig.

Unfortunately, despite his best intentions, it is also quite a disappointment, not the comeback one might have anticipated after *Trauma*. [...] There was a good film to be made here, but this isn't it.[8]

David Rooney expressed similar disappointment:

> The film kicks off with an exhilarating opening act but gradually ebbs into the domain of more commonplace psychological serial-killer chillers as the central conceit recedes. [...] The script's most unwise move is to cure Anna far too early of the artsy affliction that provides the pic's best visual gimmicks. [...] As with much of the director's work, large sections of the plot are pure hokum, and the gradual slackening of both pace and suspense in a sluggish second half only underlines the increasing silliness. [Asia] Argento is fine in her intense, terrified early scenes but progressively becomes less convincing as career cop and empowered madwoman. [...] Giuseppe Rotunno's lensing is cool and elegant, with the deep reds and blues in which Argento pics are usually drenched conspicuously absent. [...] Visual effects generally are sharp, as is the elaborately constructed soundtrack. This is compromised by Argento's usual practice of post-synching dialogue (in both Italian and English versions), but it is given immeasurable help by Ennio Morricone's creepily insistent singsong score.[9]

Prior to *The Stendhal Syndrome*, Dario had been a guest at the Rome Fantafestival in the summer of 1994. Despite the problems he was facing in both his personal and professional life, he enjoyed being feted by the fans—though he initially had mixed emotions about sharing the limelight with another guest of honor: Lucio Fulci (1927-1996). Fulci, the gifted writer and director who rose to popular prominence in the early 1980s with a string of low-budget, high-style, and very high-gore horror movies, was seen by many as Argento's chief rival in the field of Italian horror. Like so many working directors, Fulci was obliged to follow whatever was popular at the box office—and while he had actually beaten Argento to the punch when it came to *gialli* (his first, *Perversion Story/Una sull'altra*, debuted in Italy in August 1969—a full half-year before Argento made his debut), he was one of many journeymen who found himself making films in a similar style once Argento's *Bird* made its mark at the box office. Argento was none too pleased. "I always felt he had copied my signature style in his *giallo* pictures, and our paths never crossed socially or business wise."[10] Matters weren't helped any when Fulci came out with *Zombi 2*, which producers Fabrizio De Angelis (born 1940) and Ugo Tucci (born 1930) conceived as a blatant rip-off of Romero's *Dawn of the Dead*—the title even positioned it as a sequel to Romero's film, which Argento had titled *Zombi* in the Italian marketplace.

Fulci's acid tongue ensured that he let it be known in the press that he wasn't all that impressed with Dario's work, while Argento tended to take the high road and avoided talking about the older filmmaker—at least on the record. For example, Fulci once said: "I think Dario is a great artisan who considers himself an artist, as opposed to Hitchcock who was an artist who considered himself an artisan. This is the flaw which will make Argento go on repeating the same things. He's very good on the public relations side [...] Everyone thinks he's a very good writer and a very bad director, whereas, in fact, it's the other way around!"[11] By 1994, however, Fulci was in dire straits—he was suffering from a variety of health problems, including diabetes, and no producers were willing to take a chance on him, as he was regarded as a major insurance risk. His recent films had also gone over poorly; in fairness to Fulci, he did his best under very trying conditions, but it would be misleading to suggest that just about anything he made from the mid-'80s onward was representative of what he was fully capable of.

The two men—both headstrong, but with very different temperaments: Lucio, all fire and brimstone, contrasting with the cooler, moodier Dario—may well have felt a bit ill-disposed toward each other, but things took a surprising change. Fulci had injured his foot and due to his diabetes was having a difficult time healing; it necessitated him to spend much of his time in a wheelchair, which he loathed. When Argento saw the once-imposing Fulci in such a state, his heart went out to him. "His agent told me he was about to have a serious hospital operation—which the agent paid for because Fulci couldn't afford to—and I knew the best recovery therapy would be to get him working again."[12]

The idea of a collaboration between the two *maestri* of the macabre was certainly enough to work the fans up into a lather, and it also made great commercial sense. For Dario, it was an opportunity to help rebuild his business following his experience with almost complete financial ruin; for Lucio, it was a chance to finally get back in the director's chair—with the benefit of a major producer and plenty of exposure, to boot. It seemed like a win-win for all concerned, but of course, things didn't proceed smoothly. Initially Fulci and Argento settled on the idea of remaking Karl Freund's *The Mummy* (1932), and Dardano Sacchetti was drafted in to work on the script—it was a reunion of sorts, marking Sacchetti's first time working with Fulci since their falling out over *Blastfighter*, and Sacchetti's first picture with Dario since *Demons 2*. The writing proved to be problematic and the project was set aside. Fulci then hit on another classic horror property: André de Toth's *House of Wax* (1953). The film had been a huge hit internationally back in the day and it has long been rumored that it was the film's success in Italy which inspired Riccardo Freda and Mario Bava to make *I vampiri* (1957), which would become the first Italian horror film of the sound era. Argento liked the idea and arranged for them to screen copies of the de Toth film, as well as the original 1933 *Mystery of the Wax Museum*, which was the film that got the whole ball of wax rolling in the first place. Fulci and his collaborator Daniele Stroppa also hit upon the idea of using Gaston Leroux (1868-1927)'s short story "The Waxwork Museum" as their official source of inspiration, lest they run into any problems with Warner Bros. with regards to copyright infringement.[13]

According to Alan Jones, the collaboration between Argento and Fulci proved to be heated, with one aspect being a particularly touchy topic, specifically on-screen violence. Surprisingly, Fulci was not particularly interested in playing up his reputation as "The Godfather of Gore" and was more intrigued by the possibilities of making an old-fashioned, atmosphere-driven horror movie. Argento was not convinced and kept trying to increase the gore quota; the two men fought like hell over it, but Fulci was eventually left with no choice but to acquiesce.[14] Argento controlled the purse strings and was in a position to cripple the project, after all, so Fulci was not about to jeopardize his best chance of getting back into the game. Playing devil's advocate, it's easy to understand where they were both coming from. Fulci had long been regarded as terribly down-market for including so much graphic gore in his films, and a "classy" production such as this could possibly have increased his critical profile during the twilight stage of his career; on the other hand, Argento was in need of sure-fire box-office success, and he wasn't about to take chances just to massage Fulci's ego.

Unfortunately, the pre-production phase on *Wax Mask* (*M.D.C.—Maschera di cera*) dragged on interminably while Argento tinkered over post-production and promotional duties on *The Stendhal Syndrome*. Fulci became more and more desperate as the clock ticked; he was in bad shape financially and the prospect of his comeback film possibly slipping away from him was too much to bear. Argento continued to assure Fulci that they were on track and that he needed to be patient, but nobody could have foreseen what would happen next: Fulci died on Wednesday, March 13, 1996 as a result of complications from his diabetes.

Argento was then faced with the inevitable quandary, should he continue with the project without Fulci, or should he make the film and dedicate it to his memory? The latter path was chosen, but it seems that Argento himself was never seriously interested in

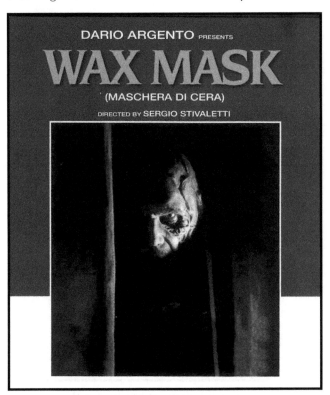

Export advertising for *Wax Mask*.

taking over directing duties himself. Instead, he turned to Sergio Stivaletti, who was already involved in the pre-production as the special make-up effects designer. Argento felt he was the only logical choice to take over the film and wasted little time in making him the proverbial offer he couldn't refuse. As Stivaletti recalled, "I was shocked when Dario called [...] I had been looking for a chance to direct and thought it would be with my own film and script. [...] I was in the right place at the right time; I accepted the offer."[15] The rest, as they say, is history. Stivaletti made some significant changes to Fulci's original script and did his best to make the film a homage while still being in his own style. He and Argento even hired Fulci's eldest daughter, Antonella, to serve as an assistant art director.

As a final sad but touching postscript to the Fulci saga, Argento, aware of the fact that Lucio died in terrible financial shape, actually paid for the funeral out of his own pocket. According to Mark Thompson Ashworth, who attended the service at the Church of the Artists located in the Piazza del Popolo in Rome, there were many people in attendance. Not many of Fulci's professional colleagues attended, but Argento and his office staff were in attendance, as were old friends like the actress Gabriella Giorgelli (who would go on to appear in *Wax Mask*) and the director Umberto Lenzi. As Mark recalled for the author, the services were held on an appropriately gloomy and rainy Saturday morning. Fulci's remains were interred in the Prima Porta Cemetery in Rome; Mario Bava (who preceded him in death by 16 years) is interred in the very same cemetery, albeit on the opposite side.

Wax Mask finally went into production on July 9, 1996, with Stivaletti nervously at the helm. He was ably assisted by Fulci's old friend and colleague, cinematographer Sergio Salvati, who helped to give the film the sumptuous, colorful look associated with Italian Gothic horrors of the 1960s. Argento again made his presence known on the set, but he was evidently pleased with what Stivaletti was doing and didn't cause the first-time director the same sort of headaches that Michele Soavi had endured on *The Church*. The loss of Fulci had been a major blow, of course, but for the time being anyway, Argento had faith that they had a winner on their hands. The filming wrapped on August 13, after which Stivaletti had his hands full with complicated post-production work, especially where the copious special visual effects were concerned.

Wax Mask opens with a bit of childhood trauma, as a little girl witnesses the brutal murder of her father; a kindly police inspector arrives later and promises to find the culprit. Fans of Argento will recognize this as the set-up for his own later *giallo*, *Sleepless*. The film then moves full force into the era of the Belle Époque in Paris, as Stivaletti and his collaborators emphasize the beauty and excess of the era to counterpoint the grisly goings-on in the story. Once again, Argento fans will recognize a similarity to one of his other films, in this instance his reviled take on *The Phantom of the Opera*. Argento may have felt that Fulci was copying him in his *gialli*, but clearly, he was not above borrowing from others, as well.

The story hews fairly closely to de Toth's model. A demented genius kidnaps various members of polite society, so that he can use their bodies in his waxworks museum. The public is fascinated by how lifelike the figures are, and for good reason. They are actually human beings coated in wax. A sick twist to the story reveals that the mad Boris Volkoff (Robert Hossein, of *Cemetery Without Crosses*) uses a special chemical compound to keep the unwilling models in a state of suspended animation while they are put on display; as such, they are aware of everything that is going on around them, but they are unable to react. One of the film's most effective sequences sees the ineffectual heroine (Romina Mondello) accidentally knocking out the hidden "feeding tube" from one of the figures, thus allowing it to regain some perfunctory body movement; it's a moment of "body horror" which wouldn't be out of place in a David Cronenberg movie.

Luridly sensational Italian advertising for *Wax Mask*.

Inspector Lanvin (Aldo Massasso, who would go on to appear in *The Phantom of the Opera* and *Sleepless*) in the film's best sequence.

According to co-writer Daniele Stroppa, "Lucio wanted this to be a very mean story, with no positive characters. He also meant to analyze the political connotations of the period, but to Sergio, the historical frame only serves as a pretext."[16] It is well known that Stivaletti made some significant changes to the script. Fulci was interested in mood and atmosphere, whereas Stivaletti (who makes a cameo appearance as a satisfied customer at a brothel) naturally tailored the material to suit his interest in special effects. As Stivaletti explained, "When I came on board, we all felt it was necessary to exploit my craft and emphasize the action. So now there are more effects-crammed sequences."[17] This manifests itself in the slightly silly finale, which contains more than a whiff of James Cameron's *The Terminator* (1984) as the exposed (literally!) Volkoff is reduced to a bloodthirsty automaton. Up until that point, however, the film is sober and well-made, even if the majority of the characters fail to register one way or another. One sequence shot apparently as Fulci intended involves a character being faced with a *doppelgänger* of sorts and climaxes with a spurt of blood spraying onto a gramophone record, which causes the needle to come to a screeching halt. It's a magnificent sequence, no matter who devised it. The film benefits from superior production design by Massimo Antonello Geleng and first-rate cinematography by Fulci's long-time collaborator Sergio Salvati. Salvati's use of shadow and vivid primary colors makes it one of the last truly rich-looking Italian horror films to date; honestly, Argento would have been wise to have employed him on his lavish remake of *The Phantom of the Opera*.

If the film falls apart during its final scenes and suffers from some less-than-convincing computer-generated effects, it still offers up ample mood and some rich imagery. One can only guess at what Fulci might have done with the film, or what it could have done to bolster his flagging career, but the film still provided him with an opportunity to attach his name to one last worthy example of a genre with which his name had become synonymous.

Commercially, *Wax Mask* proved to be yet another disappointment. The early hype surrounding the picture dissipated somewhat when Fulci passed away, and there simply wasn't the same level of excitement over an Argento-Stivaletti collaboration as there had been for the original bill of fare. Italian International Film put it out on April 4, 1997 and it failed to excite the public; it didn't even crack the top 100 in the Italian domestic box-office season, which says it all. The film's dismal response killed any hopes of a sequel, though both Stivaletti and Argento expressed some hopes of making a follow-up.[18] Once … who knows? As it stands, however, *Wax Mask* did little to solve Argento's mounting professional problems; could it be that he had lost his connection with the Italian public? As luck would have it, things were about to get even worse.

Notes:
1. Quoted from the featurette "Three Shades of Asia," included on the Blue Underground Blu-ray release of *The Stendhal Syndrome*.
2. Quoted from the featurette "Prisoner of Art," included on the Blue Underground Blu-ray release of *The Stendhal Syndrome*.
3. *Variety*, March 3, 1996.
4. http://www.hitparadeitalia.it/bof/boi/boi1995-96.htm
5. As reported on July 1, 1996 by *The San Bernardino County Sun*.
6. As reported on March 1998 by *The Record*.
7. https://www.tvguide.com/movies/the-stendhal-syndrome/review/132133/
8. Biodrowski, Steve, "*Giallo* Turns to Jello: Argento's latest thriller fails to thrill," *Cinefantastique*, Volume 27, #10, June 1996, p. 50.
9. Rooney, David, "The Stendhal Syndrome," *Variety*, February 4, 1996.
10. Jones, Alan, *Dario Argento: The Man, the Myths & the Magic* (Godalming: FAB Press, 2012), p. 237.
11. Palmerini, Luca M. and Gaetano Mistretta, *Spaghetti Nightmares* (Key West: Fantasma Books, 1997), p. 61.
12. Jones, Alan, *Dario Argento: The Man, the Myths & the Magic* (Godalming: FAB Press, 2012), p. 237.
13. Ibid.
14. Ibid.
15. Ibid, p. 238.
16. Curci, Loris, "Wax Ecstatic," *Fangoria*, #162, May 1997, p. 36.
17. Ibid.
18. Ibid, p. 38.

Chapter Eighteen:
Gothic Kitsch and Scarlet Divas

For his next project, Dario was more eager than ever to curry public favor. *The Stendhal Syndrome* had done okay, but it was far from the major hit he had been hoping for. *Wax Mask* proved to be a flop. The recent bankruptcy issues, triggered in part by an ill-advised move into the American market coupled with diminishing returns on the post-*Phenomena* pictures in the international market, was still looming in recent memory—so, putting it mildly, Argento was in need of a hit. When Silvio Berlusconi's (born 1936) company Mediaset conducted a poll among cinema viewers asking what sort of pictures they wanted to see, one of the subjects they included—based, no doubt, on the popularity of the Andrew Lloyd Webber musical—was an old chestnut: Gaston Leroux's *The Phantom of the Opera*. The response was unexpectedly positive, with an overwhelming number of people who participated in the poll saying that, yes, they'd love to see a new version mounted for the big screen. The irony should be obvious. Argento's most recent production, *Wax Mask*, was (at least nominally) based on another Leroux story—and audiences couldn't have cared less. Even so, Berlusconi's business empire encompassed Medusa, which had handled the release of *The Stendhal Syndrome* in Italy, and he also happened to be keen to get a new version of the book into production. It made perfect sense that Argento, the master of horror, should be the man to bring the story to the screen for a new generation. In addition, Berlusconi was so excited by the results of his cinema poll that he decided to throw a lot of money at the picture; the end result would become Argento's biggest production to date.

First published in serial form in *La Gaulois* from late September, 1909 through early January 1910, *Le Fantôme de l'Opéra* tells the story of a mysterious specter known as the Opera Ghost, who terrorizes the workers of the Palais Garnier opera house in Paris. When a young understudy named Christine Daaé performs in place of leading soprano Carlotta, she draws the attention of two admirers: a young aristocrat named Raoul and a mysterious admirer who claims to be the Angel of Music. The naïve Christine believes the latter to be the same character her late father had told her about when she was just a child, and she accepts his friendship and his offer to help coach her in her singing. In fact, it is the Opera Ghost himself, who warns the directors of the opera house to allow Christine to take over from Carlotta or face dire consequences. They ignore the warnings and tragedy strikes when the Phantom cuts the heavy chandelier from the ceiling, crushing at least one patron underneath it. The Phantom then abducts Christine and takes her to his lair, where he admits his true identity. He is a hideously deformed convict named Erik. Overcome with curiosity, she unmasks Erik and reveals a horrible, skull-like visage. This unhinges Erik even further and he refuses to allow her to leave his subterranean lair. She eventually convinces Erik that she will return if he allows her freedom for two weeks to tend to personal affairs in the outside world. He agrees but when he sees her confessing her love to Raoul, he becomes enraged with jealousy and he arranges to abduct her once more. After threatening to kill Raoul and everybody else with explosives, Christine agrees to marry Erik; he is so touched by her devotion to Raoul that he eventually decides to let her go free with Raoul; he subsequently dies of a broken heart and Christine keeps her word to him by arranging to bury him where he will never be found.

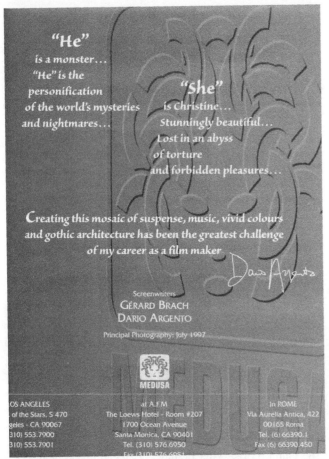

Full-page teaser ad for *The Phantom of the Opera*, which ran in *Variety*; note the way it plays the film up as Dario's most ambitious project to date.

To help adapt Leroux's story, Argento elected to go outside of his comfort zone and enlist the aid of a French screenwriter—all the better to help understand the socio-political climate in which the story was set. He decided to go for broke and reached out to Gérard Brach (1927-2006), the eccentric screenwriter who had long worked as Roman Polanski's (born 1933) screenwriting partner. Brach had begun his collaboration with Polanski with *Repulsion* (1965) and most recently they had worked together on the grossly misunderstood pitch-black comedy *Bitter Moon* (1992). Brach was also agoraphobic, which made collaborating with the Rome-based Argento a bit tricky. Argento spent much of 1997 shuttling back and forth between Rome and Paris in order to hold meetings with Brach in the latter's apartment; on the face of it, it was a major inconvenience—yet Argento was fairly effusive about the experience. "[I]t was one of the most enjoyable, if strange, relationships I've ever had with a writer."[1]

With Medusa enthusiastically footing the bill, Argento was given access to his biggest budget to date—$10 million. The money was certainly needed, as the story's scope and period setting called for greater resources than usual. Naturally, Dario looked to film at the Paris opera house—but that didn't pan out, so a deal was reached with the Budapest Opera House. The location proved to be a tremendous asset to the production—it still looked appropriate for the period, and the lavish yet tasteful décor added to the film's glossiness. Of course, the entire film couldn't be produced on location, so Massimo Antonello Geleng (born 1946), the gifted production designer on *The Church*, *The Sect*, and *The Stendhal Syndrome*, was called upon to provide designs fitting the film's Belle Époque–style milieu. This was Argento's first "costume picture" since *Le cinque giornate*, and no expense was spared with regards to recreating the period and getting the details as correct as possible. The look of the film was particularly vital and Argento decided early on that he wanted to evoke the look of the artwork of the period, as well. To photograph the picture, he elected to reach out to his *Opera* cinematographer, Ronnie Taylor; given the similarities between the two scenarios, it certainly made sense. Taylor had actually been approached to work on *The Stendhal Syndrome*, but there was a conflict in his schedule, so he was happy to have an opportunity to work with Dario again, following a decade's break. And of course, Sergio Stivaletti was also recruited to provide the elaborately conceived make-up effects—and to supplement the images where needed via CGI. The film also marked another "return to the fold" for Claudio Argento, who served as a producer for his brother for the first time since *Two Evil Eyes*.

Dario at work on *The Phantom of the Opera* in 1997, at the office of production manager Tommaso Calevi. Photo courtesy of Carla Alonzo.

The Stendhal Syndrome had arisen out of a period of fear, sadness, depression, and anger—and it showed. It could be partly owing to the fact that the film didn't perform as well as hoped and partly owing to a desire to distance himself from the unpleasant emotions that bubbled over during the making of that film, but Dario's take on *Phantom* couldn't have been more different in style and tone. There's no doubt that Gérard Brach helped to encourage a quirkier sensibility, but the *Phantom* script was positively awash in grotesque, tongue-in-cheek excess. The "origin story," absent in Leroux's book, displays an influence from Tim Burton's *Batman Returns* (1992), of all things, and the overall approach was far more comic than usual for Dario. If anything, it proved to be a little too offbeat and tongue-in-cheek, thus confusing the audience Argento was so desperately hoping to win over.

The film started shooting on January 19, 1998 and it was given a very generous shooting schedule—finally wrapping on April 17, before Sergio Stivaletti started working on post-production special effects duties. Argento found a new editor to take charge of the film:

The Unsane Cinema of Dario Argento

Anna Rosa Napoli. Napoli had previously edited Peter Del Monte's *Piccoli fuochi* (1985), which Claudio produced through Produzioni Intersound. Argento and Napoli hit it off and she would remain on board for Argento's next two projects, before they parted ways. Since then, she has become the editor of choice for Michele Soavi, for whom she is credited with such projects as the TV movies *Uno bianca* (2001) and *Il testomine* (2001) and the features *The Goodbye Kiss* (*Arrivederci amore, ciao*, 2006) and *Il sangue dei vinti* (2008). Reportedly the original edit ran well over two hours and Medusa requested that Argento get it pared down to a more workable running time; the days of allowing for a more languid Italian edit while preparing tighter versions for export were long gone. Around this time Argento talked about going to England and making a classical *giallo* in the Agatha Christie mold, but nothing ever came of it.

The action commences with a brief "origin story" sequence, in which we see a woman sobbing hysterically because she has been forced to abandon her child by her callous husband. The baby has been sent into the sewers of Paris in its basket, where it faces certain death—but miraculously it is rescued by rats, which nurse the child and provide it with some semblance of a home. To say it's a strange and unlikely start would be an understatement, yet it positions the narrative as a fairy tale rather than a conventional narrative that is to be understood on literal grounds. It's a set-up that alienates most viewers, but those who can accept it have an easier time getting into the spirit of the proceedings. The images of the child's basket floating down the stream, accompanied by the strains of the overture of *Faust* by Charles Gounod, have an oddly poetic quality. The scene is capped with a delightfully eccentric point of view shot of one of the rats looking at the child, as the baby's tiny hand reaches out and grabs hold of its whiskers. While it definitely sets up a ton of questions for the more pedantic viewers—how do rats go about raising a child? How does the child learn to speak? And so forth—it works well enough on the level on which it is intended. One's tolerance for the film is absolutely dependent on being able to "go with the flow." This is Argento's most eccentric film to date, by far, and it's almost enough to make something like *Phenomena* look positively realistic by comparison.

The action then cuts to Paris in the year 1877, as the opera house is in full swing with a production of Gounod's *Romeo and Juliet*. Argento shows off the film's lavish budget by emphasizing the period décor. The immaculate sets and art direction, the beautiful costumes, the artfully rendered lighting by Ronnie Taylor and the sensual camera movements combine to create a sense of scope. Whatever one may make of the finished film, there's no denying that the money is up there on the screen. This is one of Argento's biggest and most ambitious productions and it's clear that he was determined to make the most of the opportunity. Amid all the splendor and spectacle, there is ample room for horror and gore. As the opera stages another successful performance for a packed audience, Argento cuts to three workers in the caverns beneath the opera house. As they joke back and forth, things take a nasty turn when they accidentally happen upon the Phantom's secret lair. One of the workers is literally cut in half, and the other two are plunged into the abyss, with only the sounds of their bodies being stabbed repeatedly and their screams echoing on the soundtrack. The sudden appearance of graphic gore establishes a running theme in the film: The contrast between the opulence of the opera world with the nastiness which runs underneath it. The film is set amid "high society," and this allows Argento a chance to offer more socio-political commentary as the various figures of wealth and authority are shown to be mostly vile, corrupt and grotesque.

Unaware of what has taken place beneath the opera house, Christine Daaé (Asia Argento) takes the stage after everybody else has apparently gone home. She sings to the empty house, not realizing that she is being observed from above by a secret admirer. Christine is established early on as a much more savvy character than her counterpart in the book; she is headstrong, independent, and determined to realize her dreams. She fantasizes about taking over the role of Juliet in the opera, but for now she is forced to understudy for the grand diva Carlotta (Nadia Rinaldi). Despite her steely resolve, Christine seems to be a little unsure of herself in matters of the heart, and this leads to the central conflict which dominates the narrative thrust of the picture. Asia's performance isn't as memorable as it had been in *The Stendhal Syndrome*, but it's also not as interesting

The Paris Opera, by way of the Budapest Opera, in this Italian lobby card.

Julian Sands shows off his physique in this Italian lobby card.

a character for her to play as in her earlier films with Dario, this role relies more on her tremendous physical presence and beauty, as the camera often seems to fixate on her in a more objectified fashion.

Christine first meets the Phantom as she heads back to her dressing room. The Phantom (Julian Sands) watches her as she comes down the hall, then as she passes, she thinks she hears him saying something. "I said nothing," he says. "But I caught myself thinking about you. Thoughts that surprised me. And I'm not easily surprised." In the film's most audacious conceit, the Phantom is presented as a handsome, Byronic figure—with long flowing blonde hair and a muscular build. He doesn't have to hide behind a mask, as his features are actually quite pleasing; yet, these looks do serve as a mask, in much the same way as Alfredo Grossi's outwardly handsome and charming appearance served to mask a twisted mind in *The Stendhal Syndrome*. Early on the plan had been to give the Phantom rodent-like features, keeping with the idea of his being raised by rats, but this idea was sensibly dropped; that said, the decision to not have a horribly scarred Phantom upset many viewers—and of course it also deprives the film of the major "unmasking" scene which was so vital to the earlier adaptations with Lon Chaney and Claude Rains.

Here again, this is an idea that either works for the individual viewer, or which shoots the film down dead in its tracks. On a thematic level, it makes the film an interesting continuation of the themes and concerns of *The Stendhal Syndrome*, but in terms of shock value, it definitely invalidated the film in the minds of many fans. The dialogue between the Phantom and Christine is deliberately florid and theatrical, which seems befitting the idea of a character who has learned everything about language and social etiquette from classical literature; when we see the Phantom's lair later in the film, it's littered with old books and it's strongly implied that in educating himself, the Phantom (who is *not* identified as Erik in this adaptation) has relied strongly on a mixture of observing the behavior and attitudes of the people at the opera house and gleaning what he can from these old books. It also recalls the deliberately fruity dialogue of Brach's script for Polanski's *Bitter Moon*, which evokes the purple prose of bad erotic fiction because its protagonist/narrator is a failed writer of such fiction. Many critics have labeled the film unintentionally funny, but this rather deliberately seems to miss the point. Like it or not, *Phantom* sees Argento working in a much more tongue-in-cheek tone—as such, the humor (some of it very overt, bordering on slapstick) is anything but unintentional.

The Unsane Cinema of Dario Argento

Nadia Rinaldi is not called upon for understatement in *The Phantom of the Opera*.

Grotesque comedy is also at the heart of a major subplot involving a rat catcher named Ignace (István Bubik). Taking a cue from Monty Python, Argento is careful to differentiate his upper crust characters from the poor ones. Ignace is badly in need of a hot shower, and he appears filthy and bedraggled throughout. As played by Hungarian actor Bubik (1958-2004), the character is more vile and despicable than the creatures he makes a living exterminating; they simply act according to their nature, whereas he derives an unhealthy level of satisfaction in making his prey suffer. Bubik's performance is far from subtle—lots of salivating and eye-rolling abound—but he successfully conveys the character's wild-eyed fanaticism and gets a few chuckles along the way. While setting traps, he is suddenly compelled to stick his own hand in one of the contraptions; that's bad enough, but it gets worse when a bunch of rats swarm in and gnaw his thumb down to the bone. Here again, the emphasis on *Grand Guignol* lashings of gore is almost uncharacteristic for Argento. His earlier films certainly didn't skimp on blood and gore, it's true, but they didn't tend to wallow in excessive carnage; the violence was typically either stylized for poetic effect, or presented in a blunt, realistic and ugly fashion, as had been the case in *The Stendhal Syndrome*. Here, one gets the impression that he is using the gore to compensate for the lack of a more overtly "scary" Phantom character.

Christine continues to feel more attracted to the mysterious Phantom, and they appear to have the ability to communicate telepathically; often she will be seen to be carrying out conversations with him, even though he is nowhere near her. The psychic link between Christine and the Phantom recalls the one between Jennifer and the insect world in *Phenomena*. The Phantom also represents a kind of alternative to the mainstream world, though his schizophrenic nature makes him far from the ideal mate for her.

Christine's maid, Honorine (Coralina Cataldi-Tassoni), picks up on the difference in her personality; she recognizes that she is happier and that she seems to be lost in her own fantasy world much of the time. Honorine's interest in Christine is ambiguous. It could be that she harbors sexual desires for her, or she might just be resentful that her friend has found something that has been lacking in her own life—love. Regardless, she feels a bit of jealousy towards the attentions lavished on her, not only by the Phantom, but also by a young Baron named Raoul (Andrea Di Stefano). Cataldi-Tassoni adds wry humor to her performance, which definitely recalls her earlier role for Argento in *Opera*.

The world of the opera gives Argento ample opportunity to explore his predilection for the grotesque. Carlotta, for example, is the ultimate diva from hell. She's loud, bossy, rude, and incredibly intolerant. Like the heard-but-never-seen Mara Czekova in *Opera*, she expects everybody to satisfy her every whim. She is also very jealous of Christine, simply because the latter is younger and more conventionally attractive than she is. Nadia Rinaldi (born 1967) was well known for comedy roles, including a starring turn in Christian De Sica's

Faccione (1991), so she is ideally suited to the baroque excesses of the character; this is as close to Fellini terrain as Argento has ever ventured.

The only person she shows any affection toward is her effete servant Marc (Gábor Harsai) and this is entirely down to his totally selfless desire to serve her and satisfy her whims; he's even ready with a goblet for her to spit into after completing one of her solos in rehearsal. Marc bows and scrapes and treats her like a Queen.

The other members of the opera are a little more ambivalent and when she finds herself sidelined with a sudden case of a sore throat—the result of the Phantom putting something into her throat spray—they are only too eager to prepare Christine to go on in her place.

The various opera scenes are loaded with interesting visual details. Argento shows Edgar Degas (Ferenc Deák B.) sketching the young dancing girls, while various cutaways show the members of polite society being pampered and coddled as the opera performances are put on for their collective amusement. The period detail is impeccable and Argento's desire to evoke the artwork of the period results in some truly beautiful "still life" type images. The grotesque is never far away, however, and it's obvious in the exaggerated mannerisms and attitudes of the various "bottom feeder" types who vie for favoritism among the rich and powerful, and especially in the form of sideline characters like Pourdieu (Aldo Massasso, 1933-2013, who had just appeared as the kindly inspector in *Wax Mask* and would go on to play another policeman in *Sleepless*). Pourdieu is a wealthy, politically-connected member of the board in charge of the opera—and he's also a pedophile. He's often seen looking lustfully at the pre-pubescent dancing girls and he is basically emblematic of the worst aspects of "polite society," as he hides behind his power and privilege while carrying out unspeakable crimes without ever attracting any notice.

As the story unfolds, Christine finds herself torn between the Phantom and Raoul. Raoul is equated with the light, while the Phantom is pure darkness. He is not pure evil, however; he possesses tenderness and a sense of justice which is particularly evident when he strikes down Pourdieu before the old pedophile is able to despoil a young child. It's one of the film's most potent sequences, as the child runs to the catacombs desperately trying to avoid her would-be attacker and Argento shows the old man's shadow looming on the walls as he closes in on her. He tries to bribe the girl with chocolates and when the Phantom surprises him, there's a wonderful image of the candies being flung into the air as Pourdieu is knocked to the ground; the Phantom's bestial nature comes through as he tears the man's throat out with his bare teeth. All of this is witnessed by the traumatized

Julian Sands provides an unconventional version of the Phantom.

child—Argento incorporates a beautiful point of view shot of the action through her splayed fingers—who is then set free by the Phantom. Tellingly, her attempt to inform her teacher what has happened results in her getting slapped for telling lies.

In a way, the Phantom represents freedom from the rigid rules of society—yet his unnatural existence in the catacombs beneath the opera house is not suitable for anybody else to live with him. He truly cares about Christine and does everything in his power to protect her, but he is also seriously psychologically unhinged; not surprising given his unusual upbringing! Raoul, on the other hand, has wealth and social standing. He's a kind, thoughtful, rather bookish sort—and he, too, is marked as "different" by virtue of having a pronounced limp and needing the use of a walking stick. Christine is drawn to him but feels devoted to the Phantom; Raoul, not wanting to lose her altogether, agrees to a platonic

Christine (Asia Argento) turns to Raoul (Andrea Di Stefano) for comfort.

Italian lobby card showing the Fellini-esque visit to the Turkish Bath.

relationship, even if it's not what he really wants. Torn apart by unfulfilled desire, Raoul takes a trip with his brother (Leonardo Treviglio) to a local brothel/Turkish bath. This is another stand-out scene in the film, crammed with strange details and emphasizing the diverse shapes and forms of the human body as various people parade about completely naked; it's as frank a depiction of nudity as can be found in Argento's films up until this time, and not surprisingly the entire scene is removed from some prints of the film. As Raoul dulls his heartache with some opium, a couple of poets fight over the respective virtues of Rimbaud and Baudelaire— and in his drunken stupor, he mistakes a prostitute for Christine; there's some very overheated sexual imagery here, as he imagines her dribbling wine on her chest and rubbing her breasts in a state of erotic ecstasy. It's all an illusion, of course, and Raoul eventually snaps out of it only to collapse in tears; the character's aching love for Christine is sincerely conveyed by Andrea Di Stefano (born 1972), who gives a good performance in a tricky role.

Another subplot involves the characters of worker Alfred (David D'Ingeo, a veteran of one of the Luigi Cozzi-directed episodes of *Turno di notte*, who would go on to appear in *Scarlet Diva*) and his paramour, the scrub woman Paulette (Kitty Kéri). Alfred notices the Phantom moving through the underground and follows him; he is convinced that he has a hidden treasure and Paulette convinces him that they should go into the catacombs in search of it. Truth be told, the subplot doesn't serve much in the way of narrative function—it does nothing to further or resolve the central thrust of the story— but it does allow Argento to build some suspense and create a few nasty shock effects. As the young lovers grope their way through the seemingly endless mazes of tunnels, they become separated; Alfred is cornered by the Phantom, who assures the young man, "I'm not a Phantom. I'm a rat." Alfred's reply of "I love animals" is appropriately tongue-in-cheek, but it doesn't save him; the Phantom hurls him from one of the alcoves in the tunnel and he is impaled on top of one of the many stalagmite formations growing in the cave. Paulette arrives in time to see Alfred's mutilated body and she attempts a hasty retreat; there's great use of dynamic camerawork here as Argento alternates shifting points of view shots and we see various Steadicam views of the tunnels as the girl desperately tries to get away from the Phantom. Ennio Morricone's classy, suspenseful music adds immensely to the effectiveness of the scene, which climaxes when the Phantom corners Paulette and uses his teeth to rip the poor girl's tongue from her mouth. Again, the contrast between the stately, elegant look of the production with flourishes of over-the-top gore makes for a heady cocktail; it's not surprising, really, that the film remains so hotly debated in the Argento canon.

Of course, not everything about the film works. Despite the often-gorgeous imagery and clever variations on established tropes, there are some major stumbling blocks. The scene in which the Phantom, besotted with love for Christine, goes to the roof of the opera house and envisions images of rat-children writhing in pain in a trap, and fashion-spread-like images of Christine beckoning to him seductively is ill-conceived and badly executed; Sergio Stivaletti delivers some impressive prosthetic work, but his digital effects are well below-par and Argento would have done well to have removed the scene in its entirety.

There's also the matter of the Phantom himself. It's not so much the conception of the Phantom, however, as it is the inadequate portrayal of British actor Julian Sands (born 1958) which works against it. Sands was not the first choice for the part—Argento reportedly reached out to the likes of John Malkovich (born 1953) and Anthony Hopkins (born 1937), both of whom would have made for a very different film experience altogether—but on the face of it, he seemed to be a decent choice. His art-house connections via Ken Russell (*Gothic*, 1986) and Merchant Ivory (*A Room with a View*, 1986) were supplemented by some success in genre-oriented fare like *Warlock* (1989) and *Aracnaphobia* (1990), and his name wasn't a bad one for the all-important English-language market. He looks physically impressive and matches Argento's concept of a potentially noble creature whose scarred psyche erupts into bouts of terrifying violence, but his weak, wispy voice is all wrong for the character; not surprisingly, he comes off more convincingly in the Italian dub, where he was revoiced by another actor. Despite the best efforts of Asia and Di Stefano, the crucial romantic triangle is undercut by Sands' performance—and while he does well enough when called upon to turn vicious, he lacks the sense of mystery that the character so desperately needs.

Christine is finally lured to the Phantom's lair, where she sings for him before they succumb to carnal temptation. The Phantom's bestial qualities come to the foreground in their sex scenes, which contain implicit sodomy. The passion between the two characters is not as convincingly portrayed as it might have been; Asia and Sands don't have much in the way of chemistry, and one is left with the impression that their relationship is driven more by lust than by deeper emotional motivations.

The rat catcher comes back into the action when we see him and his little person assistant (Sandor Bese) at work on developing what can only be called a "rat mobile." The whimsical nature of the scene is underlined by Ennio Morricone's "Burlesque" theme,

The Phantom and Christine seem more in lust than in love.

Ignace (István Bubik) and his dwarf pal (Sandor Bese) could well be references to similar, yet very different, characters in the 1962 Hammer version of *Phantom*.

but the queasy mixture of the farcical and the grotesque is summed up by the images of the assistant cutting the tails off of the dead rats and stuffing them into bottles of formaldehyde; Argento's love for gross-out humor is really evident in the scenes involving the rat catcher, and to say enjoying them constitutes "an acquired taste" is definitely an understatement. Nevertheless, the duo manage to get their remarkably sophisticated piece of machinery working—and in another gloriously over-the-top scene, Argento shows the machine sucking the rats into its mechanical workings, where they are then killed and spat out for the assistant to add to his sack of "trophies." It's far more reminiscent of the films of Jean-Pierre Jeunet and Marc Caro, including *The City of Lost Children* (*La cité des enfants perdus*, 1995), or even Terry Gilliam (*Brazil*, 1985), than of anything in Argento's back catalogue—but it serves to remind the viewer that, as opposed to the deadly serious tone of *The Stendhal Syndrome*, this is far more playful in its intent. Farce gives way to gore once more when the vehicle crashes, badly injuring Ignace and decapitating his assistant in the process.

Ignace and his pal take their "rat mobile" for a spin.

Having been depicted as a source of lowbrow comedy for the better part of the film, Ignace takes on the role of villain when he spies on the Phantom making love to Christine; he finds the entire thing disgusting and sets out to "out" Christine to the public at large. Meanwhile, Christine begins to rebel against the Phantom when she discovers that he is resorting to violent methods to further her career; he threatens the opera management that catastrophe will strike if they do not allow Christine to take the lead in *Romeo and Juliet*, but they decide to call his bluff. This leads to the big "chandelier" scene, which had so impressed Dario as a boy when he saw the Arthur Lubin-directed version starring Claude Rains. The scene is played for maximum spectacle and comedy, as the patrons are crushed beneath the chandelier—while Carlotta is struck on the head by a piece of falling scenery; the image of her opening her mouth to scream in dismay at the chaos is rendered comical by the puff of dust she breathes out, an effect not unlike something from a cartoon. Christine is justifiably put off by this display of "affection," and she escapes back to Raoul, to whom she pledges her love and fidelity.

When Christine goes on stage to perform *Romeo and Juliet*, her triumph is disrupted by the sudden appearance of Ignace, who hobbles on stage, his face and clothes stained with blood from the injuries sustained from his

The Phantom's "human-trap" hallucination.

accident. He points an accusing finger at her and calls her "the Phantom's whore," at which point the Phantom swoops in and carries her back to his lair. The patrons, upset by Ignace's claims that she is in cahoots with the man responsible for so many deaths, are whipped up into a frenzy and form a mob. The finale sees the Phantom ready to kill off his rival, Raoul, but when he realizes how much Christine truly cares for him, he decides to spare him; with the mob coming and screaming for their blood, he works with Raoul to engineer their escape. Raoul and Christine make their getaway via the Phantom's boat, which he has used to get through the more inaccessible parts of the catacombs, and he stays behind to fight off the crowd; Christine cries and screams for him to join them, but he correctly asserts that this is his world—and now that it is coming down around him, he has nowhere else to go.

Ignace and the others arrive and do battle with the Phantom, who manages to kill off the rat catcher before being shot down like a wild animal. As Christine sobs, the ring he had given her as a symbol of their love drops into the murky waters; the "light" versus "dark" theme is visualized here as she and Raoul make their way into the light, while the Phantom's body sinks to the bottom of the fetid waters below. The melancholy finale is neither triumphant nor downbeat. Christine survives and it is implied that she will have a happy and loving future together with Raoul, but in killing the Phantom, society has not rid itself of a monster—he is merely a misfit whose failure to thrive is down to the inadequacies of "the normal world" above. Don't forget, he was not born a monster. He was a normal child abandoned by his parents; in sending him to his doom in the waters of the sewer, they deprived him of any chance for a normal and happy life. The Phantom is not the real villain of the piece, even if he has a propensity for violence; characters like Pourdieu and Ignace emerge as far less sympathetic figures, even if the former's social connections and wealth enable him to carry out his crimes with no fear of recrimination. The Phantom's main sin is to be "different." On that level, he never stands a chance of finding acceptance—and his romance with Christine is rendered impossible because he knows this to be true; sooner than keep her at his side and subject her to the bizarre existence to which he has become accustomed, he sets her free. On that level, at least, he proves to be sincere and selfless in his love; this allows him to emerge as a tragic anti-hero as opposed to the scar-faced monster of Leroux's book.

The Phantom of the Opera is possibly Dario Argento's most unfairly maligned and misunderstood film. The criticism that it is unintentionally funny is mystifying; it's hard to understand how any attentive viewers would believe that it was meant to be taken as a straight-faced Gothic horror film. It offers a very different style, tone, and sensibility from the dark, gritty, and despairing *The Stendhal Syndrome*; again, it almost plays as if Argento was looking to move away from that peek into the abyss. It's definitely different from anything he had made before it, which is not a bad thing; it's only his second foray into "costume melodrama" following *Le cinque giornate*, and the two films also display a similarly quirky sensibility where humor is concerned.

As mentioned above, it's certainly not a perfect film. The central romance between Christine and the

The Phantom proclaims his love for Christine in this French lobby card.

Phantom doesn't have the weight that it should and some of the digital effects are truly dismal, undercutting an otherwise very polished-looking production. Some of the shifts in tone are also not as successful as others. And yet for all its missteps, the film shows Argento bravely offering a very off-beat and highly personal take on one of the genre's most familiar chestnuts. It certainly can't be faulted on the level of ambition and the money spent on the production is visible throughout; in many respects, it's Argento's last really consistently beautiful-looking feature. He would begin to adopt a slightly colder, more realistic approach to his later films, while a subsequent foray into period horror with *Dario Argento's Dracula* would prove to be problematic. In this instance, however, his feeling for the material is very much in evidence and he manages to make his mark while delivering a hugely entertaining piece of *Grand Guignol*. The term "camp" would not be out of place here, as the film's sense of humor is very knowing, and its depiction of the over-heated and narcissistic world of the opera is absolutely relentless. If it doesn't manage to succeed in all of its goals, it is nevertheless far from the worthless failure that so many critics have labeled it as; hopefully as time moves on and more viewers begin to reassess it,

Cover art for the Italian DVD release from Medusa.

and *The Stendhal Syndrome*, *The Phantom of the Opera* seemingly signaled the demise of a great *auteur*.[2]

David Rooney pretty much hated it:

> [P]lenty of bodice-ripping, lush romanticism, gore and gross antics with rats, all of which should tickle the director's stalwart devotees. But the script's clumsy plotting, its often unintentionally hilarious dialogue and some howlingly bad acting make the already widely sold pic likely to function best as a campy video entry for irreverent genre fans.[3]

Stendhal garnered plenty of negative reviews, too, so it's not like the pans were a new thing where Argento was concerned. But the reviews were getting nastier and the stakes were also higher this time around. The big difference between *Phantom* and *Stendhal* was, it had more to lose—the earlier film had been budgeted at under $4 million, whereas the total investment this time, less advertising costs, was $10 million.

On the upside, Medusa successfully negotiated foreign sales with Movienet in Germany and Les Films de l'Astre in France—where the film was released in, respectively, early and late February 1999. In the U.S., October Films (which also handled the release of Soavi's *Cemetery Man/Dellamorte Dellamore*, 1993, David Lynch's *Lost Highway*, 1997, and Lars von Trier's *Breaking the Waves*, 1996, among others) decided to take a chance on the film—but following a limited theatrical run in June 1999, they pawned it off on A-Pix Entertainment, who released it to DVD and VHS. Sadly, the A-Pix editions were sourced from an inferior PAL format VHS transfer, thus making the film look like a cheap direct-to-video offering; if nothing else, in its proper form, it was a movie where the money lavished on it was truly evident on screen—by presenting the film in such shabby condition, A-Pix helped to perpetuate the damage already inflicted on Argento's reputation by Troma's subpar release of *The Stendhal Syndrome*, making his newest film look like a major fall from grace. Medusa had good reason to feel disappointed. Their "sure hit" turned out to be a dud, and as a point of comparison, the film made less at the Italian box office than, say, *Buena Vista Social Club* (1999), ending the 1998-1999 Italian box-office season in the 58th slot; a far cry, indeed, from the days of *Deep Red* and *Suspiria*.[4]

With *Phantom* dying a slow death in the international marketplace, Asia Argento began to have serious thoughts about walking away from acting. In truth, it

Dario's quirky take on Leroux's classic will be granted a little respect in the long run.

Medusa afforded the film a lavish ad campaign and everybody involved seemed to feel sure that they had a potential hit on their hands. It had humor, horror, a touch of spectacle, a dash of eroticism (courtesy of Asia Argento, who nevertheless had to be doubled in some scenes owing to her period-inappropriate tattoos). When the release date finally hit on November 20, 1998, history repeated itself. Like *Stendhal*, it opened well, but business dropped off sharply amid terrible reviews and bad word-of-mouth. Argento's decision to camp it up and offer a more playful take on the story didn't sit well with the purists, and despite the inclusion of some over-the-top gore and kinky sex, it seemed to satisfy hardly anybody.

There were a handful of defenders, notably Argento biographer Alan Jones, but by and large it was snubbed by critics and audiences alike. Far more typical of the response generated by the film was Ed Gonzalez at *Slant Magazine*, who described it as a "spiritless hack job" and wrote:

> *Phantom of the Opera* is a mess from the start: the transitions between scenes lack passion and Asia's lip-syncing is ludicrous at best. […] After the unfulfilled promise of *Trauma*

wasn't anything new for her. By her own admission, she chiefly went into acting as a means of establishing a deeper connection with her father—which, in fairness, did come to pass—but now that she was into her early 20s, she was looking to make a change. She had already started dabbling in directing with short subjects as far back as 1994 (with the segment "Prospettive" in the anthology film *DeGenerazione* and *A ritroso*) but by the time *Phantom* was in the can, she had decided that it was time to make a feature of her own.

Asia conceived of a semi-autobiographical story about a young actress, the product of a broken home, who endures abuse and heartache in the exploitative film industry; given some of the things she had been through (some of which wouldn't become public knowledge for 20 years), it really wasn't much of a stretch for her. She pitched *Scarlet Diva* to Dario, who decided to take a chance on the project, using it to launch the new company he was forming together with his brother Claudio, the aptly named Opera Film. As Asia would later recall in a conversation with Maitland McDonagh included on the Film Movement Blu-ray release of *Scarlet Diva*, "My father was very encouraging. He was actually the only one who was encouraging at that time." The project wasn't nearly as big and sweeping as one of Dario's own films, but the Argentos had a hard time putting together the money that was needed. Dario's recent track record didn't inspire much confidence, and there was also the matter of Asia's reputation within the admittedly sexist Italian film industry—as a headstrong, fiercely independent iconoclast, she hadn't really endeared herself to a lot of the people in power and so the idea of a film which was bound to throw some serious "shade" in their direction wasn't regarded as a major incentive.

To economize, Asia decided to shoot her feature debut on digital—and with a tiny budget in place, she began filming on September 27 1999—a mere week following her 24th birthday. A lot of the crew was comprised of technicians from *Phantom*, including editor Anna Napoli, make-up artist Barbara Morosetti, and visual effects artist Sergio Stivaletti, most of whom donated their services out of affection for Asia. Rather remarkably, the five-week shoot encompassed filming in Italy, France, the U.K., the U.S., and the Netherlands; in terms of sheer *chutzpah*, Asia was already outdoing her famous father.

The story tells of young actress Anna Battista (Asia), who struggles with self-loathing as she is repeatedly exploited by "friends," colleagues and lovers, all of whom are looking to use her in one way or another. She becomes pregnant after a dalliance with a rock star named Kirk (Jean Shepard), only to then discover that he is already married and has a son. As she spirals out of control and heads towards self-destruction, she has an epiphany that her daughter-to-be is worth living for.

Nakedly confessional and absolutely unapologetic in its approach, *Scarlet Diva* fans the flames of controversy with its mixture of frank sexuality (including a scene of unsimulated sex between Vera Gemma and Alessandro Villari) and its exploration of the way in which women are subjugated and abused by society in general—and by the film industry, in particular. Like Asia herself, Anna is tired of being marketed as a shallow sex symbol, and she has a desire to make the transition to directing her own films. At the time of its release, some of its more pointed critiques flew over the heads of most viewers—but in light of subsequent allegations by Asia that she was raped by American movie mogul Harvey Weinstein and other men in power in the industry, the film takes on additional significance. The film's most memorable and haunting sequence in this context occurs when Anna meets with American hotshot producer Barry Paar (Joe

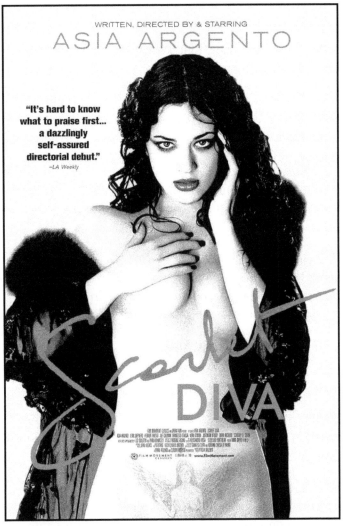

Poster art for the provocative *Scarlet Diva*; designer unknown.

The Unsane Cinema of Dario Argento   *261*

Anna (Asia Argento) tries to live out a fantasy à la Esther Williams.

Coleman, an artist and close personal friend of Asia's, making a rare acting appearance), who feigns interest in her directing project as a pretext to seduction. Paar bullies her into giving him a massage before bluntly asking her to perform oral sex on him; she tries to escape but he holds her down and says various disgusting and denigrating things to her before she's finally able to break free. The scene is clearly based on her traumatic experience with Weinstein—and by her own later admission, the film arose out of the agoraphobia which this attack brought out in her; she became terrified of leaving her apartment and spent much of her time trying to make sense of what had happened, using writing as a means of therapy.[5]

The film isn't all darkness and despair, however. In trying to numb the pain caused by her fractured home life—represented by a vivid cameo from Daria Nicolodi, who plays Anna's career-driven, drug-addicted mother—and the death of her beloved older brother—an obvious reference to the death of her half-sister, Anna Lou—Anna finds solace in the hustle and bustle of her busy existence. She smokes copious amounts of marijuana and hashish and encounters a variety of colorful characters, some of whom are as amusing as they are pathetic (including a horny Swiss journalist played by Asia's co-star from *The Stendhal Syndrome*, Paolo Bonacelli) and some of whom are obvious stand-ins for well-known industry figures (including David Brandon as a director modeled after Gus Van Sant, on the receiving end of Asia's vitriol because he worked with Weinstein on *Good Will Hunting*, 1997). There's warmth in her vaguely co-dependent relationship with her best friend Veronica (Vera Gemma, born 1970, Asia's real-life friend and the daughter of *Tenebrae*'s Giuliano Gemma; she also appeared in *The Stendhal Syndrome* and *The Card Player* in small roles), as well as ample humor as Veronica's propensity for outlandish sexual hijinks puts her into some delicate situations.

Argento doesn't make excuses for any of the film's excesses, she simply presents her life as it is, with an honesty that is truly disarming. Her final acceptance of the role of motherhood and the possibility of finding redemption in the relationship with her child ends the film on an optimistic note, though for many viewers, the events leading to that are too off-putting to endure. Argento was surely aware of that and, to her credit, she couldn't be bothered to take the edge off by soft-pedalling things; this is confrontational cinema that manages to be both vulnerable yet fearless—a potent combination, to be sure.

Scarlet Diva made its Italian theatrical debut on May 26, 2000. Critical reaction was downright hostile and the audience showed zero support; not even the suggestive ad campaign (with Asia showing off her famous angel tattoo) was enough to stir up interest among the more prurient-minded viewers. Fortunately for Dario and Claudio, the investment in the film was on the minimal side—so the combination of foreign theatrical and video sales was enough to ensure that a small profit was made. The film's failure did little to dissuade Asia from continuing to pursue her directing career—she would continue to make short subjects before directing such follow-up features as, *The Heart is Deceitful Above All Things* (2004) and *Misunderstood* (2014); the latter would cause yet another major rift between her and Dario, but they would face other challenges in the meantime.

Actress Asia Argento arrives for the awards ceremony of the 66th international film festival, in Cannes, southern France, in May 2013. Italian The actress says Harvey Weinstein the "biggest serial predator in the history," and that she has been "doubly crucified", first by the sexual violence and second by the media in TV interview. She says the abuse when she was 21 "smashed all my dreams and changed my perception of myself."

Weinstein accuser says she feels 'doubly crucified'

The Associated Press

ROME — Italian actress and filmmaker Asia Argento says being sexually assaulted by Harvey Weinstein "smashed all my dreams" and "changed the perception I had of myself."

Argento revealed for the first time in an interview published in The New Yorker magazine last week that in 1997 Weinstein forcibly performed oral sex on her at a hotel in France when she was 21 years old.

Multiple women have come forward with allegations since The New York Times first reported Oct. 5 that the since-fired movie mogul had been a subject of sexual harassment complaints for decades and paid off some of his accusers.

The 42-year-old actress told Italy's RAI state television from Berlin on Tuesday she feels "doubly crucified" since going public: first by the assault and now by hostile reactions to her story in Italy.

Italian newspaper Libero ran a scathing piece under the headline, "First they put out, and then they whine." A former parliament member said Argento should have just said "no." Comments on social media accused Argento of seeking trouble.

During the RAI interview, Argento called Weinstein one of "the biggest sexual predators in history." She also recounted Weinstein inviting her to his hotel room, chatting her up there and returning from the bathroom with a bottle of lotion and a request for a massage.

Since coming forward, the actress said that she has found something in common with other women who have been victims of sexual abuse.

"We feel guilty for being beautiful, for wearing a dress that is perhaps low-cut, or a skirt that is too short, that somehow we are the ones that bring out the animal in these men," she said.

"This is what I cannot stand any more. This is why I decided to come out with my story," Argento said.

> We feel guilty for being beautiful, for wearing a dress that is perhaps low-cut, or a skirt that is too short, that somehow we are the ones that bring out the animal in these men.
>
> — **Asia Argento**
> Italian actress, speaking about women who have been victims of sexual abuse

In March 2000, Dario was honored at the Cinequest Film Festival in San Jose, California. He may not have had much luck getting his films into the U.S. marketplace in some time, but that didn't stop the organizers from giving him the Maverick Spirit Award; the award had a special significance, as it acknowledged not only his influence on others, but also the fact that he was, in fact, an independent at heart. Dario enjoyed distinguished company for the occasion, as his fellow winners for the year included fellow directors Robert M. Young (*Triumph of the Spirit*, 1989), Jon Jost (*The Bed You Sleep In*, 1993), and Wes Craven, as well as actors Peter Fonda and Alec Baldwin.

Notes:
1. Jones, Alan, *Dario Argento: The Man, the Myths & the Magic* (Godalming: FAB Press, 2012), p. 250.
2. https://www.slantmagazine.com/film/review/the-phantom-of-the-opera
3. Rooney, David, "The Phantom of the Opera," *Variety*, November 29, 1998.
4. Thanks to Roberto Curti for the Italian box-office information.
5. Quoted from Asia Argento's commentary on the Film Movement Blu-ray edition of *Scarlet Diva*.

Chapter Nineteen: Sleepy in Turin

Following the disappointing box-office performance of *Phantom*, Dario decided it was time to return to basics. It was the same basic thing which had happened 25 years earlier with *Le cinque giornate*. The fans really weren't interested in seeing him try his hand at something so different, so after licking his wounds, he would fall back on a heavily-touted "return to the *giallo*." It worked like a charm with *Deep Red*, of course, but that was during a period when Dario's box-office clout and public persona were truly relevant; now it was the 21st century, Dario was about to turn 60, and the film scene had changed dramatically. With no other cards left to play for the time being, a new *giallo* seemed to be the only logical solution.

Dario called upon Franco Ferrini to assist him in writing the script, which he conceived as the possible beginning of a new trilogy—in the same vein as the "animal trilogy" of the early '70s. They managed to polish off an initial draft, but Dario felt something was missing. At that point, he reached out to the successful *giallo* novelist Carlo Lucarelli, whose books like *Carte Blanche* and *Almost Blue* (which was adapted into a film of the same name in 2000 by director Alex Infascelli) were such big hits with the public. Lucarelli was so thrilled by Argento's offer to come in and do some work on the script that he volunteered to do so without taking any payment.[1] It was Lucarelli who helped to flesh out the police procedural angle, as his knowledge of modern police methods was considerably more up to snuff than those of either Ferrini or Argento. From a commercial point of view, it was an inspired move, even if it indicated a growing willingness on Dario's part to not be seen as "the exclusive author" of his films—after all, Lucarelli's name had real cachet, even if his contributions to the screenplay were relatively minor. Despite his minimal involvement, Lucarelli was overjoyed to be working with Argento. "Writing with Dario Argento is so incredible that I would have done it even if we were writing The Yellow Pages!"[2] Even Asia was drafted in to lend a hand—it was she who composed the nursery rhyme which plays such a crucial role in the narrative. It doesn't appear that she was ever seriously considered for an acting role in the picture, as there really wasn't a suitable part for her; however, in short order she would be giving Dario some exciting news: She was pregnant and expecting her first child in the spring of 2001. The father was a singer by the name of Marco Castoldi (aka Morgan, of the group Bluvertigo). Dario and Daria were thrilled with the news that they were going to become grandparents, which certainly soothed whatever disappointment he may have been feeling over not being able to work with Asia on *Sleepless* as closely as he had become accustomed to collaborating with her over the past decade.

Despite the critical drubbing and disappointing box office of *Phantom*, Medusa was willing to take another roll of the dice on Dario. The film was produced through Opera Film, the latest Argento business venture, with Claudio on board as executive producer—and Medusa's involvement again guaranteed aggressive marketing and solid distribution in Italy. Since it marked a return to basics, there was ample room for Medusa to market the film as a comeback vehicle of sorts for Dario—and indeed, the posters and advertising played up the fact that the master, Argento, was back doing what he does best.

Budgeted at about $4 million, the new Argento *giallo* started filming on May 15, 2000, with location work taking place in Turin—a lucky charm of sorts for Dario, given that earlier hits like *The Cat O'Nine Tails*, *Four Flies on Grey Velvet*, and *Deep Red* had also been filmed there. The Italian title—*Non ho sonno*, which is blurred into one continuous phrase: *Nonhosonno*—translates as "I'm Not Sleepy" or "I Can't Sleep," and it refers to just one of the killer's many psychological hangups. The English title

Italian poster art for *Sleepless*; artist unknown.

Insomniac was bandied about for a while, as were several other variations, before Dario and company settled on *Sleepless*. There was ample hope early on that the film would receive the sort of exposure that Argento's previous pictures had received in the international market, but things once again didn't pan out as originally intended.

The nine-week shoot came to an end in early July 2000 and Argento again found himself working with Anna Napoli on assembling the first edit. The most important order of business in the post-production phase involved the music. Dario had enjoyed a mostly harmonious reunion with Ennio Morricone on *The Stendhal Syndrome* and *The Phantom of the Opera*, but they decided to part ways once more and the director was eager to find a new sound for his first *giallo* of the 21st century. He was initially in talks with the Serbian composer Goran Bregovich, who did indeed commence working on the picture—but there was a disagreement over money and that fell by the wayside. With the clock ticking and time wasting away, Dario decided to reach out to Claudio Simonetti—they both were at the Sitges Festival in Spain in October of 2000 when Dario broke the news. He needed a score for his new film, and he needed it in a hurry. It was a tall order, no matter how you look at it, but Dario made it borderline impossible when he suggested that the film would be the perfect opportunity to get Goblin back together. Simonetti obliged and reached out to Agostino Marangolo, Massimo Morante, and Fabio Pignatelli; as if by a miracle, they decided to set aside their differences and get together to compose the score. As Simonetti explains in the interview included in this book, it was not a happy experience, however; in-fighting continued among the members and Simonetti mostly worked with Morante, while Pignatelli and Marangolo paired off and did their own thing separately. Even so, they rose to the occasion and provided the film with a score—as well as a soundtrack release which was bound to drum up a certain measure of excitement and anticipation.

It begins in familiar fashion with a prologue, set in Turin in 1983, in which a child, Giacomo (Daniele Angius), is traumatized from seeing the brutal murder of his mother. Police Commissioner Ulisse Moretti (Max von Sydow) arrives on the scene and he assures the boy that he will find the murderer, "even if it takes me all my life." The scene is brief, but it establishes the relationship between the two characters, as well as the vow which continues to haunt Moretti over the ensuing years.

From there, the action shifts to contemporary (that is, 2000-era) Turin—and into more stylized terrain as a prostitute named Angela (Barbara Lerici) sets up an appointment with a new client. The staging is very interesting as Argento focuses in on fetishistic views of the woman's hands, mouth, and eyes—mostly via a rapid

Artwork for the vinyl release of Goblin's score.

panning shot, which isolates parts of her in the frame as she makes mindless "sexy talk" with the client on the phone. They set a date and time and the action shifts to an apartment, where Angela reacts with shock and disgust over one of the client's requests; we aren't told exactly what he had in mind, but it's clear that it must be something pretty twisted. Much of the action plays out in a stylized wide shot, with the naked prostitute standing against the wall and threatening the client with a knife; we don't see the client, save for his shadowy reflection on the wall as he waves a wad of cash, hoping to calm the girl down. She reacts as planned but the man decides that he would prefer to rest rather than continue with their assignation. He takes some pills—shades of *Tenebrae*—and hides under the covers as Angela gets dressed and ready to leave. As she's on her way out, she hears him muttering in his sleep: "I've killed lots of people … and they'll never find me." In a panic, she bolts for the door, only to knock over a cabinet containing various knives and other assorted "trophies," including a blue file; she accidentally picks up the latter while gathering her things and flees into the night. The man awakens after she slams the door and in an extended point of view shot, he discovers that the girl has discovered his awful secret.

A few things become evident early on in these scenes. For one, the film sees Argento making an aggressive bid to woo the audience by revisiting familiar turf; for another, while there are some interesting set-ups and compositions, the lighting by Ronnie Taylor is disappointingly flat, even ugly at times—a far cry indeed from his inspired work on *Opera* and *The Phantom of the*

Angela (Barbara Lerici) is terrorized by the killer aboard a train.

Opera. This continues to be the case throughout with isolated scenes standing out in a positive way amid an otherwise generally drab aesthetic. Worse, the acting and the quality of the dubbing is generally not up to par. Lerici's performance is particularly stiff and mannered, and the effect is not helped by the dismal performance of her English-dubbing vocal performer. The English dub is far and away the worst to be featured in one of the films directed by Argento—even worse than the one for *The Stendhal Syndrome*, which is at least presentable if one can get past the ruinous revoicing of Asia Argento's performance.

The next scene is the film's most celebrated set piece, as the killer follows Angela and terrorizes her as she takes a train commute back home. The setting is appropriately confined and claustrophobic, recalling the "Tram" episode of *Door into Darkness*, and it generates ample tension as the killer plays a protracted game of cat and mouse with his frightened prey. Angela takes a look at the contents of the blue file and finds a collection of gruesome Polaroids and press clippings involving a series of killings committed by a so-called "killer dwarf." The killer begins taunting Angela with a threatening phone call—the use of cell phones definitely seems indebted to the success of Wes Craven's *Scream* (1996), it must be admitted—and she seeks out the train's conductor (Aldo Delaude), who offers to provide her with protection. He ends up being rendered unconscious, however, and Angela is chased through the train as it rattles along to its final destination. Argento makes good use of the narrow passageways to generate tension and a sense of mounting hysteria as Angela tries to outwit her attacker. The use of the lights passing by the windows as the train hurtles towards the station adds to the effect, as does Goblin's throbbing rock soundtrack. It's clear from watching the scene that Argento is trying to recapture the frantic intensity of the opening of *Suspiria*; it doesn't come close to matching that towering example, but as curtain raisers go, it's certainly effective. The killer finally corners Angela and slices off a couple of her fingers before finally killing her; Argento emphasizes the loneliness of her death as she screams from behind the window of the train, the sound drowned out by the relentless clatter of the train.

Angela's friend Amanda (Conchita Puglisi) is waiting for her as the train pulls into the station. The use of heavy rain in the scene can't help but remind one of the vicious storms at the start of *Suspiria*. Angela, of course, is nowhere to be found—but Amanda finds the blue file and takes it with her, thus sealing her own fate. A less-than-helpful car park attendant (Diego Casale) offers no assistance when Amanda goes to him for guidance, and she is brutally stabbed in the throat when the killer shows up at her car to retrieve his file. Meanwhile the killer manages to drop an expensive-looking pen in the ensuing chaos, and the car park attendant—who witnesses it all—scarfs it up, looking to indulge in a bit of blackmail. There's some dynamic staging on display here, but once more the effect is undercut by a mixture of subpar acting and truly embarrassing English-language vocal performances—especially with regards to the car park attendant.

The police, represented by Inspector Manni (Paolo Maria Scalondro), prove to be a dull, unsympathetic bunch; this is a far cry from the more sympathetic and intuitive police figures of *The Bird with the Crystal Plumage* and *Tenebrae*, perhaps, but is in keeping with the more colorless, even robotic characters seen in the likes of *Phenomena* and *Trauma*. The train conductor, still recovering from the injuries he sustained from the killer, reveals that Amanda mentioned something to him about a "killer dwarf." This triggers a connection to the series of murders committed in 1983, prompting Inspector Manni to seek out the now-retired Moretti.

The reintroduction of Moretti into the plot recalls an earlier *giallo* called *The Pyjama Girl Case* (*La ragazza dal pigiama giallo*, 1978), in which Ray Milland plays a retired police inspector who is called back into action when a contemporary murder connects into a case he had been in charge of years earlier. It's not clear whether Argento (or possibly Franco Ferrini) actually saw that film and was looking to refer to it, but the similarities are striking, just the same. Manni hopes that Moretti may remember something about the killings which might offer him a lead, but the older man explains that his memory isn't what it used to be. "My memory plays me some bad tricks these days. Depending on the current, as they say." It isn't just his memory which troubles him, either; he's now prescribed medication for his heart. Moretti has grown accustomed to a solitary and sedate existence. His wife has passed away, and his only source of companionship is a parrot named Marcello. He's one of Argento's most well-rounded and instantly likable characters, and the performance by Max von Sydow (1929-2020), is one of the film's greatest assets. Von Sydow, the veteran of numerous thematically and spiritually "heavy" offerings from Ingmar Bergman, provides the film with its heart and soul. He makes Moretti into a stately and dignified reminder of the old school of police work, which stands in stark contrast to the cold and mechanical approach typified by younger men like Moretti. He also gives the character real warmth and an endearingly self-deprecating sense of humor. He has talked himself into believing that he enjoys a life of retirement, but as time goes by and he becomes more engaged, the case reinvigorates him and gives him a renewed sense of purpose. Manni, of course, is only looking to take advantage of whatever insights the old man is able to give him; when Moretti elects to come on board and actively participate in the investigation, he feels threatened and comes to regard him as an unwelcome rival of sorts.

Meanwhile the killings continue. A dancer in a local club is terrorized in the labyrinthine tunnels beneath the club before being knocked unconscious by the killer; the scene is nicely staged with plenty of shifting points of view shots as the terrified woman runs for her life, culminating with a nice piece of misdirection as the threat, which appears to be approaching from behind, proves to be in front of her. The killer then drowns the victim in a pool before clipping the nails from her fingers, as she managed to scratch him during their struggle; the close-up of the nails being brutally chopped down, with the tips of fingers being taken off with them, is one of the most squirm-inducing moments in the film—Sergio Stivaletti's prosthetic work isn't up to par in most of the murder scenes, unfortunately, but he delivers where it counts here. A cutout figure of a cat is left behind at the scene—and this, too, connects in with the series of murders from the '80s; it turns out that the dwarf who was supposedly responsible for those killings was an author of children's books who also wrote *giallo* books under a *nom de plume*—a fanciful idea, for sure, albeit one which ties back into the discussion about the connection between art and the spectator from earlier films like *Tenebrae*, *Opera*, and *The Stendhal Syndrome*. A grim nursery rhyme written by the dwarf, titled "The Death Farm," is evidently serving as the killer's template: it tells of a sleep-deprived farmer who kills off the noisy animals on his farm so that he can finally get some sleep.

The dwarf, Vincenzo De Fabritiis (Luca Fagioli), evidently committed suicide when Moretti was about to arrest him; his death seemed to signal the end of the case, but now that the killings are picking up from where

Max von Sydow as Moretti gives one of the warmest and most believable performances in the Argento canon.

Giacomo's mother (Francesca Vettori) is horrifically murdered in *Sleepless*.

they left off, Moretti and Manni are baffled. Manni is convinced it's a copycat, whereas Moretti thinks the answer is much more complicated; the differences in attitude and approach of the two men are striking, even if they are ultimately both working towards the same end. Manni barely registers as a character, while Moretti emerges as one of the most memorable characters in the Argento canon. Manni is not incompetent, but he is, as Moretti recognizes, "cold as a machine."

News of the renewed string of killings reaches the now fully-grown Giacomo (Stefano Dionisi), who is living in Rome, where he works as a waiter in a Chinese restaurant; the inadequate English dubbing rears its head once more as Giacomo's employer speaks in an embarrassing pidgin-English accent ("He clazy; good liddance!"), while the actor dubbing Giacomo also fails to compensate for Dionisi's generally listless performance. Unfortunately for the film, his character is crucial to the plot. While some of Giacomos's awkward, disconnected vibe is undoubtedly down to his fractured psyche—Dionisi fails to make the character come to life and the film suffers accordingly. Dionisi (born 1966) had been considered for the role of Marco in *The Stendhal Syndrome*, but if his work here is any indication, Dario did well to cast Marco Leonardi in his place.

When Giacomo returns to Turin, he is greeted by his old friend Lorenzo (Roberto Zibetti), who offers him a place to stay while he is visiting. Giacomo and Lorenzo are from similar backgrounds, yet they have developed in different ways. Giacomo is hard working and determined to be independent, while Lorenzo is a bit of a spoiled brat who still relies on the money and connections of his wealthy father (Gabriele Lavia in his third and final Argento role to date, though his name was briefly attached to *Dario Argento's Dracula* according to some online gossip).

Giacomo's emotional growth has been stunted by witnessing his mother's murder; adding insult to injury, he's also been essentially abandoned by his father, thus forcing him to make his own way without the support of a warm family environment. Not surprisingly, he has a history of substance abuse problems, though he's managed to get his life in order and has done his best to move on from the trauma which wrecked his childhood. Lorenzo's family is still "intact," at least as far as appearances are concerned, but there is no love visible between them. His mother (Alessandra Comerio) is ineffectual, while his father is an imposing block of ice. His needs have been met financially, but as he explains to Giacomo, he has always been viewed as something of a disappointment.

There's an ambiguously homo-erotic dimension to their relationship, evidenced by the scene in which they sit around in Lorenzo's kitchen, catching up on old times. Lorenzo has his shirt off, while Giacomo has his hanging open; nothing is ever made of this, but it arguably denotes a level of familiarity which may well go beyond simple friendship. These characters had potential to be truly interesting, but neither Dionisi nor Zibetti (born 1971) are up to the challenge; Zibetti's bizarre performance and strange vocal intonations are particularly off-putting—and in his case, the latter point can't be blamed on the dubbing, as that is his voice on the English language soundtrack.

Giacomo's return to Turin also allows him to reconnect with Gloria (Chiara Caselli), for whom he has always carried some unrequited feelings. It turns out that she feels the same, though she's temporarily encumbered with a dullard boyfriend named Fausto (Roberto Accornero). Following the beautifully detailed characterizations of Aura in *Trauma* and Anna in *The Stendhal Syndrome*, Gloria emerges as a disappointing, one-dimensional damsel-in-distress; she's arguably the least interesting female protagonist in an Argento film since Giulia in *The Bird with the Crystal Plumage*. Yet, while Suzy Kendall was able to invest Giulia with a bit of charm and vitality, Caselli (born 1967) spends the better part of the film moping and blending into the scenery. The abundance of boring characters and awkward performances takes a lot of the steam out of the film, even if Argento's quirky visual sensibility and thematic obsessions are still in evidence—albeit sporadically.

The real "meat" of the film is to be found in Moretti's relationship with the characters around him. Much of this is undoubtedly down to Max von Sydow's expert performance. Unlike a lot of the other actors, he's experienced enough to know how to underplay while still appearing engaged by the material. In the hands of a lesser actor, Moretti could well have emerged as a cliché—but von Sydow makes us care about him, and he breathes life and conviction into some awkward dialogue along the way. While talking with his old friend, Cascio (Aldo Massasso, appearing for the third and final time for Argento following roles in *Wax Mask* and *The Phantom of the Opera*), he pontificates on the differences between police work as he understood it versus how it has evolved in the 21st century. "Now the police talk about DNA, telecommunications printouts, GPS bugs. We used to say 'tailing,' now they say 'surveillance.' We used to say 'following leads,' now they say 'tactical intervention.' Listening to them talk, they sound more like marketing managers than cops." It boils down to a lot of bitter old man talk—very much of the "in my day …" variety—but von Sydow's warm and charming performance gives it weight and meaning. Moretti's contention that the human factor is missing in contemporary police work is on the money, especially when he's locking horns with a modern detective like Manni.

When he and Giacomo reconnect, Moretti starts enjoying life again; it gives him a sense of purpose. Moretti also provides Giacomo with the stable, caring parental figure he is so desperately in need of. One of the film's most low-key and beautiful sequences occurs when they share a meal of spaghetti. Argento frames the action from a low angle as the camera dollies around the dinner table; there's a lot of exposition crammed into this scene, but the combination of the intimate atmosphere and von Sydow's soothing, paternalistic delivery makes it all seem very spontaneous and natural. When he offers Giacomo some wine, he doesn't realize that the young man is on the wagon; he recovers by saying, "Well, I'd love some, but I can't—doctor's orders!"

Moretti plays up his age and weakening physical and mental condition, but he remains as sharp and intuitive as ever; unfortunately some of the clunkier moments of the scripting occasionally undercuts this, as blazingly obvious observations are given a significance that truly isn't worthy of a such a brilliant detective (the fact that it takes him so long to make the link between the animals in the nursery rhyme and the methodology of the murders is particularly difficult to swallow). Quibbles aside, *Sleepless* is at its very best when von Sydow is on screen; he anchors the film and provides it with a human center, which it desperately needs.

The murders continue and they escalate with ferocity. A particularly vicious one occurs when a waitress (Barbara Mautino) is stalked to her apartment building; Argento builds the suspense nicely as she becomes aware that she is being watched and attempts to get into her building before it is too late. A rapid Steadicam point of view shot shows the killer grabbing hold of her and smashing her face repeatedly against the marble wall, knocking out her front teeth (which are prominent, thus aligning her to a rabbit—the corresponding animal in the nursery rhyme) and killing her from sheer blunt force trauma.

The resemblance to the death of Giordani in *Deep Red* is hardly coincidental … and yet, something is seriously *wrong* here. Despite the dynamic camerawork and the thrilling musical accompaniment by Goblin, the scene doesn't work nearly as well as it should. It's tempting to lay the blame at Sergio Stivaletti's door, but in fact his prosthetics work isn't the primary culprit; the problem lies in the lighting, the staging and the editing. One can really feel the absence of Franco Fraticelli's magical hand here, as Anna Napoli's sense of rhythm pales enormously by comparison. Ronnie Taylor's atmosphere-free approach to the lighting doesn't help matters, either. With tighter cutting, more sensitive coverage and less direct lighting, the effect may have come off a lot more convincingly. As it stands, it ends up looking phony and clumsy—precisely the opposite of the artfully executed murder scenes in Dario's earlier films, many of which were executed with less in the way of production resources. In fact, the slackness in the editing becomes more and more evident as the film unfolds; Argento's earlier *gialli* tend to be beautifully paced and extremely fluid, whereas *Sleepless* definitely drags.

Argento tries introducing some comic elements, but they simply don't come off well. One particularly wince-inducing bit occurs when a group of little people are rounded up for a line-up; one recalls the line-up of "perverts" in *The Bird with the Crystal Plumage* with a smile, but here the low-brow comedy involving the little people, replete with an uncharacteristically tone-deaf "funny" music cue, seems mean-spirited and tone deaf. There are also a couple of minor characters who had the potential to function as quirky, colorful secondary players—of the variety like the pimp in *Bird* or Gigi the Loser in *The Cat O'Nine Tails*, for example—but they simply fail to register in that regard. One is the sleazy car park attendant and the other is a local bum named Leone (Massimo Sarchielli, who also appeared in *The Phantom of the Opera* and who would go on to play a similar role in *Mother of Tears*). The car park attendant is essentially there to try and blackmail the murderer, which results in his being savagely stabbed to death with the fountain pen he was using as leverage; Leone, obviously named in tribute to Sergio, ends up playing a more significant role in the last act. Sadly, all attempts at humor—save for some of von Sydow's wryly amusing line readings—feels either flat or forced; one gets the impression that Argento is trying too hard to win back his core audience, and that is symptomatic of the film's overall weakness.

The film gains some momentum in the scenes between Moretti and Giacomo, as they team up and try to solve the mystery. "What a great team we make," says Moretti. "You remember, but don't know. I know, but don't remember." Both of them suffer from a cognitive deficit: Moretti's memory is slipping away due to age, while Giacomo is sure he remembers some vital clue from when he saw his mother being butchered—yet he can't figure out what it is. The "half-forgotten clue" trope goes all the way back to *The Bird with the Crystal Plumage*, of course, but unfortunately the revelation here, when it finally comes, is a little awkward. He remembers hearing a strange whistling sound when his mother was being killed, and it's only at the end of the film that he realizes it was the killer's asthma inhaler. This rather begs the question, how was it possible for the killer to be puffing on an inhaler when his hands were surely occupied with the murder weapon (and an unusual one at that: an English horn, no less!) at the time of the killing. Here, as elsewhere, a sense of desperation starts to creep into the film: in an attempt to wow the audience with a clever final reveal, he ends up tripping over his own logic and the film starts to crumble as a result. Even so, it all barely hangs together so long as Moretti is involved in the narrative. His character clearly interests Argento the most and the film definitely springs to life whenever he is on screen.

One of the film's most hyped sequences is the so-called "swan murder," named for the corresponding animal in the nursery rhyme. Gloria is involved in a production of *Swan Lake*—she plays the harp, making her yet another in a long line of Argento's "artistic" characters—and she seems the likely target. However, the killer focuses instead on the ballerina (Rossella Lucà) in the production, due to her long, swan-like neck. Argento stages the scene in a deliberately off-beat manner, with the camera gliding along a carpeted floor—focusing on various sets of feet as people move about in a rush during an intermission in the performance. As the camera trails down the carpet, it veers off and we see the shadows of something struggling—the camera pans up and reveals the ballerina's feet shaking violently in mid-air, and suddenly her decapitated head lands on the ground with a gruesome thud. The shot is an interesting one but it's not quite the stylistic *tour de force* it has been played up to be in some circles; the punctuation point with the severed head is again undermined by Argento and Napoli holding onto the shot for a few beats too long. It's one of those conceptually interesting moments that could have blossomed into something special, but as it stands it feels a bit half-hearted—much like a "crane shot to nowhere," which evokes *Tenebrae*'s celebrated Louma crane shot with only a fraction of the energy or pizzazz.

Despite its missteps, *Sleepless* manages to be reasonably engaging for most of its running time—but Argento makes a fatal mistake in the last third when Moretti dies of a heart attack. The lead up to his death is delightful. He finally manages to crack the case and he tries to get hold of Giacomo to tell him about it, but the young man is busy making love with Gloria. As a reward for his hard work, Moretti treats himself to a cigarette ("The first since 1966!"), but his happiness is short-lived: the killer shows up at his house and triggers a fatal heart attack. Moretti's death is a blow from which the film never recovers; without him and his warm presence, the emphasis on Giacomo only serves to underline how inadequate Dionisi is in his important role. Argento's films aren't exactly revered for their complicated character dynamics, but Moretti is one of those wonderful parts—like Franco Arnò in *The Cat*

Giacomo (Stefano Dionisi) and Gloria (Ciara Caselli) make love at the left, while Barbara Mautino has a brutal encounter with the killer at the right.

O'Nine Tails—which demonstrates that he can write really interesting roles when he puts his mind to it. As noted above, characters like Giacomo and Lorenzo had potential to be interesting, but thanks to the inadequate efforts of Dionisi and Zibetti, they never really come to life; one can get past this when Moretti is around to pick up the slack, but once he is written out of the action the film takes a nosedive from which it never really recovers.

The finale is loaded with action and revelation, but it lacks the urgency and sense of suspense typical of Argento's best work. Giacomo discovers that Leone is working in tandem with the killer and he leads him and Gloria to an apartment in the city; Leone is killed before he can reveal what he knows, and it initially appears as if Lorenzo's father is the culprit. In a scene which deliberately echoes *Deep Red*, the father corners Lorenzo with a gun and blames him for everything that happens; Lavia even echoes his line "It's all your fault!" from the earlier film, though here he is in the role of the protective parent instead of the frightened and confused offspring. Ultimately the father turns the gun on himself, hoping that his death will close the door on the whole sorry affair. Lorenzo appears in time to see his father dying; one gets the impression that it's the first time the father has shown any real emotion towards his son, but as the action unfolds we begin to get a better sense of their dynamic and what possibly drove him to treat Lorenzo in such a distant and icy fashion.

Remembering the final message he received from Moretti, Giacomo pieces it together and confronts Lorenzo. He realizes that it was he who committed the murders. The fact that the killings were confined to a small neighborhood in 1983 whereas now they're being committed all over the city is the tipping point. In 1983, Lorenzo was just a child with limited access, whereas now he's an adult and can travel as he sees fit. It's a clever twist, actually, and it comes off much more successfully than the clumsy revelation involving the asthma spray. In classic Argento style, Lorenzo lets loose and admits to his misdeeds; his confession that "I'm a bad boy" is chilling, even if Zibetti's hammy acting undermines the effect somewhat. It's revealed that while the killings appear to have started anew, he continued to claim victims

The Unsane Cinema of Dario Argento

French advertising card for *Sleepless*, featuring Max von Sydow and his parrot (top), Barbara Lerici in peril (middle), and Roberto Zibetti surrounded by dead bodies.

elsewhere when his father sent him off to Geneva and then to New York to further his education. Before he can escape, however, Manni and his men arrive on the scene and Lorenzo is shot in the back of the head by a police sharpshooter. The sudden intrusion of violence is jarring and effective—and Stivaletti's splattered face effect is probably his most memorable contribution to the movie: the way the blood splatters on the camera lens gives it a queasy touch of reality, and the use of backlighting helps to sell the illusion with much more conviction than some of the earlier, comparatively botched gore effects. While the police swarm onto the scene to rescue Giacomo and Gloria, the end titles begin to run; the decision to play the titles out over the forensic work carried out by the plodding cops serves to subtly undermine their efforts, suggesting a final sardonic wink from beyond the grave by Moretti, whose use of old school intuition and logic led him to the solution long before his tech-savvy successors.

As noted above, one of the major problems with *Sleepless* can be summed up with one word: desperation. Following a string of commercial failures, the film was an all-too-obvious bid at winning over his fan base. The film takes the self-referential quality which had been creeping into Dario's work since the days of *Tenebrae* to a new level; it basically comes off as a game of "spot the homage." While this is understandable up to a point, the somewhat slapdash execution of the film does it no favors; the constant winks and nods to past triumphs only serves to remind one of how sloppy the film is by comparison. Taken on its own terms, it has some striking images and set pieces—but too much of the film feels half-hearted. Could it be that the need to revisit old terrain was a source of contention for Dario? It's difficult to say for sure, but there's something seriously "off" about the film—and no amount of references to the back catalogue of classic *gialli* can fix that.

Clocking it at just under two hours, it may not be Argento's longest film—both *Deep Red* and *The Stendhal Syndrome* run longer in their original Italian edits, for example—but it certainly feels like it is. The editing is much too slack, and the pacing is all over the place. Parts of the film breeze by with the sense of urgency one associates with Argento's best films, whereas other sections creep by in an almost glacial fashion. The last act, for example, crams in so much action and mayhem—yet it plays out in a curiously sedate, almost boring manner. The rhythm simply isn't there, no matter how hard Argento tries to surprise and shock the viewer.

The "good and bad" dichotomy is evident in so many facets of the production. In the plus category, the decision to bring back Goblin results in one of their best soundtracks; yet, the music decidedly plays better on its own as an album than as musical accompaniment to the images. Sometimes it works better than others—notably during the frenetic stalk-and-slash scene on the train—but it simply doesn't have the presence in the mix that it deserves. Ronnie Taylor's cinematography is also curiously uneven. There are some beautiful images in isolation—look at the smoky, colorful interiors of the bar where Giacomo catches up with Lorenzo and his friends, for example—but much of the photography is flat and functional; Argento's dynamic use of camerawork and his propensity for fetishistic close-ups are still very much in evidence, but without the support of the right kind of lighting, it simply doesn't come off as well as it should. This also affects the various prosthetic effects: the combination of the slack editing and the harsh lighting shows these effects up for what they are, thus undermining some potentially gruesome imagery and producing an unintentionally comical effect; for example, the vital flashback to the death of Giacomo's mother could have had a real sadistic edge, with the right sort of coverage and cutting, but as it is it plays off as clumsy and borderline inept.

It would be unfair to dismiss the film as a complete failure, however. The character of Moretti is a memorable one and Max von Sydow responds with a beautifully detailed characterization. He elevates the film and gives it real dignity. The best sequences also show Argento continuing to experiment with his already sophisticated cinematic technique. The story itself is engaging enough, even if it sometimes wanders down the wrong path. Argento had never troubled himself too much with regards to narrative absurdity, but it can be argued that he piles things on a bit much here. The whole concept of the "killer dwarf" is problematic in itself. The character of Vincenzo—glimpsed in elliptical fashion in the odd flashback, where he is played by Luca Fagioli—has some schematically interesting components (notably his dual career as a writer of children's stories and of brutal *giallo* books) but he is not afforded ample presence in the plot; he's more of a red herring or a plot device than anything else. Thus, the sudden arrival of his distraught mother (Rossella Falk), who blames Moretti for his death, is just another blind alley; it's always nice to see the elegant and refined Falk (1926-2013), but she has precious little to work with here and it's a subplot which strains an already over-burdened narrative even further. Simply put, there's a lot of good here—but it rubs shoulders with some mediocre and even subpar elements, making it Argento's most problematic and uneven *giallo* to date.

Sleepless opened in Italy on January 5, 2001. The initial box-office returns were very promising—Medusa's ad campaign paid off handsomely as audiences flocked to see Dario's "return to form." But history has a knack for repeating itself and once more that early enthusiasm lapsed into apathy as the reviews and word-of-mouth conspired to do the movie in. The fact that it wasn't a particularly expensive movie helped—it certainly didn't lose money in the long run like *Phantom* had done—but it was still far from the kind of response that Opera and Medusa had been banking on. Once again, foreign sales were spotty: Pretty Pictures acquired it for France, while Artisan Entertainment picked up the American rights. The American premiere occurred once more at the American Cinematheque in August 2001, but this was not followed by a general release. Artisan ended up dumping it on DVD and VHS in an ugly full-screen transfer; once again, it was if everybody was conspiring to make the new films look as bad as possible.

The reviews were generally negative. *TV Guide*'s critic awarded it two stars out of five and bemoaned that, despite the overall sadism, the kill scenes were executed with less audacity than usual, and described it as "less than a return to form."[3] Writing for *Cinefile*, Alberto Cassani was harsher still, saying that the film was annoying in its predictability and that;

> As a young man, Argento was an extraordinary director from a technical point of view, one of the best in Italy. This time, however, even his direction seems blurred.[4]

On the other side of the fence, however, some reviewers did see it as a major improvement following a decade in the wilderness. The BBC's Almar Haflidason, for example, wrote:

> With *Sleepless*, Dario returns to his traditional *giallo* roots, after an absence of 20 years. He shouldn't have stayed away so long because this is the type of thriller he excels in."[5]

As for the Italian release, perhaps the best that can be said for it is that it came in ahead of Wes Craven's *Scream 3* (2000) at the box office—but when they ranked as 53rd and 54th, respectively, it really wasn't much for anybody to brag about.[6]

Spanish advertising for *Sleepless*; artist unknown.

The killer's arsenal of weapons; the fetishization of weapons of violent murder goes all the way back to *The Bird with the Crystal Plumage*.

Even so, Dario's optimism remained intact, with more work ready to occupy his attention. There was also the matter of a granddaughter to consider: Asia's first-born child was born on June 20, 2001. Asia elected to name the girl Anna Lou, in tribute to her beloved late half-sister, Anna, who had died so tragically in 1994. Asia's relationship with the child's father didn't last, but she was determined to provide a warm, nurturing environment for her little girl—the sort of environment she felt she had been deprived of as a child. Dario and Daria may have been lacking as parental figures, but now that they were older and less consumed with their professional lives, they proved to be doting grandparents. Things may not have been exactly top shelf as far as his professional life was concerned—though he did collect a Lifetime Achievement Award at the Amsterdam Fantastic Film Festival (now known as the Imagine Film Festival) in April 2001—but on a personal level Dario felt happier and more content than he had done in some time.

Argento's plan for a proposed *giallo* trilogy encompassed a deal with his old associates at Cecchi Gori Films, with whom he signed a contract to develop two more projects. The first of these was *Occhiali neri* ("Dark Glasses"), which he again wrote in collaboration with Franco Ferrini. Dario outlined the basic plot in his memoirs: "A young prostitute witnesses a murder in Esquilino. All shook up, she takes her car and accidentally runs over a whole family of Asian restaurant owners: mother, father, and son. Only the young prostitute and the son survive. The glass from the exploding windshield injures her eyes and she loses her sight. They are both all alone in the world and a friendship blossoms between them. Because of the traumatic shock; she doesn't remember anything of the murder she witnessed, but the killer is on her trail. The kid becomes her eyes and she looks after him. They run all around Rome in order to survive. This is the story of *Occhiali neri*, which should have starred Asia as the young prostitute. I was interested in telling the story of two different people, who help each out and eventually become like a family."[7]

Unfortunately, while the project was in development, disaster struck: Vittorio Cecchi Gori, who had inherited the family empire from his father Mario (who passed away in 1993), filed for bankruptcy. Vittorio had already been at the center of plenty of scandals—including a highly publicized drug bust—but this was the straw that broke the camel's back. The company and all its holdings were impounded—this included any and all properties already on the slate which Cecchi Gori had purchased and put into production ... including *Occhiali neri*. Dario's dream of realizing a pair of *gialli* as part of his new contract with Cecchi Gori went down the tubes; he was particularly pleased with the *Occhiali neri* script, so the loss stung doubly bad. There was no getting around it, however. The script would remain tied up in the entire sorry Cecchi Gori scandal, so Dario was obliged to bid it *adieu* in favor of coming up with a new scenario.

Notes:
1. Jones, Alan, *Dario Argento: The Man, the Myths & the Magic* (Godalming: FAB Press, 2012), p. 285.
2. http://www.kinematrix.net/testi/lucarelli.htm
3. https://www.tvguide.com/movies/sleepless/review/137275/
4. http://www.cinefile.biz/nonhosonno-di-dario-argento
5. http://www.bbc.co.uk/films/2002/02/07/sleepless_2001_review.shtml
6. http://www.hitparadeitalia.it/bof/boi/boi2000-01.htm
7. Argento, Dario, *Peur* (France: Rouge Profond, 2018), p. 319.

Chapter Twenty: Internet *Giallo*

Owing to the need to work quickly, Argento decided to dust off an old treatment he had written with Franco Ferrini in the late '90s. Titled *Al buio* ("In the Dark"), it revolved around Asia Argento's character from *The Stendhal Syndrome*, Detective Anna Manni; curiously, Dario didn't originally intend to cast Asia in the lead—possibly owing to the grueling experience she had been through playing the character the first time. By 2002, when work was under way on redoing the *Al buio* screenplay, Dario had a change of heart and was hopeful to continue his working relationship with Asia. Before consideration could be given to the script, Argento and Ferrini worked hard to bolster what was generally regarded to be a problematic piece of screenwriting. Englishman-abroad Mark Thompson Ashworth, a resident of Rome who works in the English dialogue coaching side of the Italian film industry, was called upon to do an English translation of the script. As Mark explained in a personal correspondence, "The original screenplay was set in Venice, which obviously ups the budget considerably because of the enormous organizational difficulties involved in shooting there. Medusa later insisted the setting be moved to Rome, thus also saving on *per diems*, hotels, transportation fees, etc.—a savings they didn't invest in the other departments of the film. The killer turned out to be a minor character, so his identity was actually quite a surprise. The finale had him and Anna Mari playing a tense game of poker. She shot him through the table, which broke in half from the impact of the bullet. This was apparently lifted from an old Spaghetti Western. The script was called *Al buio*, but subtitled *Il cartaio*. I originally translated that more literally as *The Card Dealer*, which eventually became *The Card Player*. The synopsis seemed pretty modern at the time, but the actual screenplay was a bit half-baked and approximate, even though it was better than the one he actually filmed."

While *Sleepless* hadn't been the big hit everybody had been hoping for, it did well enough between the Italian box-office takings and foreign home video sales that Medusa was ready and willing to go in on Dario's newest thriller. Their involvement proved to be a bit more tentative this time around, however. All told, Argento was given a budget of $2 million—one of the paltriest he'd ever been handed. As Mark indicates in his comments about the original script versus what ended up on screen, the Venetian locales were axed early on—and some potentially exciting and colorful set pieces were lost in the process. Argento would later try to put a positive spin on this by saying he didn't "want any *Don't Look Now* pretentious association," anyway—but more than likely that was just him trying to minimize his own disappointment. Between the limited scope and budget of his "compensation prize" *giallo* and the irritation and disappointment he felt over losing *Occhiali neri*, Dario surely approached *The Card Player* (the *Al buio* moniker having been dropped) with a bit less fire and enthusiasm than usual. Even so, he still had high hopes for the project and if the pitiful budget posed some difficulties, he could use the film to prove that he was still capable of delivering the goods, even under more trying conditions than usual.

Problems continued to mount. In addition to losing the project's sense of scope, he had to do further rewrites when it became clear that Asia wasn't interested in taking part in the project. "I tried to convince my daughter, but in vain. She went to the U.S.A. to prepare the casting for her movie (*The Heart is Deceitful Above All Things*) and God knows when she'd return to Italy. This episode cracked our relationship. We didn't speak to each other for years, each of us convinced that we were in the right."[1]

Dario and Asia at the beginning of their working relationship.

The Dario-Asia rift couldn't help but evoke memories of the difficulties Dario and Daria faced in their relationship. Argento would tell Alan Jones during this period of animosity that he was frankly glad it worked out the way that it did, as dealing with his daughter had become more and more difficult; here again, however, we see Dario's wounded pride at work: sooner than admit his disappointment, it was easier to put on a fake smile and act like, in some weird way, it had all worked out for the best. With Asia out of the picture, all the connections to *The Stendhal Syndrome* were dropped—and the character's name was easily modified from Anna Manni to Anna Mari, with Stefania Rocca drafted in to play the role.

Despite Asia's absence, the family atmosphere was carried over with Claudio again serving as executive producer—Opera Film, the company he had formed with Dario around the time of making *Scarlet Diva*, co-produced the film in association with Medusa—and once again many of the familiar names and faces were drafted in to be a part of the crew.

Dario made a radical decision early on to emphasize violence and bloodshed far less than usual—whether this was a desire to do something different, a desire to curry the favor of a more mainstream audience, or simply conceding defeat in the face of an inadequate budget is open to speculation. Sergio Stivaletti would nevertheless be called upon to provide some prosthetic corpses, while a new generation of the Bava family was on-board to serve as Dario's assistant. Fabrizio ("Roy") Bava, the son of Lamberto and grandson of Mario, followed in his father's footsteps, having already passed on *Sleepless* owing to other commitments. Massimo Antonello Geleng again provided the production design and art direction, while veteran additional dialogue recording (ADR) actor and director Nick Alexander was responsible for his last English soundtrack on an Argento film; as it happens, it was one of his final projects, period, as he passed away not long after the film's release. Alexander's first picture with Dario was *Four Flies on Grey Velvet* and he had gone on to supervise the English dubs of *Deep Red*, *Suspiria*, *Phenomena*, *Demons*, *Demons 2*, *The Stendhal Syndrome*, *The Phantom of the Opera*, and *Sleepless*, in addition to doing a little extra voice work for *Inferno*, *Opera*, and *Two Evil Eyes*; quite a run! Wanting to give the film a grittier, more realistic look than usual, Argento reached out to the Belgian cinematographer Benoît Debie (born 1968), who was best known for his work for Argentine *enfant terrible* Gaspar Noé on such films as *Irreversible* (*Irréversible*, 2002). The combination of scaled-back bloodshed, greater emphasis on police procedure, a more realistic style, and even an unlikely romantic subplot all seemed to confirm that Argento was looking to reach beyond his usual fan base—a natural impulse, really, considering that his recent films hadn't performed particularly well at the box office.

The *The Card Player* filming commenced on March 10, 2003, but as reported by Alan Jones, the production shut down for two weeks in April to accommodate the Easter holidays as well as Liberation Day; filming then resumed in early May before wrapping at the end of the month. Dario would continue to tinker with the script during production, electing to change the identity of the killer and revising the ending several times in the hopes of coming up with something really spectacular. The money was tight and there simply wasn't the same opportunity (or indeed resources) available to him to experiment as he had done in the past. But despite all the adversity, the production ran more-or-less smoothly. Argento got along well with his actors and he even allowed them to ad lib and bring personal touches to their characters, something which the more control-hungry Dario of the past would've surely bristled at.

Given the script's emphasis on technology, Argento decided early on that a techno-style score would be appropriate. Claudio Simonetti was eager to provide music in that vein, and he ended up delivering his first solo score for one of Argento's films; there was no chance of a repeat of Goblin, anyway, as the group had finally, irrevocably disbanded after the tense experience of scoring *Sleepless*. The editing chores ended up being entrusted to a new face: Walter Fasano (born 1970). After parting ways with Franco Fraticelli on *The Sect*, Dario had worked with several editors—but none of them proved capable of establishing the same special bond which Fraticelli had. With Fasano, however, he

Cover art for the soundtrack release of Claudio Simonetti's score.

The police, including Anna (Stefania Rocca) and Remo (Silvio Muccino), look on helplessly as the Card Player claims another victim.

finally seemed to have found an "editing muse" who could serve him in the long run; he'd remain with Dario for the next two features, but in time he, too, would drift out of the picture. In a final irony, he'd end up enjoying greater success collaborating with Luca Guadagnino; one of the pictures they worked together on was the long-gestating remake of *Suspiria* (2018), which earned far more attention (not all of it positive!) and serious critical attention than any of Dario's later works.

The film gets down to business with speed and economy. We're introduced to Anna Mari (Stefania Rocca), an inspector with the Rome police force. Carlo (Claudio Santamaria), one of her colleagues, stops by her desk to wish her a happy birthday and give her some flowers; the gesture clearly makes her uncomfortable and she reacts with borderline rudeness. Right from the start, it's established that Anna has difficulties interacting with people on a personal level; she is very good at her job, but when it comes to social skills, she's somewhat lacking. She's not unsympathetic, however, she's merely awkward. As the story unfolds and we learn more about her, the reasons for this become more evident. Similarly, Carlo's interest in her also takes on additional significance later in the film; thus, this seemingly simple and functional opening takes on considerably more interest with repeat viewings.

It's evident from the start that the film finds Argento working in a different key than usual. Working with cinematographer Benoît Debie, he strives for greater realism than usual; the lighting is much more consistently pleasing to the eye than Ronnie Taylor's work on *Sleepless*, but it doesn't strive for the sort of rich stylization of his earlier films. The settings are functional rather than eye-catching, and for the first time the emphasis is going to be exclusively on police detection and forensic work; *Sleepless* made a step in that direction thanks to the use of Moretti as a central character—but don't forget, he was a retired cop, and after a certain point the narrative is carried by the usual amateur detective.

It doesn't take long for things to get started and Anna soon receives a strange email from a person calling himself The Card Player. The email explains that he has kidnapped a British tourist (Jennifer Poli) and that he is challenging Anna to a game of video poker, with the kidnapped girl as the stakes. The photograph of the frightened girl attached to the message is enough to convince Anna that he means business, and she tries to compel her superiors to take the message seriously. The Commissioner (Adalberto Maria Merli) refuses to authorize Anna to proceed with the game, and the tourist is killed as a result—the police are forced to watch as she expires on camera, the killer has rigged it so that her face is visible via webcam.

The Commissioner is emblematic of the staid and "by-the-book" attitude of the police force in general, whereas Anna is more adventurous. In refusing to take a risk and engage with the killer, the Commissioner effectively condemns the tourist to death. The notion of

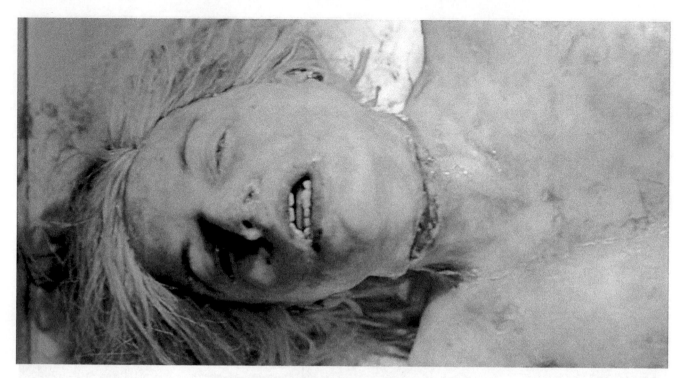

One of Sergio Stivaletti's prosthetic corpses.

reducing life and death to an online game of poker is an interesting one, but it presents the film with its biggest hurdle. Specifically, there isn't anything particularly dynamic or cinematic about the idea of a group of people huddled around a computer screen. Argento tries to compensate for this by keeping his camera active, moving in for close-ups of the various on-lookers and indulging in some striking overhead views of the action. This first death makes it abundantly clear that this will not be a conventional Argento *giallo*; bloodshed is completely de-emphasized, and the game of cat and mouse between the killer and the police carries a different kind of significance compared to an amateur working on their own without the benefit of a police arsenal behind them.

The girl's body is subsequently fished out of a lake and this allows Sergio Stivaletti a chance to show off some more prosthetic work. The fake bodies he created for the film have taken some criticism for looking phony, but there's something truly unsettling and creepy about their "alien" quality. The bodies, of course, are bereft of life and personality—they're simply empty shells, and the clinical manner in which they are presented suggests a de-romanticized approach to the violence, as the detectives and police scientists poke about the bodies looking for clues. The dehumanization makes sense in this context and Debie's lighting and Argento's coverage displays greater sensitivity than the clumsier moments in *Sleepless*, for example.

The murder results in the arrival of another significant character—John Brennan (Liam Cunningham), a detective with Interpol who has been assigned to the case owing to the victim's British citizenship. He makes his presence and authority felt early on when he storms into the police station, berating the Commissioner for refusing to engage with the killer in a bid to save the girl's life. Anna senses a kindred troubled spirit and gravitates to him right away. The interplay between Stefania Rocca (born 1971) and Liam Cunningham (born 1961) is undoubtedly one of the film's biggest strengths. Argento evidently respected what both actors brought to the table and as related by Alan Jones in his commentary on the Anchor Bay DVD release of the film, he allowed them considerably more freedom than usual when it came to ad libbing and improvisation. This shows in that their scenes have a warmth and spontaneity which is lacking in much of the rest of the film; this is a calculated move, as their relationship is the only one which carries much weight in the narrative. It's not likely that Asia would have done much better by the part than Rocca, who gives the character tremendous strength and intelligence; and Cunningham is perfectly cast in a role which could have become an awful cliché (the Irish rogue cop with a drinking problem) in the hands of a lesser actor. When Brennan storms out of police headquarters, Anna follows and tells him: "Everyone in there thinks you're an asshole." His reply of "They're right" is amusing and demonstrates the character's self-awareness, as well as his refusal to worry about making friends if it is to come at the expense of performing his job. As it happens, both Anna and John are dedicated to their work to the exclusion of having personal lives; that they find solace in each other is convincingly conveyed due to the sensitive performances of both actors.

Argento's propensity for quirky comedy comes into play when Anna and John visit the morgue, where the attendant (Claudio Mazzenga) regales them with a bit of tap-dancing and opera singing; a darker touch of humor comes when John proceeds to inspect the body, only for the attendant to refer to the dead woman as one of "my dolls." The use of colorful peripheral characters such as this is nothing new, but whether this overtly farcical character fits into the film's generally sober and serious tone is open to debate. Nevertheless, John does discover an important clue, a seed which has become lodged in the girl's nose. Here again, the emphasis on the frailty of the body gives the film a clammier quality, as opposed to the more extravagant and stylized violence and bloodshed one typically associates with Argento; the dank but clinical atmosphere of the morgue coupled with the dispassionate way in which the body is prodded and examined serves to remind one of the practical reality of death, whereby the body is reduced to so much human waste.

Another girl (Elisabetta Rocchetti, previously glimpsed in a tiny role in *Sleepless*, and soon to become one of the leads in *Do You Like Hitchcock?*) is soon kidnapped, and Anna again receives the same kind of taunting email. This time she elects to play, despite the protestations of the Commissioner; she reveals that she hates poker, though the reasons for this aren't clarified until later. Carlo agrees to step in and take her place. This is yet another scene which gains considerable interest on repeat viewings, as there's some clever misdirection going on; suffice it to say, things are not as they appear, and Carlo is not as innocent and eager to help as he presents himself to be. The game goes badly, and the girl is killed while the police look on—the use of the webcam lends a grimy, unpleasant reality to the images of the various victims meeting their demise, while the absolute lack of blood perversely undercuts audience expectation. Previous Argento films are very much concerned with the mechanics of dying, whereas this film is more of a mystery in the classical vein.

The bond between Anna and John continues to grow as they spend more time with each other. John reveals that he was a policeman in Ireland but that he was disgraced when he shot down a suspect in a robbery who turned out to be underage; sooner than remove him from duty, he was sent to the British embassy in Rome, where he's generally placed on plodding assignments. This case seems to energize his spirit, in much the same way that as the murders in *Sleepless* helped to give the retired/forgotten Moretti a sense of purpose and being in proximity with each other allows both him and Anna begin to make peace with their own long-standing emotional problems.

Anna reveals that her father had a serious gambling problem and that he ended up committing suicide by throwing himself in front of a train because of the disgrace he had brought on his family; the death by train concept recalls a key murder scene in *The Cat O'Nine Tails*, of course, but it foreshadows the finale in an interesting way as well. Both Anna and John have been traumatized and emotionally stunted because of their troubled pasts, but as they open up to one another and allow their vulnerability to become exposed, they grow stronger. They end up making love, but tellingly once it is over, John senses that Anna would rather be left alone for the rest of the night; clearly there is a limit to the amount of intimacy she can handle at this stage in the game. This isn't exactly super-original plotting, to be sure, but again the sincerity of the performances by Rocca and Cunningham make these two characters into real human beings; it is easy to sympathize with them.

As the investigation continues, Argento incorporates one of his classic tropes: John notices a strange sound on the audio recording of the second girl's murder. Inevitably this recalls *The Bird with the Crystal Plumage*, where the titular animal's squawking in the background of the threatening phone call to Inspector Morosini serves as a major clue; auditory clues also figure into the likes of *The Cat O'Nine Tails*, *Tenebrae*, and *Sleepless*, for example. John tries to isolate the sound and figure out what it could be, but it is too vague and ill-defined—it could be a gun firing or it could be a bottle of champagne being uncorked. In traditional fashion, the significance of this clue is not fully realized until the end of the picture.

Looking to increase the odds in their favor, Anna and John seek out a poker whiz named Remo (Silvio Muccino). He's well known in the city for his luck at playing online games of chance, but they're surprised when they meet him to find that he's just a shy young kid. Muccino (born 1982) gives a winning performance in the role; Remo isn't a cocky punk, but rather another lost soul of sorts who seems to drift around the city without having the benefit of a family to fall back on. Anna and John provide him with a sense of belonging, even if he is initially reluctant to put his skills to work in a life-and-death situation such as this.

The killer taunts Anna and her colleagues once more when he kidnaps another girl (Vera Gemma, who also appeared in *The Stendhal Syndrome* and *Scarlet Diva*). Remo is called in to play against The Card Player, and it soon becomes evident that his skills have not been exaggerated. Unfortunately for everybody involved, the victim decides to take her chances when she manages to wriggle free from the tape and ropes which are binding

The Card Player claims another victim.

her; she tries to make a run for it, but the killer isn't so easily outwitted. In the ensuing struggle the webcam is knocked over and Remo and the others are forced to watch helplessly as she is stabbed to death. The still, unblinking gaze of the camera is a major departure from the norm for Argento, and only convenient framing—with the killing taking place outside of the frame—prevents us from seeing the awful action as it takes place. It's a disturbing scene precisely because it relies on our imagination to fill in the gaps—and the use of sound as the girl screams while being brutally stabbed to death is tremendously effective.

The film's most accomplished suspense scene occurs when Anna is alone in her apartment and finds herself under attack by the killer. The scene is perfectly realized by Argento and Debie as Anna goes about her business as usual, only to notice a strange reflection in the glass ashtray on her coffee table; looking closer, she sees it's the face of a man wearing a ski mask. She tries to get the upper hand by drawing her gun and running outside to surprise the man—but she doesn't find anybody out there waiting for her. The use of dizzying overhead angles is particularly effective, while Claudio Simonetti's music provides exciting accompaniment to the proceedings. When Anna returns to the apartment, she gets an unwelcome surprise: the killer has broken in and has left a macabre souvenir from his most recent kill—two of the dead girl's severed fingers. Anna tries to gain the upper ground by turning off the lights, but the killer surprises her and they struggle, though he eventually disappears into the night; the use of mobile camerawork, judicious editing, and shadowy lighting adds tremendously to the effectiveness of the scene, which is arguably the most dynamic sequence in the picture. In its way it's every bit as effective as the bigger, splashier scene of murder and mayhem on the train at the start of *Sleepless*—but since it doesn't result in any bloodletting, it arguably tends to be overlooked by many critics and fans.

The killer steps up his game with his next prospective victim. He kidnaps Lucia (Fiore Argento), who happens to be the Police Commissioner's daughter. It's a calculated move, of course, and it puts additional pressure on Remo, as he is drafted in once more to try and save the young woman's life. The emphasis on card playing may not be inherently cinematic, but it does conjure memories of one of Argento's cinematic idols, Fritz Lang. One of Lang's signature works is the epic *Dr. Mabuse: The Gambler* (*Dr. Mabuse, der Spieler*, 1922), in which a criminal mastermind uses his fiendish intellect to terrorize Berlin and extort a fortune in ill-gotten gains. The killer here isn't quite that resourceful and brilliant, but the connection between the two films seems clear when one realizes the impact Lang's work has had on Argento as an artist. The whole concept of risk-taking is central to the thrust of the plot, as the willingness of characters like Anna and John to push the envelope establishes a perverse rapport with the killer; in this instance, things end happily, as Remo wins the game and Lucia is released back to her loving family. Remo pays for his collaboration with the police, however, when he is lured into an elaborate trap by the murderer. Remo tries to outwit him once more, but this time the deck is stacked against him and he is killed; Remo's death carries emotional weight because the character is so likable. The scene of his funeral is realized with a touch of visual poetry, as the vivid primary colors of the flowers in the cemetery contrast with the generally dark and almost monochromatic visual tone of the rest of the picture; even in this context, Argento is able to find something oddly beautiful in death.

Things proceed pretty quickly towards the finale, as John finally figures out the noise he heard in the background of the one recording. Every day at noon at Gianicolo (a hill located in the western part of Rome), a cannon is fired—a real-life tradition which dates back to December 1847, when the firing of the cannon signaled to local churches that it was time to sound the bells for the middle of the day. The revelation of this all-important clue allows John to narrow his search and his discovery of a rare plant which produces the seeds found on the bodies of two of the victims ultimately points him in the direction of the killer's lair. The use of the plant as a means of locating a key location is reminiscent of

Deep Red, while the visual motif of the pollen blowing through the air can't help but remind one of *The Sect*. John's instincts are correct and he actually finds the place where the killer has been broadcasting from, but he underestimates his prey. The killer has rigged a deadly booby trap, and John is killed. Argento includes a sad, wistful point of view shot as John is dying, showing the setting sun shining through some leaves, and there's no doubt that his shocking, sudden departure from the narrative is the film's biggest surprise. The death of Moretti absolutely undercut the final scenes of *Sleepless*, but in the case of this film, Anna is sufficiently engaging to hold our interest even with John out of the picture.

The finale sees Carlo taking Anna to John's aid—only for her to realize that Carlo is the very man they have been seeking. Carlo knocks her out and when she awakens, they're in an unlikely location: the railroad tracks. This gives rise to arguably the most preposterous finale of Argento's career—it's not as audaciously over the top as the final act of *Phenomena*, perhaps, but it's still within striking distance. Argento's point of reference here is another piece of silent cinema, the serial cliffhanger *The Perils of Pauline* (1914), in which Pearl White's damsel in distress is menaced by a melodramatic madman while being tied down to railroad tracks, with a train fast approaching.

In this case, the killer puts himself at risk with Anna, with whom he is in love; this connects back to the beginning of the film, in which we see Carlo sheepishly offering Anna flowers and trying to take her out on a date. Sure enough, his unrequited love, coupled with decided homicidal tendencies, has compelled him to try and catch her attention in the most extravagant of ways. The murders can therefore be seen as his twisted form of courtship, which evokes the plot of *Opera*. Using two sets of handcuffs, he locks one of his hands to the one rail, while locking one of Anna's hands to the other rail—the other hands are free to play one last game of video poker. It's a delightfully demented conceit but not surprisingly it doesn't play well for everybody. Those who can appreciate it for what it is will go with the flow, while others find it to be unforgivably goofy. The fact that Carlo has barely had a chance to register as a character is also problematic for some viewers; much like the ending of *The Cat O'Nine Tails*, one gets the sense that the identity was less important than the spectacle of his final demise. In fact, the identity of the killer reportedly changed over several drafts, which seems to confirm that hypothesis. In any event, the final "duel to the death" is nicely staged and it builds to a satisfying resolve as Anna wins the game by distracting him through various mind games, only for him to refuse to keep his end of the bargain by giving her the key to freedom. Thinking quick, Anna is able to roll over the rail, leaving Carlo sputtering in rage—before the train reduces him to nothing and severs her from the handcuff in the process. The scene climaxes with a nice touch of humor as Anna uses her gun to shoot the car stereo, which has been relentlessly blaring one of Claudio Simonetti's techno-based themes the entire time.

The film ends with a brief but significant coda. It is several weeks later and Anna (who has since been promoted to Chief Inspector due to her excellent work on the case) receives a call from her doctor, who tells her that she is pregnant. She looks puzzled at first, then a smile settles on her face. The child is the result of her brief tryst with John; he may be dead, but their love will live on through the child they've created together. It's almost a throw-away scene, but it's included for very specific reasons. Unlike the dark (or ambiguous) finales of so many earlier Argento films, *The Card Player* ends on a note of hope and optimism as Anna embraces her new role as a mother. Argento even includes the quirky "You have been watching *The Card Player*" credit, which recalls earlier films like *Suspiria* and *Deep Red*; such a credit would also feature in a couple of his later films, as well.

The Card Player is a much tighter and more focused film than *Sleepless*. It doesn't aim for the same sort of visceral shock effects, but it should not be underestimated for that reason. The deliberately drab aesthetic and emphasis on police procedure can be a little off-putting at first, but as the film unfolds and develops, it becomes considerably more engaging than its predecessor. The pacing is better, the performances are more consistent and while it isn't free of absurdity, the plot is generally

Remo (Silvio Muccino) is lured to his death.

The Unsane Cinema of Dario Argento

Turkish advertising, using the same basic artwork as the Italian.

compelling. In many respects, its approach to the central mystery is most similar to *The Cat O'Nine Tails*—and like that earlier film, it actually plays better on repeat viewings, when all the "surprises" are out of the bag, and one can better appreciate the skill and artistry with which it is assembled.

Argento's decision to back off the violence is only a problem if one believes that blood and gore are the core ingredients of an Argento film. Like *Trauma* before it, it is often undervalued for this reason. True, the film doesn't strive for the sort of flashy visual pyrotechnics of his earlier films, but there's something to be said for the pared-down approach. The film offers a welcome change of pace from the norm, and while it occasionally stumbles, it manages to tell its story with precision and economy. Add in a very good soundtrack by Simonetti and appealing central performances (it helps that there is plenty of live production audio this time, with both Rocca and Cunningham's voices being present on the English soundtrack, though the revoicing of some of the minor characters leaves something to be desired) and it emerges as the most consistently polished and successful of Argento's 21st century output for the big screen.

Medusa again gave the film a good advertising push in Italy, and the Italian theatrical premiere came on January 2, 2004. The opening numbers weren't as impressive as those of *Sleepless*, but all told the picture did steadier business; the critical reaction was negative, however, and many of the fans picked up on the "mainstream" vibe and rejected the picture as a sell-out. All told, it placed in the 51st spot for Italian theatrical releases in the 2003-2004 season[2]—not bad considering the very low budget, but still nothing to get overly excited about. And once again, foreign sales proved to be tricky. Anchor Bay acquired the film for U.S. home video release, though it made its theatrical bow stateside via the American Cinematheque on August 14, 2004. The American press was no more kind towards the film than the Italians had been, which was nothing new, of course. Reviewing the film for *The New York Times*, for example, Dave Kehr wrote, "Lately, [Argento] hasn't produced much of interest apart from his spooky, spectacularly tattooed daughter. [...] [T]he film unfolds as a tired, thoroughly conventional police procedural that might as well be titled '*CSI: Roma*.'"[3] Not surprisingly, many of the reviewers picked up on the TV crime procedural angle—and Argento's subsequent descent into the confines of the small screen seemed to signal a transition of sorts.

Prior to that transition, however, Dario started work on a very ambitious project, the long-gestating Mater Lachrymarum project, which would finally round off the "Three Mothers" trilogy. Even while post-production was under way on *The Card Player*, Argento continued to work on his outline for the film. In issue 228 of *Fangoria*, published in December 2003, Alan Jones broke the news that the project was finally inching towards becoming a reality. Argento spoke effusively about it and seemed ready to leave behind the *giallo* for a little while as he made peace with a small but important part of his cinematic legacy. Already titled *La terza madre* ("The Third Mother"), it took the place of another ill-fated but cherished project. "I'm working on the script for *The Third Mother* now. I originally planned to direct *Occhiali neri* next, but that is now dead. I will start shooting *The Third Mother* in August of 2004, and a major Hollywood studio may get involved in the financing. It will revolve around mysticism, alchemy, terrorism, and Gnosticism. So many people were tortured because the Church said that Gnosticism was heresy, and that will be the starting part of the story."[4] Before that would come to pass, however, there would be a few unexpected detours.

Notes:
1. Argento, Dario, *Peur* (France: Rouge Profond, 218), p. 320-321.
2. http://www.hitparadeitalia.it/bof/boi/boi2003-04.htm
3. https://www.nytimes.com/2004/10/06/movies/the-game-is-poker-the-stakes-are-lives.html
4. Jones, Alan, "Argento to raise *The Third Mother*," *Fangoria* #228, December 2003.

Chapter Twenty-One: Back to TV

In May 2004, at the Cannes Film Festival, Dario's new project was formally announced. As per the RAI Trade company, they had signed on to distribute a new series of made-for-TV *gialli* produced by Argento. It wasn't Dario's first foray into the world of television, of course, but it was his first time working for the small screen in nearly 20 years. Bearing in mind that the *Giallo* TV series wasn't overly successful, it pays to remember that part of the reason why Argento became such a celebrity to the Italian public was due to *Door into Darkness*. By introducing those made-for-TV thrillers, Argento reached an even larger audience than usual. Clearly, by 2004, he was in need of a boost—and so, the idea to oversee the production of a new series of tele-films seemed like a good plan. The initial concept, as outlined by Argento, was that "RAI ordered a series of seven scripts for TV, to be directed by me and some other directors. They should be thrillers, but also bear a common theme, passion for the cinema. Each episode would be based on a classic movie director from the past, where each author or director would pay homage, in their own way."[1] This meant, of course, that *The Third Mother* would have to be put on hold; Argento was still working on the screenplay, anyway, so this new project would enable him to keep the cash-flow moving as he continued to ruminate on how best to polish off his supernatural trilogy. The break also allowed him a chance to try and drum up interest from potential investors, as his conception for the film would call for a more lavish budget and shooting schedule than he had been afforded on *The Card Player*.

Argento set to work on laying out the episodes with Franco Ferrini. They worked feverishly on outlines and devoted most of their energies to the debut tele-film, which Argento decided to direct himself. The topic was an appropriate one: Alfred Hitchcock. Critics had long been comparing Dario's work to that of the master of suspense, going all the way back to *The Bird with the Crystal Plumage*. It has also been said—though nobody has ever been able to validate it—that Hitchcock, upon seeing *Deep Red*, commented, "this young Italian guy is starting to worry me."[2] It's probably apocryphal, but it's an amusing anecdote, nonetheless. Sadly, during his tenure at *Paese Sera*, Argento never had the opportunity to interview Hitchcock himself—but there's no doubt that the older man's shadow looms large where the entire suspense-thriller genre is concerned.

RAI decided early on that, sooner than take a chance on an entire series, they would wait and see how the first film performed in the ratings before commissioning Argento and Ferrini to write the balance of the episodes. Thus, while they had general outlines and ideas in place for the other installments, they were free to focus their energies on the all-important "pilot" project. The story allowed Argento to riff on some of Hitchcock's most famous films—notably *Strangers on a Train* (1951), *Rear Window* (1954), and, of course, *Psycho* (1960)—while also including plenty of references to his own back catalogue. The title, *Do You Like Hitchcock?*, made it clear that the project was intended as a valentine of sorts to Argento's "spiritual godfather."

Given how his recent films had been performing, it wasn't necessarily a shock that raising money for the project was tricky; RAI was willing to put up a minimal budget, once again somewhere in the $2 million range—with Dario and Claudio producing the feature through their Opera Film production company. The budget didn't allow for big stars and Argento compensated for this by writing the characters as younger people—film students and the like—which wouldn't call for more experienced, and therefore more expensive performers. The crew was a mixture of new and old faces. Claudio's son, Nilo, was

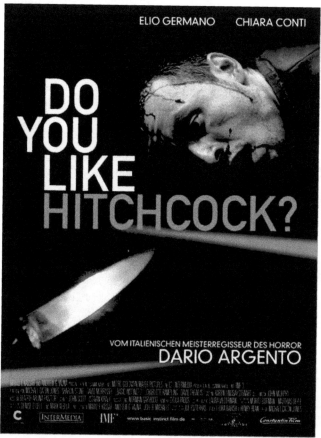

The German advertising is probably the most eye-catching that the film received anywhere it was released; designer unknown.

brought on to serve as a production assistant, and he would return in much the same capacity for Dario's next two big screen features, as well. Frederic Fasano (born 1969), the cinematographer responsible for *Scarlet Diva*, made his debut working for Dario—he, too, would be recruited for the next two big screen Argento pictures. Once again, Sergio Stivaletti was involved in the special effects side of the proceedings.

Despite the limitations of the TV format, Argento told Alan Jones that he wasn't going to hold anything back. "Upgrading the Italian TV movie has been a mission statement from the beginning, which is why I'm making *Do You Like Hitchcock?* exactly like one of my cinema movies and packing it with violence and nudity. RAI can do what they want with it after I'm finished but I'm going for it in every censorable area to make it stand out from all the network rubbish."[3] This mission statement extended to the look of the film, which Argento was determined to make as cinematic as possible. Sooner than shoot it digitally, Argento and Fasano decided to go with 35mm—and though it was made specifically for the Italian TV market, international sales were taken into consideration by filming it entirely in English.

The filming commenced on location in Turin on July 26, 2004; the schedule was tighter than usual, and the film wrapped on September 5. Once again, Walter Fasano took charge of the editing, while Dario commissioned Pino Donaggio to write a score very much in the style of Bernard Herrmann. Donaggio had already provided a score in a similar vein for *Trauma*, but whereas that soundtrack was more somber and serious, his work here proved to be more whimsical, keeping in sync with the overall tone of the film itself.

A brief prologue, set in 1990, establishes the theme of voyeurism. A little boy named Giulio (Lorenzo Federici) follows a pair of witchy-looking women

Lorenzo Federici appears as the child version of Giulio in the film's prologue.

through a forest; they end up at a cottage, where they proceed to sacrifice a chicken. A horrified Giulio looks on as the blood splatters on the face of the one woman, and he gives himself away, leading to a brief chase as they pursue him. Precisely why this scene is even in the film is unclear. It doesn't serve any real narrative function beyond establishing that the protagonist has been a voyeur since childhood; it also foreshadows a later scene in which he is again pursued after accidentally allowing himself to be caught "peeping." The use of the witches can't help but recall *Suspiria* and *Inferno*, of course, but nothing happens as a result of their inclusion in the narrative; the whole prologue is just an indulgence on Argento's part, and sadly it isn't sufficiently atmospheric or exciting to justify its existence.

The action shifts to contemporary Turin—the setting is significant in that it is one of Argento's favorite locations. He has often made claims that the magical quality of the city is partly down to the fact that witchcraft is practiced extensively there, and that there are more witches in Turin than in any other city in Italy. With that in mind, there seems to be some initial connection between the setting and the presence of the witches in the prologue, but nothing is ever made of that; it's more a matter of Dario working amid familiar surroundings and recalling the glory days of *Deep Red* than anything else.

Giulio (Elio Germano) is now residing in Turin, where he is enrolled at university studying film. His particular field of study is German Expressionism, which allows Argento a chance to pay tribute to some of his favorite films, including F.W. Murnau's *Nosferatu* (*Nosferatu, eine Symphonie des Grauens*, 1922) and Paul Wegener's *The Golem* (*Der Golem*, 1920); there are also visual nods to Fritz Lang, notably a poster for *M* (1931). The evocation of the film's fanatic lifestyle is nicely done, but sadly Giulio remains a rather dull and colorless lead character. Elio Germano (born 1980) is obviously a good deal younger than the average Argento protagonist, but he seems incapable of breathing life into Giulio and making him into a truly interesting or engaging presence. The film can't help but suffer accordingly.

The character's voyeurism comes back into play when he notices an attractive neighbor across the road, Sasha (Elisabetta Rocchetti, in her third and best role for Argento), prancing around her apartment in the nude; the impulse to watch and observe becomes all-powerful, and it gradually becomes an obsession. This emphasis on voyeurism is a commentary of sorts on the cinematic process—which is ultimately all about sitting in the dark and passively observing—but it also deliberately ties into Hitchcock's masterpiece *Rear Window* (1954); the connection becomes stronger still in the last act, when

Dario with an oversized key prop used for a tricky shot in *Do You Like Hitchcock?*.

Giulio's injuries sideline him and keep him from being an active participant. Argento apes the Hitchcock film with a wink and a nod, including a charming sequence in which Giulio glimpses insights into the lives of his neighbors as he sees an elderly man cheating at cards, a woman berating her maid for not cleaning the windows thoroughly and, most significantly, Sasha fighting with her mother (Milvia Marigliano). The tone is light and airy early on, something underlined by Pino Donaggio's playful music, but darkness begins to gradually filter in as the story unfolds.

Giulio's fixation on watching Sasha begins to have a negative impact on his relationship with his girlfriend, Arianna (Cristina Brondo). Arianna correctly calls him out for being so obsessive and inappropriate, but he can't control his impulses. Their on-again/off-again dynamic and propensity for having spats is clearly meant to be charming, but the chemistry between Germano and Brondo is virtually non-existent. That said, Brondo (born 1977) is more successful at making something out of her character. Arianna is strong-willed and fiercely independent, whereas Giulio seems to fancy himself as "the man in charge." In a way it recalls the dynamic between Marcus and Gianna in *Deep Red*, but it never does catch fire.

Giulio strikes up a friendship with Andrea (Iván Morales), a clerk at a local video store. It's a natural habitat for a character like Giulio and it has the side effect of allowing him to continue observing Sasha, since she is a frequent customer. At one point, Sasha meets Federica (Chiara Conti) while they're browsing the shelves; they "meet cute" over the Hitchcock selection, of course, and Sasha sells her on the virtues of *Strangers on a Train* (1951). There's something charmingly naïve about the idea of a couple of trendy young people bonding over a classic film in this manner; it may not be realistic, per se, but it speaks to the deep-seated cinephilia which is a part of Dario's DNA. Giulio takes note of the burgeoning friendship and it helps to fuel his already overheated imagination even further.

The plot lurches into more familiar terrain when Sasha's mother is home alone one night and somebody breaks into the apartment. In a twist on the usual trope, the killer is wearing white gloves—and the use of close-ups of the inner workings of the apartment door's lock is familiar from numerous early Argento films. The generally bland approach to staging energizes during this sequence as Argento draws upon his familiar bag of cinematic tricks, building suspense as the black-clad figure makes its way into the apartment and building to a

Dario gives the photographer the death glare; would you want to upset this man?

terrific shock effect as the killer strikes the woman's head, resulting in a welter of crimson gore. The scene is brutal, far eclipsing anything seen in *The Card Player*, and is punctuated by an effective image of the woman's bloody hand smearing blood on her window as she succumbs to her injuries. The use of graphic gore—coupled with some lingering nude scenes involving all three of the principal actresses—validates Argento's contention that he approached the film with no regards for the "delicate" sensibilities of television censorship.

The murder is witnessed by Giulio, though he doesn't get a good look at the attacker. He soon begins theorizing that Sasha is responsible and that she is using the narrative hook of *Strangers on a Train*—in which two men discuss the concept of "swapping" murders to generate the perfect alibi; problem is, one of them takes the idea literally and puts it into practice—and has enlisted Federica to assist in her diabolical scheme. Arianna tires of hearing Giulio obsessively ruminating on the topic and he is unable to find anybody who is willing to listen to him or take him seriously. Sooner than rely on others, he decides to take matters into his own hands by playing amateur detective; this allows Argento to revisit the familiar tropes of his earlier *gialli* before he started to transition to the mechanics of police work in *Sleepless* and *The Card Player*. The trouble is, neither Giulio nor the mystery he is investigating are all that interesting.

As Giulio continues to snoop around, looking for clues, he follows Federica and learns that she is being blackmailed by her boss (Giuseppe Lo Console, who would go on to appear in *Giallo* and *Dario Argento's Dracula*), because he's caught her stealing money from the company; he's been forcing her to have sex with him, but when he catches sight of Giulio peeping in at them through the apartment window, he gives chase. This obviously connects back into Giulio's traumatic childhood memory of the witches, and he's put at a distinct disadvantage when he breaks his foot falling from the balcony. The ensuing chase in a torrential downpour has the potential to be genuinely thrilling and exciting, but the lack of interest generated by the characters undermines the overall effect. Still, Argento stages the scene with energy and a touch of dark humor, as Giulio's injury gets worse and worse as he keeps slipping and falling on the slick streets. He manages to escape, but the broken foot sidelines him from being an active participant in the finale.

Things proceed in a fast-and-furious fashion in the final act. Andrea shows up at Giulio's apartment and tries to kill him in a protracted bathtub attack which manages to evoke both *Deep Red* and Hitchcock's *Psycho*, but he's chased off and is struck down and killed by a passing car. In a repeat of the ending of *Deep Red*, the case appears to have resolved itself—but then Giulio notices Federica creeping around in the apartment building. Arianna, looking to redeem herself for turning her back on Giulio earlier in the film, adopts the role of Grace Kelly in *Rear Window* by putting herself in danger in order to impress the man she loves. She sneaks across the street and tries to get a look at what Federica is up to; there's a beautiful moment when Federica hears her in the hallway and stops dead in her tracks—Argento shows a large close-up of her ear, pulling out slightly to highlight her frightened eyes before pulling out for a full figure view of her as she plots her next move. It's a small moment but it's a

Dario compares Milvia Marigliano to her dummy stand-in for her murder scene.

delicately beautiful one, expertly realized by Argento and cinematographer Frederic Fasano. The subsequent rooftop chase and struggle between Federica, Arianna, and the police inspector (Edoardo Stoppa) is crisply paced and nicely executed, but it essentially amounts to much ado about nothing. The final reveal that Federica was roped into the murder scheme by Sasha and that Andrea attacked Giulio in order to protect Sasha is no great shakes, and the whole thing resolves itself in a fairly perfunctory and inoffensive fashion with Federica being clamped in handcuffs and carted off to jail.

The film ends with an ironic coda in which Giulio is innocently looking out his window, only to catch sight of a shapely new neighbor. In spite of everything he has been through, the impulse to look remains as strong as ever; the same can be said of Argento as a professional voyeur of sorts. What will happen to Giulio beyond that is left open to speculation—all that's certain is, he hasn't changed one bit.

Do You Like Hitchcock? is very minor Argento. It pays to view it as a sort of "work in miniature." It doesn't aspire to reinvent the wheel or go for the sort of elaborate aesthetic effects typical of Argento's more ambitious big screen efforts. Taken on its own terms, as a low budget TV project, it is slick and well-crafted. Frederic Fasano's photography is clear and crisp; it doesn't come close to matching the realistic-but-artful approach of Benoît Debie's work on *The Card Player*, but it does come off better than Ronnie Taylor's sometimes slapdash work on *Sleepless*, for example. The script has some clever concepts, and the whole notion of building a thriller around a film student is a natural for a film-savvy director like Argento, but the characters are dull, and the suspense simply isn't there. The playful exploration of art vs. reality which informed so much of *Tenebrae* and *Opera* is visible once more, but it all feels a bit half-hearted and disengaged.

Matters aren't helped by the subpar English dubbing; the absence of Nick Alexander is felt, and the decision to replace the actors' voices with English accents is simply incongruous; behind the scenes clips of the actors speaking their lines in English confirm that Argento would have done better to have allowed the performers to keep their original accents instead. The end result is acceptable as a minor diversion, but ultimately it remains Argento's blandest and most disposable *giallo*.

By the time the film was ready for exhibition, RAI Trade appeared to have lost faith in the enterprise. The film was trotted out at various festivals and foreign sales deals based on Argento's fading but still recognizable name allowed it greater exposure than the usual made-for-television Italian film—but it ended up going straight to video in Italy in December 2005. Possibly the excessive

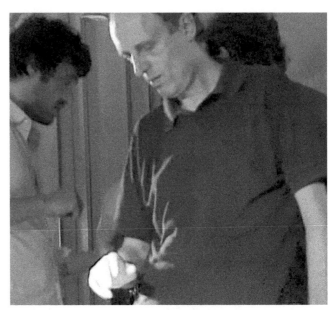

Dario dons a white glove this time, as he stands in once more for the killer.

(by TV standards) violence and nudity put RAI off of pursuing a proper Italian TV premiere, though it was screened on Italian television in August 2007, by which time Argento had lensed a further two TV projects and another feature for the big screen. Needless to say, the reaction to the film was muted and the proposed series never materialized; the treatments prepared by Argento and Ferrini would be put aside in a drawer where they could gather dust with various other projects that never managed to get off the ground. If a silver lining was to be found, it came in 2006 when the film was nominated for Best TV Film (*Millor Televmovie*) at the Barcelona Film Awards; it ended up losing out to *Coses que passen …*, directed by Silvia Munt.

Around this time, Argento was briefly attached to another portmanteau horror project—this one would also feature segments directed by Tobe Hooper (1943-2017), the *auteur* responsible for *The Texas Chain Saw Massacre* (1974), and Monte Hellman (born 1932), the indie cinema darling best remembered for directing *Two Lane Blacktop* (1971). All three men would be presenting segments based on the writing of Dennis Bartok (born 1965), a Pittsburgh native who had industry experience thanks to his work for Robert De Niro's Tribeca Productions as well as for the American Cinematheque in Los Angeles. Argento and Hooper eventually bolted from the project, but Hellman remained on board—and he was subsequently joined by Joe Dante (born 1946), the director of *The Howling* (1981), *Friday the 13th* director Sean S. Cunningham (born 1941), visual effects artist (and debuting director) John Gaeta (born 1965), and, most surprisingly, legendary *enfant terrible* Ken Russell (1927-2011), whose baroque, sexually charged visions

Cover art for the Anchor Bay DVD release of *Jenifer*; artist unknown.

had been such an inspiration to Dario on *The Phantom of the Opera*. *Trapped Ashes*, as the film was eventually known, was released in 2006; the segment Argento was to have directed, "My Twin, the Worm," was directed by Gaeta.

"My Twin, the Worm" signaled that Argento was no longer hung up on the idea of being the sole author of his work. Even more so than *Two Evil Eyes*, it indicated a new-found willingness to accept ideas from other people; to put it less charitably, it indicated that he was on his way to accepting the role of "hired gun." That his involvement in the film didn't pan out was apparently due to issues he had with the script, but he soon found himself being courted for another gig he had no hand in originating.

Mick Garris (born 1951), a life-long enthusiast of genre cinema, got his start as an interviewer and film critic—just as Dario had done long before him. He dabbled in the music scene for a number of years before finally making his way into the film industry as a receptionist at George Lucas' Star Wars Corporation. From there, he started writing and directing "making of" documentaries on genre films, including Joe Dante's *The Howling* (1981) and John Carpenter's *The Thing* (1982). With his easy-going manner, he found himself befriending many of the people he admired most in the industry, notably Steven Spielberg, John Carpenter, Joe Dante, and John Landis. After working as a story editor and writer on Spielberg's *Amazing Stories* TV series, he gradually started to gain momentum as a screenwriter before making his feature directing debut with *Critters 2* (1988). As time wore on and he became better known for his involvement in such Stephen King adaptations as *Sleepwalkers* (1992), *The Stand* (1994), and *The Shining* (1997), he continued to promote the work of his favorite genre filmmakers, all the while hoping to find a way to collaborate with all of them on an ambitious project. Thus, the concept for *Masters of Horror* was born—Garris was known for organizing dinner party get-togethers with some of the top names in modern horror, and he eventually took the idea for a *Masters of Horror* TV series to IDT Entertainment and Showtime, who reacted favorably to his proposal. His concept was relatively straightforward: each episode would be directed by one of the top names in horror. The budgets would be set at less than $2 million per episode and the schedules would be brutally short, but within those parameters, the directors would be free to let their imaginations run wild. So long as they didn't go over budget or schedule, they were granted the freedom of final cut, and the Showtime network platform ensured that they didn't need to be squeamish with regards to censorship. The regular attendees of these dinner parties—including Carpenter, Tobe Hooper, and Stuart Gordon—were eager to take part.

Argento wasn't one of the original group of directors who were invited to take part in the so-called "Masters of Horror" dinner, but he was invited along for subsequent installments. Garris was eager that Argento should be a part of his TV series as well. When the idea was pitched to him, Dario was enthusiastic; he liked the idea of having creative freedom, and the promise of "no censorship" certainly appealed to his sensibilities.

In fact, the script Garris pitched to him wasn't originally earmarked for Dario at all—*Jenifer*, adapted from a comic strip written by Bruce Jones (born 1944) and illustrated by Bernie Wrightson (1948-2017) and first published in *Creepy* magazine in 1974, was originally to have been directed by Frank Darabont (born 1959), who is best known these days as one of the creators of the hit TV series *The Walking Dead*. Darabont was uneasy with the story's graphic mixture of sex and violence and he elected to walk away from the series altogether; with most of the other directors already assigned to their own respective episodes, his departure opened the door for Argento to become involved. Argento read the script and was immediately enthusiastic. Ever since *The Phantom of the Opera*, he had begun to explore the concept of kinky sex—and *Jenifer* was certainly loaded with it. The impish, rebellious, anti-establishment flame still burned bright within Dario, so he said "yes" right away.

Garris gave Argento the same deal as all the other directors. The budget would be about $1.8 million, the shooting schedule would be 10 days, and owing to the financial incentives available to the production, it would have to be filmed in Vancouver, British Columbia. Dario was obliged to cast the piece from Rome, necessitating the casting sessions to be held via Skype, and he worked with Steven Weber—the sitcom star who adapted the Jones/Wrightson piece to script form—on some rewrites via internet as well. By the time he was able to fly to Vancouver, the preproduction period had finished, and it was time for Argento to start filming. *Jenifer* commenced its break-neck production schedule in May 2005, with Argento far from his usual resources and production personnel. Even so, the shoot proved to be a happy one. He gleefully pushed the envelope as far as he could with regards to the graphic sex and gruesome gore; not surprisingly, it proved to be one of the most lurid episodes of the entire first season.

While Dario hadn't been able to make use of any of his regular collaborators during the production, he was granted permission by Garris to commission Claudio Simonetti to write a music score. Simonetti responded with a lullaby theme which couldn't help but remind one of the score for *Deep Red*; the contrast between the idyllic, child-like music and the X-rated level of (simulated) sex and violence proved to be Argento's major contribution to the enterprise.

Jenifer begins as cop partners Frank (Steven Weber) and Spacey (Laurie Brunetti) try to enjoy a lunch break with some Chinese take-out food. Argento incorporates some interesting camera angles, including an overhead view of the two men in the car eating their food while contending with an irksome fly (shades of *Once Upon a Time in the West* and *Four Flies on Grey Velvet*), as well as a strange dolly-in towards the front windshield, which focuses in on the police light on the dashboard; the emphasis on detail over character is typical of Argento and it promises a quirky visual approach which unfortunately the balance of the episode doesn't deliver.

The monotony is disrupted when Frank sees a woman being dragged across the road by a disheveled homeless man (Kevin Crofton). Frank follows them to a clearing, where the man is preparing to kill the girl with a butcher knife. There's a nice visual flourish as Argento shows the man's deranged expression reflected in the blade of the knife, followed by a burst of violence as Frank shoots the man to death before he can kill his intended victim; the man dies saying the girl's name: Jenifer. Frank gets an added shock when he tends to Jenifer (Carrie Ann Fleming) and he gets a good look at her face. It is monstrously disfigured, with a misshapen mouth, exposed fang-like teeth and unnaturally large, pitch-black eyes. In all other respects she looks normal—attractive, even.

The experience leaves Frank badly rattled and his superior (Beau Starr) tells him it is necessary for him to see the police psychiatrist as a matter of protocol. Frank is reluctant to do so; in his mind, he's done his job and that should be the end of it. Even so, it's clear that he needs help even if he doesn't want any. Though known for playing light comedy on the TV sitcom *Wings* (1990-1997), Steven Weber (born 1961) proves quite adept at playing the conflicting emotional state of his character. It helps that he wrote the script, no doubt, but even so he manages to convey the sense of a man's gradually crumbling mental state with absolute conviction and sincerity.

As Weber discusses in his audio commentary for the Anchor Bay DVD release of *Jenifer*, he and Dario differed in some areas of the story—but he was so eager to please the director (he claims to have been a fan ever since seeing *Suspiria*) that he made adjustments to the script as requested. The most significant of the changes is with regards to Frank's family life. There isn't much about Frank's background in the short story, so Weber was obliged to embroider in order to make it work in dramatic terms. Weber felt that it made more sense for Frank to have a deeply unhappy home life: a shrew of a wife who treats him terribly, a son who wants nothing to do with him, and so on. Argento felt that it would be more satisfying on a dramatic level if his home life were basically idyllic, thus making his fall from grace all

Dario lets his new-found love of *Grand Guignol* run riot in *Jenifer*.

The Unsane Cinema of Dario Argento

Dario on location in Vancouver for *Jenifer*.

the more striking. Thus, as depicted in the film, Frank's home life is far from horrific. His wife Ann (Julia Arkos) is attractive, affectionate, and understanding. His son Peter (Harris Allan) is a typical moody and rebellious teenager, but that's not unusual in the best of families. When Frank returns home, he is sullen and moody—and he tries to take the edge off by drinking. Ann tries to reassure him that he did the right thing, but he doesn't want to talk about it; he shuts her out and becomes more and more insular. That night, Ann tries to distract him with a little sex. We learn that they've been having intimacy problems for a while and while Ann is not unkind or unsympathetic about this, she is desperate to reestablish that close physical contact with her husband. Frank reluctantly agrees, but he finds himself picturing Jenifer the entire time. The mental images of Jenifer excite him and bring out the bestial side of his nature, and he responds by forcibly attempting to sodomize Ann; she is understandably perturbed and their attempt at reconnecting ends disastrously. Weber explains on the audio commentary that the sodomy angle was something Dario brought to the scene, as he felt it cut to the nature of Frank's internal dilemma; it's certainly a surprising touch, and the overall approach to sex and sexuality is very frank—even more so than had been the case in *The Phantom of the Opera*, for example.

Frank learns that Jenifer has been sent to an institution, since she has no relatives to turn to, and he decides to rescue her. He checks her out from the facility and takes her home. Jenifer reacts to Frank like a dog trying to please its master; she licks his hand, though he tells her not to do so, and she clings to him for protection. Frank tries to pass off his feelings as brotherly concern for a poor misfit, but it soon becomes evident that his feelings aren't entirely pure and innocent. Jenifer embodies the ultimate dichotomy of attraction and repulsion: her face is horribly twisted and disfigured, but her body is immaculate and infinitely desirable. Frank makes her a makeshift bed on the couch and plans to tell his family about her in the morning, since it's already late and everybody has gone to sleep.

The next morning, all hell breaks loose when Ann and Peter see Jenifer for the first time. Frank promises to get her out of the house but begs for time to find her a suitable place to live. Ann tries to be understanding, but it's clear that the already-cracked foundation of their marriage is not going to withstand much more strain. Frank takes Jenifer with him in his car, looking for a bit of peace and quiet so he can plot his next move. Jenifer takes advantage of the secluded setting by seducing Frank. He initially tries to fight off her advances, but ultimately, he gives in. The frankness of the sex scenes is something relatively new in Argento; it signals a willingness in his later films to embrace sleaziness, something which is also evident in *Pelts*, *Mother of Tears*, and *Dario Argento's Dracula*. Carrie Ann Fleming (born 1974) is to be commended for her fearless performance as Jenifer; the role requires her to be willing to show her body and engage in some kinky and suggestive sexual acts, but it also deprives her of the ability to express herself verbally. Jenifer is completely non-verbal and the extensive prosthetic make-up effects literally masks her from conveying emotions through facial gestures as well. She relies instead on dog-like whimpers and physical gestures to convey the sense of a creature which is simultaneously vicious and innocent; she reacts according to pure instinct, and her extraordinary physique and raw sexuality enables her to seduce those around her.

Things continue to escalate when Jenifer savagely kills the family cat—a gruesome image suggestive of a wild animal killing its prey—prompting Ann and Peter to pack their bags and leave Frank. Frank continues to wallow in self-pity and his drinking gets worse. There's a nicely realized sequence where Frank staggers back from a bar, with the camera canted at an odd angle and creating a woozy visual effect; the use of harsh neon lighting gives the shot additional visual interest. Argento's visual flair is also evident in a brief dream scene which allows the viewer to finally see Carrie Ann Fleming's actual face; the use of Expressionist, colorful backdrops in this scene stands out in relief compared to the generally realistic approach adopted by Argento and cinematographer Attila Szalay.

The most audacious and controversial sequence is patterned after a parallel incident in James Whale's *Frankenstein* (1931), in which the monster (Boris Karloff) encounters a child (Marilyn Harris) who doesn't run from his hideous features. Jenifer finds such an innocent in the form of a neighbor girl named Amy (Jasmine

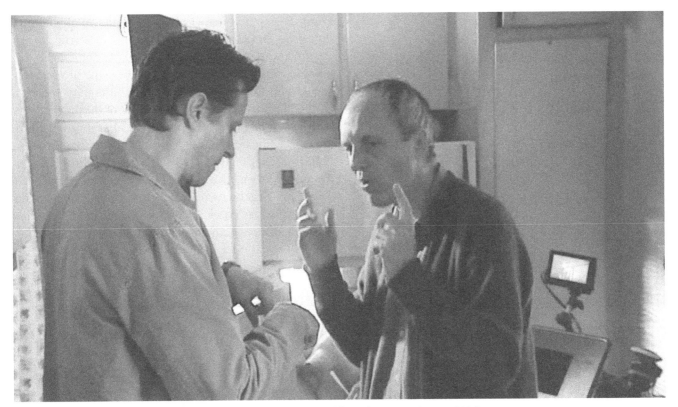

Dario discusses a scene with writer/star Steven Weber.

Chan), who invites her to play with her in her garden. The sweet, idyllic mood suggests that Jenifer has finally made an important personal connection—but Argento turns this quickly on its head when Frank comes home and finds Jenifer literally devouring the child in his basement. Jenifer's reaction is consistent with a wild dog killing another creature in the wild; she isn't doing these things maliciously; she's simply doing what comes naturally. Jenifer's taste for human flesh is beyond her control. Frank is understandably horrified, and tries to kill her, but he cannot bring himself to do so; in his own pathetic way he has become addicted to Jenifer and can't bear the idea of causing her harm. The thought of subjecting a child to such a horrific fate is about as taboo-busting as anything in Argento's work to date, and it sets the stage for some similarly twisted imagery in *Mother of Tears*.

Frank attempts to deal with the problem by hiring a man (Mark Acheson) from a circus sideshow to come and abduct Jenifer; in his mind, it's a human alternative to "putting her down," so he is able to justify it as a necessary evil. However, when he returns from his trip, Frank finds that Jenifer managed to get the upper hand; the man's dismembered corpse is now stuffed in the refrigerator. There's more dark humor evident here as this plays out like a twisted form of "peace offering" on Jenifer's part, and she is puzzled by Frank's hysterical reaction to the carnage. Starting with *The Phantom of the Opera*, Argento began crossing the line from stylish mayhem to lashings of *Grand Guignol* excess—but *Jenifer* takes things to a whole other level. Fortunately, the special make-up prosthetics work by Gregory Nicotero (born 1963) and Howard Berger (born 1964) are of a very high standard and do a convincing job of conveying the grotesque ideas in the story.

Hoping to reboot and get his head straight, Frank takes Jenifer with him to a secluded cabin in the woods. In order to make ends meet, he takes on a low-level job stocking shelves at a local convenience store; a far fall, indeed, from his earlier position in life. Frank's decline into mental collapse and alcoholism is conveyed in broad brushstrokes and that's arguably the weak spot of Weber's script. Of course, this is out of necessity. The story may have been tricky to develop into a full-fledged feature, but it arguably has too much going on to be properly conveyed in the space of one hour. This puts the film in an awkward spot, dramatically, as there's simply no way of doing justice to all the concepts it is putting forth. The emphasis on shocking sex and violence takes center stage and it never attains the sense of pathos and tragedy that it should ideally be building towards.

Jenifer claims one final victim when she seduces a teenager (Jeffrey Ballard) and tears him apart while giving him oral sex. The conflation of sex and death reaches its pinnacle here, as the hormonal teen gets his ultimate wish—at a terrible price. Frank arrives in time to see the awful aftermath and he finally decides it's time to kill Jenifer before she does more damage. The story

Dario rehearses the action for the cast and crew.

comes full circle as Frank is shot down by a hunter who catches sight of what appears to be a maniac terrorizing a defenseless woman; it's the exact same mistake that Frank had made and thus the cycle will continue unbroken.

Coming hot on the heels of the uncharacteristically restrained *The Card Player* and the incredibly bland *Do You Like Hitchcock?*, *Jenifer* couldn't have been much more surprising. For one thing, Argento's decision to work from a screenplay written by others was very much out of character; his friend George A. Romero ultimately passed on doing an installment in the series because he wanted to write his own script and not work from somebody else's ideas. For another, it finds him working completely outside of his comfort zone: it's not a *giallo*, it's not an Italian production, and it's loaded with kinky sex and nudity. Argento clearly found the experience liberating, however, and he responded to the material with boyish enthusiasm.

That's not to say that it's perfect; far from it. As noted above, the problem is one of time. There simply isn't enough time to develop the story to its full potential. The characters remain sketchy and vague. Even Frank isn't given the opportunity to really win over the viewer. Argento had managed to distill Poe into a tight and well-paced 60 minutes in his half of *Two Evil Eyes*, but here he is not as successful. Weber's script is certainly respectable enough, but there's a story with some delicious symbolic significance begging to get out, and neither he nor Argento are quite able to bring it to the foreground.

That being said, *Jenifer* is well paced, stylishly shot, and generally well-acted. After the wildly uneven English soundtracks of *Sleepless* and (to a lesser degree) *The Card Player*, to say nothing of the downright laughable one for *Do You Like Hitchcock?*, it's something of a relief to see Argento working with English-speaking actors who are allowed the opportunity to keep their own voices intact. Weber and Carrie Ann Fleming both deserve credit for their willingness to enter into the spirit of the proceedings with such feral enthusiasm and the elaborate gore effects are among the best to be featured in a latter-day Argento film. It doesn't much feel like an Argento film—save for the odd flourish, Dario was determined to respect the source material by recreating as many of the comic strip compositions as possible—but as a change of pace, it's certainly different, and it doesn't overstay its welcome.

Jenifer made its U.S. cable debut on Showtime on Friday, October 28, 2005. It was the fourth installment of the series to be aired, following on the heels of Don Coscarelli's *Incident On and Off a Mountain Road*, Stuart Gordon's *H.P. Lovecraft's Dreams in the Witch-House*, and Tobe Hooper's *Dance of the Dead*. Despite Garris' promises of no censorship, Argento was livid when he learned that his episode was cut by a few seconds, as its depiction of simulated oral sex (courtesy of a prosthetic penis) made even the brass at Showtime uneasy. Reactions to the segment were mixed; most saw it as another disappointment, but a few more enthusiastic fans applauded Argento for his fearless exploration of raw sexuality.

While reviews for the season were mixed—with Joe Dante's *Homecoming* and John Carpenter's *Cigarette Burns* earning the most acclaim—the numbers were strong enough to justify a second season. Argento was approached early on, but at that stage he had an April 2006 start date penciled in for *The Third Mother* and he was forced to decline. When *The Third Mother* started to experience growing pains, however, Argento rethought his rejection and let Garris know that, if there was a segment which was suitable for him, he'd be happy to come along for round two.

The script Argento was offered for season two was titled *Pelts*, and it was an adaptation of a short story by F. Paul Wilson (born 1946), the author of such books as *The Keep* (1981, adapted by Michael Mann for his 1983 film of the same name) and *The Tomb* (1984). The deal was precisely the same as the first time around: the same budget, the same shooting schedule, and the same location. Argento was initially reluctant to go back to Vancouver because it was in the grips of another brutally cold winter by the time the series kicked off in March 2006—but Garris postponed his episode until April, at which point things were beginning to thaw somewhat. Once again Argento was obliged to cast and collaborate with his writer (Matt Venne this time) online, and this time he elected to reach into his back catalogue by casting John Saxon in a small but important supporting role; it was their first time working together since *Tenebrae* and the two men showed great mutual respect for each other.

Venne's script originally didn't have nearly as much sleazy content as Weber's adaptation of *Jenifer*, but Argento worked with him to correct that. He felt that the story should revolve around sexual obsession as the whole idea of what people are willing to do in exchange for sexual gratification was something worth exploring. The violent content was even more extreme this time and Argento was determined to make it more of a showstopper than *Jenifer* had been. Since he didn't feel beholden to the comic strip panels designed by Wrightson for the first episode, this time he cut loose and indulged his more baroque visual sensibilities; it would prove to be his most visually extravagant offering since *The Phantom of the Opera*.

Pelts filmed in April 2006 and, like its predecessor, it enjoyed a relatively drama-free shoot. Attila Szalay, the cinematographer who shot *Jenifer*, was back in the same capacity—and working in tandem with Dario, he provided some of the most visually stunning images found in the entire run of *Masters of Horror*. The link between sex and violence was as prominent as it had been in *Jenifer*, but this time Argento was able to find a kind of macabre poetry in the excess.

The film opens with a grisly crime scene, elliptically shown as the flash of the police photographers' cameras go off. In a way, it reminds one of the use of flashbulbs as a visual motif in some of Lucio Fulci's *gialli*, notably *A Lizard in a Woman's Skin* (*Una lucertola con la pelle di donna*, 1971) and *The Psychic* (*Sette notte in nero*, 1977). The context is not explained, and the viewer is left to puzzle over what it's all supposed to mean as it transitions into a credits sequence, as various animals' skins and furs are trotted out for fetishistic display in a furrier's shop. The shop is run by Jake Feldman (Meat Loaf), who is established right off the bat as a singularly nasty piece of work. He berates and bullies his employees, many of whom appear to be illegal immigrants; he exploits the needy in order to line his own pocket, and his business comes across as the worst kind of sweat shop.

In addition to money, Jake's other obsession is sex. He is a frequent visitor at a local strip club, where he is particularly fixated on a dancer named Shanna (Ellen Ewusie). The interiors of the club allow cinematographer Attila Szalay to go deliciously over the top with garish vivid primary colors, and the scene where Jake meets with Shanna in a back room for a private dance is probably the most deliriously beautiful Argento set piece since *The Phantom of the Opera*. The use of color, camera movement, and composition is absolutely on point and it serves as a nice contrast to the seediness of the scene's content.

Shanna is accustomed to using her body to get what she wants, and she relishes the power she has over Jake. Jake is a total creep and she finds him repulsive, but she is still content to take his money and tease him; she has complete control over him, and he's looking to shift that balance of power in his favor. Jake loses control of himself and tries to force his affections on her, but Shanna is far too strong to allow that to happen—tellingly, she keeps him at bay with a chair, thus conjuring the image of a lion tamer establishing dominance over a wild beast.

The truth of the matter is, Jake doesn't care about Shanna as a person. He isn't interested in getting to know her or establishing a deep, intimate connection with her. He views her as a piece of meat. Shanna is not entirely innocent in this, either; she elects to trade her dignity and self-respect in exchange for money. Argento doesn't seem to have much sympathy for either of them, really. They're both fairly shallow and self-absorbed in their own way. Rock legend Meat Loaf (born 1947) is no novice to acting, of course—he had already proved his mettle in everything from *The Rocky Horror Picture Show* (1975) to *Fight Club* (1999)—but this is a relatively rare case of his being required to carry a feature; he

Cover art for the Anchor Bay DVD release of *Pelts*; artist unknown.

Jake (Meat Loaf) shows off his own pelt for a horrified Shanna (Ellen Ewusie) in *Pelts*.

makes no apologies for Jake's defects and embraces the character's sleazy excesses. Ellen Ewusie's background isn't as extensive, but she more than adequately fulfills the requirements of the role. They work well together and manage to convey the mutually exploitative nature of their relationship without hitting any false notes.

From there, the action switches to the woods, where "Pa" Jameson (John Saxon) and his son Larry (Michal Suchánek) are venturing out in the middle of the night to check on some traps they've laid. The setting is atmospheric and offers a nice contrast to the garish excesses of the strip club sequence. Larry expresses some concerns over going too far into the woods for fear of upsetting a local witch known as Mother Mayter—an obvious reference to the Three Mothers of Argento's then-still-incomplete trilogy. "Pa" dismisses these concerns as "bullshit," but Larry has good reason to be afraid. One of the biggest pleasures in *Pelts* is seeing the wonderful John Saxon back in Argento terrain; his role isn't a large one, but as usual he plays it with strength and conviction. "Pa" and Larry find the traps and find that they've done the trick. Argento includes a dazzling crane shot as the camera moves up for a God's eye view of the poor raccoons writhing in pain in the traps. For "Pa," it's all in a day's work and he calmly explains the best way to finish the animals off—either by stomping on them or using a bat if necessary—and they briskly go about collecting the dead animals hoping to avoid the wrath of Mother Mayter. The anti-fur message isn't hammered home with a heavy hand, but it's definitely there for those who are open to it. The images of the animals suffering in pain underline the senseless violence of the fur trade—and the fact that it's all for the sake of creating an impractical status symbol makes it even more tragic.

"Pa" calls Jake—who is busy ogling Shanna at the club—to tell him that he's got a new haul of animal pelts for sale. According to "Pa," these are extraordinary in their quality, so Jake immediately sees dollar signs and agrees to come out to meet with him the following morning. That night, however, Larry falls under a strange spell generated by the pelts. Argento is able to visualize this concept in a way that's lyrical and poetic; it could easily have come across as preposterous and even laughable, but Argento's flair for expressive imagery allows the idea to carry the appropriate weight. The effect is reinforced by one of Claudio Simonetti's most beautiful melodies. As the pelts work their magic, Larry arms himself with a metal baseball bat and proceeds to bash "Pa's" head in; the brutality of the scene is extreme even by Argento's standards, and the ensuing spray of blood on the wall can't help but remind one of Veronica Lario's demise in *Tenebrae*. Nasty as his demise is, it is soon trumped when Larry goes into the workshop below and calmly opens one of "Pa's" traps—in a state of blissful delirium, he throws himself facedown into the trap, which proceeds to slice his head in two. *Jenifer* had its share of over-the-top gore, no question, but this sequence stands out as the most elaborately outrageous scene of *Grand Guignol* in Argento's work up until this point—and there's more to come.

Jake arrives at "Pa's" house and discovers the bodies; his main focal point is the pelts, however. He sees them as the opportunity to really make his name—and to finally acquire Shanna. "Pelts like these," he says, "the sky's the limit. We can have anything our hearts desire." Jake is not motivated by love. He is a glutton who expects instant gratification; the fact that Shanna refuses to acquiesce to his desires is what keeps him coming back for more. She's clever enough to know this and uses it to her advantage.

The wonderful John Saxon makes a welcome return to Argento's films for the first time since *Tenebrae* as 'Pa' Jameson.

Shanna (Ellen Ewusie) shows off her magnificent physique to a club full of leering patrons.

He is quick to recognize the extraordinary, magical quality of the pelts and he figures they will enable him to create a fur coat that will take the fashion world by storm. There's a major fashion show coming up and he's determined to have the coat ready in time—and of course, he has his eye on Shanna to be the model. Shanna is tentative in agreeing to his proposal. She has good reason to believe it's all just an elaborate trick to get her into bed, but in theory she agrees. If the coat turns out to be as special as he claims it's going to be, she's willing to go along with him in order to gain the validation and exposure of a mainstream modeling career.

The nature of Jake's obsession becomes clearer in their dialogue. It's a major point of departure from the short story and from the original script, but as screenwriter Matt Venne explains in his audio commentary for the Anchor Bay DVD release, Argento insisted on making Jake's obsession very concrete and specific. In the story, Jake lusts after Shanna in general; he wants access to her entire body. In Argento's interpretation, he is fixated on her ass; there's no delicate way of putting it, as that's truly what it boils down to. One is reminded of the "bestial" sexuality exhibited in *The Phantom of the Opera* and *Jenifer*, but here it seems particularly relevant given the overall theme of the piece. The notion of an unhealthy obsession on a fetishized body part recalls the reference to "Berenice" in Argento's segment of *Two Evil Eyes*—and it also recalls the over-heated sexuality of Luis Buñuel in films like *Belle de Jour* (1967) and *Tristana* (1970). Jake's fixation on Shanna's backside allows him to objectify her completely. By focusing only on that one physical aspect of her, he misses connecting with her on a deeper, more emotional level. He only wants access to that one particular part—no more, no less.

Meanwhile, the pelts continue to exude a strange power over those who come into contact with them. Sergio (Emilio Salituro) feels compelled to turn his shears on himself, using them to slice his chest open; the image of the skin being cut away is gruesome enough, but Argento takes it even further by having Sergio pull out his entrails and fondle them, as well. Later, one of the seamstresses (Elise Lew) uses her needle and thread to sew her nostrils, mouth and eyes shut; she suffocates as a result. There's a sense of poetic justice in this as the various people who contribute to the making of the fur coat are claimed by the same tools they've used in the creation of the coat. Because it's developed in such a stylized way, with so much emphasis on *Grand Guignol* excess, it is easy to overlook this aspect—but it is thoughtfully incorporated into the plot and it adds a bit of depth to the proceedings.

Armed with the completed coat, Jake makes his way to Shanna's apartment. When she sees the coat, her scruples go right out the window. She gets on her hands and knees and offers Jake what he's been lusting after for so long. Their sex scene is brutal and animalistic; Jake is finally getting what he wants, and Shanna sublimates

Dario, happy at work on *Pelts*.

whatever revulsion she's feeling by focusing on the bigger picture. Tellingly, she wears the coat during their tryst; there's a nice touch where Jake, lost in the throes of passion, rubs his face all over the coat, like an animal in heat. He excuses himself to clean himself up before commencing with round two, but the pelt's influence soon distracts him. He finds a knife in the kitchen and uses it to peel away the skin on his chest and back; Meat Loaf does a brilliant job of conveying the mixture of ecstasy, delirium, and blind pain in this scene and it triggers the most gruesome and wickedly audacious finale to be found in any of Argento's films—even the demented final moments of *Mother of Tears* fails to top it in terms of sheer batshit insanity. Jake brings his bloody trophy to Shanna, calling it "My work of art," and she reacts in horror and tries to run away from him. She manages to get into the building's old-fashioned elevator, but Jake follows suit and refuses to let go of her; she gets her arm trapped in the elevator's heavy metal doors, while Jake maintains a firm grip on her ankle, and the image of the raccoons stuck in traps immediately comes to mind. Shanna ends up severing her hand to break free from the elevator door— recalling an earlier scene where a raccoon chews its paw off in order to get free from "Pa's" trap—only to die in a welter of spurting blood as she bleeds to death from her injuries. The police arrive on the scene—and the final images connect back into the opening views of the carnage, as Shanna and Jake's mutilated bodies are photographed by the police.

Along with *The Card Player*, *Pelts* is arguably the most accomplished of Argento's 21st century efforts. It manages to eclipse *Jenifer* in terms of sheer audacity, but it also feels more "complete" on a narrative level. In *Jenifer*, the attempt to chart Frank's moral decline is undermined by the compact running time; here, the short form suits it perfectly. As an exploration of a disagreeable character's willful path to self-destruction, it makes an interesting companion piece to Dario's take on "The Black Cat." The commentary on the beauty and harmony of the natural world, embodied by the animal kingdom, versus the avarice and greed of contemporary society, represented by Jake and his cronies, ties into Argento's long-running fascination with insects and wildlife. As such, it doesn't feel remotely like a "gun for hire" job, even if he didn't originate the project himself. It also offers the most jaundiced view of humanity to be found in any of Argento's films. There really isn't anybody who is worth a damn in the whole story, and the entertainment derives from one's ability to see these petty, superficial bastards taking a downward spiral as they meet their just desserts.

Crucially, it also *feels* like vintage Argento, thanks to the luminous photography and imaginative use of camerawork and music. Argento's move towards greater realism in later works like *Sleepless* and *The Card Player* goes by the wayside here as he embraces the fantastical

Dario's attention to detail is second to none, as evidenced by this shot of him combing the fur coat, so that it catches the light in just the right way.

nature of the story and plays up the stylistic aspects for all they are worth. The colorful photography is eye-catching throughout and the record levels of gore and depravity ensure that the film rattles by at a very fast clip. There really aren't any major weaknesses to complain of: it tells its story with urgency and clarity, it manages to get across the points it sets out to make, and above all, it functions as a deliriously entertaining satire of excess and greed; its commentary on the worst aspects of the human condition has bite, but it also delivers where it counts and demonstrates that Argento's flair for horrific-yet-beautiful imagery is still very much intact.

The second season of *Masters of Horror* kicked off October 27, 2006, with Tobe Hooper's version of Ambrose Bierce's *The Damned Thing*. This time Argento's episode was the sixth to be aired; prior to it, John Landis' *Family*, Ernest Dickerson's *The V Word*, Brad Anderson's *Sounds Like*, and John Carpenter's *Pro-Life* saw the series progressing very fitfully indeed. *Pelts* made its debut on December 1, 2006—and a more unlikely piece for the Christmas season would be hard to find. Reviewers remained perplexed by Dario's new-found fixation on sleazy sex and lashings of *Grand Guignol* gore, but the more sympathetic reviewers recognized the episode's aesthetic virtues.

Despite Garris' good intentions, *Masters of Horror* proved to be much too erratic and uneven for its own good; the best episodes—which certainly included *Pelts*—showed their venerated directors firing on all cylinders, but many of them felt poorly thought-out, and the presence of too many "flash in the pan" directors who were hardly deserving of "Masters of Horror" street cred helped to sink the project in its second season. Garris would rethink the format and take it to network TV, as *Fear Itself* (2008), but the added censorship did it no favors and it ended after only one season. There would later be rumors of a *Masters of Italian Horror* TV series, but that's basically all they were—rumors. Argento's name was not included in that bit of fiction, though reportedly Lamberto Bava, Umberto Lenzi, and Sergio Martino were being eyed up for it.

Notes:
1. Argento, Dario, *Peur* (France: Rouge Profond, 2018), p. 323.
2. http://hallzzz.com/alfred-hitchcock/ah/quotes-and-links/
3. Jones, Alan, *Dario Argento: The Man, the Myths & the Magic* (Godalming: FAB Press, 2012), p. 333.

Chapter Twenty-Two: Tears

The film ultimately known as *La terza madre* in Italy and as *Mother of Tears* in the U.S. endured a longer, more arduous birthing process than any of Argento's other films. Backtracking a bit, *Suspiria* had been a worldwide smash when it was released in 1977—but the animosity it generated between Dario and his partner/co-writer Daria Nicolodi proved to be permanent. Because of the film's enormous box-office success, Dario felt pressured to deliver a follow-up in relatively short order, but *Inferno* became one of the most deeply unpleasant experiences of his career. When it failed to generate the same level of commercial interest, he felt comfortable taking a break from the world of witchcraft and the supernatural.

As far back as 1984, Argento and Nicolodi let it be known that they had collaborated on a script for the third installment—but as their relationship continued to deteriorate, it became apparent that the odds of them coming together in harmony to realize what they had written were not very good. Asked in the early '90s about the status of the script, Nicolodi said, "Yes, the story is finished and as soon as the right moment comes along, even though that may be in 10 years' time, I'll pull it out of the drawer."[1] As fate would have it, that moment never came—though by the time Nicolodi said those words, she had in fact attempted to realize the screenplay without Argento's involvement. It was Nicolodi who brought Argento's friend and collaborator Luigi Cozzi a script intended to cap off the trilogy; whether this was the script she and Dario had worked on together is unclear, however, as it was reportedly written entirely by Nicolodi herself. Cozzi accepted the script but, not wishing to incur Dario's wrath, he proceeded to rewrite it from scratch. Nicolodi was displeased with the changes and left the project; she's not even credited in the finished film. *Edgar Allan Poe's The Black Cat*[2] (*Il gatto nero*, 1989), as the project became known, had absolutely nothing to do with Poe—but it works in plenty of references to Argento and the first two installments in his proposed trilogy. The story deals with the making of a horror film which somehow triggers the return of a powerful witch named Levana—the mother of sorrows. A heady but incoherent witches brew of supernatural and sci-fi elements, it includes some interesting actors (among them Caroline Munro, from Cozzi's *Starcrash*, 1978, Brett Halsey, from Mario Bava's *Four Times That Night/Quante volt ... quella notte*, 1972, and Urbano Barberini, from Dario's *Opera*) and an appropriately insistent score from Vince Tempara, but it's easy to see why the film failed to secure any kind of meaningful distribution; it was never even released in Italy, and it went straight to video in most markets. The Poe connection, incidentally, was imposed by Menahem Golan (of Golan & Globus fame), who agreed to put a stake in the film on the understanding that it would be crammed into an upcoming slate of direct-to-video Edgar Allan Poe movies he was making in association with Harry Alan Towers.

What, if anything, Argento made of the film is not known. He may not have even been aware of it as he was preoccupied with his own Poe-pourri at the time, but Nicolodi was suitably displeased and never again collaborated with Cozzi, though they maintained a personal friendship. As for Dario, he was much too busy through the early 2000s to even give much thought to revisiting the trilogy. It wasn't until 2003, when he was at work on *The Card Player*, that he started to give the idea some serious thought. It had long been supposed that Argento was holding on to the Mater Lachrymarum project as a sort of "ace in the hole." As his recent films continued to flounder at the box office, it became evident that it might be a good time to finally give the public what they had wanted for so long. Of course, there was always the chance that people had

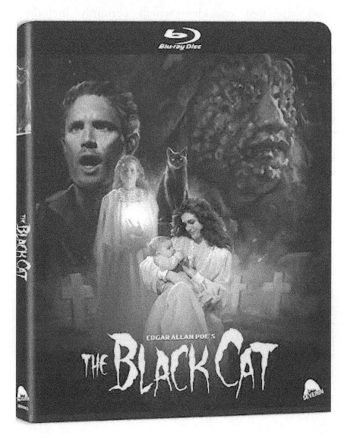

Cover art for the Severin Blu-ray of Luigi Cozzi's *The Black Cat*.

Dario on location for *Mother of Tears*.

moved on and were no longer interested—but Argento knew that time was ticking and that, if he was ever going to finish the trilogy, he needed to start giving it his serious consideration.

As it happened, his experience working on the *Masters of Horror* series proved to be beneficial in the creation of *Mother of Tears*. While *The Card Player* and *Do You Like Hitchcock?* had adopted a "less is more" attitude, especially with TV sales in mind, the *Masters of Horror* episodes permitted Dario the opportunity to cut loose and really go for broke. The two short films were loaded with kinky sex and graphic gore, and so he started to think of *Mother of Tears* along the same lines—he would go in a radically different direction from the first two films in the trilogy, which he realized would be a major gamble, but he decided to follow his instincts sooner than worry about potential audience backlash. As he continued to work on finessing the script, he found backing from Medusa—and a surprise influx of cash from an American company, Myriad Pictures. The combination of Italian and American financing meant that Argento would have access to more money than he had been working with on his last few pictures—but the sheer size and scope of the story still called for more than the resources would permit. Though he tried to appear blasé about it, Dario was well-aware that a lot was riding on the film; he tried not to concern himself with what the audience might think, but he also found himself being pulled in different directions as the various co-producers started putting their two bits in.

American screenwriters Adam Gierasch (born 1966) and Jace Anderson (born 1968) became involved when they met Dario during the post-production of *Jenifer* in the spring of 2005. Because it was a bigger project and he was really hoping to get it ample exposure in the international market, Dario decided it would be beneficial to bring an American scriptwriter into the mix—partly to help shore up the deficiencies in the dialogue, but also, hopefully, to tap into the mindset of the youth market. Gierasch and Anderson were big fans of Argento, so the offer to participate in the writing of the planned "grand finale" of the "Three Mother trilogy" seemed to be heaven sent. Gierasch commented at the time, "After speaking with Dario, he was interested in reading one of our scripts—and after he did, he asked us if we would like to do a treatment of Mater Lachrymarum! His brother Claudio then asked us to come to Rome. It was intense! Dario is such a sweet man."[3] Even at this early stage, Gierasch aptly noted that the film would be "quite different from the first two. Dario didn't want to do the same thing again. I think it's really going to be the movie that everyone is hoping for. It's a 'wow' kind of film, from the very first scene."[4]

In a report dated May 17, 2006, the website Cinematografo.it reported that, "*The Mother of Tears* will begin where *Inferno* ended, with one of the witches who manages to survive the burning of the New York apartment building, and will revolve around the investigation of a detective in charge of shedding light on the chain of mysterious murders that take place within the university. [...] [T]he film could have among its protagonists Ennio Fantastichini in the role of the detective, Chiara Caselli as a psychiatrist, Max von Sydow as a university professor with a mysterious past, and young Giordano Petri, whose character would take over the investigation after the detective character is killed."[5] If that description doesn't seem to resemble the film that emerged, there's good reason for it; the script would continue to evolve as Gierasch and Anderson worked with Argento, and many of the more ambitious ideas needed to be scaled back or indeed cut altogether when it became clear that the budget wouldn't allow for them. As for the casting—including *Sleepless* veterans Caselli and von Sydow—that appears to have been a pipe dream of sorts.

Dario enjoyed the process of working with younger, less cynical screenwriters—but the collaboration was not always a smooth one. Argento made it clear early on that he wanted the film to be separate and distinct from the first two films, and it seems as if Gierasch and Anderson had a hard time resisting the urge to reference events from the first two films; they even toyed with the idea of having Suzy Banyon, the heroine of *Suspiria*, being worked into the scenario—but Dario was reluctant to do something so on the nose and shot the idea down. There was also the matter of violence to consider. Argento was very keen on working in as much gruesome imagery as possible, but he was insistent that it should not come at the expense of narrative. Thus, the first draft completed by Gierasch and Anderson was quickly rejected because it was all gore and no plot. Nevertheless, Dario continued to believe in his American colleagues and they pressed on through it all, determined to deliver a script that would be agreeable for

If nothing else, Mother of Tears is of historical significance for reuniting Daria and Dario one last time.

all concerned; by Gierasch's reckoning, they did a total of 10 drafts on the script before Dario was satisfied.[6]

Production was due to begin at several points before things finally got off the ground on October 30, 2006. The Halloween-season timing proved to be highly appropriate as Argento was determined to make *Mother of Tears* into the strongest, most grotesque and over-the-top film of his career. Compared to the artfully designed scares of *Suspiria* and the stately tension of *Inferno*, *Mother of Tears* would go for fast paced shocks; no longer concerned with matters of good taste, Argento allowed himself to bust just about every taboo he could think of. Budgeted at about $3.5 million, the film was given an eight-week shoot, with Claudio again overseeing the production through Opera Film. The budget and schedule may have seemed lavish compared to Dario's recent forays into television, but it became evident early on that there were going to be some serious problems. The script included a lot of ambitious scenes of action and mayhem, notably a finale in which the city of Rome is overtaken and destroyed by people who've fallen under the spell of Mater Lachrymarum. Dario was thinking big, but the resources simply wouldn't allow for the kind of scope he had in mind when writing the script. Gierasch and Anderson, though still on cloud nine over their involvement in a film by one of their heroes, were as disappointed as anybody by the corner-cutting necessitated by the budgetary woes. "We begged Dario to keep the climax intact but sadly it all boiled down to economics."[7]

The casting included some welcome echoes from Argento's cinematic past. The central character of Sarah Mandy was briefly linked to the American actress Sienna Miller (*High-Rise*, 2015), but Dario decided to offer it to Asia. They had had a major falling out over *The Card Player*, but it didn't affect Asia's career any. After completing her second film as a director, *The Heart is Deceitful Above All Things* (2004), she went on to appear in such disparate fare as George A. Romero's *Land of the Dead* (2005) and Sofia Coppola's *Marie Antoinette* (2006). She had nearly worked with Romero prior to that on a couple of ill-fated projects—*The Ill* and *Diamond Dead*—but ultimately *Land* would remain their only collaboration. While in Paris to work on the thriller *Boarding Gate* (2007) in the summer of 2006, Asia decided the time had come to mend fences; Dario came to visit her, and they started talking about *Mother of Tears*. She was ambivalent about restarting their collaboration, but ultimately decided that the time was right for them to work together again.

The script also included a brief, spectral appearance by Sarah's late mother, a white witch who teaches her how to use her latent supernatural powers, and Asia told Dario that he needed to cast Daria Nicolodi in the role. Daria had already acted alongside Asia in *Viola Kisses*

Dario and Asia confer during the filming of *Mother of Tears*.

Everybody (*Viola bacia tutti*, 1998) and *Scarlet Diva*, but she had not worked directly with Dario since *Opera* in 1987. After an absence from his professional landscape of nearly 20 years, Daria agreed to partake in the filming of *Mother of Tears*; her one day on the set came on November 15, 2006, and by all accounts the reunion went smoothly enough. Another small, flashy cameo was filled by Udo Kier, the eccentric German cult icon who had previously appeared in another small role, as the well-intended psychiatrist in *Suspiria*. And Coralina Cataldi-Tassoni—whose previous collaborations with Dario included *Opera* and *The Phantom of the Opera*, in addition to *Demons 2* and the *Giallo* TV series—was brought in to appear briefly, as well.

On the technical side, Argento was back to working with familiar faces following the "fish out of water" experiences on *Masters of Horror*. Frederic Fasano was again entrusted with the cinematography, which he and Dario decided to approach in a more flat and realistic way compared to the hyper-stylized delirium of *Suspiria* and *Inferno*. Dario's nephew, Nilo, was along for the ride as production manager, while Francesca Bocca and Valentina Ferroni took care of the production design; Bocca had already worked on *Sleepless*, while Bocca and Ferroni were both involved in the design work on *Do You Like Hitchcock?*. *Mother of Tears* called for a lot of elaborate special make-up effects, and naturally Sergio Stivaletti was called upon to take charge of that department.

When the production wrapped in mid-December 2006, Argento and Walter Fasano took charge of the editing and final assembly. Claudio Simonetti was again approached to compose the soundtrack, though rather unusually in this instance, it seems as if Dario wasn't as involved in the scoring process. Perhaps he had mellowed a bit and trusted Simonetti to deliver the goods, as he always has done; or perhaps he just didn't have a particular insight into what sort of music the movie really called for. No matter how one interprets it, Simonetti's score, with its Satanic chants, is obviously indebted to Jerry Goldsmith's Oscar-winning score for *The Omen* (1976)—and compared to the iconic score for *Suspiria* or the delicately brilliant music by Keith Emerson for *Inferno*, it falls somewhat disappointingly into the realm of "scary movie" cliché.

When Dario presented the first edit to Medusa, they were horrified: according to them, the movie was much too violent; if cuts weren't made, they would encounter all sorts of censorship woes. Chances are Dario would have fought this back in the day, but at this stage he didn't have the clout or the support to weather the storm; this was precisely the sort of thing Salvatore always managed to iron out for Dario with a minimum of fuss. According to Alan Jones' *Frightfest* report, dated May 2, 2007, "the problems are all to do with the depiction of perverse sex in the witch gathering satanic scenes and one cannibal killing of a major character."[8] Argento relented and made some trims, but he did resist the mandate from Medusa to make more radical changes in order to make the film more accessibly mainstream. Of course, compared to the elegantly mysterious *Inferno*, it can't help but appear very mainstream—but Dario insisted upon staying true to his initial desire to highlight as much sleaze and depravity as possible.

The film opens with landscapers accidentally unearthing an ancient urn while doing some work on Church property. The Monsignor (Franco Leo) recognizes the significance of the urn and arranges to have it passed on to a historian named Michael Pierce (Adam James), who works at the Museum of Ancient Art in Rome. When the urn is delivered to the museum, Michael is not there—but Giselle (Coralina Cataldi-Tassoni) and her assistant Sarah Mandy (Asia Argento) decide to get a head start on investigating its contents. It soon becomes apparent that *Mother of Tears* is cut from a very different cloth and sensibility compared to *Suspiria* and *Inferno*; this is as it should be, really, but the differences aren't necessarily for the better. The sense of mystery and dread which pervaded the opening of the earlier films is nowhere to be found; the set-up is clunky, and it continues in a similar vein. *Suspiria* had the benefit of a simple but lucid narrative, while *Inferno*'s more esoteric and dreamy approach gave it the feel of a nightmare. By contrast, this final installment stubbornly and willfully pursues a very different path—but one doesn't get the impression that it was one worth taking. The opening scenes deliver little in the way of atmosphere and Argento's recent forays into *Grand Guignol* with the *Masters of Horror* series appears to have emboldened him to take the violence to even more graphic extremes. Giselle pays for her curiosity when the evil spirits unleashed by opening the urn manifest in the form of some grotesque-looking demons who set upon her and kill her off in a painfully protracted fashion. In a moment worthy of *Pelts*' exploration of "body horror," the demons gut Giselle and use her intestines to strangle her; it's gross, without a doubt, but it doesn't come close to recapturing the sheer dizzying terror of the opening of *Suspiria* or the creeping sense of dread of *Inferno*'s opening scenes. Sarah witnesses the tail end of what has happened and attempts to make a run for it, but a monkey—the demons' familiar—makes it difficult for her; the use of the monkey recalls *Phenomena*, and sure enough there will be other nods to that film in the climax, as well. At the time of its release, *Phenomena* stood out as Argento's least-controlled work to date, but compared to the spirited but hopelessly clumsy delirium of *Mother of Tears*, it looks like a masterclass.

The police, represented by Detective Enzo Marchi (Cristian Solimeno) and his partner Detective Lissoni (Robert Madison), are called to investigate Giselle's gruesome murder. Sarah reports what she saw, and the two men are understandably skeptical. As it happens, Sarah even doubts her own senses; she is not a natural believer in the supernatural, though she undergoes a radical change as the story develops. The police were notable in their absence in *Suspiria* and *Inferno*, and the scenes involving them in *Mother of Tears* confirm that this had been a good move on the part of Argento and Nicolodi. The attempt at merging the world of magic with the more pragmatic and plodding "mainstream" world is not very successful; if anything, the addition of the police only serves to further clutter an already overbusy narrative. There's some attempt at generating wry humor in the interplay between Marchi and Lissoni, thanks in large part to Cristian Solimeno (born 1975)'s deadpan performance, but it doesn't work very well.

In a way, it seems churlish and unfair to criticize *Mother of Tears* for not being what we think it should be. The fact remains, Dario elected to follow a very different path in completing his trilogy—it's clearly a calculated move on his part, and in a way there's a lot to admire in that. Yet, whereas the first two films had been elegant, mysterious, and beautifully baroque, too much of *Mother of Tears* feels flat, listless, and downright ugly. Argento and cinematographer Frederic Fasano completely abandon the vivid colors of the first two films in favor of a more grounded and "realistic" aesthetic; given that so much of the narrative is set in the real

Giselle (Coralina Cataldi-Tassoni) and Sarah (Asia Argento) discover the sacred tunic in *Mother of Tears*.

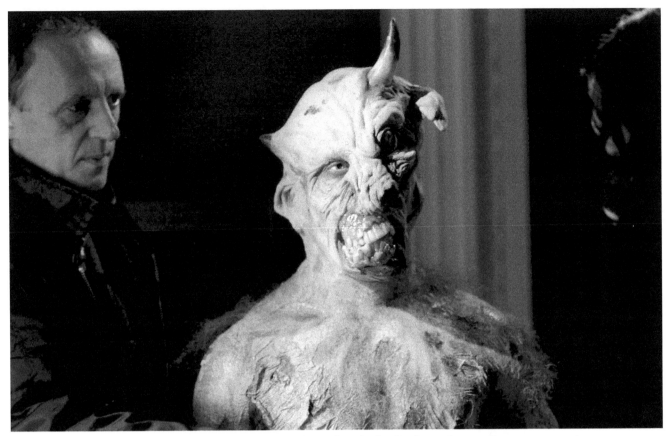

Dario seems pleased with Sergio Stivaletti's demonic creation.

world, whereas the first two were centered on their respective "damned houses," this actually makes sense. The drab opening scenes come as a really unpleasant surprise for those expecting something in the same vein, but—emboldened by his recent forays into the world of excess on *Masters of Horror*—Argento tries compensating for this by dramatically upping the sex and gore factor. *Suspiria* and *Inferno* had been basically sexless movies; they're dark twisted fables in which the protagonists feel disconnected from the real world and from mundane everyday concerns like sex and relationships. Whether it's "fair" or not, it's virtually impossible not to compare the film to its predecessors—but even on its own very different terms, with its specific goals and ambitions in mind, it's clear from the outset that there is something seriously amiss here.

The unleashing of the evil spirits allows Mater Lachrymarum (Moran Atias) to regain her strength. She summons her disciples from all over the globe and holds twisted sacrificial rites and orgies in her subterranean lair. The primary source of her power is an ancient tunic which is adorned with esoteric symbols. It's not a bad idea, but again it suffers from bad execution. The tunic looks like it was picked off the rack from the local K mart and the ancient symbols appear to have been applied with a glitter gun. In playing up the sexual angle, Argento also has Mater Lachrymarum strutting about a good deal of the time in the nude—save for a pair of fetishistic high heels, of course. Israeli model-turned-actress Moran Atias (born 1981) does what is asked of her and appears to have entered into the spirit of the proceedings with enthusiasm, but she doesn't come close to capturing the character's menace or power. Without wanting to be too unkind, she comes off more like a softcore actress trying to channel a *film noir femme fatale*; we

Moran Atias spends much of her screen time naked in *Mother of Tears*.

The Unsane Cinema of Dario Argento

see much too much of her and the mystique and magic is dispelled as a result.

Now that Mater Lachrymarum is gathering her strength, she unleashes a flood of irrational violence on Rome. Argento conveys this with economy. We see a mother pushing her child in a baby stroller, only to stop, remove the baby from the carriage and throw it over a bridge; a man stabs another man for no reason; people begin fighting each other and destroying property, all for no apparent reason. The concept is akin to the second fall of Rome, but it calls for considerably more money and production resources than Dario had at his disposal; he does his best to make the idea work, but it comes off as penny-pinching and it doesn't manage to evoke the sort of cosmic chaos and horror that Argento is clearly striving for. Given the practical realities of the production, he probably would have done well to have scaled back the concept a bit, but evidently, he was set on realizing the idea as best as possible under the circumstances. Thus, much of the epic destruction is conveyed via news reports and cut-away glimpses of random acts of violence. In a way, it's not too far removed from the way George A. Romero had conveyed the sense of a global apocalypse in his living dead movies, but for whatever reason it just doesn't come off as convincingly here.

It's established also that in addition to their professional relationship, Sarah and Michael have a romantic relationship as well. Asia Argento's performance is curiously flat and disengaged; she doesn't manage to recapture the intensity of her earlier performances for her father, though much of that is undoubtedly down to the weakness of the material. The relationship between her and Michael doesn't carry any weight and as played by Adam James (born 1972), Michael fails to register as a significant character. He has a son named Paul (Luca Pescatore), and it's shown in broad brushstrokes that he is a doting father and that Sarah is attached to him as a stepmother figure, but no effort is made to play that angle up. This is unfortunate, because when Paul is abducted by Mater Lachrymarum's minions, it fails to generate any sense of suspense or horror. In a repetition of the shocking death of the little neighbor girl in *Jenifer*, Paul is sacrificed and devoured as part of a baroque cannibal feast; the scene is bathed in the sort of garish red lighting one might expect to see a good deal of in the film, but it doesn't pack the visceral punch that it should. Paul is glimpsed too quickly to register as a character and the scene itself verges on camp as the acolytes cower in the presence of Mater Lachrymarum's awesome power; again, given the failure of Argento and Atias to really sell the character's power and villainy, this is almost to be expected. The death of the child in *Jenifer* is shocking

Mater Lachrymarum (Moran Atias) and her followers rejoice.

The witches revel in *Mother of Tears*.

and upsetting; the death of Paul in *Mother of Tears* simply isn't.

Asia's best moments in the film are the more "human" ones. One of the most affecting moments occurs when Sarah is alone in her room, tearfully looking through various mementos and family pictures. It's revealed that she lost both her parents when she was just a small child, and this allows Asia to work through the theme of parental loss/abandonment which has been a focal point in so many of her own films as a director. She has often indicated that her childhood was not a happy one and that both Dario and Daria were too focused on their respective careers to really be there for her when she needed them; her relationship with Dario has been complex, to say the least, though there's undoubtedly a strong bond between the two of them. Even so, it's not surprising that scenes like this bring out the best in her—Argento shows her as she looks over old pictures of her mother and father; the former is "played" by Daria Nicolodi, while Dario elects to keep himself off camera by using a picture of his brother Claudio to stand in for the father figure. In scenes such as these, where her raw emotions are allowed to come to the surface, Asia reminds us of what a powerful and deeply affecting actress she can be. Alas, the script burdens her with too many clunky lines and she doesn't seem engaged enough to do much about that.

The witches themselves are another problem. For whatever reason, Dario elected to depict them as catty Goth types. They strut around laughing and being obnoxious, but they look about as threatening as a group of kids hyped up on too much sugar. It's another example of showing too much; the minions of Mater Tenebrarum in *Inferno* are seldom seen beyond the usual close-ups of hands in black gloves. Too much of *Mother of Tears* comes off as vaguely campy, but it's unclear whether it's *meant* to be funny or not. It's definitely true that a more camp sensibility started to filter into Argento's work after the dark and despairing *The Stendhal Syndrome*, but here it feels out of place and misguided—that is if it's even intended at all.

Sarah finds herself being menaced by the witches while trying to shake off the police as she makes her way out of the city in search of Michael, who has gone in search of Paul. The scene lacks rhythm and it falls back on the "if you can't think of a way out of it, go with magic" approach, as the spirit of Sarah's mother communicates to her that if she concentrates and uses her latent powers, she will be saved. Sarah's skepticism finally crumbles away, and she is able to render herself invisible, thus escaping from the police—and she subsequently kills one of the witches (Jun Ichikawa) in self-defense. Sarah's transition from passive observer to active participant recalls the "rite of passage" aspect of *Suspiria*, and Asia is admittedly more convincing as a committed woman of action than as a bookish and self-doubting skeptic.

With the police off her tail and the witches temporarily set back by the loss of one of their own, Sarah makes her way to the home of Father Johannes (Udo Kier, in his first Argento film since *Suspiria*), a renowned exorcist. While there, she makes the acquaintance of a woman

Dario appears to share the audience's disbelief in the tunic prop.

named Marta (Valéria Cavalli), who introduces herself as a friend of her late mother's. Marta explains that Sarah's mother was a powerful white witch who inflicted serious harm on Mater Suspiriorum, who got her own back by killing her and her husband; Sarah has always been under the impression that they had died in an accident, but that isn't quite accurate. This is the most overt attempt by Argento and his co-writers to connect in with the earlier films, though subsequent references to Varelli and his book "The Three Mothers" ensures that *Inferno* gets a name-check as well. Marta is nicely played by Valéria Cavalli (born 1959), who emerges as the film's most interesting character. She embodies all that is good and positive about the world of magic and the occult. She is also one of the few truly selfless and empathic characters to be found in the film. As such, she's inevitably being set up for a gruesome demise. As for Father Johannes, the role provides Udo Kier (born 1944) with a nice little cameo; he isn't exactly subtle,

Father Johannes (Udo Kier) makes a splashy exit.

but then again subtlety isn't what *Mother of Tears* is all about. Johannes is introduced in a state of distress. His health has been seriously compromised by the sudden burst of evil and violence which is affecting Rome, and he is now performing daily exorcisms, which has been a terrible strain on his heart. He provides Sarah (and the audience) with a bit of back story about the Three Mothers but before he is able to play a more important role in the narrative, he is unexpectedly murdered by his housekeeper Valeria (Barbara Mautino, the "bunny" murder victim from *Sleepless*). The murder of Father Johannes is the most brutal and shocking moment in the film; he's established as an important savant figure, so one doesn't expect him to be removed from the narrative so quickly. The emphasis on the destruction of his body by the possessed Valeria recalls the viciously prolonged and detailed murders in *Jenifer* and *Pelts*; it's one of the few moments in the film that really does pack a visceral wallop.

Sarah flees with Marta back to the latter's house, where she learns more about her mother—and about her own latent powers. Marta convinces her to open her mind to the possibilities of the supernatural and in a lovely moment, she blows a special dust into the room, which reveals the presence of spirits moving about. It's a lyrical and poetic moment in a film that's sorely lacking in lyricism. In a moment typical of the infuriatingly uneven nature of the movie, the beauty is soon undercut by a well-intended but hopelessly clumsy intrusion. Sarah's mother appears and spouts some gibberish intended to motivate her and give her strength. It's lovely seeing Nicolodi again, but there's no denying that she is very badly used in the film; some of the less sympathetic fans have referred to her character as "Obi Wan Nicolodi," and for good reason. The use of old school green screen effects looks hokey and, worst of all, she is not given anything really interesting to say or do. It's fitting that she should have played a part in the finale of the trilogy she had such a big hand in creating, but one wishes that she and Dario could have put aside their differences and worked together on the script instead. In any event, the character arc with Sarah is now complete and she comes to embrace the powers she has been carrying inside of her for so many years; communicating with her mother allows her to set aside some unresolved grief and anger, and Sarah is able to move into the finale as a stronger, more centered person. Thematically it all makes sense— it's just the clumsiness of the execution that gets in the way.

Things soon lurch back into the grotesque when Marta and her lover Elga (Silvia Rubino) are targeted by Mater Lachrymarum and her followers. The scene is unusually troubling as it represents a rare instance where

Mater Lachrymarum (Moran Atias) oversees the sadistic murder of Marta (Valéria Cavalli).

Argento's flair for the vicious and the grotesque crosses the line into out-and-out bad taste. The two women are shown making love in bed, only to be disturbed by the arrival of Mater Tenebrarum's chrome-domed lackey (Clive Riche). He stabs Elga with a dagger, then uses a medieval torture device to gouge out the woman's eyes. Things take a nastier turn when he uses a long, phallic device and rams it through Marta's vagina, as she lays dying, Mater Lachrymarum licks the tears from Marta's face—the connection between sex and violence is queasy enough as it is, but to establish Marta as a lesbian, only to then have her brutally dispatched in such a sexually symbolic way is arguably taking things too far. It could be argued that the point is to criticize the brutality of toxic masculinity, but realistically speaking it comes off like Argento indulging in cheap shock effects for their own sake.

Sarah escapes from Marta's house and makes her way to the home of an alchemist named Guglielmo De Witt (Philippe Leroy). In order to establish whether her motives are as pure, De Witt uses a special spray to incapacitate Sarah before looking at her eyes through a special, green magnifying glass. It's one of the few really magical moments in the film as De Witt's use of his arcane knowledge steers the film away from the more overt use of monsters and gore for shock value. The presence of Philippe Leroy (born 1930) is one of the film's most welcome surprises; a veteran of numerous Italian genre items of the '60s and '70s (including *The Castle of the Living Dead/Il castello dei morti vivi*, 1964, the film which first enabled Argento to interview genre icon Christopher Lee), he brings the sort of weight and gravitas to his role that is in short supply in much of the cast. Unfortunately, like Udo Kier, his efforts are undermined by the brevity of screen time. Even so, his main scene is a good one and it hints at the elegance, refinement and sense of wonder that the film could have conveyed had Argento not elected to steer the material in such a different direction. De Witt imparts vital information about the Three Mothers and explains that his home once belonged to the architect Varelli, who designed the houses for the three mothers. He provides Sarah with a copy of the famous book about the mothers and this allows Argento to quote the opening of *Inferno* as the camera tracks along with the text as Sarah reads from it. The book provides a clue as to the location of Mater Lachrymarum's lair, so Sarah sets out in search of it. Her taxi ride through the city recalls the earlier trips taken by Suzy in *Suspiria* and by Sarah in *Inferno*; it's one of the few moments where Claudio Simonetti's

Sarah (Asia Argento) wanders into a demonic orgy during *Mother of Tears'* deranged climax.

regrettably cliché-driven symphonic soundtrack comes to life (the track itself is called "The Three Mothers Book"), though it's kind of a shame that the late Fulvio Mingozzi (who passed away in 2000) was unable to complete the trifecta by driving the car himself.

When Sarah finds the house in question, Argento and Fasano briefly toy with the sort of bold primary colors associated with the first two installments; it's short-lived, however, and the finale plays out in the same rather drab and ordinary visual style that is to be found in most of the film. It's not that Fasano's work is *bad*, by any means; but compared to the hyper-stylized approaches of Luciano Tovoli and Romano Albani, it comes off as awfully plain. That said, Argento indulges himself with an impressive Steadicam shot as the camera follows Sarah into the house and follows her as she investigates it for clues; it runs about four minutes and it's about as "showy" a piece of technique as Argento allows himself in the picture. Sarah is eventually surprised by Detective Marchi, who has been following her, and together they make their way into the catacombs underneath the house. It's here that the film becomes positively unhinged as Argento delights in depicting the various perverse rites being carried out in Mater Lachrymarum's name. It's a sort of bargain basement evocation of Bosch, really, as we see what appears to be a woman eating entrails out of another woman's anus, two lovers bound by barbed wire and licking the blood from each other's wounds (shades of the deaths of Liz and her lover in *Demons*), and various other bizarre images. Mater Lachrymarum manages to get hold of Marchi and her minions set about torturing him, while Sarah hides and plots her next move. De Witt and his assistant (Paolo Stella) are also in the process of being tortured to death, and they expire amid plenty of gore and hysteria as things build to a fever pitch. Mater Lachrymarum appears wearing the magic tunic and her followers display an almost orgasmic reaction to her presence; Dario originally included a kinky bit where she literally sprays them with a "golden shower," but Medusa wouldn't allow it, so that bit was ultimately removed.[9]

Thinking quick, Sarah uses a lance to remove the tunic from Mater Lachrymarum and plunges the sacred garment into the fire; the destruction of the tunic causes all hell to break loose. The building begins to shake, as if the bowels of hell are opening beneath them, and Mater Lachrymarum is impaled while her followers perish around her. Sarah and the injured Marchi flee to safety, but Sarah plunges into a pit full of offal and floating body parts—another clear visual nod to *Phenomena*. They finally emerge, *Alice in Wonderland*-style, from a hole in the

Asia ends up in a fetid pit of body parts and maggots, just as Jennifer Connelly had done over 20 years prior in *Phenomena* (below).

ground above them; just like Suzy at the end of *Suspiria*, they can do nothing but laugh—they've survived, though whether their sanity is still intact is open to interpretation.

Argento's decision to avoid repeating himself may well have been motivated by the trauma he continues to feel over *Inferno*. While *Inferno* has long been embraced as one of his best films, for many years Dario had a hard time discussing it because of so many bad memories. Thus, *Mother of Tears* couldn't possibly have been any more different in style or tone. On the one hand, Argento is to be commended for having the conviction to follow his instincts; but the question becomes, were his instincts correct in this instance? As mentioned earlier, it seems unfair to attack the film for not living up to what one wants it to be; all films deserve to be judged on their own merits. However, it is difficult to do that here because of the link to two earlier artistic triumphs. Whether one prefers *Suspiria* or *Inferno* is beside the point; but does anybody favor *Mother of Tears* over its predecessors? Not likely.

That being said, the film is not without merit. There are sequences that display Argento's aesthetic sensibility. The overall absurdity of the piece can be a lot of fun to watch, provided one is in the right frame of mind. The mixture of alchemy, witchcraft, demons, and magic is a heady one and there are moments—the "powder puff" sequence comes to mind—where it really does manage to achieve the odd poetic effect. Some of the shock effects are brilliantly done. It's also a relatively fast-paced movie, though admittedly it functions better as a series of set pieces than as a unified whole.

The major problems with the film can be summed up in four points: the script is a mess, the style is all wrong for the subject matter, the campy tone (intended or not) undercuts its ability to frighten, and the budget simply doesn't allow for Argento to successfully realize the more ambitious conceits. Of all these issues, the script is the hardest one to justify. Given the amount of time he had to think about this project, it's frankly shocking that Argento went along with such a half-baked and often insipid piece of writing. Some of the ideas had potential, but it's too "busy" and the combination of prosaic *Angels and Demons*-style investigatory material with schlock horror tropes makes for an unhappy marriage. The sheer exuberance with which Argento executes the more outlandish visual ideas helps, but on the whole the film is an unworthy and unsatisfactory conclusion to an otherwise extraordinary trilogy.

Mother of Tears made its world premiere at the Toronto International Film Festival shortly before midnight on September 7, 2007—Dario's 67th birthday, in fact. The screening was a bit of a fiasco owing to some technical issues and Asia would later recall being a bit revolted by some of the film's over-the-top imagery. It went into general release in Italy on October 31, 2007—a full year following the start of production, which allowed ample time for Stivaletti and *Masters of Horror*'s Lee Wilson to sort out the many digital effects. That latter factor ended up causing serious strife among the Argento brothers, however, as the film ended up going over budget because of all the expensive post-production tinkering; it put a

Dario demonstrates the "powder puff" scene in *Mother of Tears.*

U.S. advertising for *Mother of Tears*, in the *LA Times*, dated June 6 2008.

strain on an already complex relationship, but there was still much worse in store.

Advance publicity played up the hype for all it was worth, but the backlash against the film was fairly instantaneous. In a repeat of past failures, the opening numbers were promising—but ultimately it ended up coming in at a very disappointing 82nd in the Italian box-office rankings for the 2007-2008 season.[10] Myriad negotiated a deal with Dimension Extreme, a subsidiary of the Weinstein Company, who decided to give the film a limited theatrical release in the U.S.: it opened at the Nuart Theatre in West Los Angeles on June 6, 2008 where it played for a week; that same date also saw it opening in New York and in Boston, followed by scattered screenings in various venues. It played on June 13 in Philadelphia, July 4 at the Music Box Theater in Chicago, July 11 in Atlanta and St. Louis, and so on. Owing to the film's excessive gore and sexual imagery, it was denied an official rating and was put out uncut and unrated. Argento's name no longer commanded much interest in the international marketplace and the film—his "ace in the hole," which seemed like a ready-made winner—ended up going straight to video in many markets.

The critical response was mostly negative, of course, though some of the critics admired the film's sheer audacity. Nathan Lee, in *The New York Times*, referred to the film as:

> [S]illy, awkward, vulgar, outlandish, hysterical, inventive, revolting, flamboyant, titillating, ridiculous, mischievous, up-roarious, cheap, priceless, tasteless, and sublime. And that's *before* the evil monkeys and sniggering Japanese harpies start running amok.[11]

Variety's Dennis Harvey agreed, calling it "a cheesy, breathless future camp classic."[12] On the other hand, Jim Ridley of *The Village Voice* opined, "It's painful to watch the Hieronymus Bosch of '70s horror sink this low."[13] Michael Phillips of the *Chicago Tribune* was more mixed, awarding it two-and-a-half stars and writing:

> The Italian horror veteran Dario Argento marches to his own blood-soaked, wild-eyed drummer, and the more we endure such things as *Hostel II* and *Saw III*, the better even a second-shelf Argento picture looks by comparison. *Mother of Tears* may not stand tall in Argento's body of viscera-laden work, but this final chapter of a loosely defined trilogy is refreshingly old school in its trashiness.[14]

Stephen Whitty, writing for the *Atlanta Constitution*, called it "a stylish gorefest for Argento fans only," and wrote:

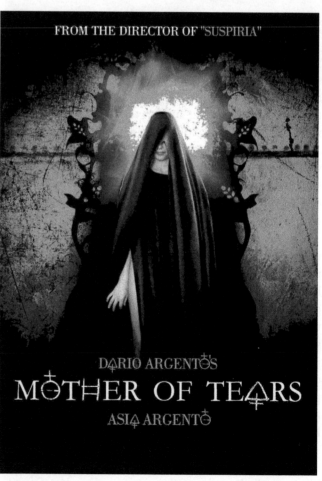

U.S. poster art for *Mother of Tears*; artist unknown.

[T]here is something undeniably compelling about the way this film unfolds, with its mix of '60s Hammer-horror crypts and '70s Eurotrash staples (including Udo Kier as a shaky exorcist). But the gore is simply midnight-movie disgusting. And the ending is rushed and flat—as if it had been tacked on by another hand. A severed one, of course."[15]

Argento was never particularly concerned about what the critics thought about his work, but the middling box-office receipts came as a major disappointment; he had no more aces up his sleeve, no other long-gestating projects to tease his fan base with.

Even as *Mother of Tears* was floundering and being torn limb-from-limb by the critics, honors continued to role in—albeit gradually. The Flaiano Prizes (*Premi Flaiano*), established in 1974 and named in honor of the great Italian screenwriter Ennio Flaiano (1910-1972), who collaborated with Federico Fellini on such gems as *La dolce vita* (1960) and *8½* (1963), selected Dario as one of the recipients of their Career Award. The other lifetime honorees for the year included the Indian actor Kabir Bedi, Italian actress Stefania Sandrelli, and American actor Willem Dafoe. The irony of being honored by such distinguished institutions while his stock in the critical and popular communities continued to decline was surely not lost on Dario.

Following the release of *Mother of Tears*, Asia seemed prepared to settle down somewhat. She married the director Michele Civetta (born 1976) on August 27, 2008, in the city of Arezzo in Tuscany. Both Dario and Daria were present for the ceremony. As it happens, the young couple were already expecting their first child together—and their son Nicola Giovanni Civetta was born on September 15, 2008. Asia's marriage to Michele would ultimately end in divorce in 2013.

Scene from *Profondo rosso: Il musical*.

By far the oddest project connected to Argento during this time, however, was the stage production of *Profondo rosso: Il musical*. Yes, indeed, somebody, somewhere thought it would be a good idea to reinterpret Argento's 1975 *giallo* masterpiece as a piece of musical theater. In truth, one can understand the idea of trying to stage a piece of musical theater in the Argento style—perhaps even a musical of *Suspiria* would make some sort of sense in this context. It wasn't the first time a genre film had been retooled in this fashion, either. There had been a musical adaptation of Stephen King's *Carrie* in 1988, for example, though it was an expensive flop[16], while Roman Polanski staged (to great acclaim) a musical version of his horror-comedy classic *The Fearless Vampire Killers* (*Dance of the Vampires*, 1967); known as *Tanz der vampire*, it opened in 1997 in Vienna and ended up being staged in numerous European cities.

With this in mind, it's easy to see why the idea of adapting Argento into this context seemed like a potential winner. *Profondo rosso*, however, proved to be a strange concept. It was the brainchild of director Marco Calindri and writer Marco Daverio, who approached Dario for his blessing; he gave them the go-ahead and even agreed to lend his name to the production by appearing in some promotional videos designed to drum up interest in the production. Michel Altieri (Mark), Silvio Specchio (Gianna), Claudio Lobbia (Giordani), and Maria Maddalena Trani (Carlo's mother) headed the cast, and Claudio Simonetti provided the music and songs. Notices for casting calls were out in April 2007 and the first performance took place in Novara, at the Teatro Coccia[17], on Sunday, October 7, 2007. An

Dario is all smiles at the wedding of Asia to Michele Civetta; Daria is at the right and Asia's daughter Anna Lou Castoldi is at the front.

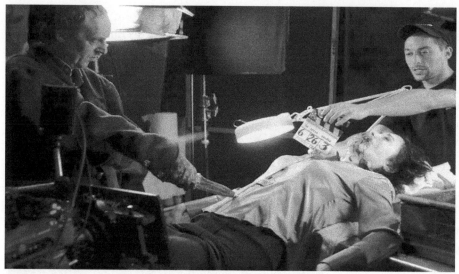

Dario once again stands in for the killer, as he prepares to eviscerate former girlfriend Coralina Cataldi-Tassoni in *Mother of Tears*.

ambitious tour was planned encompassing many major venues throughout Italy, including Halloween dates in Turin (where Argento shot part of the film back in 1974), but as Luigi Cozzi related to the author, "it was such a total flop that after just a few performances, all dates were cancelled."

Meanwhile, in 2008, talks of a remake of *Suspiria* started to float around social media. In March, it was officially announced that David Gordon Green, the director of the hit comedy *Pineapple Express* (2008), was slated to direct the picture. By August, it was announced that Natalie Portman had joined the film as a co-producer and that she would play the lead role—but ultimately, she left the film in favor of another macabre dance academy picture, Darren Aronofsky's *Black Swan* (2010). Argento let it be known that he was against the idea of a remake, but he had no way of blocking it from being made. In any event, for the time being at least, the remake of *Suspiria* collapsed into nothing; through 2011 and 2012, David Gordon Green let it be known that he was still trying to get the project off the ground, but by 2013 it was officially dead in the water. Argento was relieved by the news, but that wouldn't be the end of the matter.

Notes:
1. Palmerini, Luca M. and Gaetano Mistretta, *Spaghetti Nightmares* (Key West: Fantasma Books, 1997), p. 116.
2. The film is also known as *Demons 6: De Profundis*, in an obvious bid to shoehorn it into Dario's *Demons* franchise.
3. http://www.fangoria.com/news_article.php?id=5168
4. Ibid.
5. https://www.cinematografo.it/news/set-pronto-per-argento/
6. Jones, Alan, *Dario Argento: The Man, the Myths & the Magic* (Godalming: FAB Press, 2012), p. 364.
7. Ibid, p. 365.
8. http://www.frightfest.co.uk/2ndmay2007.html
9. Jones, Alan, *Dario Argento: The Man, the Myths & the Magic* (Godalming: FAB Press, 2012), p. 348.
10. http://www.hitparadeitalia.it/bof/boi/boi2007-08.htm
11. https://www.nytimes.com/2008/06/06/movies/06arge.html
12. Harvey, Dennis, "*Mother of Tears: The Third Mother*," *Variety*, September 8, 2007.
13. Ridley, Jim, "The Mother of Tears: Dario Argento Clowns Himself," *The Village Voice*, June 3, 2008.
14. Phillips, Michael, "Director offers more than gore," *The Chicago Tribune*, July 2, 2008.
15. Whitty, Stephen, Tears fall for skills wasted on gorefest," *The Atlanta Constitution*, July 11, 2008.
16. The musical version of *Carrie* would be revived to much more financial success and critical acclaim in 2012.
17. As fate would have it, Argento returned to the Teatro Coccia in 2013 to stage his version of Verdi's *Macbeth*.

Moody promotional advertising for *Mother of Tears*. Note the misspelling of *Suspiria*.

Chapter Twenty-Three: Hired Gun

Just as *Mother of Tears* was being premiered in Italy, Dario received a script from an American writing team. Jim Agnew and Sean Keller wrote *Giallo* as a tribute to Dario Argento and arranged to submit it to their idol through Asia Argento's American agents. Dario read the script and thought it had real potential; he contacted Agnew and Keller with some script changes he had in mind and they happily accommodated his wishes. And thus, it came to be that *Giallo* followed in the tradition of his *Masters of Horror* entries by becoming the first feature film Dario directed which he had absolutely no hand in originating.

In blunt terms, it indicated his transition from *auteur* to gun for hire—not an entirely shameful thing, of course, when one considers the practical reality behind the way that, say, Mario Bava had spent much of his career. It was a significant thing, however, in that Argento had always rejected the idea of making films he hadn't written himself; he often has mentioned how Dino De Laurentiis asked him to take a crack at adapting some Agatha Christie stories or how Stephen King was keen to have him make a version of *Salem's Lot*. Back in the '70s and '80s, a project like *Giallo* would have been absolutely unthinkable. In 2007, however, it no longer seemed like such a bad idea. No doubt part of it was a matter of settling into a more sedate frame of mind in his twilight years—he didn't feel as if he had so much to prove anymore, so to speak. But there's no doubt that the desperation to get back into the international market colored his thinking, as well. Don't forget he had already reached out to American screenwriters to help him realize *Mother of Tears*—and while that didn't end up going as planned, the idea of a ready-made thriller with some ties to the American marketplace seemed attractive at that moment in time. Dario discussed it with Claudio, and they decided to make it their next project under their Opera Film banner.

A cash infusion was obtained early in 2008 when Hannibal Pictures negotiated a deal to handle international sales for the picture, while Lionsgate ended up nabbing the U.S. theatrical and home video rights. Budgeted in the same realm as *Mother of Tears*, it was announced to have a pretty impressive cast, including Asia Argento as the heroine, Ray Liotta as the cynical detective, and Vincent Gallo as the killer, who suffers from hepatitis C—thus tying in to the whole "yellow" theme. Adrien Brody, the Oscar-winning star of Roman Polanski's *The Pianist* (2002), took an interest in the film when his then-girlfriend Elsa Pataky was cast in a key role. Brody decided that he'd like to play the detective role, and he given that his name was more prominent than that of Liotta, it was quickly arranged for him to do so. Things started to become more complicated when Asia dropped out of the picture; it was assumed by some that she wasn't keen to work with Vincent Gallo, as they had been formerly romantically linked, but in fact she was pregnant with her son at the time, and her casting would have been impractical under those circumstances. Gallo, meanwhile, dropped out of the picture, as well; Argento's "all-star *giallo*" was starting to lose a bit of its commercial luster.

At this stage, Brody decided to get involved in the production of the film and took on the mantle of co-producer—and with his clout, he was in a better position to call the shots where the creative decisions were concerned, even more so than Dario himself. The two men expressed mutual admiration, however, and apparently, they enjoyed working together, even if the project itself ended up becoming a sore point for them both. Brody came up with the idea of playing the killer himself—making it the first time in Argento film history that an actor took on dual roles. Sooner than let it be known that he was playing both parts, however, Brody elected to play the killer with the addition of plenty of prosthetics and a cheesy wig—under the name of Byron Deidra. With Asia out of the picture, Brody used his connection with Polanski to persuade the latter's wife, French star Emmanuelle Seigner, to play the heroine.

Giallo didn't just find Dario working from somebody else's writing—he was also in no position to really

Dario was thrilled to be working with Adrien Brody, but *Giallo* proved to be far from a joyous experience.

The Unsane Cinema of Dario Argento

commandeer the material in his usual style. Brody's involvement in the picture went well beyond that of the usual leading man, and the need to get the film properly financed meant that a number of other companies (including Aramis Films and Media Films) had a say in all the major artistic decisions, as well. Dario did his best to soldier on and make the best of it, but it became clear early on that he wasn't going to be functioning in the manner to which he had become accustomed. If there was any consolation to be found, it was surely in the presence of Frederic Fasano, who returned as cinematographer—for what would prove to be his final collaboration with Argento to date.

The filming commenced in Turin on May 12, 2008, and it was scheduled for an uncommonly rushed four weeks, finally wrapping on June 19. The production was kept pretty closely guarded and even Argento's biographer, Alan Jones, was not permitted on set. Brody's method acting intensity extended to his control over the shoot, which he was determined to keep away from the prying eyes of the press. Perhaps part of that was a desire to keep his dual casting under wraps, but regardless there was something fishy about the whole enterprise from early on.

After the filming wrapped in June, Argento found himself working with a new editor, Roberto Silvi. Silvi was no novice, however. He'd been editing features since the late 1970s, and his résumé included everything from John Huston's *Wise Blood* (1979) and William Peter Blatty's *The Ninth Configuration* (1980) to *Tombstone* (1993) and *The Three Burials of Melquiades Estrada* (2005). It's unclear whether the use of Silvi was due to Brody's involvement, as it broke the run of feature editing credits by Walter Fasano, but in any event Argento soon found himself overruled where the final cut was concerned, anyway. Argento had had difficulties in the past on films like *Trauma* and *Mother of Tears*, of course, but this marked a new low. He was basically overruled and the final cut was taken out of his hands completely. He had discussed scoring duties with Claudio Simonetti, who excitedly announced his involvement in the picture … only to then learn that Brody had hired a cheaper alternative, Marco Werba (born 1963). Werba delivered a perfectly efficient score, but Simonetti felt offended by the snub, even if it really wasn't Argento's fault.

The story opens as a pair of foreign exchange students head out with some of their fellow classmates for a night of high culture at the opera. They quickly tire of the opera and decide to sneak off to a club instead. The one girl, Keiko (Valentina Izumi), eventually decides to return to her apartment for some rest. Heading out into the rain, she hails a taxi—but it soon becomes evident that the driver is up to no good, and they eventually pull over to a secluded side street, where the driver subdues her with a sedative. The opening shows some potential. Some of the images are striking, notably a slow dolly-in on the taxi as Valentina screams for help which is punctuated by the view of her pressing her face and hands against the glass when she is attacked—a not-unfamiliar image in Argento's work and one which is still effective.

The fifth day of filming on *Giallo*, with Emmanuelle Seigner and Adrien Brody.

Keiko (Valentina Izumi) prepares for more torture while Celine (Elsa Pataky) looks on in horror.

Keiko eventually awakens in a grubby industrial setting; her hands and ankles are bound, and she has no idea where she is or how long she's been there. Worse still, she's not alone. The taxi driver looms over her, excitedly taking snapshots of her as she struggles and begs to be set free—and another girl lies on a metal table; she's been terribly mutilated and has already died from her wounds. The atmosphere is exceedingly grimy and seedy and at this stage in the game, the killer retains some mystique and power since he's pretty much kept in the shadows; that will soon change, however, and the film never recovers once it does.

In the midst of this horror, a model named Celine (Elsa Pataky) is getting ready to go on stage when she receives a phone call from her older sister Linda (Emmanuelle Seigner). Linda is a flight attendant and she's arrived in Turin, where she plans to stay with Celine for a few days. Their plans are disrupted when Celine leaves the fashion studio and ends up in the wrong taxicab. In a repetition of what had just happened to Keiko, Celine realizes that she's being abducted—but since she is on the phone with Linda while it's happening, she's able to alert her sister that something is going wrong before the cell signal is lost. Elsa Pataky (born 1976) adds a touch of spunk and vitality to her pitifully under-written role; we don't get to know much about her, however, and she spends much of the film being tortured and tormented by her captor. When she ends up in the killer's lair, Keiko is already deposited on the same metal table previously occupied by her "predecessor," and it's clear that they're both in for a bad time of it.

Linda goes to the police to report Celine's abduction, but the desk sergeant (Giancarlo Judica Cordiglia) explains that she has no proof that the girl has been taken against her will—and since she hasn't even been missing for 24 hours, there is nothing they can do. He does, however, point her in the direction of Inspector Enzo Avolfi (Adrien Brody), an eccentric rogue cop who seems to function independently from the rest of the police. Avolfi is introduced as a brusque sort; he's isolated from the rest of the force in his own lair in the basement—and one can't help but be reminded of the killer on that level. As it happens, the two men share a lot of similarities—and it's this reason that undoubtedly compelled Brody to do double duty by playing both characters. Brody (born 1973) had done remarkable work for Spike Lee in *Summer of Sam* (1999) and for Polanski in *The Pianist*, so his participation was reason enough to give Dario and his fan base some hope for the picture.

Unfortunately, Avolfi is a caricature, while the less said about his work as the killer (aka Flavio Volpe), the better. Avolfi is a lone wolf; he has no family and he doesn't work with a partner, either. He seems utterly devoted to his job and it's explained that he usually sleeps in his office, as well. There was some potential for an interesting, quirky characterization, but Brody and Argento elect to play up the character's macho posturing and the film suffers for it. Eccentric or not, Avolfi does

The Unsane Cinema of Dario Argento

get results, so Linda opens up to him and tells him about what is going on with Celine. When she mentions that she was in a taxi when the abduction occurred, his interest is peaked; he curtly dismisses Linda and tells her to wait by the phone for more news. After she leaves, he looks at Celine's picture and mutters, "So beautiful. He hates beautiful things."

Things start to take a turn for the worse when we start spending more time with the killer in his lair. As played by Brody, the killer is a figure of grotesque comedy; the problem is, it's evidently not meant to be funny. He loves to taunt his victims, talking gibberish with a Chico Marx accent, and he's also prone to sucking on a pacifier while masturbating to pictures of his handiwork. The psychosexual hangups of Argento's peak period *giallo* killers were anything but amusing; they managed to function as legitimately threatening villains. The same can't be said for Brody, who plays the part with all the subtlety of a pantomime bad guy. The fact that the killer is suffering from hepatitis C, which gives him jaundice, adds to the grotesque factor; and in order to try and conceal his real identity, Brody is fitted out with a wig and heavy-duty prosthetic appliances supplied by Sergio Stivaletti. It all comes off like an elaborate practical joke and if indeed there was any real hope of pulling one over on the audience, it is much too heavy-handed to be successful. In allowing Brody the room to overact so badly,

For whatever reason, Adrien Brody thought it would be a good idea to pull double duty by playing the killer, known as Giallo because of his jaundiced complexion; the effect is more comical than frightening.

Argento effectively ruins any opportunity for the film to work as a suspenseful or scary enterprise. That said, there is still a slight edge to the sadism—as evidenced in the scene where the killer takes a pair of shears to Keiko's lip; Argento actually pans away from the action for once, but that is probably for the best—the effects work seen in the film is very uneven, whereas here the audience is able to piece together the action for themselves. The theme of the killer's hatred of beauty is probably the most successful element of the story; in emphasizing his grotesque appearance, Argento and his writers provide him with a motive which is simultaneously horrible and logical. In addition, his deteriorating physical condition provides him with an impetus to try and save himself, even if he is completely rejected by society at large. In the hands of a more sensitive actor, all of this could have been oddly sympathetic— but the killer never convinces as a character because he's depicted with all the conviction of a bad joke.

As Avolfi continues his investigation, he finds himself being followed by Linda. Linda refuses to sit idly by and wait for him to call, so he reluctantly allows her to tag along with him. Emmanuelle Seigner (born 1966) had given fine performances for her husband, Roman Polanski, in such films as *Frantic* (1988) and *Bitter Moon* (1992), but her performance here is decidedly uneven; she is effective at conveying the character's mounting sense of worry for her baby sister, but she struggles with some of the clunkier lines of dialogue. Her attempt to initiate a romantic relationship with Avolfi seems particularly forced under the circumstances, but fortunately he is too set in his ways to allow himself to indulge in such a distraction. Linda at least registers more strongly as a character than, say, Gloria in *Sleepless*, but she's still not nearly as interesting or engaging as the better-written female characters in Argento's filmography. As such, one of the most profoundly disappointing things about the film is seeing such a potentially interesting group of actors waste their talent on subpar material. Indeed, the same can be said of Argento himself.

It turns out that both Avolfi and the killer are the products of childhood trauma. Avolfi tells Linda that when he was a young child, he saw his mother (Daniela Fazzolari) being savagely murdered by an intruder; he was shipped off to New York for a period, but after getting into trouble one too many times, he was shipped back to Turin. There, he found the man (Giuseppe Lo Console, previously seen in *Do You Like Hitchcock?* and soon to reappear for Argento in *Dario Argento's Dracula*) responsible for his mother's murder—armed with a club and a knife, he took the law into his own hands and exacted revenge. As for the killer, he was the product of an unwanted pregnancy by an IV drug user—she abandoned him at a local orphanage, and the drugs in his system because of her drug use caused him to turn yellow when he was just a little boy. Thus, he has spent his entire life being regarded as a freak. The two men are therefore linked by their respective childhood traumas; the difference is, Avolfi has managed to channel his heartache and rage into productive work, while the killer uses his bitterness as an excuse to target beautiful young women. Argento's expressive visual style is mostly absent in *Giallo*, but it does show up sporadically during these flashback scenes, with their heightened color and unusual camera movements; elsewhere, much of the film is shot in the same murky, grimy visual style as the average "torture porn" movie of the period, such as *Saw* (2004) or *Hostel* (2005).

The killer eventually tires of toying with Keiko and he wraps her up in a plastic shroud (shades of Mario Bava's quirky *giallo Five Dolls for an August Moon / 5 bambole per la luna d'agosto*, 1970), leaving her for the police to find. Avolfi arrives on the scene and manages to record her final words—they're in Japanese, so he is unable to understand, but he gets a Japanese informer (Taiyo Yamanouchi) to translate it for him. It turns out that she was telling Avolfi that the man was yellow; he and Linda eventually figure out that this could mean jaundice, and he checks the local transplant clinics to see if he can find any leads. Sure enough, the killer happens to be there and Avolfi hones in on him, but he manages to get away. A nurse (Barbara Mautino, in her third role for Argento following *Sleepless* and *Mother of Tears*) provides him with information on the suspect, including his name (Flavio Volpe) and address. What's particularly striking about all of this is how very *unexciting* it all is; because the killer is so utterly comical and ridiculous, it's impossible to take him seriously, while Avolfi's posturing doesn't exactly make him an endearing hero, either.

Things pick up briefly as Avolfi makes his way into Volpe's lair; there's some nice backlighting effects courtesy of Frederic Fasano as Avolfi investigates the property, and the clever use of cross-cutting provides the film with its best instance of misdirection as we're led to believe that Avolfi is in the same location as the killer and Celine. As it happens, however, Celine is being kept in a separate location, so Avolfi's sense of triumph is short-lived.

There's also a reasonably exciting chase scene when Celine breaks free from the killer and runs to safety; Pataky's endearingly strong-willed characterization makes the viewer root for her to be successful, and there's a nice transition from the grubby interiors of her makeshift prison into the bright, vivid colors of the outside world when she finally gets out. The killer gets the upper hand once more, however, and she soon finds herself locked up again.

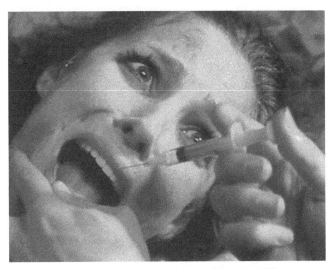

Celine (Elsa Pataky) is tortured by the killer.

The finale sees the killer surprising Linda in her apartment. He's desperate to get out of town and get access to medical help, since Avolfi destroyed his medication supply during his investigation of his house; in exchange for her help in getting out of Turin, he promises to provide her with the information as to Celine's whereabouts. Linda agrees, but Avolfi, consumed with his own selfish need to bring the killer to justice, makes an unwelcome appearance. He chases the killer to the roof and in the ensuing struggle, the killer falls through a plate glass skylight—the image of him holding on for dear life as the glass embedded in the metal structure shreds his hands recalls the finale of *The Cat O'Nine Tails*; Linda begs him to tell her where her sister is, but he refuses and plummets to his death. Avolfi is confident that the killer would never have told her what she wanted to know, but Linda is furious. "You're just like him! Why did I trust you?!" As Avolfi walks away, shattered by the loss of the one friend who believed in and trusted him, the sounds of Linda's sobs and cries of condemnation echo through the night. Ideally, this would have provided the film with its perfect ambiguous final image, but it cuts to a brief coda in a parking garage, where Celine is trapped in the trunk of one of the cars. A cop patrolling the garage hears her cries and comes to the rescue; the image of blood dripping from the back trunk leaves it unclear as to whether she will survive or not, but it feels like a pat and unnecessary addition after the more profoundly affecting image of Avolfi walking away in shame from what should have been his moment of triumph.

The bad publicity generated by the production woes led most viewers and critics to dismiss *Giallo* sight unseen. The truth is, taken on its own merits, it's not a particularly awful film; but make no mistake, it's not a good one, either. On the surface, it seems to provide Argento with an ideal opportunity to make his most "meta" statement on the genre which made his name—

Cover for the Italian DVD release; the close-up of Brody's eyes comes close to giving the game away where his stunt casting is concerned!

but there is very little invention or innovation to be found here. The story plods along without any particular rhythm and Argento's staging seems curiously flat and listless.

Adrien Brody's indulgent appearance as Avolfi and the killer is another major stumbling block. It's unclear whether he decided it was in his best interests to send the material up, or whether he really was trying to do something sincere and it got lost along the way. Nevertheless, his broad take on the material undercuts its effectiveness at every turn; the contrast between the killer and the detective had potential, but Brody seems to be lampooning it; if he doesn't believe in it, then how is the audience supposed to do so? Had the original casting of Ray Liotta and Vincent Gallo worked out, who knows—the film might have come off a lot better.

Argento's flair for atmosphere and the macabre is briefly glimpsed in a few scenes and striking set-ups, but overall it plays like it could have been made by anybody. In effect, it seems more like an imitation from a well-meaning but talent-deprived fan. It's not a particularly badly made movie—Fasano's photography is professional if impersonal, and it looks slick enough to pass muster—but it is curiously inert. Just why Argento elected to undertake the project is not immediately clear.

Perhaps he felt that the combination of his name and legacy with a trendy cast list could get him back into the international market. If that was the intent, it sadly blew up in his face; it remains the one film he has effectively disowned owing to all the behind-the-scenes double dealing and drama.

Giallo made its first appearance at the 2009 Cannes Film Festival, on May 13, where it was screened out-of-competition in the hopes of attracting some buyers. The reaction was overwhelmingly negative; Dario didn't even attend the festival, having already decided that he wanted to wash his hands of the whole sorry affair. Not long after that first disastrous screening, word started to get around that there were some serious lawsuits brewing in connection to the production. It was eventually revealed that neither Brody nor Argento had been properly compensated for their work on the film and that, while the budget looked perfectly good and proper on paper, little of the money had been made available where it was needed. Brody and Argento took the producers to court and, as these things tend to, the proceedings dragged on and on. Ultimately, in 2011, the lawsuit was settled in favor of Brody and Argento, though precisely how they were compensated has never been revealed; Dario, for his part, pretty much refuses to discuss the film in general—and he certainly hasn't shown any desire to talk about the legal woes, either.

In the midst of the acrimony, *Giallo* ended up going straight to video in Italy—and pretty much everywhere else in the world. Until the lawsuit was settled, Brody tried to block video companies from using his likeness to promote the film—though the American DVD release did so, anyway. There were a handful of theatrical releases, in places like Romania (in May 2010) and Japan (in September 2010), but few distributors were willing to take a chance on putting the film into theaters.

The Italian DVD premiere was delayed until November 2010, by which point the film acquired the

Japan was one of the few places where *Giallo* played in theatres.

The Romanian theatrical poster utilized the same bland imagery as most other territories.

reputation as the lowpoint in Dario's career. Curiously, a belated Italian theatrical release was granted after the video release, under the title of *Giallo/Argento*; it did lousy business. The critics were predictably unimpressed; while *Mother of Tears* had been savaged by most critics, it at least garnered grudging admiration from some reviewers, who admired the film's cheerful lack of good taste. No such good will could be mustered for *Giallo*, however. *The Guardian*'s Mark Kermode wrote that it:

> [D]oes nothing to enhance the reputation of Italy's former horror *maestro*. On the contrary, with its sub-*Saw* leering gore and crassly unimaginative exploitation aesthetic, this looks more like the work of a hacking fan boy than the father of stylishly extreme modern cinema.[1]

Variety's Leslie Felperin put it succinctly, saying "this serial killer story plays like a work for hire that no one had much fun working on."[2]

Argento's stock may have been plummeting, but he took solace in being feted at the Capri Hollywood International Film Festival in 2010, where he and several other veterans of the film industry (including director Jerzy Skolimowski, actor/director Enrico Montesano, and actress Sandra Milo) were given the Capri Legend Award. A similar honor was bestowed on him in November 2011 when he was given the Lifetime Achievement Award at the Cinemanila International Film Festival in Taguig City in the Philippines. Honors such as this helped to keep Argento visible, but they carried a mixed message of sorts. By honoring him for a lifetime's worth of work, they seemed to imply that there wasn't much left in store. Dario was by no means ready to rest on his laurels, however, even if his next projects made some wish that he would do just that.

In May 2010, at the Cannes Film Festival, Claudio Argento made a surprising announcement. He was producing a remake of *Deep Red*—in the newly fashionable 3D format, no less. He approached George A. Romero with an offer to direct; Romero was initially agreeable, as he liked the idea of working in 3D and was frankly grateful to have a chance to do something outside of his iconic living dead realm. The internet was abuzz with mixed emotions over the project, but by August of that year, it was all over. As Romero explained, "I was approached by Dario's brother, Claudio Argento, and the last time I worked with those guys they were together and still speaking to each other. And I found out now they're not, and Claudio calls me and asked me to do it, and he initially said that Dario was involved, and I said, 'well, I'd like to talk to him about it.' And the other numbers I had for Dario were old and no good anymore, and finally a friend gave me a contact for Dario, and I wrote to him and he said no, he wasn't involved and he didn't appreciate the idea that Claudio was doing it so I said, 'well hey man, then I'm out.'"[3] The idea of remaking the film was eventually dropped, though the friction generated by it and the experience of making *Giallo* put yet another wedge between the brothers Argento which has yet to fully heal.

Ironically, at the same time Claudio was flogging his Romero-directed 3D remake of *Deep Red* at Cannes, Dario was also represented at the festival, where it was formally announced that he was going to direct a 3D version of Bram Stoker's *Dracula*. Up until that time, the idea of Dario tackling such a project had been a closely guarded secret—but given that Claudio is family, it's entirely possible that he was wise to what was going on and, in a classic case of "what you can do, I can do better," he decided to throw caution to the wind and tell everybody that he was making a 3D horror extravaganza of his own.

The project was the brainchild of Roberto Di Girolomo, the owner of FilmExport Group, and producer Giovanni Paolucci. Looking to try and bolster the flagging

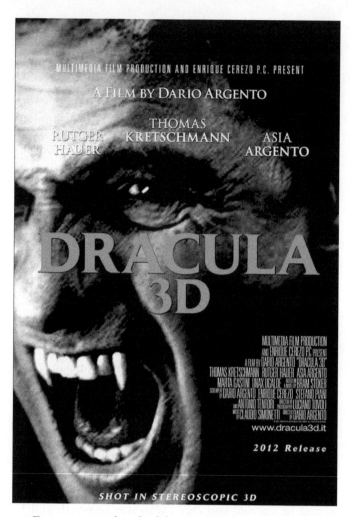

Teaser promotional ad for *Dario Argento's Dracula*.

Italian cinema scene, Di Girolomo and Paolucci started brainstorming and tried to come up with an idea that had real commercial potential. Inspired by the success of films like *My Bloody Valentine 3D* (2009), they decided that 3D would have to be a part of the equation. There was also a renewed interest in vampires thanks to the success of the *Twilight* franchise, so why not go back to where it all began by mounting a new adaptation of Stoker's book? Neither Di Girolomo nor Paolucci had ever worked with Argento before, but they decided that he would be the perfect name to galvanize the project and give it even more commercial validity. As it happened, Dario was actively looking for his next subject—the *Giallo* debacle had resulted in the dissolution of Opera Film and there were no projects on the horizon. As such, Di Girolomo and Paolucci happened to luck into approaching him at just the right time.

In truth, Dario had never expressed the slightest interest in making a version of *Dracula*. His own approach to horror had always been more modern. True, he and Cozzi had pitched a new version of *Frankenstein* back in 1973, but until the remake of *The Phantom of the Opera*, Argento had always stayed well clear of the Gothic. The failure of *Phantom* seemed to confirm that Argento wasn't particularly well-suited to the period Gothic milieu, but he wasn't about to let that deter him. If there was one thing that truly appealed to him in this proposal, it was the opportunity to work in 3D. Dario had already dabbled in just about every kind of new technology which had come down the pike, so he was keen to experiment with 3D, as well. "3D is a very interesting discipline to work in, so much so it's difficult to go back to 2D because you see everything so flat."[4] He studied Hitchcock's use of the medium in *Dial M for Murder* (1954) and decided to use it, rather than the schlockier variety of "comin' at ya!" techniques favored by most filmmakers, as his model. When it became clear that the technology had evolved to a place where he really could make proper extensive use of it, he enthusiastically signed on to direct.

Argento refamiliarized himself with Stoker's book and also drew particular inspiration from Terence Fisher's 1958 version of *Dracula* starring Christopher Lee as the Count and Peter Cushing as Dr. Van Helsing. "I suppose Hammer's *Dracula* is my touchstone up to a point—and I am trying to make my spin on Bram Stoker as classic as that. Terence Fisher's masterpiece positioned Dracula and Van Helsing as two sides of the same coin and I went down that route too."[5] In writing the script, Argento found himself working with three new collaborators: the film's co-producer Enrique Cerezo, TV veteran Stefano Piani, and Antonio Tentori, whose earlier works included Lucio Fulci's self-referential *Cat in the Brain* (*Un gatto nel cervello*, 1990). Precisely how the four divided their work is not clear, but Argento seemed to be satisfied with the fruits of their labors. All told, their take on Stoker's tale was less revisionist than his earlier spin on *Phantom*, but there was still something of a playful approach evident in some of the more outrageous concepts and set pieces.

Between the period setting and all the trappings that called for and the use of 3D and extensive visual effects, it was clear that the picture needed a fairly sizable budget. Di Giacomo and Paolucci, for all their wide-eyed enthusiasm, couldn't muster all that was needed, so further funding was secured from Spanish producer Enrique Cerezo of Enrique Cerezo Producciones and French producer Sergio Gobbi of Les Films de l'Astre. For the first time in years, Dario had no hand in producing the picture himself; on the plus side, this meant that he didn't have to worry himself over the financing beyond needing to be assured that the resources promised to him would really materialize. All told, the budget was set at a little under $8 million—making it one of the more expensive films of his career.

Argento reached out to some of his favorite past collaborators to bring their special talents to the project. Massimo Antonello Geleng made a long-overdue return to the Argento filmmaking family and provided the film with some impressive set designs and art direction. Sergio Stivaletti had his hands full with the various elaborate visual effects dreamed up by Argento—notably Dracula's shape-shifting skills, which result in his taking the form of a swarm of flies in one scene ... and an oversized praying mantis in another. Mario Bava once said that the lighting in a horror film accounts for 70% of its effectiveness, since it creates the requisite atmosphere. Bava certainly knew what he was speaking of, and Argento made the sensible decision to recruit Luciano Tovoli to light the picture—it was their first time working together since *Tenebrae*, though Argento had attempted to secure his services for *Opera*. Tovoli's aesthetic sensibility was far better suited to the film's Gothic atmosphere than the more reality-based Frederic Fasano, and Argento fans the world over overreacted with enthusiasm when they learned that he was attached to the project.

In casting the film, Argento largely decided to go with younger actors with whom he had no experience; however, the role of Lucy (Westenra in the book, but renamed as Kisslinger in the film for reasons best known to Argento) seemed ideally suited to Asia. They had nearly worked together on *Giallo*, but that didn't pan out; *Dario Argento's Dracula* (or *Dracula di Dario Argento* on Italian prints; the film is informally known as *Dracula 3D*, but that is not the actual on-screen title) would therefore mark their first film together since *Mother of Tears*. Asia later told Alan Jones that the project appealed to her because it was a supporting part and therefore only demanded 10 days of her time.[6] It's just as well that they got together for the film when they did—her third feature directorial offering, the partly-autobiographical *Misunderstood* (*Incompressa*, 2014), would tear open the old wounds between her and Dario, resulting in yet another prolonged rift.

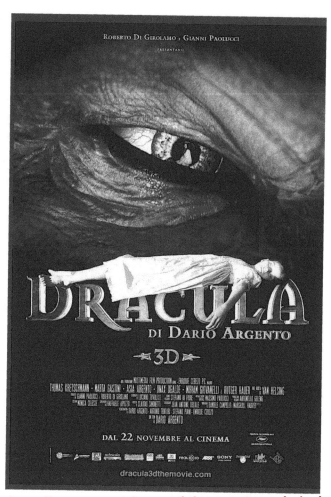

The Italian poster art is one of the worst ever devised for an Argento film, which is perhaps appropriate. Artist unknown.

The decision to cast Rutger Hauer as Van Helsing was an inspired touch, though rumors abounded that Gabriele Lavia (who had appeared in *Deep Red*, *Inferno*, and *Sleepless*) was under consideration for the part as well. The all-important role of Dracula proved to be uncommonly difficult to cast—Argento wanted to get a name actor to help the film's commercial chances, but he was also cognizant of the reality that Dracula called for a very special kind of screen presence. After much hemming and hawing over offering it to Vincent Gallo—and ultimately passing on him for fear that the eccentric actor/director might overpower him on set; was this collateral damage from the experience of having Adrien Brody as producer and star on *Giallo*, one wonders?—he finally decided to offer the part to German actor Thomas Kretschmann, who had appeared so memorably as the brutal psychopathic killer Alfredo Grossi in *The Stendhal Syndrome*. Kretschmann was an unusual choice, yet he managed to respond with a quietly dignified performance.

Dario and Asia discuss a scene on location for *Dario Argento's Dracula*.

There was also the matter of location work to consider. *Dario Argento's Dracula* would rely on a lot of atmospheric exterior locations and Argento originally

Thomas Kretschmann and Mara Gastini go over a scene with Dario.

considered going back to Budapest, where *The Church* and *The Phantom of the Opera* had been filmed. The most important location, of course, was Castle Dracula. Argento finally found the location he was searching for in Turin, of all places—the Castle of Montalto Dora proved to be an ideal substitute for the Count's lair, while the town of Ricetto in Candello, in the Piedmont region, provided the ideal location for the village being affected by the vampire's nefarious activities. Il Torchio, a restaurant in Ricetto, provided the location for the village inn. The nature reserve in Baraggio, in Biella, would stand in for the forests of Carpathia. The use of these locations saved the production a pretty penny—thus freeing Geleng to work his magic where real locations couldn't be secured.

The 11-week shoot commenced in May 2011. Argento and Tovoli stressed over the use of 3D in the early stages of production, but as time went on, they found themselves getting more used to the format. It proved to be a challenge for the actors, too, in that they had to be mindful of their precise positioning in every frame to ensure that the technology was being exploited to its full advantage. Having been disappointed by Francis Ford Coppola's big budget *Bram Stoker's Dracula* (1992), Argento was sure to emphasize horror over romance—though the old "reincarnated love" angle from H. Rider Haggard's *She* (1886-1887), recycled in everything from *The Mummy* (1932) to *Blacula* (1972), did manage to rear its unwelcome head in his treatment, as well. Sooner than focus on the Count mooning over his lost love, however, he decided to offer up plenty of gore and a heaping helping of sleaze, as well. Technical challenges notwithstanding, the production proceeded smoothly enough and came in on schedule.

For the post-production phase, Argento needed to find an editor who was well-versed in the new 3D technology. In fact, Marshall Harvey, Dario's editor on *Jenifer*, was drafted early on and played an active role during the filming. Argento and Tovoli needed to be sure that what they were shooting was achieving the desired technical effects, so Harvey—whose experience with 3D goes back to working with Joe Dante on *The Hole* (2009)—was basically editing scenes as the film progressed. By the time it was finished filming, a rough cut was already in place—and thus, Stivaletti and a veritable army of visual effects technicians were free to focus on completing the various transformations and gore effects. Dario decided to go with the tried-and-true where the music was concerned and he asked Claudio Simonetti to compose the soundtrack; in a repeat of *Mother of Tears*, however, he seemed to be less inclined to involve himself in the scoring than he had in the past—and Simonetti responded with a lush symphonic score with heavy-duty use of the Theremin.

The film gets off on the wrong foot with some less-than-convincing digital effects work, as the camera swoops down from above and glides through the village which is adjacent to Castle Dracula. By way of full disclosure, having not been fortunate to have seen the film projected in 3D, it's entirely possible that scenes such as this have an effectiveness which is stripped away by the less-forgiving dimensions of 2D; some Argento enthusiasts who have seen the film in 3D have assured the writer that, at the very least, the format is used very well indeed.

In the first of many digressions from Stoker's novel—Argento's possessory credit on the American print is fair; this really isn't Bram Stoker's *Dracula*—a character

Prior to becoming a vampire, Tanja (Miriam Giovanelli) enjoys a tryst with her lover (Christian Burruano).

named Tanja (Miriam Giovanelli) is introduced. Despite it being Walpurgis Night—the night when all the spirits of evil are supposed to be in full power—she leaves the safety of her home in order to meet her lover, Milos (Christian Burruano). In the film's first instance of over-ripe exploitation, the two make love in a cottage, with little left to the imagination of the viewer. The increase in sexploitation imagery in Argento's latter day work sinks to an all-time low here; it plays out like soft-core porn and it feels extremely out of place. One can hardly help but see this as a cynical move on Argento's part, as if he is hoping that the increase in sex and sleaze will help to connect with the modern audience. The sexual component was vital to the thematic concerns of something like *Pelts*, for example, but here it's simply window dressing.

Tanja is afraid to walk home and asks Milos to accompany her, but he is more worried about his wife finding out about their tryst. Abandoned by her lover, she makes her way through the creepy forest; there's some very atmospheric nighttime photography courtesy of Luciano Tovoli and Argento gets good use out of graceful camera movements and high angles which suggest the presence of something watching the young woman from up above. Her fears are confirmed when a large owl swoops down—the owl transforms into the figure of Count Dracula (Thomas Kretschmann), who sinks his fangs into the girl's throat.

This is the first example of the Count's transformative powers and it's one of the few truly imaginative touches introduced into the scenario by Argento; his long-standing fascination with the natural world, symbolized by animals and insects, manifests itself throughout the film as Dracula shape-shifts into a variety of unusual forms. The concept of a vampire turning into a wolf or a bat is nothing new, of course, but Argento gets further eccentric mileage out of the idea than any other filmmaker who preceded him in this subgenre. Unfortunately, the digital effects by Sergio Stivaletti and company aren't always up to par, thus undermining the effectiveness of some of the transformations. The transition from owl-to-vampire is nicely done, however, and ends the opening "teaser" on an appropriately off-kilter note.

All the good will built up by the attack on Tanja soon dissipates with the introduction of Jonathan Harker (Unax Ugalde), as he arrives in town via train. The use of green screen backdrops and hopelessly artificial-looking digital effects can be charitably described as naïve—but far from evoking a kind of fairy tale vibe, they merely serve to render the introduction of an important character utterly ludicrous. The presence of a pesky fly bothering Jonathan as he asks for directions to the castle recalls earlier Argento films like *Four Flies on Grey Velvet* and *Phenomena*, but it does little to make up for the air of slipshod quality which bedevils so much of the movie.

Jonathan stops off in town while making his way to Castle Dracula, and there he meets Lucy Kisslinger (Asia Argento), who is established as the best friend of

Unax Ugalde as Jonathan Harker at work in Dracula's library.

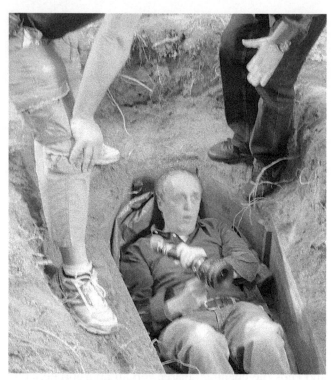
Dario gets cozy on the set of *Dracula*.

his wife, Mina. Lucy is disappointed to see that Mina is not with him, but as he explains she is detained for a few days and is expected to arrive at the end of the week. Lucy represents the more "modern" woman; she is strong-willed and independent and despite attracting the attention of several suitors, she refuses to settle for the sake of comfort or appearance. Even so, the role is thinly written, and Asia comes off poorly in it; by this stage, her reluctance to continue acting is more obvious than ever. The most interesting aspect of her character is how she unwittingly helps to set the tragedy in motion. It's on her advice that the Count has hired Jonathan to work for him, thus opening the door for him and his wife Mina to become immersed in his world. Lucy does so without malice. Her father, the town mayor (Augusto Zucchi), sings the praises of the Count and has assured Lucy that he has done a lot of good for the area; thus, she has every reason to believe that working for the Count would be a step in the right direction for Jonathan. Like so much in the script, however, it remains under-developed as an idea; Lucy never seems to come to this realization herself and she's ultimately reduced to a minor sideline victim rather than a fully fleshed-out human being.

Jonathan's journey to the castle evokes aspects of the F.W. Murnau (*Nosferatu/Nosferatu, eine Symphonie des Grauens*, 1922) and Werner Herzog (*Nosferatu the Vampyre/ Nosferatu: Phantom der Nacht*, 1979) adaptations, but doesn't come close to recapturing that sense of magic and atmosphere. Much more successful is a scene in which Tanja's grave is unearthed by Milos and a couple of cohorts. Tovoli's lighting is particularly effective in the nighttime exteriors, and Argento incorporates some striking low camera angles from inside the coffin. Before Milos is able to stake Tanja, a psychotic villager named Renfield (Giovanni Franzoni) attacks—he bites the ear off of one of the men and uses a shovel to split Milos' skull open. He is finally arrested and taken to prison, where he's held in anticipation of a public execution. Renfield is depicted rather differently than he had been in the book. Argento retains the idea of his being a loyal subject of Dracula, but the idea of the character eating insects in order to feed on their blood and life-force is notable in its absence. Maybe with the emphasis on Dracula adopting the form of various insects, Argento figured it was just as well to drop that idea from his adaptation.

When Jonathan arrives at the castle, Argento follows the typical *Dracula* story as he finds the place apparently deserted, only to find a note from his employer advising him that he is away for the day and that a meal has been left out for him. Argento was fortunate indeed to gain access to the Castle of Montalto Dora—it adds a tremendous amount of production value and provides the film with a primary setting that is both realistic and appropriately stylized. As explained by set decorator Silvia Guglielmetti in the behind the scenes documentary included on the IFC Blu-ray release of the film, Argento was very specific in wanting a pared down approach to the set dressing; sooner than embrace the idea of opulence and excess as he had done in *The Phantom of the Opera*, here he goes for a different ambience—as if suggesting that the Count's presence has drained the world around him of life and vitality. The aesthetic is simple and direct—functional as opposed to being "over-stuffed." Argento's roving camera prowls and finds interesting angles as Jonathan explores the castle; in scenes such as this, the old magic is evident once more. When Jonathan sits down to eat, he is suddenly joined by Tanja. She is coquettish in her demeanor, but before she is able to make a move on Jonathan, they find themselves suddenly joined by Dracula himself. Thomas Kretschmann, who had made such a terrific impression as the psychotic Alfredo Grossi in *The Stendhal Syndrome*, brings real dignity and gravitas to his characterization as Dracula. Like so many of the previous screen Draculas, from Max Schreck and Béla Lugosi to Christopher Lee and Frank Langella, he does not hew at all to the description of the Count in Stoker's text; instead he appears as a handsome, dignified man dressed entirely in black—that aspect is at least consistent with Stoker, and Argento avoids cliché by not having him wear a cape or a cloak.

Kretschmann's performance has been criticized as fatally low-key by some, but he provides the film with the stately center it so desperately needs; there is nothing remotely camp about his interpretation and he manages to hold his head high even as the film crumbles around him. It's worth noting that Argento's model for some of these early scenes is the series of Dracula films produced by Hammer Films in the '50s, '60s, and '70s. The whole concept of Jonathan coming to the castle to serve as the Count's librarian is straight out of Terence Fisher's *Dracula* (aka *Horror of Dracula*, 1958), while the distillation of the Count's trio of vampire brides into a single disciple named Tanja is cribbed from Roy Ward Baker's *Scars of Dracula* (1970). Unfortunately, in terms of overall quality, his take is considerably closer to the latter than it is to the former.

The introductory scene of Dracula with Jonathan allows Argento and Kretschmann to trot out variations on the old favorite tropes. He turns down dinner, saying, "I never eat … in the evening," and when he hears the wolves baying in the distance it prompts him to say the classic "Listen to them, the children of the night …" speech. Moments like this find Argento paying homage to the literary source, but overall the approach is anything but reverential. When Dracula leads Jonathan to his library, Argento and Tovoli create some gorgeous images—the art direction is beautifully detailed, and the use of framing is absolutely precise. The color and depth of clarity in the image work in perfect harmony in sequences such as this, whereas in other sections of the film the amount of light needed for the 3D effects coupled with the use of digital instead of 35mm tends to make the film look too harsh and overly bright.

When Jonathan retires to his room for the night, he is suddenly visited by Tanja. She makes a more overt play for him this time and strips naked in order to entice

Miriam Giovanelli bares more than just her fangs as Tanja.

him. Miriam Giovanelli (born 1989) is something of a fan favorite—if that's the right word—based on her willingness to embrace the more sexual aspects of the material; she provides the movie with some of the most "in your face" moments of raw sexuality to be found in any of Argento's films, but like just about everybody else her efforts aren't properly supported by the material. The character is strictly one-dimensional and while Giovanelli enters in the spirit of the proceedings with breathless enthusiasm, one can't help but feel badly for the way she is so obviously being exploited in the hopes of selling a few extra tickets; Tanja remains a cartoonish vamp, in both senses of the term, and she is far too cartoonish on that level to function as a credible menace.

When Tanja bites Jonathan on the throat, Dracula makes a dramatic appearance and flings her across the room; Argento was obviously hoping to evoke the savage fury and energy of the comparable scene in Fisher's *Dracula*, but the unconvincing effects again rear their

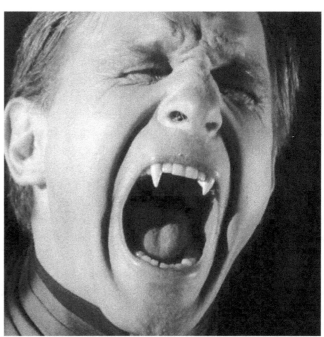

The Count sprouts fangs.

unwelcome head and the end effect is more comic than thrilling. Dracula snarls that Jonathan belongs to him before sinking his fangs into the young man's throat. If we regard vampirism as a symbolically sexual condition, then Dracula's willingness to go after male and female victims adds a pansexual dimension to the character.

Things continue to follow the tried-and-true route as Dracula frees Renfield and sets his eyes on Lucy, hoping to use her friendship with Mina to lure the latter into his trap. Dracula's seduction of Mina is convincingly played by both Kretschmann and Asia, adding a kinky sexual element to the proceedings, but Asia continues to be badly treated by the material. She soon grows weak and

Marta Gastini and Asia Argento prepare for a scene.

dies. Prior to har death, however, she enjoys some time being reunited with Mina (Marta Gastini). Mina refuses to leave her side when Lucy falls ill, even though she is anxious to be reunited with Jonathan; one of the film's more notorious moments occurs when she helps Lucy with her bath. The nudity involving Asia is not exactly shocking, but viewers continue to struggle with feeling uncomfortable over the idea of her father being behind the camera during sequences such as this. Mina notices a pair of bite marks on Lucy's leg, behind her knee, but Lucy dismisses it as an insect bite; in a sense, given the Count's shape-shifting abilities, that's not so far from the truth.

Mina's concerns over Lucy and Jonathan prompts her to have a nightmare—and the scene definitely recalls the harshly over-lit, bleached out sleepwalking scenes in *Phenomena*. The unnaturally exaggerated colors and use of bright white light is striking, but the more unforgiving nature of digital vs. 35mm undermines the dreamy atmosphere somewhat. Nevertheless, there's a nice moment when Mina sees a body being savaged by a wolf, only to then realize that the body is her own. All told, there is far more visual creativity and panache evident in sequences such as this than can be found in the entirety of *Giallo* or *Do You Like Hitchcock?*, for example.

Lucy finally talks Mina into taking her leave so that she can be rejoined with her husband. When Mina arrives at the castle, she finds Dracula waiting for her; he claims that Jonathan has gone away on an errand, and he plays at being the perfect host. Kretschmann is particularly good as the suave, well-mannered nobleman and Marta Gastini (born 1989) is quite good in her role. She's emblematic of the more demure and submissive type of woman of the period, whereas Lucy points to the stronger and independent-minded woman of the future. Dracula is obviously attracted to her, but Mina manages to leave the castle with her virtue—and her implicitly unspoiled blood—still intact. The attempt to affix a love story to the film is one of Argento's clumsiest missteps. Stoker's book is anything but a love story—Dracula is evil, pure and simple, and Mina is simply another "meal" for him in a long chain of victims. Why Argento decided it was necessary to dust off the "reincarnated love" angle from both the Dan Curtis-directed *Dracula* (1973) and the more recent Francis Ford Coppola hit *Bram Stoker's Dracula* is open to speculation; it could be another cynical ploy to curry audience favor—don't forget the romantic vampire approach of *Twilight* was all the rage at the time—but its inclusion feels arbitrary and forced. If there's a silver lining to be found, it's that Argento and Kretschmann don't overlook this aspect of the plot; their take on Dracula is much too dignified and austere to allow for any scenes of overbaked melodrama and weepy soul-searching.

When Mina returns to the village, she is greeted with terrible news: Lucy has succumbed to her illness. There's a touch of poetry in the image of Lucy's pale white body laid out for her friends and family to see—and this is soon trumped by one of the most beautifully realized visual flourishes in the film, when Mina visits the village Priest (Franco Ravera) in his church. The use of color and lighting is particularly accomplished here, as light streams in through the stained glass windows. For all its missteps, *Dario Argento's Dracula* at least has the benefit of some truly tasteful and exquisite cinematography courtesy of one of Argento's most gifted collaborators, Luciano Tovoli. It's a pity that the 3D technology necessitated filming in digital, but if one can get past the unusual look and texture of the format, there really is much to appreciate on a purely aesthetic level. The Priest proves to be utterly ineffectual—a common trope in the Hammer horror films so beloved by Argento—but he promises to reach out to someone who may be able to assist her.

Dracula (Thomas Kretschmann) goes in for Mina (Marta Gastini)'s... throat.

Far and away the most interesting narrative element introduced by Argento and his collaborators is the concept of the town elders being in cahoots with the Count. Argento has often toyed with political themes in his work. While it would be a mistake to think of him as a "political filmmaker" (at least in the sense that we tend to think of Elio Petri or Francesco Rossi or Damiano Damiani, for example), it would be equally unfair to suggest that socio-political commentary is completely absent in his work. In *Dario Argento's Dracula*, this element manifests itself in the theme of the council turning a blind eye to Dracula's misdeeds in exchange for the money and financial prosperity he brings to the area. It's a delicious concept and a very pointed metaphor for the idea of a corrupt aristocracy bleeding the working classes dry. In the film's most accomplished set piece, the town elders assemble in the town hall in order to discuss breaking their pact with the Count; they've decided that they've had enough of the violence he has been inflicting on them and that the time has come to double cross him. Unbeknownst to them, he is silently watching and listening in the form of a swarm of flies—suddenly the window flings open and the flies come in and transform into the Count. It's one of the better visual effects in the movie—note the way the flies on the Count's face seem to dissolve into his skin—and the ensuing scene is a great showcase as he goes from politely perturbed ("You were wrong to turn against me.") to homicidal with rage as he sprouts fangs and claws and makes mincemeat of the entire assembly. There's a touch of classic flashy Argento mayhem when the Count compels Lieutenant Delbruck (Francesco Rossini) to turn his own pistol on himself; the use of ultra-slow-motion as the bullet enters the bottom of his mouth and travels upwards is reminiscent of *Four Flies on Grey Velvet* and *The Stendhal Syndrome*, and the ensuing spray of blood and guts underlines Argento's late period fondness for overstated *Grand Guignol*. It's a fantastic sequence, energetic and stylishly realized, and the film could have used a lot more scenes like it; unfortunately, nothing which follows comes close to matching its impact.

At this point, Dr. Abraham Van Helsing (Rutger Hauer) enters the story. He is established early on as a bit off-key—he's an outsider and he comes across as odd and socially awkward. This is a major contrast to the more assertive portrayals of the character in previous versions, notably Peter Cushing in the Hammer films. It's easy to mistake this as disinterested acting on the part of Rutger Hauer (1944-2019), but a closer viewing reveals that this was clearly deliberate on his part. Van Helsing is the classic savant figure whose knowledge of the undead helps to bring the story to a successful resolution, but he is by no means an infallible or invincible antagonist to the

The late Rutger Hauer as Doctor Van Helsing.

undead; he ends up being seriously injured on more than one occasion and there is a sense of fearful trepidation about him that makes him into a more vulnerable heroic figure. The casting of Hauer is one of the film's most inspired touches—he's the first actor to be the right age and nationality to do justice to the character as written by Stoker, even if fidelity to the text is the last thing on Argento's mind.

Van Helsing visits Lucy's crypt, hoping to get to her before she returns as a vampire. Mina follows him there and they are soon surprised when Lucy arrives bearing the body of a little girl (Simona Romagnoli) to whom she used to give piano lessons. Asia is in her element as a feral vampire, but unfortunately, she barely has a chance to do anything before being set on fire by a lamp flung at her by Van Helsing. The inadequate digital effects again undermine the intended effect and Asia's exit from the film is as arbitrary as it is undignified; it would have been

Mina (Marta Gastini) and Dr. Van Helsing (Rutger Hauer) attend to Lucy's little victim (Simona Romagnoli).

Dracula (Thomas Kretschmann) goes for the jugular of a soldier (Marco Mancia).

to the film's benefit if she had been given a little more screen time in vampire mode, as she really does make a terrific impression, but alas it was not to be. Mina is understandably rattled by what has happened and Van Helsing encourages her to leave while he attends to her child victim. Argento's willingness to kill off a child character reminds one of the death of the neighbor girl in *Jenifer* and the death of Paul in *Mother of Tears*, but this time he elects for restraint as Van Helsing stakes the child off camera; her screams tell us everything we need to know.

The story continues to progress along familiar lines as Van Helsing fills in Mina on the nature of vampires, while Dracula is sent into a rage when he learns of Lucy's destruction. Tanja attempts to kill Van Helsing, but he is able to impale her with his golden crucifix; meanwhile Dracula makes his way to the Kisslinger home where

The film's most notorious and outrageous conceit: Dracula as a giant praying mantis.

he plans to abduct Mina. In the film's most infamous sequence, he adopts the guise of a giant praying mantis and kills Lucy's father, who has been standing guard outside of Mina's bedroom. The concept of Dracula taking the form of a giant insect is quirky, to say the least; maybe with the right production resources and technical expertise, it could have worked as a piece of surrealism—but with the subpar effects evident in the film, it comes off as completely laughable. Scenes such as this make it difficult to reconcile that the film is the work of the same man who directed *Deep Red* and *Inferno*. Dracula manages to take Mina from the home, thus setting the stage for the finale.

Van Helsing tries to enlist the aid of the village priest, but the priest is too frightened to do so. The frequently over-ripe dialogue comes to a memorable head here as the priest tries to justify his cowardice by shrieking, "You do not know what he is capable of! He is evil! *Evil!*" The priest finally has a change of heart and agrees to help, but his death is a foregone conclusion. Dracula confesses his love to Mina, explaining that she is the spitting image of his deceased wife, Dolingen de Gratz. She tries to resist but is ultimately placed under his spell. After finding and destroying the now-undead Jonathan, Van Helsing and the priest do battle with Renfield; the priest is killed, but Van Helsing manages to slit the madman's throat before setting his sights on the Count.

The climax is set in the forest where Dracula takes Mina to the grave of his wife, there he plans to initiate her into the ranks of the undead. He is interrupted by the arrival of Van Helsing, who tries to destroy the Count with his homemade silver bullets. Van Helsing isn't fast enough, and Dracula starts beating him savagely; in this version, it's Mina who saves the day—she snaps out of her spell and uses the gun on Dracula, who disintegrates into a pile of ashes. The decision to sideline Van Helsing and have Mina emerge as the hero of the piece is an interesting one which goes against the tradition established in most of the earlier versions—but it does tie in to the finale of the Murnau and Herzog versions, wherein Mina sacrifices herself for the greater good. Not content with a cut-and-dry finale, Argento includes a brief coda in which the ashes assemble in the air and come at the camera in the shape of a wolf; it could be a way of conveying the notion that evil cannot be obliterated, but on a more cynical level it also leaves the door open for a sequel.

There's something perversely fascinating about great directors making legitimately bad films. Argento had certainly come close to this level with *Mother of Tears* and *Giallo*, but his take on *Dracula* emerges as his one truly monumentally awful movie. It's painfully evident that this sort of Gothic milieu does not play to his strengths

Dracula (Thomas Kretschmann) and Mina (Marta Gastini) visit the grave of the Count's dead wife.

as an artist; at least with *Phantom* he managed to deliver an appealingly personal take on an old chestnut—here it's as if he is too disengaged to be bothered. The script is a mess, the performances are largely inadequate, and the emphasis on elaborate visual effects is positively suicidal. Without the appropriate resources to realize the outlandish ideas, they come off as inept and unintentionally funny. So much of the film feels utterly uninspired, as if Argento simply couldn't find a way of putting his stamp on the material.

That's not to say that the film is utterly without merit. Kretschmann, Hauer, and Gastini all deliver solid performances. Tovoli's cinematography is occasionally brilliant; the unforgiving nature of the digital medium takes some getting used to, but some of the images (notably the castle interiors and the nighttime exteriors) really are breathtaking. Argento's flair for the medium comes through in a few sequences—notably the confrontation between the Count and the town elders—

Jonathan (Unax Ugalde) goes over to the dark side.

and this is enough to confirm that, given the right material, he is still capable of delivering the goods.

Unfortunately, *Dario Argento's Dracula* is not a feather in Dario's cap; one can only hope that if he manages to get another project off the ground, it's a film he feels real passion for. In promoting the picture he put on a positive face and said that it was a story he had long wanted to bring to the screen—but the truth is, this is absolutely not the sort of film he would have consented to make when his career was in better shape. While it allowed him the opportunity to experiment with 3D (surely his major incentive in accepting the proposal), the film sees him squandering his unique talents and abilities

The crew prepares for the scene in which Tanja (Miriam Giovanelli) returns from the dead.

Dario and Marta Gastini on the set of *Dario Argento's Dracula*.

Dario and Asia attend the premiere of *Dario Argento's Dracula* at the Cannes Film Festival, 2012.

on a piece of subject matter for which he has very little feeling. The steady decline evident in his 21st century output finally reached critical mass with the epic triple fail of *Mother of Tears*, *Giallo*, and *Dario Argento's Dracula*; if there is to be more as Dario enters his 80s, hopefully it will do something to repair the bad will generated by these epic misfires.

Dario Argento's Dracula was selected for inclusion in the 2012 Cannes Film Festival—not that it would be in competition, but it would nevertheless be given a special premiere screening in the hopes of attracting buyers. The screening took place on May 19, 2012, and like the Cannes screening of *Mother of Tears* which preceded it, it was beset with technical woes; once the film finally finished, the audience showed no enthusiasm whatsoever. Clearly the film was in danger—and yet, it managed to secure better theatrical exposure than most of his recent films. Bolero Film put it out in Italy on November 22, 2012, while the Spanish release through Filmax came even earlier on November 9. IFC Films acquired the film for the American market, and sensing midnight movie status, they elected to give it a brief theatrical run. The results were pretty much disastrous across the board. In the U.S., for example, it made a grand total of $8,139—$3,085 of which was culled from the opening weekend. And in Italy, it became Dario's second film in a row to fail to make the top 100 at the Italian box office—the difference being that the problem-plagued *Giallo* had been dumped and given very little exposure, whereas *Dario Argento's Dracula* was an obvious bid at currying public favor. Fortunately for everybody involved, the video sales helped somewhat, but *Dracula* was fated to become Dario's biggest bomb to date.

The critics had a field day trashing it. David Rooney in *The Hollywood Reporter* described it as "a tired rehash," and lamented the "hilarious cheesy score" and "so-so digital effects."[7] Peter Sobczynski, of Roger Ebert.com, awarded it two out of five stars and wrote:

> From a technical standpoint, there are impressive contributions from two longtime collaborators, cinematographer Luciano Tovoli and composer Claudio Simonetti, and the retro production design is equally striking. However, Argento wastes their considerable efforts on a story that he never seems especially interested in telling in the first place. [...] Kretschmann is perhaps the least terrifying version of *Dracula* to come along since Leslie Nielsen, Gastini and Giovanelli are pretty blanks (though the latter will no doubt become a favorite of followers of Mr. Skin), and Ugalde seems

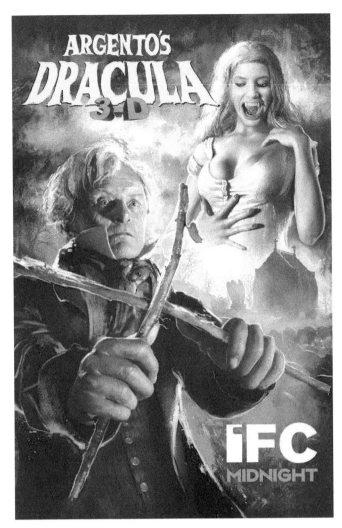

U.S. poster art, with heavy-duty emphasis on Hammer; artwork by Anthony Palumbo.

to have based his performance on the one that Keanu Reeves almost gave in *Bram Stoker's Dracula* and fails to live up to those standards. […] I found myself wondering why Argento didn't choose to properly exploit his daughter's alluringly feral persona by simply casting her as Dracula and going from there.[8]

And *Variety*'s Rob Nelson described the film as "a near-two-hour joke that ought to have been funnier."[9] Rather remarkably, in light of such overwhelming negativity, it was actually nominated for the Audience Choice Award at the Chicago International Film Festival in 2013, but it lost out to David Frankel's *One Chance*; that being said, it appears as if every film entered into the competition (including the eventual Best Picture winner at the 2014 Academy Awards, Steve McQueen's *12 Years a Slave*) were given a nomination in that category.

Dario Argento's Dracula did absolutely nothing to restore Argento's luster in the eyes of his fan base. Many fans insisted upon writing him off as "washed up," though inevitably there is always the chance that the *maestro* may return to form if the right project were to come along. That may well be the equivalent to whistling past the graveyard, perhaps, but given his impressive résumé, it would take more than a few bad pictures to truly diminish Dario's standing in genre cinema history.

Notes:
[1] https://www.theguardian.com/film/2011/jul/17/giallo-unknown-country-kermode-dvd
[2] https://variety.com/2009/film/markets-festivals/giallo-1200474916/
[3] https://bloody-disgusting.com/news/21392/george-romero-on-why-he-wont-be-directing-deep-red-3-d-remake/
[4] Jones, Alan, *Dario Argento: The Man, the Myths & the Magic* (Godalming: FAB Press, 2012), p. 383.
[5] Ibid, p. 385.
[6] Ibid, p. 373.
[7] https://www.hollywoodreporter.com/review/dario-argento-dracula-3d-cannes-326991
[8] https://www.rogerebert.com/reviews/dracula-3d-2013
[9] https://variety.com/2012/film/markets-festivals/dario-argentos-dracula-117947598/

International sales flyer for *Dario Argento's Dracula*.

The Unsane Cinema of Dario Argento

Chapter Twenty-Four: Reflections in a *Giallo* Eye

The years following *Dario Argento's Dracula* have seen a mixture of heartache and potential projects vanishing into thin air. On a personal level, he suffered a major loss on March 14, 2013, when his mother Elda passed away. "My mother left us gradually. About 90 years old, she had lots of difficulties in simply moving around, but her last moments were quiet. It became much worse in the last two or three weeks, when first she stopped talking, and then she stopped eating. When I came to visit her, she barely recognized me; she just stared at me with hostility. It was clear that the end was approaching. The nurse told the family that she was not in pain, so we all met at her deathbed: Floriana, Claudio, and myself. On March 14, 2013, she stopped breathing. She passed at home, quietly, close to her children."[1]

Dario's relationship with Elda had always been complex and riddled with mixed emotions, but they had become closer after Salvatore's death in 1987. It was Elda's background in photography which made a vivid impression on Dario as a child and influenced his aesthetic sensibility; they may have been opposed in many areas, including politics, but he was aware of what a vital role she had played in his life and he took the loss hard. Dario was already closing in on his 73rd birthday, but it didn't matter; to suddenly find himself without a parent shook him badly. "Every day in this world, people lose their parents. Parents are not eternal, they usually go before their children. Their passing should be accepted from a rational point of view. But it is painful, no matter how old you are."[2] Dario himself had a checkered past when it came to parenting, but he continued to be on good terms with Fiore—and his next bit of drama with Asia was still off in the distance. He also found some solace in his new role as grandfather, doting on Asia's children whenever she brought them around to see him.

In September 2014, Dario's friend and collaborator Luigi Cozzi set out to direct his first feature film in nearly 30 years: *Blood on Méliès' Moon*. Cozzi got quite a few of his friends in the Italian film scene to do cameos and naturally he couldn't resist extending an offer to Argento, as well. On Halloween night of 2014, when Argento stopped by the "Profondo Rosso" shop to meet with fans and sign copies of his newly-released autobiography, he gave Cozzi some time and did a small cameo appearance for the film. Cozzi would continue to tinker with *Blood on Méliès' Moon* until February 2016, at which point he finally decided he had enough material to assemble the picture; it was presented at various film festivals (including the Brussels International Fantastic Film Festival in Belgium and the Arbertoir Horror Festival in the U.K.) throughout 2016. It was warmly received at the Sitges Film Festival in 2016, where it inspired a standing ovation. Kim Newman caught the film at the Trieste Science+Fiction Festival and shared his thoughts on his blog: "I saw only the latest cut (111 minutes) of Luigi Cozzi's bizarre, epic semi-home movie, which has been screened in longer and shorter versions. I'm assuming it's finished, but wouldn't be surprised if the genial *auteur* enthusiast keeps tinkering with it for years. A sort of mock-documentary, it offers some parallels with the much tauter *Fury of the Demon* (2016) by positing a connection between a fragment of a lost Georges Méliès movie and a magical attempt to avert an impending asteroid apocalypse. [...] It's even further off the mainstream path than *The Black Cat* (1989), Cozzi's last completed feature."[3]

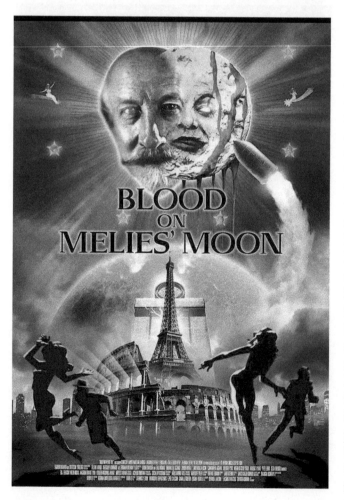

Poster art for Luigi Cozzi's return to directing; artist unknown.

Cover for the Italian DVD release of *Macbeth*.

The killing of Duncan allowed Dario to restage an iconic image from *Deep Red*.

With no film work on the plate, Dario accepted an offer from the Teatro Coccia in Novara to stage his first proper opera as part of their 2013-2014 season. The selection of Verdi's *Macbeth* surely struck a special nerve with Dario, as it was the very same opera he had featured in *Opera* nearly 30 years earlier. He approached the assignment with vigor and enthusiasm, determined to bring his trademarked violent imagery to the proceedings; one violent set piece even manages to quote one of the murders from *Deep Red*. The production was staged in October 2013 and while critical response was mixed, it certainly went over better than most of his recent film productions. One of the performances was even captured on video and subsequently was made available on Blu-ray, thus allowing the diehard fans a chance to see an honest-to-goodness Argento opera. Argento subsequently staged the opera again at the Teatro Verdi in Pisa in late March 2015.

Dario enjoyed the experience of staging *Macbeth*, and he would follow it up with other engagements in a similar vein. In early 2015, he was approached by the Teatro Carlo Felice in Genoa with another opera: Gaetano Donizetti's *Lucia di Lammermoor*. The show opened to strong notices in February 2015. Then in October 2017, he staged a very pared down and minimalist performance of *Salomè* by Giuseppe Magrino at the Basilica Superiore di San Francesco in Assisi, Umbria; compared to the more elaborate productions of *Macbeth* and *Lucia di Lammermoor*, it lacked in spectacle, but Dario again found himself energized by the process of staging a live performance.

The three witches as envisioned by Dario.

Dario appears on stage to take a bow with the cast.

The Unsane Cinema of Dario Argento

Cover for the Italian edition of Dario's memoirs.

In the midst of the opera work, Argento also found time to pen his memoirs. *Paura* was released in time for Halloween in 2014 and it allowed Argento a chance to talk about his life in candid terms. The book is not written from the perspective of a man who is ready to hang it all up, however; if anything, he makes it abundantly clear that he still has stories he wants to tell. Even so, it's clear from reading it that he realizes that the "golden period" is over and that the more lavish lifestyle he had lived as a young man had been overtaken, as is so often the case in old age, by quiet and contemplation. "For a few years now, I have lived alone about Corso Trieste in a flat. I frequently meet a person who is very important to me. Thanks to her I feel serene, and I am thankful every day. Whenever I can, I continue to travel or meet my daughters. Fiore stopped the fashion business and is now into *grande cuisine* […] Asia continues to pursue her career in the cinema. Each of them thinks that I love the other more, but I loved them both to my fullest. I accomplished myself through them, and to know that they found their own ways makes me very happy."[4]

It all hasn't been opera and meditation, however. In June 2014, Argento was announced as the director of an upcoming project titled *The Sandman*. Written by David Tully and based on the classic horror story by E.T.A. Hoffmann, it was to have been a Canadian/German co-production between KCUS Productions and Shivertownroad Films. The project was one of many announced as part of a slate of projects through the Frontières International Co-Production Market. An official website was launched for the film at thesandmanfilm.com—where the story was outlined thus: "*The Sandman* tells the story of a young student in the city who struggles to forget his childhood trauma at the hands of the serial killer dubbed 'The Sandman.' As a child the student killed The Sandman years ago, on Christmas Eve, after witnessing the murder of his mother. This memory is repressed until he sees the beautiful young woman who lives in the apartment across the way dying at the hands of that same masked killer. We follow our protagonist to find out who is the real killer. This is a story of voyeurism and obsession and is a direct homage to *giallo* films of the past."

All told, it smacked a bit of *Giallo*, with Argento being recruited to direct a film in the Argento style which originated in the hands of others. Rock legend Iggy Pop was signed to play the title character and an Indiegogo campaign was launched online in October 2014 to help raise added funding for the picture. Close to $200 grand was raised, and then… crickets. In an interview with *Indiewire* in August 2016, Dario said, "Iggy Pop keeps asking, 'How long do we have to wait on this film?' Honestly it's not my fault. This film is a co-production between many different producers in different countries. They apparently can't agree on a number of different things, including where to shoot, locations, things like that. It goes on and on. I know it's been dragging on.

Promotional teaser art for the ill-fated *The Sandman*; artist unknown.

Time goes by and they haven't reached an agreement. I must say that I myself have been thinking about some other projects in the meantime. I still need to work on them, think about them."[5] To date, *The Sandman* remains unproduced; perhaps tellingly, the film's official website now lists the movie as "Dario Argento presents *The Sandman*," suggesting that, if it ever does get off the ground, Argento may not be serving in a directorial capacity after all.

In April 2015, the French company Atlantique Productions and the Italian company Cattleya announced a plan to make a TV series based around *Suspiria*. The idea was to use Thomas De Quincey's writings as the inspiration for a 12-part series titled *Suspiria de Profundis*. As outlined by Nancy Tartaglione, "De Quincey is the main character, styled as a new Sherlock Holmes, the producing partners say. The story will explore psychological fantasies of evil and attempt to solve fearful mysteries. It will be set in London and Rome between the end of the 19th and the beginning of the 20th centuries."[6] Argento was not slated to direct or write the series, but his name was attached as an artistic supervisor; the planned series eventually stalled. Whether audiences would have been receptive to the concept of a now-obscure 19th century writer solving occult mysteries is open to speculation.

That wasn't the end of the road where *Suspiria* was involved. The long-gestating David Gordon Green remake was officially dead by 2013, but it refused to stay buried. Argento was less than thrilled when it was announced the Luca Guadagnino (born 1971), the acclaimed *auteur* responsible for *A Bigger Splash* (2015) and *Call Me by Your Name* (2017), was going to make his own remake of *Suspiria*.

Guadagnino formally announced the project at the Venice Film Festival in September 2015 and Argento let it be known to whoever would listen that he was opposed to the idea. "What's really absurd—really unbelievable—is that I have never, ever been asked about it. I mean, I never got a call or anything, asking me about casting, locations, whatever. I know nothing about this project except what I read in the papers. I repeat: I have never, ever been asked about it. […] But honestly, I do think it would be better if it wasn't remade."[7] Matters weren't helped when Guadagnino's screenwriter, David Kajganich, admitted that he wasn't a fan of the original movie. "I'm not a fan of the original *Suspiria*, to be honest. I'm a fan of it as an art piece, but as a narrative, it makes almost no sense."[8] While it's easy to sympathize with Argento's frustration over not being involved in the process of remaking his most famous film, the outraged indignation voiced by the fan community was more than a little excessive.

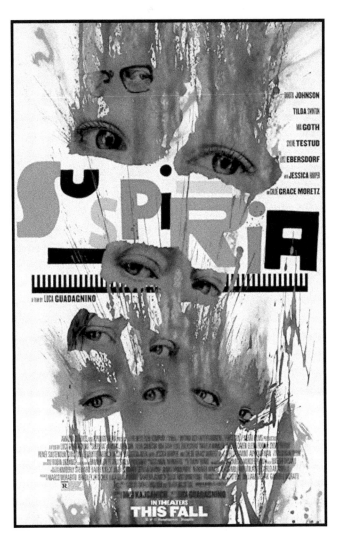

Poster for Luca Guadagnino's ambitious remake of *Suspiria*; **artist unknown.**

Regardless, Guadagnino was undaunted by the potshots Argento and the fans took at him and he pushed ahead with the project anyway. Filming commenced on Halloween of 2016 and lasted until early March 2017. With a budget of $20 million and a trendy cast headed by Tilda Swinton and Dakota Johnson, Guadagnino's *Suspiria* had a lot more going for it than any of Argento's own recent films; no doubt that was the deepest cut of all, even if he never vocalized it.

The controversy among the fan base generated considerable word of mouth and the film finally emerged, following a lengthy post-production process, at the Venice Film Festival in September 2018. Word of mouth was mixed, but not in the way that, say, word of mouth had been mixed with regards to *Mother of Tears*; most of the critics of Argento's film agreed that it was a bit of a fiasco, but it managed to coast by on sheer audacity. By contrast, Guadagnino's film was obviously very well-crafted and serious in intent, the work of a still vital *auteur*, yet it went so far astray from Argento and Nicolodi's original concept that it left people confused.

Avant garde imagery in the remake of *Suspiria*.

Amazon provided the film with a limited theatrical release in time for Halloween of 2018, while the Italian theatrical release was set for January 2019. Argento remained ambivalent about the entire enterprise, but it arguably drew more positive attention to him and his cinematic legacy than most of his own recent films had done. Guadagnino made sure to credit both Argento and Nicolodi for their original screenplay, and Dario was given a token "associate producer" credit, though as already noted, he had absolutely nothing to do with the picture whatsoever.

The new version follows the same basic template established by Argento and Nicolodi, but it is developed in a very different way. This is confirmed by the fact that it runs nearly an hour longer than the original film. Set in Berlin in 1977, it begins with Pat Hingle (Chloë Grace Moretz) making a visit to her psychiatrist, Dr. Klemper (Tilda Swinton, disguised in lots of prosthetics and billed as Lutz Ebersdorf), where she has a terrifying meltdown over pressures at the Tanz Dance Academy. Pat disappears but is subsequently accused of being involved in the terrorist activities which are rocking Berlin during the Baader-Meinhof period. Susie Bannion (Dakota Johnson) arrives from America just in time to take Pat's place, and she makes a vivid impression on Madame Blanc (Swinton, again) who grants her admission to her program owing to her extraordinary dancing skills. Strange events begin to unfold and Susie's friend Sara (Mia Goth) comes to believe that witchcraft is being practiced there behind closed doors. Susie discovers extraordinary powers within herself in a surprising variation on the film's original climax.

Few horror films of the past 20 years have been as profoundly polarizing as Guadagnino's *Suspiria*. Beginning with the fact that Argento was openly opposed to it being made in the first place, many fans were ready to attack the film sight unseen. Sooner than deliver a carbon copy of the film Dario had made—which would have been an exercise in futility—Guadagnino elected to take the material in a radical new direction. The look of the film is deliberately drab, but it is by no means aesthetically displeasing; the visual scheme suits this fresh take on the material, and the gradual introduction of vivid reds is highly appropriate given the slow burn approach which builds to a bloody and brutal climax.

Early on, a great deal of attention was generated by a particularly brutal sequence involving the character of Olga (Elena Fokina). The scene in question is beautifully staged by Guadagnino and expertly edited by Argento's old collaborator Walter Fasano, but whether it would impress a hardcore horror audience in the same way that it affected the more genteel crowd who generally embrace works by directors like Guadagnino is open to speculation. Certainly nothing in the film is as over the top as the violence seen in late period Argento works like *Jenifer*, *Pelts*, and *Mother of Tears*—but the scene packs more of a wallop because it takes place in a more controlled environment; the "anything goes" approach

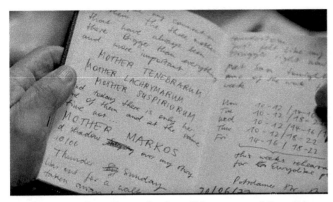

A cryptic clue about the horrible secret of *Suspiria*.

adopted by Argento in much of his later work tends to be a bit broad and tongue-in-cheek, whereas the scene in *Suspiria* is legitimately distressing because of the emphasis on the pain being suffered by the character.

Though imperfect—at two-and-a-half hours, it's much too long, and the more grotesque elements of the finale don't quite gel with the austere tone of the rest of the picture; additionally the casting of Swinton in multiple roles comes off like an obnoxious stunt, though she certainly gives a good account of herself as Madame Blanc—it is a far more worthy and dignified continuation of the mythology established by Argento and Nicolodi than *Mother of Tears* had been. That said, it's easy to understand why so many critics were nonplussed by the end result: with its deliberate pacing and odd combination of the art-house and the grindhouse, it simply isn't a movie that was designed to be an "audience pleaser."

2017 marked a period of new pain and controversy for the Argento clan when Asia told Ronan Farrow in an interview with the *New Yorker* that she had been raped by disgraced movie mogul Harvey Weinstein in 1997. Weinstein, the Oscar-winning producer of such hits as Quentin Tarantino's *Pulp Fiction* (1994) and Martin Scorsese's *Gangs of New York* (2002), was already in the midst of some pretty heavy-duty accusations by various women accusing him of improper conduct and sexual assault. Asia threw her hat into the ring and became a very visible and outspoken part of the #metoo and #timesup movements, which were designed to draw attention to years and years of unspoken misuse of power by male authority figures. The decidedly conservative and chauvinistic Italian press had long held a condescending attitude towards Asia thanks to her "I don't give a fuck what you think about me" attitude, and they wasted no time lobbing unkind comments in her direction, even going so far as to blame her for what had happened to her. The experience prompted her to move, for a time, to Germany. Dario spoke up on her behalf when the topic was broached to him but generally did his best to keep a low profile as the media circus continued to play itself out.

In June 2018, Asia suffered a major loss when her boyfriend, the celebrity chef, Anthony Bourdain committed suicide at the age of 61. Bourdain had long suffered from depression, though he and Asia, who began dating in 2016, reportedly had a loving relationship. Things reached critical mass in August 2018, when *The New York Times* published an article in which the actor Jimmy Bennett (who had appeared with Asia as her on-screen son in *The Heart is Deceitful Above All Things*) alleged that Asia sexually assaulted him when he was only 17 years old. Asia denied the allegations but the fall-out was immediate; it was alleged that she paid Bennett hush money to keep the story from reaching the press, and even her friend Rose McGowan, another abuse survivor and perhaps the most visible member of the #metoo movement, lashed out against her, doing irreparable harm to their friendship. In an interview with *La Stampa*, Dario theorized that Weinstein was somehow responsible for these allegations. "I'm only making assumptions, but certainly, since Asia decided to make her accusation there have been violent reactions, even in Italy, by politicians. […] Everything that is happening puts me in a negative state of mind, it is a sequence of unpleasant events."[9] Asia, who was then lined up to serve as a celebrity judge on the popular TV show *X Factor Italy*, was fired from her gig; she was replaced by the musician Lodo Guenzi of the group *Lo stato sociale*. Precisely what will happen with Asia's career once the dust settles is open to speculation, but in the meantime she has continued her acting career and she also plans to continue with her new passion: directing.

Asia Argento stars in the forthcoming *Sans Soleil*, a sci-fi drama directed by Banu Akseki now in post-production.

The Unsane Cinema of Dario Argento

In the midst of all this family turmoil, Dario kept his creative juices going by accepting an offer to pen the story for the latest issue of *Dylan Dog*. Created by Tiziano Sclavi (born 1953), the comic first appeared in October 1986 and it has earned a loyal following. It served as the inspiration for Michele Soavi's *Dellamorte Dellamore/Cemetery Man* (1993), so it seems only too fitting that Argento should also become a participant in Sclavi's universe. Titled *Profondo Nero*, the Argento-written issue (#383) went on sale in July 2018, and it proved to be more of a popular success than any of his recent forays into the cinema.

At the time of the writing of this book, Dario has teased that he is looking to develop a new *giallo* for the cinema; if that falls through, it could always end up being made on a smaller scale for television. In March 2019, he also indicated that he is working on a film to be "divided into eight episodes." Whether that indicates that it will take the form of a serial or a self-contained anthology is open to speculation. If it comes to pass, the as-yet-untitled project is to be distributed via Netflix or Amazon Italy.[10]

The night of March 26 2019 also saw Dario being feted at the prestigious David di Donatello awards—essentially, the Italian equivalent to the Academy Awards. Argento was awarded a "Special David" for his contribution to the cinema; actress Uma Thurman (*Pulp*

Dario is feted at the David di Donatello Awards on March 26, 2019.

Fiction, 1994) and set decorator Francesca Lo Schiavo (*Gangs of New York*, 2002) were also honored. Dario received a well-deserved standing ovation and during the course of his good-natured acceptance speech, he reminded everybody that he was never once nominated for a David during the course of his career—but that this honor was a step in the right direction.[11]

Late March 2019 also saw Argento attaching his name to a rather unusual project: a video game. Clod Studio collaborated with Dario in developing a new game titled *Dreadful Bond*. A Kickstarter was established to bring the project to fruition and early reaction to the trailer created to promote it has been generally positive. Argento is credited as "artistic director" and he appears to have enjoyed developing the narrative for the game, which revolves around a mysterious mansion with a violent history.[12] In fact, this is not Dario's first foray into the world of gaming: he also voiced the character of Doctor Kyne in the Italian version of the video game *Dead Space*.

In late August 2019, Dario attended *Frightfest* in London, where he was interviewed by his old friend/biographer, Alan Jones. As always a gracious and amusing interviewee, Dario reflected on his career—but the evening wasn't all about looking towards the past. He confirmed to the crowd that he is planning his next film, and that it would be a *giallo*—but not just any *giallo*. Evidently the legal issues surrounding his screenplay *Occhiali neri* ("Dark Glasses") have at last been resolved, and he is attempting to finally bring the project to the screen. Hopefully it comes to pass as it remains "the one that got away" among the various projects he was most keen to realize.

On October 11, *Variety* also reported that Dario is set to direct a TV series titled *Longinus* for BIM Production and Publispei. Described as Argento's "most ambitious TV project," it is supposed to deal with a series of murders which are "suspended between the real and the supernatural." As reported by *Variety*, "the title of the

Cover for issue #383 of *Dylan Dog*, written by Dario Argento.

Promotional teaser for Dario's long-awaited film *Occhiali neri*—its future remains uncertain.

series appears to reference the name given to the Roman soldier who pierced the side of the crucified Jesus with a lance to make sure that Jesus was dead."[13] It's all a bit vague and ambiguous at this stage, but if it comes to be, the series is being pitched to the international market.

Through the latter stages of 2019 and into the early months of 2020, Dario was actively involved in preproduction on the long-awaited *Occhiali neri*. Rumors circulated online that the group Daft Punk was set to compose the score, though the producers subsequently denied this.[14] To photograph the film, Argento sought out his old friend and collaborator Luciano Tovoli. Asia was once again enlisted to appear, though in early May 2020 it was announced online that Stacy Martin (*Nymphomaniac*, 2013) had been signed to play the lead.[15] Despite being absent from the screen for the better part of a decade, it finally seemed as if Dario was poised to realize his dream project. Unfortunately the emergence of a real-life horror story—the COVID-19 pandemic—put the brakes on the project, but Argento and the producers remain optimistic that conditions may improve sufficiently to allow the film to move forward by October 2020. Time will tell.

Now that he's poised to enter his 80s, the grand old man of Italian horror is showing no signs of wanting to retire. As such it seems only fitting to allow him the final word: "I'll stop making films when I no longer have anything to say—but that moment is still far away."[16]

Notes:
1. Argento, Dario, *Peur* (France: Rouge Profond, 2018), p. 346.
2. Ibid.
3. https://johnnyalucard.com/2016/11/06/trieste-sf-festival-review-blood-on-melies-moon/
4. Argento, Dario, *Peur* (France: Rouge Profond, 2018), p. 353.
5. https://www.indiewire.com/2016/08/dario-argento-interview-suspira-remake-2016-locarno-film-festival-1201714247/
6. https://deadline.com/2015/04/django-suspiria-drama-series-atlantique-cattleya-dario-argento-miptv-1201406287/
7. https://www.indiewire.com/2016/08/dario-argento-interview-suspira-remake-2016-locarno-film-festival-1201714247/
8. https://www.dreadcentral.com/news/281968/suspiria-remake-screenwriter-doesnt-like-argentos-original-film/
9. https://www.hollywoodreporter.com/news/dario-argento-defends-daughter-asia-sexual-assault-allegations-1136625
10. https://bloody-disgusting.com/movie/3550366/dario-argentos-next-project-film-divided-eight-episodes/
11. https://variety.com/2019/film/news/matteo-garrone-dogman-big-winner-italy-david-di-donatello-awards-1203174521/
12. https://bloody-disgusting.com/video-games/3552574/trailer-dario-argento-artistic-director-upcoming-video-game-dreadful-bond/
13. https://variety.com/2019/tv/global/dario-argento-direct-horror-series-longinus-suspiria-1203367191/
14. https://www.screendaily.com/news/dario-argento-producers-deny-reports-daft-punk-to-score-dark-glasses/5149383.article
15. https://www.quotidiano.net/magazine/dario-argento-coronavirus-1.533975
16. Argento, Dario, *Peur* (France: Rouge Profond, 2018), p. 349.

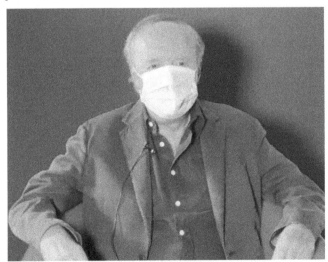

Dario joined the rest of the world in a real-life horror story: the COVID-19 pandemic.

Chapter Twenty-Five: Argento's Legacy—A Collection of Essays

The Witches and the One Percent—The Political Subtext of Dario Argento's films, 1971-1980
by Jennifer Kellow-Fiorini

After watching an uncut Italian print of *Suspiria* in New York City this past summer, I turned to two young guys sitting next to me and I asked them what they thought of it. Immediately, they said, "The witches—they're a symbol of the one percent!" Precisely my thoughts during the same screening. In *all* the books and essays I have read on this film, and there have been many, no one ever makes this connection—they never really get past the witches/fairy tale thing. There are those who would argue that Argento is essentially an apolitical filmmaker, but politics have always been pervasive in Italy, so to suggest that the politics of wealth and the capitalistic acquisition of money and power (money being a vehicle of power and vice versa) have some bearing on aspects of Argento's work seems very reasonable. And these first-time viewers in their 20s, got this message immediately. It begs the questions, why would an American audience pick up on this idea now? And, is Argento an apolitical filmmaker, as many have suggested? To address these questions, I needed to look further into interviews with the director about his life, artistic influences, his films leading up to *Suspiria*, and Italian culture at the time he created these films.

In Italian cinema class, our professor discussed how directors actively making films during the Second World War, and those born during that time, made frequent inferences in their films about political corruption. Much of this kind of commentary goes unnoticed by those outside of Italian culture. Italy's transformation after the war happened very quickly—the fastest of any country to date after a world war—and too much, too soon gave rise to pervasive corruption. Italy's inability to ever really become "unified"—it has only been a unified country in the technical sense for 150 years—also didn't help. When studying Argento's work, I found many references to money, greed, and corruption in his films.

The end of the Second World War brought the rise of neorealism in both literature and cinema in Italy. For 20 years Italians had lived under Fascist dictatorship, which meant that anyone living and working in Italy would have done so under the eye of the Fascist party. Films made during this period were anti-Hollywood. The government tried, and ultimately failed, to create a uniquely Italian and Fascist culture by banning American cinema and putting money into Italian films where they could control the messages. Many directors, who would become neorealist filmmakers, had been working under the Fascist party. As the Second World War came to a close, those directors sought to capture the realities of post-war Italy and the problems the country and its people faced. With the Fascists gone, they had more freedom but little or no money with which to make films, and it was out of financial necessity that they took their cameras to the streets and utilized their surroundings to tell Italian stories. Both novelists and directors in the post-war era sought to create a new literary and cinematographic language that would allow them to deal poetically with the problems of the times they were living in. Vittorio De Sica (*Ladri di biciclette/Bicycle Thieves*) stated that his neorealist films reflected "Reality transposed into the world of poetry." This was the generation of *auteurs* would successfully give way to the next generation of Italian filmmakers, including Dario Argento.

It wasn't until the birth of the Spaghetti Western and the sword and sandal, or *peplum* films, of post-war Italy in the late 1950s and early 1960s that genre films with a distinctly Italian style became popular. Prior to this period such films were rare in Italy, but as the Italian movie industry hit its peak, Italian filmmakers wanted to break into the international market. In order to get this kind of distribution, most countries needed American financers, which meant they had to make films that held some appeal to American audiences while retaining their own cultural identity. In the mid-1960s, Italy's film industry was second only to Hollywood, and with the downturn of the Hollywood studio system, American money suddenly became available to Italy. This would lay the groundwork for the enormous popularity of genre films in Italy. They would make their way to the Italian market with great success, leading directors to experiment with other genres such as police crime thrillers, or *poliziottesco*, and the *giallo*.

Though Riccardo Freda and Mario Bava are credited with ushering the *giallo* from the pages of books to the medium of film we know today, the popularity of *giallo* would really take off in 1970. Italy did not make many horror films, at least as Italians define horror. The focus of *giallo* films is serial killers with all manner of psychological and sexual problems, but they are not otherworldly creatures such as vampires, werewolves, or zombies. This is a very crucial distinction that is usually passed over by critics either because many *giallo* directors also made horror films or because, for an American audience, *giallo* falls somewhere between the slasher film and the thriller. In fact, between 1958 and 1970, it is important to note that horror films made up only one percent of the films made in Italy. Having film roots in neorealism, Italian filmmakers seem to feel more at home depicting the monstrous side of humanity rather than allowing a supernatural being to take the blame for the evil in the world. They often refer to a serial killer in the news as "mostro" when not using the English term "serial killer."

Gialli usually have an outsider trying to catch the killer—the opposite of the police crime dramas created in the same era. Police thrillers focused on corruption within the police department, the mafia, and even in government. In a *giallo* film, it is usually an outsider rather than a detective attempting to solve a crime because the police, as portrayed in these films, were ineffective, lazy, and/or corrupt.

In Bava's 1970 *giallo Hatchet for the Honeymoon* (*Il rosso segno della follia*), for example, psychopathic killer John Harrington diverts the cops by showing them a scene from the director's own film, *Black Sabbath* (*I tre volti della paura*, 1963), playing on Harrington's television as explanation for the screams that rouse the officers, while his wife's freshly-hacked body succumbs to death just out of sight. Inspector Russell asks Harrington, "So you like horror films?" The inspector goes on to answer his own question: "I don't find them very entertaining. I keep thinking reality is more terrifying than fiction." The horror film playing on the television is from the segment "I Wurdulak," a folk tale about vampires in Eastern Europe. It's no coincidence that this is the only story in the anthology that is completely supernatural, with no real-life killer at its core. When you understand this cultural proclivity, it becomes obvious that Bava is warning the audience not to invest fear in make-believe monsters, while failing to see the real monsters, like Harrington, hiding in plain sight. Another example of the real-life monster idea can be found in the horror film *Castle of Blood* (*Danza macabra*, 1964) directed by Sergio Corbucci and Antonio Margheriti. The film opens with a young journalist named Alan Foster conversing with none other than American author Edgar Allan Poe in a tavern. Foster is offered a wager to stay the night in a haunted castle. He tells Poe that he respects his genius, but "Nobody ever returns from the dead as in your stories, I admit that I'm afraid, yet I'm not afraid of the dead—it's the living, oh yes, my fear is of the living—they're the ones who can harm us, you must agree." These two examples show that the classic American

Mario Bava's *Hatchet for the Honeymoon* offers a grimly comic take on *giallo* tropes; artwork by EB.

horror film wasn't always a comfortable cultural fit for Italians. There were far too many real-life monsters that were considered much scarier.

Genre films in general are typically thought of as pure throwaway entertainment, and this is possibly a big reason that references of political or social critique in Argento's films have gone unnoticed. Americans in particular have a tendency to view foreign-made genre films as if they exist only in the context of American films. Maitland McDonagh touches on this in her book *Broken*

The Unsane Cinema of Dario Argento

Mirrors/Broken Minds: The Dark Dreams of Dario Argento. McDonagh cites a review by Richard Cohen in *Women's Wear*: "It is apparently time for Italian filmmakers to turn their knock-off talents to the crime-melodrama done in the fashion of Alfred Hitchcock ... Argento gets in a lot of the little touches but, like the Italian makers of Westerns, he gets them all cockeyed." She goes on to assert the obvious problems with this statement. The first being that Hitchcock is himself a foreign director who worked in his native Britain making thrillers for 20 years before coming to America. The second is the assumption that "there is only one right way to make movies, and that's the way we make them in America." Who's to say that a thriller made in a country outside of America should be held to an American standard? Audiences outside of Italy miss the critique on society that gives depth to these films because it is specific to Italian culture at the time the films were made. For Italians, including social critique in their films, a holdover from the powerful influence of post-war neo-realism, is simply a part of their culture.

In Peter Bondanella's book, *A History of Italian Cinema*, he writes, "Other film genres (the *Commedia all'italliana*, the Spaghetti Western, even the greatest art films of the time) quite often contained political or ideological messages at least as subtext, if not their primary purpose, as did more avowedly engaged works of art. The frequent thematic emphasis on the relationships of fathers and sons quite obviously treated questions of authority or rebellion that linked to current events. In general, most of these works approached the Italian state and its institutions (schools, the police, the bureaucracy, the judiciary) with negative opinions ranging from harsh criticism to outright rejection. Regardless of their specific ideological position or their individual style, these films remained true to the essential heritage of Italian neorealism: they cast a critical eye on the society that the films reflected, and in so doing, broadened the very idea of the cinema as 'entertainment.' This created a civic function for the movies in Italy, defining film as a public forum in which hotly debated social issues could be communicated through artistic means in an often uncomfortable but ultimately healthy marriage of convenience."

It is in Argento's second film, *The Cat O'Nine Tails*, that he first casts a critical eye on a corrupt upper class and various social/political institutions. Although Argento expressed disappointment with this film, he effectively uses the story line to take jabs at contemporary society. While this is not the main point of the film, once you notice this, it is hard to ignore, especially because of the consistency in which political and cultural criticisms appear in his body of work created between 1970 and 1982. Because *The Cat O'Nine Tails* contains many of these reoccurring critiques, I will refer to this film in more depth and point out some of the more obvious scenes from Argento's other films of this period.

A genetic research lab called the Terzi Institute is the backdrop of *The Cat O'Nine Tails*. In keeping with *giallo* tradition, wealth, espionage, and government secrets are a fertile breeding ground for a corrupt cast of characters. Also traditional are its three amateur sleuths—Franco Arnò, a blind man, his 10-year-old niece, Lori, and a reporter named Giordani. Professor Terzi runs a government research program dealing with genetics, in particular pinpointing an XYY chromosome said to denote criminal tendencies in humans. When reporter Giordani comes to the institute to cover a robbery committed in the film's opening, he asks another reporter what goes on at the institute. The man replies, "genetic research, they even perform those pre-matrimonial examinations for people with cash who want to keep their offspring of high quality." In this early scene, Argento makes it a point to let the audience know that of course the wealthy will be the only ones that truly benefit from this science, leaving us to draw our own conclusions as to what that means for "regular people."

The next day Arnò's niece Lori sees the man's death on the front page of the newspaper. She remembers him as the man in a car parked outside their apartment building before the robbery. As Lori describes the violent image to her uncle, the audience can clearly see the headlines. The headlines of *Paese Sera*, a newspaper Argento once wrote for, reference the bombings of the Red Brigade, a terrorist group formed in 1970 which had begun random bombings, robberies, and assassinations that would keep citizens in a state of fear until 1980. It's disturbing that 10-year-old Lori must describe such graphic violence for her blind uncle, but violence was a reality for both children and adults living in 1970s Italy. Argento uses the newspaper image to bring this harsh reality to his *giallo* in a quasi-neorealist way. Arnò and Lori eventually team up with reporter Giordani to solve the case.

After Giordani's photographer co-worker is killed looking into a lead for him, he goes to the police to make a statement. He waits a long time to talk to the cops, illustrating the languid pace and inefficiency of government-run offices in Italy. While he's waiting, a cop sits around telling Giordani about his wife's recipe for sauce. It's a long-running joke that this officer constantly talks about his wife's cooking when he should be solving crimes.

Many of Argento's films during this period of his career feature civil servants who are blissfully unaware of what is going on around them. Another example occurs in *Deep Red*, when two garbage men are shown laughing and talking unaware, until it's too late, that Carlo is being dragged to his death when his pants leg gets hooked to the back of their truck. Then there is the "pervert" mailman the girls complain about in *Four Flies on Grey Velvet* who is attacked and beaten by Michael Brandon when he mistakes him for the killer.

Midway through *The Cat O'Nine Tails*, reporter Giordani talks to a scientist from the institute who tells him that the government's plan is to test children for the XYY triad and isolate them from the general population to prevent future criminals. He further explains to Giordani, "We are on our way to developing a new wonder drug which will solve the problem of hereditary diseases and malformations once and for all." This theme fits with the cold perversity found in *giallo* films, but both of these breakthroughs in science could easily parallel the Nazi's attempt to breed an Aryan race, especially to someone who was born during World War II. It isn't lost on Argento that only wealthy, privileged people will benefit from this costly new science. When Giordani hires an ex-con on parole to crack open a safe, Argento utilizes this plot point as both comic and middle finger to "the Man."

We meet "Gigi the loser" in a pool hall performing a stream of curses as an audience looks on. The joke is that signs on the wall, shown predominately throughout the scene, specifically say, "It is forbidden to spit and yell." Of course, Gigi has done precisely the opposite for a majority of the scene. Unfortunately, the signs are not subtitled for the scene leaving only Italian speaking audience members to fully understand the joke.

The harshest insults in *The Cat O'Nine Tails* are leveled at Anna, Terzi's beautiful young daughter. When Giordani meets her after walking unannounced into the Terzi home, she flirts with him, and he responds, "Look at you sitting there like an aristocratic child trying to show off your legs." In the Italian language version, his comment demonstrates contempt for her wealth in a very direct manner. In Italian, he essentially calls her a wealthy bitch. Clearly Argento has never been a fan of the upper class.

After finishing his "animal trilogy," Argento was offered the chance to produce four one-hour television features for RAI network in the form of a series called *La porta sul buio/Door into Darkness*. A highlight of this series is the episode "Il Tram," a stylish mystery/thriller about murder on a city tram. Enzo Cerusico stars as detective Giordani. Cerusico's detective feels like an extension of the director himself when he snaps his fingers, all controlled nervous energy, the wheels of his mind spinning as he closes in on the killer. In the final scene, the director's voice, speaking through Giordani, delivers a passionate statement about who he believes are society's worst criminals. Giordani and officer Morini share some parting thoughts about the killer. Morini says, "Murderers are never intelligent—cunning, quick, astute, ferocious, maybe, but never intelligent. An intelligent man doesn't take these kind of risks, only a foolish criminal does." Giordani responds, "There are also intelligent criminals. They own cars and luxury villas. They even seem like honest people. They also commit crimes. When they show us their hands, they are always white, clean, immaculate."

Cerusico would co-star in Argento's next feature, *Le cinque giornate*. *Le cinque giornate* is the director's least seen film, and it is his only overtly political film. Of this film Argento has said, "It's a strange little film, and one that reflected the times and my political influences. Although it was set at the dawn of Italian Independence it still reflected contempary issues." *Le cinque giornate* stars Adriano Celentano as Cainazzo, a thief set free from jail during the Italian revolution when an errant cannonball knocks down his cell wall. Enzo Cerusico plays his sidekick, Romolo. As a divided Italy strives to unify and rid itself of Austrian rule, a number of powerful interest groups attempt to secure "the largest piece of the pie" while selling the people a lie in the form

Italian 2 *foglio* poster for *The Cat O'Nine Tails*; artist unknown.

.of liberty and democracy in order to get them to fight their wars, endorse whatever ideals suit their endgame, and move their furniture. Our two protagonists are Cainazzo, a cynical, world-weary thief, and Romolo whose boyish innocence represents the everyman of the Italian people. Cainazzo and Romolo wander the streets of Milan meeting various aristocrats, revolutionaries, and clergy along their journey.

Cainazzo is a common thief, and while he is much smarter than Gigi the loser from *The Cat O' Nine Tails*, they have both made their living picking locks. Once again Argento puts criminal behavior into two categories: the street criminal who is just trying to get by and the white-collar criminals who exploit the middle class on a much larger scale for their own benefit. Cainazzo hears that his former partner in crime, Zampino, has become a hero of the revolution and has been dubbed "Liberty" by both the people and the freedom-fighting patriots. He has achieved mythical status, the kind that resides in a history viewed through rose-colored glasses. He is the representation of the Liberty that Cainazzo and Romolo are looking for both literally and metaphorically. Sightings of the elusive Liberty drive the two men forward through the plot until Cainazzo is finally able to confront him in the film's final scenes.

Argento pulls no punches in this film. His depictions of the aristocracy, clergy, and phony politicians are merciless as he gleefully skewers them in scene after scene. He never shrinks away from harsh truths, as when Cainazzo and Romolo fall asleep in a library and are roused by a man who asks them what they think they will get from this "glorious tri-colored affair?" Cainazzo of course replies, "Liberty!" The man laughs saying, "What other nonsense have they put in your head? You have been tricked because you are desperate, naïve, and act without thinking. You do the killing while they divide the pie. In the end they will leave you nothing. One day, a long time from now, you will pay dearly for believing them." It isn't so much that the protagonists act without thinking, but that the contrived chaos constantly bombarding them makes stopping to think a luxury. After all, they have just fallen asleep out of sheer exhaustion in a library.

Cainazzo's cynicism is counter balanced by Romolo's innocent nature. In this very uneven film, Enzo Cerusico as Romolo, creates an endearing and likable character that is crucial to the emotional arch of the story. When Romolo is involved in an altercation with Italian soldiers and is executed, Cainazzo can no longer deny what is going on in his country. He finally tracks down Zampino and finds him working for the Austrians who Italian patriots have been fighting and dying to remove from power. Zampino declares, without remorse, that he's been playing both sides and is only loyal to himself and the highest bidder. He tells Cainazzo what he already knows but can't yet admit—there is no revolution and no real liberty. They are stories created by the real men in power to exploit the masses for their own gain. In a scene illustrating how people rationalize corruption, Zampino attempts to seduce Cainazzo with an offer to get rich working with him, and warns that if he doesn't, all he will always be is a "poor thief." In the late '60s and early '70s, corruption that eroded much of the best of Italy at the expense of the majority of the Italian people had already begun and this, in part, is what Argento is alluding to when he says the film is a parallel between the Italian revolution and the early 1970s. In the film's final moments, Cainazzo wanders in a daze of disillusionment, grief, and anger. He suddenly realizes he is standing on a makeshift stage in the center of the street and is asked to share his experience of this great historical moment—the Austrians have left the country, but there is no real victory because corrupt people remain in power. He looks out at the crowd in disbelief as a man urges him to "speak up so the people can hear you." Laughing through anger and tears he yells at the naïve crowd, "*c'hanno fregato!*" (They have screwed us!)

With his detour from *giallo* finished, Argento returned to the genre that made him famous with the filming of *Deep Red* in 1975. The film would triumph as the best *giallo* of the decade, simultaneously setting the bar and signaling the end of the *giallo* craze that began with Argento's initial success in 1970, *The Bird with the Crystal Plumage*.

Once again Argento was looking to break new ground with his next project. After *Le cinque giornate* and prior to *Deep Red*, Argento and Luigi Cozzi had attempted to write a version of *Frankenstein* set in the early days of Hitler's Germany using the Monster to draw parallels to Nazism. They failed to secure enough interest from both Universal Pictures and Hammer Film Preductions, so the entire project was shelved. However, the idea of evil in tandem with Nazi Germany didn't completely die. Clearly parts of this idea would live on in one of Argento's few "horror" films, 1977's *Suspiria*, and its follow up, *Inferno*.

Suspiria is sometimes incorrectly referred to as a *giallo* film. It is a horror film, but also is the culmination of much of the political and cultural commentary Argento has used in his previous films— greed, corruption, and the abuse of power. He also uses references to Hitler and the Nazis in the form of the film's locations. Like other Italian filmmakers of his generation, Argento needed real-world horror to ground the *Suspiria* fairy tale because, as we have discussed, Italians liked their horror grounded in the real world, not fairy tale imaginings. World War II was still very vivid for those born during the war. Argento's father was a promoter of films for the Italian government and he has said that his mother and uncle's photography were important influences in the forming of his visual style. His uncle in particular was hand-picked by Mussolini to document the Fascist party during their time in power. No doubt this greatly influenced Argento to create shots of large looming spaces that make one feel the omnipotence of the witches in the same manner that the Fascist party built massive buildings like Milan's train station as a constant reminder of their power. In fact, Bertolucci utilizes very similar visual cues in his 1970 film about a man who willingly works for the fascist party—*The Conformist/Il conformista*.

Before I had a deeper understanding of Italian culture, it had always bothered me that *Suspiria* creates the worst possible stereotype for its witches. Having grown up in a fairly religious area of the Midwest, but being open-minded, I had friends who were Wiccan. *Suspiria*'s definition of witches is the most negative kind, and the film's claim that the witches' "reason for being" is to obtain a great amount of wealth, had always been particularly perplexing because Wicca is about being one with nature, not material gain. However, it makes complete sense when you think of them as the manifestation of Argento's definition of evil—they possess the traits of Nazis, white-collar criminals, and other nefarious characters.

Suspiria is an allegorical, very grim fairy tale about a young American dancer named Suzy Banyon who travels to Freiburg, Germany, to attend the world famous Tanz Akademie. She arrives in a thunderstorm on the same night that another student named Pat leaves the school and is murdered. Madame Blanc and her henchwoman, Mrs. Tanner, run the school. Suzy makes friends with Pat's former roommate, Sara, and soon comes to believe that the school may be a front for a very powerful witch, Helena Marcos, and her coven. However, Helena Marcos is only one of three powerful witches known collectively as The Three Mothers who reside in New York, Rome, and Freiburg, infecting the world with evil. Argento famously based the mythology of *Suspiria* on both the writings of Thomas De Quincey (*Confessions of an English Opium Eater*) and a story his girlfriend, Daria Nicolodi, shared with him about her grandmother's experience at an Arts school that secretly taught black magic.

After her friend Sara disappears, Suzy contacts Doctor Frank Mandel, a friend of Sara's, who happens to have studied the occult, to see if he could shed some light on both Sara's disappearance and the mystery of the school. Mandel suggests that Sara was mentally ill, and, further, that belief in the occult is brought on by "broken minds, not broken mirrors." He then suggests Suzy speak to his colleague, Professor Milius, who has written the definitive book on the subject entitled "Paranoia or Magic." Instead of writing off the supernatural completely as mental illness—as some other films have (notably Nevenka in Mario Bava's *The Whip and the Body/La frusta e il corpo*, 1963, who it turns out is not plagued by a ghost but by her own sexual obsession, or the aforementioned *Hatchet for the Honeymoon*'s John Harrington, a film that remains ambiguous as to whether the ghost of his wife is real or a manifestation of his mental illness) when Professor Milius is questioned by Suzy about the existence of witches, he says, "They are malefic, negative, and destructive. Their knowledge of the occult gives them tremendous power. They can change the course of events and people's lives, but only to do harm. Their goal is to accumulate great personal wealth, but that can only be achieved by causing injury to others."

Here Argento blurs the line between fairy tale witches, greed of those in power, and real-life monsters of the Nazi party. 2017's Synapse release of *Suspiria* included the featurette, "Suzy in Nazi Germany," showing the locations used in *Suspiria* that were also locations of historical importance for Hitler and the Nazi Party. Argento was so specific that in Alan Jones' book, *Mondo Argento*, the director is quoted as saying, "In *Suspiria*, when the blind man goes into the beer hall, he sits at the exact same table where the famous Munich speech was given that heralded the start of the Nazi

Madame Blanc (Joan Bennett) represents the one percent in *Suspiria*.

The Unsane Cinema of Dario Argento

movement. I have a fondness for automatic writing like that, whether the audience gets it or not." I believe that Argento wasn't completely comfortable with portraying random, supernatural evil in his film. After all many more people have suffered at the hands of the Nazis than from a witch's curse, making the horror more relatable for the director and the audience.

Money and greed come up constantly in the film. For example, on her first day at the Tanz Akademie another dancer offers to sell Suzy an extra pair of shoes and is clearly disappointed when Suzy isn't interested in spending the money. Olga tells Suzy she must pay 50 marks up front for her room. Once Suzy comes back to live at the school full-time, Suzy's friend Sara says to her, "Did they shake you up with all that about money? Don't worry it's a regular thing here." Olga makes a lurid comment about a handsome young dancer named Mark when she say's "He's cute, but he's got no money—and he never has any money for room and board, that's why that bitch Tanner has him under her thumb. She gives him 1,001 things to do …" Poor Mark is trapped due to lack of money and therefore owned by the witches. Most men have a fear of being cuckolded, but Mark's plight is sure to strike terror in the heart of any Italian man!

Suzy mentions to Sara that Pavlos, the school's handyman, has been eyeing her beautiful lighter and warns her to not let it out of her sight. Sara says that she's noticed it too but doesn't think he's a thief. Poor Sara couldn't have been more wrong. When Suzy finds Sara's mutilated body in the final 10 minutes of the film, Pavlo can be seen looking for Suzy in the hallway, using Sara's lighter to illuminate the corridor. It's a vicious petty act, and Argento makes sure his audience sees it.

While *Suspiria* uses a fairy tale archetype to get its story across and focuses on the concentrated power

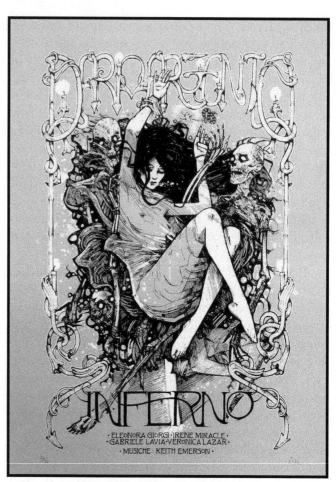

Artwork for *Inferno* by Malleus, a trio of artists, Poia, Lu and Urlo, known mostly for rock art posters.

of an elite evil power or group, *Inferno* attempts to explain more of the mythology surrounding the "Three Mothers" trilogy. This is the last film in this timeline that we will look at and is the second film in the trilogy that begins with *Suspiria*.

Inferno takes place in the cities ruled by the other two witches—Rome and, more predominately, New York. German settings are gone and there is less focus on the "group" dynamic of the coven as seen in *Suspiria*, but there are still references to the foul corruption of the uber-wealthy. What seems like a throwaway scene involving Alida Valli, whose character barely has a name, it becomes more important once we understand the themes Argento plays with throughout his film work.

In the film, John (Countess Elise's butler) and the woman who runs the building (Alida Valli's character, Carol the caretaker) are found rifling through the Countess' things after someone has killed her. A full moon seems to illuminate the evil people in and around the large Gothic building that Mater Tenebrarum (Mother of Darkness of the Three Mothers) dwells in. The building is a physical manifestation of her evil. Under this full moon, three characters simultaneously commit

Death goes up in flames at the end of *Inferno*.

horrible acts. John brags while counting her money: "The Countess, that bitch, she thought she had hidden it so well. It took me all of 15 minutes to find it." They plan to call her husband and tell him that she has suddenly left so that they can keep her money and jewelry. Carol says she knows that "the bitch isn't coming back." Either Carol killed her or made sure that some evil within the house killed the Countess. She then says, "Now it's our turn to enjoy life. Now we are going to live it up like the Countess Elise and all the other rich bastards." Moments later both she and the butler are murdered. Carol might have thought she knew how to control and direct the energy of Mater Tenebrarum, but soon she is in over her head, as if her own evil is directed back onto her in the moonlight. Like Kazanian who has drowned cats and is then stabbed and eaten by rats, Carol meets a horrible end when she discovers John's dead body, eyes torn out of their sockets. She stumbles backward onto a candle setting fire to the massive curtains that quickly engulf her in their flames as she falls to her death through a glass skylight. As Mater Tenebrarum's power starts to reach its apex, evil people in and around the building act on their wicked impulses and are discarded by the Mother of Darkness after she has fed on their greed and corruption.

In America in the 1970's, culturally we were preoccupied with issues like divorce, birth control, and women's new power in the workplace, and fears surrounding these issues worked its way into much of our horror films. After all, America is a country founded by Puritans, and we still tend to prefer our horror with a decidedly supernatural slant. In short, the pure fantasy side of *Suspiria* and *Inferno* were much better selling points to an American audience. However, in 2018, the concepts of globalization and the one percent have been in the forefront of thought and discourse, not only in America, but also in many parts of the world. So, is it not so surprising that some of Argento's more personal politics are being picked up on by an entirely new generation? This is exciting to witness, as there are lessons to be learned here that are very relevant to today's audience and generations to come.

Argento's views created a framework on which to hang his films. As a savvy filmmaker, he knows to put the emphasis on a thrill ride for the viewer, but that is not to say that his films are devoid of meaning. I hope that this will help to finally put to bed the notion that Argento's films are nothing more than beautiful but empty set pieces.

A (former) singer/dancer, and lover of all things strange, Jennifer Fiorini holds a degree in Advertising Design from the Fashion Institute of Technology where she also studied Italian language, cinema, and fashion in film. Nocturnal at heart, you're likely to find her at midnight screenings with her Mondo Culto film family. Jennifer lives in New York City and Turin, Italy.

Suspiria was a huge hit the world over, including Japan as can be seen in this pressbook for the film.

Works Cited:
Bondanella, Peter, *A History of Italian Cinema*, (New York: Continuum International Publishing Group, 2009)
Jones, Alan, *Dario Argento: The Man, the Myths & the Magic* (Godalming: FAB Press, 2016)
Jones, Alan, *Mondo Argento*, (London: Midnight Media Publishing, 1996)
McDonagh, Maitland, *Broken Mirrors, Broken Minds: The Dark Dreams of Dario Argento* (Minneapolis: University of Minnesota Press, 2010)

Argento's Music
by Randall D. Larson

The films of Dario Argento are acclaimed as much for their unique and superbly integrated musical scores as they are for their stylistic visual inventions and audacious storylines. As author Howard Hughes wrote in *Cinema Italiani* (2011), "though Bava was a *giallo* pioneer, Dario Argento remains the genre's *maestro*."[1] "What sets Dario apart from all the other directors I've worked with is the great care he takes with the score," remarked Goblin's Claudio Simonetti. "He believes the music is very important, so he follows it closely."[2]

Cover for the Cinevox release of Metti, una sera a cena.

The director has described his working relationship with composers in this 2009 online interview: "I've worked with many, many musicians," he said. "With Morricone, sometimes we like to do the music before shooting. I go to his house, he composes and plays in my presence and if it's good, we do the film and he finishes the score. With Pino Donaggio, it's the same thing. With Goblin or with Claudio Simonetti, it's different. For *Profondo rosso* (*Deep Red*), we meet in my house nearly every night and they introduce me to the work of the day, and it inspires me to do the next scene. It was very important. For *Suspiria* we collaborated on the music—it was good to do it before shooting. Also, on *The Card Player* it was just Claudio Simonetti doing electronic music, which was very interesting ... It's a great adventure the music in that film; not so well known by everybody."[3]

Argento's first three films formed what has been called the Animal Trilogy by virtue of their titles: *The Bird with the Crystal Plumage* (*L'uccello dalle piume di cristallo*) *The Cat O'Nine Tails* (*Il gatto a nove code*), and *Four Flies on Grey Velvet* (*4 mosche di velluto grigio*). To score these films, Argento brought in celebrated composer Ennio Morricone, who had composed the scores to five of the films Argento had written or co-written prior to his directorial debut (*Comandameni per un gangster*, *Once Upon A Time In The West/C'era una volte il west*, *One Night at Dinner/Metti, una sera a cena*, *The 5-Man Army/Un esercito di 5 uomini*, and *Season of the Senses/La stagione dei sensi*). The variety of approach in each of those scores surely gave Argento a good idea of the composer's abilities. Argento had met Morricone through his father, Italian producer Salvatore Argento. "Morricone was a friend of my father's, and we were neighbors too," Argento recalled in a 1999 interview. "My father asked him to read the script of my first film. He liked it a lot and decided to do the music for it."[4]

By selecting Morricone to compose these seminal *giallo* films, Argento forged an ideal partnership that linked his own stylistic visual storytelling style with the composer's uniquely designed and oft-experimental musical approach which, for these three films, presented an ideal collaboration between the audio and visual design that pervades each of those movies.

Morricone is an innovative chameleon whose shape-shifting compositions have traveled through every genre, intensified hundreds of movies, enhanced every emotion, and captured almost every species of music imaginable. He has referred to his *giallo* scores as "traumatic music" and "meditations on fear and tension."[5] He crafted "simple sounds that combine repetitive rhythmic motifs, or ostinato ... with improvised, often discordant, cries on top," wrote one commentator. "In this music, like so much of his work elsewhere, Morricone perfectly realizes a merger of the logical, the physical, and the emotional into the most human of sounds."[6]

The Bird with the Crystal Plumage inaugurated a musical style that would develop and keep all three films in stylistic sync, merging the melodic with the mysterious and providing viewers/listeners with emotions of both delight and disturbance. "In *The Bird with the Crystal Plumage* the refrain has a 'beat lullaby' feel to it ... In *The Cat O'Nine Tails* it has a distinctly renaissance atmosphere ... and in *Four Flies on Grey Velvet* it becomes almost sacred," wrote soundtrack producer Claudio Fuiano. "Here Morricone's music and Argento's images match each other perfectly."[7] *Bird* opens with the sweet melody of the "Crystal Plumage" lullaby, very softly intoned by the lovely voice of Morricone's most favored vocalist, Edda Dell'Orso, over a gentle rhythm from a jangly acoustic guitar; its enchanting sequence of la-la's will be joined by male vocalists for the cue's second half, energized by hand drums, bells and chimes, along with organ and/

or harpsichord. The breezy folk-ish melody will be set in stark contrast to the chaotic jazz-inflected tension theme, "Fraseggio senza struttura" ("Phrases without Structure") which is associated with the killer's presence, whether on or off-screen. This is one of Morricone's most chaotic and free-form motifs, drawn from the composer's love of modern, free jazz as a trumpet player in his youth, and is an untamed and partially improvised synthesis of musical sound that forms a stridently uneasy sonic mélange; it nearly constitutes an assault on the ears but appropriately keeps the audience very much on edge. This motif, as blogger Ed Chang has aptly described in his carefully-curated blogspot of detailed film music analysis, *cuebycue*, is a "jazz-rock fantasia featuring free jazz drums and muted trumpet, female 'la-la'/sighing ornaments and synth/computer, all using elements of "Phrases Without Structure," but played *with* structure (i.e., a rhythmically-tight episodic structure, with more unison ensemble presentations of the atonal tension theme and with accented rhythmic cadences)."[8] Elsewhere in the score Morricone will add female and male sighs as well as quasi-orgasmic female gasps to denote a potential victim's terror and perhaps suggest the killer's psycho-sexual homicidal intent.

While the main theme allows audience engagement through its melodic cadences, the tension theme builds a palpable discordance which, via its female vocalisms, creates a sense of fragile intimacy that connects the audience with the terror and plight of the prey. It's a structure that Morricone would follow again in *The Cat O'Nine Tails*, setting a pleasant melodic theme against a much more incongruous instrumental substance. Edda Dell'Orso's voice is heard in both categories, serenely siren-like in the score's main "groove" theme, and more abstractly in the free-form tension material. As Chang described, "In this film, Morricone incorporated clipped, syncopated bass grooves (with simple drum rhythms on brushes and hi-hat) to support newly composed selections of rhythmically floating "phrases" (atonal themes/motifs, ostinato patterns, ambient textures, et cetera) using similarly unconventional instrumentation."[9]

Four Flies on Grey Velvet continued the trend with a similarly conceived score mixing a poignant theme for voice and celeste (or harpsichord) called "Come un madrigal" ("Like a Madrigal") and a number of discordant, avant-garde and jazzy pieces. Additionally, with the main character being a rock drummer, Morricone created a number of drums cues that are put to good use; the title music, for example, in which the character rehearses with his band, is a feral source cue for electric guitar, drum kit, and Hammond organ as a male singer intones wordlessly and wildly. As well as infusing the suspense moments, Dell'Orso's vocals creates a delicate fragrance for the film's bathtub love scene. In addition to Dell'Orso's solo vocalisms, the score also features Morricone's oft-used choir, I Cantori Moderni di Alessandroni.

"This concept of groove structures to support avant-garde thriller textures would continue into many more classic Morricone-scored *giallo* films (such as in Massimo Dallamano's 1972 *What Have You Done To Solange?/Cosa avete fatto a Solange?*) and have a lasting influence on the genre itself," noted Chang.[10] Anne Billson, writing about *giallo* films in an article for *The Telegraph* in 2013, notes that "the *giallo* sound is typically an intoxicating mix of groovy lounge music, nerve-jangling discord, and the sort of soothing lyricism that belies the fact that it's actually accompanying, say, a slow-motion decapitation."[11] This intrinsic style of scoring is something that can be traced back to Morricone's scores for The Animal Trilogy.

Morricone described his technique for the tension music, and its contrast with his gentler melodic music, in these films thusly: "I created a framework for the orchestra soloists and then I directed them in gestures ... We didn't have a precise meter, so it was a bit complicated. This was one of the first cases where I applied this technique. I applied it to only 18 or 19 other films. Then I stopped because I thought that this type of traumatic music was very acceptable for Dario Argento's films but for other films that were less traumatic the music did not fit. It didn't work because it was too much. It might distract the audience. So naturally in *The Cat O'Nine Tails*, *Four Flies on Grey Velvet*, and *The Bird with the Crystal Plumage*, in order to balance this audacious, jarring, and traumatic music, I wrote ... more simple themes, almost childish."[12]

This release from DRG offered choice cuts from Ennio Morricone's scores for Dario's first three films.

The Unsane Cinema of Dario Argento

As it turned out, Argento was not completely happy with Morricone's score for *Four Flies on Grey Velvet*, describing how Morricone "had composed music I didn't like, and I asked him to change it … I had to finish directing the music myself because Morricone walked out on me …"[13] Argento claims to have considered having the British rock band Deep Purple replace some of the music he didn't like in *Four Flies on Grey Velvet*[14] but nothing came of it, and whatever musical changes Argento wanted were made in the editing room.

From Morricone's perspective, he had this to say: "At one point the father of Dario Argento, Salvatore, who was the producer, came to me and said, 'You know, Ennio … you've been composing the same music for all three films now. There is no difference. They all sound alike.' I said, 'No, it's not that they're alike. The style is the same but there is a progression. If you're not musically educated enough to grasp the meaning of that, it would be better if you resort to another composer. If you think that I repeat myself then you don't understand what I have done.' And, in fact, they did work with someone else for a while … but Dario Argento later called me himself so that we could work together again."[15]

Argento's thoughts about using a rock band, Deep Purple, to write a film score would come into play for his next horror film, *Deep Red*, when he came into contact with a newlyformed band called Goblin. But in the meantime, Argento was busy developing a mystery/thriller anthology series for RAI Radiotelevision Italiana, called *Door into Darkness* (*La porta sul buio*). Of its four episodes, he wrote and directed two of them ("The Tram"/"Il tram" and "Eyewitness"/"Testimone oculare"), while Luigi Cozzi and Mario Foglietti helmed the other two. A jazz pianist and composer named Giorgio Gaslini (1929-2014) was hired to compose each episode's music score. Gaslini had been scoring films in Italy since the early 1960s; and he'd composed a couple of traditional horror films, *La lunga notte di veronique* (1966, aka *But You Were Dead*) and *Night of the Devils* (1972, *La notte dei diavoli*), an adaptation of Tolstoy's "The Family of the Vourdalak" story, as well as the *giallo* film *So Sweet, So Dead* (1972, *Rivelazioni di un maniaco sessuale al capo della squadra mobil*). His title theme music for *Door into Darkness* was a short, aggressive mélange that opened with a squealing violin and plodding footsteps from a tom-tom drum that opened into a frantic piano riff beneath heavily imposing violin chords that conveyed a strong prelude of anxiety.

"The Tram" is a stylish whodunit in which a young woman is murdered on a crowded city tram without anyone else noticing the crime; the police inspector recreates the incident in order to find out the killer's identity, at his own peril. Gaslini's score is spare but effective, built around pastiches of a jazz idiom: a garish rally of brass for the newspaper montage about the killing, swaths of big band, a touch of modern jazz as the crime reconstruction plays out, and some misterioso violins to reflect the detective's pondering. Gaslini used a similar approach for the other three episodes—for example in Luigi Cozzi's "The Neighbor" we have the shrill cry of paired flutes and jazzy horns when a dead body is found, and discordant, abrasive clusters of musical sound which add to the jarring mood of the episode. In "Eyewitness," about a woman who discovers a murder that no one believes, Gaslini uses chaotic trills from a solo flute for the woman's rush from the scene to inform police; solo and multiple flutes, as well as ferociously aggressive drumming, escalates her panic when she is threatened by the murderer. In the final tale, "The Doll," about an insane asylum patient who escapes and goes on a killing spree, Gaslini reprises his piercing, sharp flutes and adds bass guitar notes counterpointed against jagged piano arpeggios as potent suspense figures. When the man stalks a woman in a toy store, discordant music box notes over furious drumming and electric bass notes evokes growing menace yet suitable to the setting, returning to the frantic flutes motif as the man follows the woman home.

Gaslini also scored Argento's period comedy *Le cinque giornate* and had begun composing music for *Deep Red* (*Profondo rosso*) when Argento became enamored with a newly-formed progressive rock band named Goblin. "Giorgio Gaslini started composing the *Deep Red* music but during the shooting I had the exact melodies and themes I wanted in my brain," Argento said. "Gaslini didn't seem to understand the new spirit of the film and

This rare 1973 vinyl includes some of Gaslini's music for *Door into Darkness*.

the soundtrack he presented to me was awful. I had three months to come up with an alternative, and after flying to London to see if Pink Floyd were interested—they weren't—started asking Roman musician friends of mine for ideas."[16]

In 1975, Goblin (originally named Oliver and then Cherry Five), consisted of Claudio Simonetti (keyboards), Massimo Morante (guitars), Fabio Pignatelli (bass), and Walter Martino (drums and percussion—replaced by Agostino Marangolo midway through the *Deep Red* sessions). Argento was impressed by two demo tracks Simonetti submitted and signed the band to score the film, working with them in the studio to familiarize them with the requirements of recording music for movies. Because of Argento's close involvement with the band during the *Deep Red* sessions, the music credits read "The Goblins with Dario Argento" for both *Deep Red* and *Suspiria*.

In *Deep Red*, the band's music wound up replacing or rerecording most of what Gaslini had composed. Gaslini had "started recording several parts with an orchestra, including the lullaby of the girl ('School at Night')," Simonetti said. "But Dario said, 'I want more rock in the film.' So, we had to arrange Giorgio Gaslini's music. However, Gaslini had problems with Dario and he left the film. Dario arrived and said 'Gaslini will not be with us anymore, so we need the main themes for the film—you try!'"[17] Only three of Gaslini's motifs remained in the film when it was released, "School at Night," "Deep Shadows," and "Gianna," re-arranged and electrified by the band.

"Goblin's music adds immeasurable pumped-up frisson to the sleek tone of *Deep Red* and their soundtrack is a genre watershed," wrote Alan Jones in *Dario Argento: The Man, the Myths & the Magic*.[18] Goblin had been influenced by prog bands of the 1970s such as Gentle Giant, King Crimson, Emerson, Lake & Palmer, and Deep Purple. The band's guitar and Moog synthesizer sound for *Deep Red* is derived from those influences, whereas the music for *Suspiria* defined a more cinematic sensibility, focused on a haunting lullaby theme of their own which has become one of the genre's most pervasive and memorable horror ostinatos, and a sinister anthem to *Suspiria*'s cruel witch, Mater Suspiriorum, the Mother of Sighs. "When [Dario] called us to do the film he said, 'This is not about a serial killer or the typical Italian *giallo*, but a film that talks about witches. I need music that always lets the audiences feel that witches are there, even if there is nothing on the screen.' We recorded *Profondo rosso* in just 10 days, but … for *Suspiria* we stayed in the studio for almost three months. We experimented with different ethnic instruments like a Greek bouzouki and Indian tabla, and we used a lot of different synthesizers

Cover art for the expanded 2-disc edition from Cinevox.

like the Mellotron and the big system 55 of Moog [the Moog Modular System 55 Synthesizer, consisting of a number of up to 36 modules mounted in a large cabinet]."[19]

In addition to the main theme's 14-note melody, played on a synthesizer keyboard, the more aggressive and discordant segments of the score add harsh, breathy voices, reflective of the film's title, which means "whispers" in Italian. The *Suspiria* score "is a true wonder in eliciting subconscious reactions to accompany the visuals," wrote Louis Paul in *Italian Horror Film Directors*. "Viewed with the aid of an advanced home audio visual system, this is more readily apparent when the music reaches wild crescendos with actual whispered words filling the middle range. Listen carefully and you'll often hear the word 'witch' whispered in an almost subliminal manner during the finale."[20]

"Goblin [delivered] plenty of original material for *Suspiria*," wrote "progcroc" in a 2016 online article about Goblin's film music. "Their dissonant cacophony of whispers, screams, strangulated synthesizer and found percussion [provided] the perfect accompaniment to Argento's all-out visual, visceral assault. Just as the witches' murderous daggers are wielded in close-up by the director's own skinny hands, so it is Simonetti's voice that can be heard throughout the picture, muttering lines from the folk poem 'Three Witches Sitting in a Tree.'"[21]

"I think that the real Goblin sound is in *Suspiria*," said Simonetti, who was the band's primary composer. "In *Suspiria* we created something really new. If you listen to *Suspiria* and then *Profondo rosso* there is nothing to compare one to the other. It sounds like two different bands."[22]

The Cinevox release of Goblin's music for *Dawn of the Dead*.

After *Suspiria*, Argento collaborated with George A. Romero on the script for his zombie movie sequel, *Dawn of the Dead*. Argento helped finance the independent venture in exchange for international distribution rights, for which he made his own editorial cuts and supplied its own soundtrack from Goblin, which created a new musical score that replaced most of the library music that Romero had compiled for his American release version. Romero wound up using three of the Goblin tracks in his own English-language theatrical cut. Both versions of the film are unique in their own way, structurally and musically (Argento's cut was released in Europe as *Zombi*). Goblin's music provided an effective counterpoint to Romero's vivid scenes of flesh-eating zombies invading an abandoned shopping mall. Their music is desolate and brutal, built around pulsating prog rock rhythms and textures, both electric and acoustic. "There was a new release in the States of the film with our music after the first distribution with the traditional music," noted Simonetti.[23]

After *Zombi*, Goblin disbanded. Argento, continuing his affection for progressive rock, hired British keyboardist Keith Emerson to score 1980's *Inferno*. Emerson, one third of the progressive rock supergroup Emerson, Lake & Palmer and one of the first rock musicians to exploit the Moog synthesizer as a featured instrument, had just begun a solo career after the trio disbanded in 1980 when Argento approached him to create the score for *Inferno*. "Composing soundtracks was an avenue I was eager to explore and as I did love horror movies I thought [*Inferno*] was the perfect opportunity to see what I could do," Emerson said. "We assembled a 90-piece orchestra and it all came to me pretty quickly, really. I wanted to get a motif happening, so whenever something awful was about to occur, it would be signaled by a piano riff."[24]

Being a keyboard player, the majority of Emerson's score is piano based, sometimes counterpointed against strings or synth, which lends a stimulating sonic atmosphere as the characters explore the complicated, colorful, and often abstract landscape inside the strange witch house in New York. Emerson played his keyboards live with the orchestra, conducted by Godfrey Salmon, in sync with the picture during the recording sessions. "Godfrey kept me in check, and if I was a bit late or slow, I'd speed up my playing while he conducted the orchestra to keep in rhythm with me."[25]

A heavy cathedral-type organ accompanies Sara's visit to the *Biblioteca Filosofica* library with its massive stacks of ancient books rising to ceiling level, while a misterioso of violins follows her into the vaults during her ill-fated attempt to purloin a rare copy of Varelli's *The Three Mothers*; a tarantella for piano and orchestra accompanies the hungry rat-death of bookseller Kazanian. Verdi's "*Va, pensiero*," from his opera "*Nabucco*," is featured in the film (a performance by the *Orchestra Sinfonica Nazionale della RAI* licensed from the record label Fonit Cetra) as a source cue played during a musicology lecture attended by Mark and Sara; at Argento's request, Emerson arranged the Verdi piece into a fast-moving scherzo in 5/4 time for piano, synth, and drums, which is heard over Sara's harrowing taxi ride to the *Biblioteca*. Emerson also provides a raucous choral-and-keyboard theme for *Inferno*'s witch, Mater Tenenbrarum, the Mother of Darkness. Emerson went on to score a couple of Hollywood action thrillers, returning to Rome in 1989 to score Michele Soavi's *Dèmoni* sequel, *The Church* (1989, *La chiesa*), which Argento co-scripted and co-produced.

When Argento made *Tenebrae* (Latin for "Darkness") in 1982 he was adamant of having the Goblin sound for its score. Simonetti therefore arranged for three of its original members to join him and score Argento's film. Bass player Fabio Pignatelli had begun a new album under the Goblin name with new musicians, so *Tenebrae*'s score was credited to simply Simonetti/Pignatelli/Morante to avoid conflicts with the other Goblin. "*Tenebrae* is kind of a different soundtrack, comparing to what we did before," Simonetti explained. "It was the beginning of the '80s and after the split of Goblin I started working with dance music … when Dario asked us to do the soundtrack for *Tenebrae*; we decided to use electronica and a drum machine … [which created] fusion between electronica and rock."[26] The pulsating main theme, opening with a throbbing series of synth chords that almost sound like moaning voices, which segues into the steady disco beat of the drum machine contrasted strikingly against Morante's blistering hard rock guitar solos, dramatically integrated with Pignatelli's driving bass and Simonetti's piercing synths. The result was an effective modern-retro musical style to the film. It's especially effective during Argento's acclaimed two-and-a-half-minute plus tracking shot across the roof and walls of the modernistic house that preludes the murder of the lesbian couple within. Simonetti also used a vocoder (an audio processor that captures elements of an audio signal to blend the human voice with a synthesizer producing a harmonized performance of what is being sung) in *Tenebrae* to "say the word '*paura*' (fear) in the main track."[27]

The harsh electronic sounds of *Tenebrae* marked Goblin's last real collaboration with Argento until *Sleepless*, even if they weren't billed as such.

Like Morricone's music for The Animal Trilogy, the music of Goblin has equally created a triptych of remarkable audiovisual interaction with their music for *Deep Red*, *Suspiria*, and *Tenebrae*. Simonetti would continue to score several other films for Argento as director or producer (14 projects as of *Dracula*), but these three, with their deceptively simple recurring themes, have become iconic film scores in their own right. "Definitely one of the reasons for our success are the repetitive melodies," Simonetti said. "Each soundtrack written by us has its own peculiarities, especially in the choice of arrangements and instruments. In *Deep Red*, we used the church organ, Moog, clavicembalo [harpsichord], acoustic and electric guitars; in *Suspiria*, we played the celesta, big Moog, and ethnic instruments; while in *Tenebrae*, we used the vocoder and drum machine."[28]

The music for *Phenomena* brought about the collaboration between several rock musicians—Simonetti and Pignatelli were on board; Argento brought in British rocker Simon Boswell after seeing him play in a club in Rome, and Boswell brought with him the Goth rock singer known as Andi Sex Gang; former Rolling Stones bassist Bill Wyman, joined by guitarist/songwriter Terry Taylor, came in and composed the "Valley" music, heard beneath the film's main title as the story's first fatality meets her doom when she enters the wrong cabin to seek help. "'Valley' wastes no time establishing the mood and the doom of *Phenomena*'s introductory victim as its cascading lead synth 'horn' evokes a chilling alpine loneliness amidst great spaces and a melancholy, haunted vulnerability," described online columnist Ben Simington.[29] The same music is arranged with a driving tempo later in the film. Argento also muscled in three licensed tracks from Iron Maiden ("Flash of the Blade"), Motörhead ("Locomotive"), and (sans credit) Frankie Goes to Hollywood ("Two Tribes") that play over three scenes.

"When he directed *Phenomena*, Dario wanted to keep up with the changing Hollywood times," Simonetti said. "Most soundtrack albums around this time (*Top Gun* for example) were filled with pop songs geared towards chart success and crossover promotion. Dario wanted to assemble his own version of that trend, the reason why Bill Wyman, Andi Sex Gang, Motörhead, and Iron Maiden were included."[30]

"I worked with Claudio Simonetti and Fabio Pignatelli for a few days, but things did not go smoothly. How could they? They had scored [three of] Dario's previous movies on their own," Simon Boswell remarked of his experience on the film. "We decided to split into separate studios to accomplish the score. I contributed about three themes plus two rock songs that I wrote and performed with Andi Sex Gang. With this, my first attempt at film music, I essentially created a collage of unlistenable sounds, feedback guitar, violin harmonics, the scrape of a plectrum down the strings of my Strat, and the wailing and moaning of green-haired Andi Sex Gang (that cue was for the scene where Jennifer Connelly's character plunges into a pit of maggot-infested body parts). When Dario first sat down and listened to it, the aural equivalent of running your fingernails down a blackboard, he pronounced it: 'Beautiful!' I can't tell you how many avenues opened up in my head at that point in time!"[31]

Phenomena inaugurated a second career for Boswell, scoring films—mostly in the horror genre and often in Italy—such as Lamberto Bava's *Demons 2* (*Dèmoni 2*; produced by Argento) and *Demons 5* (1990, *La maschera del demonio*), and went on to score Hollywood films as well, including Clive Barker's *Lord of Illusions* (1995), Richard Stanley's *Hardware* (1990) and *Dust Devil* (1992), among others.

The primary themes for *Phenomena* were composed and performed by Goblin's Simonetti and Pignatelli, including the main "Phenomena" theme with its soaring female vocals, "Jennifer," a valiant rocker for the main character performed on keyboard and bass, an associated keyboard riff for "Jennifer's Friends," and the wildly atmospheric "The Wind" with its whooshing synths and wildly intoned soprano voice.

A similar amalgamation of composers created the soundtrack for Argento's *Opera*, in which a young opera singer is stalked by a deranged fan who wants her for himself. Argento brought back Simonetti along with Wyman and Taylor, plus electronica and ambient music pioneer Brian Eno, collaborating here with his brother Roger, and a couple of songs licensed from Italian metal band Gow (here using the pseudonym Steel Grave) and Sweden's Norden Light. Steel Grave's "Knights of the Night" is used during the killer's murder of Stefano; and then the sympathetic piano and soprano vocals of Simonetti's "Opera" escorts a released, but terrified, Betty outside into the rain. "In *Opera*, I tried to give this very ferocious film a contrast to the violence with the sweetness of the opera itself," Simonetti said. "In fact, the piece 'Opera' is very sweet, very delicate."[32] In contrast, Simonetti's rock instrumental "Crows" accompanies the whirlwind attack of the freed crows into the audience where they swarm upon and reveal the identity of the killer.

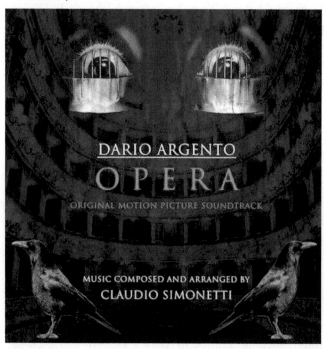

Cover art for the vinyl release of Simonetti's music for *Opera*, from Rustblade.

"I tried to divide the movie into various sections," Argento explained. "Each section I gave to a different musician ... Brian Eno composed the biggest chunk—I think he actually composed about 45 minutes, although I didn't use it all. And then [the] others each composed a different kind of music to match each different situation." Brian and Roger Eno provide much of the film's ambient tension through eerie suspended synth patterns, while Simonetti's contribution is a more aggressive component of sustained rock and roll vibe.

The dreamlike synth percussion and keyboard of Wyman and Taylor's "Black Notes" is heard during the killer's flashback of killing a woman he's held captive at the bottom of a stone staircase. Brian and Roger Eno's "Balance" sets an nervous tension when the killer slashes Betty's costume until he's disturbed by the escape of the crows from their cages; their "White Darkness" resonates with somnambulant ambiance as cast and crew discuss recent circumstances with the investigating Inspector Santini; and "From the Beginning" sets up a wonderful nervous tension just before the killer murders costume designer Giulia, while the deadly act itself is accompanied by Norden Light's "No Escape." Each of the pieces, or variations of them, are used elsewhere in the film. Gow's raucous "Steel Grave" is heard after Betty escapes from the killer using the air vents in the apartment house, and hurries out into the streets to find a refuge, while their "Knights of the Night" is reprised to accompany Betty's flight from the cabin in the film's controversial coda.

Opera has a very rich musical underscore, though its variety of musical styles makes the music work best in individual scenes rather than as an integrated audiovisual whole. Verdi's *Macbeth*, being the opera performed by the company in the film, is frequently heard, of course; in fact in one early scene, seguing from the report that diva Mara Czecova has been struck by a car to understudy Betty receiving a threatening phone call from the black-gloved killer, it's Verdi's dramatic underscore from *Macbeth* that resonates menacingly across the soundtrack. Some of the arias from the opera, played on Betty's tape recorder in her apartment, also serve as underscore to several tense sequences set therein.

In 1987, Argento created a mini-anthology series called *Gli incubi di Dario Argento* ("The Nightmares of Dario Argento"). Broadcast as part of Enzo Tortora's *Giallo* TV program, the series consisted of nine three-minute long vignettes, introduced and sometimes narrated by Argento and concluding with a kind of shock ending. The series had no original music, but rather consisted of library and licensed tracks. Its main title music, for example, was a brief two-note phrase edited from the opening fanfare of Richard Strauss' "Also

Sprach Zarathustra," best known contemporaneously as the opening and closing music from Kubrick's *2001: A Space Odyssey*. Music for its episodes consisted of cues from various Argento's films—you'll hear a bit of Morricone's *The Bird with the Crystal Plumage* in the grisly birthday party episode, "*La Strega*"/"The Witch"), the soprano vocals of "The Wind" from Simonetti's *Phenomena* waxes urgently in the final episode, "*L'incubo di chi voleva interpretare "l'incubo" di Dario Argento*"/"The Nightmare of the One Who Tried to Interpret Dario Argento's Nightmares.'" The haunting violin figure and dark, 'meowing" processed vocalization from Simon Boswell's "Maggots," also from *Phenomena*, is used as generic suspense music in each of the episodes, and portions of Simonetti's "Jennifer" (*Phenomena*, again) and "Opera" (from *Opera*) are heard here and there. Franco Micalizzi's "The Action Theme," a library track from the BMG Production Music library, was also licensed for use in the series. Several other licensed (or not) songs, including Michael Jackson's "Bad" and Italian metal band Accept's "Fast as a Shark" (previously used in the Argento produced *Demons*) are also heard in single episodes.

Argento rejoined forces with George A. Romero in *Two Evil Eyes* (*Due occhi diabolici*), in which each director spun a sinister cinematic story based on the tales of Edgar Allan Poe. Argento chose "The Black Cat," although his film actually merges a number of Poe references into a new narrative. This film was the first of three films in which Argento worked with composer Pino Donaggio, a former popstar in the 1960s who received genre cinematic acclaim in the mid-1970s when he scored a suspenseful swath of horror films—first for Nicolas Roeg (*Don't Look Now*) and then with newly minted directors Brian De Palma (*Carrie, Dressed To Kill*), Joe Dante (*Piranha, The Howling*), and David Schmoeller (*Tourist Trap, Crawlspace*).

Donaggio, who incidentally composed the score for Lucio Fulci's own *The Black Cat* in 1981, gave the score for *Two Evil Eyes* a sonic mix of pop-rhythms and more traditional orchestral film scoring. His opening theme "Dreaming Dreams" is a compelling soft rock ballad featuring a double-tracked female singer (uncredited) over a drum-heavy synthpop underbelly. Perhaps somewhat reminiscent of Morricone's theme song from *The Bird with the Crystal Plumage*, its melody is reprised orchestrally elsewhere in the film, including a variation, called "Shadyside," given a vivid jazz rendition for rhythm section. Most of the film, however, features Donaggio's signature spine-tingling string writing familiar from his De Palma and Dante scores.

Donaggio also scored Argento's next film, 1993's *Trauma*, which like *Two Evil Eyes*, was filmed in America.

Dario Argento presents *La Chioma di Berenice* Lifetime Achievement Award to composer Pino Donaggio.

In between the composer had written the music for Michele Soavi's *The Sect* (*La setta*), which Argento had also produced. *Trauma* has a more classically-structured orchestral score than *Two Evil Eyes*, very much in the Bernard Herrmann vein which influenced Donaggio back in the '70s. It does feature a song, "Ruby Rain" (lyrics by Paolo Steffan and sung by Laura Evan), which is heard late in the film in the scene where boyfriend David believes Aura has been drowned in a lake and, grief-stricken, swims out to try and recover her; the song also segues out of the reggae band heard at the film's end to play through the end titles. The song is an especially poignant one, a grieving ode to a lost love, adding a poignant bit of emotive sympathy to an otherwise suspenseful score.

"I remember meeting [Pino] in a hotel in Venice," Argento described how he worked with Donaggio in *Trauma*. "[I listened] to what he had already done on his computer. I told him at what points in my opinion the soundtrack had to be modified. I think it would take a little more rhythm in some passages. I walked away for a couple of hours and on my way back to the hotel, Pino had already made the planned changes, and I think he did a good job."[33]

Donaggio returned four films later to score Argento's made-for-TV mystery thriller *Do You Like Hitchcock?*. This film too contains a main pop tune with a sultry female-voice, not unlike "Dream of Dreams," but its wordless vocals serves more of an instrumental role here than the lyric content of the earlier film. Donaggio's string writing, almost always modeled after that of Bernard Herrmann for his many Hitchcock scores, fits both the tone and the title of this mystery thriller; if not via Herrmann's well-known chord progressions then definitely via his deft violin phrasing and the strings' atmospheric tonal range. "I asked composer Pino Donaggio to come up with a typical Bernard Herrmann violin-heavy score," Argento said.[34] Donaggio accommodated but only in part—he also incorporates the anachronistically un-

Herrmannesque idiom of contemporary electronics and seductive vocals to identify the voyeurism of main character Giulio, while the frantic pace of at least one of the murder scenes is energized by the ferocious attack of multiple horns accompanied by the distinct robotic beat of a drum machine.

In a 2017 interview with the Italian website cinecitta.com, Donaggio reports that he had a very good experience working with Argento, adding, "But only in *Trauma* I managed to remain coherent as I used to do with De Palma. Argento slips from pop music to jazz improvisation. He has an idea and just exits from the soundtrack line."[35]

After completing *Trauma* in 1993, Argento decided it was time to reconnect with Morricone, and asked him to score *The Stendhal Syndrome* (*La sindrome di Stendhal*) a psychological thriller about the growing connection between a serial killer and the police officer on his trail, who happens to be afflicted with the titular psychosomatic disease that causes hallucinations when she is exposed to works of fine art. So, the film's climax, of course, plays out in a huge art museum. The score mixes voices with the music, random and converging excerpts of normal conversation as well as the kind of sexual moans Morricone had used in Argento's *The Bird with the Crystal Plumage*, which create a very disorienting and unsettling atmosphere, especially when contrasted against a ringing, piercing synth tonality.

"When I read the script, the music I subsequently wrote came immediately to mind," Morricone explained. He noted his use of music-noise in his scores for Argento's Animal Trilogy, "in which harsh sounds [were] melded with traditional strings … but in the new story there were paintings, classical material. So, I had a natural impulse to write some music that would create a certain classical atmosphere … [I] had an intuition that my music would give the film a certain classicism, in line with the powerful presence of the paintings."[36]

One motif used for the officer's hallucinatory moments consists of four slowly climbing notes, followed by four slowly returning, repeated over and over, heard from strings over harpsichord or celeste, and also from sung female "la-las," which build a disorienting pattern enhancing the character's dizziness and delirium in the art museum; the up-and-down melodic pattern is somewhat along the lines that Bernard Herrmann crafted in his *Vertigo* (1958) music, and the effect is similarly bewildering. Morricone exploits this fact by adding increased volume and velocity, a strident drum beat, brassy punctuation, to create an almost nightmarish quality.

In 1997 Argento produced Sergio Stivaletti's affectionate homage to wax museum horror films, *Wax Mask* (*Maschera di cera*). Stivaletti brought in his own composer, Maurizio Abeni, who he had worked with previously and would again afterwards.

Back on home territory the following year, and

Cover for the Italian CD release from Image Music; Morricone's final score for Argento proved to be his most lush and melodic.

with Morricone once more, Argento, having teased the tale with *Opera*, ambitiously embarked to make his own version of the actual classic horror melodrama, *The Phantom of the Opera* (*Il fantasma dell'opera*). Said Morricone: "When I did *The Stendhal Syndrome* and later *The Phantom of the Opera*, I changed the style because [Dario had] also changed his style. He told a more in-depth story by focusing less on certain types of horrifying things that were in the other three films I did."[37] This score is formulated with a dichotomy of sublime melancholy and rhythmic, relenting oppression. In both melody and tone, his main theme is reminiscent of his wistful melody from *Once Upon A Time in America*, a soft and gentle motif for strings over piano. The theme is associated with Christine, who becomes enamored by—and entangled with—the phantom denizen of the catacombs. Similar sustained strings are associated with the phantom, but where of course Christine's music is pretty and fragile, the phantom's motif is laced with malevolence and darkness. Music from the tombs, essentially, it will jolt to life with an abrupt jostle of strings and percussion, and as suddenly it morphs back into mysterioso and then is gone.

Christine's rival, Carlotta, the diva for whom she understudies (and who is the unfortunate victim of much of the phantom's menace as he seeks to promote Christine into her place in the opera company), is associated with a slow wash of violins over a pulsing twang from, first, pizzicato violin and later electric bass. The climax brings all the players together, wherein Morricone reorients his suspense music: bold descents of brass over fast strokes of strings drive the film's crescendo, after which it spirals into a quiet downward tonality as the phantom submerges below the subterranean waves of the river. For the film's operatic moments (Argento described these classical pieces as "the real engine of the film"[38]), Morricone adapted excerpts from "Carmen," Gounod's "Faust" and "Romeo and Juliet" which had been selected by the director.

Another reunion occurred when Argento returned to *giallo* territory with 2001's *Sleepless* (*Nonhosonno*), with a reassembled Goblin—back in form with its basic *Dawn of the Dead* line-up: Agostino Marangolo, Massimo Morante, Fabio Pignatelli, and Claudio Simonetti. Actually, Argento had originally sought Serbian composer Goran Bregovich to score this film, because his music for director Emir Kusturica's Yugoslavian films had impressed him (Argento: "I thought experimenting with his themes would be interesting. Ennio Morricone always wrote victim music to my mind and Goblin seemed always to be on the villain's side. Something in between was intriguing…")[39] Bregovich wrote out a few cues, but when his fee became too hefty for Argento's taste, the director called on Simonetti and asked if he could reform Goblin's *Deep Red/Suspiria* line-up and create the music for *Sleepless*. "So, I contacted my friends and they agreed," Simonetti recalled. But "it was very hard to work together again … because we hadn't played for 22 years and we were not ready to play together again."[40]

Cover for the Cinevox release of Dario's long-awaited reunion with Goblin.

The film had to do with an elderly retired police detective and a young amateur sleuth who team up to find a serial killer whom has resumed a killing spree after a 17-year hiatus. The use of a heavy rock score fit the story and Argento's *giallo* style of filming it, in addition to providing an elegant power ballad for the film's romantic scenes, replete with soaring soprano vocals. The style of 1970s-era Goblin with their traditional mix of electric guitar, arpeggiated keyboards, bass and drums shines through every so often, although the sound is heavier and broader in scope. "It was great to work with Goblin again," Argento said. "What I needed from them was a nervous and edgy music score that could unsettle [the audience]. This is in contrast with some of my other movies where I used Ennio Morricone for his ability to create an epic feel through his music."[41]

Simonetti returned alone to score Argento's next *giallo*, *The Card Player* (*Il cartaio*), in which a Roman policewoman teams up with a British Interpol agent to find a serial killer who is abducting and killing young women and showing it over an Internet web cam. This film as well as its score were largely inspired by Gaspar Noé's 2002 French crime drama, *Irréversible*, which had been scored by Thomas Bangalter (one half of the French house music duo Daft Punk). Argento asked Simonetti to emulate its score. "Claudio Simonetti also has dance music in his past, so I asked him, rather than Goblin, to compose the score," Argento remembered. "I'm not talking rap or Euro-disco but a House/Garage carpet of music that is continually in the background fading in and out at the right moments to heighten the fright. I want to summon up hysteria and spine-tingling nervousness through a repetitive beat."[42]

"When he called me to write the soundtrack for *Il cartaio*, Dario, given the style of his thriller, asked me to do a totally computerized electronic sound, made with keyboards, synthesizers, drum machine, and also using typical "techno" music of contemporary European electronic music," Simonetti explained. "Also, for the first time I found myself writing music during the making of a film, from the very start. I've been on set several times and I watched Dario shooting, and this helped me to get into the spirit of the film."[43]

Simonetti also scored both of the episodes that Argento directed for the America *Masters of Horror* television series (2005-2007), *Jenifer* and *Pelts*. Simonetti played electric bass and guitar as well as keyboards on both scores, which were primarily synth-driven compositions to evoke tension and some aural anxiety, but enhanced by bringing in a four-player violin section and child voice for *Jenifer* to provide a sympathetic motif for the feral, bestial woman of the title, and a female singer and drummer for *Pelts*, whose cruel backwoods

Cover for the Italian CD release through the Deep Red label.

hunter protagonist faces a grisly lesson in raccoon/furrier social politics. Both hour-long episodes have their suspense flavored and jolted by Simonetti's scores, with *Jenifer* in many levels echoing the keyboard articulations and voicings of *Deep Red* while *Pelts* reflects in its violin harmonics another classic score for a horror film involving skin removal and wearing: Bernard Herrmann's *Psycho*. Both episodes end with massive chaotic discordances worthy of their resolutions.

When Argento belatedly made the third movie in his Three Mother triptych, *Mother of Tears* (*La terza madre*), Simonetti composed a massive score replete with electronics, a small ensemble of strings and brass, and a sizeable choir. The instruments enhanced Simonetti's keyboards and vice-versa providing a thickly conveyed score that fit the large scale of Argento's saga of the denouement of Mater Lachrymarum and her cannibal cabal. It's a thickly textured work, and more orchestral-sounding in timbre than Simonetti's previous electronics-based scores. To add enhanced power to the music, Simonetti added in a chorus of guttural chants, reflecting a set of Evil Commandments paralleling but reversing biblical text, to be uttered by the three awakened demons. The chants were devised by dialogue coach Lynn Swanson and actor Clive Riche ("Man in the Overcoat") and given to Simonetti to write into the score.

Argento's 2009 thriller, *Giallo*, based for the first time on someone else's script, was something of a shift in both its story and its treatment. It's also unique in the Argento canon for being scored in a classic symphonic tradition, by classically trained and focused composer Marco Werba (*Zoo*, *Darkness Surrounds Roberta*, *Dead on Time*). Werba's music for *Giallo* is a departure from the electronic rhythm-based scores of some of Argento's earlier films. "I met with Dario several times to discuss the music style that would best fit the needs of the film," said Werba. "I thought that the film had equal qualities to the Hitchcock and De Palma masterpieces. For this reason, I suggested to the director to write a symphonic film score which would increase the quality of the film to a first-class level. Argento gave me freedom to write for his film as I felt was best. He only asked me to compose a specific music theme for the first scenes in which a taxi is driving through the city like a shark searching for prey. I tried to create a theme that had the same aura as the John Williams, *Jaws* theme. I only used it for the main titles and the taxi scenes." Werba created a number of themes for the characters and their interactions, including a long, dramatic sequence in which a would-be victim escapes from the killer's house in search of freedom ... "In this sequence I created an epic music motif, starting with strings and harp and going into a large orchestra with the horns playing the main theme."[44] Werba's score was the winner of the "Fantasy and Horror Award" at the 2010 Fantafestival in Rome.

Simonetti's last score for Argento, to date, is for the director's ambitious *Dracula*. He reflected the story's filmic sensibility with a score that is heavy on Gypsy violin, rugged runs of piano, highly reverberated clusters of harp notes, and eerie wails from a Theremin (the first use of this classic horror/science fiction instrument in an Argento score). In contrast to the simpler melodies of the early Goblin scores, the music of *Dracula* is thick with atmosphere that takes its substance from horror cinema's musical legacies—with sonic elements reflective of the Universal and Hammer eras, as well as the initial Argento era of electronic horror scoring, creating a sonic texture that carries the legacy of Goblin into the present day.

In a 2015 interview, Simonetti was asked to contrast the music for modern horror films with that of those classic eras of horror moviemaking. "Music for horror films has really changed from 1940 to now, surely also has the relevant acoustics, which were sometime very rock orientated. But I honestly love to be closed off to the old style, especially in *Dracula* ... where I tried to recreate the typical atmosphere of the Hammer films, even though it was with modern sound."[45]

Simonetti and all the others are members of a rare group of film composers and musicians who have left profound and memorable musical accomplishments in their music for the unique cinematic world of Dario Argento.

Randall D. Larson wrote his first soundtrack album review in 1972 and hasn't stopped writing about movie music yet. He went on to become the editor/publisher of CinemaScore: The Film Music Journal *in the 1980s, senior editor for* Soundtrack Magazine *in the 1990s, and served as a film music columnist for* Cinefantastique *magazine from 1982 to 1999. A specialist on horror & science fiction film music, he is the author of* Musique Fantastique: 100+ Years of Fantasy, Science Fiction & Horror Film Music *and* Music from the House of Hammer. *He currently writes articles on film music and sf/horror cinema, and has written liner notes for nearly 300 soundtrack CDs. Randall can be contacted at via https://musiquefantastique.com/*

Multiple segments from Dario Argento, The Man, the Myth & the Magic *(available from www.fabpress.com/) are quoted with permission of Alan Jones, with thanks.*

Notes:
1. Hughes, Howard, *Cinema Italiano*, London: I.P. Taurus & Co., 2011, p. 228.
2. Quoted from the featurette "Conducting Dario Argento's *Opera*," included on the Anchor Bay DVD release of *Opera*.
3. http://www.electricsheepmagazine.co.uk/features/2009/07/03/interview-with-dario-argento/
4. Bendoni, Daniel, notes to *The Stendhal Syndrome* soundtrack album (DRG Records CD, 1999), p.5.
5. Douglas Payne, notes to *Morricone Giallo* soundtrack compilation album (U.K.: Bella Casa/Cherry Red Records CD, 2007), p. 5.
6. Payne, Douglas, notes to *Morricone Giallo*, p. 5.
7. Fuiano, Claudio, notes to *4 mosche di velluto grigio* soundtrack album, Cinevox, 2007, p. 2.
8. Chang, Ed, "The Bird with the Crystal Plumage," http://cuebycue.blogspot.com/2016/06/the-bird-with-crystal-plumage-morricone.html (discussing album track 3).
9. Chang, last paragraph of blog.
10. Ibid.
11. Bilson, Anne, "Violence, Mystery and Magic: How to Spot a *Giallo* Movie." *The Telegraph*, Oct. 14, 2013.
12. Quoted from the featurette "Music for Murder," included on the Blue Underground Blu-ray release of *The Bird with the Crystal Plumage*.
13. Jones, Alan, *Dario Argento: The Man, the Myths & the Magic*, (Godalming: FAB Press, 2012), p. 40.
14. Ibid, p. 65.
15. Traynor, Cian, "A Peculiar Kind of Music: Ennio Morricone Interviewed," http://thequietus.com/articles/ 19432-ennio-morricone-interview
16. Jones, Alan, *Dario Argento: The Man, the Myths & the Magic*, (Godalming: FAB Press, 2012), p. 65.
17. Colegate, Mat, "Claudio With A Chance of Pain: Simonetti On *Profondo rosso*, posted at http://thequietus.com/articles/17023-claudio-simonetti-interview
18. Jones, Alan, *Dario Argento: The Man, the Myths & the Magic*, (Godalming: FAB Press, 2012), p. 65.
19. Yanick, Joe, "Legendary Horror Score Composer Claudio Simonetti is Still a Phenomena," https://noisey.vice.com/en_us/article/64yxyp/simonetti-interview-demons-life-after-goblin
20. Paul, Louis, *Italian Film Directors*, (Jefferson: McFarland & Co., 2005), p. 48.
21. "progcroc:" "Goblin Up the Years ... Claudio Simonetti interviewed in 2006," posted online March 22, 2016 at https://houseoffreudstein.wordpress.com/2016/03/22/profondo-simonetti-claudio-simonetti-interviewed-in-2006/
22. Colegate, Mat, "Claudio With A Chance of Pain: Simonetti On *Profondo rosso*, posted at http://thequietus.com/articles/17023-claudio-simonetti-interview
23. https://crypticrock.com/interview-claudio-simonetti-of-goblin
24. Jones, Alan, *Dario Argento: The Man, the Myths & the Magic*, (Godalming: FAB Press, 2012), p. 115-116.
25. Ibid, p. 116.
26. Quoted from the "A Composition for Carnage: Claudio Simonetti on *Tenebrae*" featurette included on the Arrow Video Blu-ray edition of *Tenebrae*.
27. http://thethinair.net/2015/10/interview-claudio-simonetti/
28. O'Connor, Anthony, "Claudio Simonetti: Music to Die For," https://www.filmink.com.au/claudio-simonetti-music-die/
29. Simongton, Ben, "Lost Sounds and Soundtracks. Dario Argento's *Phenomena*," https://mubi.com/notebook/postomes/lost-sounds-and-soundtracks-dario-argentos-phenomena
30. Jones, Alan, *Dario Argento: The Man, the Myths & the Magic*, (Godalming: FAB Press, 2012), p. 79.
31. Larson, Randall D., "Lord of Musical Illusions: A Conversation with Simon Boswell" *Soundtrax*, May 2009
32. Quoted from the featurette "Conducting Dario Argento's *Opera*," included on the Anchor Bay DVD release of *Opera*.
33. D'Elia, Donato, "Interview with Dario Argento, from the Sandman project to the Rome Film Festival," posted online Oct. 21, 2015.
34. Jones, Alan, *Dario Argento: The Man, the Myths & the Magic*, (Godalming: FAB Press, 2012), p. 335.
35. Stefanutto Rosa, Stefano, "Pino Donaggio: From Sanremo to Brian De Palma," https://news.cinecitta.com/EN/en/news/104/71813/pino-donaggio-from-sanremo-to-brian-de-palma.aspx
36. Bendoni, Daniel, notes to *The Stendhal Syndrome* soundtrack album (DRG Records CD, 1999), p. 3-4.
37. Quoted from the featurette "Music for Murder," included on the Blue Underground Blu-ray release of *The Bird with the Crystal Plumage*.
38. Notes to *The Phantom of the Opera* soundtrack album (DRG Records CD, 1999), p. 6.
39. Jones, Alan, *Dario Argento: The Man, the Myths & the Magic*, (Godalming: FAB Press, 2012), p. 290.
40. "progcroc:" "Goblin Up the Years ... Claudio Simonetti interviewed in 2006," posted online March 22 2016 at https://houseoffreudstein.wordpress.com/2016/03/22/profondo-simonetti-claudio-simonetti-interviewed-in-2006/
41. Haflidason, Almar, http://www.bbc.co.uk/films/2002/02/08/dario_argento_sleepless_interview.shtml
42. Jones, Alan, *Dario Argento: The Man, the Myths & the Magic*, (Godalming: FAB Press, 2012), p. 306.
43. Notes to *Il cartaio* soundtrack album, Simonetti prods. S.a.s. 2004, p. 6-7.
44. Larson, Randall D., April 5, 2009.
45. http://thethinair.net/2015/10/interview-claudio-simonetti/

Inside Out: Reinterpreting *The Stendhal Syndrome*
by Michael Mackenzie

At the time of its release, critical responses to Dario Argento's *The Stendhal Syndrome* (*La sindrome di Stendhal*) were less than effusive. A "poorly acted, over-the-top, and generally out-of-control bloodbath" was the verdict of Jonathan Rosenbaum in the *Chicago Reader*. "Flimsy, facile identity psychodrama," declared *L.A. Weekly*'s Hazel-Dawn Dumpert, who also took time to condemn "its horrific and typically misogynistic violence." In *Variety*, David Rooney described much of the plot as "pure hokum," and decried the "increasing silliness" of the "sluggish second half." Even the Argento faithful weren't keen to muster up much in the way of a defense. Maitland McDonagh, who penned the first serious study of the maestro's films in the seminal *Broken Mirrors/Broken Minds* (1991), expressed disappointment at its failure to capture "the baroque heights of *Opera* and *Tenebrae*," while Alan Jones, who has arguably done more over the years to champion Argento than any other critic, was even more withering in his assessment, declaring it "a doggy bag of leftover ideas from the maestro's Pizza Paura takeaway."

It wasn't supposed to be like this. Prior to its release, *The Stendhal Syndrome* was hotly anticipated as Argento's triumphant return to his native Italy, newly unfettered after the frustrations of working within the U.S. production system with the uneven George A. Romero collaboration *Two Evil Eyes* (*Due occhi diabolici*) and the ambitious but deeply flawed *Trauma*. The prevailing wisdom was that the *maestro*'s creative voice had been reined in by cowardly American producers (a theory given credence by Argento's own comments on the matter), and so his homecoming was accompanied by expectations of a return to the *Grand Guignol* highs of his golden period: the fluid, mobile camerawork of *Opera*, the lurid colors of *Suspiria* and *Inferno*, the bold, stylized violence of *Tenebrae* (*Tenebre*), and the classic *giallo* plotting of *Deep Red* (*Profondo rosso*) and the Animal Trilogy. What audiences got, however, was a film that was far more muted and reflective in its approach to violence, style, and characterization than anything previously seen from Argento: more Bergman than Bava.

The reviews quoted above fall, broadly speaking, into two categories. On the one hand, we have critics unfamiliar with Argento's work objecting to the idiosyncrasies his long-term followers have long taken for granted: the questionable dubbing, the brutal violence, the often-dreamlike logic. On the other, we see those used to the director's usual stylistic exuberance expressing confusion and disappointment in the face of a lack of the vicarious thrills of a *Deep Red* or even a *Cat O'Nine Tails* (*Il gatto a nove code*). For *Stendhal* occupies a curious place in Argento's filmography, both radically different to its predecessors while at the same time adapting and re-exploring the same themes and obsessions to which Argento has repeatedly returned throughout his lengthy career. It is in respect of the latter that I think the film is most interesting, for in spite of its more superficial differences, it is nonetheless part of a common thread which runs all the way back to his first feature, *The Bird with the Crystal Plumage* (*L'uccello dalle piume di cristallo*). With this essay, my aim is to tease out the relationship between *Stendhal* and Argento's directorial debut, arguing that, despite seeming on the surface to have little in common, they are in fact very much two sides of the same coin, approaching the same scenario in different ways and, in effect, bringing their maker's career full circle.

Detective Anna Manni (Asia Argento) arrives in Florence, hunting a serial rapist who has recently begun killing his victims. While responding to a tip-off at the Uffizi Gallery, she becomes stricken by the Stendhal syndrome, a condition which causes those afflicted to be overpowered by works of great art. Her quarry, the charismatic Alfredo Grossi (Thomas Kretschmann), witnesses her collapse and follows her back to her hotel room, where he overpowers and rapes her. Anna escapes, but Alfredo remains at large, and he ultimately follows her to her hometown of Viterbo, where he kidnaps her and subjects her to another harrowing assault. Eventually, Anna is able to break free and overpower Alfredo, whose mutilated body she tosses into the nearby river.

Anna again tries to return to normal life, changing her appearance and beginning a relationship with a French student, Marie (Julien Lambroschini). However, she remains plagued by memories of her ordeal, and grows convinced that Alfredo (whose body was never found) is still alive and stalking her. She subsequently finds Marie murdered, sending her into a spiral of despair. Meanwhile, her psychologist, Dr. Cavanna (Paolo Bonacelli), discovers the truth: That Alfredo is indeed dead and that Anna herself was responsible for Marie's murder, having assumed the mantle of her tormenter's identity. Cavanna confronts Anna at her home, but she kills both him and her colleague and ex-lover Marco (Marco Leonardi) before fleeing into the street, where, overcome by her multiple conflicting identities, she collapses in a fit of despair and insanity. As the credits roll, the last we see of Anna is her being carried through the streets by her former colleagues, now a broken and empty shell.

There is an argument, with which I have some sympathy, that Argento has been remaking the same film throughout his career. It's possible to overstate the case somewhat, but there's no denying that a common set of themes, character types, and plot devices persist throughout his filmography and that, with the exceptions of the "Three Mothers" trilogy, the lamentable *Dario Argento's Dracula*, and his ill-fated historical comedy *Le cinque giornate*, all his films have adhered, to varying degrees, to the classic cinematic *giallo* template established by Mario Bava with his pioneering works *The Girl Who Knew Too Much* (*La ragazza che sapeva troppo*, 1963) and *Blood and Black Lace* (*6 donne per l'assassino*, 1964), and popularized by Argento himself with *The Bird with the Crystal Plumage*. Of all his subsequent films, *Deep Red* is the one that is most obviously a re-telling of his directorial debut, substituting Tony Musante's frustrated writer with David Hemmings' uptight jazz pianist and an attacker mistaken for a victim with a mirror reflection mistaken for a painting. That said, echoes of these conventions recur throughout Argento's work: the vast majority of his protagonists are outsiders connected to the arts in some way, and even *Suspiria*'s half-heard clue about "secret irises" is, in its own way, a reworking of *Bird*'s misunderstood "primal scene" (to borrow a turn of phrase from Freud).

At first glance, making *The Stendhal Syndrome* fit this framework seems like something of a stretch. For one thing, there's no mystery to the killer's identity to unravel: Alfredo is revealed as the murderous rapist Anna has been pursuing within the opening 15 minutes—a move which could hardly have failed to disappoint viewers who'd turned up anticipating a classical *giallo* whodunit. For another, unlike any of Argento's previous films (save perhaps *Tenebrae*, which pulls off a vaguely similar sleight of hand, albeit with a far less jarring shift in pace and tone), *Stendhal* has a distinctive two-part structure, splitting the narrative into two halves which we might call "Before Alfredo" and "After Alfredo." When Anna turns the tables on Alfredo and kills him at the film's midpoint, any notion that *Stendhal* is going to adhere to the conventions of a standard serial killer thriller is promptly jettisoned, leaving us—and Anna—in an odd sort of limbo where the film seems to have lost its *raison d'être* and can only limp along to its bloody conclusion, half-heartedly paying lip service to the rather unconvincing notion that—shock, horror!—Alfredo might still be alive and continuing his campaign of terror against Anna.

To better understand *Stendhal*'s relationship to Argento's more traditional *gialli*, we must take a step back and break these films down into their structural components. Doing so reveals that *Stendhal*'s two-part structure is less unique than one might assume at first

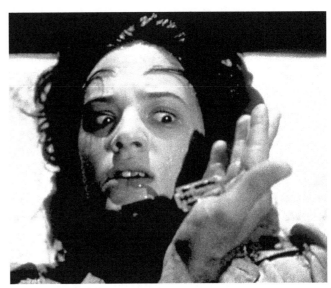

Alfredo (Thomas Kretschmann) demonstrates his inability to feel pain to a horrified Anna Manni (Asia Argento).

glance. In fact, *all* Argento's other films exhibit this same narrative split; the difference is in how they go about structuring it. Every Argento *giallo*—indeed every *giallo* in which the killer's motive is rooted in a past trauma as opposed to something more banal like a plot to seize the protagonist's inheritance money—is effectively two stories rolled into one. There is the "before" story, in which, at some point prior to the film beginning, a character endures a horrific ordeal which leaves them permanently damaged and consumed by murderous tendencies. Then there is the "after" story, the phase which takes place in the present day during the film proper, in which the character's latent madness is reawakened and they embark on a murder spree until they are identified and apprehended or themselves killed.

For my part, it took me several viewings to realize that, for all its structural differences, *Stendhal*'s story was the same one to which Argento has returned time and again throughout his career. The key breakthrough for me lay in the realization that I was approaching the character of Anna all wrong. Anna is unusual in that she occupies a dual function as both protagonist and antagonist—a role she shares with another iconic Argento character, novelist-turned-killer Peter Neal in *Tenebrae*. During my initial viewings, I focused primarily on the "protagonist" side of her role, in which respect she has little in common with Argento's typical "accidental eyewitness" anti-heroes. She doesn't, for example, witness a crime and fail to understand the significance of a key clue; nor does she conform to the archetype of the Bohemian artist abroad.

The "eureka" moment for me came when, a number of years ago, I was researching my PhD thesis on representations of gender in the *giallo*, and more specifically the chapter focusing on those that feature a female protagonist—or, as I've termed them elsewhere, "F-*gialli*." There is insufficient space here to detail my findings in full,[1] but broadly speaking my conclusion, after having watched and spent more time thinking about *gialli* than any sane person would, was that, in the typical *giallo*, female characters are presented as a "problem" to be solved—a challenge to the traditional, male-dominated social order that needs to be neutralized before equilibrium can be restored. This remains true whether the character in question is the protagonist, as with Julie Wardh (Edwige Fenech) in Sergio Martino's iconic *The Strange Vice of Mrs. Wardh* (*Lo strano vizio della Signora Wardh*, 1971), or the villain, as with the majority of Argento's 1970s films. As such, the most important aspect of any female character in a *giallo* is not whether she is the heroine or the villain: it is that she is a woman.

The article which led to this epiphany was "Caging Women's Rage", an analysis by Frank Burke of *The Bird with the Crystal Plumage* which takes the radical (and arguably provocative) step of recasting the film's villain, deranged serial killer Monica Ranieri (Eva Renzi), as the film's heroine, presenting her violence as a triumphant fightback against the violence inflicted on her by a cruel, male-dominated society. This reading, of course, glosses over the fact that most of Monica's victims are themselves women, which severely undercuts the notion that her actions strike a blow against patriarchal tyranny. As a result, I think Burke's argument is more effective as an interesting thought experiment than as a literal interpretation of the film. The idea of Monica as heroine stuck with me, however. In his own mind, even the most brutal dictator or genocidal maniac believes he's doing the right thing: as screenwriting guru Christopher Vogler put it in *The Writer's Journey*, "Every villain is a hero of his or her own story." And, if such a philosophy can be applied to Lex Luthor or the Joker, then why not to the killers in *gialli* as well? Suddenly, I realized I had been reading *Stendhal* all wrong, and that Anna Manni's most direct analogue in *Bird* was not that film's protagonist—amateur sleuth Sam Dalmas (Tony Musante)—but rather the deranged and damaged Monica.

At this stage, it might be helpful to revisit the basic plot of *Bird*, restructuring it into a more linear fashion by splitting it into distinct "before" and "after" phases, and shifting the emphasis from protagonist to antagonist:

BEFORE: As a young girl, Monica is subjected to a brutal sexual assault by a knife-wielding maniac. She survives the ordeal, but the trauma leaves her mind permanently scarred.

AFTER: Several years later, the now adult Monica encounters a painting by the artist Berto Consalvi (Mario Adorf) depicting her assault. This awakens a dormant psychosis in her and, rather than identifying with the representation of herself in the painting, she instead aligns herself with her attacker. She embarks on a series of murders of young women, recreating her own assault, until finally being apprehended by the police.

In his report from the *Stendhal* set in 1995, Alan Jones revealed that one of the projects Argento had considered after the disappointing critical and commercial fortunes of *Trauma* was a remake of *The Bird with the Crystal Plumage*. While Jones describes this proposal, much like concurrent plans to produce an updated version of *Der Golem* or a big budget Spaghetti Western, as having fallen by the wayside, I would argue that Argento actually *did*, in effect, end up remaking *Bird*—just not in the literal sense that most people understand by the term "remake." The primary difference between the two films is one of structure and perspective as opposed to plot, and, if we recast *Bird* as Monica's story rather than Sam's, the parallels between her and Anna Manni are clear. Both films, boiled down to their core essentials, are the story of a woman who is brutalized by a male attacker, survives her ordeal but is driven mad by what she experienced, and at a later point snaps and begins committing murders herself, having subsumed a part of her attacker's identity into her own. In *Bird*, several years elapse between the initial attack on Monica and her embarking on her own killing spree, whereas in *Stendhal*, the interval between Anna vanquishing Alfredo and committing her first murder (that of her boyfriend Marie) appears to be one of mere weeks. In almost every other respect, however, the narratives of *Bird* and *Stendhal* run parallel to one another, even concluding in much the same manner, with the delirious Monica/Anna subdued and carried off by police officers toward an uncertain future. It's tempting to envisage an unfilmed post-credits

German lobby card for *The Bird with the Crystal Plumage*, showing Monica (Eva Renzi) in distress.

coda in which a psychologist-for-hire attempts to explain Anna's behavior in a series of cod-psychoanalytical musings under the harsh glare of television studio lights, much like the puffed-up Professor Rinaldi (Giovanni Di Benedetto) in *Bird*'s final scene.

In essence, then, *Stendhal* takes the classical Argento *giallo* formula—a person, usually a woman, is subjected to some form of appalling psychosexual trauma, and the resulting psychosis leads to her embarking on a murder spree—and turns on its head, re-ordering it in a linear fashion and, in so doing, laying bare what these films are ultimately all about. For, as much as Argento's *gialli* were made to entertain, there is a common thread running through them—a way of viewing the world, if you like—that gives them a degree of depth and thematic richness beyond those of the majority of his contemporaries. That's not to say that all other *gialli* were devoid of substance. For instance, with his "schoolgirls in peril" *gialli*—*What Have You Done to Solange?* (*Cosa avete fatto a Solange?*, 1972) and *What Have They Done to Your Daughters?* (*La polizia chiede aiuto*, 1974)—Massimo Dallamano explored the exploitation of minors and the fraught relationships between them and their parents, while Lucio Fulci used settings as disparate as the swinging London of *A Lizard in a Woman's Skin* (*Una lucertola con la pelle di donna*, 1971) and the backwards southern Italian village of *Don't Torture a Duckling* (*Non si sevizia un paperino*, 1972) to convey his bleakly misanthropic view of humanity. But neither of these filmmakers returned to the same preoccupations with the sort of frequency and consistency exhibited by Argento—and not just because neither of them virtually dedicated their careers to the *giallo* in the way Argento has. Simply put, there is a thematic consistency to Argento's work matched by no other *giallo* director, and across all his *gialli* from the '70s through to the '90s, the image of the abused woman who turns to violence herself recurs with remarkable consistency.[2]

As the victim turned serial killer, Anna Manni's character journey is one shared by any number of previous (and subsequent) Argento villains, from the initial trauma in her hotel room to her eventual apprehension by her police colleagues. For instance, Nina Tobias (Mimsy Farmer) in *Four Flies on Grey Velvet* (*4 mosche di velluto grigio*) was physically and emotionally abused by her father, who, angry that he ended up with a daughter rather than a son, raised her as a boy and beat her to drive the "weakness" out of her. At the film's climax, we discover that the various murders she committed are part of a campaign waged against the film's protagonist, Nina's husband Roberto (Michael Brandon), who bears a strong resemblance to her late father. The father is therefore the cause of her psychosis, while the husband (albeit through no fault of his own) reinforces it. Similarly, Adriana Petrescu (Piper Laurie) in the aptly named *Trauma* is compelled to kill as a result of a botched medical procedure, performed by Dr. Lloyd (Brad Dourif), which resulted in the decapitation of her baby. Frau Brückner (Daria Nicolodi) in *Phenomena* (1985) kills to cover up the murders of her deformed son, the product of her rape by an inmate at an insane asylum. Even Marta (Clara Calamai) in *Deep Red*, while ostensibly not a victim in the conventional sense, is railing against male oppression of a sort, albeit of a far more benign variety than any of the other examples: in the flashback towards the end of the film which reveals what really happened during the primal scene, we discover that her present-day killing spree is committed in order to cover up her murder of her husband after (it is implied) he tried to have her committed.

Stendhal, then, is far from a wholesale *volte-face* from the films that preceded it—and yet it still manages to feel wholly different. The pleasures of watching this film—if indeed "pleasures" is the right word—seem almost diametrically opposed to those of his '70s and '80s *gialli*. Above all else, the violence in *Stendhal* simply isn't "fun." Whereas the "violence numbers" (as Aaron Smuts has described the various murder sequences in *Deep Red*) were undoubtedly among the main selling points of his earlier films, it's difficult to derive any enjoyment from the brutal rapes and murders depicted here. In stark contrast to the almost operatic nature of, say, *Suspiria*'s opening double murder or the masterful "bullet through the keyhole" shot in *Opera*, *Stendhal*'s violence is squalid, ugly, and degrading, and the psychological marks it leaves on its victims linger long after the outer scars have faded. The sight of Anna, after being raped for the first time, standing in front of a hospital mirror hacking off her hair with a pair of surgical scissors has no equal in the *gialli* of the '70s and points to a degree of introspection not previously demonstrated by the director. Only in the scene of Anna's turning of the tables on Alfredo, in which she punctures his neck with mattress springs, rams her finger into his eye and shoots him several times, are we invited to actively "enjoy" any of the violence, and even this is more of a cathartic release *à la I Spit on Your Grave* (Meir Zarchi, 1978) after the abuse to which we've witnessed him subjecting her earlier. The cinematography, too, reinforces this new, understated approach. If I had to describe it with a single word, it would be "dignified." Giuseppe Rotunno, in his sole collaboration with Argento, delivers lighting and camerawork that are impeccable on a technical level and yet rarely call attention to themselves. We're a long way from the arch style of *Tenebrae* or the gaudy Technicolor of *Suspiria*. It's almost as if Argento is saying to us: "You've had your fun, but this is how it *really* is."

Opinions differ as to precisely when Argento's "golden age" came to an end. Some hold that it concluded as early as 1982 with *Tenebrae*, while I myself would contend that his uninterrupted run of masterpieces and near-masterpieces which began with *Deep Red* in 1975 ultimately came to an end with *Opera* in 1987. There is, however, a growing school of thought which holds that *The Stendhal Syndrome* represents his last truly great movie. The film has undergone considerable reappraisal since its rather tepid reception in 1996, with English-speaking audiences in particular warming considerably to it with the advent of DVD releases featuring the Italian dub—a far superior affair to its English counterpart. There is also, it has to be said, the small matter of the majority of Argento's films since the turn of the millennium having been disappointing to say the least, prompting many to look more kindly on his '90s output in retrospect. In addition, thanks to the vast array of books and articles that have been written about his work over the last couple of decades, as well as the explosion in communication between like-minded fans facilitated by the growth of the internet, audiences today have a far greater understanding of how *Stendhal* fits into its director's portfolio with regard to his recurring themes and obsessions.

If we accept, at least in the broadest sense, that a common thread runs through Argento's filmography and that most (if not all) of his subsequent films have been variations on the same framework established in *The Bird with the Crystal Plumage*, then it is tempting to suggest that the reason his post-*Stendhal* work has felt disappointing and even by-the-numbers is that, with *Stendhal*, he said everything he had left to say. Having turned the formula he'd mined so fruitfully in his earlier films inside out, laying bare its inner workings, there was nowhere left to go with the material. The only options at his disposal were to throw caution to the wind and reinvent himself, perhaps by moving into a different genre altogether, or to keep doing the same thing with diminishing returns. Given that he had built his entire career on successfully reworking the same overarching formula with subtly different permutations, it is perhaps understandable (though no less regrettable) that he opted for the latter.

Critic Julian Grainger has described *Deep Red* as the "final word on the subject," and certainly it would be fair to say that, at the time of its release, its status as the *giallo* to end all *gialli* was close to unassailable. (It's telling that, beyond 1975, the genre, whose popularity had already waned considerably after the frenzied levels of production it had enjoyed at the beginning of the decade, all but ceased to exist as an ongoing concern.) Argento subsequently returned to the *giallo* throughout the following decade, taking it in new and unexpected directions with the self-referential *Tenebrae* and to a lesser extent *Opera*. However, I would argue that it was with *The Stendhal Syndrome* that he finally and conclusively reached the destination toward which he had originally set out a quarter of a century earlier when a young American writer wandering the nocturnal streets of Rome happened to glance through the window of a gallery and witness a woman grappling with a figure in black ....

Michael Mackenzie is an author and freelance Blu-ray/DVD producer. He has overseen home video releases of films by several acclaimed directors, including recent remastered editions of Dario Argento's The Bird with the Crystal Plumage, The Cat O'Nine Tails, Deep Red, *and* Phenomena, *all from Arrow Video. His first novel,* In the Silence, *was published in September 2018 by Bloodhound Books.*

Works Cited:
Burke, Frank, "Dario Argento's *The Bird with the Crystal Plumage*: Caging Women's Rage", in Anette Burfoot and Susan Lord (eds.), *Killing Women: The Visual Culture of Gender and Violence*, (Waterloo: Wilfrid Laurier University Press), p. 197-217.
Dumpert, Hazel-Dawn, *The Stendhal Syndrome, L.A. Weekly*.
http://web.archive.org/web/20010709210552/http://www.laweekly.com/film/film_results.php3?showid=749&searchfor=&searchin=all&Sumbit.x=59&Sumbit.y=19.
Grainger, Julian, "Deep Red," in Chris Gallant (ed.), *Art of Darkness: The Cinema of Dario Argento*, (Revised Edition. Godalming: FAB Press), p. 49–63.
Jones, Alan, *Profondo Argento: The Man, the Myths & the Magic*, (Godalming: FAB Press, 2004).
McDonagh, Maitland, "The Stendhal Syndrome," *TV Guide*. http://www.tvguide.com/movies/the-stendhal-syndrome/review/132133.
Rooney, David, "The Stendhal Syndrome," *Variety*.
http://variety.com/1996/film/reviews/the-stendhal-syndrome-1200445110.
Rosenbaum, Jonathan, "The Stendhal Syndrome," *Jonathan Rosenbaum*
http://www.jonathanrosenbaum.net/2000/06/the-stendhal-syndrome.
Smuts, Aaron, "The principles of association: Dario Argento's *Profondo rosso (Deep Red*, 1975)," *Kinoeye* Vol. 2 #11.
http://www.kinoeye.org/02/11/smuts11.php.
Vogler, Christopher, The Writer's Journey: Mythic Structure for Writers, (Third Edition. Studio City: Michael Wiese Productions, 2007).

Notes:
1. Though if you feel so inclined, you can read the whole thing at http://theses.gla.ac.uk/4730.
2. If there is an exception to this rule, it is *The Cat O'Nine Tails*—an atypically testosterone-fueled entry that Argento himself long regarded as his weakest film, considering it to be "too American." The world of *Cat* very much belongs to men and their problems, and the female characters—Anna Terzi (Catherine Spaak), Bianca Merusi (Rada Rassimov), and young Lori (Cinzia De Carolis)—are far more conventional victims than is typical of the women in Argento's films. Perhaps this lack of his usual preoccupations explains his indifference towards the end result.

Tenebrae & *Opera*: Dario Argento's 1980s *Gialli*—A Thematic Comparison
by Rachael Nisbet

In the examination of the career of Italian horror thriller director Dario Argento, one can examine a marked change in the director's thriller output in the 1980s. Adapting to the changing cinematic and social landscape of the decade, Argento built on his established work in the thriller genre in the 1970s while incorporating new elements and ideas into his films reflecting the cinematic and popular cultural trends of the era. By embracing a more overtly sexualized approach to thematic ideas already present in his *oeuvre*, Argento was able to explore ideas about the human condition, sexuality, and voyeurism through a 1980s postmodernist, self-referential lens exemplified in his key work in the thriller genre of the decade: *Tenebrae* and *Opera*. Through the examination of these two films as companion pieces in Argento's filmography, we can see the development of the aforementioned ideas as well as the evolution of the *giallo* as a genre as a whole as Argento played with its form, setting in motion a new era for the Italian thriller.

One of the most prevalent themes in Argento's *gialli*, alongside the horror genre as a whole, is the act of voyeurism. Throughout his career Argento has explored the intersection between the act of voyeurism and horror cinema, utilizing and manipulating the act of watching to illustrate and highlight key themes and ideas throughout his work. Voyeuristic themes in the Italian thriller cinema of the 1960s and 1970s were indebted to the psychosexual thrillers of the early 1960s, in particular, Alfred Hitchcock's *Psycho* (1960) and Michael Powell's *Peeping Tom* (1960) and Argento's early work in the thriller genre reflects this, utilizing many of the same thematic and visual cues as his predecessors. In Argento's first feature film, *The Bird with the Crystal Plumage*, the director explores voyeuristic themes and Freudian psychosexual concepts against a backdrop of violent imagery, engaging with voyeuristic motifs in relation to the *mise en scène*. Post-*The Bird with the Crystal Plumage*, Argento continued to explore such concepts culminating in his 1975 *giallo* redefining work *Deep Red*, a film that revels in the concept of spectacle and the spectator instilled with a visual style reflective of the act of voyeurism itself.

However, it is not until Argento's *gialli* of the 1980s that we begin to see the director engage with the concept of voyeurism in a more overtly self-referential way that feels heavily directed at his audience. In *Tenebrae* and *Opera* Argento extends his examination of voyeurism beyond ideas that relate to the characters and narrative elements within his films to include commentary that directly relates to the viewer and their personal engagement with his cinema; exploring the symbiotic relationship between consumer, media and creator. Argento uses voyeurism to highlight the viewer's participation in his work highlighting the importance of this connection and the wider reaching implications in an often wry, tongue in cheek way.

The concept of voyeurism is prevalent throughout *Tenebrae* and is established in the film's initial scenes in which Luciano Tovoli's roaming camera voyeuristically captures Argento's characters in a way that feels exposed and predatory; infiltrating their private moments. *Tenebrae* engages with the notion that everyone is a voyeur; we see frequent shots of characters looking out of windows, watching other people and surveying the world around them. There's a sense of paranoia that runs throughout the film and there's a constant feeling that the characters within *Tenebrae* are being watched—either shown through anonymous characters surveying the central characters or through the film's camera work which feels intrusive in nature. Argento directs *Tenebrae* in such a way that we the audience feel acutely aware of being a voyeur, always detached from what's happening

Japanese pressbook for *Tenebrae*.

on screen. The use of architecture is particularly effective in creating this sense of voyeuristic paranoia as characters move between buildings that feel exposed via the use of glass, long windows and high ceilings as typified in the architecture of Cristiano's house. Argento frequently uses architecture, disorientating and distant angles and sterile locations to detach his audience from the film while engaging his audience in the film's thematic ideas, posing questions about their complicity in the horror film in a wider context. *Tenebrae* is a film that intentionally forces its viewer to question their role as a consumer of fiction. His thematic critiques aimed squarely at his audience.

The act of watching is crucial to understanding *Tenebrae*. The characters within the film are frequently shown to be observers or observees often switching between these two roles. This helps to instill the film with a sense of paranoia, but it also serves to establish a sense of ambiguity—suggesting that any one of the film's characters may have nefarious motives, manipulating and orchestrating events from behind the scenes. Characters continuously watch one another as they take on dualistic roles as both voyeur and the subject of the voyeur's gaze; particularly evident in the characters of Peter Neal and Cristiano Berti. Gianni witnesses Berti's murder, the murderer watches Tilde through her bedroom window, Bullmer feels a presence as he waits in the piazza, Jane senses she is being watched as she navigates the underground car park; the characters of *Tenebrae* are constantly stalked and observed as they navigate the fractured world they inhabit seemingly unable to escape from prying eyes. The camera itself often prowling the landscape like a supernatural force surveying its prey, particularly evident in the double murder scene that takes place at Tilde and Marion's house.

Argento utilizes the male gaze in order to further illustrate the voyeuristic themes of *Tenebrae*. In the scene in which shoplifter Elsa is introduced, we see her viewed by anonymous faces from a highrise building, as she enters a department store. She is watched through the windows as she browses by a middle-aged businessman. Immediately Argento introduces this concept of voyeurism, exaggerating it to an uncomfortable level as we are forced to examine our own predatory view of Elsa. Elsa tries to remain undetectable when she steals a copy of *Tenebrae* but is spotted by security, unable to shift prying eyes away from her. Elsa is continuously watched by those around her and Argento uses voyeurism in Elsa's murder to misdirect the audience; we are so concerned with the vagrant watching Elsa through her apartment window that we do not see her attacker come from behind. It could be argued that Argento has a certain sense of awareness in the scenes involving Elsa, perhaps a commentary on the way in which the audience and director objectifies the female body. We are acutely aware of the male gaze in relation to Elsa as she is watched and lusted after by various men. Argento plays with the concept of the audience as a voyeur forcing them to examine how they view his female characters contrasted against further scenes in which the male gaze is inverted i.e. in the flashback dream sequences.

The voyeuristic tendencies played out in *Opera* skew slightly differently to the ones portrayed in *Tenebrae* as they tend to look at the act of watching as a collective experience as well as an individual one. The act of watching is deemed as something collective and Argento illustrates this point through the prevalence of media as well as the opera itself. Televisions are frequently on display throughout the film and we often see characters receive information relating to the world they reside within via television broadcast; for example in the scene in which Mira finds out about Betty's involvement in the opera or when Betty finds out that Inspector Santini is alive via a news report. Characters are frequently fixated on televisions, viewing one another through a lens. The television screens give the impression of a constructed reality as well as acting as an all-seeing eye. This idea of collective viewing is exemplified in the opera itself in which the audience watches the production of *Macbeth* later on actively taking part in its performance when Betty interrupts the performance in her plan to identify the killer.

Like with *Tenebrae*, *Opera* features voyeuristic camera work that both detaches and engages its audience with what is happening on stage. This is frequently achieved through POV shots; Betty is presented in the film's introduction via a POV shot through a grate in her room. Betty is often observed through the grate in her bedroom; a red herring as her voyeur turns out to be her nextdoor neighbor, little girl Alma. Betty's real stalker observes her on a much larger scale through the stage of the opera. Argento misdirects his audience by alluding to Betty's stalker hiding in the shadows when he is in plain sight. Argento arguably utilizes voyeuristic elements in *Tenebrae* not to obscure his killer, who is fairly easy to identify, but to highlight his audience's complicity in the act of voyeurism itself. Expertly demonstrated in the killer's sadistic torture of Betty in which he pins needles under her eyes forcing her to watch his murderous actions. The film's central image of an eye propped up with needles is a direct commentary on Argento's audience as well as his critics; he is forcing his audience to watch, to be complicit in his violent opera going as far as to feature a shot in which we are positioned as Betty, the camera showing the needles in front of the audience's eyes. Eyes are a frequent motif throughout the film shown in the close-ups of crow's eyes, a shot of Betty through opera glasses and another through the peep hole of a door; Argento continuously reminds us that we are the viewer, that we are not divorced from what is happening on screen.

While voyeurism has always been a key theme and motif of the *giallo*, Argento leans on this idea in a more heavy-handed fashion in the 1980s and in such a way that forces introspection on his audience. *Tenebrae* and *Opera* force the audience to examine their complicity in his cinema. The theme of voyeurism becoming more blatant in *Opera* than in *Tenebrae* as Argento continues to develop self-referential ideas about his work at the tail end of the 1980s.

What's particularly compelling about *Tenebrae* and *Opera* as comparison pieces in Argento's *oeuvre* is their deliberate focus on female sexuality with both films feeling far more overtly sexual than Argento's previous work. In the mid-to-late 1970s, Italian thrillers became far more sexual in nature evidenced in films such as *The Sister of Ursula* (*La sorella di Ursula*, 1978), *Play Motel* (1979), and *Giallo a Venezia* (1979) which had a sleazier, more sexual feel that that of the *gialli* of the golden era. Argento's *gialli* of the 1980s arguably embodied the trend for more eroticized thrillers which became prevalent during this period, featuring far more nudity and sex than in his earlier work. Yet the more sexualized themes in *Tenebrae* and *Opera* go beyond serving as mere titillation instead exploring female sexuality and power as key themes and motivations for a killer's rage.

Tenebrae features two pivotal flashback scenes which explain the root cause of Peter Neal's murderous rage. In the initial flashback we see a young woman (Eva Robin's) lure a group of young men onto a beach, exposing her naked breasts to entice them. The men gather round the woman in an act of worship as she eagerly paws at them. When a young Peter Neal approaches and strikes her, presumably to chastise her for her sexual display, the woman orders the men to chase after him. Neal is tackled to the beach, pinned down by the men and orally raped by the girl's red high heel, the camera cuts to a long shot of the woman and the group of men pile on Neal in a scene that visually reads as a gang rape. This scene is significant not only in terms of its connection to Neal's novel *Tenebrae* and his murderous crimes, but also in its depiction of female sexuality. The girl on the beach is orchestrating this act, using her sexuality to influence the young men into carrying out her bidding, enacting punishment on Neal who does not comply. While it's fairly common to see the act of rape carried out in the *giallo* and Italian genre cinema as a whole, it is unusual to see a woman enacting a rape against a man, an idea that Argento explores once again in his 1996 thriller *The*

Arguably the defining Argento image: Betty (Cristina Marsillach) is forced to watch as the killer goes about his work.

Stendhal Syndrome. While it is evident that Eva Robin's character exhibits cruelness in her humiliation of Neal, setting in motion Neal's murderous rage, it is important to note that Argento depicts a female character with sexual agency and control. The girl on the beach is sexually dominant, not the men around her.

The depiction of a group of half-naked men worshiping at the feet of a young woman also feels significant. In a genre that is known for an abundance of sex and female nudity, Argento instead depicts young male characters as faceless bodies, vessels for the pleasure of Eva Robin's character. In this scene, Argento subverts the horror genre by depicting men as sexualized objects used for the pleasure of a woman as opposed to the genre's predilection for displaying women as sex objects for men. In doing so, Argento not only shows the sexual power exhibited by Robin's' character but also displays an awareness of the misogynistic accusations that have plagued his work and the horror genre as a whole. In *Tenebrae*, both women and men are viewed voyeuristically.

The idea of female sexual dominance is echoed earlier in *Tenebrae*, shown through the character of shoplifter Elsa. As previously discussed, Elsa is watched by various people as she enters and browses a department store viewed voyeuristically by those around her. Elsa's beauty is shown to enrapture those around her; she is the embodiment of a siren, seemingly drawing men towards her captured under her spell. However, Elsa is seemingly aware of her beauty and sex appeal and uses this to escape a shoplifting conviction, promising the middle-aged store detective that she'll be available to him at her address later on. Elsa departs the store by hitching a ride with a young man once again showing her ability to extract favors from men. Like with the example of Eva Robin's character, Elsa uses her sexuality to her own advantage. While her sexuality and great beauty is shown to be somewhat of a hindrance in terms of the unwanted attention she is given, it is also shown to be an asset—a way of Elsa enacting control and persuasion over the men she encounters. For this reason, like with the girl on the beach, Elsa must be punished for exhibiting sexual dominance and weaponising her sexuality to her own advantage.

These examples illustrate that in *Tenebrae*, women are shown to exhibit sexual control and agency and are not shown to be sexually passive but sexually dominant, also illustrated in bisexual Marion who picks up a man and Maria who rejects her date. In both *Tenebrae* and *Opera*, female sexuality fuels the respective murderer's desire to murder. In *Tenebrae*'s case, the sexual humiliation of Peter Neal at the hands of the girl from the beach and in *Opera*, Santini's sexual impotency and rejection by his lover. Whether the audience or Argento subscribe to Cristiano Berti's idea that his victim's behavior is reprehensible/deviant is somewhat irrelevant, what is important is that the women in *Tenebrae* are choosing to exert sexual control which makes them remarkably less passive than many of the women depicted in the *giallo*. Whilst many of the characters in *Tenebrae*, and to a lesser extent *Opera*, may be considered problematic in terms of their depiction as cruel temptresses, it is still somewhat refreshing to see a frank depiction of female sexuality in the context of the Italian thriller. Female sexuality is key to the themes at the heart of these films providing more than just window dressing for the audience.

Opera continues this exploration of female sexuality through the characters of opera singer Betty and her deceased mother. Like with *Tenebrae*, Argento does not necessarily depict female sexuality in a positive light, but by portraying a woman who is the driving force behind a sexual relationship, *Opera* shows a certain sense of female sexual autonomy. In *Opera*, Betty's mother is not the victim but the instigator in her relationship with Inspector Santini and is shown to be a callous and cruel woman. In the relationship between Betty's mother and Santini, it is Santini who takes the feminine role; indulging in sex games and rituals to fulfil his partner's sexual desires in the hope that she will reciprocate his own. In the scene in which Santini and Betty's mother's relationship is revealed, Argento depicts it as fantasy-like, merging reality and fantasy together in order to evoke a romanticized feel that indicates Santini's feelings of sexual longing and romanticism. The motif of the monstrous mother is one that is present throughout many of Argento's films and in *Opera* it is used to great effect with Betty's mother's monstrous, depraved, violent fantasies and actions manifesting in her sexuality. The nurturer is inverted, thus becoming the destroyer. Whilst mothers are often depicted as warm and caring altruistic beings, in *Opera* and in the wider context of Argento's career, they are depicted as selfish and sexually motivated; shown to be as sexually-minded as their male counterparts. This is certainly true in both the case of Betty's mother and the mother of Betty's neighbor, Alma. Again, whilst it could be argued that Argento's depiction of female sexuality could be perceived as negative, these characters demonstrate female sexual autonomy and dominance that is not often depicted in motherhood. Argento rejects the idea that motherhood is equated to altruism, sacrifice, and purity, instead depicting the mothers of *Opera* as cruel and callous—the counterparts of male sexual deviance and villains of the genre.

The depiction of *Opera*'s protagonist, Betty and her own understanding of her sexuality is shown to be a central theme throughout the film and is contrasted against her mother's sexually deviant behavior. We understand Betty and her mother to be women who are in many ways, diametrically opposed despite their surface level similarities. By contrasting the meek virginal Betty against her monstrous mother, Argento highlights different, arguably extreme, sides of female sexuality. The wicked nature of Betty's mother is more apparent through the innocence of Betty's character. One of the film's most engaging aspects is Betty's development as a character and whether she will fully take on the form of her mother, manipulated by Santini who is determined to redo his relationship with Betty's mother with Betty. *Opera*'s ending shows Betty rejecting her mother's influence, instead choosing to be "good" taking a different path seemingly in line with the established positive tropes of womanhood—becoming a nurturer; at one with nature, demonstrating pure altruistic traits. *Opera*'s ending signifies that Betty is not her mother's daughter despite being positioned as such by Santini. Whilst *Opera* touches on the darkness that Betty could easily succumb to, she is presented throughout the film as virginal and childlike in a dark and cynical world.

The *giallo* is often typified by the genre's examination of the relationship between sex and violence and the psychosexual themes that are often prevalent throughout, typically exhibited as the killer's fundamental motivation for their crimes. Whilst psychosexual themes and eroticized violence are prevalent throughout Argento's work prior to the 1980s, these elements arguably became more overt in the 1980s with sexual themes presented as overarching narrative elements in both *Tenebrae* and *Opera*. The sexual element in Argento's 1980s *gialli* is presented through the aforementioned ideas about female sexuality, power and dominance but also through Argento embracing concepts and visuals that feel far more fetishistic in nature than in his previous cinematic offerings.

The fetishistic element of Argento's work and the *giallo* is taken further in both *Tenebrae* and *Opera* fused with BDSM elements. The 1980s saw BDSM culture shift further into the mainstream popularized with fetishistic imagery employed in films, fashion and music videos, and Argento's films embraced this trend in their depiction of the intersectionality between sex and violence as well as through visual motifs typically associated with the subculture. In *Tenebrae* the striking image of the girl on the beach penetrating a young Peter Neal's mouth with a stiletto heel in an act of oral rape has a fetishistic feel with a heavy emphasis on the patent red shoes throughout the film. The patent red heels become a fetish like object both acting as a signifier of Neal's sexual humiliation while simultaneously acting as a perverse way of Neal taking back sexual control from the women who have wronged him. The heels, as worn by the girl on the beach, representing female sexuality literally stomping over a man. As par the course with the *giallo* as a genre, we see Argento continue the Italian thriller's tradition of fetishizing the blade; the straight edged razor once again used to swipe away at a woman's life and her sexuality. Neal and Berti's punishment enacted through a phallic object.

While fetishistic elements are clearly evident in *Tenebrae* and show Argento bringing a more overt form of fetishism into his work, *Opera* successfully builds on these ideas, becoming one of Argento's most sexualized films. *Opera* explores ideas of sadomasochism which came to prominence in 1980s culture and became somewhat fashionable at time as evidenced through cultural trends in fashion and music as well as in films such as William Friedkin's *Cruising* (1980). There's a fetishistic element to the killer's torturing of Betty in *Opera*; whilst Betty is traumatized by her capture, the killer remarks that Betty is "not frigid at all—you're a bitch in heat" after he's tied her up with ropes—a direct contrast to the virginal Betty shown in the previous scene. Inspector Santini assumes that Betty shares her mother's predilection for bondage like practices, an idea that is explored throughout the film culminating in Betty's rejection of her mother's lust for violent sexual degradation. Ropes and restraints are frequently used in the film's set pieces taking on a fetishistic feel; Betty's unwilling participation in the murders feeling akin to indulging in an extreme form of BDSM role-play. Flashback scenes to Betty's mother draw parallels to the murders taking place in the modern day and in the full reveal of Betty's mother's story the audience fully understands the significance of the killer's torturous games, realizing that they are in fact a manifestation of BDSM games played by Betty's mother and Santini, once again blurring the line between sex and violence in *Opera*.

BDSM elements are also displayed in *Opera* through costuming, which signifies the connection between

Eroticism seeps into Argento's work in *Tenebrae*: Eva Robin's appears as the girl in the fetish heels.

Betty and her mother. As Betty assumes the role of Lady Macbeth, she also takes on the character of her opera singer mother. Betty changes from an almost childlike tearful teenager clutching her teddy bear to an accomplished opera starlet donned in an almost fetish-like outfit made up of chains, studs, and PVC like material. The transformative nature of the opera positions Betty as an assertive and powerful individual who immediately commands the attention of Santini who now views her as her mother's daughter, forging a sexual connection between the two women in his mind. The connections between Lady Macbeth and Betty's mother are apparent as both women are master manipulators who exert control over their lovers in order to carry out their own cruel and selfish desires. By juxtaposing Betty as a childlike teen with her role as Lady Macbeth, Argento reflects the duality of her character and the duality of Betty and her mother. By costuming Betty in an opera costume that borrows from BDSM in fashion, *Opera* signifies these ideas demonstrating why Santini's murderous impulses have been rekindled and the connection between BDSM styled sex practices, Santini and Betty's mother.

By adopting more overtly fetishistic BDSM elements in both *Tenebrae* and *Opera*, Argento instills his 1980s *gialli* with themes that are far more overtly sexual in nature embracing the decade's pop cultural fascination with the dark side of sexuality.

The *gialli* of the 1960s and 1970s were synonymous with the modernist movement reflecting the radical social changes that took place within the mid-to-late 20th century. The *gialli* produced during the golden age of the Italian thriller tended to critique modernity whilst simultaneously reveling in its trappings. However, as modernism began to wane in the 1960s and 1970s, the postmodernist movement gained traction marking a radical departure from the ideas presented through modernism acting as somewhat of a rejection of the ideals of the movement. As a result, the 1980s marked a new era for filmmakers, divorced from the modernist aesthetics and thematic ideas that characterized the *gialli* of the 1960s to early 1970s. Filmmakers began to embrace postmodernist concepts, ideas and aesthetics in their work and as a result, films of the era became more reflexive, self-aware and embraced a certain sense of irony in their adoption of postmodernist thought.

During the 1980s Argento played with postmodernist ideas, infusing his work with meta elements that embodied the self-aware, referential nature of postmodernist film. These ideas materialize in both *Tenebrae* and *Opera* as well as in Argento's *Gli incubi di Dario Argento* series which aired on RAI 2 in 1987. In *Tenebrae* and *Opera*, Argento uses meta elements as a way of wryly referencing his body of work as a director but more importantly, he uses this idea to offer a critique of his audience and critics acknowledging his reputation as a filmmaker and the criticisms often levelled at his films. These criticisms are frequently presented through the character of Peter Neal in *Tenebrae* and Marco the director in *Opera*, with both characters acting as mouthpieces for Argento while also representing Argento's critics' exaggerated perception of him as a man and as a director.

Tenebrae was influenced by Dario Argento's own experiences of being stalked and harassed by an obsessed fan which gives the film a highly personal feel acting as an exploration of the relationship between Argento's fictional work and its apparent real-world implications. Argento uses *Tenebrae* as a vehicle for addressing criticisms of his work, particularly in relation to his depiction of violence and the resulting real-world accountability his critics have bestowed upon him. This gives *Tenebrae* a self-referential quality as the character of Peter Neal becomes a mouthpiece for Argento the man and the director; Neal as the embodiment of both Argento's critics' perception of him as well as Argento's own musings of his relationship between reality and fiction and his societal role as a director of horror films.

Catholic television host Cristiano Berti is positioned as a manifestation of Argento's critics. The scene in which Neal is pre-interviewed by Berti is of great importance as it acts as a direct commentary on the misconceptions about Argento's work from his critics. Peter Neal, a substitute for Argento, challenges Berti's statements about *Tenebrae* as a novel "about human perversion and its effects on society" stating that the novel goes beyond such ideas. The two men discuss what they consider to be deviant behavior with both Berti and Neal interpreting the text in radically different ways due to their differing world views. This conversation echoes previous criticisms against Argento's work while simultaneously preempting the inevitable criticisms that will arise on the release of *Tenebrae* the film. This scene is pivotal in understanding Argento's thoughts on his role as a creator of fiction and the misinterpretation of his work—it acts as a defense, a plea to critics that he is not who they paint him to be; ironically, subverted in the film's final act when Peter Neal the author is revealed to be the killer. Prior to this pivotal scene with Berti, Neal engages with journalist and family friend, Tilde, about his work as an author, again fielding criticisms about his character in relation to his work. Tilde challenges Neal on the sexism in his novel and when Neal points out to Tilde that she knows him and should know he is not a misogynist, she curtly tells him that she's talking about his work—a statement which again highlights the connection between the author of a piece of fiction and the fiction itself. It's clear that in this scene, Argento is mulling over the relationship between a fictional work and its author. Argento knows he is not the man that his work would lead people to believe yet if his audience is only aware of his work and not him as a man does this matter?

By naming Peter Neal's novel *Tenebrae*, Argento highlights the connection between his film and the titular novel at its heart demonstrating that they are intrinsically linked; in order to fully understand the intention of *Tenebrae* the film one must understand Neal's *Tenebrae*. *Tenebrae* is an examination of a creator's personal accountability for his work and it's telling that Argento's script features two murderers; the author and the critic suggesting that there's a sense of mutual accountability. While Argento (framed as Neal) does not wholly position himself as responsible for the actions of a fan, he acknowledges the symbiotic relationship between the creator and the consumer and as a result *Tenebrae* feels like Argento acknowledging that he cannot completely divorce himself from his work and its real-world implications. Argento knowingly and wryly acknowledges a certain amount of culpability, he accepts that there is a certain level of darkness to his work that cannot be separated from Argento the individual. One's intention does not live in a vacuum, feeding back into the idea that once a piece of art has been put into the public domain, the creator loses a sense of control over their ideas and intentions.

While Argento muses over his level of culpability and societal obligation to produce work that is deemed morally acceptable in *Tenebrae*, he also rejects the onus put on his films in regards to their influence on society.

In one of the film's most memorable quotes, Peter Neal asks Detective Germani: "If a man is killed by a Smith & Wesson revolver, do you go to the head of Smith & Wesson?" In this key statement, Argento chastises his critics for singling his films out as sole perpetrators of violence posing the question of why culpability is placed on films but not weapons. This statement has particular relevance when we consider *Tenebrae*'s placement on the video nasties list in the U.K.; 39 films deemed as obscene and harmful to the British general public thus proving Argento's criticisms of his work being detrimental to society.

Like with Peter Neal in *Tenebrae*, in *Opera* Argento once again uses a character as a stand-in for himself. Argento continues to address the accusations of misogyny and violence in his work in a semi-satirical fashion following on from the self-referential themes and commentary on his work presented within *Tenebrae*.

Opera was conceived during a tumultuous period in Argento's career developed off the back of his failed attempt to stage an opera alongside his creative involvement and direction of a horror themed fashion show for Italian fashion house Trussardi in 1986. Argento's experiences in other creative fields proved to be a significant influence on *Opera*; a film that depicts the inner workings of a production and the issues that often arise behind the scenes. *Opera* continues on from themes established in *Tenebrae* showing a heightened awareness of Argento's societal role as a filmmaker and the supposed negative influence of his work reflecting growing criticisms of the horror genre in the 1980s.

In one scene in *Opera*, Marco the director says, "I think it's unwise to use movies as a guide for reality." This is a vastly important statement in the examination of *Opera* in relation to Argento's personal relationship with his films, their audience, and his critics. Through the character of Marco, Argento rejects the concept of his films having a sense of moral obligation or culpability highlighting the absurdity of holding a film accountable for the behavior of an individual. The idea of citing the horror film as a factor in criminal behavior is shown to be absurd when we consider the greater importance of one's upbringing. This is shown not only through the character of Betty and her relationship and understanding of her deceased mother but also through Betty's neighbor, the young girl Alma and her mother. Argento also highlights in his ending that there is always a choice to be made highlighting the importance of individual responsibility.

Just as *Tenebrae* features a novel within a film, *Opera* features an opera inside of a film. By featuring a fictional work inside of both films, Argento is able to examine the relationship between a fictional source and the characters and narrative within his films at large. Again, displaying intertextual ideas that are at the heart of postmodernist thought. *Macbeth*, which we the audience are familiar with as a real-life play and opera, exemplifies the key themes at the heart of *Opera*. By understanding *Macbeth* as an opera, we as the audience unlock the reading of *Opera*.

Tenebrae takes a different approach as we the audience are not familiar with the novel at the heart of the film, discovering its meaning as the film's narrative unravels. However, references to another well known work, Arthur Conan Doyle's *The Sign of Four* lays the groundwork for uncovering the conundrum at the center of the film. *Tenebrae*'s opening scene in which a narrator reads a passage from the novel *Tenebrae* also sets the tone for the events that transpire throughout the film as Peter Neal embraces his murderous rage. Like with *Opera*, Argento uses our understanding of other texts in order to understand key themes in his own work embodying a self-referential postmodernist sensibility throughout his work.

By reading *Tenebrae* and *Opera* as companion pieces one can examine the evolution of the *giallo* as it adapted towards a more 1980s sensibility. Argento's *gialli* of the decade rewrote what the Italian thriller was for a 1980s audience, straying from many of the previously established tropes of the genre to produce thriller films that were an engaging mixture of classic *giallo* elements and more contemporary horror fare. It is evident that *Tenebrae* and *Opera* represent postmodern readings of the genre with meta elements that were heavily influenced by Argento's own personal experiences, feeling self-referential and self-aware in nature. Argento also utilized sexual themes, particularly in regards to frank depictions of female sexuality in order to create *gialli* far darker in tone than his previous work. By reinventing the *giallo* through these two key texts, Argento embodied the 1980s as an era whilst remaining true to his directorial vision as a director of thriller cinema. It is through this evolution of the genre that we can appreciate Argento's ability to reinvent the genre that he helped bring to prominence.

Rachael Nisbet is an Edinburgh-based writer specializing in Italian genre cinema, with a slant towards style and gialli. *She maintains a blog at* http://hypnoticcrescendos.blogspot.com

Chapter Twenty-Six: The Interviews

Dario Argento Interviewed by Rob Ruston

Author's Note: Dario Argento is not particularly fond of revisiting his old films. I am very grateful to him for kindly donating his time to meet with Rob in order to answer these questions, which are intended to give a sort of generalized overview of his life in the cinema. I am also very grateful to Rob for agreeing to set up this interview and for the time and energy he put into transcribing it—and then helping me to edit, proof-read, and generally put it into readable form.

I grew up in a city famous for its rain, where old, industrial factories loomed and where long winter's nights led to gray days. Like many of my friends, I longed for a bit of color.

Don't get me wrong, Manchester in the 1980s was an extraordinary place. We're justifiably famous for our amazing music, world-famous nightclubs, and legendary northern hospitality. We're a kind and generous bunch, albeit constantly wet when we go out.

Growing up I got the best of the '80s. School holidays consisted of gaming arcades, the Roxy Cinema (which I frequented often) and browsing round record and VHS video stores. Manchester is a big city for a kid, but one that's easy to lose yourself in: lots of places to explore and new things to discover. And that meant I could explore my first love: horror movies.

I don't remember the exact moment when I fell in love with the macabre and magical, but I remember my mum allowing me to stay up quite late at the weekends when the BBC regularly screened classic horror films. I loved to be scared. This became almost ritualistic. My mum would prepare a late supper for me and then go to bed. Universal and Hammer films were always on one of the four late night channels.

In 1980, I was filled with glee when I saw the cover of the Radio Times that summer. The writhing, horned monster from *Night of the Demon* (1957) glared up at me alongside Peter Cushing, who was starring in *The Ghoul* (1974). While the other kids at school were obsessed with football, I was obsessed with *House of Hammer* magazine. Hand drawn werewolves, demons, and goblins were penciled into my exercise books.

Then one night in August 1985 I saw a film that changed everything. A rumor had gone around school about a horror film marathon at a cinema in Manchester City Centre. Four or five films showing back to back. Being only 15 years old, naturally my mother strictly forbade this. Regardless, I was still going. I pretended to go to bed, waited until she did the same, and then I climbed out of my bedroom window to catch the night bus into the city. My friend's dad worked at the cinema. And, there, sandwiched in between Raimi and Romero, was Dario Argento's *Phenomena*, screened that night as *Creepers*.

From the minute I saw the opening shot of the school bus arriving on the Swiss pass, the wind frantically blowing on the soundtrack, the Danish tourist lost and alone, I was transfixed. Suddenly these extraordinary scenes led to an amazing crane shot, the camera slowly gliding up through the windswept pine branches, accompanied by Terry Taylor and Bill Wyman's haunting score. Here was a dark fairy tale like no other. I'd never seen anything quite like it. The next day I immediately went out and bought the soundtrack on vinyl. Soon after, I owned Palace's VHS release. My obsession with Argento had begun.

While Manchester is a liberal city, the country was at war with itself. Strikes, unemployment and censorship abounded, overseen by a woman who ruled Old Blighty with an iron fist. There was a war against left-wingers, libertarians, feminists, and the LGBT community—and horror—the tabloid's bogeyman. I had to resort to terrible pirate copies to discover *Tenebrae*, *Suspiria*, *Inferno*, and *The Bird with the Crystal Plumage*. In some way those fourth generation tapes made these masterpieces even more alluring, more mysterious. It also makes rediscovering them with every new release and new crystal-clear print a revelation.

But God, how I fell in love with Argento's work! He affected me like no other horror director. I'd also discovered *gialli* for the first time and longed to visit Italy more than ever. From Roman amphitheaters to towering cathedrals, exquisite landscape and world-famous art, there are lots of reasons why people visit Italy. I wanted to experience all those things. But Dario was why I bought my first plane ticket there.

Eventually, it was the early days of social media that led me to reach out to the people in Argento's circle who had inspired me. I was surprised and flattered by their kindness and generosity when it came to welcoming me into their world.

One of the most outstanding and significant people I would go on to meet is Carla Alonzo, who was previously a PA and secretary to Dario. An amazing woman and now a close friend. In the summer of 2014, I had the opportunity to visit Rome on my own for the first time. Here I would visit some of the enchanting filming locations from Dario's cinema. I'd explore the city's beautiful landmarks and famous architecture. It was like stepping through the screen.

Naturally, the Profondo Rosso store was high on my list of priorities. Here I met Luigi Cozzi and his wonderful partner Letizia. I'd already befriended Claudio Simonetti a year earlier and one of the best experiences on this visit was seeing *Deep Red* screened at an open-air cinema at the Eutropia festival, L'Altra Città with my friend Giulia. Goblin performed the score live on a stage directly below the screen. Later I had the wonderful opportunity to meet the likes of Sergio Stivaletti, Fiore Argento, and Franco Bellomo. I also became friends with actor Franco Trevisi, who appeared briefly in *Phenomena*. A wonderful and very funny man!

Eventually, I met Dario himself.

It wasn't until June 2016 that I met Dario for the first time in Trastevere. The experience was both exciting and nerve wrecking. I was with my partner, Roberto. Dario was making an appearance at Piazza S. Cosimato, after which he was literally mobbed by the crowd, to the deafening chants of "*Maestro! Maestro! Maestro!*" from adults and teenagers alike. The public adore him in Italy. Eventually the crowd subsided. Fortunately, I had a prized possession with me—a Japanese *Phenomena* theater program—and I shakily handed it to him for a signature. He was about to go in his favorite restaurant. A photo opportunity followed. It was a brief meeting but the first of many.

I began to visit Rome frequently. I met Dario in more intimate settings. One particularly memorable evening was at the screening of Polanski's *Rosemary's Baby*, again in Trastevere. We drank wine and smoked a lot and talked about Polanski, the shock of the Manchester terrorist bombing (which had occurred a few weeks before), and his upcoming projects. This was a dream come true to me, as you can imagine.

I'd struck up a friendship online with author Troy Howarth. We regularly discussed Argento and his films. Troy told me he felt inspired to write a book on Dario and would I be willing to collaborate? Absolutely! My first task was to secure an interview with the man himself. We were at a screening of *Phenomena*, again in Trastevere in late July 2017 when we approached Dario and asked him if he would allow me to interview him for the book, and Dario immediately answered yes. Even better, the interview would be conducted at his home. Troy had already provided the questions. The following Tuesday, a very hot sunny day in Rome, Carla accompanied me to his apartment.

Interviewer Rob Ruston with Dario Argento.

Dario welcomed us at the door into a spacious and (fortunately) heavily air-conditioned apartment. The living room was decorated with beautiful antique furnishings and relics that once belonged to Dario's mother. A huge bookcase took up a whole wall in the room, filled with books, DVDs, and awards, some of which I recognized instantly. The original snow globe from *The Stendhal Syndrome* sat on one of the shelves. I felt a *fission* of pride when I saw that a Cthulhu statue that I had gifted him on the previous Halloween was also amongst the trophies. We relaxed and the interview proceeded. It was one of the most joyous moments of my life.

A final word. I know I've been incredibly lucky to have experienced all this. I still remember the young boy in the rainy city who once saw a film of such transcendent color, passion, and beauty he wanted to know more. Come and walk the streets of Rome and drink in the atmosphere and history that inspired Argento. And get inspired yourself. As the great man demonstrated, there is poetry and beauty in all things. You just have to let the light shine on it.

Rob Ruston: *Dario, when did you first fall in love with movies?*
Dario Argento: It's a long story. I have some memories of when I was very young. I remember I was on vacation in the mountains with my family. I remember I would go and see the films … summer films, in the open air, old

films. I remember one time, one film, I was very young—*Phantom of the Opera* (1943) directed by Arthur Lubin and starring Peter Lorre ... no! Claude Rains. For me, it was a great discovery. I felt such great emotion.

RR: *And this was at an open-air cinema where you saw it for the first time?*

DA: Yes. It was very important for me because it helped me to discover something different from the other stories—the usual stories they teach you at school or the usual films I'd seen before. I was shocked to find such films! But it wasn't terrifying to me, you understand? No, these films moved me. I was very enthusiastic. I said to myself, "This is a marvelous, marvelous world that I have discovered."

RR: *These were very different?*

DA: Yes, the films moved me; it was marvelous. Then after this, I discovered a very important book. I don't remember my age; I know I was very young. I was sick during the summer months for three or four months. Every morning all the family leaves. My brother and sister went to school. My father and mother were at work. I was home alone and I would go in to my father's library. I read everything *(laughs)*.

RR: *Horror literature?*

DA: All kinds of literature, from Shakespeare to Robert Louis Stevenson. Everything! And then I found a book of Edgar Allan Poe's stories; this was another very important moment in my life because I discovered another beautiful mind. I discovered very strange things, but I liked it and was quite enchanted.

RR: *And this left a huge impression on you?*

DA: Yes, very much. It stayed inside me. It was very profound. Then another important moment was when my father took me to a theater close to my house; this was important. One summer they had a season of horror films, which was not usual at all. Every day they showed a different film. My father wasn't interested in this at all.

RR: *Your father didn't like horror films?*

DA: No, he considered them stupid things *(laughs)*. Anyway, he gave me a free pass. I had a free ticket to go every day to the cinema; and every day, I went! I saw all the panorama and landscape of marvelous films—very old and famous films.

RR: *Did you spend time alone there?*

DA: Yes, watching old films like *Frankenstein* (1931).

RR: *Me, too, but I think the earliest ones I saw were the Hammer films. Maybe something like* The Brides of Dracula.

DA: These were much older films, of course.

RR: *I think my favorite silent films were* The Cabinet of Dr. Caligari *(1919) and* Nosferatu *(1922).*

DA: Yes, *The Cabinet of Dr. Caligari* and films like *Vampyr* (1932); so many films. This is my education in horror films. Later on, I went to France to study—to Paris. I would go to the *cinémathèque* and it was great to see the old masterpieces there. I studied in the morning and in the afternoon, I would see the old films. It was very important to me, for my education. I was very influenced by the Expressionist German films; all those dark shadows. The cinematography was very complicated and imaginative.

RR: *At this time were you imagining that one day you would direct?*

DA: No, I was just enjoying the films. Not once was it in my mind to be a director; I just enjoyed seeing the films. The story of my education in movies continued when I started to work for a newspaper, *Paese Sera*.

RR: *Do you have any favorite memories of working for* Paese Sera *and interviewing any actors and directors?*

DA: Yes, I was very enthusiastic; I worked with great enthusiasm. It was marvelous to interview famous actors and directors. I started doing minor jobs at the newspaper. Then the film critic at the newspaper—I was his assistant—became sick. The director of the paper asked me to take over as the critic, at least for a short while. I was very young, around 21 years old. I became the youngest critic in Italy. So I started to write, and to see films and write about them. The critic's illness lasted for some time, so I became the critic at the paper for a long period of time. I considered films differently than the usual critic, since I was younger. I followed the French magazine *Cahiers du Cinéma*. These were some of the best moments of my life about films. It was a marvelous time.

RR: *You worked on the scripts of some Spaghetti Westerns?*

DA: Yes, I decided that I wanted to write myself. I wrote some things that were accepted; I worked in genres like the Spaghetti Western and war films. There was a film about a strange romantic relationship [Note: *Metti, una sera a cena*, 1969]. I wrote some films, but not many.

RR: *Did you ever think about directing one yourself?*

DA: No, I liked to write. Writing is good for me. It's important: when I write, it is just me and a blank piece of paper. I can be alone in my mind, in my dreams—alone, with no distractions. As I wrote the scripts, the films appeared in front of me—like a reel of film. I could see the stories appearing in front of me.

RR: *How did you collaborate with Bernardo Bertolucci in writing the story for* Once Upon a Time in the West?

DA: We worked together for about four months. We worked with Sergio Leone at first, then on our own.

RR: *How would you describe your first day on the set of* The Bird with the Crystal Plumage?

DA: Before I started the film, I did the storyboards and shooting list. On the set, for me, it was easy, because it was right there, on the page. The only thing that was not good was my relationship with the actor ...

RR: *Tony Musante?*

DA: Yes, Musante. No, not a good relationship. From the first day until the last day, we argued. (*Dario mimics arguing.*) You see, he thinks I'm a nobody and he's the big star from the Actor's Studio. He had something to say about everything.

RR: *Fortunately, the film turned out magnificent. So Musante insisted on making changes?*

DA: Yes. He wanted to change the idea, but I still was very strong and determined. I wouldn't allow this.

RR: *How was it to work with Enrico Maria Salerno?*

DA: Much better! Yes, he was a good person. My only problem was with Musante.

RR: *Next came* The Cat O'Nine Tails. *Were you happy with it?*

DA: Yes.[1]

RR: *What are your memories of working with Karl Malden and James Franciscus in the movie?*

DA: Karl Malden was marvelous! A great actor. A wonderful person. He taught me lots of things about American movies.

RR: *His character added heart to the movie…*

DA: Yes.

RR: *How was Catherine Spaak?*

DA: She was … good.

RR: Four Flies on Grey Velvet *was the first time you worked with Luigi Cozzi. How did that come about?*

DA: At that time, Luigi [Cozzi] was obliged to be a soldier [Note: national service]. It's not like today; it didn't matter whether he wanted to be a soldier or not. He was in the military in Rome. He was aware of my work and he came to see me. He was very young. We spoke and I could see that he was very intelligent. He liked music, like me, and we went to concerts in those days to see groups like Genesis; very famous groups of the time. We became friends. Then he was my assistant on *Four Flies*.

RR: *What made you decide to go into television with* Door into Darkness?

DA: My father suggested I should do something for television. I was interested in a new experience. We did four episodes, but it was difficult because, for one, the director [Note: Argento's former assistant Roberto Pariante, on the episode titled "The Doll."] was no good. I ended up doing it myself. The series was a big success because it was something nobody had tried before. For the first time my ideas made it on to television. National television.

RR: *How did* Le cinque giornate *come about? Was it difficult for you to adjust to working in the "period" context?*

DA: I do not remember difficulties in the actual making of the film.

RR: Deep Red *is such an ambitious film; were you trying to "outdo" yourself?*

DA: Yes, the film was very ambitious. I had made a trilogy of *gialli*, now I wanted to go ahead with something different. Something more psychological. Something very different. I was much more mature. I had more experience. Also, I added some humor.

RR: *Yes, the first cut of the film I saw had all the humor intact. There was more comical interaction between David Hemmings and Daria Nicolodi, which was cut from a lot of other versions. What memories do you have of David Hemmings?*

DA: Yes, he was a great person. I liked him a lot. When he was young, he was a singer—an opera singer. He performed in the famous [Benjamin] Britten opera, which was adapted from the Henry James book *The Turn of the Screw*.

RR: *I didn't know that he was a singer.*

DA: Yes, when he was much younger. We became good friends. He was a really marvelous person.

RR: *How did the idea of making* Suspiria *come into being?*

DA: After *Deep Red*, I knew I had to do something different.

RR: Deep Red *was a huge success.*

DA: Yes, it was. I remembered, before making *Suspiria*, that horror was my first love. I wanted to do a supernatural film. I chose the story of witches because there aren't so many films about witches. I wanted to do something new. I toured around in Europe to find the inspiration for a story about witches. Then I wrote the story. This is my most famous film outside of Italy. I am famous for this film, especially in the United States and Japan.

RR: *And of course,* Deep Red *became well known in Japan as* Suspiria 2.

DA: Yes, it was.

RR: *What made you seek out Luciano Tovoli as the cinematographer?*

DA: I saw some of the films he had photographed before, especially *Profession: Reporter* (*The Passenger*, 1975); his photography was wonderful. I knew he would be perfect for my film. I wanted different colors.

RR: *And different colors is what we got!*

DA: Yes! Red, gold, blue, green … like in the films of Walt Disney, especially *Snow White* (1937). The same sort of colors; that is what I wanted. He did marvelous work.

RR: *Yes, they are very vibrant and dream-like.* Inferno *was the last film Mario Bava worked on. What are your memories of him?*

DA: Yes, I spent a lot of time working closely with him. He gave me lots of advice. Not so much advice about the film, but advice about special effects. Wonderful special effects.

RR: *Yes, particularly the matte paintings he did on glass.*

DA: Yes, on very big sheets of glass. There were great paintings on glass. Actually, it was crystal. Crystal is perfect. Glass is not so perfect. Also, crystal is better for the light. Very important.

RR: *Is it true that you entrusted scenes to Bava whilst you were ill?*
DA: No, no; Bava was my assistant on *Inferno*.[2]
RR: *There has always been a rumor that you were ill and that Bava directed some scenes, like the underwater scene with Irene Miracle.*
DA: No, that isn't true at all.
RR: *What made you cast Leigh McCloskey?*
DA: I found him in Los Angeles. We were in Los Angeles because 20th Century Fox was involved in the picture. I was there for the casting of Irene Miracle. It was my idea to have a swimming pool with the furniture in it; a sunken room. I needed a very good swimmer. Irene was a wonderful swimmer.
RR: *I believe Irene could hold her breath for very long periods.*
DA: Yes! Because of this, I chose her. She was perfect.
RR: *One of the most memorable scenes, of course, is the underwater scene. That scene always amazed me.*
DA: Yes, one of the best scenes in *Inferno*. I was very happy with it. (*Smiles*)
RR: *Now we come to* Tenebrae. *How did you come up with the idea? With the story?*
DA: (*Thinks hard*) That is a long story …[3]
RR: Tenebrae *is one of my favorite films, as you know. It's very important to me.*
DA: Me, too. It is one of my perfect *giallo* films. Perfect for me.
RR: *People are surprised when I say I prefer* Tenebrae *to* Deep Red. *As beautiful as* Deep Red *is,* Tenebrae *is very special to me. It's very clinical looking.*
DA: Yes, marvelous photography. It was like a black-and-white film. I tried to do a perfect *giallo*. An unbelievable *giallo* (*laughs*). I worked for months and months on this film. Also, it has the quotation from Sherlock Holmes.
RR: *Yes, "When you have eliminated the impossible, whatever remains, however improbable, must be the truth." Was that from* The Hound of the Baskervilles?
DA: No, but the same phrase occurs in maybe three or four of the stories.[4] It was the perfect explanation of the work of the investigator.
RR: *The Goblin score was excellent. Really astonishing*
DA: Yes, very much so.
RR: *There are so many great scenes in this film, notably the death of John Saxon's character in broad daylight at La Terrazze, one of many* Tenebrae *locations I have visited …*
DA: Yes, that is one of my favorite scenes, when he dies. Because, it is silent. There are no lines spoken. No words. He just watches. He's an American agent who only thinks about money and there he is, in the sun, watching life go by. Maybe he has forgotten something about life; maybe he has forgotten that life is good.
RR: Tenebrae *lacks any landmarks of Rome. I always liked your comment that, it is maybe Rome in the future, with less population. It is a bit futuristic.*

DA: Yes, the world of *Tenebrae* is very empty. It is a different world. For me, it is like a science fiction film!
RR: *What are your memories of working with John Saxon and Anthony Franciosa?*
DA: John Saxon was a wonderful collaborator—so much so that I specifically asked for him on one of the *Masters of Horror* episodes I did, *Pelts*. It was wonderful working with him the second time, too. As for Anthony Franciosa, I do not have any positive memories of him. He was difficult and did not seem to participate in the life of the film. He was also very capricious.
RR: Phenomena *is one of your most unusual films. How did you come up with the idea for this film?*
DA: Well, *Phenomena* started when I was on vacation with my mother on the island of Giannutri, a very small island. There was no TV reception; we just had a radio. One day, we heard the news of a story in Germany, where the police found a killer by studying the flies and maggots at a crime scene. It stayed with me, and when I returned to Rome a few days later, I started studying books on the subject. I also discovered the works of the famous Professor [Marcel] Leclerq. He was French. I went to Paris to speak with him. If you had a gun and it went off—*bang*—the sound vibrations would kill the insects. If you found certain insects who had died in this way near a crime scene, you could determine that a shot was fired—or even *when* it was fired. Of course, it's a lot more complicated than that. There were many interesting stories. He was a very good person. I learned a lot from him. This began the inspiration for *Phenomena*: insects solving a crime or a murder.
RR: Phenomena *sort of combines the supernatural with the giallo. Like* Suspiria, *it is set in a girls' school.*
DA: I wanted to work with very young people. At that time, my daughter Fiore was 13. And Jennifer Connelly was divine. She was also only around 13 or so.
RR: Phenomena *was the first Argento film that I saw at the cinema. I had never seen young actresses go through so much in a drama. Jennifer Connelly fell into a huge pit full of maggots and body parts; she endured lots of things. I felt I could relate to Jennifer Corvino, too, because like so many young people I was having a hard time fitting in at school. The father figure was absent from the home. It hit me on so many different levels.*
DA: Yes, this is also something that happened in my real life. It was personal. Very personal. When Jennifer talks of how her parents separated on Christmas, this happened to me. Separation. My ex-wife. There was a phone call and that was that! Yes, I put it into the film; my own experience.
RR: Opera *is probably your most extravagant giallo. Was it significantly more expensive than your other films?*
DA: Yes, many producers participated, and I had much more money to spend. For this film, that was very

important. For me, it is one of my best films. The music and the cinematography …

RR: *There are some beautiful interior shots of the opera in this film.*

DA: Yes, marvelous! Some beautiful shots. Yes, everything—and the crows!

RR: *The ravens as animals solving the crime almost seems a nod to* Phenomena. *And of course, we end up back in Phenomena territory at the end of the film.*

DA: Yes, we do (*smiles*).

RR: *How did you get to collaborate with Ronnie Taylor?*

DA: I met him when I directed a Fiat commercial in Australia.

RR: *A car commercial?*

DA: Yes, it was a very good collaboration. We were friends immediately.

RR: *The use of heavy metal music is interesting in* Phenomena *and* Opera.

DA: In *Opera*, we had the gentle aria. I wanted to add something stronger. Heavy metal is something very strong; very loud. It's a sound that assaults the senses. It creates tension for these scenes.

RR: *What made you decide to come to America to make* Two Evil Eyes *and* Trauma?

DA: *Two Evil Eyes* was because of George Romero. We are good friends, very good friends. We talked about doing a film together. We discussed maybe bringing in some other directors and doing a film in four different episodes, all from tales by Edgar Allan Poe. As a tribute to our master. It was going to be me, George, John Carpenter, and Stephen King. We chose the stories we wanted to adapt. The first to leave the project was Stephen King. His adaptation was going to be "The Tell-Tale Heart." He said that he was too busy writing his books, so he decided to stop before completing his script; he never did direct another film. John Carpenter was enthusiastic about the project, then he was offered lots of money for an important film; so, we agreed on doing two episodes, George and me.

RR: *And you have Harvey Keitel on board for your episode … Were you happy with it?*

DA: Ah, yes, Harvey Keitel. A great actor. A wonderful worker. Yes, I was happy with it.

RR: *Was* Trauma *a good shoot, too?*

DA: I decided to make *Trauma* in the United States because of *Two Evil Eyes*. I enjoyed the experience very much. It was a pleasure to work there. So, I decided to make *Trauma* there, with my daughter (Asia). It was my first film with my daughter.

RR: *It's a very good film.* The Stendhal Syndrome *is your darkest movie; was it your intention to make it so dark?*

DA: Yes, it was. The collaboration with Graziella Magherini was very important. She is a great professor of psychology. Then I collaborated with Franco Ferrini on developing the story. It was great.

RR: *It's a very good and complex story. How was it directing Asia? She endured quite a lot in that role; was it difficult?*

DA: Sometimes it was. Some moments were—for me and for her.

RR: *Now this is an interesting question that Troy wanted me to ask you: in an interview in the 1990s, Christopher Lee mentioned he was involved in a documentary you were directing.…*

DA: Yes.

RR: *Really? Troy can find no information on it. Do you have any recollection of this project?*

DA: Very little. It happened, yes. But it was for television. It was at a film festival. I asked him (Christopher Lee) if it was possible to do a documentary, to tell me about his life story. He said yes, okay.

RR: *Christopher Lee mentioned it, and nobody can find the footage anywhere.*

DA: No, it disappeared. It was shown on television at that time.

RR: *At least we know it actually happened now and it isn't just another rumor.*

DA: Yes, it's true.

RR: The Phantom of the Opera *is another ambitious film. Was it deliberately tongue-in-cheek because* Stendhal *had been so dark?*

DA: Yes, with some moments of comedy.

RR: *Were you happy with* Phantom?

DA: Yes. Also, because it took me back to my first film as a child—my memory of seeing *Phantom of the Opera*.

RR: Sleepless *marks your return to the* giallo; *can you explain your collaboration with Carlo Lucarelli on the screenplay?*

DA: Carlo Lucarelli and I worked together on the script. I was at his house, then he came to my hotel in Turin. We worked well together. We became very good friends—great friends.

RR: *And Max von Sydow?*

DA: Yes, we also became good friends. A great actor and a gentleman. He was marvelous.

RR: The Card Player *is more police procedural; what made you try something in that mode?*

DA: I decided to film in the neighborhoods of Rome. Around Rome, rather than in the center.

RR: *You shot in place like* Gianicolo *and* Trastevere; *I've visited most of the locations where it was shot. It's much less violent than your other thrillers.*

DA: Yes. No, it wasn't a violent film compared to the others. Also, I chose a very different style of photography for this film. Benoît Debie was the cinematographer. He's from Belgium. We shot it as much as possible with natural light. It was a new style for me.

RR: *How was your experience making your two* Masters of Horror *episodes for American TV?*

Dario directs Michal Suchánek in the lead-up to his big death scene in Pelts.

DA: A marvelous experience, very good. In Canada. Also, in Los Angeles.

RR: *Your episodes were* Jenifer *and* Pelts. *How did you feel when* Jenifer *was the only episode censored by the network?*

DA: *Jenifer* wasn't cut for TV. The DVD is also the uncut version. As far as I know, they didn't touch it.⁵

RR: *It took you a long time to complete the Three Mothers trilogy with* Mother of Tears.

DA: Yes, many years.

RR: *Was the finished film what you had had in mind?*

DA: It was the same. I know these films—my other trilogy. I like revisiting these stories. I love them because they are like a prophecy *(laughs)*.

RR: *One scene in particular that I liked was after the taxi ride to the house, when the camera follows Asia into the house. The score was very good there, too.*

DA: Yes, it's a good scene.

RR: *What made you try your hand at a Gothic horror subject like* Dracula?

DA: Because somebody asked me to make *Dracula* in 3D. It was very interesting to me, 3D. Also, I am very interested in new technology. It was a big temptation for me to do something in 3D.

RR: *I remember reading about your curiosity with using CGI. You had wanted to do a particular effect with the pills going down the throat in* Phenomena, *but the technology wasn't there yet; so, you were finally able to do the effect with CGI in* The Stendhal Syndrome.

DA: Yes, and now I wanted to try 3D. Also, it is important for me because the first time I saw a film in 3D, I thought, 'This is marvelous!' I wanted to try it.

RR: *And then you directed your first opera,* Verdi: Macbeth, *in 2015. How did you find the experience?*

DA: You've seen it?

RR: *Well, I own the Blu-ray.*

DA: *(surprised)* It's on Blu-ray? Well, *Macbeth* was a very good experience. It created a great scandal, this version, because I included nudity. It is also very violent. One scene in particular came straight from *Deep Red*.

RR: *Yes, the scene with the window; I spotted it immediately!*

DA: Very good!

RR: *You followed that up with another opera,* Salomè; *was that as enjoyable an experience for you?*

DA: *Salomè* was presented in the church of San Francesco di Assisi, in between frescoes painted by Giotto and by Cimabue. It was recommended to me by the friars of the convent, so as not to betray the tradition of the church. There were no sets and the singers performed in their own contemporary clothing. It was very different from *Macbeth*, which was presented in an opera with great sets and costumes.

RR: *And finally: you have been talking about an upcoming project for television—a TV series based on* Suspiria. *How is that progressing?*

DA: I think it will still take some time before that sees the light of day. I do not know when work will begin on it.

RR: *Okay, well fingers crossed—I know the fans are anxiously awaiting it!*

DA: Yes!

RR: *Thank you so much for doing this and inviting me here, Dario; it means a lot to me.*

DA: *Prego*!

Notes:

1. For years, Dario expressed dissatisfaction with the film. His attitude towards the picture appears to have softened with the distance of time.
2. Argento evidently misunderstood the question. Mario's son Lamberto was his assistant on *Inferno*; it has been reported by numerous sources that Argento, ill with hepatitis, entrusted some second unit scenes to Mario Bava to direct. There has never been a precise break-down of what these scenes might have been.
3. Dario trailed off here. It could be that the memory of some of the unpleasant events which inspired the film (outlined in the text of this book) was something he wasn't eager to discuss in detail.
4. Though accredited to *The Hound of the Baskervilles* in the film, it actually is from *The Sign of Four*.
5. *Jenifer* was the only episode censored for broadcast on Showtime and Argento went on record at the time stating that he was upset about the cuts. Interested readers can consult his video interview on the Anchor Bay DVD where he discusses his feelings on the subject.

Fiore Argento interviewed by Rob Ruston

The following interview with Dario's eldest daughter/sometimes-collaborator, Fiore, took place at Piazza Mincio on Friday, June 15, 2018. Fiore has our sincere thanks for making time for this interview.

Rob Ruston: Ciao *Fiore! First. I would like to say how grateful I am that you have met me today, particularly under the current circumstances.*
Fiore Argento: No, thank you!
RR: *I'll start by asking you about your childhood. As a child, when did you first become aware that your father was a famous film director?*
FA: I always knew my father was a film director but, when I was very small, I didn't know what that meant exactly. Growing older, when I was eight years old, I decided I wanted to live with my father. At that point, I started going on set and I began to realize what kind of job he did. It was not the set of a horror movie. Later, when I was a little older, I visited the set of one of his horror films and it was explained to me that, all the blood, it was not real, that it was fake. It was fiction.
RR: *So, it was clear to you at a very young age that what you saw on set wasn't real? That it was "make believe"?*
FA: Yes! But, even now, to see the movies, even after watching them 200 times, I still get scared!
RR: *Was it difficult growing up in the spotlight or did you get to enjoy a relatively quiet childhood?*
FA: My childhood was very normal. We went to school, we played sports. As a kid everything was normal. It was when I became a teenager that something changed. I played the role in *Phenomena*.
RR: *What sets do you remember visiting?*
FA: I remember, very vividly, visiting the set of *Suspiria*. Many, many times. I remember being very scared and my father would try to console me. I was friends with all the actors. Yes, *Suspiria* I recall perfectly! *Deep Red* I don't really remember. For *Inferno* I wasn't there because it was shot in New York.[1] I was present on the set of *Tenebrae*, most of the time. It was very exciting and, because I was older, I understood what was going on much more. *Suspiria* scared me more because I was so young at the time.
RR: *We're the same age so I think you would've been around 12 years old when your father shot* Tenebrae, *one of my favorites. But it wasn't until 1984 that you first acted for Dario in* Phenomena. *What was it like being directed by your father?*
FA: Well, firstly, it wasn't one of my dreams to become an actress. My father offered me the role of Vera Brandt, the tourist, in *Phenomena*. I was very flattered that my father asked me to do this and I said okay. I prepared for the role with Daria (Nicolodi). She helped me a lot because even all the screaming that I had to do in that scene wasn't easy, you know? Lots of screaming!
RR: *Lots of screaming* and *lots of running!*
FA: (Laughs) Yes! It was very difficult
RR: *Poor Vera's hand was skewered onto a door frame with an enormous pair of scissors and then she was chased through the waterfalls*[2] *before being stabbed and decapitated!*
FA: Yes—a very difficult scene to shoot. Also, my father's behavior was very different to what I was used to. He was not the sweet father I knew before. He acted very differently. He was like another person. I was an actress, not a daughter. The first day on the set I was almost shocked!
RR: *So, you were treated in a professional manner maybe?*
FA: Yes, professional. It was very strange to me. But I love his professionalism. He is a perfectionist. He has a vision, an idea in his head and he expects the actor to do everything step by step. He tells the actor exactly what he wants. Many other film directors don't have a clear idea of what they want and so they (the actors) maybe feel lost and confused. They don't know what to do. My father always knows exactly what he wants them to do
RR: *What do you remember about Jennifer Connelly?*
FA: We were very good friends. We were the same age when we shot the movie. She was great! Later, when I went to New York, to university, we met again.
RR: *At the time did you have any serious aspirations to become an actress or did you realize that it was something you didn't want to pursue?*
FA: Acting was something that happened, and I went through with it. It wasn't my dream to become an actress. Like I said before, I was very flattered, but I wasn't sure that acting would be my career
RR: *Were all your scenes shot in Switzerland or were any scenes shot here in Italy?*
FA: All my scenes were shot on location in Switzerland.

Fiore poses for Rob Ruston near Piazza Mincio.

Dario and Fiore.

RR: *The next film you appeared in was* Demons *by Lamberto Bava. What was Lamberto like to work for compared to your father?*

FA: Totally different! They are two completely different people. It was very stressful working on *Demons*. In fact, after *Demons*, my mother didn't give me permission to work anymore until I was older.

RR: *The film was shot here in Italy with exteriors shot in Berlin?*

FA: Yes, here in Italy

RR: *And, of course, you're still good friends with Guido Baldi after all these years, your onscreen boyfriend who played Tommy. I bumped into you both, strangely enough, at a cinema last year here in Rome!*

FA: Yes, but we were friends before *Demons*. He is the son of actress Macha Méril. We were friends before and we are still friends today although we don't see each other as much as we used to.

RR: *Lamberto's father is, of course, Mario Bava. Do you ever remember meeting Mario?*

FA: No, never. I never met him. I don't know, maybe when I was *very* small.

RR: *Any memories of the co-stars of* Demons*?*

FA: Yes, we were a group of people every day on the set, so we all became friends. Urbano Barberini …

RR: *Ahh, yes, the very handsome Urbano …*

FA: Yes, very handsome. In fact, we are still friends today. The others, at that time, we were very close because we were always on the set together

RR: *And this was shortly after* Phenomena*…*

FA: Yes. Almost one year later

RR: *After* Demons*, you stepped away from acting. What made you decide to abandon acting? We touched on this briefly earlier …*

FA: My mother. My mother didn't want me to continue and when you're underage you need permission from both parents. Both parents had to sign. My mother decided she didn't want me to work. She wanted me to enjoy my teenage years, my childhood. Also, I was living with Asia and she was super motivated! More than me. So, I didn't have this passion for acting that she had. I thought maybe I need to do something else

RR: *Asia was becoming active as an actress around that time. Did you two have a competitive streak as kids? Or were you always close?*

FA: No, we were always close and there was no competition. She had this incredible passion that I never had. If she had to do a role that involved her needing to lose 15 kilos, she did it! She was very dedicated. So, I decided to leave her to her work, and I pursued another career. I had my passion for fashion, for designing clothes. That's what I really wanted to do.

RR: *It's been said that you also appeared in* Trauma, *the giallo your father made in America; is there any truth to this?*

FA: No, no! I never appeared in the film at all! I don't know where that rumor came from? It is not me! Also, my hair was very dark at the time, not blonde. It was totally different. I was in New York at the time studying, yes. I also visited the set many times. But, no, that wasn't me.

RR: *You worked as a production manager for your father on* The Stendhal Syndrome. *How challenging was that? Is it a job you'd ever consider doing again?*

FA: I was the assistant production manager on the movie. It was incredibly challenging. For a while I was contemplating to work behind the scenes for my father. It was incredibly challenging, yes, but a great experience.

RR: *And, of course, you provided support on set for Asia, particularly during her difficult scenes, some of which were quite brutal.*

FA: Yes. I also provided support and took care of all the other actors, too. I knew how to talk to them. I helped them with their roles. I enjoyed working with them on this film very much.

RR: *Any particular memories of filming* The Stendhal Syndrome*?*

FA: Everything! Florence, the Uffizi, the paintings, the art …

RR: *Yes, I visited there. Truly beautiful.*

FA: I'll tell you a strange thing. Before the film, I went to visit a friend in Athens. She was doing her Master's Degree there. She was studying all day so I would explore and walk through Athens by myself. I visited the Parthenon, the Acropolis. I had a strange experience there. I phoned my father and I told him: "I have the Stendhal Syndrome!" And he said: "What?!" I said: "Yes, I went at 10 o'clock in the morning and now they are kicking me out at 6 o'clock in the evening!" And my father replied: "Fantastic!" I was looking at the statues and they were breathing to me! It's like they were alive. I was shocked by this. Then, of course, my father went to make the movie.

RR: *I think great works of art can have a strange overwhelming effect on us sometimes.*

FA: Yes, definitely!

RR: *What made you decide to return to acting with* The Card Player? *Did your father approach you about it early on?*

FA: Yes, my father told me about a role he had specifically written for me [Lucia Marini, the police inspector's daughter] and that he wanted me in the movie. He also asked if I would design my own clothes. He wanted me to wear very bright white clothes in the film and have very blonde hair. He wanted me to be the 'light' in the movie, a movie which focused on such dark subject matter. My character would also survive and escape the killer.

RR: *Out of all the films you've appeared in, which is your favorite? And which performance are you the happiest with?*

FA: I don't know because they were all shot at different ages. It's difficult to say. With *The Card Player* I was more mature so I experienced the film in a different way. *Phenomena* was also at a different stage in my life as I was very young. They are all very different films, made at different times, and I experienced and approached each one very differently. But I love to work with my father each time.

RR: *Tell us a little about your fashion design. When did you decide that this is what you wanted to do for a living?*

FA: It began when I bought my first *Vogue* magazine when I was 10 or 11 years old. I always had a great passion for fashion. Also, my first boyfriend, my first love, was involved in fashion and he used to take me to fashion shows in Milan. In the 1980s, I studied at the Fashion Institute of Technology. And so, I pursued my career in fashion and opened my own company.

RR: *Does being part of a famous family ever cause problems for you in Italy?*

FA: No, although when I was younger, I liked it when I moved to America where nobody knew that I was the daughter, the sister, or the niece. When you are younger you want to find yourself. And then I realized I was loved even if nobody knew I was the daughter or the sister or the niece and so on. From that moment on, I no longer cared, and things didn't bother me.

RR: *Do people sometimes recognize you in Italy?*

FA: In Rome? Yes, sometimes. It happened to me a few months ago. It was very cold at the time and I was completely covered wearing a long coat, scarf, sunglasses and a hat. I was walking Julie, my dog, near my home and a young guy, a total stranger, stops me and he asks, "Are you Fiore Argento?!" I was shocked! How did you recognize me?? (*Laughs*)

Asia Argento poses with big sister Fiore at the premiere of *The Stendhal Syndrome.*

RR: *Would you ever consider going back into filmmaking in any capacity, be it as an actress or even as a director? Is it something that has ever crossed your mind?*

FA: I think it has to be here, in your heart, the need to act or direct. It needs to come naturally. It's not my obsession. With Asia, it is different.

RR: *Of course, aside from acting, Asia has also directed. She's produced. films, TV, music videos…*

FA: Yes, she's great. In fact, I helped her with the production of her Indochine music video. A very unusual camera was used in the video, one that attaches to your forehead. Amazing video!

RR: *What's your favorite film directed by your father? Are you a fan of horror movies?*

FA: Naturally, I love the classics like *Suspiria* and *Inferno*. Fabulous! But even *Sleepless* was incredible to me. I don't know, maybe because I spent so much time on the set of that movie. I love that movie. I intended to stay one week during shooting, but I ended up staying one month! Also, *The Phantom of the Opera*. I spent a great deal of time on that set, too. Yes, I like horror movies. I like to be scared. They scare me but it's an emotion I love to feel!

Notes:
1. Fiore is mistaken. Apart from a week's worth of location filming in New York City in April 1979, the entire film was shot in Italy.
2. The Thurfälle in Unterwasser, Switzerland, to be precise.

Sally Kirkland Interviewed by Troy Howarth

Sally Kirkland as the sultry Eleonora in Dario's segment of *Two Evil Eyes*, "The Black Cat."

The following interview with actress Sally Kirkland (Eleonora in *Two Evil Eyes*) was conducted on November 29, 2018. Mark Savage has my thanks for facilitating the interview, and Ms. Kirkland has my thanks for her kindness in talking to me about her work experience with Argento.

Troy Howarth: *Well let me start by saying thank you for taking the time to talk about your experiences making* Two Evil Eyes *with Dario Argento.*
Sally Kirkland: You're welcome. I honestly don't have a lot of information about the film, but I'll do my best!
TH: *First things first: how did you become involved in* Two Evil Eyes?
SK: It was through my agents at William Morris. They packaged it. They basically told me I had the job and gave me a start date. I didn't even have to audition for it.
TH: *Were you aware of who Dario Argento was when you were cast?*
SK: Not at that time, no. I mean, I had heard the name—but I didn't know his work, not at that time. Since then I've become more aware, obviously.
TH: *Well, this was actually his first American-made project …*
SK: I know! Amazing.
TH: *Do you happen to remember how long you were on the picture?*
SK: No, but I can't imagine it was more than a just a few days.
TH: *How did you find working with Dario? Was he able to communicate much in English or did he use an interpreter?*

SK: I didn't have any problems communicating or working with him, but whether he just spoke broken English or if he had somebody helping him, I honestly can't remember. I just know he made everything feel very easy.
TH: *The film was shot in Pittsburgh; do you have any memories of being there?*
SK: I honestly don't remember too much about Pittsburgh. I was just glad to be working. I do remember going to the Andy Warhol Museum; I had known Andy and I enjoyed that. It was a good time.
TH: *You shared screen time with Harvey Keitel; what are your memories of him?*
SK: Harvey is a long, long-time friend of mine. He and I go back to the days of studying under the same acting teacher—Frank Corsaro was both Harvey's and my acting teacher. That's going all the way back to around 1961 or '62. He may have been one of the first people I knew in show business, actually.
TH: *Was this the first time acting with him?*
SK: I think we had done some scenes together at the Acting Studio.
TH: *Was there a lot of ad libbing allowed?*
SK: Not that I remember.
TH: *Did you get to interact with any of the other actors, like Madeline Potter or Martin Balsam?*
SK: Well, I knew Martin from the Actor's Studio, but I didn't meet Madeline that I can remember.

Harvey Keitel, Sally Kirkland and Dario take a break on the set of *Two Evil Eyes*.

TH: *Did you ever get to see the finished film and, if so, what did you think of it?*
SK: That's a good question … I know I've seen clips of my work in it. I don't think I saw the whole thing in completion, though.
TH: *What did you think of what you saw?*
SK: I was very proud of it. He let me do my own costumes. The hair and the costumes were by me and approved by him. I came in with my hair already done and the black-and-white striped shirt was mine and the jewelry, too. They had their makeup person do me up, but I brought a lot of my own stuff to it.
TH: *Do you have any favorite memories connected with the shoot?*
SK: Nothing specific, really. I mean, I had a terrific time. Dario was incredibly respectful. I loved working with Harvey; he was my friend for so many years and I just loved working with him. As I learned who Dario was, what a genius he was, I thought, "Oh my God, I'm so proud to be a part of his film legacy."
TH: *Do you recall his specific methods in working with the actors—was he very specific, or did he leave you a lot of room to do your thing?*
SK: No, he had a vision of what he wanted. I do remember telling him that I photograph best from the left side and he made a point of acknowledging that and keeping that in mind.
TH: *Obviously it's just a small part, but you make a strong impression; it calls to mind the old expression about there not being any small roles, just small actors …*
SK: Yeah! It was a real pleasure. I only ran into him once since that time—I can't remember where. But fans from all over, like you, seem to be curious. So, I'm glad I'm a small part of his cinematic legacy.
TH: *Are you a horror fan in general or is it not your cup of tea?*
SK: No, no, I'm interested in them. I did *The Haunted* (1991), did you see that one?
TH: *Yes, indeed!*
SK: I got a Golden Globe nomination for that. I like doing horror—good horror, anyway.
TH: *Well, I guess that about wraps it up; I appreciate your taking the time to revisit the film with me!*
SK: I'm sorry I don't remember more, but I was thrilled to do it. Again, when people explained who Dario was and how respected he was in the film community—I was very impressed. I really had a blast. I wonder if Harvey had anything to do with my being in it?
TH: *I guess that's possible, based on what you've told me!*
SK: Maybe. But anyway, thank you, Troy—and good luck with your book!

Henrik Möller Discusses *Trauma* with T.E.D. Klein

Henrik Möller is a filmmaker/podcaster from Sweden and a long-time fan of Mr. T.E.D. Klein. Henrik interviewed Mr. Klein for his podcast "Udda Ting" in 2017, and one of the many topics they touched on was his problematic collaboration with Dario on *Trauma*; the following comments represent Mr. Klein's very candid and humorous memories of the experience. My thanks to both Henrik and Mr. Klein for agreeing to share these comments in this context.

Henrik Möller: *Can you tell me how you got involved in the writing of Dario Argento's* Trauma*? Many view it as Argento's first bad film—what happened?*

T.E.D. Klein: Oy! So, I have the honor to have written Argento's first bad film? Well, I can't argue with that.

I was brought in—through [agent] Kirby McCauley, bless him—to write a script based on, if memory serves, a 12-page, or maybe 16-page, untitled treatment by Argento and one or two associates. It seemed to me excessively, at times even ludicrously, violent and somewhat incoherent. Like, for no particular reason, a young boy character ended up hanged. I saw my task, in part, as trying to make the story a bit more logical and believable, but also to add, if I could, some notions here and there that struck me as unnerving. I had seen three or four of Argento's films and had been quite riveted by them, especially by *Suspiria*. His English, I found when I met him, was somewhat limited—that was another reason I'd been hired, as this was to be his first full-length American feature—but he was an eccentric, colorful character, and I felt fortunate to be working with him. We spent a couple of days in Pittsburgh together, looking over possible locations; it's an area, of course, where George Romero had shot his zombie films and where Jonathan Demme had shot *The Silence of the Lambs*. I remember, while there, being somewhat uneasy, as I was also, at the time, editing a monthly crime magazine and had concealed from the staff where I was going. Later, I gather, Argento considered filming in New Orleans. Alas, the movie ended up being shot in Minneapolis, one of the least atmospheric cities in America, for a depressingly tiny budget, and an elaborate opening scene I'd dreamed up, involving a death at a construction site, was simply never filmed. I'd thought it was rather neat, but it was obviously way too expensive.

In general, once I'd begun writing, a typical face-to-face encounter with Argento consisted of me bringing him a scene I'd written, pleased with my own cleverness, and him reading it, nodding, and—with an appropriate hand gesture—saying, deflatingly, "Ah, yes. You cut, yes?" In the end, a lot of material did get cut—maybe not enough! But there was some connecting tissue, some necessary exposition that also got cut, leaving a few plot points unexplained and confusing. Finally—and forgive me for trying to shift some of the blame—Argento was prey to sudden enthusiasms and had a habit of latching onto ideas from whatever he'd just seen or read and urging me to incorporate them into the story, occasionally at the expense of logic. For example, at some point—I forget when—I found myself having to introduce a side plot about anorexia, because Dario had seen some sort of documentary about it and felt sorry for the girls, or perhaps just attracted to them. I remember that while we were putting together the script, he saw *Shadows and Fog*—a very strange Woody Allen film—and immediately wanted to work some elements from it into ours. And then one day he saw Hitchcock's *Shadow of a Doubt* and was influenced by that as well. At one point, he wanted to add a talking lizard (maybe there *is* one in the film now; I forget), and he did an amusing imitation of it in a high, piping voice. In the end, my friend Andy Sands, one of the production crew, summed up the film's problems by saying, "Too much plot, too little time." I've never watched the damned thing all the way through. One small, pleasant memory: getting to take Argento's 17-year-old daughter, Asia, who would star in the film, out to lunch when she came to New York.

HM: *Do you recall anything about the original opening of the film? I believe it was intended to set up the killer's motivation, but as you say, it was dropped for budgetary reasons.*

TK: As best I can remember, Dario's original treatment involved a mysterious killer who's running around lopping off heads. And the origin of the killer's lunacy—as we learn at the end—lies in some traumatic incident years before in which ... was it a baby's head that was cut off in a botched obstetric procedure? That seems to ring a bell. At any rate, Dario's treatment never addressed the question of why the psychopath at the heart of the mystery would suddenly begin murdering people after years of living a peaceful, law-abiding life.

So I had this idea for opening the movie with a bizarre fatal accident at a construction site, a sort of Rube Goldberg affair, in which some object balanced on one of the topmost girders—a heavy bucket, a block of concrete, whatever—tips over and falls, snapping an attached cable whose end gets yanked through a pulley and goes whipping through the air at great speed, slicing off some luckless worker's head. I'd once heard about something similar happening on an aircraft carrier. And I imagined the head bouncing down a series of platforms, level after level, like a ball bearing in a pinball game, until it drops onto the sidewalk below and comes rolling up to the feet of what seems an ordinary passing pedestrian—who will turn out, in the end, to be the murderer. But we don't entirely see this passerby—we just see a close-up of the person's shoes, I think, coming to a stop beside the head, and we hear some sort of scream—a scream of horror but also, perhaps, of ... well, not recognition, exactly, but of remembering. For this would be the incident—a jarring flashback, more or less, to the original incident in the hospital—that would awaken long-buried memories and set the murderer off. I may even have suggested that the severed head—like guillotined heads have been reputed to do—might look up and mouth some sort of silent message.

I guess I should have realized that the scene would be too complicated to film, but I thought Dario might find the idea amusing and give it a try. It seemed like the sort of thing that might appeal to him. And so far as I know, he actually considered doing it, until he found himself working with a much smaller budget than he'd expected.

T.E.D. Klein

Irene Miracle Interviewed by Rob Ruston

The following interview with actress Irene Miracle was conducted via email on March 9, 2018; follow-up questions were completed on April 8, 2018. I provided the questions and Rob took care of interviewing and following up with Irene Miracle. The author wishes to extend his gratitude to both Irene Miracle and Rob Ruston for making this interview possible.

Rob Ruston: *How did your role in* Inferno *come about? Do you recall your first meeting with Dario and your impressions of him as a director?*

Irene Miracle: I had just received my Golden Globe for *Midnight Express* and was looking to the next film to focus my passions on. A call came in to meet an Italian director at 20th Century Fox. After a long wait, a lanky man with dark, curly hair, stepped cautiously into the room. "This is Irene Miracle," said my agent, while the thin wiry man inched shyly towards me. He fastidiously began to examine my hair, my hands, and then looked intensely into my eyes. "Irene, this is Dario." He cupped his leaning face into his hand, the corner of his mouth curled into smile. I smiled back. He leaned over to whisper to his father (the film's producer), then gave me another quick look over and I got the part of Rose! I was off to Rome!

RR: *Do you remember Mario Bava directing any of your scenes?*

IM: Yes, of course. Aside from rumors that Mario directed much of the film, one can see the evidence of his aesthetic stamp everywhere. I was so young, so happy to be working, so happy to be in Rome. I wasn't so focused on who was directing me as much as how to make sense out of the story. I wanted to find truth in Rose, to find what was hidden beneath the lines of her dialogue and story. Without that deeper narrative to sink my teeth into I instead found solace in the underwater sequences with Mario. It was the hottest of summers in Rome that year, so apart from the frustration that I wasn't given much to emotionally immerse myself into, I did find the physical immersion into that large pool extremely refreshing.

RR: *Mario's son, Lamberto Bava, was Argento's assistant on the film; are you sure you don't mean he was there, as opposed to Mario?*

IM: Surely Lamberto had a strong presence on the shoot, but it is Mario that lights up my memory most clearly after all this time. Considering the sensuality and poetry, which is typical of Mario's other work, my underwater scenes very much reflect Mario's influence, as do other more abstractly lit scenes I'm in. My sense was that Lamberto and Mario were close and thus worked in harmony on the set.

RR: *Any recollections of Sacha Pitoëff?*

IM: Sacha and I only had one night on the set together. He was quiet and kept to himself, as I am apt to do when I'm in character. At that time, I wasn't aware of my luck, to be working with such legends as Pitoëff and Alida Valli. *The Third Man* (1949, starring Alida Valli) is one of my all-time faves.

RR: *Did you find the script confusing?*

IM: It always seemed like we were making things up as we went, " off the cuff," trying to row a boat in the dark, without oars. As a result, I didn't take the film seriously, but I was getting paid to work on a film, I was in Rome, and I was grateful to be a part of something special.

Later, it was somewhat of a shock to me that *Inferno* had become such a cult classic. At the time I felt like just another pretty face, without the tools to reflect my true value. But then, in the end, it's what is unspoken that sheds the most light on any story. Perhaps that's Dario's greatest gift—shedding light on the unspoken. At the time, I couldn't imagine the film making sense to anyone. Who knew?

RR: *Is it true that further scenes were shot that didn't make it into the final cut?*

IM: I do recall some scenes at Central Park during our New York shoot, where I (Rose) find Sacha Pitoëff's body being fed upon by a congress of rats.[1] It was a particularly creepy scene so go figure why it was excluded from the final cut, unless it was a matter of time constraint and simply having to economize to keep the film at an appropriate length for theaters.

RR: *What was the atmosphere like on set?*

IM: I was treated with grace and respect. Everyone was very loving, supportive, and amicable. It is a great privilege to work in the film biz and the atmosphere of the cast and crew reflected that. My only regret is not having had more time with Dario. I had the sense he was going through a rough emotional patch in those days and felt sadness that I couldn't turn that around in some way.

RR: *What did you think of the finished film?*

IM: Dario brings off a wild and beautiful magic trick. I appreciate the underwater scenes, which have a lovely aesthetic quality. I am not usually a fan of the horror genre—but I love any stories that pull at my heart, or strives to be political or

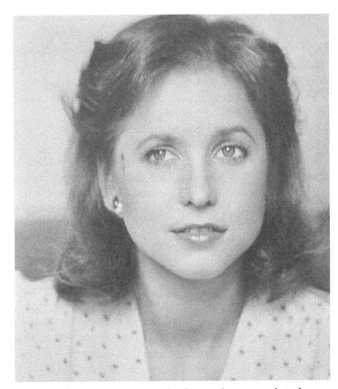

Behind the scenes portrait from the set of *Inferno*, provided by Irene Miracle.

Behind the scenes candid from the set of *Inferno*, provided by Irene Miracle.

spiritually significant. Fantasy and horror in the right hands can reach such heights. Ann Rice's Lestat novels do this, and I love *Penny Dreadful*, the recent HBO series starring Eva Green and Josh Hartnett, which was exceptional for its humanity and poetry. By contrast, though, anything that is gratuitously violent or spilling over with gore leaves me repulsed. I'm proud of my work in *Inferno*, which magnetized some wonderful people like Dario and the Bava's into my life, not to mention the many fans—beautiful spirits—that I've befriended over the years as a result of making it.

RR: *How was working with Argento compared to working with Aldo Lado on* Night Train Murders*?*

IM: One cannot compare, of course, but Argento was introspective, complicated, and tender. I'd say Lado was more interactive, sociable, and inclusive.

RR: *How was your murder scene orchestrated?*

IM: Very simply. The only preparation I needed to do for it was the usual prosthetic process of making a rubber mask of my face—so that when the guillotine slices my character's head off, I'd be ready for my close-up! My least favorite/uncomfortable part of the shoot, with all the sticky dyed-sugar they used for blood in those days.

RR: *Is there anything else connected to the film that you'd like to mention?*

IM: Most definitely! Giancarlo de Leonardis, my hair stylist on the film, deserves an Oscar for his contribution to *Inferno*. Shortly after we'd already shot most of my scenes in New York, I started finding clumps of hair on my pillow in the morning. It was horrifying, so much so that I started to count the strands. One morning it was 300, another morning it was 400 and so forth. I later learned that Dario thought I had some terminal illness and that I'd deceived him to get the part. There were even rumors that I'd died, after the film's release because of that whole fiasco. What I did eventually learn is that my hair loss was a result of having had a very high fever during a bout of the flu only a short time before getting signed onto the film.

Fast forward, back to New York—Giancarlo had a brilliant idea. He took me to one of the world's leading natural hair Boutique's. I'd never seen so much hair, or so many colors of hair. He picked out over 100 colors, repeatedly matching my hair to swatches of hair lining the walls. By the time we started hair and make-up on our first day of our shoot in Rome, he surprised me with his ingenious invention.

He'd tied all of these various hundreds of colors of hair to tiny little springs, each about an inch long. He could then expand the coils and let them spring onto my own hair, making it look thick while not detecting any kind of extensions or bulky effect as my hair moved around in the water. Brilliant for the underwater scenes! Giancarlo is a genius, truly! He was the first to try something like that on a film shoot, and I believe it's become an industry standard ever since. Understandably, Giancarlo has earned his own notoriety in the film biz and had gone on to work on many impressive bigger budget films.

RR: *What are you up to now?*

IM: I've written a film for myself to direct, called *Guest of the King*, based on Jon Cole's memoir, *Bangkok Hard Time*. You could say it bears a strong surface resemblance to *Midnight Express*, because it tells the story of Jon's time in a Thai prison for the crime of drug-smuggling. But it describes a much more spiritual journey. The hero's only way out of the hell he's made for himself will not involve a dramatic escape, the way it did for Billy Hayes. There's no angelic girlfriend like the one I played, who drops in to show off her breasts and smuggle him a pack of money! The female in this case is a fellow prisoner, a beautiful "Ladyboy"—still physically a male, but outwardly and in his soul a woman—who in a Platonic way awakens in Jon a Buddhist perspective, a quest for higher consciousness, an acceptance of life the way Buddha directs, that will win him a pardon from Thailand's King. This is the only way out of any Thai prison. For a man who earns it, the effect is more positive than any trick-escape.

RR: *What stage of production are you in?*

IM: We're in the pre-production phase and in the midst of attaching actors. I've recently returned from Thailand, where I scouted locations, talked to production houses and found my ideal Ladyboy. We're looking to shoot this baby by winter/spring of 2018/2019. Wish me luck!

Notes:
1. If indeed this is true, then the script for *Inferno* must have evolved considerably during the filming. In the film as it stands, Pitoëff's character is killed off long after Rose has already exited the narrative.

Claudio Simonetti Interviewed by Rob Ruston

The following interview was conducted on the Via dei Gracchi, in Rome, on Wednesday, June 13, 2018. I provided Rob with the questions and he was kind enough to meet with Claudio on my behalf. He and Claudio both have my sincere thanks for the wonderful interview.

Rob Ruston: *Thank you for meeting me today Claudio! It's good to see you again.*

Claudio Simonetti: Yes, the same for me!

RR: *So, Claudio, let's start with you telling us a little about your childhood …*

CS: I was born in Brazil. My father worked there for over 30 years. He was a very popular musician, just like in Italy. I grew up in San Paola and I began studying piano when I was eight years old, even if at the time I didn't like it so much! I preferred to play with my friends outside of course! Then my family came back to Italy when I was around 11 years old. At 14, I started to play the piano again. I studied at Santa Cecilia, a very important school of music here in Rome. I studied piano and composition there. I was very lucky to have grown up in Brazil, a wonderful place to grow up in the '50s and '60s. They didn't have the same problems there back then as they do today. At that time, it was a country where everyone smiled! The people were very happy all of the time! A great place. So, I have Brazil inside of me, even if I don't like the football or like to play Brazilian music! (*Laughs*). Yes, I'm a rock musician but I love the feel and move of the Brazilian people, even if I do write the scores for horror films! That's why I work a lot with disco music because I have this feeling inside of me. So, I had a great childhood, a very happy childhood. I don't remember anything bad about it. I was very lucky, I think, especially to have a father like mine.

RR: *When did you first discover your love of music? You've already mentioned that you started to play the piano when you were very young …*

CS: Yes, the piano at eight years old. My father tried very hard to teach me at an early age, but I never really began to appreciate music until I heard bands like The Rolling Stones in the 1960s. This is the real reason why I play, because of this type of music. Then I started to play the guitar at maybe 13 or 14 years old. But I changed my vision of music after I started to listen to different bands. The most important band to me was Procol Harum. This band made a huge impression on me. When I heard "A Whiter Shade of Pale" it was incredible! When I heard the organ sound I thought it was very beautiful. So, this inspired me to play the keyboards again, starting with the piano. I grew up with bands like Emerson, Lake & Palmer, Genesis—all this music influenced me. Each band had their own style. They were very different to each other. I was very lucky to be 20 years old in the prog rock period, to experience all of this at such a young age. All this music was very important to me. This is what I think is missing now. Today there is nothing new. It's very difficult to create a new sound. Something like Pink Floyd or The Rolling Stones will never exist again. I'm glad I experienced them.

RR: *How did you come into Dario Argento's circle?*

CS: I met Dario Argento when he had finished the filming of *Deep Red*. He had asked a very famous Italian composer, Giorgio Gaslini, to do the music. The first three films were, of course, by Ennio Morricone. *Le cinque giornate*—"The Five Days"—was composed by Gaslini. So, Dario asked Gaslini to compose the music for *Deep Red*. Gaslini started recording his music with the orchestra and it was a very traditional sound. And Dario heard it and said he wanted something different. We were very lucky because we were on the same record label that was shared by many important composers of that time, composers of many important films of the '60s and '70s, including Dario's. Dario spoke to our producer, Carlo Bixio, saying he would like to have a band like Deep Purple or Pink Floyd for his film. Carlo says to him, "No, listen, before you choose these bands. Why don't you listen to these guys whose music I produce in Rome." And so, Gaslini left the film. Dario came to us and said we don't have the musician but, more importantly, we are missing a band! So, you try to do this. So we created the music of *Deep Red*—"Death Dies," "Mad Puppet," and so on—and this is why *Deep Red* has two different scores within the film, including the lullaby which is Giorgio Gaslini's. It's interesting because you have the traditional orchestra along with the rock. This was our first experience with Dario Argento.

RR: *We mentioned Cherry Five before. Can you explain the change of the band name from Cherry Five to Goblin?*

CS: No, we never actually changed the name because we considered ourselves two different bands. When we started to record the Cherry Five album, we had a singer and a different drummer. When we recorded *Deep Red*, we had no singer and we used another drummer. So, we were actually two different bands. The producers said, "We'll use the name Cherry Five for the album we are recording now, but for *Deep Red*, we will use a different name." They decided to call us Goblin.

RR: *What was the experience like recording the soundtrack of* Deep Red?

CS: It was a strange experience because Dario had contacted us to do the music for the film, but he told us we didn't have much time. It had to be finished in the next two months. So, we completed the soundtrack in 10 days! At the time, we had no idea that the soundtrack would be such a huge success. So, we finished working on the film and went back to work as Cherry Five. We didn't expect to sell one million copies of the *Deep Red* album in a matter of months! It was a big surprise to us. It was an unexpected success.

RR: *How specific was Dario about the type of music he wanted for* Deep Red?

CS: We listened to a lot of music at his house. He told us that this is the sound he wanted for his film. I remember one day, after that, we went to my little studio and we recorded the main theme. Then the next day we went to the main studio and Dario listened to the theme and he said okay, let's do it. We decided to use an organ to create a very unique style. I recorded the soundtrack in the studio behind a huge church in Rome, the Sacro Cuore di Maria. I knew there was this enormous organ in the church, designed by Vincenzo Mascioni, and I thought, "Wow, why don't we use this 15 thousand pipe organ for the soundtrack?" I used the same organ later for *Tenebrae*. Of course, in 1975, there weren't any digital keyboards. Now, thanks to digital, I can play the sound of a real organ on stage but back then this wasn't possible. Now I can use my iPad to produce the sound of a perfect organ, an organ as good as the one in Saint Peter's! That's how it came about that we used the organ. It's a strange connection of the themes. If Gaslini hadn't left the production, who knows how different things would be? It would be a different film maybe and also a very different life for me. The success of this film changed my life completely, of course. For the first time I was a soundtrack composer. It's something I never planned to do, compose for films. It was very unexpected. And this led to the big success of *Suspiria* a few years later.

RR: *With* Suspiria, *it's been said that Argento had you record the melodies before the film had even began shooting. What was the process like?*

CS: Yes, we did do that, but it didn't work. We started recording the soundtrack and Dario used something—but just while he was shooting, to create ambience on set. I was still in the studio when they completed the film. We did some themes but nothing that was used in the finished film. We recorded a score, but we decided that it wasn't good enough to be used for the final film. We changed it completely.

RR: *So, it's not true that Dario used the* Suspiria *soundtrack on set to 'unsettle' the actors during filming?*

CS: Yes, Dario played the music on set—but not the *Suspiria* score that we all know. It was a different score altogether, the original themes we did. Anyway, we never used it, and shortly after the tapes were lost. Vanished! The real *Suspiria* score came later. We went into the studio and it took almost two months to create the soundtrack. Dario said he wanted music that would make the audience feel that the witches of the film were always present, even if they weren't on the screen at the time. This is what we wanted to achieve.

RR: *Did you or any of the band members get to visit the set of* Suspiria?

CS: Yes, we visited together. Maybe two times. It was mainly filmed at De Paolis studios here in Rome. All the interiors, the school and so on, were shot in Rome. Even the exteriors of the school itself, the Akademie, were shot here. That was also a set.

RR: *What made you decide to use the bouzouki for the soundtrack?*

CS: The bouzouki belonged to Massimo (Morante). He bought it in Greece years before. He loved it and he bought it! The main witch of *Suspiria*—Helena Markos—was Greek, so we thought it would be a good idea to use it. It's a typical Greek instrument. Dario agreed. And we also used the Indian tabla (*imitates the sound*). Fabio (Pignatelli) had the tabla at his home. We also used a lot of sequencers. We rented a Moog System 55 because it had a lot of sequencers inside, but we never knew how to use it. We contacted a music engineer, Felice Fugazza, who specialized in electronic music and he knew how to use it. I knew how to turn it on but that was about it! So, we used a lot of electronic and ethnic instruments. We also used a celeste.

RR: *How would you describe the evolution of the sound of Goblin, from* Deep Red *to* Suspiria?

CS: I think they're two completely different projects, both very different from each other. Deliberately different. If you listen to both soundtracks separately, you would never tell they are the same band. I always keep this kind of mood when I write, the same when we did *Tenebrae*. *Tenebrae* is more rock disco, for example. The sound is very different. I like to change things. We used a drum machine for that, not a real drummer.

RR: *When you did* Dawn of the Dead, *did you ever meet Romero?*

CS: No, never. Dario came to Rome and he said he would be distributing this film in Europe and in Italy. I remember, for the first time, we went to Claudio Argento's home and we watched *Night of the Living Dead*, on 16mm. We then watched the original American version of *Dawn*. We were asked to compose new music as the original music was very bad and very boring. We recorded the soundtrack, with Dario, here in Rome. It wasn't until two years ago that I got to meet George. I was very lucky. It was shortly before he died. It was at the Lucca Festival in Tuscany. I spent the entire afternoon and evening with George and his wife. We talked a lot. He was a wonderful person. I asked him why he used that type of music for his film. He said he wanted the film to have a vintage '50s feel to it. He also said the film was better with the music of Goblin, even if he never called us again! (*Laughs*). So, the film was originally released with the original soundtrack then, when they released it again, it was with the Goblin music. The first version was a successful film in America but, afterwards, even more successful with our music. I remember I was in New York and I read on the screen music by The Goblin! (*Laughs*). Yes, I saw the film in New York, I remember. And two years ago, I visited the mall that was used in the film. They also did a big show at the mall [the Monroeville Mall, just east of Pittsburgh, PA] featuring all the actors from the movie.

RR: *I believe you met the lovely Gaylen Ross recently?*

CS: Yes, she came to see my show in New York. She's a very nice person. You know what she said? She said this is the first time she's heard my music in the film! She's only seen the original version. This is the first time she watched the Argento version. Also, another actor came to see us when we played in Pittsburgh, David Crawford. We had an idea at one point to perform *Dawn of the Dead* live in the mall but there were problems and we were not able to do it.

RR: *Did you enjoy working with Enzo G. Castellari on his film* The Heroin Busters?

CS: Yes, I did two films with him. Yes, *La via della droga* (*The Heroin Busters*) in 1977, which starred David Hemmings, and *I nuovi barbari* (*The New Barbarians*) in 1983. A good guy. Tarantino loves him! Castellari directed the original *The Inglorious Bastards* back in 1978 which, of course, Tarantino later remade.

RR: *Troy is very fond of the score you did for* Buio omega, *aka* Beyond the Darkness. *Do you remember how that project came about and were you happy with the end results?*

CS: No, that wasn't me. I left the band in 1978. This was a little later, maybe 1979. I don't know anything about it.

RR: *Was there ever any talk at all about doing the follow up to* Suspiria, Inferno?
CS: No because Dario loved Keith Emerson and just before the film was made, Goblin no longer existed. So, Keith was brought on-board to do the music. A beautiful soundtrack.

RR: *Yes, a wonderful soundtrack. Can you explain why* Tenebrae *is not credited to Goblin?*
CS: Because, after the split of the band, Fabio Pignatelli continued as Goblin with different members and he'd signed a contract with the record label. So, when we did *Tenebrae*, it was not possible to use the name "Goblin" for legal reasons. So that's why *Patrick* and *Buio omega* was done with other members, but not with Morante. The only thing we could do was use our real names. Of course, a drummer wasn't used. Like I said earlier, we used a drum machine for that recording.

Dario poses with Claudio Simonetti in the 1980s.

RR: *Can you explain what Goblin did on* Phenomena *and what you did by yourself?*
CS: Yes, because when the film was made, in 1984, I had a contract for Claudio Simonetti as a solo artist. Pignatelli had come to the end of his contract with Goblin, with the new line up. So, we remained together, me and Fabio. I said, "Okay, I will write the main theme and I will use my own name because I have a contract with you, but if you want I will do something together with Fabio so the only two members of Goblin used there was just me and Pignatelli. Fabio did very good work. He was very good with a computer, and he was one of the best players. Together we recorded together in my studio. I did the main theme as Simonetti even if Cinevox records released it as "Phenomena by Goblin." The main theme was by me.

RR: *There have been quite a few versions of that soundtrack out there. One release just featured the music by Simonetti and Goblin and another release featured various artists such as Bill Wyman and Terry Taylor, The Andi Sex Gang and so on. I used to own the various artists' vinyl, as* Creepers, *distributed on the Heavy Metal Worldwide label. It's a very special soundtrack to me because that's the first Argento film I saw and it's also the first time I heard your music.*
CS: *Phenomena* was the first Argento film you saw?

RR: *Yes. I saw it at a late-night screening at a cinema in Manchester. I remember the screening very well. Aside from the visuals, the soundtrack stood out to me. Obviously, your main theme along with "Sleepwalking," "The Wind," and "Jennifer." I also liked "Jennifer's Friends," a track that was never featured in the film but was included on the OST. The Bill Wyman/Terry Taylor track "Valley" also made a huge impression.*
CS: We used a beautiful soprano voice on there.

RR: *Yes. It was wonderful that the soundtrack was later reissued with all the previously unreleased scores and unused material. A great soundtrack. Now, with* Opera, *you wrote a great many beautiful pieces of music for the film. Did Dario instruct you to write melodies that would contrast with the violent imagery?*

CS: Yes. I think sometimes this contrast works, like the lullaby in *Deep Red*. We have violent scenes with soft music, along with the heavy metal.

RR: *The contrast also works well in numerous other Italian works, such as Riz Ortolani's wonderful score for* Cannibal Holocaust, *along with his score for* Don't Torture a Duckling *by Fulci, most notably "Quei giorni insieme a te," a vocal track which plays during Florinda Bolkan's infamous chain-whipping scene. A beautiful score.*
CS: I've never seen it!

RR: *Really? You must! It's an incredible film and one of Fulci's best. What was it like working on the Argento-produced* Demons *and* The Church?
CS: Well *La chiesa* (*The Church*) was scored by Pignatelli, along with Keith Emerson and Philip Glass. I worked on *Dèmoni* (*Demons*), of course. Also, Romero's *Martin*, known as *Wampyr* in Italy. So, I did the soundtrack for Lamberto Bava's film even though I didn't really have much contact with him.

RR: *How did working with Lamberto compare to working with Dario?*
CS: Well I can't really compare as I only dealt with Dario. Dario was the producer and he, more or less, decided on the kind of music. So Lamberto approved it but I never had a great deal of contact with him.

RR: *Any memories of doing* Conquest *for Lucio Fulci?*
CS: Lucio Fulci, the same, as I never really had contact with him. Fulci had problems with the producer. The producer left the film, as Fulci argued with him a lot! I worked a lot with the editor on that film. We decided what music to use. But Fulci I never met in my entire life. I met his daughter Antonella, but never him!

RR: *Tell us about reuniting Goblin for* Sleepless. *Was it a happy experience?*
CS: Not a happy experience! Actually, quite bad! (*Laughs*) Dario told me that he had finished this film. We were at the Sitges festival at the time. He said, "Why don't we try to reunite Goblin for this film?" The film was shot in Torino and it was also a thriller, so it seemed like a perfect idea to

The Unsane Cinema of Dario Argento

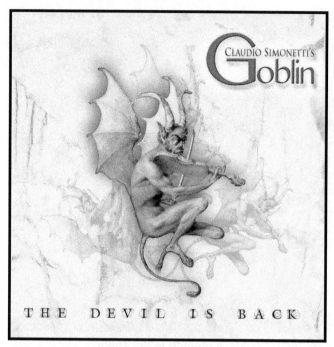

Federica Simonetti's cover design for one of the non-film albums from Claudio Simonetti's Goblin.

him. So, I tried to reunite the band, but this was difficult from the beginning. It was a great soundtrack but, even when we were recording, two of us were in one studio and two in another. It was almost impossible. Probably because, after almost 20 years, we changed as musicians, you know? Massimo and I were more attached to rock and Agostino and Fabio were into something different; they don't like rock. So, it was a very hard thing to do.

RR: *Regardless of all of that, it turned out to be a great soundtrack. I remember how excited fans were at the time when they heard you were back in the studio. Are you happy with the result?*

CS: Yes, of course.

RR: *The score for* Mother of Tears *was very different from the music of* Suspiria. *Did Dario deliberately encourage you to go for something completely different?*

CS: No, I said to Dario I think this film is not in the same fashion as *Suspiria*. So that's why a decided to use a choir and a big orchestra. I needed the sound to be more powerful. I needed something very different, a very different sound altogether.

RR: *How was the experience of providing the scores to the American made-for-TV movies* Jenifer *and* Pelts?

CS: This was great! It was a really good experience. Dario was in America and he shot these films. He did each one in 10 days.

RR: *Dario told me he really enjoyed the whole experience in America. He loved making those episodes …*

CS: Yes, and I remember recording this music in my studio and I sent it to the American editor.

RR: *Did you watch the films beforehand?*

CS: Yes, I watched them. They sent me the episodes and I wrote the music. But Dario was very busy at the time with other projects, so I did it all by myself. Both. I sent the music and the editor said that it was very good. Dario just listened to the results, which was different from the way we worked before. Dario trusts me. The same goes for *Dracula*. I decided the music there too. Dario left me to it completely.

RR: *Both scores are very different to each other.* Jenifer *was quite melodic in its style …*

CS: I wanted to pay homage to Bernard Herrmann, the composer of *Psycho*. For some scenes, I used a similar style. A similar theme. But not in *Pelts*.

RR: Dracula *was your most recent film with Dario. You used the Theremin very extensively in the score. Was there any particular reason for that?*

CS: Yes, because I love the Theremin! The Theremin sound was very typical of the vampire films of the 1950s. One of my favorite soundtracks of the '50s is Bernard Herrmann's score for *War of the Worlds*.[1] He used the Theremin. I thought it was an unbelievable sound! Danny Elfman also used it for Tim Burton's *Mars Attacks*.

RR: *Has working with Dario changed much down through the years?*

CS: Yes, it's a little different but we still have a good relationship. He always calls me. I would've loved the opportunity to work on *The Sandman* with him but nothing progressed with that. To work with Iggy Pop would've been an incredible experience too, I'm sure! Nothing happened with that, which is a shame. It's always a great experience to work with Dario. We travel a lot together and attend a lot of festivals. We are very good friends and we have a good relationship.

RR: *You've composed a lot of horror, thriller, science fiction, action films and many more. Is there any genre that you haven't composed for that you'd like to tackle?*

CS: Well I've also done comedies and many TV series too. I've worked with many other directors on lots of dramatic films. I've had a very varied career. But, actually, if I have to tell you the truth, I don't like to work anymore with horror movies. It's always the same you see. I don't have any new ideas for them. So, I would like to do something different. I have many proposals for these films, from many independent film makers, but I always say no now.

RR: *What were the last films you worked on?*

CS: I recently worked on two films. One was *Prigioniero della mia libertà*, starring Giancarlo Giannini, a drama based on a true story about a man who was wrongfully jailed for 23 years until he was proven innocent. The other film was Ruggero Deodato's *Ballad in Blood*. So, these kinds of films I like because *Ballad in Blood* is a film *noir*, it's not a thriller or a horror movie. It's very well done. It's also based on a true story about an American girl, Amanda Knox, who was accused of killing her roommate in Tuscany in 2007.

RR: *Claudio, that's everything! Thanks again for meeting me for lunch today. I've really enjoyed our chat. Troy sends his gratitude for your contribution to the book. No doubt I'll see you at the Union Chapel gig in London.*

CS: It's been a pleasure, Rob.

Notes:
1. Claudio is thinking of Herrmann's score for *The Day the Earth Stood Still* (1951); *The War of the Worlds* (1953) was scored by Leith Stevens.

Luciano Tovoli Interviewed by Troy Howarth

While talking with Don May, Jr., the president of Synapse Films, about recording an audio commentary for their then-upcoming Blu-ray release of *Suspiria*, I inquired about talking with Luciano Tovoli for this book. Don was kind enough to provide me with *Maestro* Tovoli's email address, and I was delighted to find that he was ready, willing and eager to talk about his association with Dario Argento. The following questions were answered via email on June 17, 2017. My thanks to Don for helping to arrange this and, of course, to *Maestro* Tovoli for taking the time to talk about this chapter of his very distinguished career.

Troy Howarth: *Were you familiar with Dario Argento prior to working on* Suspiria?

Luciano Tovoli: No. I was, however, familiar with the fact that his films were immensely successful!

TH: *Argento said that he was originally going to use Luigi Kuveiller to film* Suspiria, *as he had already filmed* Deep Red *and* Le cinque giornate *for Argento, but Kuveiller said the strong colors he wanted to achieve were "impossible." How did you feel when Argento first came to you with this project; did you worry that you might not be able to achieve the kind of color he was looking for?*

LT: At that time, I did not know at all about the proposition Argento had made to Luigi Kuveiller for *Suspiria*, nor did I know that Kuveiller had refused him. I worried only that, not being familiar with horror films, probably I was not apt to collaborate with him. It was not a problem of experimenting with the kind of bold colors he had in mind. I had always been of the mindset that I needed to be ready to experiment with photography, and my past work with Antonioni provided me with a solid background in that respect.

TH: *The airport scene in* Suspiria *was filmed at the same location that was used in Antonioni's* The Passenger; *did you recommend this location to Argento?*

LT: No, I did not recommend this specific airport. That was decided upon by the production, and it was easy for me to go along with it.

TH: *Did you have any difficulties filming on location in Munich on* Suspiria? *Do you have any memories of the locations, like the BMW building for example?*

LT: We shot at the BMW building on the first day of shooting, so I remember the normal tension of every first day of shooting as in every film.

TH: Suspiria *was an unusual assignment for you at this time, as you had not photographed a film in this style ... did you find it stressful or difficult achieving the results Argento was looking for? Was utilizing the 3-strip Technicolor processing system difficult?*

LT: In all the years before and since *Suspiria* no other films have been photographed in exactly this extreme style! No, I did not feel any unusual stress. I was quite excited once we really decided, thanks to the photographic test I completed on my own to experiment with these bold colors, that we would definitely do the film together. Also, I have always held the goal and the illusion that every film should be visually different from the previous one. This does not mean at all that I have *always* accomplished this very ambitious goal or illusion—with *Suspiria* it just added to the overall challenge. But shooting *The Passenger* with Michelangelo Antonioni was not just a Sunday picnic, either! When it came to using the Technicolor processing system, it was a remarkably simple and logical process; every step was understandable, and for me Technicolor remains the best color system in film history.

TH: *How was Argento to work with on set? Did he storyboard his shots, or did he work with you on the set to find the framing and shots he was looking for?*

LT: Argento has always been as a great director has to be. He is sure of himself and he is ready at the same time to integrate his vision with the input of the collaborators he carefully chose to work with him! I do not remember about any storyboards. Argento was working on the frames and directing the actors, and I was responsible for the colors and the lighting.

TH: *Do you have any memories of the cast, including Jessica Harper, Stefania Casini, Alida Valli, and Joan Bennett?*

LT: All the actors were perfectly cast, and their behavior on the set made them a pleasure to be around.

TH: *What was the most difficult shot you had to achieve in* Suspiria?

LT: In terms of lighting, it was certainly the finale, with the explosions and the colored lightning.

TH: *You next worked with Argento on* Tenebrae *in 1982; did Argento approach you about photographing* Inferno, *which was the follow-up to* Suspiria?

LT: Yes, it was originally intended that we would work together again on *Inferno*, but the film was delayed several times and I had a previous contract with another production. So, I proposed to Argento that he should employ my collaborator Romano Albani as the cinematographer. Dario accepted this, and it was my pleasure to connect them.

TH: Tenebrae *is shot in a very different style compared to* Suspiria: *very bright and with a strong pastel color scheme. Was this something specific that Argento wanted from the beginning?*

LT: If the cinematographer has the full trust of a director, he is not merely the executor of the director's orders. On *Suspiria*, under the influence of Argento's important suggestions, I decided to utilize only primary colors plus, on occasion, little splashes of yellow—with Argento's general approval, of course! Again, on *Tenebrae*, we both decided together to avoid a kind of *Suspiria #2* and make other choices. Dario then proceeded on his work as the director, and I proceeded on my work as the cinematographer—almost independently, in a kind of perfect and magical collaboration. It wasn't a matter of so many words or consultations or briefings or debriefings. The shooting of a film often advances on its own like a highspeed train (mostly in terms of new ideas coming forth every day), and we all are quite busy trying to just remain on board. This extends, I think, to Argento himself—who was the main "ideas generator," of course!

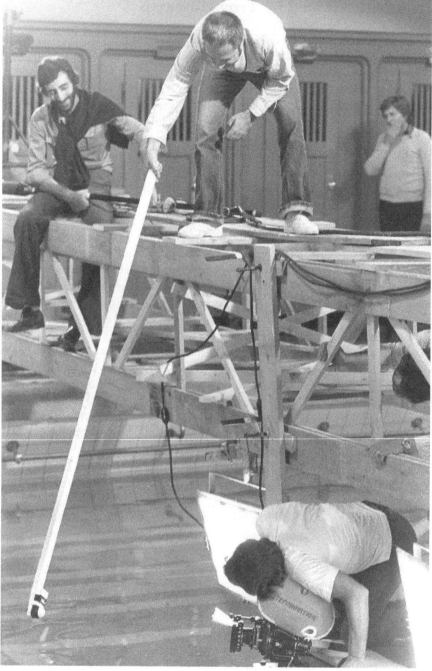
Tovoli taped his light meter to a pole to get a reading for the pool scene in *Suspiria*.

TH: *The film includes a famous scene with the Louma Crane, which is quite spectacular ... do you recall the filming of this shot, and if so, was it difficult to get the desired effect? Did it take a lot of takes?*

LT: I introduced the Louma from France, where I had previously used it in the filming of Christian De Chalonge's film *The Roaring Forties* (*Les quarantièmes rugissants*, 1982). I introduced Argento to the use of this then-new instrument. It wasn't really so difficult to utilize, but it did require perfect preparation—which is really the real secret of every complicated shot. Not so many takes; maybe five. Argento's conception of the shot he had in mind was very clear.

TH: *Whereas* Suspiria *is a supernatural movie,* Tenebrae *is set in a more realistic environment. Would you say that this approach was easier or more difficult, or was it about the same from your point of view?*

LT: I think both presented the same degree of difficulty. Once you find a style, you have to remain true to it, not allowing yourself to be influenced by outside elements which can contaminate your vision. This is the real challenge: to remain true to your vision and that of your director. Practical difficulties can be solved more or less easily.

TH: *Do you recall anything of working with the actors, including Anthony Franciosa, Giuliano Gemma, John Saxon, and Daria Nicolodi?*

LT: I have always been very interested in seeing how the actors do their job, and of course part of my job is to add value to their work through the use of lighting and color. What I remember of these actors is their professionalism and their kindness.

TH: *Argento's assistants on this film were Lamberto Bava, the son of Mario Bava, and Michele Soavi. Both went on to become successful directors. Do you remember much about them?*

LT: They were very different, thanks to their backgrounds—Lamberto was apparently more down-to-earth, coming from the famous Mario, whereas Michele was coming from a more literary background, as his father is the famous Giorgio Soavi. Michele was new to the film world, so they had slightly different attitudes towards their work—but they were both nice and talented guys, as they proved not much later on in their own films.

TH: *Is there a particular image or sequence in* Tenebrae *of which you are especially proud?*

LT: Sorry if I say I am proud of the whole of *Tenebrae*, and of its cinematographic consistency! Yes, the nighttime scene with the girl and the dog in the park, which is so fully and totally unrealistically lit, is my preferred sequence—but just because I want to be nice to you and make an impossible choice.

TH: *You did not work again with Argento for 30 years ... did you keep in touch with him during this time? Did he approach you about doing any other films during this time?*

LT: Yes, we stayed in touch and we almost made the film *Opera* together, but then something in my schedule did not work out and I was obliged to decline. Argento chose as my substitute the great Ronnie Taylor, which of course made me very proud!

TH: *How did your involvement in* Dracula *come about?*

LT: With an Argento phone call, as usual!

TH: *I imagine that filming in 3D posed a lot of difficulties—did you enjoy using this process?*

LT: I enjoyed it immensely; I truly regret that this system has been abandoned in favor of the quite stupid run on high-definition systems!

TH: *Had Argento's method of working changed in the 30 years since you last worked with him?*

LT: No, Argento hasn't changed at all. He's the same charming man, great friend, and great artist! A real pleasure to work with! We spent a minimum of 30 unforgettable dinners together during the shooting time of *Dracula*, as we were alone in the same hotel; the full crew lodged together in another hotel. For the both of us, it was a period of great amusement, cultural analysis—and not only about film in general or the film we were doing, but also on the history of art in general, as well as politics. We actually went out alone to a forest on a Sunday to do an unplanned scouting tour, without even telling the rest of the production, and we almost were washed away and even possibly drowned by this incredible storm and heavy downpour; it was a frightening experience, as Argento narrates in his beautiful book *Paura*.

TH: *There are some very beautiful images in* Dracula, *composed in a more classical, Gothic style compared to your earlier films with Argento. Did you enjoy the challenge of lighting the film in this fashion?*

LT: As I mentioned earlier, my main goal has always been to define a specific style on all the films I have ever worked on. The script comes first, the choice of the locations later, the choice of the actors, and the choice of costumes— they all help to define in advance a possible visual style that the cinematographer shouldn't try to fight against. The main "idea generator" on a film is of course the director, and our cinematographic work consists mainly of harmonizing all the above already very carefully chosen elements—and to add, if the talent permits, a final visual form, a final decisive touch in terms of vision. Having said that I do not want, of course, to subtract anything from the directors or from the production designers or from the costumes designers—but by virtue of the fact that we are making a film, the cinematographer does tend to dominate, to some extent, the finalization of all the elements that have been assembled. This is very different from the stage, for example, where these talents could work without the presence of a cinematographer or an editor—two very specific cinematographic talents.

TH: *Did you have any particular influence with regards to how you lit* Dracula? *Did you and Argento refer back to older horror films, or were you working without any specific frames of reference?*

LT: We had no references in terms of visual inspiration, but we did pay special attention to the mastery of 3D by Hitchcock in *Dial M for Murder*.

TH: *Do you have any particular scenes or images in* Dracula *that you were particularly pleased with?*

LT: No, not any scene in particular. I am quite happy with the entire film. I do not like to play the unsatisfied guy who reacts by minimizing the people who appreciate his work! Fake modesty makes me crazy! I am highly proud of all three films I have made with Dario Argento!

TH: *This was your first time working with Argento while he was directing his daughter Asia ... how did they collaborate on the set and what is your opinion of Asia as an actress?*

Dario and Tovoli stage Jessica Harper on the set of *Suspiria*.

LT: There is a scene with Asia where she is surprised by Dracula, who appears amid some lightning, framed from above. Well, I like that scene and Asia was perfect, as she is in the other scenes. She is a very interesting actress—and a very interesting person too!

TH: *Looking back over your films with Argento, what are your opinions on the three films? I imagine* Suspiria *is your favorite, but how do the other films compare from your point of view?*

LT: Apparently *Suspiria* is the fan favorite and has remained so for 40 years! For that simple reason I have a tendency to defend *Tenebrae* and *Dracula*—and each one for different reasons.

TH: *You have been involved in the restoration of* Suspiria *for the upcoming Synapse Blu-ray and DVD editions; can you comment on how you felt the film has been treated on home video? Other versions have had a lot of problems in terms of color timing and so forth. Do you feel that this new transfer is absolutely correct for the first time ever?*

LT: It has been a great pleasure collaborating with Synapse on their restoration of *Suspiria*. Donald May, the company CEO and a passionate expert, put forth all the necessary efforts to properly restore the vivid colors, which are the film's signature. There are so many positive and serious elements to make this last restoration surely the best ever done and the closest to the original theatrical presentation. What has been done in the past will remain in the past, with its errors and its sometimes-unperceived inadequacies, but what Synapse has achieved will be a definitive presentation for many years to come.

Postscript: The Synapse Blu-ray of Suspiria *was released, to much acclaim, in 2017; Luciano Tovoli reminisces in greater detail about the experience of making the film in the book* On Suspiria and Beyond: A Conversation with Luciano Tovoli, *published by Artdigiland in 2017.*

Bibliography

The following are books about and/or pertaining to Dario Argento and his films. They were not all referred to in the writing of this book, but they are all worth seeking out if you are interested in the subject.

Argento, Dario, *Paura* [English version: *Fear*] (Rome: Einaudi, 2014; Godalming: FAB Press, 2019)
Curti, Roberto, *Italian Gothic Horror Films, 1970-1987* (Jefferson: McFarland & Company, Ltd., 2017)
Curti, Roberto, *Italian Gothic Horror Films, 1980-1989* (Jefferson: McFarland & Company, Ltd., 2019)
Frayling, Christopher, *Once Upon a Time in the West: Shooting a Masterpiece* (London: Reel Art Press, 2019)
Frayling, Christopher, *Spaghetti Westerns: Cowboys and Europeans from Karl May to Sergio Leone* (London: I.B. Taurus, 1998)
Frayling, Christopher, *Sergio Leone: Something to Do with Death* (London: Faber and Faber, 2000)
Gallant, Chris, ed., *Art of Darkness: The Cinema of Dario Argento* (Godalming: FAB Press, 2003)
Gili, Jean A., *Elio Petri* (Rome: Cinecittà Holding, 2000)
Grant, Kevin, *Any Gun Can Play: The Essential Guide to Euro-Westerns* (Godalming: FAB Press, 2011)
Hemmings, David, *Blow Up: And Other Exaggerations* (London: Robson Books, 2004)
Jones, Alan, *Dario Argento: The Man, the Myths & the Magic* (Godalming: FAB Press, 2012)
McDonagh, Maitland, *Broken Mirrors, Broken Minds: The Dark Dreams of Dario Argento* (London: Sun Tavern Fields, 1991)
Murray, John B., *Brett Halsey: Art or Instinct in the Movies…* (Baltimore: Midnight Marquee Press, 2008)
Rigby, Jonathan, *Christopher Lee: The Authorised Screen History* (Richmond: Reynolds & Hearn, Ltd., 2007)
Rigby, Jonathan, *Euro Gothic: Classics of Continental Horror Cinema* (Cambridge, Signum Books, 2017)
Stagni, Piercesare and Valentina Valente, ed., *On Suspiria and Beyond: A Conversation with Luciano Tovoli* (Dublin: Artdigiland, 2017)
Williams, Tony, ed., *George A. Romero Interviews* (Jackson: University Press of Mississippi, 2011)

Online sources cited:

Anderson, Artison, "*Dario Argento Defends Daughter, Claims 'An Air of Conspiracy' Over Allegations*," https://www.hollywoodreporter.com/news/dario-argento-defends-daughter-asia-sexual-assault-allegations-1136625
Blackford, James, "*George A. Romero: The Sight & Sound Interview*," https://www.bfi.org.uk/news-opinion/sight-sound-magazine/interviews/george-romero-sight-sound-interview
Bogani, Giovanni, "*Dario Argento: Bolletino del virus piu saventoso di tanti miei film*," https://www.quotidiano.net/magazine/dario-argento-coronavirus-1.5133975
Cassani, Alberto, "*Nonhosonno*" *di Dario Argento*, http://www.cinefile.biz/nonhosonno-di-dario-argento
Crawford, Travis, "*Everything in this Film is Autobiographical, But Then Again Everything Is Not*": *Asia Argento on Her Debut Feature, Scarlet Diva*, https://filmmakermagazine.com/105305-everything-in-this-film-is-autobiographical-but-then-again-everything-is-not-asia-argento-on-her-debut-feature-scarlet-diva/#.XBQuX_ZFyUk
Decker, Sean, *Scripters talk Argento's Mother of Tears*, http://www.fangoria.com/news_article.php?id=5168
Ebert, Roger, *Bird With Crystal Plumage*, https://www.rogerebert.com/reviews/bird-with-crystal-plumage-1970
Ebert, Roger, *Four Flies on Grey Velvet*, https://www.rogerebert.com/reviews/four-flies-on-grey-velvet-1972
Eggersten, Chris, *George Romero On Why He WON'T Be Directing 'Deep Red' 3-D Remake!*, https://bloody-disgusting.com/news/21392/george-romero-on-why-he-wont-be-directing-deep-red-3-d-remake/
Felperin, Leslie, *Giallo*, https://variety.com/2009/film/markets-festivals/giallo-1200474916/
Fessenden, Marissa, *How Forensic Scientists Once Tried to "See" a Dead Person's Last Sight*, https://www.smithsonianmag.com/smart-news/how-forensic-scientists-once-tried-see-dead-persons-last-sight-180959157
FL, *Tenebrae*, https://www.timeout.com/london/film/tenebrae
Gonzalez, *The Phantom of the Opera*, https://www.slantmagazine.com/film/review/the-phantom-of-the-opera
Goodfellow, Melanie, "*Dario Argento producers deny reports Daft Punk to score 'Dark Glasses'*," https://www.screendaily.com/news/dario-argento-producers-deny-reports-daft-punk-to-score-dark-glasses/5149383.article
Haflidason, Almar, *Sleepless* review, https://www.tvguide.com/movies/sleepless/review/137275/
Kehr, Dave, *The Game Is Poker; The Stakes Are Lives*, https://www.nytimes.com/2004/10/06/movies/the-game-is-poker-the-stakes-are-lives.html
Kermode, Mark, *Mark Kermode's DVD round-up*, https://www.theguardian.com/film/2011/jul/17/giallo-unknown-country-kermode-dvd
Kohn, Eric, *Dario Argento Says the Remake of 'Suspiria' Shouldn't Happen & His Iggy Pop Movie Is Delayed*, https://www.indiewire.com/2016/08/dario-argento-interview-suspira-remake-2016-locarno-film-festival-1201714247/
Laurenzi, Laura, *Asia Argento e la passione per l'obiettivo. 'Con le foto ho messo a fuoco la mia vita,'* https://www.repubblica.it/spettacoli/people/2013/09/07/news/asia_argento-66047992/
Lee, Nathan, *Supernatural Stew, Served with Camp*, https://www.nytimes.com/2008/06/06/movies/06arge.html
Lust, Markus, *Dario Argento Dreams Up Your Nightmares*, https://www.vice.com/en_us/article/7b74x9/interview-dario-argento

M., Chris, An Interview with Daniela Giordano, https://www.spaghetti-western.net/index.php/Interview_with_Daniela_Giordano

McDonagh, Maitland, *The Stendhal Syndrome review*, https://www.tvguide.com/movies/the-stendhal-syndrome/review/132133/

Nelson, Rob, *Dario Argento's Dracula*, https://variety.com/2012/film/markets-festivals/dario-argento-s-dracula-1117947598/

Newman, Kim, *Trieste S+F festival review—Blood on Méliès' Moon*, https://johnnyalucard.com/2016/11/06/trieste-sf-festival-review-blood-on-melies-moon/

Pritchard, Tiffany, Rome: Dario Argento and William Friedkin deliver candid retrospective, https://www.screendaily.com/rome/rome-dario-argento-and-william-friedkin-deliver-candid-retrospective/5095816.article

Pulici, Davide, *Tutto quello che avreste voluto su L'uccello dalle piume di cristallo*, http://www.nocturno.it/l-uccello-dalle-piume-di-cristallo/

Rooney, David, *Dario Argento's Dracula 3D: Cannes Review*, https://www.hollywoodreporter.com/review/dario-argento-dracula-3d-cannes-326991

San Pietro, Elena, ed., *Kinematrix Meets Carlo Lucarelli*, http://www.kinematrix.net/testi/lucarelli.htm

Sobczynski, Peter, *Dracula 3D*, https://www.rogerebert.com/reviews/dracula-3d-2013

Sprage, Mike, *Suspiria Remake Screenwriter Doesn't Like Argento's Original Film*, https://www.dreadcentral.com/news/281968/suspiria-remake-screenwriter-doesnt-like-argentos-original-film/

Squires, John, *Dario Argento's Next Project is "A Film Divided into Eight Episodes,"* https://bloody-disgusting.com/movie/3550366/dario-argentos-next-project-film-divided-eight-episodes/

Squires, John, *Dario Argento Was the Artistic Director of Upcoming Video Game 'Dreadful Bond,'* https://bloody-disgusting.com/video-games/3552574/trailer-dario-argento-artistic-director-upcoming-video-game-dreadful-bond/

Tartaglione, Nancy, *'Django,' 'Suspiria De Profundis' Series In Works from Atlantique & Cattleya*, https://deadline.com/2015/04/django-suspiria-drama-series-atlantique-cattleya-dario-argento-miptv-1201406287/

Viale, Valerio, *In Conversation with Sergio Donati: Once Upon a Time... Italy Made Great Cinema!*, https://italoamericano.org/story/2015-12-24/sergio-donati

Vivarelli, Nick, *Dario Argento to Direct Horror Series 'Longinus' for Wild Bunch-Owned BIM and Publispei*, https://variety.com/2019/tv/global/dario-argento-direct-horror-series-longinus-suspiria-1203367191/

Vivarelli, Nick, *Matteo Garrone's 'Dogman' Is Big Winner at Italy's David di Donatello Awards*, https://variety.com/2019/film/news/matteo-garrone-dogman-big-winner-italy-david-di-donatello-awards-1203174521/

Unsigned, *Two Evil Eyes*, https://www.tvguide.com/movies/two-evil-eyes/review/128146/

Unsigned, *Niente Rigoletto per Dario Argento*, https://ricerca.repubblica.it/repubblica/archivio/repubblica/1985/04/24/niente-rigoletto-per-dario-argento.html

Unsigned, *Set pronto per Argento*, https://www.cinematografo.it/news/set-pronto-per-argento/

Unsigned, *Sleepless* review, https://www.tvguide.com/movies/sleepless/review/137275/

Filmography

As actor only:

Scusi, le e favorevole o contrario?
Release date: December 23, 1966 (Italy)
Director: Alberto Sordi; Screenplay: Alberto Sordi and Sergio Amidei; Producer: Fono Roma; Cinematography: Benito Frattari; Camera Operator: Guglielmo Vincioni; Editor: Antonietta Zita; Music Composer/Conductor: Piero Piccioni; Art Director: Ezio Altieri; Costumer Designer: Bruna Parmesan; Assistant Director: Gualtiero Licastro and Giulio Paradisi
Technical specs and running time: 35mm; 2.35:1 (Techniscope), color; 129 minutes
Cast: Alberto Sordi (Tullio Conforti); Anita Ekberg (Olga, the Baroness); Bibi Andersson (Ingrid); Tina Aumont (Romina); Giulietta Masina (Anna); Silvana Mangagno (Emanuela); Mirella Panphili (Fiorella Conforti); Laura Antonelli (Piera Conforti); Paola Pitagora (Valeria Conforti); Mario Pisu (Baron Renato Santambrogio); Caterina Boratto (Agnese Frustalupi); Nino Besozzi (Camillo Tasca); Maria Quasimodo (Baroness Cornianu); Eugene Walter (Igor); Anna Mazzanti (Carmen); Leontine Snell (Monti); Wendy D'Olive (French call-girl); Antonio Gallo (Son); Jacques Herlin (Bergerac); Dario Argento (Altar boy)

Giallo (TV series)
Production date/Release date: Late September 1987 through January 1988
Show Director: Enzo Gatta; Show Creator: Enzo Tortora; Show Writers: Oreste Del Buono, Laura Grimaldi, Dardano Sacchetti and Marco Troppea; Series Music: Manuel De Sica
Recurring roles: Enzo Tortora, Gabriella Carlucci (Presenters); Dario Argento (Himself); Coralina Cataldi-Tassoni (Dario Argento's assistant)

Innocent Blood
Production date: January 13 through mid-April 1992
Release date: September 25, 1992 (U.S.A.)
Director: John Landis; Screenplay: Michael Wolk; Producer: Leslie Belzberg, Lee Rich, Jonathan Sheinberg, and Michael Wolk (Warner Bros.); Cinematography: Mac Ahlberg; Editor: Dale Beldin; Assistant Editor: James Andrykowski and Destiny Borden; Music: Ira Newborn; Additional Music: Johnny Lehmann and Herb Miller ("Night"), Johnny Mercer and Harold Allen ("That Old Black Magic," performed by Frank Sinatra), Cole Porter ("I've Got You Under My Skin," performed by Frank Sinatra), James Bernard ("Music from *Dracula* (1958)"), O.V. Hirsch ("Too Far Gone," performed by Sturm & Twang), Prince ("Get Off," performed by Prince & The New Power Generation), Carl Sturken and Evan Rogers ("Sexitivity" and "I Wanna Make Love to You"), Jon Secada ("I See Your Smile," performed by Gloria Estefan); Production Design: Richard Sawyer; Costumer Designer: Deborah Nadoolman; Assistant Director: Nicholas Mastandrea; Special Make-up Effects: Darren Perks and Steve Johnson's XFX; Special Effects: Syd Dutton; Special Visual Effects: Bill Taylor
Technical specs and running time: 35mm; 1.85:1, color; 112 minutes
Cast: Anne Parillaud (Marie); Anthony LaPaglia (Joe Gennaro); Robert Loggia (Sallie 'The Shark' Macelli); David Proval (Lenny); Don Rickles (Emmanuel 'Manny' Bergman); Rocco Sisto (Gilly); Tony Sirico (Jacko); Tony Lip (Frank); Kim Coates (Ray); Marshall Bell (Marsh); Leo Burmester (Dave Flinton); Rohn Thomas (Coroner); Angela Bassett (U.S. Attorney Sinclair); Luis Guzmán (Morales); Tom Savini (News photographer); Gil Cates, Jr. (Dog Boy); Charlie Gomorra (Gorilla); Lamont Arnold (Morgue desk man); Yancey Arias (Coroner's assistant); David Early (Reporter); Forrest J. Ackerman (Stolen car man); Elaine Kagan (Frannie Bergman); Michael Ritchie (Night watchman); Bernard Hocke (Motel clerk); Sam Raimi (Roma Meats man); Dario Argento (Paramedic); Marina Durell, Linnea Quigley (Nurses); Teri Weigel, Lisa Ann Baker, Christina Jiménez, Christina Bowers, Kim Currow, Christina Diaz, Kim Melton, Robin Place, Regan Kerwin, Tracy Rolen, Tammy Ulm, Katrina Witt, Maribe Zolli (Melody Lounge dancers); Michael Wolk (Surgeon); Ron Roth (Gus); Vic Notto (Tommy); Jerry Lyden (Vinnie); Rick Avery (Cab driver); Bob Minor (Bus driver); Phil Nardozzi, Christian Stavrokis (Melody Lounge patrons)

Il cielo è sempre più blu
Alternate titles: *Bits & Pieces*
Production date: 1995, Release date: February 2, 1996 (Italy)
Director: Antonello Grimaldi; Screenplay: Daniele Cesarano and Paolo Marchesini; Producer: Domenico Procacci, Maurizio Totti and Gianluca Arcopinto (Colorado Film Production/Fandango); Cinematography: Alessandro Pesci; Editor: Angelo Nicolini; Music Composer/Conductor: Enzo Favata; Production Design: Giada Calabria; Costume Designer: Antonella Amato, Alessandra Covelli and Maria Camilla Righi; Assistant Director: Daniele Cesarano
Technical specs and running time: 35mm; 1.85:1, color; 110 minutes
Cast: Asia Argento (Nicoletta); Luca Barbareschi (The fence); Monica Bellucci (The other girl); Margherita Buy (Traffic warden); Roberto Citran (Nicoletta's cousin); Enrico Lo Verso (Mailman); Ivano Marescotti (Jogger); Alessandro Haber (The killer); Francesca Neri (Student); Carlo Croccolo (Lonely middle-aged man); Silvio Orlando (The mechanic); Sergio Rubini (Taxi driver); Antonio Catania (Prison guard); Remo Remotti (Grandfather); Monica Scattini (Bar owner); Gigio Alberti (Psychiatrist); Fabrizio Moroni (Betti, the engineer); Dario Argento (Man confessing to Franciscan monk)

Tutti pazzi per amore (TV series)
Episode title: "*Quando due si lasciano*"—Broadcast date: May 24, 2010
Episode director: Riccardo Milani; Production Company: Publispei and Rai Fiction; Episode cinematography: Roberta Allegrini; Episode camera operator: Daniele Proietti; Episode editor: Patrizia Ceresani and Francesco Renda; Episode music: Luca Antonini; Episode assistant director: Francesco Capone
Cast: Claudia Alfonso (Viola); Luca Angeletti (Giulio Pierantoni); Dario Argento (Ugo); Giuseppe Battiston (Dr. Freiss); Alessio Boni (Adriano); Laura Calagni (Nina Balestrieri); Piera Degli Esposti (Clelia); Irene Ferri (Rosa); Francesca Inaudi (Maya); Antonia Liskova (Laura Del Fiore); Neri Marcorè (Michele Brunetti); Nicole Murgia (Cristina Giorgi); Carlotta Natoli (Monica); Brenno Placido (Emanuelle Balestrieri); Ariella Reggio (Aunt Sofia); Marina Rocca (Stefania Del Fiore); Carla Signoris (TV presenter); Emilio Solfrizzi (Paolo Giorgi); Pia Velsi (Aunt Filomena)

100 pallottole d'argento (TV series)
Broadcast date: August 2012 through May 2013
Role: Himself/host
Series director: Giorgio Amato; Series writer: Luigi Cozzi; Series cinematography: Paolo Mancini; Series cameraman: Giorgio Abbruzzetti and Antonio Conte; Series music: Cesare Ranucci Rascel and Emiliano Rubbi
Cast: Dario Argento (Himself)

Blood on Méliès' Moon
Production date: filmed sporadically from September 2014 through February 2016; Argento's scenes were shot in October 2014.
Release date: 2016
Director: Luigi Cozzi; Screenplay: Luigi Cozzi and Giulia Leone; Screen story: Luigi Cozzi, Alexandre Jousse and Giulia Leone; Producer: Maria Letizia Sercia; Second Unit Director: Alexandre Jousse; Music: Simone Martino; Special Effects: Jean Manuel Costa
Cast: Brahim Ahmadouche (Gormak); Barbara Magnolfi (Barbara);

Philippe Beun-Garbe (Professor Pierpoljakos); David Traylor (Méliès); Dario Argento (Himself); Lamberto Bava (Himself); Antonio Tentori (Himself); Luigi Cozzi (Himself); Fabio Giovannini (Himself)

Documentaries specifically about Dario Argento:
Note: This does not include the various interviews and featurettes included on the DVD and Blu-ray editions of Argento's films.

Il mondo dell'orrore di Dario Argento
Alternate title: *Dario Argento's World of Horror*
Release date: 1987
Director/Writer: Michele Soavi
Interviewees: Dario Argento, Luciano Tovoli, Keith Emerson

Dario Argento: Master of Horror
Release date: 1991
Director: Luigi Cozzi; Writer: Luigi Cozzi and Fabio Giovannini
Interviewees: Dario Argento, Sergio Stivaletti, Luigi Cozzi, Pino Donaggio, Michele Soavi, Madeline Potter, Tom Savini, Fabio Giovannini

Il mondo di Dario Argento 3: Il museo degli orrori di Dario Argento
Release date: 1997
Director/Writer: Luigi Cozzi
Interviewees: Dario Argento, Daria Nicolodi, Claudio Simonetti, Riccardo Freda, Antonella Vitale, Tom Savini

Dario Argento: An Eye for Horror
Release date: 2000
Director: Leon Ferguson; Writer: Charles Preece
Interviewees: Dario Argento, Daria Nicolodi, Asia Argento, Fiore Argento, Claudio Argento, Michael Brandon, Mark Kermode, Tom Savini, Alan Jones, Jessica Harper, John Carpenter, Claudio Simonetti, Alice Cooper, Maitland McDonagh, Keith Emerson, William Lustig, George A. Romero, Piper Laurie, Luigi Cozzi

Screenwriting and Producing credits:
A note on screenwriting credits: The films in this section are limited to those which carry Argento's name; it's entirely possible that he had a hand in a number of other scripts which were produced, but which didn't carry his name for one reason or another. Some sources, for example, indicate that he had a hand in the writing of the very obscure Western-comedy *Man Called Amen* (*Così sia*, aka *They Called Him Amen*, 1972—which should not be confused with *A Man Called Amen* (*O tutto o niente*, 1968) directed by Guido Zurli), which was written and directed by Alfio Caltabiano; given that Argento and Caltabiano collaborated on *Comanadamenti per un gangster*, it's not impossible that Dario had some input on this script as well; given that it was produced after his ascent to fame via his first works as a director, Argento may even have asked Caltabiano to do him a favor and not include his name in the credits, fearing that the critics might see it as his taking a step backwards professionally. Alternatively, it's just as possible that he had nothing to do with the film and that somebody, somewhere got the wrong information and ran with it. In any event, Argento's name is not on the credits—and so it is not included here.

The early (pre-*Bird*) screenwriting credits are presented in order of theatrical release, which inevitably differs from the order in which Dario worked on these films.

A note on producing credits: This includes only the films on which Argento is credited as a producer. Seda Spettacoli produced (or co-produced) several off-beat films in the '70s which carry the name of Salvatore Argento, but Dario himself is not credited; there is no reason to believe that he was actively involved in these films, so they are not included in this context. Dario had no direct involvement in the production of *Suspiria* (2018), but it is included in this context because he is credited for his original screenplay.

Qualcuno ha tradito (Italy/France)
Alternate titles: *Every Man is My Enemy*
Release date: December 29, 1967 (Italy); August 14, 1968 (France)
Director: Francesco Prosperi [as Frank Shannon]; Screenplay: Francesco Prosperi and Giovanni Simonelli, with the collaboration of Dario Argento and Raimondo Del Balzo; Producer: Tiki Film; Cinematography: Sante Achilli; Editor: Ruggero Mastroianni; Music Composer/Conductor: Piero Piccioni; Dubbing Director (English version): Gene Luotto
Technical specs and running time: 35mm; 1.85:1, color; 88 minutes
Cast: Robert Webber (Tony Costa); Elsa Martinelli (Laureen); Jean Servais (Jean); Pierre Zimmer (Gabriel Blondell); Marina Berti (Ann); Franco Giornelli (Koko Herman); Ennio Balbo [as William Bosh] (The Professor); Emilio Messina (Willie); Umberto Raho (Drug dealer)

Oggi a me ... domani a te! (Italy)
Alternate titles: *Today We Kill, Tomorrow We Die!*; *Today It's Me ... Tomorrow It's You!*
Release date: March 28, 1968 (Italy); November 19, 1968 (Germany); November 23, 1968 (Japan); June 11, 1969 (France); March 8, 1971 (Spain); June 1971 (U.S.A.)
Filmed at: Elios Studios, Rome, with location work in Lazio (Italy).
Director: Tonino Cervi; Screenplay: Tonio Cervi and Dario Argento; Producer: Produzione Atlas Consorziate/Splendida Film/Rewind Film; Cinematography: Sergio D'Offizi; Camera Operator: Giuseppe Gatti and Remo Grisanti; Editor: Sergio Montanari; Assistant Editor: Roberto Gianandrea and Marcello Olasio; Music Composer/Conductor: Angelo Francesco Lavagnino; Production Design: Carlo Gervasi; Costume Designer: Giorgio Desideri; Assistant Director: Mauro Sacripanti
Technical specs and running time: 35mm; 1.85:1, color; 95 minutes
Cast: Brett Halsey [as Montgomery Ford] (Bill Kiowa); Bud Spencer (O'Bannion); William Berger (Francis 'Colt' Moran); Wayde Preston (Jeff Milton); Jeff Cameron (Moreno); Tatsuya Nakadai (James Elfego); Franco Borelli [as Stanley Gordon] (Bunny Fox); Dana Ghia [as Diana Madigan] (Mirana Kiowa); Teodoro Corrà [as Dorro Corra] (Gun seller); Victoriano Gazzara [as Vic Gazzara] (Gambler); Aldo Marianecci (Barber); Michele Borelli (Prison Director); Umberto Di Grazia (second in command); Franco Pechini (Prison Director); Nazzareno Natale (Comanchero); Remo Capitani (Publican); Lina Franchi (Bunny's girl); Pietro Torrisi (Bill); Riccardo Petrazzi, Renzo Pevarello, Aysanoa Runachagua, Rinaldo Zamperla (Comancheros)

Comandamenti per un gangster (Italy/Yugoslavia)
Release date: May 22, 1968 (Italy); August 10, 1968 (Japan); December 20, 1968 (Germany), Filmed on location in Yugoslavia.
Director: Alfio Caltabiano; Screenplay: Dario Argento and Alfio Caltabiano; Producer: Salvatore Argento (Avala Film/Prodi Cinematografica/Triumph Film 67); Cinematography: Milorad Markovic; Camera Operator: Emilio Varriano; Editor: Eugenio Alabiso; Assistant Editor: Ada Grimaldi; Music Composer: Ennio Morricone; Music Conductor: Bruno Nicolai; Additional Music: "Solo Nostalgia," written by Ennio Morricone and Audrey Nohra, performed by Jane Relly; Art Director: Luciana Marinucci; Assistant Director: Nicola Balini
Technical specs and running time: 35mm; 1.85:1, color; 96 minutes (92 minutes, 90 minutes)
Cast: Ljuba Tadic [as Lee Tadic] (Northon); Alfio Caltabiano [as Al Norton] (Five Cents); Dante Maggio [as Dan May] (Old Man); Rade Marcović [as Rade Markon] (Alberto Torio, "Santo"); Olivera Vukotic [as Olivera] (Regina Westling)

Commandos (Italy/Germany)
Alternate titles: *Chacales del desierto*; *Himmelfahrtskommano El Alamein*; *Sullivan's Marauders*
Release date: November 19, 1968 (Italy); July 21, 1969 (France); August 8, 1969 (Germany); August 9, 1969 (Japan); September 1, 1969 (Spain)

Filmed on location in Sardinia (Italy).
Director: Armando Crispino; Screenplay: Lucio Battistrada, Armando Crispino, Stefano Strucchi, and Dario Argento; Screen story: Menahem Golan, Don Martin, and Artur Brauner; Producer: Henryk Chroscicki, Alfonso Sansone, and Artur Brauner (Central Cinema Company Film/G.G.I. SpA Rome/Produzione Intercontinentale Cinematografica); Cinematography: Benito Frattari; Camera Operator: Silvio Fraschetti; Editor: Daniele Alabiso; Music Composer/Conductor: Mario Nascimbene; Production Designer: Alberto Boccianti

Technical specs and running time: 35mm; 2.35:1 (Cromoscope), color; 112 minutes (98 minutes, 95 minutes, 88 minutes, 82 minutes)

Cast: Lee Van Cleef (Sergeant Sullivan); Jack Kelly (Captain Valli); Giampiero Albertini (Aldo); Marino Masé (Italian Lieutenant Tomassini); Joachim Fuchsberger [as Akim Berg] (Oberleutnant Heitzel Agen, "Professor"); Götz George (Oberleutnant Rudi); Pier Paolo Capponi (Corbi); Ivano Staccioli (Rodolfo, the radio man); Marilù Tolo (Adriana); Heinz Reincke (Offizier Hanz); Helmut Schmid (Sergeant Miller); Otto Stern (Sergeant Braumann); Pier Luigi Anchisi (Riccio); Gianni Brezza (Marco); Duilio Del Prete (Bruno); Emilio Marchesini (Antonio); Biagio Pelligra (Carmelo); Lorenzo Piani (Bianca); Giacomo Piperno (Vincenzino); Romano Puppo (Dino); Franco Cobianchi (Abu Ali); Mario Feriazzo (Sergeant on watch); Mauro Lumachi (Italian truck driver); Gianni Pulone (Mario); Giovanni Ivan Scratuglia (Italian soldier)

La rivoluzione sessuale (Italy)
Alternate titles: *La révolution sexuelle*; *Seid nett aufeinander*
Release date: November 21, 1968 (Italy); January 16, 1970 (Germany); June 24, 1970 (France)
Director: Riccardo Ghione; Screenplay: Riccardo Ghione and Dario Argento; Based on: *Die Sexualität im Kulturkampf* by Wilhelm Reich; Producer: Roberto Palaggi and Italo Zingarelli (West Film); Cinematography: Alessandro D'Eva; Editor: Attilio Vincioni; Music Composer/Conductor: Teo Usuelli; Production Designer: Giulio Cabras; Costume Designer: Maria Gelmetti; Assistant Director: Anna Maria Sbordoni

Technical specs and running time: 35mm; 1.85:1, color; 92 minutes

Cast: Riccardo Cucciolla (Emilio Missiroli); Laura Antonelli (Liliana); Ruggero Mitti (Giorgio Segre); Marisa Mantovani (Marcella Segre); Christian Aligny (Cesare); Maria Luisa Bavastro (Nanna); Giulio Girola (Dino Segre); Andrés José Cruz (Tony); Lorenza Guerrieri (Rita); Guy Heron (Marco)

C'era una volta il West (Italy/U.S.A.)
Alternate titles: *Once Upon a Time in the West*; *Il était une fois dans l'Ouest*; *Spiel mir das Lied vom Tod*; *Hasta que llegó su hora*
Production date: April 1 through August 10, 1968
Release date: December 20, 1968 (Italy); May 28, 1969 (U.S.A.); August 14, 1969 (U.K.); August 14, 1969 (Germany); August 27, 1969 (France); October 4, 1969 (Japan); January 29, 1970 (Spain)
Filmed at: Cinecittà Studios and Centro Sperimentale, Rome, with location work in Guadix, La Calahorra, and Almería (Spain), and Monument Valley, Arizona (U.S.A.).
Director: Sergio Leone; Screenplay: Sergio Leone and Sergio Donati; Screen story: Dario Argento, Bernardo Bertolucci, and Sergio Leone; Producer: Bino Cicogna and Fulvio Morsella (Rafran Cinematografica/San Marco/Paramount Pictures); Cinematography: Tonino Delli Colli; Camera Operator: Franco Di Giacomo; Editor: Nino Baragli; Assistant Editor: Andreina Casini and Carlo Reali; Music Composer/Conductor: Ennio Morricone; Production Designer: Carlo Simi; Costume Designer: Carlo Simi; Assistant Director: Adolfo Aristarain and Salvatore Basile; Make-up: Alberto De Rossi and Giannetto De Rossi; Special Effects: Eros Bacciucchi; Dubbing Director (English version): Mickey Knox

Technical specs and running time: 35mm; 2.35:1 (Techniscope), color; 177 minutes (165 minutes, 145 minutes)

Cast: Claudia Cardinale (Jill McBain); Charles Bronson (Harmonica); Henry Fonda (Frank); Jason Robards (Cheyenne); Gabriele Ferzetti (Mr. Mortimer); Frank Wolff (Brett McBain); Paolo Stoppa (Sam); Woody Strode (Stony); Jack Elam (Snaky); Al Mulock (Knuckles); Keenan Wynn (Sheriff); Lionel Stander (Bartender); Dino Mele (Harmonica as a boy); Claudio Mancini (Harmonica's brother); Marco Zuanelli (Wobbles); Simonetta Santaniello (Maureen McBain); Enzo Santaniello (Timmy McBain); Stefano Imparto (Patrick McBain); Michael Harvery (Frank's lieutenant); Benito Stefanelli (Frank's lieutenant); Ricardo Palacios (Train conductor); Aldo Sambrell (Cheyenne's lieutenant); Conrado San Martín (Vecino); Salvatore Basile, Bruno Corazzari, Lorenzo Robledo (Cheyenne's gang); Aldo Berti, Frank Braña, Saturno Cerra, Spartaco Conversi, Paolo Figlia, John Frederick, Antonio Molino Rojo, Fabio Testi (Frank's gang); Don Galloway, Frank Leslie, Enrico Morsella, Umberto Morsella (Frank's gang in flashback); Raffaela Leone, Francesca Leone (Girls at Flagstone station)

Une corde, un colt… (France/Italy)
Alternate titles: *Cemetery Without Crosses*
Production date: January 8, 1968 through March 30, 1968
Release date: January 25, 1969 (France); April 19, 1969 (Italy); February 27, 1970 (Germany)
Filmed on location in Almería (Spain).
Director: Robert Hossein; Screenplay: Robert Hossein, Claude Desailly, and Dario Argento (uncredited on French prints); Producer: Jean-Pierre Labatut and Jean-Charles Raffini (Loisirs du Monde/Les Films Copernic/Fono Roma); Cinematography: Henri Persin; Camera Operator: Gilles Bonneau; Editor: Marie-Sophie Dubus; Assistant Editor: Andrée Davanture; Music Composer: André Hossein; Additional Music: "The Rope and the Colt," music by André Hossein, lyrics by Hal Shaper, performed by Scott Walker, conducted by André Lafosse; Production Designer: Jean Mandaroux; Costume Designer: Rosine Delamare; Assistant Director: Tony Aboyantz and Lucio D'Attino; Special Effects: Rosine Delamare

Technical specs and running time: 35mm; 1.66:1, color; 90 minutes

Cast: Robert Hossein (Manuel); Michèle Mercier (Maria Caine); Guido Lollobrigida [as Lee Burton] (Thomas Caine); Daniele Vargas [as Daniel Vargas] (Will Rogers); Serge Marquand (Larry Rogers); Pierre Hatet (Frank Rogers); Philippe Baronnet (Bud Rogers); Pierre Collet (Sheriff Ben); Ivano Staccioli, José Canalejas (Vallee's brothers); Béatrice Altariba, Maria Gustafsson (Saloon women); Michel Lemoine (Eli Caine); Anne-Marie Balin (Diana Rogers); Charly Bravo (Sam Vallee); Álvaro de Luna (Deputy Sheriff); Benito Stefanelli (Ben Caine); Simón Arriaga, Saturno Cerra, Fabio Testi (Rogers' ranch hands); Cris Huera (Hotel desk clerk)

Metti, una sera a cena (Italy)
Alternate titles: *One Night at Dinner*; *Love Circle*; *Disons un soir à dîner*; *Supongamos que una noche, cendando…*
Release date: April 3, 1969 (Italy); July 9, 1970 (France); November 16, 1971 (U.S.A.)
Director: Giuseppe Patroni Griffi; Screenplay: Dario Argento, Giuseppe Patroni Griffi, and Carlo Carunchio; Based on a play by Giuseppe Patroni Griffi; Producer: Euro International Film/Red Film/San Marco; Cinematography: Tonino Delli Colli; Camera Operator: Franco Di Giacomo; Editor: Franco Arcalli; Assistant Editor: Gabriella Crisanti and Olga Pedrini; Music Composer: Ennio Morricone; Music Conductor: Bruno Nicolai; Production Designer: Giulio Coltellacci; Assistant Director: Carlo Carunchio

Technical specs and running time: 35mm; 2.35:1 (Techniscope), color; 125 minutes

Cast: Jean-Louis Trintignant (Michele, the husband); Florinda Bolkan (Nina, the wife); Lino Capolicchio (Rick, Nina's lover); Tony Musante

(Max, the actor); Annie Girardot (Giovanna); Silvia Monti (Actress at press conference); Carla Mignone [as Milly] (Singer); Adriana Asti (Stepdaughter); Titina Maselli (Mother); Ferdinando Scarfiotti (Son); Claudio Carrozza (Baby); Nora Ricci (1st actress); Mariano Rigillo (Comedian); Antonio Jaia (Young actor); Enrica Bonaccorti (Young actress playing Pirandello)

Probabilità zero (Italy)
Alternate titles: *Probability Zero*; *Les heros ne meurent jamais*; *Operation Red Point*
Release date: May 7, 1969 (Italy)
Director: Maurizio Lucidi; Screenplay: Dario Argento, Maurizio Lucidi, Giuseppe Mangione, and Vittorio Vighi; Screen story: Dario Argento; Producer: Salvatore Argento (Aurigo 68); Cinematography: Aldo Tonti; Editor: Alberto Gallitti; Music Composer: Carlo Rustichelli; Music Conductor: Bruno Nicolai; Assistant Director: Aldo Lado; Special Effects: Carlo De Marchis
Technical specs and running time: 35mm; 1.85:1, color; 95 minutes
Cast: Henry Silva (Duke); Luigi Casellato (Carlo 'Charlie' Sardi); Riccardo Salvino (Hans Liedholm); Katia Christine (Kristy); Marco Guglielmi (Captain Kreuz); Ezio Sancrotti (Captain Simon Schulz); Pietro Martellanza [as Peter Martell] (Sam the Brit); Franco Giornelli (John McHarding); Vittorio André (Professor Schwartz); Renato De Carmine (Major Holst); Paolo Magalotti (Tall bearded OSS officer); Fulvio Mingozzi (British intelligence officer); Alfonso Giganti (Nazi); Bill Vanders (OSS officer)
English dubbing credits: Marc Smith (Captain Kreuz); Edward Mannix (Various roles)

La legione dei dannati (Italy/Spain/Germany/Switzerland)
Alternate titles: *Battle of the Commandos*; *La légion des damnés*; *Todeskommando Atlantik*; *Die zum Teufel gehen*; *La brigada de los condenados*
Production date: January through February 1969
Release date: August 12, 1969 (Italy); April 17, 1970 (Germany); June 17, 1970 (France)
Director: Umberto Lenzi; Screenplay: Dario Argento, Rolf Grieminger, Eduardo M. Brochero [as Eduardo Manzanos], and Ugo Moretti; Screen story: Stefano Rolla and Romano Maschini; Producer: Bruno Bolognesi (Tritone Cinematografica/Eguiluz Films/Hape Film Company GmbH); Cinematography: Alejandro Ulloa; Camera Operator: Mario Sbrenna; Editor: Giese Rohm; Music Composer/Conductor: Marcello Giombini; Production Designer: Piero Filippone; Costumer Designer: Luciano Sagoni; Assistant Director: Wolf Duschi and Jaime Bayarri; Special Effects: Fernando Pérez and Pablo Pérez
Technical specs and running time: 35mm; 2.35:1 (Cromoscope), color; 95 minutes (94 minutes)
Cast: Jack Palance (Colonel Charlie MacPherson); Thomas Hunter (Captain Kevin Burke); Curd Jürgens (General von Reilow); Wolfgang Preiss (Colonel Ackerman); Claudio Hundari [as Robert Hundar] (Private Raymond Stone); Helmuth Schneider (Private Sam Schrier); Guido Lollobridgida [as Lee Burton] (Private Tom Carlyle); Aldo Sambrell (Sergeant Karim Habinda); Diana Lorys (Janine); Franco Fantasia (Schiwers); Gérard Herter (SS Lieutenant Hapke); Mirko Ellis (Captain Adler); Bruno Corazzari (Private Frank Madigan); Antonio Molino Rojo (Private Albert Hank); Lorenzo Robledo (Private Bernard Knowles); Luis Induni (Pierre, Janine's lover)

Un esercito di 5 uomini (Italy)
Alternate titles: *The 5-Man Army*; *The 5-Man Army*; *5 hommes armés*; *Un ejército de 5 hombres*; *Die fünf Gefürchteten*
Release date: October 16, 1969 (Italy); February 20, 1970 (U.S.A.)
Director: Don Taylor [Italo Zingarelli directed almost the entire film without credit]; Screenplay: Marc Richards and Dario Argento; Producer: Italo Zingarelli (Tiger Film); Cinematography: Enzo Barboni; Camera Operator: Sergio Bergamini; Editor: Sergio Montanari; Music Composer: Ennio Morricone; Music Conductor: Bruno Nicolai; Art Director: Enzo Bulgarelli; Costume Designer: Enzo Bulgarelli and Luciano Sagoni; Assistant Director: Stefano Rolla
Technical specs and running time: 35mm; 1.85:1, color; 105 minutes
Cast: Peter Graves (Dutchman); James Daly (Augustus); Bud Spencer (Mesito); Nino Castelnuovo (Luis); Tetsuro Tamba (Samurai); Claudio Gora (Esteban); Carlo Alighiero (Gutierrez); Giacomo Rossi Stuart (Mexican General); Daniela Giordano (Maria); Dan Sturkie (Carnival Barker); José Torres (Mexican spy); Marino Masé (Railroad man); Annabella Andreoli (Perla); Artemio Antonini (Prison warden); Fortunato Arena (Execution squad commander); Dante Cleri (Pueblo mayor); Don Taylor, Steffen Zacharias (Poker players); Luigi Bonos (Priest); Pietro Torrisi (Mexican officer); Bruno Ariè, Omero Capanna, Paolo Figlia, Franco Pasquetto, Angelo Susani, Franco Ukmar, Sergio Ukmar (Mexican soldiers)

La stagione dei sensi (Italy/Germany)
Release date: October 22, 1969 (Italy)
Filmed on location in Calabria (Italy).
Director: Massimo Franciosa; Screenplay: Barbara Alberti, Dario Argento, Peter Kintzel, and Franco Ferrari; Screen story: Amedeo Pagani; Producer: Roberto Palaggi and Italo Zingarelli (A&P Film/Rapid Film/West Film); Cinematography: Alessandro D'Eva; Camera Operator: Carlo Fiore; Editor: Sergio Montanari; Assistant Editor: Nadia Bonifazi; Music Composer/Conductor: Ennio Morricone; Production Designer: Giuseppe Aldrovandi; Assistant Director: Ezio Palaggi
Technical specs and running time: 35mm; 1.85:1, color; 94 minutes
Cast: Udo Kier (Luca); Laura Belli (Monica); Edda Di Benedetto (Claudia); Eva Thulin (Michele); Susanne von Sass (Marina); Gaspare Zola (Peter); Ugo Adinolfi (Marco)

Dawn of the Dead (U.S.A./Italy)
Alternate titles: *Zombi*; *Zombies*
Production date: November 13, 1977 through the end of February 1978
Release date: September 1, 1978 (Italy); February 12, 1979 (Spain); March 13, 1979 (Japan); April 20, 1979 (U.S.A.); August 2, 1979 (West Germany); March 9, 1980 (U.K.); May 11, 1983 (France)
Filmed at: Monroeville Mall, with location work in and around Pittsburgh, Pennsylvania (U.S.A.).
Director: George A. Romero; Screenplay: George A. Romero; Script Consultant: Dario Argento; Producer: Richard P. Rubinstein, Claudio Argento, Dario Argento, Alfredo Cuomo, and Donna Siegel (Dawn Associates/Laurel Group); Cinematography: Michael Gornick; Editor: George A. Romero; Assistant Editor: Kenneth Davidow; Editor (Italian Version): Piero Bozza; Music: Goblin (Claudio Simonetti/Fabio Pignatelli/Massimo Morante/Agostino Marangolo); Additional Music (Non-European version only): Pierre Arvay ("Desert De Glace"), Herbert Chappell ("The Gonk"), Electric Banana [The Pretty Things] ("Cause I'm a Man"), Paul Lemel ("Cosmogony Part 1," "Dramaturgy"), Simon Park ("Figment," "Sun High"), Derek Scott ("Scarey 1," "Scarey 2," "Fugarock"), Barry Stoller ("Tango Tango"), Reg Tilsley ("We Are the Champions"), Jack Trombey ("Mask of Death"), Simon Park ("Figment"), and Eric Towren ("Sinestre"); Set Decoration: Josie Caruso and Barbara Lifsher; Costumer Designer: Josie Caruso; Assistant Director: Christine Forrest; Special Make-up Effects: Tom Savini
Technical specs and running time: 35mm, 1.33:1 (shot open matte; sometimes screened in 1.85:1), color; 127 minutes (119 minutes [Argento edit]; 139 minutes [Cannes edit])
Cast: Ken Foree (Peter Washington); David Emge (Stephen Andrews, aka "Fly boy"); Scott H. Reiniger (Roger DeMarco, aka "Trooper"); Gaylen Ross (Francine Parker, aka "Fran"); David Crawford (Dr. James Foster); Richard France (Dr. Millard Rausch, the scientist with the eye patch); David Early (Mr. Sidney Berman, the talk show host);

Howard Smith (TV commentator); Daniel Dietrich (Dan Givens); Fred Baker (Commander); James A. Baffico (Wooley); Jese Del Gre (Old priest); Rod Stouffer (Young officer on roof); Tom Savini, Pasquale Buba, Tony Buba, William George [as "Butchie"], Dave Hawkins, Tom Kapusta, Rudy Ricci, Marty Schiff, Joe Shelby, Taso Stavrakos, Nick Tallo, Larry Vaira (Motorcycle gang); Sharon Hill (Zombie nurse); Mike Christopher (Hare Krishna zombie); Clayton Hill (Sweater zombie); Jay Stover (Zombie with gun); Tommy Lafite (Miguel, tenement zombie); Jim Krut (Helicopter zombie); Conchita Lazarus (Zombie nun); Lenny Lies (Machete zombie); John Paul (Bald zombie at fueling station); Lee Cummings (Zombie in swimming trunks); John Harrison (Department store zombie who gets screwdriver in the ear); George A. Romero (TV director); Christine Forrest (Assistant director); Clayton McKinnon, John Rice, Ted Bank, Randy Kovitz, Patrick McCloskey, Joseph Pilato (Officers at dock); John Amplas (Latino gang member on roof)

Dèmoni (Italy)
Alternate titles: *Demons*; *Démons*
Production date: June through July 1985
Release Date: October 4, 1985 (Italy); April 26, 1986 (Japan); May 30, 1986 (U.S.A.); October 1, 1986 (France); January 1987 (U.K.); August 24, 1987 (Spain).
Filmed at: De Paolis Incir Studios, Rome, with location work in Berlin (Germany).
Director: Lamberto Bava; Screenplay: Dario Argento, Lamberto Bava, Dardano Sacchetti, and Franco Ferrini; Screen story: Dardano Sacchetti; Producer: Dario Argento (DACFILM); Cinematography: Gianlorenzo Battaglia; Editor: Franco Fraticelli; Assistant Editor: Piero Bozza; Music: Claudio Simonetti; Additional Music: Accept ("Fast as a Shark"), The Adventurers ("Send My Heart"), Billy Idol ("White Wedding"), Pretty Maids ("Night Danger"), Mötley Crüe ("Save Our Souls"), Saxon ("Everybody Up"), Rick Springfield ("Walking on the Edge"), Go West ("We Close Our Eyes"), Edvard Grieg ("In the Hall of the Mountain King," from *Peer Gynt*), Gioachino Rossini ("The Thieving Magpie"); Production Designer: Davide Bassan; Costume Designer: Marina Malavasi and Patrizia Massaia; Assistant Director: Michele Soavi; Special Make-up Creations: Sergio Stivaletti; Special Make-up and Effects: Rosario Prestopino; Dubbing Director (English version): Nick Alexander
Technical specs and running time: 35mm; 1.66:1, color; 88 minutes
Cast: Urbano Barberini (George); Natasha Hovey (Cheryl); Karl Zinny (Ken); Fiore Argento (Hannah); Paola Cozzo (Kathy); Bobby Rhodes (Tony, the pimp); Fabiola Toledo (Carmen, Tony's companion); Nicoletta Elmi (Ingrid, the usherette); Stelio Candelli (Frank); Nicole Tessier (Ruth, Frank's wife); Alex Serra (Werner, the blind man); Geretta Geretta [as Geretta Giancarlo] (Rosemary, Tony's companion); Guido Baldi (Tony, Hannah's boyfriend); Enrica Maria Scrivano (Liz, Werner's daughter); Claudio Spadaro (Liz's lover); Michele Soavi (Masked man/"Jerry" in the horror film); Pasqualino Salemme (Ripper, head gang member); Bettina Ciampolini (Nina, blonde gang member); Giuseppe Cruciano (Hot Dog, gang member); Peter Pitsch (Baby Pig, gang member); Sally Day (Carla, blonde victim); Eliana Hoppe ('Edith' in the horror film); Jasmine Maimone ("Nancy" in the horror film); Marcello Modugno ('Bob' in the horror film); Giovanni Frezza (Kirk, the kid on the jeep with the shotgun); Janis Martin (Blonde girl in the jeep); Goffredo Unger (Jeep driver); Lamberto Bava (Bearded man at subway); Emanuela Zicosky (June)
English dubbing credits: Nick Alexander (Frank—"international" English dub only); Victor Beard (Tony, the pimp); Russel Case (Ripper)

Dèmoni 2 (Italy)
Alternate titles: *Demons 2*; *Démons 2*
Production date: May 26 through June 22, 1986
Release date: October 9, 1986 (Italy); February 13, 1987 (U.S.A.); March 25, 1987 (France); July 9, 1987 (West Germany); September 18, 1987 (U.K.); April 17, 1987 (Spain)
Filmed at: De Paolis Incir Studios, Rome, with location work in Rome (Italy).
Director: Lamberto Bava; Screenplay: Dario Argento, Lamberto Bava, Dardano Sacchetti, and Franco Ferrini; Producer: Dario Argento and Ferdinando Caputo (DACFILM); Cinematography: Gianlorenzo Battaglia; Editor: Franco Fraticelli and Piero Bozza; Assistant Editor: Fabrizio Fraticelli, Alessandro Gabriele, and Roberto Priori; Music: Simon Boswell; Additional Music: The Smiths ("Panic"), Gene Loves Jezebel ("Heartache"), The Cult ("Rain"), Fields of the Nephilim ("Power"), The Art of Noise ("Backbeat"), Peter Murphy ("Blue Heart"), Dead Can Dance ("De Profundis"), Love & Rockets ("Kundalini Express"), Pierce Turner ("How it Shone"), Caduta Massi ("Blood and Flame"), The Producers ("Live in TV"); Art Direction: Davide Bassan; Costume Designer: Nicola Trussardi; Assistant Director: Fabrizio Bava; Mechanical creations and transformations: Sergio Stivaletti; Special Make-up Effects: Rosario Prestopino; Dubbing Director (English version): Nick Alexander
Technical specs and running time: 35mm; 1.66:1, color; 91 minutes (82 minutes)
Cast: David Knight (George); Nancy Brilli (Hannah, David's wife); Coralina Cataldi-Tassoni (Sally); Asia Argento (Ingrid Haller); Bobby Rhodes (Hank); Virginia Bryant (Mary, the prostitute); Anita Bartolucci (Woman with dog); Antonio Cantafora (Mr. Haller, Ingrid's father); Luisa Passega (Helga Haller, Ingrid's mother); Davide Marotta (Tommy as a demon); Marco Vivio (Tommy); Michele Mirabella (Prostitute's client); Pasqualino Salemme (Security guard); Maria Chiara Sasso (Ulla, party-goer with camera); Dario Casalini (Teddy, Ulla's boyfriend); Andrea Garinei (Young party-goer waiting for Jacob); Bruno Bioltta (Jacob); Yvonne Fraschetti (Jacob's girl); Lorenzo Gioielli (Jake); Angela Frondaroli (Susan, bodybuilder); Caroline Christina Lund (Jennifer, bodybuilder); Marina Loi (Kate, party-goer); Fabio Poggiali (Muller, bodybuilder); Eliana Hoppe ('Pam' on TV show); Pascal Persiano ("Joe" on TV show); Robert Chilcott ("Bob on TV show); Stefano Molinari (Demon on TV); Lamberto Bava (Sally's father); Annalie Harrison (Sally's mother); Pasquele Valente (Tommy's father); Kim Rhone (Tommy's mother); Luca De Nardo, Silvia Rosa, Monica Umena, Lorenzo Flaherty (Party-goers); Furio Bilotta, Giovanna Pini (Jacob's passengers)
English dubbing credits: Victor Beard (Hank)

La chiesa (Italy)
Alternate titles: *The Church*; *Demons 3*; *El engendro del diablo*
Production date: September 4 through November 19 1988
Release date: March 10, 1989 (Italy); August 18, 1990 (Japan); August 22, 1990 (U.S.A.); June 12, 1992 (Spain)
Filmed at: Elios Studios, Rome, and R.P.A. Studios, Rome, with location work in Rome (Italy), Hamburg (Germany), and Budapest (Hungary).
Director: Michele Soavi; Screenplay: Dario Argento, Franco Ferrini, and Michele Soavi; Screen story: Dario Argento and Franco Ferrini; Producer: Dario Argento, Mario Cecchi Gori, and Vittorio Cecchi Gori (ADC Films/Cecchi Gori Group Tiger Cinematografica/Reteitalia); Cinematography: Renato Tafuri; Camera Operator: Alessandro Carlatto; Editor: Franco Fraticelli; Assistant Editor: Piero Bozza; Music Composer: Goblin [Fabio Pignatelli] ("La Chiesa," "Possessione," "Lotte") and Keith Emerson ("The Church Main Theme," "The Possession," "The Church Revisited"); Additional Music: Philip Glass ("Floe," performed by Martin Goldray; "Civil Wars," performed by Goblin/Fabio Pignatelli), Zooming on the Zoo ("Go to Hell"), Definitive Gaze ("The Wire Blaze"), Simon Boswell ("Imagination"); Production Designer: Massimo Antonello Geleng; Costume Designer: Maurizio Paiola; Assistant Director: Filiberto Fiaschi; Special Effects: Renato Agostini; Special Effects Creations: Sergio Stivaletti and Barbara Morosetti; Dubbing Director (English version): Nick Alexander

Technical specs and running time: 35mm; 1.66:1, color; 102 minutes
Cast: Tomas Arana (Evan); Barbara Cupisti (Lisa); Hugh Quarshie (Father Gus); Fedor Chaliapin, Jr. (The Bishop); Giovanni Lombardo Radice (The Reverend); Asia Argento (Lotte); Antonella Vitale (Bridal model); Roberto Corbiletto (Hermann, Lotte's father); Alina De Simone (Lotte's mother); Clair Hardwick (Joanna); Roberto Caruso (Freddie, Joanna's boyfriend); Olivia Cupisti (Mira, Dark Ages witch with the mark of the devil on her foot); Gianfranco De Grassi (Dark Ages accuser); Lar Jorgensen (Bruno, groom model); John Karlsen (Heinrich); Katherine Bell Marjorie (Heinrich's wife); Riccardo Minervini, Matteo Rocchietta (School boys); Micaela Pignatelli (Fashion photographer); Patrizia Punzo (Miss Brückner, the teacher); Enrico Osterman (The torturer); John Richardson (The architect); Michele Soavi (Policeman)

English dubbing credits: Wendee Lee (Lisa); Theodore Lehmann (The Bishop); Marbry Steward (Lotte); Bill Capizzi (Hermann, Lotte's father)); Michael McConnohie (Reverend); Edie Merman (Bridal model); Robert V. Barron (Heinrich); Lara Cody (Joanna); David Thomas (Bruno, groom model); J.C. Henning (Miss Brückner, the teacher); Melora Harte (Fashion photographer); Robert Axelrod (Dark Ages accuser); Kerrigan Magan (The architect); Jeff Winkless (The torturer)

La setta (Italy)
Alternate titles: *The Sect*; *The Devil's Daughter*; *Demons 4*
Production date: September 20 through November 16, 1990
Release date: March 1, 1991 (Italy); October 18, 1991 (U.S.A.); June 5, 1992 (Spain)
Filmed at: De Paolis Incir Studios, Rome, with location work in Frankfurt (Germany).
Director: Michele Soavi; Screenplay: Dario Argento, Giovanni Romoli, and Michele Soavi; Producer: Dario Argento, Mario Cecchi Gori, Vittorio Cecchi Gori, and Andrea Tinnirello (ADC Films/Penta Film/Silvio Berlusconi Communications); Cinematography: Raffaele Mertes; Camera Operator: Camillo Sabatini; Editor: Franco Fraticelli; Assistant Editor: Andrea Benedetti; Music: Pino Donaggio; Additional Music: America ("A Horse with No Name"), John Kander and Fred Ebb ("Tomorrow Belongs to Me," sung by Kelly Curtis), W.L. Wilson and B.S. Mason and D.R. Pfrimmer ("Don't Leave Me Alone"); Production Designer: Massimo Antonello Geleng; Costume Designer: Vera Cozzolino; Assistant Director: Marco Guidone; Make-up Effects: Rosario Prestopino; Special Effects: Massimo Cristofanelli; Fantasy Creatures: Sergio Stivaletti and Barbara Morosetti; Dubbing Director (English version): Nick Alexander
Technical specs and running time: 35mm; 1.85:1, color; 115 minutes
Cast: Kelly Curtis (Miriam Kreisl); Herbert Lom (Moebius Kelly); Maria Angela Giordano (Kathryn); Michel Adatte (Frank); Tomas Arana (Damon); Carla Cassola (Dr. Pernath); Angelika Maria Boeck (Claire Henri); Giovanni Lombardo Radice (Martin Romero); Niels Gullov (Mr. Henri); Donald O'Brien (Justice Jonathan Ford); Yasmine Ussani (Samantha); Dario Casalini (Mark, a hippy); Paolo Pranzo (Steven); Richard Sammel (Jack, truck driver); Ralph Bola Mustapha (2nd truck driver); Erica Sinisi (Sara); Fabio Saccani (Bald pick-pocket); Vincenzo Regina (Male nurse); Giovanna Rotellini, Chiara Mancori (Midwives); Carmela Pilato (Sect member); Michele Soavi (Magician on TV)

M.D.C.—Maschera di cera (Italy/France)
Alternate titles: *Wax Mask*; *La máscara de cera*; *Le masque de cire*
Production date: July 9 through August 13, 1996
Release date: April 4, 1997 (Italy); December 6, 1997 (Japan); December 10, 1997 (France)
Filmed at: Cinecittà Studios, Rome, with location within Rome (Italy).
Director: Sergio Stivaletti; Screenplay: Lucio Fulci and Daniele Stroppa; Screen story: Dario Argento, Lucio Fulci, and Daniele Stroppa; Based on: "The Waxwork Museum" by Gaston Leroux; Producer: Dario Argento, Giuseppe Colombo, and Fulvio Lucisano (Mediaset/France Film International/Cine 2000); Cinematography: Sergio Salvati; Camera Operator: Franco Bruni (Italy) and Jean-François Gondre (France); Editor: Paolo Benassi; Assistant Editor: Flora Elisa Algeri Bricoli and Letizia Caudullo; Music Composer/Conductor: Maurizio Abeni; Production Designer: Massimo Antonello Geleng; Costume Designer: Stefania Svizeretto; Assistant Director: Federica Ciciarelli, Simone Di Carlo, and Michele Salimbeni; Special Effects and Computer Graphics: Sergio Stivaletti; Dubbing Director (English version): Robert Rietty
Technical specs and running time: 35mm; 1.85:1, color; 98 minutes
Cast: Robert Hossein (Boris Volkoff); Romina Mondello (Sonia Lafont/Marta Volkoff); Riccardo Serventi Longhi (Andrea Conversi); Gabriella Giorgelli (Francesca, Sonia's aunt); Umberto Balli (Alex, Volkoff's assistant); Aldo Massasso (Inspector Lanvin); Gianni Franco (Inspector Palazzi); Antonello Murru (Museum caretaker); Daniele Auber (Luca); Romano Iannelli (Pathologist); Stefania Fidotti (Anna); Rosa Pianeta (Anna's mother); Sonia Topazio (Nurse); Massimo Vanni (Victor, Marta's second husband); Omero Capanna (The monster); Sabrina Pellegrino (Elena); Giuseppina Lo Vetro (The madame); Luca Memè (Giovanni); Goffredo Unger (The puppeteer); Loretta Cester (Girl in waiting room); Salvatore Cammuca (Gypsy); Maria Asiride, Ginevra Cassini, Caterina Cuomo, Angela D'Ambra, Federica Leuter, Antonella Sannite, Elena Marchesina, Michela Paolucci, Elisabetta Rocchetti, Andreina Sirena (Prostitutes); Sergio Stivaletti (Brothel client)

English dubbing credits: Robert Rietty (Boris Volkoff)

Scarlet Diva (Italy)
Production date: September 27 through October 30, 1999
Release date: May 26, 2000 (Italy); January 24, 2001 (France); February 23, 2002 (Japan); August 9, 2002 (U.S.A.)
Filmed on location in Rome and Naples (Italy), Paris (France), London (England), Los Angeles (U.S.A.), and Amsterdam (Netherlands).
Director: Asia Argento; Screenplay: Asia Argento; Producer: Dario Argento, Claudio Argento, Gianluca Curti, Stefano Curti, and Adriana Chiesa Di Palma (Opera Film); Cinematography: Frederic Fasano; Editor: Anna Rosa Napoli; Assistant Editor: Francesca Genevois and Maria Cristina Marra; Music: John Hughes; Additional Music: Lory D, Mauro Ruvolo and Stefano Curti ("Supernatural"), Lory D and Mauro Ruvolo ("Ghettoverse," "Granulator K.," "Fantasy Drums"), Jean Shepard, Mauro Ruvolo and Stefano Curti ("Illusion," "Passing Through"), Fred Buscaglione ("Che bella sosa sei"), Dimitri Tiomkin, Ned Washington and Nina Simone ("Wild is the Wind"); Production Designer: Alessandro Rocca; Costume Designer: Susy Mattolini; Assistant Director: Alessia Cerasaro and Massimo Sagramola; Visual Effects Supervisor: Sergio Stivaletti; Mechanical Effects: David Bracci; Special Effects Production Supervisor: Barbara Morosetti
Technical specs and running time: Mini DV (Standard Definition); 1.85:1, color; 91 minutes
Cast: Asia Argento (Anna Battista); Jean Shepard (Kirk Vaines); Herbert Fritsch (Aaron Ulrich); Gianluca Arcopinto (Dr. Pascuccia); Joe Coleman (Mr. Paar); Francesca d'Aloja (Margherita); Daria Nicolodi (Anna's mother); Justinian Kfoury (J-Bird); Jesse B. Weaver [as Schooly D.] (Hash-Man); Luce Caponegro [as Selen] (Quelou); Alessandro Villari (Hamid); Paolo Bonacelli (Swiss journalist); Leo Gullotta (Dr. Vessi); David D'Inego (Adam); Vanessa Meadows [as Vanessa Crane] (Luke Ford); Jeff Alexander (Tyrone); David Brandon (Director); Robert Sommer (Cesare, the actor); Gloria Pirrocco (Anna as a child); Leonardo Servadio (Alioscia as a child); Deborah Restante (Simona); Massimo De Lorenzo (Drunk); Giovanna Papa (Fast food woman); Taiyo Yamanouchi (Japanese man); Angelica Di Majo (Piercing girl); Fabio Camilli (Pierre); Peppe Lanzetta (Maurizio)

Suspiria (Italy/U.S.A.)
Production date: October 31, 2016 through March 10, 2017
Release date: September 1, 2018 (Venice Film Festival); October 4, 2018 (Sitges International Fantastic Film Festival); October 11, 2018 (Film Festival Cologne); October 16, 2018 (London Film Festival); October 22, 2018 (Beyond Fest); October 26, 2018 (U.S.A.); October 31, 2018 (Germany); November 14, 2018 (France); November 16, 2018 (U.K.); December 5, 2018 (Spain); January 1, 2019 (Italy); January 25, 2019 (Japan)
Filmed at: Grand Hotel Campo dei Fiori in Varese (Italy) [Dance academy interiors], with location work in Berlin (Germany).
Director: Luca Guadagnino; Screenplay: David Kajganich; Based on: story and screenplay by Dario Argento and Daria Nicolodi; Producer: Luca Guadagnino, David Kajganich, Brad Fisher, Francesco Melzi d'Eril, Marco Morabito, Gabriele Moratti, William Sherak, Silvia Venturini Fendi, Michael Frenschkowski, Natalie Galazka, Stefano Spadoni, Carlo Antonelli, Lauren Beck, Josh Godfrey, Roberto Manni, Stella Savino, Kimberly Steward, James Vanderbilt, Massimiliano Violante, and Claudio Argento (Frenesy Film Company/Videa/First Sun/MeMo Films/Mythology Entertainment/Amazon Studios/K Period Media); Cinematography: Sayombhu Mukdeeprom; Second Unit Cinematography: Carolina Costa; Editor: Walter Fasano; Assistant Editor: Alessio Franco, Marco Costa, and Linda Taylor; Music Composer: Thom Yorke; Music Conductor: Hugh Brunt; Additional Music: Jackson Browne ("Fairest of the Season," performed by Chloë Grace Moretz), Bernhard Potschka and Herwig Mitteregger ("Auf'm Friedhof," performed by Nina Hagen Band), Harmonica ("De Luxe (Immer Wieder)"), Kristian Hoffman ("Total Eclipse," performed by Klaus Nomi), Erhard Bauschke und sein Orchester and Rudi Schuricke ("Komm doch in meiner Arme"), Johnny Hess and Paul Misraki ("Vous qui Passez sans me Voir," performed by Jean Sablon), Werner Richard Heymann ("Das Lied vom Einsman Mädchen," performed by Angela Winkler), Johannes Brahms ("Brahms' Lullaby," performed by Ingrid Caven); Production Designer: Inbal Weinberg; Costume Designer: Giulia Piersanti; Second Unit Director: Ferdinando Cito Filomarino; Assistant Director: Luca Lachin and Rickie-Lee Roberts; Special Effects Supervisor: Franco Ragusa; Visual Effects Producer: Virginia Cefaly; Visual Effects Supervisor: Luca Saviotti; Make-up: Sonia Cedrone and Paola Cristofaroni; Prosthetic Make-up: Mark Coulier, Andrea Leanza (Coulier Creatures FX), Lorenzo Tamburini, and Valentina Visintin
Technical specs and running time: 35mm; Super 35 (1.85:1); color; 152 minutes
Cast: Dakota Johnson (Susie Bannion); Tilda Swinton (Madame Blanc/Helena Markos/Dr. Josef Klemperer [as Lutz Ebersdorf]); Angela Winkler (Miss Tanner); Mia Goth (Sara); Elena Fokina (Olga); Chloë Grace Moretz (Patricia); Doris Hick (Frau Sesame); Vanda Capriolo (Alberta); Malgorzata Bela (Susie's mother/Death); Alex Wek (Miss Millius); Jessica Batut (Miss Mandel); Clémentine Houdart (Miss Boutaher); Ingrid Caven (Miss Vendegast); Sylvie Testud (Miss Griffith); Jessica Harper (Anke Klemperer); Fabrizia Sacchi (Pavla); Brigitte Cuvelier (Miss Kaplitt); Renée Soutendijk (Miss Huller); Christine Leboutte (Miss Balfour); Vincenza Modica (Miss Marks); Marjolaine Uscotti (Miss Daniels); Charo Calvo (Miss Killen); Sharon Campbell (Miss Martincin); Elfriede Hock (Miss Mauceri); Iaia Ferri (Judith); Gala Moody (Caroline); Sara Sguotti (Doll); Olivia Ancona (Marketa); Anne-Lise Brevers (Sonia); Halla Thordardottir (Mascia); Stephanie McMann (Siobhan); Marjon Van der Schot (Janine); Maria Bregianni (Sadie); Josepha Madoki (Liza Jane); Navala Niku Chaudhari (Marianne); Karina El Amrani (Hermione); Mikael Olsson (Agent Glockner); Fred Kelemen (Agent Albrecht); Greta Bohacek (Young Susie); Joel-Dennis Bienstock (Mennonite Priest)

Films and TV as director:
L'uccello dalle piume di cristallo (Italy/West Germany)
Alternate titles: *The Bird with the Crystal Plumage*; *The Gallery Murders*; *The Phantom of Terror*; *Das Geheimnis der schwarzen Handschuhe*
Production date: August 25 through mid-October 1969
Release date: February 27, 1970 (Italy); June 12, 1970 (U.S.A.); June 24, 1970 (West Germany); March 8, 1971 (U.K.); June 20, 1971 (France)
Filmed at: Incir—De Paolis Studios, Rome, with location work in and around Rome (Italy).
Director: Dario Argento; Screenplay: Dario Argento (and uncredited Aldo Lado); Based on: *The Screaming Mimi* by Fredric Brown (uncredited); Producer: Salvatore Argento (Seda Spettacoli/CCC Filmkunst); Cinematography: Vittorio Storaro; Camera Operator: Enrico Umetelli and Arturo Zavattini; Editor: Franco Fraticelli; Assistant Editor: Cesarina Casini and Sergio Fraticelli; Music Composer: Ennio Morricone; Music Conductor: Bruno Nicolai; Production Designer/Costume Designer: Dario Micheli; Assistant Director: Roberto Pariante; Dubbing Director (English version): Robert Rietty
Technical specs and running time: 35mm; 2.35:1 (Cromoscope), color; 96 minutes
Cast: Tony Musante (Sam Dalmas); Suzy Kendall (Julia); Enrico Maria Salerno (Inspector Morosini); Eva Renzi (Monica Ranieri); Umberto Raho (Alberto Ranieri); Renato Romano [as Raf Valenti] (Carlo); Mario Adorf (Berto Consalvi); Giuseppe Castellano (Monti); Pino Patti (Faiena); Gildo Di Marco (Garullo, the pimp); Werner Peters (Antiques dealer); Rosita Torosh (4th victim, bedroom); Fulvio Mingozzi (Policeman); Karen Valenti (5th victim, elevator); Gianni Di Benedetto (Professor Rinaldi); Reggie Nalder (Assassin in yellow); Maria Tedeschi (Old lady in the fog); Nestore Cavaricci (Fruit vendor); Filippo La Neve (Street cleaner); Annamaria Spogli (3rd victim, opening titles)
English dubbing credits: Robert Rietty (Rietty appears to have dubbed the majority of the male characters, with the exception of Tony Musante, who did his own dubbing. It sounds as if he dubbed such characters as Inspector Morosini, Alberto Ranieri, Carlo, Faiena, Garullo, the antiques dealer, and the assassin in yellow, among others.)

Il gatto a nove code (Italy/West Germany/France)
Alternate titles: *The Cat O'Nine Tails*; *Die neunschwänzige Katze*; *Le chat à neuf queues*; *El gato de las nueve colas*
Production date: September through October 1970
Release date: February 12, 1971 (Italy); May 21, 1971 (U.S.A.); June 6, 1971 (U.K.); July 15, 1971 (West Germany); August 9, 1971 (France); December 16, 1971 (Spain)
Filmed at: Cinecittà Studios, Rome, with location work in Rome and Turin (Italy).
Director: Dario Argento; Screenplay: Dario Argento; Screen story: Dario Argento, Dardano Sacchetti, and Luigi Collo; Producer: Salvatore Argento (Seda Spettacoli/Terra-Filmkunst/Labrador Films); Cinematography: Erico Menczer; Camera Operator: Roberto Brega; Editor: Franco Fraticelli; Assistant Editor: Cesarina Casini and Sergio Fraticelli; Music Composer: Ennio Morricone; Music Conductor: Bruno Nicolai; Production Designer: Carlo Leva; Costume Designer: Carlo Leva and Luca Sabatelli; Assistant Director: Roberto Pariante; Dubbing Director (English version): C.D.S.
Technical specs and running time: 35mm; 2.35:1 (Techniscope), color; 112 minutes (90 minutes)
Cast: James Franciscus (Carlo Giordani); Karl Malden (Franco Arnò); Catherine Spaak (Anna Terzi); Cinzia De Carolis (Lori, Franco's niece); Tino Carraro (Professor Fulvio Terzi); Rada Rassimov (Bianca Merusi); Horst Frank (Doctor Braun); Pier Paolo Capponi (Police Superintendent Spimi); Werner Pochat (Manuel); Ugo Fangareggi (Gigi the loser); Aldo Reggiani (Doctor Casoni); Carlo Alighiero (Doctor Calabresi); Tom Felleghy (Doctor Esson); Emilio Marchesini (Doctor Mombelli); Umberto Raho (Manuel's ex-

lover); Vittorio Congia (Righetto, the photographer); Corrado Olmi (Morsella); Fulvio Mingozzi (Policeman); Pino Patti (Barber); Jacques Stany (Professor Manera); Stefano Oppedisano (Taxi driver); Gianni Di Benedetto (Chief of Police Salmi); Margherita Horowitz (Lori's babysitter); Ada Pometti (Telephone operator); Marie Louise Sinclair (Starlet at train station); Franco Ukmar (Policeman)

4 mosche di velluto grigio (Italy/France)
Alternate titles: *Four Flies on Grey Velvet*; *4 mouches de velours gris*; *4 Moscas sobre terciopelo gris*; *Vier Fliegen auf grauem Samt*
Production date: July 12 through early September 1971
Release date: December 17, 1971 (Italy); May 19, 1972 (West Germany); August 4, 1972 (U.S.A.); February 11, 1973 (U.K.); June 21, 1971 (France)
Filmed at: Incir—De Paolis Studios, Rome, with location work in Turin, Milan, and Rome (Italy).
Director: Dario Argento; Screenplay: Dario Argento; Screen story: Dario Argento, Luigi Cozzi, and Mario Foglietti; Producer: Salvatore Argento (Seda Spettacoli/Universal Productions France); Cinematography: Franco Di Giacomo; Camera Operator: Giuseppe Lanci; Editor: Françoise Bonnot; Assistant Editor: Bruno Bianchini and Sergio Fraticelli; Music Composer: Ennio Morricone; Music Conductor: Bruno Nicolai; Production Designer: Enrico Sabbatini; Assistant Director: Roberto Pariante; Special Effects: Cataldo Galiano; Dubbing Director (English version): Nick Alexander
Technical specs and running time: 35mm; 2.35:1 (Techniscope), color; 104 minutes
Cast: Michael Brandon (Roberto Tobias); Mimsy Farmer (Nina Tobias); Jean-Pierre Marielle (Gianni Arosio); Bud Spencer (Godfrey, aka 'God'); Francine Racette (Dalia); Marisa Fabbri (Amelia, the maid); Calisto Calisti (Carlo Marosi); Oreste Lionello ('The Professor'); Fabrizio Moroni (Mirko); Stefano Satta Flores (Andrea); Gildo Di Marco (The mailman); Corrado Olmi (Porter); Costanza Spada (Maria); Dante Cleri (Coffin salesman); Guerrino Crivello (Rambaldi, the neighbor); Ada Pometti (Amelia); Tom Felleghy (Police Commissioner Pini); Sandro Dori (1st Funeral exhibition attendant); Pino Patti (2nd Funeral exhibition attendant); Gianni Di Benedetto (Funeral exhibition attendant); Jacques Stany (Psychiatrist); Fulvio Mingozzi (Music studio manager); Leopoldo Migliori (Musician); Shirley Corrigan (Girl at party); Luigi Cozzi (Masked man in theater)
English dubbing credits: Marc Smith (Gianni Arosio); Edward Mannix (Godfrey/Postman/Carlo Marosi); Gene Luotto ('The Professor'); Charles Howerton (Andrea); Nick Alexander (Music studio manager)

La porta sul buio (Italy) (TV series)
Alternate title: *Door into Darkness*
Production date: last week of August/first week of September 1972 (*Il tram*); second and third weeks of September 1972 (*Il vicino di casa*); last week of September/first week of October 1972 (*Testimone oculare*); second and third weeks of October 1972 (*La bambola*)
Broadcast dates: September 4, 1973 (*Il vicino di casa*); September 11, 1973 (*Il tram*); September 18, 1973 (*La bambola*); September 25, 1973 (*Testimone oculare*).
Director: Dario Argento (*Il tram* and [uncredited] *Testimone oculare*), Luigi Cozzi (*Il vicino di casa* and [uncredited] *La bambola*), Roberto Pariante (*Testimone oculare*), and Mario Foglietti (*La bambola*); Screenplay: Dario Argento (*Il tram*), Dario Argento and Luigi Cozzi (*Testimone oculare*), Luigi Cozzi (*Il vicino di casa*), and Mario Foglietti and Marcella Elsberger (*La bambola*); Producer: Dario Argento (Seda Spettacoli); Cinematography: Elio Polacchi; Editor: Amedeo Giomini (*Il tram*, *La bambola*, and *Testimone oculare*) and Alberto Moro (*Il vicino di casa*); Assistant Editor: Piero Bozza; Music Composer/Conductor: Giorgio Gaslini; Production Designer: Dario Micheli
Technical specs and running time: 16mm; 1.33:1 TV, color

Cast: (*Il vicino di casa*): Aldo Reggiani (Luca); Laura Belli (Stefania); Mimmo Palmara (The Neighbor); (*Il tram*): Enzo Cerusico (Commissario Giordani); Paola Tedesco (Giulia); Pierluigi Aprà (Main Suspect); Emilio Marchesini (Marco Roviti); Luciana Lehar (Prostitute); Tom Felleghy (Distinguished older Man); Fulvio Mingozzi (Policeman); Maria Tedeschi (Elderly nurse); Salvatore Puntillo (Heavy-set man with mustache); Gildo Di Marco (Man with cold); (*La bambola*): Robert Hoffmann (Doctor); Mara Venier (Daniela Moreschi); Gianfranco D'Angelo (Commissario); Erika Blanc (Elena Moreschi); Umberto Raho (Psychiatrist); (*Testimone oculare*): Marilù Tolo (Roberta Leoni); Riccardo Salvino (Guido Leoni); Glauco Onorato (Police inspector); Altea De Nicola (Anna); Gino Pagnani (Man at restaurant); Gianfranco Barra (Policeman talking to Dario Argento)

Le cinque giornate (Italy)
Unofficial alternate title: *The Five Days of Milan*
Production date: June 18 through late August 1973
Release date: December 20, 1973 (Italy)
Filmed at: ICET—De Paolis Studios, Milan, with location work in Rome and Milan (Italy).
Director: Dario Argento; Screenplay: Dario Argento, Luigi Cozzi, and Vincenzo Ungari; Producer: Claudio Argento and Salvatore Argento (Seda Spettacoli); Cinematography: Luigi Kuveiller; Camera Operator: Antonio [Nino] Annunziata; Editor: Franco Fraticelli; Assistant Editor: Piero Bozza and Sergio Fraticelli; Music Composer/Conductor: Giorgio Gaslini; Production Designer: Giuseppe Bassan; Costume Designer: Elena Mannini; Special Effects: Aldo Gasparri; Assistant Director: Sofia Scandurra
Technical specs and running time: 35mm; 2.35:1 (Techniscope), color; 122 minutes
Cast: Adriano Celentano (Cainazzo); Vincenzo Cerusico (Romolo Marcelli); Marilù Tolo (The Countess); Luisa De Santis (Pregnant woman); Glauco Onorato (Zampino); Carla Tatò (The widow); Sergio Graziani (Baron Tranzunto); Salvatore Baccardo (Garafino); Tom Felleghy (Mariano, the Countess' servant); Fulvio Mingozzi (Man at debate); Ugo Bologna (Official at victory celebration); Emilio Marchesini (Prisoner); Ivana Monti (Woman raped by Tranzunto); Stefano Oppedisano (Man at debate); Dante Maggio (Old man in jail); Dario Argento (Bandaged man with Baron Tranzunto)

Profondo rosso (Italy)
Alternate titles: *Deep Red*; *The Hatchet Murders*; *Les frissons de l'angoisse*; *Rojo oscuro*; *Rosso—Die Farbe des Todes*; *Suspiria Part 2*
Working title: *La tigre dai denti a sciabola*
Production date: September 9 through the end of December 1974
Release date: March 7, 1975 (Italy); October 31, 1975 (Spain); June 9, 1976 (U.S.A.); August 17, 1977 (France); September 23, 1978 (Japan)
Filmed at: De Paolis Incir Studios, Rome, with location work in Turin and Rome (Italy).
Director: Dario Argento; Screenplay: Dario Argento and Bernardino Zapponi; Producer: Claudio Argento and Salvatore Argento (Seda Spettacoli); Cinematography: Luigi Kuveiller; Camera Operator: Ubaldo Terzano; Editor: Franco Fraticelli; Assistant Editor: Piero Bozza; Music Composer/Conductor: Giorgio Gaslini ("Wild Session," "Deep Shadows," "School at Night," "Gianna") and Goblin [Claudio Simonetti/Fabio Pignatelli/Massimo Morante/Walter Martino/Agostino Marangolo] ("Profondo rosso," "Death Dies," "Mad Puppet"), performed by Goblin; Production Designer: Giuseppe Bassan; Costume Designer: Elena Mannini; Assistant Director: Stefano Rolla; Special Effects: Germano Natali and Carlo Rambaldi; Dubbing Director (English version): Nick Alexander
Technical specs and running time: 35mm; 2.35:1 (Techniscope), color; 127 minutes (105 minutes, 98 minutes)
Cast: David Hemmings (Marcus Daly); Daria Nicolodi (Gianna Brezzi); Gabriele Lavia (Carlo); Glauco Mauri (Professor Giordani);

Macha Méril (Helga Ulmann); Giuliana Calandra (Amanda Righetti); Clara Calamai (Marta, Carlo's mother); Eros Pagni (Superintendent Calcabrini); Furio Meniconi (Rodi); Nicoletta Elmi (Olga, Rodi's daughter); Piero Mazzinghi (Bardi); Aldo Bonamano (Carlo's father); Liana Del Balzo (Elvira, Amanda's housekeeper); Geraldine Hooper (Massimo Ricci, Carlo's lover); Jacopo Mariani (Young Carlo); Fulvio Mingozzi (Agent Mingozzi); Salvatore Puntillo (Heavy cop with mustache); Vittorio Fanfoni (Cop taking notes); Piero Vida (Fat cop with frizzy hair); Dante Fioretti (Police photographer); Lorenzo Piani (Fingerprint cop); Franco Vaccaro (Pietro Valgoi, man at psychic conference); Salvatore Baccaro (Fruit vendor); Bruno Di Luia (Concerned man in bathroom)

English dubbing credits: Carolyn De Fonseca (Gianna Brezzi); Marc Smith (Professor Giordani); Cicely Browne (Marta); Ted Rusoff (Superintendent Calcabrini); Geoffrey Copleston (Bardi); Edward Mannix (Rodi); Nick Alexander (Newscaster); Lewis E. Ciannelli (Pietro Valgoi)

Suspiria (Italy)
Production date: July 26 through early November 1976
Release date: February 1, 1977 (Italy); May 5, 1977 (West Germany); May 18, 1977 (France); June 11, 1977 (Spain); June 25, 1977 (Japan); July 28, 1977 (U.K.); August 10, 1977 (U.S.A.).
Filmed at: De Paolis Incir Studios, Rome, with location work in Munich and Bavaria (Germany).
Director: Dario Argento; Screenplay: Dario Argento and Daria Nicolodi; Producer: Claudio Argento and Salvatore Argento (Seda Spettacoli); Cinematography: Luciano Tovoli; Camera Operator: Idelmo Simonelli; Editor: Franco Fraticelli; Assistant Editor: Piero Bozza and Roberto Olivieri; Music Composer/Conductor: Goblin (Claudio Simonetti/Fabio Pignatelli/Agostino Marangolo/Massimo Morante); Production Designer: Giuseppe Bassan; Costume Designer: Pierangelo Cicoletti; Assistant Director: Antonio Gabrielli; Special Effects: Germano Natali; Dubbing Director (English version): Nick Alexander
Technical specs and running time: 35mm; 2.35:1 (Technovision, anamorphic), color; 98 minutes (92 minutes)
Cast: Jessica Harper (Suzy Banyon); Stefania Casini (Sara); Alida Valli (Miss Tanner); Joan Bennett (Madame Blanc); Flavio Bucci (Daniel); Miguel Bosé (Mark); Barbara Magnolfi (Olga); Susanna Javicoli (Sonia, Pat's friend); Eva Axén (Pat Hingle); Rudolf Schündler (Professor Milius); Udo Kier (Dr. Frank Mandel); Giuseppe Transocchi (Pavlos); Margherita Horowitz (Teacher); Jacopo Mariani (Albert, Madame Blanc's nephew); Fulvio Mingozzi (Taxi driver); Franca Scagnetti (Cook); Renato Scarpa (Professor Werdegast); Serafina Scorceletti (second cook); Renata Zamengo (Caroline); Alessandra Capozzi, Salvatore Capozzi, Diana Ferrara, Cristina Latini, Alfredo Raino, Claudia Zaccari (Dancers); Lela Svasta (Helena Markos, Mater Suspiriorum)
English dubbing credits: William Kiehl (Narrator; Narrated by Dario Argento on the Italian soundtrack); Sylvia Faver (Sara); Carolyn De Fonseca (Olga); Frank Von Kuegelgen (Dr. Frank Mandel); Geoffrey Copleston (Professor Milius); Edward Mannix (Taxi driver)

Inferno (Italy)
Alternate titles: *Horror Infernal—Feuertanz der Zombies*
Production date: May 21 through late August 1979; this was preceded by a week's filming in New York (Manhattan and Central Park, U.S.A.), in April 1979
Release date: February 7, 1980 (Italy); April 2, 1980 (U.S.A.); April 16, 1980 (France); June 1, 1980 (Spain); September 12, 1980 (West Germany); September 13, 1980 (Japan); September 1980 (U.K.)
Filmed at: De Paolis Incir Studios, Rome, and Elios Studios, Rome, with location work in Rome (Italy) and New York City (U.S.A.).
Director: Dario Argento; Screenplay: Dario Argento and (uncredited) Daria Nicolodi; Producer: Claudio Argento and Salvatore Argento (Produzioni Intersound); Cinematography: Romano Albani; Camera Operator: Idelmo Simonelli; Editor: Franco Fraticelli; Music Composer: Keith Emerson; Music Conductor: Godfrey Salmon; Additional Music: Giuseppe Verdi ("Nabucco: Va, pensiero"); Art Director: Giuseppe Bassan; Costume Designer: Massimo Lentini; Assistant Director: Lamberto Bava; Special Effects: Germano Natali and (uncredited) Mario Bava; Dubbing Director (English version): Neil Robinson
Technical specs and running time: 35mm; 1.85:1 (Technovision), color; 106 minutes
Cast: Leigh McCloskey (Mark Elliot); Irene Miracle (Rose Elliot); Eleonora Giorgi (Sara); Daria Nicolodi (Elise De Longvalle Adler); Sacha Pitoëff (Kazanian); Alida Valli (Carol); Veroniza Lazar (The Nurse/Mater Tenebrarum); Gabriele Lavia (Carlo); Feodor Chaliapin, Jr. ('Professor Arnold'/Dr. Varelli); Leopoldo Mastelloni (John, the butler); Ania Pieroni (Mater Lachrymarum); James Fleetwood (Cook); Rosario Rigutini (Man); Ryan Hilliard (Shadow); Paolo Paoloni (Music teacher); Fulvio Mingozzi (Taxi driver); Luigi Lodoli (Bookbinder); Rodolfo Lodi (Old Man in Library)
English dubbing credits: Edward Mannix (Kazanian); Carolyn De Fonseca (Carol); Brett Morrison ('Professor Arnold'/Dr. Varelli)

Tenebre (Italy)
Alternate titles: *Tenebrae*; *Unsane*; *Shadow*; *Tenebre—Der kalte Hauch des Todes*
Working title: *Sotto gli occhi dell'assassino*
Production date: May 3 through July 16, 1982
Release date: October 28, 1982 (Italy); April 27, 1983 (France); May 19, 1983 (U.K.); June 11, 1983 (Japan); February 17, 1984 (U.S.A.); October 12, 1984 (West Germany); November 23, 1984 (Spain)
Filmed at: Elios Studios, Rome, with location work in Rome (Italy) and New York (U.S.A.).
Director: Dario Argento; Screenplay: Dario Argento (George Kemp credited only on English-language prints); Producer: Claudio Argento and Salvatore Argento (Sigma Cinematografica); Cinematography: Luciano Tovoli; Camera Operator: Giuseppe Tinelli; Editor: Franco Fraticelli; Assistant Editor: Piero Bozza and Roberto Priori; Music Composer/Conductor: Claudio Simonetti, Massimo Morante, and Fabio Pignatelli (as Simonetti-Morante-Pignatelli); Production Designer: Giuseppe Bassan; Costume Designer: Pierangelo Cicoletti and Franco Tomei; Assistant Director: Lamberto Bava and Michele Soavi; Make-up: Pierantonio [Pierino] Mecacci; Dubbing Director (English version): Robert Rietty
Technical specs and running time: 35mm; 1.85:1, color; 101 minutes (91 minutes)
Cast: Anthony Franciosa (Peter Neal); Daria Nicolodi (Ann); Giuliano Gemma (Captain Germani); John Saxon (Bullmer); Mirella D'Angelo (Tilde); Christian Borromeo (Gianni); John Steiner (Cristiano Berti); Eva Robin's [Robins, aka Roberto Coatti] (Girl on the beach); Lara Wendel (Maria Alboretto); Veronica Lario (Jane Miccaro, Peter's wife); Ania Pieroni (Elsa Manni); Carola Stagnaro (Inspector Altieri); Mirella Banti (Marion, Tilde's girlfriend); Ennio Girolami (Store detective); Fulvio Mingozzi (Mr. Alboretto, the porter); Marino Masé (John, Peter's chauffeur); Gianpaolo Saccarola (Autopsy doctor); Isabella Amadeo (Bullmer's secretary); Ippolita Santarelli (Prostitute stalked by the killer); Michele Soavi (Maria's boyfriend/Man with girl from beach in swimming pool flashback); Lamberto Bava (1st elevator repair man)
English dubbing credits: David Graham (Detective Giermani); Theresa Russell (Ann); Adrienne Posta (most of the female characters, including Tilde, Maria, and Jane)

Phenomena (Italy)
Alternate titles: *Creepers*; *Fenomina*

Production date: Early August through the end of October 1984; the second unit began their work on June 18, 1984
Release date: January 31, 1985 (Italy); June 12, 1985 (France); June 22, 1985 (Japan); August 2, 1985 (U.S.A.); April 18, 1986 (U.K.)
Filmed at: De Paolis Incir Studios, Rome, with location work in Zurich (Switzerland).
Director: Dario Argento; Screenplay: Dario Argento and Franco Ferrini; Producer: Dario Argento (DACFILM); Cinematography: Romano Albani; Camera Operator: Stefano Ricciotti; Music Composer/Conductor: Goblin [Claudio Simonetti/Fabio Pignatelli] ("Jennifer," "The Wind," "Sleepwalking," "Jennifer's Friends," "The Monster Child"), Claudio Simonetti ("Phenomena"), Simon Boswell ("The Maggots"), Bill Wyman & Terry Taylor ("Valley," "Valley Bolero"); Additional Music: Iron Maiden ("Flash of the Blade"), Motörhead ("Locomotive"), Andi Sex Gang ("The Naked and the Dead," "The Quick and the Dead," and "You Don't Know Me," all written by Simon Boswell), Frankie Goes to Hollywood ("Two Tribes"); Editor: Franco Fraticelli; Assistant Editor: Piero Bozza, Sergio Fraticelli, and Roberto Priori; Production Designer: Maurizio Garrone, Nello Giorgetti, Luciano Spadoni and Umberto Turco; Costume Designer: Giorgio Armani, Marina Malavasi and Patrizia Massaia; Assistant Director: Michele Soavi; Special Optical Effects: Luigi Cozzi; Special Make-up Effects: Sergio Stivaletti and Maurizio Garrone; Dubbing Director (English version): Nick Alexander
Technical specs and running time: 35mm; 1.66:1, color; 116 minutes (110 minutes; 83 minutes)
Cast: Jennifer Connelly (Jennifer Corvino); Donald Pleasence (Professor John MacGregor); Daria Nicolodi (Frau Brückner); Dalila Di Lazzaro (Headmistress); Patrick Bauchau (Inspector Rudolf Geiger); Federica Mastroianni (Sophie); Fiore Argento (Vera Brandt); Fiorenza Tessari (Gisela Sulzer); Mario Donatone (Morris Shapiro); Francesca Ottaviani (Nurse); Alberto Cracco (Bank teller); Michele Soavi (Kurt, Geiger's assistant); Franco Trevisi (Real estate agent); Gaspare Capparoni (Karl); Antonio Maimone (Dr. Grubach); Davide Marotta (Pattau, Brückner's son); Fausta Avelli, Marta Biuso, Sophie Bourchier, Paola Gropper, Ninke Hielkema, Mitzy Orsini, Geraldine Thomas (School girls); Fulvio Mingozzi (Mr. Sulzer); Tanga (Inge)
English dubbing credits: Carolyn De Fonseca (Frau Brückner); Nick Alexander (Real estate agent)

Opera (Italy)
Alternate titles: *Terror at the Opera*; *Terror in der Oper*; *Opéra*; *Terror en la ópera*
Production date: May 25 through the beginning of September 1987
Release date: December 19, 1987 (Italy); February 11, 1989 (Japan); August 31, 1990 (U.S.A.)
Filmed at: De Paolis Incir Studios, Rome, with location work in Parma (Regio Theatre) and Rome (Italy), and Lugano (Switzerland).
Director: Dario Argento; Screenplay: Dario Argento and Franco Ferrini; Producer: Dario Argento, Mario Cecchi Gori, and Vittorio Cecchi Gori (ADC Films/Cecchi Gori Group Tiger Cinematografica/RAI Radiotelevisione Italiana); Cinematography: Ronnie Taylor; Camera Operator: Antonio Scaramuzza; Second Unit Cinematography: Renato Tafuri and Luca Robecchi; Second Unit Camera Operator: Enrico Maggi; Second Unit Director: Michele Soavi; Music Composer/Conductor: Claudio Simonetti ("Opera," "Craws," "Confusion), Bill Wyman & Terry Taylor ("Opera Theme," "Black Notes"), Brian Eno & Roger Eno ("White Darkness," "Balance," "From the Beginning"); Additional Music: Gow [as Steel Grave] ("Knights of the Night" and "Steel Grave"), Norden Light ("No Escape"), Giuseppe Verdi ("Macbeth" and "Lady Macbeth [Vieni t'affreti]," from *Macbeth*; "Amami Alfredo" and "Sempre libera," from *La Traviata*, Giacomo Puccini ("Un bel dì vedremo" from *Madame Butterfly*), Vincenzo Bellini ("Casta Diva," from *Norma*), Pino Daniele ("Boys in the Night"); Editor: Franco Fraticelli; Assistant Editor: Piero Bozza, Alessandro Gabriele and Roberto Priori; Production Designer: Davide Bassan (opera set designed by Gianmaurizio Ferncioni); Costumer Designer: Francesca Lia Morandini; Assistant Director: Antonio Gabrielli and Paolo Zenatello; Special Effects: Renato Agostini; Animatronic Effects: Sergio Stivaletti; Animatronic Effects Assistant: Barbara Morosini; Chief Make-up Effects: Rosario Prestopini; Make-up Artist: Franco Casagni; Dubbing Director (English version): Robert Rietty
Technical specs and running time: 35mm; 2.35:1 (Super 35) [1.78:1 version also made available], color; 107 minutes (95 minutes)
Cast: Cristina Marsillach (Betty; singing dubbed by Elizabeth Norberg-Schulz); Ian Charleson (Marco); Urbano Barberini (Inspector Alan Santini); Daria Nicolodi (Mira); Coralina Cataldi-Tassoni (Giulia); Antonella Vitale (Marion); William McNamara (Stefano); Barbara Cupisti (Signora Albertini); Antonio Iuorio (Baddini); Francesca Cassola (Alma); Carola Stagnaro (Alma's mother); Maurizio Garrone (Maurizio, the raven trainer); Cristina Giachino (Maria, the assistant director); György Győriványi (Miro); Peter Pitsch (Mara Czekova's assistant); Bjorn Hammer (1st cop); Sebastiano Somma (2nd cop); Michele Soavi (Inspector Daniele Soave)
English dubbing credits: Robert Rietty (Inspector Alan Santini—original English dub only; the character was revoiced for the more common final English dub)

Gli incubi di Dario Argento (Italy) (TV series)
Production date: the end of September 1987 through the first week of January 1988
Broadcast dates: the end of September 1987 through the first week of January 1988
Director: Dario Argento; Screenplay: Dario Argento; Producer: Dario Argento (RAI Radiotelevisione Italiana); Cinematography: Pasquale Rachini; Editor: Piero Bozza; Art Direction: Maurizio Garrone; Special Make-up Effects: Sergio Stivaletti
Technical specs and running time: 35mm; 1.33:1 TV, color
Cast: "Gli incubi" segments hosted by Dario Argento

Due occhi diabolici (Italy)
Alternate titles: *Two Evil Eyes*; *Deux yeux maléfiques*; *Los ojos del diablo*
Working titles: *Edgar Allan Poe*; *Metropolitan Horrors*
Production date: July 10 through September 12, 1989 (the first 22 days were devoted to Romero's half, with the remaining 32 days going to Argento's segment)
Release date: January 25, 1990 (Italy); November 9, 1990 (Spain); October 25, 1991 (U.S.A.); July 8, 1992 (France)
Filmed at: entirely filmed on location in Pittsburgh, Pennsylvania (U.S.A.). Locations for Argento's segment include 954 Beech Avenue in Pittsburgh (Roderick and Madeline's house), "Le Mardis Gras," located at 731 Copeland Street in Pittsburgh ("South of Heaven" bar), Market Square and South Side in Pittsburgh. Prologue filmed in Baltimore, Maryland (U.S.A.).
Director: George A. Romero ("The Facts in the Case of Mr. Valdemar") and Dario Argento ("The Black Cat"); Screenplay: George A. Romero ("The Facts in the Case of Mr. Valdemar") and Dario Argento and Franco Ferrini ("The Black Cat"); Producer: Claudio Argento, Dario Argento, and Achille Manzotti (ADC Films/Gruppo Bema); Cinematography: Peter Reniers ("The Facts in the Case of Mr. Valdemar") and Giuseppe ['Beppe'] Maccari ("The Black Cat"); Camera Operator: Frank Perl; Music Composer: Pino Donaggio; Music Conductor: Natale Massara; Editor: Pasquale [Pat] Buba; Assistant Editor: Ray Boniker, John S. Bich, and Lorenzo Franco; Production Designer: Cletus Anderson; Costume Designer: Barbara Anderson; Assistant Director: Nicholas Mastandrea; Second Unit Director: Luigi Cozzi and Nicola Pecorini; Special Make-up Effects: Tom Savini and Kevin McTurk; Interpreter: Bert Bell;

Dialogue Coach: Kenneth Gargaro
Technical specs and running time: 35mm; 1.85:1, color; 120 minutes
Cast: ("The Facts in the Case of Mr. Valdemar"): Adrienne Barbeau (Jessica Valdemar); Ramy Zada (Dr. Robert Hoffman); Bingo O'Malley (Ernest Valdemar); E.G. Marshall (Steven Pike); Tom Atkins (Detective Grogan); Christine Forrest (Nurse); Jeff Howell (Policeman); Chuck Aber (Mr. Pratt); Barbara Byrne (Martha); Anthony DiLeo, Jr. (Taxi driver); Mitchell Baseman (Boy at zoo); Larry John Myers (Old man); ("The Black Cat"): Harvey Keitel (Rod Usher); Madeleine Potter (Annabel); John Amos (Detective Inspector LeGrand); Sally Kirkland (Eleanora); Martin Balsam (Mr. Pym); Kim Hunter (Mrs. Pym); Holter Ford Graham (Christian); Julie Benz (Betty); Lou Valenzi (Editor); Peggy Sanders (Young policewoman at crime scene); J.R. Hall (2nd policeman); Scott House (3rd policeman); Jeffrey Wild (Delivery man); Laurene Charters (Bonnie); Ted Worsley (Desk editor); James G. MacDonald (Luke); Jonathan Adams (Hammer); Tom Savini (The monomaniac); Jonathan Sachar (Officer Brian)

Trauma (Italy/U.S.A.)
Working title: *Aura's Enigma*
Production date: August 3 through September 26, 1992
Release date: March 12, 1993 (Italy); April 8, 1994 (Japan)
Filmed at: filmed entirely on location in Minneapolis and St. Paul, Minnesota (U.S.A.).
Director: Dario Argento; Screenplay: Dario Argento and T.E.D. Klein; Screen story: Dario Argento, Franco Ferrini, and Gianni Romoli; Producer: Dario Argento, Chris Beckham, T. David Pash, and Andrea Tinnirello (ADC Films/Overseas FilmGroup); Cinematography: Raffaele Mertes; Camera Operator: Kirk Gardner; Music Composer: Pino Donaggio; Music Conductor: Natale Massara; Editor: Bennett Goldberg; Assistant Editor: Jim Schermerhorn; Production Designer: Billy Jett; Costume Designer: Leesa Evans; Assistant Director: Rod Smith; Special Make-up Effects: Tom Savini, Greg Funk, Will Huff, and Christopher Martin; Physical Effects Supervisor: Paul Murphy; Dialogue Coach: Paul Draper; Romanian language coach: Michael Lupu
Technical specs and running time: 35mm; 2:35:1 (Technovision, anamorphic), color; 111 minutes (106 minutes)
Cast: Asia Argento (Aura Petrescu); Christopher Rydell (David Parsons); Piper Laurie (Adriana Petrescu); Frederic Forrest (Dr. Leopold Judd); Laura Johnson (Grace Harrington); Cory Garvin (Gabriel Pickering); Dominque Serrand (Stefan Petrescu); Brad Dourif (Dr. Lloyd); James Russo (Captain Travis); Ira Belgrade (Arnie); Hope Alexander-Willis (Linda Quirk); Sharon Barr (Hilda Volkman); Isabell Monk (Georgia Jackson, the chiropractor); Terry Perkins (Mrs. Pickering); Tony Saffold (Ben Aldrich); Peter Moore (Mark Leneer); Lester Purry (Sergeant Carver); David Chase (Sid Marigold); Jacqueline Kim (Alice); Rita Vassallo (Rita); Stephen D'Ambrose (Pale man); Bonita Parsons (Prime woman); Gregory Beech (Deaf man); Kevin Dutcher (John Miller, the timid man); Kathy Quirk (Gare Grayson); E.A. Violet Boor (Mrs. Potter); Les Exodus, Onesmo Kibira, Innocent Mafalingundi, Charles Petrus, Lance Pollonais (Reggae band)

La sindrome di Stendhal (Italy)
Alternate titles: *The Stendhal Syndrome*; *Le syndrome de Stendhal*; *Das Stendhal Syndrom*; *El síndrome de Stendhal*
Production date: July 17 through September 15, 1995
Release date: January 26, 1996 (Italy); July 19, 1996 (American Cinematheque); March 25, 1998 (Spain)
Filmed at: Cinecittà Studios, Rome, with location work in Viterbo, Florence, and Rome (Italy).
Director: Dario Argento; Screenplay: Dario Argento; Screen story: Dario Argento and Franco Ferrini; Based on: *La sindrome di Stendhal* by Graziella Magherini; Producer: Dario Argento, Giuseppe Colombo, and Walter Massi (Medusa Film/Cine 2000); Cinematography: Gisueppe Rotunno; Camera Operator: Giovanni Fiore Coltellacci; Second Unit Cinematography: Roberto Girometti; Music Composer/Conductor: Ennio Morricone; Editor: Angelo Nicolini; Assistant Editor: Carla Furnari; Production Designer: Massimo Antonello Geleng; Costume Designer: Lia Francesca Morandini; Assistant Director: Nicolò Bongiorno, Fabrizio Campanella, Filipo Macelloni and Daniele Persica; Second Unit Director: Luigi Cozzi; Special Visual and Digital Effects: Sergio Stivaletti; Special Effects: Giovanni Corridori & Co.; Special Make-up Effects: Franco Casagni; Dubbing Director (English version): Nick Alexander
Technical specs and running time: 35mm; 1.85:1, color; 120 minutes (113 minutes)
Cast: Asia Argento (Assistant Inspector Anna Manni); Thomas Kretschmann (Alfredo Grossi); Paolo Bonacelli (Dr. Cavana); Marco Leonardi (Marco Longhi); Julien Lambroschini (Marie Bale); Luigi Diberti (Inspector Manetti); John Quentin (Anna's father); Sonia Topazio (Victim in Florence); Lucia Stara (Shop assistant); Franco Diogene (Victim's husband); Veronica Lazar (Marie's mother); Lorenzo Crespi (Giulio); Vera Gemma (Policewoman); John Pedefferi (Hydraulic engineer); Mario Diano (Coroner); Eleonora Vizzini (Anna as a child); Maximilian Nisi (Luigi); Leonardo Ferrantini (Alessandro); Sandro Giordano (Fausto); Cinzia Monreale (Mrs. Grossi); Michele Kaplan (Grossi's son); Laura Piattella (40-year-old woman); Vincenzo Uccellini (40-year-old woman's son); Elena Bermani (30-year-old woman); Luca Camilletti (Hotel porter); Graziano Giusti (2nd coroner); Monica Fiorentini (Doctor in Florence); Giancarlo Tedori (Doctor in Florence); Antonello Murru (Police officer #1); Marna Del Monaco (Dining car stewardess); Maria Grazia Nazzari ("Night Watch" victim)
English dubbing credits: Teresa Pascarelli (Assistant Inspector Anna Manni)

Il fantasma dell'opera (Italy/Hungary)
Alternate titles: *The Phantom of the Opera*; *Das Phantom der Oper*; *El fantasma de la ópera*; *Le fantôme de l'Opéra*
Production date: January 19 to April 17, 1998
Release date: November 20, 1998 (Italy); February 3, 1999 (France); Febaruary 25, 1999 (Germany); June 18, 1999 (U.S.A.)
Filmed at: Mariassy Studio, Budapest (Hungary), with location work in Pertosa caves (Salerno, Italy), Paris (France), and Budapest, including the Budapest Opera House (Hungary).
Director: Dario Argento; Screenplay: Dario Argento and Gérard Brach; Based on: *Le Fantôme de l'Opéra* by Gaston Leroux; Producer: Claudio Argento, Giuseppe Colombo, and Áron Sipos (Medusa Film/Cine 2000); Cinematography: Ronnie Taylor; Camera Operator: Marco Pieroni; Music Composer/Conductor: Ennio Morricone; Additional Music: Charles Gounod ("Faust: Overture—Act 1 & The Elves Chorus," "Romeo and Juliet: Act 1 & Duet"), Léo Delibes ("Lakmé: Air des clochettes," "Sylvia: Intermezzo & Slow Waltz"), Georges Bizet ("Carmen: L'amour est un oiseau rebelle"), Frederic Chopin ("Vivace: Mazurka No. 5 in B Flat Major—Op. 7 no 1"), Maurizio Guarini and Cinzia Cavalieri ("Tour Keys"); Editor: Anna Napoli; Assistant Editor: Emanuela Di Giunta and Maria Cristina Marra; Production Designer: Massimo Antonello Geleng and Csaba Stork; Costume Designer: Ágnes Gyarmathy; Assistant Director: Péter Rácz; Special Visual Effects: Sergio Stivaletti; Special Effects: Péter Szilágyi and Iván Pohárnok; Mechanism of Mechanical Creatures: David Bracci; Mechanism of rat-hunting machine: Simon Blades; Singing Teachers: Lilian Zafred (for Asia Argento) and Stefania Magnifico (for Nadia Rinaldi); English Adaptation: Georgina Caspari; Dubbing Director (English version): Nick Alexander
Technical specs and running time: 35mm; 1.85:1, color; 103 minutes (99 minutes)

Cast: Julian Sands (The Phantom); Asia Argento (Christine Daaé; singing dubbed by Raffaella Milanesi); Andrea Di Stefano (Baron Raoul De Chagny); Nadia Rinaldi (Carlotta Altieri); Coralina Cataldi-Tassoni (Honorine); István Bubik (Ignace, the rat catcher); Lucia Guzzardi (Madame Giry); Aldo Massasso (Pordieu); Zolta Barabas (Poligny); Gianni Franco (Montluc); David D'Ingeo (Alfred); Kitty Kéri (Paulette); John Pedefferi (Dr. Princard); Leonardo Treviglio (Jerome De Chagny); Massimo Sarchielli (Joseph Buquet); Luis Molteni (Nicolaud); Enzo Cardogna (Marcel); Antonio Pupillo (Gustave); Domenica Coppolini (Carlotta's mother); Zsolt Anger (Waiter); Sandor Bese (Dwarf); Rodrigo Crespo (Father); Iván Dengyel (Martin); Ferenc Deák B. (Edgar Degas); David Drucker (Kiki); Gábor Harsai (Marc); Tibor Nemes (Mephisto); Róbert Szabó Benke (1st poet); Zoltán Rajkai (2nd poet); György Szakaly (Ballet master); Balázs Tardy (Longuet); Dénes Ujlaky (Papin)

Nonhosonno (Italy)
Alternate titles: *Sleepless*; *Le sang des innocents*; *Insomnio*
Production date: May 15 through July 2 2000
Release date: January 5, 2001 (Italy); August 3, 2001 (American Cinematheque); March 13, 2002 (France); March 30, 2002 (Japan)
Filmed at: Euphon Studios, Turin, with location work in Turin (Italy).
Director: Dario Argento; Screenplay: Dario Argento and Franco Ferrini, with the collaboration of Carlo Lucarelli; Screen story: Dario Argento and Franco Ferrini; Producer: Claudio Argento and Dario Argento (Medusa Film/Opera Film/Tele+); Cinematography: Ronnie Taylor; Camera Operator: Roberto Brega; Music Composer/Conductor: Goblin (Claudio Simonetti/Agostino Marangolo/Massimo Morante/Fabio Pignatelli); Additional Music: Luca Morino and Fabio Barovero ("Mi casa tu casa"), Luca Morino, Fabio Barovero and Giovanni Sanfelci ("Gwami Moloko"), Cecilia Chailly ("Autumn Window"), Pyotr Ilyich Tchaikovsky ("Swan Lake"), Fabrizio Fornaci ("Quicksilver"); "Death Farm" nursery rhyme written by Asia Argento; Editor: Anna Napoli; Assistant Editor: Alessandro Di Cola and Maria Cristina Marra; Production Designer: Massimo Antonello Geleng; Costume Designer: Susy Mattolini; Assistant Director: Riccardo Cannone; Special Visual Effects: Sergio Stivaletti; Special Effects Production Supervisor: Barbara Morosetti; Special Mechanical Effects: David Bracci; Dubbing Director (English version): Nick Alexander
Technical specs and running time: 35mm; 1.85:1, color; 117 minutes
Cast: Max von Sydow (Ulisse Moretti); Stefano Dionisi (Giacomo); Chiara Caselli (Gloria); Roberto Zibetti (Lorenzo); Gabriele Lavia (Mr. Betti); Rossella Falk (Laura de Fabritiis); Paolo Maria Scalondro (Manni); Roberto Accornero (Fausto); Barbara Lerici (Angela, the train victim); Conchita Puglisi (Amanda); Guido Morbello (Detective); Massimo Sarchielli (Leone); Diego Casale (Beppe); Alessandra Comerio (Mrs. Betti); Aldo Massasso (Cascio); Elena Marchesini (Mel, "the kitten"); Barbara Mautino (Dora, "the rabbit"); Brian Ayres (District Attorney); Daniele Angius (Giacomo as a child); Robert Camero (Marco); Luca Fagioli (Vincenzo de Fabritiis); Daniela Fazzolari (Maria Luisa); Aldo Delaude (Train conductor); John Pedefferi (Police officer); Francesco Benedetto (Porter); Renato Liprandi (Stationmaster); Elisabetta Rocchetti (Waitress); Rossella Lucà (Mara, "the swan"); Antonio Sarasso, Piero Marcelli (Coroners); Giuseppe Minutillo (Dwarf); Giancarlo Colia (Adolfo Farina); Francesca Vettori (Giacomo's mother)
English dubbing credits: Greg Snegoff (Giacomo)

Il cartaio (Italy)
Alternate titles: *The Card Player*
Working title: *Al buio: Il cartaio*
Production date: March 10 through May 28, 2003
Release date: January 2, 2004 (Italy); August 14, 2004 (American Cinematheque)
Filmed at: Teatri di Posa Studios, Rome, with location work in Rome, Lazio, and Venice (Italy).
Director: Dario Argento; Screenplay/Screen story: Dario Argento and Franco Ferrini; Producer: Claudio Argento and Dario Argento (Opera Film/Medusa Film); Cinematography: Benôit Debie; Camera Operator: Alessandro Bolognesi; Music Composer/Conductor: Claudio Simonetti; Editor: Walter Fasano; Assistant Editor: Maria Cristina Marra and Sarah McTeigue; Production Designer: Massimo Antonello Geleng and Marina Pinzuti Ansolini; Costume Designer: Patrizia Chericoni and Florence Emir; Assistant Director: Fabrizio Bava; Special Effects: Maurizio Corridori, Danilo Bollettini, and Franco Ragusa; Special Visual Effects: Sergio Stivaletti; Special Mechanical Effects: David Bracci; Plastics Creator: Barbara Morosetti; Dialogue: Jay Benedict and Phoebe Scholfield; Dialogue Coach: Lynn Swanson; Dubbing Director (English version): Nick Alexander
Technical specs and running time: 35mm; 1.85:1, color; 103 minutes
Cast: Stefania Rocca (Anna Mari); Liam Cunningham (John Brennan); Silvio Muccino (Remo); Claudio Santamaria (Carlo Sturni); Adalberto Maria Merli (Police Commissioner); Fiore Argento (Lucia Marini); Cosimo Fusco (Berardelli); Mia Benedetta (Francesca); Giovanni Visentin (C.I.D. Chief); Claudio Mazzenga (Mario); Conchita Puglisi (Marta); Micaela Pignatelli (Professor Terzi); Luis Molteni (Pathologist); Carlo Giuseppe Gabardini, Alessandro Mistichelli, Francesco Guzzo (Anti-Hackers); Pier Maria Cecchini (Flying squad chief); Jennifer Poli (Christine Girdler, 1st victim); Elisabetta Rocchetti (2nd victim); Irene Quagliaretta (2nd victim's friend); Vera Gemma (3rd victim); Ulisse Minervini (Alvaro); Antonio Cantafora (Vice Squad Chief Marini); Mario Opinato (Inspector Morgani); Gualtiero Scola (Crime scene investigator); Robert Madison (Gustavo); Emanuel Bevilacqua (Slot Machine Arcade Owner); Robert Dawson (Embassy employee); Adriana Fonzi Cruciani (Bunny); Carla Fonzi Cruciani (Bunny's sister); Elena Falgheri (Teacher); Michele Pellegrini (Young man); Isabella Celani (Doctor); Lynn Swanson (C.I.D. wife)
English dubbing credits: Robert Steiner (Remo)

Ti piace Hitchcock? (Italy/Spain) (TV movie)
Alternate titles: *Do You Like Hitchcock?*; *Vous aimez Hitchcock?*
Production date: July 26 through September 5, 2004
Broadcast date: August 24, 2007
Filmed at: Lumiq Studios, Turin, with location work in Turin (Italy).
Director: Dario Argento; Screenplay/Screen story: Dario Argento and Franco Ferrini; Producer: Carlo Bixio, Joan Antoni González, Fabrizio Zappi, Claudio Argento, and Miguel Ángel González (Opera Film/Genesis Motion Pictures/RaiTrade/Televisió de Catalunya/Institut del Cinema Català/Film Commission Torino-Piemonte); Cinematography: Frederic Fasano; Camera Operator: Giovanni Gebbia; Music Composer/Conductor: Pino Donaggio; Editor: Walter Fasano; Assistant Editor: Claudio Misantoni and Irma Misantoni; Production Designer: Francesca Bocca and Valentina Ferroni; Costume Designer: Fabio Angelotti; Assistant Director: Leopoldo Pescatore; Special Visual Effects: Sergio Stivaletti; Dialogue Coach: Lynn Swanson; Dubbing Director (English version): John Ireland
Technical specs and running time: 35mm; 16x9 TV, color; 93 minutes
Cast: Elio Germano (Giulio); Chiara Conti (Federica Lalli); Elisabetta Rocchetti (Sasha Zerboni); Cristina Brondo (Arianna); Iván Morales (Andrea); Edoardo Stoppa (Inspector); Elena Maria Bellini (Rosanna, Giulio's mother); Horacio José Grigatis (Rosanna's fiancé); Giuseppe Lo Console (Federica's boss); Milvia Marigliano (Sasha's mother); Giampiero Perone (Alvaro); Antonio Mazzara (Cleaning man); Anna Varello (Cleaning lady); Carla Gambino (Barbona); Lorenzo Federici (Giulio as a boy); Alessandra Magri, Emanuela Cuglia (Witches); Lynn Swanson (Chiropodist); Nicola Rondolino (Priest)

Jenifer (U.S.A./Canada) (*Masters of Horror* TV series)
Production date: May 2005
Broadcast date: November 18, 2005
Filmed on location in Vancouver (Canada).
Director: Dario Argento; Screenplay: Steven Weber; Based on a story by Bruce Jones; Producer: Mick Garris, Keith Addis, Morris Berger, Steve Brown, Ben Browning, Andrew Deane, Adam Goldworm, John W. Hyde, Lisa Richardson, Tom Rowe, and Pascal Verschooris (IDT Entertainment/Nice Guy Productions/Industry Entertainment/Province of British Columbia Production Services Tax Credit/Reunion Pictures); Cinematography: Attila Szalay; Camera Operator: Bradley S. Creasser and Richard Wilson; Music Composer/Conductor: Claudio Simonetti; Editor: Marshall Harvey; Assistant Editor: David Reale; Production Designer: David Fischer; Costume Designer: Lyn Kelly; Assistant Director: Trevor Ralph; Special Make-up Effects: Howard Berger and Gregory Nicotero (KNB EFX Group); Special Effects Coordinator: Wayne Szybunka; Visual Effects Producer: Lisa Sepp-Wilson (Anthem Visual Effects); Visual Effects Supervisor: Lee Wilson and Sébastien Bergeron (Anthem Visual Effects)
Technical specs and running time: 35mm; 16x9 TV, color; 58 minutes
Cast: Steven Weber (Frank Spivey); Carrie Anne Fleming (Jenifer); Brenda James (Ruby); Harris Allan (Pete); Beau Starr (Chief Charlie); Laurie Brunetti (Spacey); Kevin Crofton (Homeless man); Julia Arkos (Ann Wilkerson); Jasmine Chan (Amy); Matt Garlick (Institute guard); Mark Archeson (Sideshow owner); Cynthia Garris (Rose); Jeffrey Ballard (Young Jack); Brad Mooney (1st friend); Riley Ruckman (2nd friend); Jano Fransden (Hunter)

Pelts (U.S.A./Canada) (*Masters of Horror* TV series)
Production date: April 2006
Broadcast date: December 1, 2006
Filmed on location in Vancouver (Canada).
Director: Dario Argento; Screenplay: Matt Venne; Based on a story by F. Paul Wilson; Producer: Mick Garris, Keith Addis, Morris Berger, Steve Best, Steve Brown, Ben Browning, Andrew Deane, Adam Goldworm, John W. Hyde, Lisa Richardson, Tom Rowe, and Pascal Verschooris (Starz!/Nice Guy Productions/Industry Entertainment/IDT Entertainment); Cinematography: Attila Szalay; Camera Operator: Peter Wilkie and Richard Wilson; Music Composer/Conductor: Claudio Simonetti; Editor: Jacqueline Cambas; Assistant Editor: Nathan Atkins and Edo Brizio; Assistant Director: Ian Samoil; Production Designer: David Fischer; Costume Designer: Lyn Kelly; Special Make-up Effects: Howard Berger and Gregory Nicotero (KNB EFX Group); Special Effects Coordinator: Wayne Szybunka; Digital Effects Producer: Lisa Sepp-Wilson (Anthem Visual Effects); Visual Effects Supervisor: Lee Wilson and Sébastien Bergeron (Anthem Visual Effects)
Technical specs and running time: 35mm; 16x9 TV, color; 58 minutes
Cast: Meat Loaf Aday (Jake Feldman); Ellen Ewusie (Shanna); John Saxon (Jeb 'Pa' Jameson); Michal Suchánek (Larry Jameson); Link Baker (Lou Chinaski); Brenda McDonald (Mother Mayter); Emilio Salituro (Sergio); Elise Lew (Sue Chin Yao); Shawn Hall (Bouncer); Sylvesta Stuart (Beefy bouncer); Melissa Gonzalez (Mira); Darren E. Scott (Agent); Chuck Duffy (Detective); Kelvin Lum (Cop); Angela Case (Dancer in hallway); Idiko Ferenczi (Attractive woman); Angela Fong, Ashley Laventure (Dancers)

La terza madre (Italy/U.S.A.)
Alternate titles: *Mother of Tears*; *Mother of Tears—La troisième mère*; *La madre del mal*
Production date: October 30 through December 17, 2006
Release date: October 31, 2007 (Italy); June 6, 2008 (U.S.A.); April 25, 2009 (Japan)
Filmed at: Cinecittà Umbria Studios, Terni, with location work in Rome, Turin, and Terni (Italy).
Director: Dario Argento; Screenplay: Dario Argento, Jace Anderson, and Adam Gierasch [The Italian credits also list editor Walter Fasano and Simona Simonetti, the sister of Claudio Simonetti, but this was purely for quota purposes]; Producer: Dario Argento, Claudio Argento, Giulia Marletta, Tommaso Calevi, Kirk D'Amico, and Lee Wilson (Medusa Film/Opera Film/Myriad Pictures/Sky Cinema/Film Commission Torini-Piemonte); Cinematography: Frederic Fasano; Camera Operator: Giovanni Gebbia; Music Composer/Conductor: Claudio Simonetti; Additional Music: "Mater Lacrimarum," music by Claudio Simonetti, vocals by Dani Filth, performed by Daemonia (Claudio Simonetti/Bruno Previtali/Federico Amorosi/Titta Tani); Editor: Walter Fasano; Assistant Editor: Sarah McTeigue; Assistant Director: Leopoldo Pescatore; Second Unit Director: Nicola Rondolino; Production Designer: Francesca Bocca and Valentina Ferroni; Costume Designer: Ludovica Amati; Special Visual Effects: Sergio Stivaletti; Visual Effects Producer: Lisa Sepp-Wilson (Anthem Visual Effects); Special Visual Effects Supervisor: Lee Wilson and Sébastien Bergeron (Anthem Visual Effects); Prosthetic Make-up Artist: Carlo Diamantini; Dialogue Coach: Lynn Swanson
Technical specs and running time: 35mm; Super 35; 2.35:1, color; 102 minutes
Cast: Asia Argento (Sarah Mandy); Cristian Solimeno (Detective Enzo Marchi); Adam James (Michael Pierce); Moran Atias (Mater Lachrymarum); Valéria Cavalli (Marta Colussi); Philippe Leroy (Guglielmo De Witt); Daria Nicolodi (Elsa Mandy); Udo Kier (Father Johannes); Coralina Cataldi-Tassoni (Giselle Mares); Robert Madison (Detective Lissoni); Jun Ichikawa (Katerina); Tommaso Banfi (Father Milesi); Paolo Stella (Julian); Silvia Rubino (Elga); Clive Riche (Bald man in overcoat); Massimo Sarchielli (Hobo); Barbara Mautino (Valeria); Gisella Marengo (1st catacombs witch); Marica Coco (2nd catacombs witch); Diego Bottiglieri (Indian); Franco Leo (Monsignor Brusca); Claudio Fadda (1st demon); Roberto Donati (2nd demon); Gianni Gatta (3rd demon); Luca Pescatore (Paul Pierce); Alessandro Zeme (Luigi); Antonio Pescatore (Plainclothes Detective); Stefano Fregni (Taxi driver); Simonetta Solder (Young mother); James Kelly Caldwell (TV announcer); Simone Sitta (Witch guide); Daniela Fazzolari, Alessandra Magrini, Camila Gallo, Maria Biondini, Federica Botto, Serena Brusa, Eleanora Marcucci, Eleanora Misti, Rebecca Perlati, Ivana Zimbaro, Araba Dell'Utri (Witches)

Giallo (Italy/U.S.A.)
Alternate titles: *Giallo/Argento*
Production date: May 12 through June 19, 2008
Release date: With the exception of various festival screenings, the film went straight to video.
Filmed on location in Turin (Italy).
Director: Dario Argento; Screenplay: Jim Agnew, Sean Keller, and Dario Argento; Producer: Claudio Argento, Donald A. Barton, Adrien Brody, Tommaso Calevi, Aitana de Val, Luis de Val, Billy Dietrich, Patricia Eberle, Oscar Generale, Nesim Hason, John S. Hicks, Lisa Lambert, Martin McCourt, David Milner, Simona Politi, Rafael Primorac, and Richard Rionda Del Castro (Hannibal Pictures/Giallo Production/Opera Films/Footprint Investment Fund/Media Films); Cinematography: Frederic Fasano; Camera Operator: Gianni Aldi; Music Composer/Conductor: Marco Werba; Editor: Roberto Silvi; Additional Editing: Edo Brizio; Assistant Director: Fabrizio ('Roy') Bava; Second Unit Director: Jim Agnew; Production Designer: Davide Bassan; Costume Designer: Stefania Svizzeretto; Special Make-up Effects: Sergio Stivaletti; Special Visual Effects: Chris Ervin (VdlocityApe FX); Dialogue Coach for Emmanuelle Seigner: Gail de Courcy-Ireland; Dubbing Director (Italian version): Jessica Loddo
Technical specs and running time: 35mm; 1.85:1, color; 92 minutes
Cast: Adrien Brody (Inspector Enzo Avolfi/Giallo [as Byron Deidra]); Emmanuelle Seigner (Linda); Elsa Pataky (Celine); Robert Miano

(Inspector Mori); Valentina Izumi (Keiko); Sato Oi (Midori); Luis Molteni (Sal); Taiyo Yamanouchi (Toshi); Daniela Fazzolari (Sophia, Enzo's mother); Nicolò Morselli (Young Enzo); Giuseppe Lo Console (Butcher); Anna Varello (Butcher's wife); Franco Vercelli (Cabbie); Lorenzo Pedrotti (Delivery boy); Farhad Re (Designer); Barbara Mautino (Nurse); Silvia Spross (Russian woman); Cesare Scova (Shopkeeper); Lynn Swanson (Tour guide); Massimo Franceschi (Coroner); Andrea Redavid (1st officer); Alberto Onofrietti (2nd officer); Lorenzo Iacona (Investigator); Giancarlo Judica Cordiglia (Desk Sergeant); Salvatore Rizzo (Security Guard)

Dracula di Dario Argento (Italy/France/Spain)
Alternate titles: *Dario Argento's Dracula*
Production date: May 30 through late July 2011
Release date: November 22, 2012 (Italy); October 4, 2013 (U.S.A.); November 27, 2013 (France); March 8, 2014 (Japan)
Filmed on location in Candello, Ivrea, and Birella (Italy).
Director: Dario Argento; Screenplay: Dario Argento, Enrique Cerezo, Stefano Piani, and Antonio Tentori; Based on: *Dracula*, by Bram Stoker; Producer: Enrique Cerezo, Roberto Di Girolomo, and Giovanni Paolucci (Enrique Cerezo Producciones Cinematográficas S.A./Film Export Group/Les Films de l'Astre); Cinematography: Luciano Tovoli; Camera Operator: Roberto Marsigli; Music Composer/Conductor: Claudio Simonetti; Additional Music: "Kiss Me Dracula," music by Claudio Simonetti, lyrics and vocals by Silvia Specchio; Editor: Marshall Harvey and Daniele Campelli; Assistant Director: Leopoldo Pescatore; Production Designer: Claudio Cosentino; Costume Designer: Monica Celeste; Visual Effects and Stereoscopic Supervisor: John Attard; Visual Effects: Rebel Alliance International, Video Masterwork Films and Film Maker; Visual Effects and On-Set Supervisor: Raffaele Apuzzo; Prosthetic Make-up Effects: Apocalypsis; Special Effects Designer and Supervsior: Sergio Stivaletti
Technical specs and running time: Digital; 2.35:1 (Non-anamorphic), Dual strip 3D, ARRIRAW (source format)/Digital Intermediate (master format), color; 110 minutes.
Cast: Thomas Kretschmann (Dracula); Rutger Hauer (Van Helsing); Marta Gastini (Mina Harker); Asia Argento (Lucy Kisslinger); Unax Ugalde (Jonathan Harker); Miriam Giovanelli (Tanja); Maria Cristina Heller (Jarmila); Giovanni Franzoni (Renfield); Augusto Zucchi (Andrej Kisslinger); Christian Burruano (Milos); Giuseppe Lo Console (Zoran); Riccardo Cicogna (Janek); Franco Guido Ravera (Priest); Francesco Rossini (Lieutenant Delbruck); Eugenio Allegri (Innkeeper); Nicola Baldoni (Smith); Alma Noce (Marika); Luca Fonte (1st soldier); Marco Mancia (2nd soldier); Tonio Pandolfo (Station master); Simona Romagnoli (Innkeeper's wife); Piero Passatore (Van Helsing's assistant)

Miscellaneous directing projects:
Jennifer (Music video)
Director: Dario Argento. Starring Jennifer Connelly, Elena Pompei, and Claudio Simonetti. Cinematography: Romano Albani. Editor: Piero Bozza. Assistant Editor: Roberto Priori.

Trussardi Action (Fashion show)
Staged by Dario Argento at Castello Sforzesco in Piazza del Cannone, Milan, on March 9, 1986.

Fiat Croma (TV commercial)
Filmed in Australia in 1987. Director of Photography: Ronnie Taylor. Running time: 30 seconds.

Glade Pyramid (TV commercial)
Filmed in U.S.A. in 1992. Running time: 30 seconds.

Verdi: Macbeth (Opera by Giuseppe Verdi)
Based on *Macbeth* by William Shakespeare
Staged by Dario Argento at Teatro Coccia in Novara, Piedmont, in October of 2013.

Lucia di Lammermoor (Opera by Gaetano Donizetti)
Based on *The Bride of Lammermoor* by Sir Walter Scott
Staged by Dario Argento at the Teatro Carlo Felice in Genoa, in March of 2015.

Salomè (Opera by Giuseppe Magrino)
Based on *Salome* by Oscar Wilde
Staged by Dario Argento at Basilica Superiore di San Franesco in Assisi, Umbria, in October of 2017.

Mooted directing/producing projects:
Montesa 1970 Written by Dario Argento and Dardano Sacchetti.

Frankenstein 1973 Written by Dario Argento and Luigi Cozzi.

Oltre la morte 1980 Written by Dario Argento.

Three Mothers project 1984 Written by Dario Argento and Daria Nicolodi.

Rigoletto 1985 Opera staged by Dario Argento; it was cancelled after extensive preparation.

Undici 1988 Written by Dario Argento and Franco Ferrini.

Untitled Spaghetti Western 1993.

The Bird with the Crystal Plumage 1993 (Remake).

Dario Argento: Sei delitti, sei città 1993 (TV series) Argento would have produced the series and directed an episode, along with Lamberto Bava, Michele Soavi, and Luigi Cozzi.

The Golem 1993 Produced by Dario Argento. Written by Franco Ferrini.

The Mummy 1994/95 Produced by Dario Argento. Directed by Lucio Fulci. Written by Dario Argento, Lucio Fulci, and Dardano Sacchetti.

NP: North Point 1995 Adaptation of the novel written by Mahoko ('Banana') Yoshimoto. Japanese co-production.

Occhiali neri [*Black Sunglasses*] 2001 Written by Dario Argento and Franco Ferrini. (Though as noted in the text, Argento is attempting to finally move forward with this project as of the summer of 2019.)

Trapped Ashes (segment "My Twin, the Worm") Argento dropped out and the segment was directed instead by John Gaeta.

The Sandman 2014 Written by David Tully.

Videography: The Films
Compiled by Bryan Martinez

The following videography is not intended to be definitive. The releases cited were compiled with U.S./U.K. versions in mind. Other releases are indicated as "Imports" (Germany, France, Japan, Australia, etc.). The various bootleg and public domain editions have not been included. The (highly subjective) notations about the best available editions were provided by Troy Howarth; they are intended to help guide fans through the maze of multiple editions available on some of the more popular titles. Films without a particular "stand out" release are not given any such notation.

Qualcuno ha tradito [Every Man is My Enemy]
No official English-friendly release.

Oggi a me ... domani a te! [Today We Kill, Tomorrow We Die!]
VHS
    Imports only
DVD
    2002 VCI
Blu-ray
    Imports only

Comandamenti per un gangster
No official English-friendly release.

Commandos
VHS
    1985 Prism Home Video
    1989 Interglobal Home Video
    1989 MSD Video LTD
DVD
    2002 Passion Productions
    2004 Digiview Productions
    2018 AFA Entertainment LLC

La rivoluzione sessuale [The Sexual Revolution]
No official English-friendly release.

C'era una volt il West [Once Upon a Time in the West]
VHS
    1997 Paramount
Laserdisc
    1994 Paramount
DVD
    2003/2010 Paramount
Blu-ray
    2011/2017 Paramount
Note: The 2011/2017 Paramount Blu-ray remains the best edition.

Une corde, un colt... [Cemetery Without Crosses]
VHS
    1982 Techno Video
DVD
    ` 2015 Arrow Video
Blu-ray
    2015 Arrow Video
Note: The 2015 Arrow Video Blu-ray remains the best edition.

La legione dei dannati [Battle of the Commandos]
VHS
    1991 Republic Entertainment

Un esercito di 5 uomini [The Five Man Army]
DVD
    2012 Warner Archive

Probabilità zero
DVD
    2017 Code Red

La stagione dei sensi [Season of the Senses]
No official English-friendly release.

Metti, una sera a cena [The Love Circle]
No official English-friendly release.

L'uccello dalle piume di cristallo [The Bird with the Crystal Plumage]
VHS
    1986 United Home Video
    1986/1998 (re-release) VCI
DVD
    1999 VCI
    2005 Blue Underground
    2011 Arrow Video (Reformatted by Vittorio Storaro to 2:1 aspect ratio)
    2018 Arrow Video
Blu-ray
    2009 Blue Underground
    2013 VCI
    2017 Arrow Video (Limited Edition Blu-ray/DVD combo)
    2018 Arrow Video (Standard Edition)
Note: The 2017/2018 Arrow Video Blu-ray remains the best edition.

Il gatto a nove code [The Cat O'Nine Tails]
VHS
    1980s Hollywood Select
    1980s Simitar Entertainment
    1990 Summit International
DVD
    2001 Starz/Anchor Bay
    2004 Miracle Pictures
    2007 Blue Underground
Blu-ray
    2013 Arrow Video
    2011 Blue Underground
    2015 Blue Underground (Identical to the 2011 release, included as part of the three film "Dario Argento Collection")
    2018 Arrow Video (Limited and Standard Edition Blu-ray/DVD combo)
Note: The 2018 Arrow Video Blu-ray remains the best edition.

4 mosche di velluto grigio [Four Flies on Grey Velvet]
VHS
    1982 Silver Star
    1980s Virtual Assassin
DVD
    2009 Mya Communication/Ryko
    2012 Shameless Entertainment
Blu-ray
    2012 Shameless Entertainment

Note: *The Koch Media Blu-ray/DVD combo (Germany, 2012) remains the best edition.*

La porta sul buio [Door Into Darkness]
DVD
- 2009 Mya Communication

Le cinque giornate
No official English-friendly release.

Profondo rosso [Deep Red]
VHS
- 1984 HBO Home Video
- 1990s Redemption
- 2000 Starz/Anchor Bay

Laserdisc
- Imports only

DVD
- 2000 Starz/Anchor Bay
- 2001 Starz/Anchor Bay (Double film release with *Tenebrae* as "Dario Argento Collection, Volume 3")
- 2007 Blue Underground
- 2011 Arrow Video

Blu-ray
- 2011 Blue Underground (Includes both the director's cut and the shorter "international" export cut)
- 2015 Blue Underground (Identical to the 2011 release, included as part of the three film "Dario Argento Collection")
- 2011 Arrow Video (Includes both the director's cut and the shorter "international" export cut)
- 2016 Arrow Video (Standard Edition and Limited Edition, both remastered, includes both the director's cut and the shorter "international" export cut; U.K. release)
- 2018 Arrow Video (Standard Edition and Limited Edition, both remastered, includes both the director's cut and the shorter "international" export cut; U.S. release)

Note: *The 2016/2018 Arrow Video Blu-ray remains the best edition.*

Suspiria
VHS
- 1988 Magnum Entertainment
- 1990s Entertainment In Video
- 1998 Fox Lorber

Laserdisc
- 1989 Magnum/Image Entertainment
- Multiple imports

DVD
- 2001 Starz/Anchor Bay
- 2007 Blue Underground

Blu-ray
- 2012 Nouveaux
- 2018 Umbrella Entertainment
- 2017 Synapse Films (Limited Steelbook Edition)
- 2018 Synapse Films (Standard Edition)
- 2019 Cult Films

Note: *The 2017/2018 Synapse Films Blu-ray remains the best edition.*

Dawn of the Dead [Zombi]
Beta
- 1978 Thorn EMI Video

VHS
- 1983/1996 Thorn EMI Video
- 1987 HBO/Cannon Video
- 1989 HBO/Weintraub
- 1992 Republic Video
- 1996/1999 Starz/Anchor Bay

Laserdisc
- 1989 Image Entertainment
- 1993 Republic Pictures Home Video
- 1996 Elite Entertainment (Standard Edition and Collector's Edition of the Cannes Edit)

DVD
- 1997 Starz/Anchor Bay (Cannes Edit)
- 1999 Starz/Anchor Bay (20th Anniversary Special Extended 'Hybrid' Edit)
- 2004 Starz/Anchor Bay (Director's Cut)
- 2004 Starz/Anchor Bay (Ultimate Edition, includes all three official edits of the film)
- 2010 Arrow Video (Includes all three official edits of the film)
- Multiple imports

Blu-ray
- 2007 Starz/Anchor Bay (Director's cut)
- 2010 Arrow Video (Includes all three official edits of the film)
- 2020 Second Sight (Includes all three official edits of the film)

Note: *The 2004 Starz/Anchor Bay Ultimate Edition box set, the 2017 Midnight Factory/Koch Media Blu-ray set (Italy, 2017), and the 2020 Second Sight Blu-ray remain the best editions. All three of these editions contain the three official edits of the film; the Midnight Factory/Koch Media set includes a 4K edition of the Argento edit.*

Inferno
VHS
- 1985 Key Video
- 1999 CBS Fox Home Media
- 2000 Starz/Anchor Bay

Laserdisc
- 1983 CBS/FOX Video

DVD
- 2000 Starz/Anchor Bay
- 2001 Starz/Anchor Bay (Identical to the 2000 release, included with *Phenomena* as "Dario Argento Collection, Volume 1")
- 2007 Blue Underground
- 2010 Arrow Video
- 2011 Blue Underground

Blu-ray
- 2010 Arrow Video
- 2011 Blue Underground
- 2015 Blue Underground (Identical to the 2011 release, included as part of the three film "Dario Argento Collection")
- 2013 Arrow Video
- 2014 Arrow Video (Steelbook Edition)

Note: The 2011/2015 Blue Underground edition and the Camera Obscura/Koch Media Blu-ray/DVD combo (Germany, 2012) remain the best editions.

Tenebre [Tenebrae]
VHS
    1987 Fox Hills Video (Released as *Unsane*)
    1999 Starz/Anchor Bay
Laserdisc
    1998 The Roan Group
DVD
    1999 Starz/Anchor Bay
    2001 Starz/Anchor Bay (Single disc release, as well as double film release with *Deep Red* as "Dario Argento Collection, Volume 3")
    2008 Starz/Anchor Bay (Included as part of the five film "Dario Argento Collection" steelbook release)
    2011 Arrow Video
Blu-ray
    2011 Arrow Video
    2013 Arrow Video (Steelbook Edition)
    2015 Arrow Video (Standard Edition)
    2016 Synapse Films (Lmited Edition Steelbook Blu-ray/DVD combo and Standard Edition)

Note: The 2013/2015 Arrow Video and 2016 Synapse Films Blu-ray remain the best editions.

Phenomena [Creepers]
VHS
    1985 Media Home Entertainment (Released as *Creepers*)
    1996 Palace Premiere (Released as *Creepers*)
    1999 Starz/Anchor Bay
Laserdisc
    1998 The Roan Group
DVD
    2005 Legacy Entertainment
    1999 Starz/Anchor Bay
    2001 Starz/Anchor Bay (Identical to the 1999 release, included with *Inferno* as "Dario Argento Collection, Volume 1")
    2008 Starz/Anchor Bay (Single disc edition, or as part of the five film "Dario Argento Collection" steelbook release)
    2011 Arrow Video
    2017 Synapse Films
    2018 Arrow Video
Blu-ray
    2011 Arrow Video
    2017 Arrow Video (Limited Edition, includes both *Phenomena* and *Creepers*)
    2018 Arrow Video (Standard Edition, includes both *Phenomena* and *Creepers*)
    2016 Synapse Films (Limited Edition Steelbook, includes both *Phenomena* and *Creepers*)
    2017 Synapse Films (Standard Edition, includes both *Phenomena* and *Creepers*)

Note: The 2016/2017 Synapse Films and 2017/2018 Arrow Video Blu-rays remain the best editions.

Dèmoni [Demons]
VHS
    1986 New World Video
    1991 StarMaker Entertainment Inc
    1999 Starz/Anchor Bay
Laserdisc
    1998 The Roan Group
DVD
    1999 Starz/Anchor Bay
    2001 Starz/Anchor Bay (Identical to the 1999 release, included with *Demons 2* as "Dario Argento Collection, Volume 2")
    2007 Ascot Films
    2012 Arrow Films
    2014 Synapse Films
Blu-ray
    2012 Arrow Films (Standard Edition and Limited Edition Steelbook, included with *Demons 2*)
    2013 Synapse Films (Limited Edition Steelbook)
    2014 Synapse Films (Standard Edition)

Note: The 2013/2014 Synapse Films Blu-ray remains the best edition.

Dèmoni 2 [Demons 2]
VHS
    1988 Imperial Entertainment Corp.
    1999 Starz/Anchor Bay
Laserdisc
    1998 The Roan Group
DVD
    1999 Starz/Anchor Bay
    2001 Starz/Anchor Bay (Identical to the 1999 release, included with *Demons* as "Dario Argento Collection, Volume 2")
    2012 Arrow Films
    2014 Synapse Films
Blu-ray
    2012 Arrow Films (Standard Edition and Limited Edition Steelbook, included with *Demons*)
    2013 Synapse Films (Limited Edition Steelbook)
    2014 Synapse Films (Standard Edition)

Note: The 2013/2014 Synapse Films Blu-ray remains the best edition.

Opera
VHS
    1988 First Release Home Entertainment
    1991 South Gate Entertainment
DVD
    2001 Starz/Anchor Bay
    2007 Blue Underground
    2010 Arrow Video (Includes the director's cut and the shortened U.S. edit)
    2012 Arrow Video (As part of the box set "Dario Argento: The Neo Giallo Collection")
Blu-ray
    2018 Scorpion Releasing (Standard Edition)
    2019 Scorpion Releasing (Deluxe Edition, includes 2.35 and 1.78 aspect ratios, Cannes and International English dubs, and the director's cut and the shortened U.S. edit)
    2019 Cult Films

Note: The 2019 Scorpion Releasing Blu-ray and the 2019 Cult Films Blu-ray/DVD combo remain the best editions.

Gli incubi di Dario Argento (Giallo: la tua impronta del venerdi)
No official English-friendly release.

La Chiesa [The Church]
VHS
    1991 South Gate Entertainment
DVD
    1999 Starz/Anchor Bay
Blu-ray
    2017 Shameless Entertainment
    2018 Scorpion Releasing (Standard and Limited Special Edition)
Note: The 2018 Scorpion Releasing Blu-Ray remains the best edition.

Due occhi diabolici [Two Evil Eyes]
VHS
    1993 Video Treasures
DVD
    2010 Arrow Video
Blu-ray
    2016 Blue Underground
    2019 Blue Underground (Remastered Special Edition Blu-ray/DVD combo)
Note: The 2019 Blue Underground Blu-ray/DVD combo remains the best edition.

La setta [The Sect]
VHS/Laserdisc
    1991 Republic Pictures (Released as *The Devil's Daughter*)
DVD
    2016 Shameless Entertainment
Blu-ray
    2016 Shameless Entertainment
    2018 Scorpion Releasing (Standard Edition and Limited Special Edition)
Note: The 2018 Scorpion Releasing Blu-ray and the Koch Media Blu-ray/DVD combo (Germany, 2016) remain the best editions.

Trauma
VHS
    1993 World Vision Home Video, Inc.
DVD
    2002 Tartan Video
    2005 Starz/Anchor Bay
    2008 Starz/Anchor Bay (As part of the five film "Dario Argento Collection" steelbook release)
Blu-ray
    Imports only

La sindrome di Stendhal [The Stendhal Syndrome]
VHS
    1999 Troma Team Video
DVD
    1999 Troma Team Video
    2007 Blue Underground
    2010 Arrow Video
    2012 Arrow Video (As part of the box set "Dario Argento: The Neo Giallo Collection")
Blu-ray
    2016 Blue Underground
    2018 Blue Underground (Remastered Special Edition Blu-ray/DVD combo)
Note: The 2018 Blue Underground Blu-ray/DVD combo remains the best edition.

La maschera di cera [Wax Mask]
VHS
    2000 Image Entertainment
Multiple imports
DVD
    2000 Image Entertainment
Blu-ray
    2017 CAV Distributing
    2019 Severin Films
Note: The Severin Blu-ray remains the best edition.

Il fantasma dell'opera [The Phantom of the Opera]
VHS
    2000 Unapix
DVD
    1999 Allumination
Blu-ray
    2020 Scorpion Releasing
Note: The Scorpion Releasing Blu-ray remains the best edition.

Scarlet Diva
DVD
    2002 Shriek Show
Blu-ray
    2018 Film Movement Classics

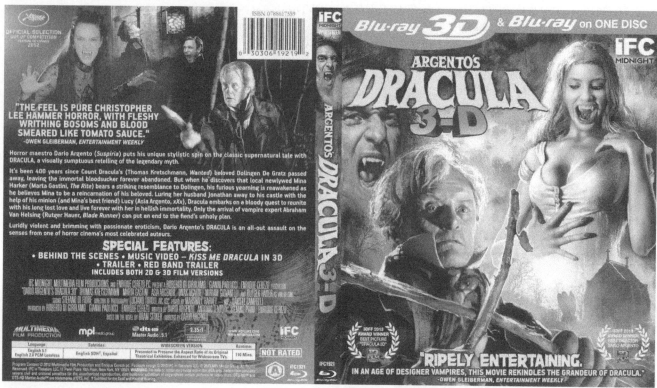

Nonhosonno [Sleepless]
VHS
    2001 Artisan
DVD
    2001 Artisan
    2009 Arrow Video
    2012 Arrow Video (As part of the box set "Dario Argento: The Neo Giallo Collection")
Blu-ray
    2020 Scorpion Releasing

Note: The Scorpion Releasing Blu-ray remains the best edition.

Il cartaio [The Card Player]
DVD
    2005 Starz/Anchor Bay
    2008 Starz/Anchor Bay (As part of the five film "Dario Argento Collection" steelbook release)
    2004/2010 Arrow Video
    2012 Arrow Video (As part of the box set "Dario Argento: The Neo Giallo Collection")
Blu-ray
    2019 Scorpion Releasing

Note: The Scorpion Releasing Blu-ray remains the best edition.

Ti piace Hitchcock? [Do You Like Hitchcock?]
DVD
    2006 Starz/Anchor Bay
    2008 Starz/Anchor Bay (As part of the five film "Dario Argento Collection" steelbook release)
Blu-ray
    Imports only

Masters of Horror [Jenifer/Pelts]
DVD
    2007 Starz/Anchor Bay (Season 1, Vol. 2: *Jenifer*)
    2007 Starz/Anchor Bay (*Pelts*)
Blu-ray
    2007 Starz/Anchor Bay (Season 1, Vol. 2: *Jenifer*)

La terza madre [Mother of Tears]
DVD
    2008 Dimension Extreme
    2008 StudioCanal
Blu-ray
    Imports only

Giallo
DVD
    2010 Maya Home Entertainment
Blu-ray
    Imports only

Dracula di Dario Argento [Dario Argento's Dracula]
DVD
    2014 MPI/IFC Home Video
    2014 Spirit Entertainment
Blu-ray
    2014 MPI/IFC Home Video

Bryan Martinez is a Chicago-based filmmaker and a passionate fan of Italian cult cinema—and of Dario Argento, in particular. His short films, including Gelato Giallo *(2015) and* My Friend Lisa *(2017), are openly indebted to Dario Argento. Bryan's passion for* giallo *cinema led him to create* The Giallo Room *show, which comes as highly recommended.*

Discography: The Soundtracks
Compiled by Jimmie Gonzalez

This discography is not intended to be comprehensive, but it should hopefully provide guidance with regards to most of the significant soundtrack releases; many of these are out of print and command high prices—shop wisely! These releases encompass all the films directed, written and/or produced by Dario Argento; it does not include the films he has appeared in as an actor.

A note on formatting: under label/release info, the individual releases are broken down by label name/ country/ format /year of release.

Qualcuno ha tradito [*Every Man is My Enemy*]
Theatrical release date: 1967
Composer: Piero Piccioni
Original label: Avanz/ Japan/ CD/ 1997
Note: To date, there has not been an official soundtrack release. However, tracks from the score show up on the compilations "Splendido al Piccioni" (Avanz/ Japan/ CD/ 1995) and "Splendido il Piccioni Vol. 2" (Avanz/ Japan/ CD/ 1997).

Oggi a me... domani a te! [*Today We Kill, Tomorrow We Die!*]
Theatrical release date: 1968
Composer: Angelo Francesco Lavagnino
Label/release info: EVB/ France/ LP/ 1988; EVB/ France/ CD/ 1988; Digitmovies/Italy/ CD/ 2009
Note: A remastered version of the title theme is available on the limited edition blue vinyl compilation, "Bud Spenser di musica" (Sugar/ Italy/ LP/ 2017)

Comandamenti per un gangster
Theatrical release date: 1968
Composer: Ennio Morricone
Label/release info: Cam/Italy/ LP/ 1968; CAM/ Italy/ CD/ 1992; GDM/ Italy/ CD/ 2011; Dagored/ Italy/ LP/ 2015 (Limited edition on grey with red splatter vinyl)
Note: The GDM release from 2011 is the most complete. Selections from the score have also been included in such compilations as "Ennio Morricone: Gangster Movies" (The Ultimate CD/ Italy/ CD/ 2010).

Commandos
Theatrical release date: 1968
Composer: Mario Nascimbene
Label/release info: Cinevox/Italy/ LP/ 1968

La rivoluzione sessuale [*The Sexual Revolution*]
Theatrical release date: 1968
Composer: Teo Usuelli
Label/release info: Beat Records/ Italy/ CD/ 2018

C'era una volt il West [*Once Upon a Time in the West*]
Theatrical release date: 1968
Composer: Ennio Morricone
Label/release info: RCA Original Cast/ Italy/ 7"/ 1968; RCA/ France/ LP/ 1969; RCA/ Italy/ 45 RPM/ 1969; RCA/ France/ 45 RPM/ 1969; RCA/ Italy/ LP/ 1970; Duse/ Italy/ 45 RMP/ 1970; Ariola/ Germany/ 45 RPM/ 1971; RCA/ Italy/ LP/ 1971; RCA/ U.S./ LP/ 1972; RCA/ Netherlands/ LP/ 1973; RCA/ Japan/ LP/ 1974; RCA/ France/ LP/ 1981; RCA/ U.S./ CD/ 1989; BMG/ France/ CD/ 1989; BMG/ Japan/ CD/ 1994; RCA/ Italy/ CD/ 1999; RCA/ France/ CD/ 2003; GDM/ Italy/ CD/ 2005; GDM/ Italy/ LP/ 2014
Note: Selections from the score have also been included in a variety of compilations, including "The Ennio Morricone Chronicles" (BMG/ Japan/ CD/ 2000), "Ennio Morricone Anthology" (BMG/ U.S./ CD/ 1995), "A Fistful of Sounds" (Camden/ U.K./ CD/ 1999), and "Ennio Morricone—The Complete Collection" (GDM/ Italy/ CD/ 2008).

Une corde, un colt... [*Cemetery Without Crosses*]
Theatrical release date: 1969
Composer: André Hossein
Label/release info: CGD/ Italy/ LP/ 1969; Philips/ France/ LP/ 1969
Note: Selections from the score are also included in the release "Bandes Originales des Films de Robert Hossein" (Écoutez le Cinéma!/ France/ CD/ 2004).

La legione dei dannati [*Battle of the Commandos*]
Theatrical release date: 1969
Composer: Marcello Giombini and Piero Piccioni
Note: To date, there has been no soundtrack release.

Un esercito di 5 uomini [*The Five Man Army*]
Theatrical release date: 1969
Composer: Ennio Morricone
Label/release info: Ariete/ Italy/ LP/ 1969; Ariete/ Italy/ 45 RPM; 1969; Duse/ Italy/ LP/ 1977; Film Score Monthly/ U.S./ CD/ 2009; Ariete/ Italy/ LP/ 2018
Note: The 2009 release from Film Score Monthly is the most complete. The score has also been paired with selections from Morricone's score for *Blood Link* (*Extrasensorial*, 1982) on at least two occasions (Duse/ Italy/ CD/ 1994; Beat/ Italy/ CD/ 2001).

Probabilità zero
Theatrical release date: 1969
Composer: Carlo Rustichelli
Label/release info: Cinevox/ Italy/ LP/ 1969; Saimel/ Spain/ CD/ 2011 (Limited edition)

La stagione dei sensi [*Season of the Senses*]
Theatrical release date: 1969
Composer: Ennio Morricone
Label/release info: Ariete/ Italy/ LP/ 1969; Carossello/ Italy/ LP/ 1969; Halidon/ Italy/ LP/ 2009
Note: The score is also included in the release "*Teorema / La Stagione dei sensi / Vergogna schifosi*" (Fin de Siècle/ Sweden/ CD/ 2008). Tracks from the score are included in such compilations as "Edda Dell'Orso's Voice" (Bella Casa/ U.K./ CD/ 2007), "Morricone Bossa" (Cinedelic/ Italy/ CD/ 2006), "Women in Lounge" (Cinedelic/ Italy/ CD/ 2005), "Mondo Morricone" (Royal Ear Force/ Germany/ CD/ 2003), and "...A Tutto Beat" (Cinedelic/ Italy/CD/ 2002).

Metti, una sera a cena [The Love Circle]
Theatrical release date: 1969
Composer: Ennio Morricone
Label/release info: Cinevox/ Italy/ LP/ 1969; Cinevox/ Italy/ 45 RPM/ 1969; A&M/ Italy/ 45 RPM/ 1969; CBS/ U.K./ LP/ 1970; Cinevox/ Italy/ LP/ 1980; Cinevox/ Italy/ CD/ 1987; Cinevox/ Italy/ CD/ 1997; Dagored/ Italy/ LP/ 2001 (Limited edition); Cinevox/ Italy/ CD/ 2006; Cinevox/ Italy/ CD/ 2015; AMS/ Italy/ LP/ 2015 (Limited edition on blue, white, and transparent green swirl vinyl)

Note: The 2015 Cinevox release is the most complete edition. Selections from the score have been released as part of various compilations, including "Musica per film" (DFV/ Italy/ CD/ 2001), "The Sacred and the Profane" (BMG/ Italy/ CD/ 1999), "Morricone Bossa" (Cinedelic/ Italy/ CD/ 2006), and "Ennio Morricone Deluxe Edition" (Cinevox/ Italy/ CD/ 2005).

L'uccello dalle piume di cristallo [The Bird with the Crystal Plumage]
Theatrical release date: 1970
Composer: Ennio Morricone
Label/release info: Capitol/ U.S./ LP/ 1970; Cerberus/ U.S./ LP/ 1981; Cinevox/ Italy/ CD/ 1991; Cinevox/ Italy/ CD/ 1998; Cinevox/ Italy/ CD/ 2008; AMS/ Italy/ LP/ 2014; Cinevox/ Italy/ CD/ 2016

Note: The Cinevox releases from 2008 and 2016 are the most complete editions. The 1991 release from Cinevox pairs the score with selections from *Four Flies on Grey Velvet*. Selections from the score were also issued along with selections from *The Cat O'Nine Tails* and *Four Flies on Grey Velvet* for "An Ennio Morricone-Dario Argento Trilogy" (DRG/ U.S./ CD/ 1995), which also includes an audio interview with Argento. Selections from the score are also included in various compilations, including "An Ennio Morricone Anthology" (DRG/ U.S./ CD/ 1995), "Puro Vivo Argento" (Cinevox/ Italy/ CD/ 2005), and "Dario Argento" (Mediane/ Italy/ CD/ 2007). Digital versions, not available in any other format besides the 1970 Capitol Records LP can be found in the bonus materials on the 1999 VCI Entertainment DVD release of the film.

Il gatto a nove code [The Cat O'Nine Tails]
Theatrical release date: 1971
Composer: Ennio Morricone
Label/release info: General Music/ Italy/ 45 RPM/ 1971; GSF/U.S./ LP/ 1978; Point/ Italy/ CD/ 1994; Dagored/Italy/ LP/ 2000; Dagored/ Italy/ CD/ 2000; GDM/ Italy/ CD/ 2006; AMS/ Italy/ LP/ 2014

Note: The GDM release from 2006 is the most complete release. Selections from the score were also issued along with selections from *The Bird with the Crystal Plumage* and *Four Flies on Grey Velvet* for "An Ennio Morricone-Dario Argento Trilogy" (DRG/ U.S./ CD/ 1995), which also includes an audio interview with Argento. Selections from the score are also included in various compilations, including "An Ennio Morricone Anthology" (DRG/ U.S./ CD/ 1995), "Puro Vivo Argento" (Cinevox/ Italy/ CD/ 2005), and "Dario Argento" (Mediane/ Italy/ CD/ 2007).

4 mosche di velluto grigio [Four Flies on Grey Velvet]
Theatrical release date: 1971
Composer: Ennio Morricone
Label/release info: Cinevox/ Italy/ 45 RPM/ 1971; Cinevox/ Italy/ CD/ 1991; Cinevox/ Italy/ CD/ 1999; Dagored/ Italy/ LP/ 2001; Cinevox/ Italy/ CD/ 2007; AMS/ Italy/ LP/ 2013

Note: The 1991 release from Cinevox pairs the score with selections from *The Bird with the Crystal Plumage*. The 2007 Cinevox release is the most complete edition. Selections from the score were also issued along with selections from *The Bird with the Crystal Plumage* and *The Cat O'Nine Tails* for "An Ennio Morricone-Dario Argento Trilogy" (DRG/ U.S./ CD/ 1995), which also includes an audio interview with Argento. Tracks from the score have also shown up on various Argento and Morricone compilations, including "Ennio Morricone Deluxe Edition" (Cinevox/ Italy/ CD/ 2005), "Ennio Morricone—The Complete Edition" (GDM/ Italy/ CD/ 2008), "I film della violenza" (RCA/ Italy/ LP/ 1975), "Puro Vivo Argento" (Cinevox/ Italy/ CD/ 2005), and "Dario Argento" (Mediane/ Italy/ CD/ 2007).

La porta sul buio [Door into Darkness]
TV broadcast date: 1973
Composer: Giorgio Gaslini
Label/release info: Produttori Associati/ Italy/ 7"/ 1973

Note: Music from the series is included as bonus track on the Lucertola Media CD release of Gaslini's score for *Le cinque giornate*.

Le cinque giornate
Theatrical release date: 1973
Composer: Giorgio Gaslini
Label/release info: Cinevox/ Italy/ LP/ 1973; Lucertola Media/ Germany/ CD/ 1997

Note: The Lucertola Media release also includes music from *La porta sul buio* as bonus tracks.

Profondo rosso [Deep Red]
Theatrical release date: 1975
Composer: Goblin and Giorgio Gaslini
Label/release info: Cinevox/ Italy/ LP/ 1975; CNR/ Netherlands/ LP/ 1976; Cinevox/ Italy/ LP/ 1980; Cinevox/ Italy/ CD/ 1991; Nexus/ Japan/ CD/ 1995; Cinevox/ Italy/ CD/ 1996; Cinevox/ Japan/ CD/ 2000; Dagored/ Italy/ LP/ 2001; Cinevox/ Italy/ CD/2006 (double disc); Death Waltz/ U.S./ LP/ 2018 (Double disc set, one transparent orange, the other transparent purple)

Note: The 2006 double-disc Cinevox edition includes both the original 1975 soundtrack album as well as the complete film score including different takes on the familiar themes. Tracks from the soundtrack have also been released as part of various different Argento and/or horror movie tribute compilations, as well as various Goblin "greatest hits" releases. These include "The Goblin Collection 1975-1980 Vol. II" (DRG/ U.S./ CD/ 1998), "Goblin: Their Hits, Rare Tracks and Outtakes Collection" (DRG/ U.S./ CD/ 1995), "Goblin Greatest Hits" (Cinevox/ Italy/ CD/ 1987), and "The Horror Films Collection" (DRG/ U.S./ CD/ 1995). There is also a special 40th anniversary edition performed by "Claudio Simonetti's Goblin" which was issued as a limited-edition red vinyl and CD (Rustblade/ Italy/ CD&LP/ 2015). There is also a soundtrack release for the ill-fated *Profondo rosso—il musical* (Cinevox/ Italy/ CD/ 2008).

Suspiria
Theatrical release date: 1977
Composer: Goblin
Label/release info: Cinevox/ Italy/ LP/ 1977; Attic/ Canada/ LP/ 1977; Barclay/ France/ LP/ 1977; EMI/ Japan/ LP/ 1977; Cinevox/ Italy/ LP/ 1980; Cinevox/ Italy/ CD/ 1987; Cinevox/Japan/ CD/ 1993; Cinevox/ Italy/ CD/ 1997; Dagored/ Italy/ LP/ 2000; Anchor Bay/ U.S./ CD/ 2001; Cinevox/ Italy/ CD/ 2007; Rambling Records/ Japan/ CD/ 2009; Death Waltz/ U.S./ LP/ 2017 (Limited edition red, blue, and yellow vinyl variants); Cinevox/ Italy/ 2017 (Deluxe "ultra-limited peacock" box set edition on red vinyl or standard limited edition on black vinyl; both contain a bonus CD version and a DVD exploring the creation of the soundtrack); Synapse/ U.S./ CD/ 2017

Note: Tracks from the soundtrack have also been released as part of various different Argento and/or horror movie tribute compilations, as well as various Goblin "greatest hits" releases. These include "The Goblin Collection 1975-1980 Vol. II" (DRG/ U.S./ CD/ 1998), "Goblin: Their Hits, Rare Tracks and Outtakes Collection" (DRG/ U.S./ CD/ 1995), and "Goblin Greatest Hits" (Cinevox/ Italy/ CD/ 1987). The Anchor Bay CD was included as a bonus in their special limited edition DVD release of *Suspiria*. A remastered and expanded soundtrack, containing tracks not included in the original 1977 release, is also included as a bonus CD in the Synapse Films limited edition steelbook Blu-ray release of *Suspiria*.

Dawn of the Dead [*Zombi*]
Theatrical release date: 1978
Composer: Goblin
Additional composers (non-European cut): Pierre Arvay, Herbert Chappell, Roland de Cande, Even de Tissot, Gordon Grant, Don Harper, Paul Lemel, Keith Papworth, Simon Park, Derek Scott, Barry Stoller, Reg Tilsley, Jack Trombey, Walter Warren
Label/release info: Cinevox/ Italy/ LP/ 1978; Polydor/ Germany/ LP/ 1978; Varese Sarabande/ U.S./ 1979; Cinevox/ Italy/ LP/ 1980; Polydor/ France/ LP/ 1983; King Records/ Japan/ CD/ 1994; Cinevox/ Italy/ CD/ 1998; Cinevox/ Japan/ CD/ 2000; Dagored/ Italy/ LP/ 2001; Cinevox/ Italy/ CD/ 2012; Cinevox/ Italy/ CD/ 2006; Rambling Records/ Japan/ CD/ 2014; Waxwork/ U.S./ LP/ 2018 (Limited edition in grey; Limited edition in green with double CD included); Waxwork/ U.S./ CD/ 2018 (2 disc set)

Note: The CD release titled "Unreleased Incidental Music from George A. Romero's *Dawn of the Dead*" (Trunk Records/ U.K./ CD/ 2004; Trunk Records/ U.K./ LP/ 2004) includes all of the library cues used by Romero for the American release of the film; it does not contain any of the cues written by Goblin especially for the film. The Limited Edition Oxblood Red vinyl (Svart Records/ Finland/ 2018) is a Live Soundtrack Experience recorded in Helsinki on May 24th 2017 by "Claudio Simonetti's Goblin."

Inferno
Theatrical release date: 1980
Composer: Keith Emerson
Additional composers: Giuseppe Verdi ("Va, pensiero" from *Nabucco*)
Label/release info: Cinevox/ Italy/ LP/ 1980; Ariola/ German/ LP/ 1980; Barclay/ France/ LP/ 1980; Cinevox/ Italy/ CD/ 1989; Jimco/ Japan/ CD/ 1992; Cinevox/ Italy/ CD/ 1997; Cinevox/ Italy/ CD/ 2006; Waxwork/ U.S./ LP/ 2018 (Double disc expanded release)

Note: The various soundtrack releases include music written by Emerson which is not included in the finished film; it does not, however, include the recording of "Va Pensiero." The 2006 release from Cinevox and the Waxwork LP are the most complete recordings of the score available. Selections from the score have also been included in various compilations, including "Keith Emerson at the Movies" (Castle/ U.K./ CD/ 2005), "Puro Vivo Argento" (Cinevox/ Italy/ CD/ 2005), and "Dario Argento" (Mediane/ Italy/ CD/ 2007).

Tenebre [*Tenebrae*]
Theatrical release date: 1982
Composer: Claudio Simonetti, Massimo Morante, and Fabio Pignatelli
Additional composers: Kim Wilde ("Take Me Tonight") [US theatrical release only]
Label/release info: Cinevox/ Italy/ LP/ 1982; Nexus/ Japan/ LP/ 1982; That's Entertainment/ U.K./ LP/ 1983; Cinevox/ Italy/ CD/ 1996; Cinevox/ Japan/ CD/ 2000; Dagored/ Italy/ LP/ 2001; Cinevox/ Italy/ CD/ 2006; Cinevox/ Italy/ CD/ 2012; Waxwork/ U.S./ LP/2018 (Double disc "Blood Red and Straight Razor Silver")

Note: None of the releases include the Kim Wilde song; it was appended to the film by the U.S. distributor without the consent of Argento or the composers. Selections from the score have also been included on various compilations, including "Goblin The Awakening" (Bella Casa/ U.K./ CD/ 2012), "The Best of Goblin, Vol. 1" (Cinevox/ Italy/ CD/ 2000), "Puro Vivo Argento" (Cinevox/ Italy/ CD/ 2005), and "Dario Argento" (Mediane/ Italy/ CD/ 2007).

Phenomena
Theatrical release date: 1985
Composer: Goblin, Claudio Simonetti, Simon Boswell, Fabio Pignatelli, Bill Wyman & Terry Taylor
Additional composers: Iron Maiden ("Flash of the Blade"), Motörhead ("Locomotive"), Andi Sex Gang ("The Naked and the Dead," "The Quick and the Dead," and "You Don't Know Me," all written by Simon Boswell), Frankie Goes to Hollywood ("Two Tribes")
Label/release info: Cinevox/ Italy/ LP/ 1985; Enigma/ U.S./ LP/ 1985; Victor Musical Industries/ Japan/ LP/ 1985; Heavy Metal World Wide/ U.K./ LP/ 1986; Cinevox/ Italy/ CD/ 1987; SLCS/ Japan/ CD/ 1992; Cinevox/ Italy/ CD/ 1997; Cinevox/ Italy/ CD; 2007; Cinevox/ Italy/ CD/ 2012; Waxwork/ U.S./ LP/ 2018

Note: The Cinevox CD releases from 1997, 2007 and 2012 only include the instrumental pieces written for the film by

Simonetti, Pignatelli, and Goblin. The Cinevox CD from 1987 and the SLCS release from 1992 includes "Phenomena" (Simonetti), "Jennifer," "The Wind," "Sleepwalking," and "Jennifer's Friends" (Goblin), "Valley" (Wyman & Taylor), "The Maggots" (Boswell), "Flash of the Blade" (Iron Maiden), "The Quick and the Dead," "You Don't Know Me" and "The Naked and the Dead" (Andi Sex Gang), and "Locomotive" (Motörhead); the Enigma vinyl and the Heavy Metal vinyl include much the same track list, however the former also includes "Transmute" (Goblin) in place of "You Don't Know Me," while the latter includes "Follie" (Goblin). The Victor Musical Industries vinyl also includes the same play list, as well as "Transmute," "Follie" and "Cranky Sound I (Effect)" (Simonetti). Selections from the score have also been included on various compilations, including "Goblin: Their Hits, Rare Tracks and Outtakes Collection" (DRG/ U.S./ CD/ 1995), "The Best of Goblin, Vol. 1" (Cinevox/ Italy/ CD/ 2000), "Puro Vivo Argento" (Cinevox/ Italy/ CD/ 2005), and "Dario Argento" (Mediane/ Italy/ CD/ 2007).

Dèmoni [Demons]
Theatrical release date: 1985
Composer: Claudio Simonetti
Additional composers: Accept ("Fast as a Shark"), The Adventurers ("Send My Heart"), Billy Idol ("White Wedding"), Pretty Maids ("Night Danger"), Mötley Crüe ("Save Our Souls"), Saxon ("Everybody Up"), Rick Springfield ("Walking on the Edge"), Go West ("We Close Our Eyes"), Edvard Grieg ("In the Hall of the Mountain King," from *Peer Gynt*), Gioachino Rossini ("The Thieving Magpie")
Label/release info: RCA/ Italy/ LP/ 1985; Victor/ Japan/ CD/ 1986; Deep Red/ Italy/ CD/ 2003; Rustblade/ Italy/ LP/ 2015 (Limited edition blue vinyl); Rustblade/ Italy/ LP/ 2015 (Limited edition tin box with bonus CD and video clips); Rustblade/ Italy/ LP/ 2016 (Limited edition "puke green" vinyl); Rustblade/ Italy/ CD/ 2015 (includes two video clips)
Note: The Deep Red CD release includes only the Simonetti music plus re-recordings by "Simonetti Horror Project" and "Daemonia," as well as the original music video by Michele Soavi and a TV spot featuring Argento and Simonetti. The Victor release contains the Simonetti music as well as "Everybody Up" (Saxon), "Walking on the Edge" (Rick Springfield), "Night Danger" (Pretty Maids), and "Fast as a Shark" (Accept). Tracks from the score have also been released as part of various compilations, including "Evil Tracks" (RCA/ Italy/ CD/ 1991), and "Music from Dario Argento's Horror Movies" (Vivi/ Italy/ CD/ 1993). A special "remixed" version was released in 2019 through Rustblade on CD as well as a limited edition black vinyl LP.

Dèmoni 2 [Demons 2]
Theatrical release date: 1986
Composer: Simon Boswell
Additional composers: The Smiths ("Panic"), Gene Loves Jezebel ("Heartache"), The Cult ("Rain"), Fields of the Nephilim ("Power"), The Art of Noise ("Backbeat"), Peter Murphy ("Blue Heart"), Dead Can Dance ("De Profundis"), Love & Rockets ("Kundalini Express"), Pierce Turner ("How it Shone"), Caduta Massi ("Blood and Flame"), The Producers ("Live in TV")
Label/release info: Ricordi Int/ Italy/ LP/ 1986; Apollon/ Japan/ LP/ 1987; Apollon/ Japan/ CD/ 1990; Rustblade/ U.K./ CD/ 2019; Rustblade/ U.K./ LP/2019 (Limited edition red vinyl); Rustblade/ U.K./ LP/ 2019 (standard black vinyl)
Note: A cut from the score was included on the compilation "I films di Dario Argento" (Cinevox/ Italy/ CD/ 1991).

Opera
Theatrical release date: 1988
Composer: Claudio Simonetti, Bill Wyman & Terry Taylor, Simon Boswell, Brian Eno & Roger Eno
Additional composers: Steel Grave ("Knights of the Night" and "Steel Grave"), Norden Light ("No Escape"), Giuseppe Verdi ("Macbeth" and "Lady Macbeth [Vieni t'affreti]," from *Macbeth*; "Amami Alfredo" and "Sempre libera," from *La Traviata*, Giacomo Puccini ("Un bel dì vedremo" from *Madame Butterfly*), Vincenzo Bellini ("Casta Diva," from *Norma*); Pino Daniele ("Boys in the Night")
Label/release info: Cinevox/ Italy/ LP/ 1987; Cinevox/ Italy/ CD/ 1987; Cinevox/ Italy/ LP/ 1988; Cinevox/ Italy/ CD/ 1991; Anchor Bay/ U.S./ CD / 2001; Deep Red/ Italy/ CD/ 2003; Rustblade/ Italy/ LP/ 2017 (Limited edition colored vinyl); Rustblade/ Italy/ CD/ 2017
Note: The original Cinevox releases did not include any of Claudio Simonetti's pieces for the film; instead, they contained the music by Bill Wyman & Terry Taylor, Simon Boswell, Brian Eno & Roger Eno, and all of the incidental pieces, with the exception of the heavy metal music by Steel Grave. The Anchor Bay CD was part of a special edition DVD box set of the film; it contained Claudio Simonetti's music for the film, as well as "Steel Grave" and "Knights of the Night" (Steel Grave). The Deep Red CD release also contains the Simonetti/Steel Grave pieces, as well as various re-recordings performed by "Simonetti Horror Project" and "Daemonia." Tracks from the score have also been released as part of various compilations, including "Puro Vivo Argento" (Cinevox/ Italy/ CD/ 2005), "Music from Dario Argento's Horror Movies" (Vivi/ Italy/ CD/ 1993), and "Dario Argento" (Mediane/ Italy/ CD/ 2007).

La Chiesa [The Church]
Theatrical release date: 1989
Composer: Goblin, Keith Emerson
Additional music: Philip Glass ("Floe," performed by Martin Goldray; "Civil Wars," performed by Goblin), Zooming on the Zoo ("Go to Hell"), Definitive Gaze ("The Wire Blaze"), Simon Boswell ("Imagination")
Label/release info: Cinevox/ Italy/ LP/ 1989; Avanz/ Japan/ CD/ 1999; AMS/ Italy/ LP/ 2015 (Limited edition)
Note: The Avanz CD release includes all of the Goblin and Emerson music, as well as "Floe" (Glass), "Go to Hell" (Zooming on the Zoo) and "The Wire Blaze" (Definitive Gaze). The Cinevox and AMS releases includes the pieces by Goblin and Emerson, as well as "Go to Hell" (Zooming on the Zoo) and "The Wire Blaze" (Definitive Gaze). Selections from the score have also been included in various compilations, including "Keith Emerson at the Movies" (Castle/ U.K./ CD/ 2005), and "Goblin: Their Hits, Rare Tracks and Outtakes Collection" (DRG/ U.S./ CD/ 1995).

Due occhi diabolici [***Two Evil Eyes***]
Theatrical release date: 1990
Composer: Pino Donaggio
Label/release info: Ricordi/ Italy/ LP&Cassette/ 1990; Blue Underground/ U.S./ CD/ 2019
Note: The score received its worldwide CD debut as part of the special edition Blu-ray/DVD release of *Two Evil Eyes* from Blue Underground.

La setta [***The Sect***]
Theatrical release date: 1991
Composer: Pino Donaggio
Additional composers: America ("A Horse with No Name"), John Kander and Fred Ebb ("Tomorrow Belongs to Me," sung by Kelly Curtis), W.L. Wilson and B.S. Mason and D.R. Pfrimmer ("Don't Leave Me Alone")
Label/release info: Cinevox/ Italy/ LP/ 1991; Cinevox/ Italy/ CD/ 1992; Cinevox/ Italy/ CD/ 2019
Note: The additional songs are not included in the soundtrack release; however, a piece of music by Keith Emerson, titled "Candace," is included—it is not from *The Sect*, but it was written for the Lucio Fulci film *Murder Rock* (*Murderock—uccide a passo di danza*, 1984). Music from the score has also been included on various compilations, including "Puro Vivo Argento" (Cinevox/ Italy/ CD/ 2005). The 2019 release from Cinevox includes a number of previously unreleased tracks.

Trauma
Theatrical release date: 1993
Composer: Pino Donaggio ("Ruby Rain" sung by Laura Evan, lyrics by Paolo Steffan)
Label/release info: Cinevox/ Italy/ CD/ 1993; Cinevox/ Italy/ CD&Cassette/ 2004
Note: The 2004 release is the most complete. Music from the score has also been included on various compilations, including "Puro Vivo Argento" (Cinevox/ Italy/ CD/ 2005), and "Dario Argento" (Mediane/ Italy/ CD/ 2007).

La sindrome di Stendhal [***The Stendhal Syndrome***]
Theatrical release date: 1996
Composer: Ennio Morricone
Label/release info: Image Music/ Italy/ CD 1996; DRG/ U.S./ CD/ 1999

M.D.C.: La maschera di cera [***Wax Mask***]
Theatrical release date: 1997
Composer: Maurizio Abeni
Label/release info: Screen Trax/ Italy/ CD/ 1997; Digitmovies Italy/ CD/ 2003

Il fantasma dell'opera [***The Phantom of the Opera***]
Theatrical release date: 1998
Composer: Ennio Morricone
Additional composers: Charles Gounod ("Faust: Overture"), Léo Delibes ("Lakmé: Air des clochettes"), Georges Bizet ("Carmen: L'amour est un oiseau rebelle")
Label/release info: Image Music/ Italy/ CD/ 1998; DRG/ U.S./ CD/ 1999
Note: The CD release includes only the music composed by Ennio Morricone for the film; the additional pieces are not included. Music from the film is also included in the compilation "Ennio Morricone: 50 Movie Theme Hits" (GDM/ Italy/ CD/ 2005).

Scarlet Diva
Theatrical release date: 2000
Composer: John Hughes
Label/release info: Hefty Records/ U.S.A./ CD/ 2001; Sergent Major Company/ France/ CD/ 2001

Non ho sonno [***Sleepless***]
Theatrical release date: 2001
Composer: Goblin
Additional composers: Luca Morino and Fabio Barovero ("Mi casa tu casa"), Luca Morino, Fabio Barovero and Giovanni Sanfelci ("Gwami Moloko"), Cecilia Chailly ("Autumn Window"), Pyotr Ilyich Tchaikovsky ("Swan Lake"), Fabrizio Fornaci ("Quicksilver")
Label/release info: Cinevox/ Italy/ CD/ 2000; Cinevox/ Italy/ CD/ 2017; Cinevox/ Italy/ LP/ 2011 (Limited Edition Yellow Vinyl)
Note: The CD release includes only the music composed by Goblin for the film; the additional pieces are not included. Music from the score is also included in such compilations as "Puro Vivo Argento" (Cinevox/ Italy/ CD/ 2005), and "Dario Argento" (Mediane/ Italy/ CD/ 2007).

Il cartaio [***The Card Player***]
Theatrical release date: 2004
Composer: Claudio Simonetti
Label/release info: Deep Red/ Italy/ CD/ 2004
Note: Music from the score is also included in the compilations "Puro Vivo Argento" (Cinevox/ Italy/ CD/ 2005), and "Dario Argento" (Mediane/ Italy/ CD/ 2007).

Ti piace Hitchcock? [***Do You Like Hitchcock?***]
TV broadcast date: 2005
Composer: Pino Donaggio
Label/release info: Quartet/ Spain/ CD/ 2013
Note: The CD includes the entire score, as well as Donaggio's unused tribute to Hitchcock titled "Homage to Hitchcock."

Jenifer / Pelts ("Masters of Horror" episodes)
TV broadcast date: 2006/2007
Composer: Claudio Simonetti
Label/release info: Simonetti Music/ U.S./ CD/ 2008 (Both scores on the same CD)

La terza madre [***Mother of Tears***]
Theatrical release date: 2007
Composer: Claudio Simonetti ("Mater Lacrimarum" sung by Dani Filth and performed by Daemonia)
Label/release info: Deep Red/ Italy/ CD/ 2007

Giallo
Theatrical release date: 2009
Composer: Marco Werba
Label/release info: Kronos/ Germany/ CD/ 2010

Dracula di Dario Argento [***Dario Argento's Dracula***]
Theatrical release date: 2012
Composer: Claudio Simonetti ("Kiss Me Dracula" sung by Silvia Specchio)
Label/release info: Deep Red/ Italy/ CD/ 2012

Jimmie Gonzalez is a Las Vegas-based filmmaker and DJ. He has parlayed his passion for Italian horror into his work in music (under the moniker "Cinema Therapy") and film—his movie The Red Man (2015) wears its Italian genre influences proudly on its sleeve.

Index

A note on index entries: titles of films and TV episodes, short-and-long-form writing, publications, song titles, and works of art explicitly referenced within the body of the text are italicized. English-language titles are referenced wherever applicable. Only a few select well-known alternate English titles are included.

1,000 Eyes of Dr. Mabuse, The, 24, 42
12 Years a Slave, 331
2001: A Space Odyssey, 355
39 Steps, The, 57
8 ½, 97
A ritroso, 261
Abbott and Costello Meet Frankenstein, 88
Abbott, Bud, 93
Accornero, Roberto, 269, 407
Acheson, Mark, 291, 408
Ackerman, Forrest J., 61, 396
Addormentarsi, 205
Adjani, Isabelle, 120
Adorf, Mario, 56, 362, 402
Adventures of Baron Munchausen, The, 207
Agnew, Jim, 313, 408
Albani, Romano, 143, 148, 167, 184, 308, 391, 404, 405, 409
Albero dalle foglie rosa, L, 131
Alberti, Barbara, 44, 399
Aldrich, Robert, 41
Alessandrini, Carlo, 33, 34
Alessi, Francesco, 49
Alexander, Nick, 187, 188, 276, 287, 400, 401, 403, 404, 405, 406, 407,
Alexander: The Other Side of Dawn, 145
Alexander-Willis, Hope, 230, 406
Alice in Wonderland, 176, 308
Alien, 189
Alighiero, Carlo, 66, 67, 399, 402
Alinari, 82
Allan, Harris, 290, 408
Almost Blue, 264
Also Sprach Zarathustra, 354
Altieri, Michel, 311
Amare e morire, 205
American Werewolf in London, An, 185
Amidei, Sergio, 25, 396
Amos, John, 212, 213, 217, 406
Amour Braque, L', 180
Amplas, John, 145, 400
Anderson, Brad, 297
Anderson, Jace, 299, 300, 408
Andi Sex Gang, 353, 389, 405, 417
Angels & Demons, 142
Angius, Daniele, 265, 407
Anonymous Venetian, The, 39, 52, 53
Antoine et Sébastien, 131
Antonioni, Michelangelo, 102, 116, 158, 193, 391
Aracnaphobia, 257
Arana, Tomas, 208, 220, 401
Arcalli, Franco, 39, 398
Argento, Asia, 18, 111, 112, 115, 128, 130, 136, 170, 181, 188, 189, 192, 204, 206, 208, 224, 225, 226, 227, 228, 229, 233, 234, 235, 236, 237, 238, 239, 241, 242, 243, 244, 245, 246, 252, 255, 257, 260, 261, 262, 263, 264, 266, 274, 275, 276, 278, 300, 301, 302, 304, 305, 308, 309, 311, 313, 321, 323, 324, 325, 326, 327, 330, 331, 332, 334, 337, 339, 360, 361, 377, 378, 380, 381, 384, 393, 396, 397, 400, 401, 406, 407, 408, 409
Argento, Beatrice, 20
Argento, Claudia, 20
Argento, Claudio, 18, 19, 20, 91, 95, 97, 98, 109, 111, 113, 131, 133, 137, 138, 139, 152, 164, 166, 191, 211, 218, 233, 251, 252, 261, 262, 264, 276, 283, 299, 300, 305, 313, 319, 332, 388, 397, 399, 401, 402, 403, 404, 405, 406, 407, 408
Argento, Domenico, 18
Argento, Fiore, 10, 11, 50, 66, 86, 130, 167, 169, 170, 171, 172, 180, 181, 184, 185, 204, 224, 233, 235, 280, 332, 334, 373, 376, 379-381, 397, 400, 405, 407
Argento, Floriana, 18, 19, 20, 21, 23, 332
Argento, Laudomia, 18
Argento, Nilo, 20, 283, 301
Argento, Salvatore, 11, 18, 19, 20, 30, 31, 40, 48, 49, 59, 63, 72, 74, 83, 90, 91, 95, 97, 109, 111, 113, 114, 131, 138, 139, 152, 166, 180, 191, 301, 332, 348, 350, 397, 399, 402, 403, 404
Arkos, Julia, 290, 408
Armani, Giorgio, 167, 405
Aronofsky, Darren, 312
Art of Noise, 188, 400, 418
Atias, Moran, 303, 304, 307, 408
Attenborough, Richard, 192
Autopsy, 32
Avati, Pupi, 180
Axén, Eva, 117, 118, 404
Babbo Natale, 206
Baker, Rick, 185
Baker, Roy Ward, 325
Baldi, Guido, 185, 380, 400
Baldwin, Alec, 263
Balestrini, Nanni, 90
Ballad in Blood, 390
Ballad of Cable Hogue, The, 93
Ballard, Jeffrey, 291, 408
Balsam, Martin, 217, 382, 406
Bambino rapito, Il, 206
Bangalter, Thomas, 357
Barbeau, Adrienne, 213, 406
Barberini, Urbano, 185, 198, 200, 298, 380, 400, 405
Barker, Clive, 211, 354
Baron Blood, 117, 189
Barr, Sharon, 229, 406
Bartok, Dennis, 287
Bartoli, Francesco, 106
Bassan, Giuseppe, 98, 100, 113, 117, 128, 142, 403, 404
Battle of the Commandos, 29, 41-42, 399, 410, 415
Bauchau, Patrick, 171, 175, 177, 405
Bava, Fabrizio, see Bava, Roy
Bava, Lamberto, 138, 139, 159, 170, 180, 182, 183, 184, 185, 186, 187, 188, 189, 190, 203, 205, 207, 208, 209, 210, 220, 223, 276, 297, 353, 376, 378, 380, 385, 386, 389, 392, 397, 400, 404, 409
Bava, Mario, 11, 12, 13, 14, 15, 16, 22, 24, 29, 31, 47, 53, 55, 59, 61, 64, 79, 83, 87, 100, 106, 117, 124, 128, 138, 139, 141, 146, 174, 183, 187, 189, 199, 206, 222, 247, 248, 276, 298, 313, 317, 321, 340, 341, 345, 348, 360, 361, 375, 376, 378, 380, 385, 386, 392, 404
Bava, Roy, 188, 276, 400, 407, 408
Beatrice Cenci, 65
Bed You Sleep In, The, 263
Bedi, Kabir, 311
Before the Revolution, 26, 48, 97
Belgrade, Ira, 229, 406
Bell'Antonio, Il, 184
Belle de Jour, 111, 295
Beneath the Planet of the Apes, 65
Bennett, Jimmy, 337
Bennett, Joan, 118, 119, 127, 345, 391, 404
Berenice, 216, 295
Berger, Howard, 291, 408
Berger, William, 30, 397
Bergman, Ingmar, 267, 360
Berkeley, Busby, 184
Berlusconi, Silvio, 152, 161, 250, 401
Bertolucci, Bernardo, 14, 26, 27, 28, 34, 36, 38, 39, 46, 48, 97, 119, 123, 202, 345, 374, 398
Bertolucci, Giovanni, 38
Bese, Sandor, 257, 258, 407
Best of Youth, The, 236
Beyond the Darkness, 148, 388
Beyond, The, 122
Bianca, Uno, 252
Bianchi, Andrea, 183
Bible... In the Beginning, The, 24
Bicycle Thieves, 340
Bierce, Ambrose, 297
Big Chill, The, 168
Bigger Splash, A, 335
Biodrowski, Steve, 245
Bird with the Crystal Plumage, The, 11, 41, 44, 46-61, 63, 64, 66, 72, 73, 75, 80, 84, 88, 102, 103, 105, 106, 108, 110, 112, 122, 125, 127, 129, 152, 156, 159, 175, 180, 191, 198, 220, 232, 233, 267, 269, 270, 274, 279, 283, 344, 348, 349, 355, 356, 360, 361, 362, 364, 365, 372, 374, 375, 402, 409, 410, 416
Bitter Moon, 251, 253, 316
Black Alibi, The, 74, 77
Black Belly of the Tarantula, 62
Black Cat, The (1934), 120
Black Cat, The (1980), 211
Black Cat, The, 211-219, 227, 231, 296, 355, 382-383, 405, 406
Black Rainbow, 204
Black Sabbath, 199, 341
Black Sunday, 187, 139, 189
Black Swan, 312
Black Veil for Lisa, A, 44
Blacula, 322
Blade in the Dark, A, 183
Blanc, Erika, 89, 403

Blastfighter, 182, 183, 247
Blatty, William Peter, 314
Blood and Black Lace, 53, 79, 139, 199, 361
Blood for Dracula, 119, 123
Blood on Méliès' Moon, 12, 332, 396
Bloodstained Butterfly, The, 47, 62
Blow-Up, 102, 193
Bluvertigo, 264
Boarding Gate, 300
Bob and Carol and Ted and Alice, 38
Bocca, Francesca, 301, 407, 408
Body Double, 190
Bogart, Humphrey, 78
Bogdanovich, Peter, 14
Bohème, La, 184
Bolkan, Florinda, 38, 39, 52, 389, 398
Boll, Franz Christian, 80
Bolognini, Mauro, 184
Bonacelli, Paolo, 239, 242, 262, 360, 401, 406
Bondanella, Peter, 342
Bonnot, Françoise, 83, 403
Bordini, Carlo, 109
Borromeo, Christian, 154, 156, 161, 404
Borsalino, 61
Bosch, Hieronymous, 308, 310
Bosé, Miguel, 127, 404
Boswell, Simon, 168, 188, 353, 355, 400, 405, 417, 418
Bottin, Rob, 185
Bouchan, Patrick, 183
Boulting, John, 70
Boulting, Roy, 70
Bourdain, Anthony, 337
Bozza, Piero, 109, 110, 134, 135, 179, 399, 400, 403, 404, 405, 409
Brach, Gérard, 251, 253, 406
Brady Kids, The, 44
Bram Stoker's Dracula, 322, 326, 331
Brandon, David, 205, 262, 401
Brandon, Michael, 28, 74, 75, 76, 77, 78, 81, 82, 83, 84, 85, 343, 363, 397, 403
Brauner, Artur, 48, 398
Brazil, 258
Breaking the Waves, 260
Bregovich, Goran, 265, 357
Brides of Dracula, The, 374
Brilli, Nancy, 188, 400
Britten, Benjamin, 375
Brody, Adrien, 313, 314, 315, 316, 318, 321, 408
Broken Mirrors/Broken Minds: The Dark Dreams of Dario Argento, 70, 360
Brondo, Cristina, 285, 407
Bronson, Charles, 34, 35, 398

Brothers Grimm, The, 207
Brothers Kip, The, 80
Brown, Fredric, 46, 78, 402
Bruegel, Pieter, 236
Brunetti, Laurie, 289, 408
Buba, Pasquale, 212, 400, 405
Bubik, István, 254, 258, 407
Bucci, Flavio, 121, 127, 404
Buena Vista Social Club, 260
Buñuel, Luis, 16, 111, 295
Buona fine e miglior principio, 206
Burial Ground, 183
Burning, The, 212
Burruano, Christian, 323, 409
Burton, Tim, 12, 251, 390
Cabinet of Dr. Caligari, The, 374
Cain, James M., 105
Calamai, Clara, 105, 109, 110, 363, 404
Calandra, Giuliana, 106, 404
Calevi, Tommaso, 251, 408
Calindri, Marco, 311
Calisti, Calisto, 75, 80, 84, 403
Call Me by Your Name, 335
Caltabiano, Alfio, 30, 31, 397
Cameron, James, 249
Cammell, Donald, 234
Campanile, Pasquale Festa, 62, 63
Canby, Vincent, 60, 110
Candelli, Stelio, 187, 400
Cantafora, Antonio, 189, 400, 407
Cantori Moderni di Alessandroni, I, 349
Capolicchio, Lino, 38, 39, 52, 102, 399
Capparoni, Gaspare, 183, 405
Capponi, Pier Paolo, 33, 70, 398
Caravaggio, 137, 236
Card Player, The, 9, 57, 88, 189, 262, 275-282, 283, 286, 287, 292, 296, 298, 299, 300, 348, 357, 377, 381, 407, 414, 419
Cardinale, Claudia, 18, 34, 35, 398
Cardona, Jr., René, 131
Carioca tigre, 131
Carnevali, Roberto, 87
Carnimeo, Giuliano, 131
Caro, Marc, 258
Carpenter, John, 12, 14, 17, 59, 80, 106, 170, 207, 211, 222, 288, 292, 297, 377, 397
Carraro, Tino, 67, 402
Carrie (musical), 311, 312
Carrie, 177, 231
Carte Blanche, 264
Casa dello Stradivari, La, 206
Casale, Diego, 266, 407
Casale, Gioia, 86
Casale, Marisa, 23, 25, 29, 34, 40, 49, 50, 64, 66, 74, 75, 83,

86, 87, 130, 181
Casaro, Renato, 164, 203
Case of the Scorpion's Tail, The, 62
Casella, Alfredo, 96
Casella, Yvonne, 112
Caselli, Chiara, 269, 271, 300, 407
Casini, Stefania, 57, 119, 123, 127, 391, 404
Cassani, Alberto, 273
Cassola, Francesca, 199, 405
Castellari, Enzo G., 43, 155, 388
Castelnuovo, Nino, 42, 43, 44, 399
Castle of Blood, 341
Castle of the Living Dead, The, 24, 307
Castoldi, Anna Lou, 233, 274, 311
Castoldi, Marco, 264
Cat in the Brain, 320
Cat O'Nine Tails, The, 33, 48, 54, 55, 62-73, 74, 76, 80, 84, 88, 98, 100, 103, 108, 110, 138, 143, 171, 174, 191, 206, 242, 264, 270, 271, 279, 281, 282, 317, 342, 343, 348, 349, 360, 364, 375, 402, 410, 416
Cataldi-Tassoni, Coralina, 15, 188, 189, 198, 205, 254, 301, 302, 312, 396, 400, 405, 407, 408,
Cavalli, Valéria, 306, 307, 408
Cave of the Golden Rose, The, 189
Cecchi Gori, Mario, 190, 191, 192, 203, 204, 207, 209, 219, 222, 274, 400, 401, 405
Cecchi Gori, Vittorio, 190, 191, 192, 203, 204, 207, 209, 219, 222, 274, 400, 401, 405
Celentano, Adriano, 20, 90, 91, 92, 93, 94, 95, 178, 343, 403
Cemetery Without Crosses, 29, 36-37, 248, 398, 410, 415
Cerezo, Enrique, 320, 409
Ceroli, Anna Lou, 229, 233, 262, 274
Ceroli, Mario, 110
Cerusico, Enzo, 88, 92, 93, 95, 343, 344, 403
Cervi, Tonino, 29
Chaliapin, Jr., Feodor, 146, 147, 208, 401, 404
Chan, Jasmine, 290, 408
Chandler, Raymond, 46, 75
Chaney, Lon, 253
Chang, Ed, 349
Charleson, Ian, 151, 192, 193, 195, 196, 200, 405
Child's Play, 230
Chorus Line, A, 192
Christie, Agatha, 16, 46, 151, 211, 252, 313

Church, The, 12, 140, 141, 147, 195, 207-210, 218, 219, 220, 221, 222, 224, 248, 251, 322, 352, 389, 400, 413, 418
Cicala, La, 166
Cicogna, Marina, 38
Cigarette Burns, 292
Cinque giornate, Le, 11, 17, 19, 20, 83, 88, 89, 90-95, 96, 97, 98, 109, 111, 113, 142, 157, 173, 178, 218, 251, 259, 264, 343, 344, 350, 361, 375, 387, 391, 403, 411, 416
City of Lost Children, The, 258
Civetta, Michele, 311
Civetta, Nicola Giovanni, 311
Clément, René, 61
Cléry, Corinne, 206
Clockwork Orange, A, 57, 93, 196
Close Friends, 228
Clouzot, Henri Georges, 41
Cohen, Richard, 342
Cole, Jon, 386
Coleman, Joe, 262, 401
Collo, Luigi, 62, 63, 64, 73, 402
Comandamenti per un gangster, 9, 30-31, 49, 397, 410, 415
Comerio, Alessandra, 268, 407
Commandos, 29, 31-33, 42, 70, 87, 397-398, 410, 415
Conan Doyle, Arthur, 88, 146, 161, 371
Concerto d'Aranjuez, 128
Confessions of an Opium Eater, 345
Conformist, The, 34, 38, 48, 345
Connelly, Jennifer, 168, 170, 171, 172, 173, 180, 309, 353, 376, 379, 405, 409
Contempt, 24
Conti, Chiara, 285, 407
Cook, the Thief, His Wife & Her Lover, The, 204
Coppola, Francis Ford, 14, 322, 326
Coppola, Sofia, 300
Corbucci, Sergio, 44, 52, 90, 131, 166, 341
Cordiglia, Giancarlo Judica, 315, 409
Corman, Roger, 212, 213
Corrigan, Shirley, 79, 403
Corsaro, Frank, 382
Corvino, Paola, 187
Coscarelli, Don, 292
Coses que passen..., 287
Costa-Gavras, 83
Costello, Lou, 93
Costner, Kevin, 222
Coxhead, Martin, 122
Cozzi, Luigi, 2, 11-12, 61, 63, 71, 74, 75, 76, 78, 79, 83, 85, 86, 88, 90, 95, 96, 100, 142, 168, 204, 205, 206, 210, 212,

222, 235, 256, 298, 312, 320, 332, 344, 350, 373, 375, 396, 397, 403, 405, 406, 409
Cozzo, Paola, 185, 400
Craven, Wes, 12, 211, 222, 263, 266, 273
Crawford, David, 388, 399
Crawford, Travis, 181
Crawlspace, 355
Crazies, The, 131
Creepers, see *Phenomena*
Creepy, 288
Crispino, Armando, 31, 32, 87, 398
Crist, Judith, 73
Crittenden, John, 39
Crivello, Guerrino, 77, 403
Crofton, Kevin, 289, 408
Cronenberg, David, 188, 248
Cruising, 369
Cucciolla, Riccardo, 33, 398
Cult, The, 188, 400, 418
Cunningham, Liam, 278, 279, 282, 407
Cunningham, Sean S., 177, 222, 287
Cuomo, Alfredo, 132, 133, 137, 399
Cupisti, Barbara, 208, 401
Curse of Frankenstein, The, 111
Curtis, Dan, 326
Curtis, Jamie Lee, 221
Curtis, Kelly, 220, 221, 222, 401, 419
Cushing, Peter, 80, 111, 320, 327, 372
D'Angelo, Mirella, 155, 159, 164, 206, 404
Dafoe, Willem, 311
Daft Punk, 339, 357
Dallamano, Massimo, 44, 166, 349, 363
Dalton, Timothy, 95
Daly, James, 42, 43, 399
Damiani, Damiano, 68, 327
Damned Thing, 297
Dance of the Dead, 292
Dances with Wolves, 222
Dante, Joe, 222, 287, 288, 292, 322, 355
Darabont, Frank, 288
Dario Argento: The Man, the Myths & the Magic, 10, 351
Dario Argento's Dracula, 17, 91, 121, 240, 259, 268, 286, 290, 316, 319-331, 332, 361, 409, 414, 419
Dario Argento's World of Horror, 207, 397
Dark Shadows, 119, 213
Darkness Surrounds Roberta, 358
Darnton, Nina, 149
David, 237
Davis, Desmond, 63

Dawn of the Dead (2004), 136
Dawn of the Dead, 19, 131-137, 148, 182, 211, 213, 246, 352, 357, 388, 399-400, 411, 417-418
Day of the Dead (2008), 136
Day of the Dead, 135, 136
Day of the Dead: Bloodline, 136
Day the Earth Stood Still, The, 390
De Angelis, Fabrizio, 246
De Bernardinis, Mario, 116
De Carolis, Cinzia, 64, 66, 70, 364, 402
De Chalonge, Christian, 392
De Fonseca, Carolyn, 146, 404, 405
De Laurentiis, Dino, 16, 18, 24, 150, 151, 313
De Leonardis, Giancarlo, 386
De Neef, Ronald, 187
De Nicola, Altea, 89, 403
De Niro, Robert, 119, 287
De Palma, Brian, 14, 114, 163, 177, 190, 218, 222, 231, 355, 356, 358
De Quincey, Thomas, 112, 335, 345
De Sica, Christian, 255
De Sica, Vittorio, 340
De Toth, André, 247, 248
Dead Are Alive, The, 31
Dead on Time, 358
Dead Poets Society, 218
Deák B., Ferenc, 255, 407
Death Occurred Last Night, 47
Death Weekend, 111
Debie, Benoît, 276, 277, 278, 280, 287, 377, 407
Deep Purple, 83, 350, 351
Deep Red, 12, 13, 14, 54, 55, 56, 58, 59, 68, 74, 75, 90, 96-111, 112, 113, 115, 116, 119, 121, 122, 123, 124, 127, 128, 129, 135, 136, 137, 138, 140, 143, 146, 147, 152, 154, 155, 156, 160, 163, 166, 169, 178, 193, 206, 217, 223, 225, 226, 227, 228, 230, 231, 246, 260, 264, 269, 271, 272, 276, 281, 283, 284, 285, 286, 289, 319, 321, 328, 333, 342, 344, 348, 350, 351, 353, 357, 358, 360, 361, 363, 364, 365, 373, 375, 376, 378, 379, 387, 388, 389, 391, 403-404, 411, 412, 416-417
DeGenerazione, 261
Del Balzo, Raimondo, 28, 397
Del Monte, Peter, 20, 252
Delaude, Aldo, 266, 407
Delitto in rock, 206
Dell'Orso, Edda, 348, 349, 415
Dellamorte Dellamore, 220, 221, 223, 260, 338
Delli Colli, Tonino, 35, 38-39,

398
Demons (book), 183
Demons 2, 188-190, 191, 198, 209, 218, 224, 247, 276, 301, 353, 400, 412, 418
Demons, 12, 95, 106, 170, 180, 182-188, 198, 206, 207, 208, 209, 210, 218, 276, 308, 355, 380, 389, 400, 412, 418
Deodato, Ruggero, 14, 166, 390
Depardieu, Gérard, 119
Deray, Jacques, 61
Desailly, Claude, 37, 398
Designated Victim, The, 41
Devilfish, 183
Di Benedetto, Giovanni, 363, 402, 403
Di Girolomo, Roberto, 319, 320, 409
Di Lazzaro, Dalila, 171, 173, 405
Di Marco, Gildo, 55, 77, 88, 402, 403
Di Stefano, Andrea, 254, 255, 256, 257, 407
Diaboliques, Les, 41
Dial M for Murder, 320
Dial: Help, 166
Diamond Dead, 300
Diary of the Dead, 136
Diberti, Luigi, 237, 243, 406
Dickerson, Ernest, 297
Dionisi, Stefano, 268, 269, 270, 271, 407
Dirty Dancing, 203
Dirty Dozen, The, 41
Discreet Charm of the Bourgeoisie, The, 111
Disney, Walt, 113, 375
Do You Like Hitchcock?, 20, 218, 279, 283-287, 292, 299, 301, 316, 326, 355, 407, 414, 419
Dobbins, Richard, 129
Dolce vita, La, 46, 311
Doll, The, 86, 89, 350, 375, 403
Don't Look Now, 167, 177, 275, 355
Don't Torture a Duckling, 137, 363, 389
Donaggio, Pino, 190, 218, 221, 225, 226, 228, 284, 285, 348, 355, 356, 397, 401, 405, 406, 407, 419
Donati, Sergio, 28, 398
Donatone, Mario, 175, 405
Donizetti, Gaetano, 333, 409
Donner, Richard, 142
Door into Darkness, 11, 17, 55, 86-90, 104, 109, 142, 204, 266, 283, 343, 350, 375, 403, 411, 416
Dostoyevsky, Fyodor, 183
Douglas, Michael, 153
Dr. Mabuse: The Gambler, 280

Dr. No, 47
Dr. Strangelove, or: How I Learned to Stop Worrying and Love the Bomb, 214
Dr. Zhivago, 72
Dracula (1958), 111, 320, 325, 396
Dracula (1973), 326
Dracula (1979), 13
Dracula (novel), 319, 320, 323
Dracula 3D, see *Dario Argento's Dracula*
Dressed to Kill, 163, 355
Duck You Sucker, 28, 34, 36, 85, 92, 94
Dudgeon, Elspeth, 105
Dumpert, Hazel-Dawn, 360
Dunwich Horror, The, 24
Dust Devil, 354
Dwellings of the Philosophers, 140
Dylan Dog, 338
È di moda la morte, 205
E.T.: The Extra-Terrestrial, 164
Eastwood, Clint, 16, 29
Easy Rider, 62
Ebert, Roger, 60, 85
Edelstein, David, 180
Edgar Allan Poe's The Black Cat, 298, 332
Ekberg, Anita, 46, 396
Elam, Jack, 28, 34, 75, 398
Element of Crime, The, 180
Elfman, Danny, 390
Elmi, Nicoletta, 106, 400, 404
Emerson, Keith, 140, 146, 148, 150, 209, 301, 352, 389, 397, 400, 404, 417, 418, 419
Emerson, Lake & Palmer, 148, 351, 352, 387
Emge, David, 133, 399
Eno, Brian, 354, 405, 418
Eno, Roger, 354, 405, 418
Er più: storia d'amore e di coltello, 90, 131
Erasmus of Rotterdam, 117, 145
Eternal Fire, 180
Eva Man, 157
Evan, Laura, 355, 419
Evasa, L', 206
Every Man is My Enemy, 28-29, 30, 67, 397, 410, 415
Ewusie, Ellen, 293, 294, 295, 408
Executive Suite, 145
Exorcist, The, 115, 125, 129, 137
Eyewitness, 86, 87, 89-90, 93, 104, 350, 403
Fabbri, Marisa, 77, 403
Faccione, 255
Facts in the Case of Mr. Valdemar, The, 211, 213, 405
Fagioli, Luca, 267, 273, 407
Falk, Rossella, 273, 407
Fall of the House of the Usher,

422 **MURDER BY DESIGN**

The, 214
Family, 297
Famous Monsters of Filmland, 61
Fangareggi, Ugo, 67, 402
Fangoria, 13, 185, 186, 282
Fantastichini, Ennio, 300
Fantozzi, 110
Farmer, Mimsy, 74, 76, 81, 83, 84, 85, 104, 363, 403
Farrow, Ronan, 337
Fasano, Frederic, 284, 287, 301, 302, 308, 314, 317, 318, 321, 401, 407, 408
Fasano, Walter, 276, 284, 301, 314, 336, 402, 407, 408
Fast as a Shark, 206, 355, 400, 418
Faust, 252, 357, 406, 419
Fazzolari, Daniela, 316, 407, 408, 409
Fear Itself, 297
Fearless Vampire Killers, The, 92, 93, 311
Federici, Lorenzo, 284, 407
Felleghy, Tom, 88, 402, 403
Fellini, Federico, 22, 46, 96, 97, 234, 242, 255, 256, 311
Fellini's Casanova, 234
Felperin, Leslie, 319
Fenech, Edwige, 362
Fenomeni di Moda Trussardi Action, 190
Ferrantini, Leonardo, 239, 406
Ferreri, Marco, 22
Ferri, Umberto, 210
Ferrini, Franco, 166, 167, 182, 191, 196, 201, 202, 207, 211, 219, 223, 234, 238, 244, 264, 267, 274, 275, 283, 287, 377, 400, 405, 406, 407, 409
Ferroni, Valentina, 301, 407, 408
Ferzetti, Gabriele, 34, 39, 398
Fessenden, Marissa, 80
Fight Club, 293
Finestra sul cortile, La, 205
Finis Gloriae Mundi, 140
Fisher, Terence, 111, 320, 325
Fistful of Dollars, 26, 35, 36, 44, 166
Five Dolls for an August Moon, 206, 317
Five Man Army, The, 29, 30, 42-44, 47, 49, 78, 348, 399, 410, 415
Flaiano, Ennio, 311
Flash of the Blade, 172, 205, 353, 405, 417
Fleming, Carrie Ann, 289, 290, 292, 408
Foglietti, Mario, 74, 85, 86, 89, 350, 403
Fokina, Elena, 336, 402
Fonda, Bridget, 234
Fonda, Henry, 34, 35, 398

Fonda, Peter, 263
Footloose, 168
For a Few Dollars More, 35, 166
Ford, John, 22, 28
Foree, Ken, 133, 399
Forrest, Frederic, 229, 406
Four Flies on Grey Velvet, 11, 12, 28, 30, 38, 55, 58, 66, 67, 68, 71, 72, 74-85, 88, 89, 90, 96, 100, 103, 104, 110, 143, 161, 167, 169, 187, 199, 213, 236, 264, 276, 289, 323, 327, 343, 348, 349, 350, 363, 375, 403, 410, 416
Fragasso, Claudio, 151
Fragment of Fear, 102
Franchi, Franco, 47
Franci, Laura, 183
Franciosa, Anthony, 152, 153, 154, 155, 156, 162, 163, 194, 376, 392, 404
Franciscus, James, 64, 65, 68, 71, 72, 375, 402
Franco, P., 47, 63
Frank, Horst, 69, 402
Frankenstein (1931), 290, 374
Frankenstein and the Monster from Hell, 95
Frankenstein, 78, 79, 95, 320, 344, 409
Frankie Goes to Hollywood, 353, 405, 417
Frantic, 316
Franzoni, Giovanni, 324, 409
Fraticelli, Franco, 49, 54, 56, 71, 83, 109, 128, 148, 153, 167, 192, 195, 213, 220, 235, 269, 276, 400, 401, 402, 403, 404, 405
Freda, Riccardo, 11, 13, 29, 59, 167, 247, 340, 397
French Connection, The, 115
Friday the 13th, 56, 177, 212, 222, 287
Friedkin, William, 16, 115, 125, 137, 369
Fright Night, 180
From Russia with Love, 47
Fruet, William, 111
Frumkes, Roy, 133
Fuchsberger, Joachim, 33, 398
Fuiano, Claudio, 348
Fulcanelli, 140, 141, 144, 147, 208
Fulci, Lucio, 9, 13, 14, 15, 16, 29, 37, 65, 83, 87, 122, 137, 138, 163, 165, 180, 182, 183, 194, 203, 207, 211, 246, 247, 248, 249, 293, 320, 355, 363, 389, 401, 409, 419
Fungi from Yuggoth, 228
Fury of the Demon, 332
Gaeta, John, 287, 409
Gallo, Vincent, 313, 318, 321

Gangs of New York, 16, 337, 338
Gargaro, Ken, 212, 406
Garris, Mick, 288, 289, 292, 297, 408
Garvin, Cory, 228, 406
Gaslini, Giorgio, 88, 109, 350, 351, 387, 388, 403, 416
Gaspari, Rodolfo, 35
Gastini, Marta, 322, 326, 327, 329, 330, 409
Geleng, Massimo Antonello, 249, 251, 276, 321, 322, 400, 401, 406, 407
Gemma, Giuliano, 156, 262, 392, 404
Gemma, Vera, 261, 262, 279, 406, 407
Gentle Giant, 351
Geretta, Geretta, 185, 186, 188, 400
Germano, Elio, 284, 285, 407
Ghione, Riccardo, 33, 398
Ghoul, The, 111, 372
Giallo (2009), 71, 286, 313-319, 320, 321, 326, 328, 330, 334, 358, 409-410, 414, 419
Giallo a Venezia, 111, 367
Giallo Natale, 206
Giallo: la tua impronta del venerdì, 189, 195, 198, 204-207, 283, 301, 354, 396, 413
Giannini, Giancarlo, 390
Gierasch, Adam, 299, 300, 408
Gilliam, Terry, 207, 258
Giordana, Marco Tullio, 236
Giordano, Daniela, 43, 399
Giordano, Sandro, 239, 406
Giorgelli, Gabriella, 248, 401
Giorgi, Eleonora, 142, 144, 404
Giovanelli, Miriam, 323, 325, 329, 330, 409
Girardot, Anne, 38, 399
Girdler, William, 187
Girl Who Knew Too Much, The, 11, 47, 53, 361
Girolami, Ennio, 155, 404
Giubbetto rosso, 206
Glass, Philip, 209, 389, 400, 418
Gobbi, Sergio, 320
Goblin, 59, 99, 101, 106, 109, 115, 116, 121, 122, 128, 129, 135, 136, 137, 140, 146, 148, 151, 153, 163, 168, 206, 209, 265, 266, 269, 272, 276, 348, 350, 351, 352, 353, 354, 357, 358, 373, 376, 387, 388, 389, 390, 399, 400, 403, 404, 405, 407, 416, 417, 418, 419
Godard, Jean-Luc, 14, 24
Golan, Menahem, 298, 398
Goldberg, Bennett, 225, 406
Goldsmith, Jerry, 301
Golem, The, 284, 362, 409
Gonzalez, Ed, 260
Good Will Hunting, 262

Good, the Bad and the Ugly, The, 26, 27, 35, 36
Goodbye Kiss, The, 252
Gordon, Stuart, 288, 292
Goth, Mia, 336, 402
Gothic, 257
Gounod, Charles, 252, 357, 406, 419
Grainger, Julian, 364
Grandi Cacciatori, 215
Graves, Peter, 42, 43, 44, 399
Graziani, Sergio, 94, 403
Green, David Gordon, 312, 335
Green, Eva, 386
Greenaway, Peter, 204
Gremlins 2: The New Batch, 222
Griffi, Giuseppe Patroni, 38, 39, 194, 398
Grim Reaper, The, 26, 97
Guadagnino, Luca, 277, 335, 336, 402
Guarino, Ann, 39
Guenzi, Lodo, 337
Guest of the King,
Guglielmetti, Silvia, 324
Gurdjieff, G.I., 145
Guyana: Cult of the Damned, 131
H.P. Lovecraft's Dreams in the Witch-House, 292
Haflidason, Almar, 273
Haggard, H. Rider, 322
Haller, Daniel, 24
Halloween (1978), 13, 59, 80, 88, 170, 222
Halloween II, 106
Halsey, Brett, 29, 30, 206, 298, 397
Hannibal, 236
Hardware, 354
Hardy, Oliver, 93
Harper, Jessica, 114, 116, 118, 119, 123, 125, 126, 127, 130, 391, 393, 397, 402, 404
Harris, Marilyn, 290
Harsai, Gábor, 255, 407
Hartnett, Josh, 386
Harvey, Dennis, 310
Harvey, Marshall, 322, 408, 409
Hatchet for the Honeymoon, 100, 106, 124, 341, 345
Hatchet Murders, The, see *Deep Red*
Hate for Hate, 43
Hauer, Rutger, 321, 327, 329, 409
Haunted, The, 383
Hawks, Howard, 16
Hayden, Sterling, 44
Hayes, Billy, 386
He's Worse Than Me, 178
Heart is Deceitful Above All Things, The, 262, 275, 300, 337
Heat, 245

Heavy Metal, 205
Hellman, Monte, 287
Hemmings, David, 99, 100, 102, 104, 105, 107, 109, 110, 154, 193, 361, 375, 388, 403
Heroin Busters, The, 388
Herrmann, Bernard, 206, 218, 225, 284, 355, 356, 358, 390
Herzog, Werner, 120, 324, 328
High-Rise, 300
Hill, Debra, 106
Hill, Terence, 93
History of Italian Cinema, A, 342
Hitchcock, Alfred, 12, 13, 14, 16, 22, 51, 53, 55, 56, 57, 59, 60, 86, 97, 144, 149, 217, 225, 226, 228, 246, 283, 284, 285, 286, 320, 342, 355, 358, 365, 384, 393
Hitler, Adolf, 121, 344, 345
Hodges, Mike, 204
Hoffmann, E.T.A., 334
Hoffmann, Robert, 89, 403
Holden, William, 44
Hole, The, 322
Holland, Tom, 180
Honey, I Shrunk the Kids, 204
Hooper, Geraldine, 105, 404
Hooper, Tobe, 57, 287, 288, 292, 297
Hopkins, Anthony, 257
Hopper, Dennis, 62
Hopper, Edward, 109
Horror Express, 80
Horror of Frankenstein, The, 95
Horse With No Name, A, 221, 401, 419
Hossein, Robert, 29, 36, 37, 248, 398, 401
Hostel II, 310
Hostel, 317
Hound of the Baskervilles, The, 376, 378
House by the Cemetery, The, 165
House of Wax, 247
Hovey, Natasha, 185, 400
Howling, The, 185, 287, 288, 355
Hugo, Victor, 184
Hunnicut, Gayle, 102
Huston, John, 16, 24, 314
I Spit on Your Grave, 363
Iacono, Angelo, 98, 111, 170
Ichikawa, Jun, 305, 408
Idol, Billy, 187, 400, 418
Iguana with the Tongue of Fire, The, 62
Ill, The, 300
Immagine e Strategia, 235, 244
Impronta dell'assassino, L', 206
Incident On and Off a Mountain Road, 292
Incident, The, 51
Incubi di Dario Argento, Gli, 198, 204, 354, 370, 405, 413
Incubo di chi voleva interpretare l'incubo di Dario Argento, L', 205
Indiana Jones and the Last Crusade, 218
Indiana Jones and the Temple of Doom, 179
Induni, Luis, 42
Inferno, 10, 15, 36, 106, 108, 112, 123, 124, 138-151, 153, 154, 155, 164, 165, 176, 178, 183, 184, 187, 191, 194, 203, 208, 276, 284, 298, 299, 300, 301, 302, 303, 305, 306, 307, 309, 321, 328, 344, 346, 347, 352, 360, 372, 375, 376, 378, 379, 381, 385, 386, 389, 391, 404, 411, 412, 417
Inglorious Bastards, The, 388
Ingrassia, Ciccio, 47
Innocent Blood, 223, 396
Invisible Ray, The, 80
Iron Maiden, 169, 172, 205, 353, 405, 417
Irreversible, 276, 357
Italian Horror Film Directors, 351
Iuorio, Antonio, 193, 405
Izumi, Valentina, 314, 315, 409
James, Adam, 302, 304, 408
James, Henry, 375
Jano, 179
Javicoli, Susanna, 117, 118, 404
Jaws, 358
Jenifer, 288-292, 293, 294, 295, 296, 299, 304, 306, 322, 328, 336, 357, 358, 378, 390, 408, 414, 419
Jeunet, Jean-Pierre, 258
Jodorowsky, Alejandro, 20, 211
Johnny Guitar, 27
Johnson, Dakota, 335, 336, 402
Johnson, Laura, 227, 406
Johnston, Joe, 204
Jolie, Angelina, 97
Jones, Alan, 10, 22, 41, 44, 91, 131, 165, 167, 168, 170, 192, 210, 224, 233, 247, 260, 276, 278, 282, 284, 302, 314, 321, 338, 345, 351, 359, 360, 362, 397
Jones, Bruce, 288, 408
Jost, Jon, 263
Juliet of the Spirits, 97
Kajganich, David, 335, 402
Karloff, Boris, 24, 80, 290
Kaufman, Lloyd, 245
Keep, The, 292
Kehr, Dave, 282
Keitel, Harvey, 212, 214, 215, 217, 218, 377, 382, 383, 406
Keller, Sean, 313, 408
Kelly, Grace, 286
Kelly, Jack, 32, 398
Kendall, Suzy, 54, 104, 269, 402
Kermode, Mark, 319, 397
Kidnapping, 30
Kiehl, William, 115, 404
Kier, Udo, 119, 125, 301, 305, 306, 307, 311, 399, 404, 408
Kill, Baby... Kill!, 189
King Crimson, 351
King, Stephen, 57, 211, 288, 311, 313, 377
Kinski, Klaus, 215
Kintzel, Peter, 44, 399
Kirkland, Sally, 10, 215, 216, 382-383, 406
Klein, T.E.D., 9, 223, 224, 232, 384, 406
Knight, David, 188, 400
Komeda, Krzysztof, 209
Kramer vs. Kramer, 149
Kretschmann, Thomas, 236, 237, 240, 241, 245, 321, 322, 323, 324, 325, 326, 328, 329, 330, 361, 406, 409
Kubrick, Stanley, 16, 57, 93, 196, 214, 355
Kühne, Wilhelm Friedrich, 80
Kurosawa, Akira, 16, 30, 40, 122
Kuveiller, Luigi, 94, 98, 100, 113, 391, 403
Lado, Aldo, 46, 386, 399, 402
Lagerfeld, Karl, 184
Lambroschini, Julien, 241, 360, 406
Land of the Dead, 136, 300
Landi, Mario, 141
Landis, John, 223, 288, 297, 396
Landscape with the Fall of Icarus, 236
Lang, Fritz, 16, 23, 24, 42, 48, 118, 125, 280, 284
Langella, Frank, 324
Lario, Veronica, 152, 161, 162, 294, 404
Last Emperor, The, 203
Last Tango in Paris, 34
Laurel, Stan, 93
Laurie, Piper, 226, 231, 232, 363, 397, 406
Lavia, Gabriele, 101, 143, 268, 271, 321, 403, 404, 407
Lazar, Veronica, 146, 404, 406
Leclerq, Marcel, 170, 181, 376
Lee, Christopher, 24, 80, 186, 307, 320, 324, 377
Lee, Nathan, 310
Lee, Spike, 315
Leigh, Janet, 144
Lennon, John, 76
Lenzi, Umberto, 38, 41, 42, 44, 248, 297, 399
Leo, Franco, 302, 408
Leonardi, Marco, 238, 242, 268, 360, 406
Leone, Sergio, 11, 22, 26, 27, 28, 29, 34, 35, 36, 37, 51, 75, 85, 91, 92, 93, 94, 100, 128, 166, 168, 270, 374, 398
Leopard Man, The, 77, 85
Leopard, The, 212, 234
Lerici, Barbara, 265, 266, 272, 407
Leroy, Philippe, 307, 408
Lew, Elsie, 295, 408
Lewton, Val, 77
Lies, Lenny, 135, 400
Lionello, Oreste, 78, 403
Liotta, Ray, 313, 318
Lisa and the Devil, 128
Little Sister, The, 75
Little, Robbie, 225
Lizard in a Woman's Skin, A, 62, 293, 363
Lizzani, Carlo, 22
Lo Console, Giuseppe, 286, 316, 407, 409
Loaf, Meat, 293, 294, 296, 408
Lobbia, Claudio, 311
Locomotive, 175, 353, 405, 417
Lollobrigida, Gina, 18
Lom, Herbert, 220, 221, 401
Lombardo, Goffredo, 47, 48, 49, 59, 62, 63
Lombardo, Gustavo, 47
Longinus, 338-339
Lord of Illusions, 354
Loren, Sophia, 18
Lorre, Peter, 374
Lost Highway, 260
Lovecraft, H.P., 24, 228
Loy, Nanni, 91
Lualdi, Antonella, 19
Lubin, Arthur, 258
Lucà, Rossella, 270, 407
Lucarelli, Carlo, 264, 377, 407
Lucas, George, 14, 122, 288
Lucas, Tim, 139
Lucherini, Enrico, 151
Lucia di Lammermoor, 333, 409
Lucidi, Maurizio, 41
Lugosi, Béla, 80, 120, 141, 324
Lumet, Sidney, 110
Lunga notte di Veronique, La, 350
Lustig, William, 138, 397
Luxardo, Alfredo, 18
Luxardo, Daniele, 19
Luxardo, Elda, 18, 105, 191, 332
Luxardo, Elio, 18
Luxardo, Margherita, 18
Lynch, David, 12, 260
Macaroni, 187
Macbeth, 191, 192, 194, 195, 197, 200, 312, 333, 354, 366, 369, 371, 378, 405, 409, 418,
Maccari, Giuseppe, 212, 405
Madison, Robert, 302, 407, 408
Magherini, Graziella, 238, 377, 406
Magnificent Seven, The, 30

Magnolfi, Barbara, 119, 120, 127, 396, 404
Magrino, Giuseppe, 333, 409
Maimone, Antonio, 173
Malcolm, Derek, 180
Malden, Karl, 64, 65, 66, 71, 72, 73, 375, 402
Malkovich, John, 257
Malleus, 234, 346
Maltese Falcon, The, 24
Man Who Knew Too Much, The, 56
Mancia, Marco, 328, 409
Manhattan Baby, 182
Maniac, 138
Manitou, The, 186, 187
Mann, Michael, 245, 292
Marangolo, Agostino, 265, 351, 357, 399, 403, 404, 407
Margheriti, Antonio, 11
Mariani, Jacopo, 119, 127, 404
Marie Antoinette, 300
Marielle, Jean-Pierre, 78, 79, 403
Marigliano, Milvia, 285, 286, 407
Marsillach, Cristina, 192, 193, 194, 196, 199, 200, 201, 202, 367, 405
Martin, 134, 145
Martino, Luciano, 182, 183
Martino, Sergio, 13, 182, 297, 362
Martino, Walter, 109, 351, 403
Maschini, Romano, 41, 399
Mascioni, Vincenzo, 388
Maslin, Janet, 129
Masque of the Red Death, The, 211, 214
Massaccesi, Aristide, 207
Massasso, Aldo, 249, 255, 269, 401, 407
Mastelloni, Leopoldo, 146, 404
Masters of Horror, 155, 288-297, 299, 301, 302, 303, 309, 313, 357, 376, 377, 408, 414, 419
Masterton, Graham, 187
Mastroianni, Federica, 171, 405
Mastroianni, Marcello, 171
Mauri, Glauco, 100, 403
Mauriat, Paul, 128
Mautino, Barbara, 269, 271, 306, 317, 407, 408, 409
May, Don, Jr., 391, 392
Mazzenga, Claudio, 279, 407
Mazzinghi, Piero, 100, 404
McCabe, Bruce, 129
McCauley, Kirby, 384
McCloskey, Leigh, 142, 145, 147, 376, 404
McDonagh, Maitland, 10, 70, 215, 245, 261, 341, 342, 360, 397
McGowan, Rose, 337

McNamara, William, 196, 197, 199, 405
McQueen, Steve, 331
Medusa, 236
Melville, Jean-Pierre, 83
Memoirs of an Invisible Man, 211
Menczer, Erico, 64, 402
Menello, Riccardo, 72
Meniconi, Furio, 106, 404
Mercenary, The, 52
Merchant Ivory, 257
Mercier, Michèle, 37, 398
Méril, Macha, 100, 380, 404
Merli, Adalberto Maria, 277, 407
Mertes, Raffaele, 221, 232, 401, 406
Metti, una sera a cena, 37-40, 49, 51, 52, 76, 102, 348, 374, 398-399, 410, 416
Micalizzi, Franco, 355
Midnight Express, 385, 386
Milius, John, 14
Milland, Ray, 267
Miller, Sienna, 300
Milo, Sandra, 319
Mindswap, 78
Mingozzi, Fulvio, 41, 88, 116, 142, 171, 308, 399, 402, 403, 404, 405
Miracle, Irene, 10, 139, 140, 141, 142, 376, 385-386, 404
Misunderstood, 262, 321
Möller, Henrik, 9, 141, 384
Mondadori, Arnoldo, 99, 204
Mondello, Romina, 248, 401
Monk, Isabell, 225, 406
Montesa, 62, 63, 409
Montesano, Enrico, 319
Monti, Ivana, 94, 403
Morales, Iván, 285, 396, 407
Morante, Massimo, 109, 153, 159, 265, 351, 352, 353, 357, 388, 389, 399, 403, 404, 407, 417
Moretz, Chloë Grace, 336, 402
Moroni, Fabrizio, 79, 396, 403
Morosetti, Barbara, 261, 400, 401, 407
Morricone, Ennio, 31, 35, 39, 44, 49, 56, 57, 59, 65, 66, 71, 75, 78, 82, 83, 128, 206, 207, 218, 234, 235, 236, 246, 257, 265, 348, 349, 350, 353, 355, 356, 357, 387, 397, 398, 399, 402, 403, 406, 415, 416, 419
Morrison, Jim, 206
Morrissey, Paul, 119
Moses the Lawgiver, 174
Mother of Tears, 17, 20, 36, 121, 127, 148, 176, 189, 199, 270, 290, 291, 296, 298-312, 313, 314, 317, 319, 321, 322, 328, 330, 335, 336, 337, 358, 378,

390, 408, 414, 419
Mötley Crüe, 187, 400, 418
Motörhead, 169, 175, 353, 405, 417
Muccino, Silvio, 277, 279, 281, 407
Mulock, Al, 34, 398
Mummy, The (1932), 247, 322, 409
Munro, Caroline, 298
Munt, Silvia, 287
Murder Obsession, 167
Murder on the Orient Express, 110
Murnau, F.W., 284, 324, 328
Musante, Tony, 38, 39, 51, 52, 53, 54, 59, 76, 154, 194, 361, 362, 374, 375, 398, 402
Mussolini, Benito, 18, 154, 345
My Bloody Valentine 3D, 320
My Dear Killer, 87
Mystery of the Cathedrals, The, 140
Nabucco (Va, pensiero), 143, 352, 404
Nakadai, Tatsuya, 30, 397
Naked Ape, The, 63
Nalder, Reggie, 56, 57, 402
Nannuzzi, Armando, 131
Napoli, Anna Rosa, 252, 261, 265, 269, 270, 401, 406, 407
Narrative of Arthur Gordon Pym of Nantucket, The, 217
Nascimbene, Mario, 33, 398, 415
Natali, Germano, 140, 403, 404
Neighbor, The, 86, 88, 403
New Adventures of Gilligan, The, 44
New Barbarians, The, 388
New York Ripper, The, 163, 165, 182
Newman, Kim, 180, 332
Nicolai, Bruno, 83, 397, 398, 399, 402, 403
Nicolini, Angelo, 235, 396, 406
Nicolodi, Daria, 90, 96, 97, 98, 102, 103, 104, 109, 110, 112, 114, 115, 116, 120, 121, 127, 128, 138, 141, 144, 145, 146, 149, 150, 154, 156, 164, 168, 171, 172, 177, 178, 192, 193, 194, 195, 201, 206, 227, 233, 262, 298, 300, 302, 305, 306, 335, 336, 337, 345, 363, 375, 379, 392, 397, 401, 402, 403, 404, 405, 408, 409
Nicotero, Gregory, 291, 408
Nielsen, Leslie, 330
Night Has a Thousand Eyes, 74
Night of the Demon, 372
Night of the Devils, 350
Night of the Living Dead (1990), 136
Night of the Living Dead, 131,

133, 388
Night Porter, The, 44
Night Train Murders, 386
Night Watch, The, 237
Nighthawks, 109
Nightmare on Elm Street 2: Freddy's Revenge, A, 179
Ninth Configuration, The, 314
Noé, Gaspar, 276, 357
Norden Light, 354, 405, 418
Nosferatu (1922), 284, 324, 374
Nosferatu the Vampyre (1979), 120, 324
Nostalgia punk, 205
Nothing Left to Do But Cry, 179
O'Malley, Bingo, 213, 215, 406
Occhiali neri, 274, 275, 282, 338, 339, 409
Old Dark House, The, 105
Oldfield, Mike, 140
Olmi, Corrado, 67, 88, 89, 403
Oltre la morte, 151, 409
Omen, The, 129, 137, 142, 301
On the Waterfront, 66
Once Upon a Time in America, 34, 36, 166, 168, 356
Once Upon a Time in the West, 27-28, 29, 31, 34-36, 37, 38, 39, 49, 51, 74, 75, 77, 128, 166, 289, 348, 374, 398, 410, 415
Onorato, Glauco, 89, 93, 403
Opera, 12, 15, 59, 67, 75, 100, 101, 108, 113, 121, 138, 150, 155, 156, 185, 189, 191-204, 207, 208, 209, 214, 218, 222, 223, 226, 228, 251, 254, 265, 267, 276, 281, 287, 298, 301, 321, 333, 354, 355, 356, 360, 363, 364, 365-371, 376-377, 389, 392, 405, 412, 418
Original Ghostbusters, The, 44
Ossessione, 105
Oswald, Gerd, 46
Ottaviani, Francesca, 173
Paese Sera, 22, 23, 25, 29, 37, 40, 51, 65, 104, 283, 342, 374
Pagani, Amedeo, 44, 399
Pagni, Eros, 103, 404
Palance, Jack, 41, 42, 399
Palma, Angelo, 151
Palumbo, Anthony, 331
Paolella, Domenico, 43
Paolucci, Giovanni, 319, 320, 409
Pareles, Jon, 180
Pariante, Roberto, 86, 375, 402, 403
Partner, 34, 123
Pasolini, Pier Paolo, 14, 27
Passenger, The, 116, 158, 375, 391
Pataky, Elsa, 313, 315, 317, 408
Patrick Still Lives, 141
Patrick, 148, 151, 389

Patti, Pino, 55, 67, 402, 403
Patton, 66
Paul, Louis, 351
Paura, 334
Peeping Tom, 159, 365
Pelts, 155, 290, 292-297, 302, 306, 323, 336, 357, 358, 376, 378, 390, 408, 414, 419
Penny Dreadful, 386
Pensione paura, 44
Périer, Jean-Marie, 131
Perils of Pauline, The, 281
Perkins, Anthony, 204
Perversion Story, 246
Pescatore, Luca, 304, 408
Peters, Werner, 51, 55, 402
Petri, Elio, 61, 84, 96, 327
Petri, Giordano, 300
Phantom of the Opera (1943), 19, 113, 191, 374
Phantom of the Opera, The (novel), 131, 201, 250, 251
Phantom of the Opera, The, 91, 92, 189, 248, 249, 250-261, 265, 266, 269, 270, 276, 288, 290, 291, 293, 295, 301, 320, 322, 324, 356, 377, 381, 406-407, 413, 419
Phantom of the Paradise, The, 114
Phenomena, 12, 13, 17, 59, 80, 98, 103, 124, 146, 148, 166-181, 184, 185, 187, 191, 194, 197, 200, 201, 202, 204, 206, 207, 210, 218, 222, 237, 250, 252, 254, 267, 276, 281, 302, 308, 309, 323, 326, 353, 354, 355, 363, 364, 372, 373, 376, 377, 378, 379, 380, 381, 389, 404-405, 411, 412, 417
Phillips, Michael, 310
Piani, Stefano, 320, 409
Pianist, The, 313, 315
Piccoli fuochi, 151, 252
Pieroni, Ania, 142, 146, 154, 155, 404
Pignatelli, Fabio, 109, 153, 159, 168, 265, 351, 352, 353, 354, 357, 388, 389, 399, 400, 401, 403, 404, 405, 407, 417
Pineapple Express, 312
Pink Floyd, 109, 204, 351, 387
Pirates, 92
Pitoëff, Sacha, 141, 144, 385, 386, 404
Pitsch, Peter, 187, 400, 405
Pitt, Brad, 97
Placido, Michele, 228
Planet of the Apes, The, 65
Play Motel, 111, 367
Pleasence, Donald, 13, 170, 171, 172, 173, 174, 180, 405
Poe, Edgar Allan, 14, 16, 61, 120, 135, 211, 212, 214, 216, 217, 292, 298, 341, 355, 374, 377, 405
Polanski, Roman, 16, 83, 92, 93, 120, 158, 209, 251, 253, 311, 313, 315, 316, 373
Poli, Maurice, 206
Pontecorvo, Gillo, 22
Pop, Iggy, 334, 390
Portman, Natalie, 312
Possession, 153
Postman Always Rings Twice, The, 105
Potter, Madeleine, 214, 216, 217, 382, 397, 406
Powell, Michael, 120, 157, 159, 365
Preiss, Wolfgang, 42, 399
Pressburger, Emeric, 120, 157
Prestopino, Rosario, 185, 186, 200, 400, 401
Price, Vincent, 183, 186
Prigioniero della mia libertà, 390
Private Life of Sherlock Holmes, The, 61
Probability Zero, 40-41, 46, 399
Profondo rosso: Il musical, 311
Pro-Life, 297
Property is No Longer a Theft, 96
Prosperi, Francesco, 28, 397
Psychic, The, 182, 293
Psycho, 55, 144, 206, 217, 283, 365
Puglisi, Conchita, 266, 407
Pulp Fiction, 337, 338
Pyjama Girl Case, The, 267
Quarshie, Hugh, 208, 401
Quentin, John, 239, 406
Quilici, Folco, 131
Racette, Francine, 77, 82, 84, 403
Raho, Umberto, 29, 57, 69, 89, 397, 402, 403
Raiders of the Lost Ark, 206
Rains, Claude, 253, 258, 374
Rashomon, 122
Rassimov, Rada, 69, 364, 402
Rather Complicated Girl, A, 68
Ravera, Franco, 326, 409
Rear Window, 228, 283, 284, 286
Reason to Live, A Reason to Die, A, 133
Rebolledo, José Ángel, 180
Red River, 27
Red Shoes, The, 120, 123, 157
Redgrave, Vanessa, 193
Reed, Rex, 39
Reggiani, Aldo, 70, 402, 403
Regreso de Eva Man, El, 157
Reich, Wilhelm, 33, 398
Reiniger, Scott H., 133, 399
Rembrandt, 237
Reniers, Peter, 212, 405
Renzi, Eva, 52, 53, 58, 362, 402
Repulsion, 251
Rhodes, Bobby, 188, 400
Rich Man, Poor Man, 145
Richards, Marc, 44, 399
Riche, Clive, 307, 358, 408
Rickles, Don, 223, 396
Rider on the Rain, 61
Ridley, Jim, 310
Rigoletto, 184, 190, 191, 409
Rinaldi, Nadia, 252, 254, 255, 406, 407
Rings of Fear, 166
Rivoluzione sessuale, La, 33-34, 47, 398, 410
Roaring Forties, The, 392
Robards, Jason, 31, 34, 35, 398
Robe, The, 122
Robin's, Eva, 157, 367, 369, 404
Rocca, Stefania, 276, 277, 278, 279, 282, 407
Rocchetti, Elisabetta, 279, 284, 401, 407
Rocky Horror Picture Show, The, 293
Roeg, Nicolas, 167, 177, 355
Roi s'amuse, Le, 184
Rolla, Stefano, 41, 399, 403
Rolling Stones, The, 168, 353, 387
Romagnoli, Simona, 327, 409
Rome. 2072 AD: The New Gladiators, 182
Romeo and Juliet, 39, 252, 258, 357, 406
Romero, George A., 12, 19, 131, 132, 133, 134, 135, 136, 137, 138, 145, 182, 200, 211, 212, 213, 214, 217, 218, 219, 246, 292, 300, 304, 319, 352, 355, 360, 372, 377, 384, 388, 389, 397, 399, 400, 405, 418
Romoli, Gianni, 219, 223, 401, 406
Room with a View, A, 257
Rooney, David, 246, 260, 330, 360
Rosemary's Baby, 120, 209, 219, 373
Rosenbaum, Jonathan, 360
Ross, Gaylen, 133, 388, 399
Rossetti, Dante Gabriel, 148
Rossi, Francesco, 96, 327
Rossini, Gioachino, 93
Rossini, Renato, 206
Rosso, Enrico Colombatto, 106
Rotunno, Giuseppe, 212, 234, 242, 245, 246, 363, 406
Roy Colt & Winchester Jack, 87
Rubino, Silvia, 306, 408
Russell, Ken, 184, 257, 287
Russo, James, 232, 407
Rydell, Christopher, 226, 228, 230, 406
Sacchetti, Dardano, 10, 62, 63, 64, 73, 96, 138, 182, 183, 247, 396, 400, 402, 409
Sailing Home, 44
Salem's Lot, 57, 313
Salerno, Enrico Maria, 52, 53, 152, 375, 402
Salmon, Godfrey, 352, 404
Salomè, 333, 378, 409
Salvino, Riccardo, 89, 399
Sambrell, Aldo, 42, 398, 399
Sammy, 205
Sandman, The, 334, 335, 390, 409
Sandrelli, Stefania, 311
Sands, Andy, 384
Sands, Julian, 253, 255, 257, 259, 407
Sangue dei vinti, Il, 252
Sans Soleil, 337
Santa Sangre, 20, 151, 211
Santamaria, Claudio, 277, 407
Sarchielli, Massimo, 270, 407, 408
Satta Flores, Stefano, 78, 403
Satyricon, 96
Savini, Tom, 12, 133, 134, 135, 186, 212, 214, 216, 223, 224, 226, 231, 232, 235, 396, 397, 399, 406
Saw III, 310
Saw, 317, 319
Saxon, 206, 400, 418
Saxon, John, 77, 154, 155, 156, 161, 163, 293, 294, 376, 392, 404, 408
Scagnetti, Franca, 119, 404
Scalondro, Paolo Maria, 267, 407
Scarlet Diva, 256, 261-263, 276, 279, 284, 301, 401
Scarlet Street, 118
Scarpa, Renato, 120, 404
Scars of Dracula, 325
Schmoeller, David, 355
Schrader, Paul, 14
Schreck, Max, 324
Schündler, Rudolf, 125, 404
Sciotti, Enzo, 169, 182, 219
Scorsese, Martin, 14, 16, 184, 337
Scott, Ridley, 189, 236
Scream 3, 273
Screaming Mimi, The, 46, 74, 78, 402
Sea of Love, 218
Searchers, The, 27
Sect, The, 83, 95, 208, 218, 219-222, 223, 225, 232, 233, 245, 251, 276, 281, 355, 401, 413, 419
Seigner, Emmanuelle, 313, 314, 315, 316, 408, 409
Sentinel, The, 129, 137
Serra, Alex, 183, 400
Serrand, Dominique, 226, 406
Seven Blood-Stained Orchids,

41
Seven Samurai, The, 30, 40
Shakespeare, William, 374, 409
She, 322
Sheckley, Robert, 78
Shelley, Mary, 79
Shining, The (1997), 288
Shivers, 188
Shocker, 222
Sholder, Jack, 179
Shwanzer, Karl, 125
Sign of Four, The, 371, 378
Silva, Henry, 40, 41, 399
Silvi, Roberto, 314, 408
Simi, Carlo, 35, 398
Simonelli, Giovanni, 28, 397
Simonelli, Idelmo, 148, 404
Simonetti, Claudio, 10, 109, 128, 148, 153, 159, 168, 169, 174, 187, 192, 197, 202, 265, 276, 280, 281, 282, 289, 294, 301, 308, 311, 314, 322, 330, 348, 351, 352, 353, 354, 355, 357, 358, 373, 387-390, 397, 399, 400, 403, 404, 405, 407, 408, 409, 417, 418, 419
Simonetti, Federica, 390
Siskel, Gene, 85, 129
Sister of Ursula, The, 367
Skolimowski, Jerzy, 319
Sleepless, 57, 88, 248, 249, 255, 264-274, 275, 276, 277, 278, 279, 280, 281, 282, 286, 287, 292, 296, 300, 301, 306, 316, 317, 321, 353, 357, 377, 381, 389, 407, 414, 419
Sleepwalkers, 288
Smiths, The, 188, 400, 418
Snow White and the Seven Dwarfs, 113, 123, 375
So Sweet, So Dead, 350
So Sweet... So Perverse, 38
Soavi, Giorgio, 392
Soavi, Michele, 159, 167, 169, 170, 171, 199, 207, 208, 209, 210, 212, 219, 220, 221, 222, 223, 248, 252, 260, 338, 352, 355, 392, 397, 400, 401, 404, 405, 409
Sobczynski, Peter, 330
Sogni e biscogni, 188
Solimeno, Cristian, 302, 408
Sordi, Alberto, 25, 26, 396
Sounds Like, 297
Soupy Sales Hour, The, 44
Spaak, Catherine, 64, 67, 68, 71, 104, 364, 375, 402
Specchio, Silvio, 311, 409, 419
Spencer, Bud, 30, 42, 43, 44, 78, 81, 93, 397, 399, 403
Spielberg, Steven, 14, 164, 179, 218, 288
Spirits of the Dead, 96
Sposarsi è un po' morire, 206
Springfield, Rick, 187, 400, 418

Stagecoach, 27
StageFright, 207, 208, 209
Stagione dei sensi, La, 44, 45, 49, 348, 399, 410, 415
Stalag 17, 42
Stamp, Terence, 76
Stand, The, 288
Stander, Lionel, 36, 398
Stanley, Richard, 141, 354
Star Wars, 122, 206
Stara, Lucia, 240, 406
Starcrash, 12, 298
Starr, Ringo, 76
Stato sociale, Lo, 337
Steel Grave, 354, 405, 418
Steffan, Paolo, 355, 419
Steiner, John, 158, 161, 404
Stella, Paolo, 308, 408
Stendhal Syndrome, The, 12, 108, 163, 234-246, 247, 250, 251, 253, 254, 258, 259, 260, 262, 265, 266, 267, 268, 269, 272, 275, 276, 279, 305, 321, 324, 327, 356, 360-364, 367, 373, 377, 378, 380, 381, 406, 413, 419
Stendhal, 238
Steno, 151
Stevens, Leith, 390
Stevenson, Robert Louis, 374
Stivaletti, Sergio, 167, 185, 186, 187, 189, 235, 237, 248, 249, 251, 257, 261, 267, 269, 272, 276, 278, 284, 301, 303, 309, 316, 321, 321, 323, 356, 373, 397, 400, 401, 405, 406, 407, 408, 409
Stoker, Bram, 17, 319, 320, 323, 324, 326, 327, 409
Stone, Oliver, 153
Stoppa, Edoardo, 287, 407
Storaro, Vittorio, 48, 57, 59, 65, 402, 410
Strange Vice of Mrs. Wardh, The, 362
Strangers on a Train, 283, 285, 286
Strauss, Richard, 355
Streetcar Named Desire, A, 65
Strega, Le, 205
Strode, Woody, 34, 398
Stroppa, Daniele, 247, 249, 401
Sturgeon, Theodore, 79
Sturges, John, 30, 40
Suchánek, Michal, 294, 378, 408
Summer of Sam, 315
Survival of the Dead, 136
Suspiria (2018), 277, 335-337, 397, 402
Suspiria de Profundis, 112, 335
Suspiria, 13, 15, 21, 36, 57, 59, 95, 98, 106, 108, 112-130, 131, 136, 137, 138, 140, 141, 142, 144, 146, 147, 148, 149,

150, 152, 153, 154, 155, 157, 160, 164, 167, 169, 171, 172, 174, 175, 176, 178, 180, 187, 190, 192, 194, 197, 207, 222, 232, 236, 238, 260, 266, 276, 281, 284, 289, 298, 300, 301, 302, 303, 305, 307, 309, 311, 312, 335, 340, 344, 345-346, 347, 348, 351-352, 353, 357, 360, 361, 363, 364, 372, 375, 376, 378, 379, 381, 384, 388, 389, 390, 391, 392, 393, 404, 411, 417
Swanson, Lynn, 358, 407, 408, 409
Swinton, Tilda, 335, 336, 337, 402
Symeoni, Sandro, 97
Szalay, Attila, 290, 293, 408
Tafuri, Renato, 209, 400, 405
Tales of Terror, 212
Tamba, Tetsuro, 42, 43, 399
Tanz der Vampire, 311
Tarantino, Quentin, 16, 337, 388
Tartaglione, Nancy, 335
Taxi fantasma, Il, 207
Taylor, Don, 29, 42, 43, 44, 399
Taylor, James, 76
Taylor, Ronnie, 191, 192, 199, 200, 251, 252, 265, 269, 272, 277, 287, 377, 392, 405, 406, 407, 409
Taylor, Terry, 168, 169, 192, 202, 353, 354, 372, 389, 405, 417, 418
Tea with Mussolini, 236
Teal, Vanni, 32
Tedesco, Paola, 88, 403
Tell-Tale Heart, The, 211, 377
Tempara, Vince, 298
Tenant, The, 83, 158
Tenebrae, 57, 58, 77, 88, 98, 103, 105, 108, 146, 152-165, 166, 169, 175, 178, 183, 191, 192, 194, 195, 198, 200, 206, 207, 214, 217, 222, 227, 235, 240, 242, 262, 265, 267, 270, 272, 279, 287, 293, 294, 321, 352, 353, 360, 361, 363, 364, 365-371, 372, 376, 378, 379, 388, 389, 391, 392, 393, 404, 411, 412, 417
Tentori, Antonio, 320, 397, 409
Tepepa, 133
Terminator, The, 249
Terror at the Opera, see *Opera*
Tessari, Duccio, 26, 47,
Testament of Dr. Mabuse, The, 125
Testomine, Il, 252
Texas Chain Saw Massacre, The, 287
There's Always Vanilla, 131
They Call Me Trinity, 44, 93
They Have Changed Their Faces, 105
Thing, The, 185, 207, 288
Third Man, The, 385
Thompson, Howard, 85
Three Burials of Melquiades Estrada, The, 314
Thunderball, 47
Today We Kill, Tomorrow We Die!, 29-30, 78, 206, 397, 410, 415
Tolo, Marilù, 32, 33, 87, 89, 90, 91, 93, 94, 95, 96, 97, 104, 111, 114, 398, 403
Tomb, The, 292
Tombstone, 314
Topaz, 59
Topazio, Sonia, 237, 401, 406
Torn Curtain, 55
Torosh, Rosita, 55, 60
Tortora, Enzo, 204-205, 354, 396
Totò, 47
Tourist Trap, 355
Tovoli, Luciano, 9, 113, 116, 121, 123, 124, 128, 130, 148, 153, 158, 160, 163, 192, 308, 321, 322, 323, 324, 325, 326, 329, 330, 339, 365, 375, 391-393, 397, 404, 409
Toxic Avenger, The, 245
Tram, The, 55, 86, 88-89, 343, 350, 403
Trani, Maria Maddalena, 311
Transocchi, Giuseppe, 119, 127, 404
Trap, The, 194
Trapped Ashes, 288, 409
Trauma, 10, 17, 19, 58, 103, 121, 167, 218, 221, 223-233, 234, 235, 237, 244, 245, 246, 260, 267, 269, 282, 284, 314, 355, 356, 360, 362, 363, 377, 380, 384, 406, 413, 419
Treasure of the Sierra Madre, The, 24
Treversari, Fabio, 140
Treviglio, Leonardo, 256, 407
Trevisi, Franco, 373, 405
Trinity Is Still My Name, 84
Trintignant, Jean-Louis, 38, 39, 76, 398
Tristana, 295
Triumph of the Spirit, 263
Trussardi, Nicola, 190, 371, 400, 409
Tucci, Ugo, 246
Tucky Buzzard, 168
Tully, David, 334, 409
Tunnel sotto il mondo, Il, 61
Turn of the Screw, The, 375
Turno di notte, 12, 30, 195, 205, 206, 256
Twilight, 320, 326
Twisted Nerve, 70
Twitch of the Death Nerve, 31,

64
Twlight Zone, 223
Two Evil Eyes, 12, 135, 211-219, 223, 225, 233, 245, 251, 276, 288, 292, 295, 355, 360, 377, 382-383, 405-406, 413, 419
Two Lane Blacktop, 287
Ugalde, Unax, 323, 323, 329, 331, 409
Ullmann, Linn, 168
Ullmann, Liv, 168
Ulmer, Edgar G., 120
Undici, 210, 409
Ungari, Vincenzo, 90, 142, 403
Unsane, see *Tenebrae*
Urlatori all sbarra, 87
Ustinov, Peter, 170, 184
V Word, The, 297
Valerii, Tonino, 87
Vallejo, Boris, 209
Valli, Alida, 18, 21, 118, 119, 127, 146, 346, 385, 391, 404
Vampiri, I, 247
Vampyr, 374
Van Cleef, Lee, 26, 32, 33, 44, 398
Van Sant, Gus, 262
Vanzina, Carlo, 151
Vanzina, Enrico, 151
Venne, Matt, 292, 293, 295, 408
Verdi, Giuseppe, 143, 146, 149, 184, 191, 195, 312, 333, 352, 354, 378, 404, 405, 409, 417, 418
Vermen, Il, 205
Verne, Jules, 80
Vertigo, 356
Vettori, Francesca, 268, 407
Via delle streghe, 206
Victory Out of Time, 211
Videodrome, 188
Villari, Alessandro, 261, 401
Viola Kisses Everybody, 301
Visconti, Luchino, 22, 87, 105, 234
Vitale, Antonella, 151, 195, 209, 210, 397, 401, 405
Voices, 102
Von Sydow, Max, 265, 267, 269, 270, 272, 273, 300, 377, 407
Von Trier, Lars, 180, 260
Wait Until Dark, 47
Wakeman, Rick, 140
Walbrook, Anton, 120
Walken, Christopher, 154
Wall Street, 153
Wallace, Bryan Edgar, 48
Wallace, Edgar, 45, 48, 125
War of the Worlds, 390
Warlock, 257
Wax Mask, 37, 247-249, 250, 255, 269, 356, 401, 413, 419
Waxwork Museum, The, 247
Webber, Andrew Lloyd, 250
Webber, Robert, 28, 29, 397

Weber, Steven, 289, 290, 291, 292, 293, 408
Weegee, 214
Wegener, Paul, 284
Weiler, A.H., 72
Weinstein, Harvey, 245, 261, 262, 337
Welles, Orson, 170
Wendel, Laura, 153, 159, 160, 404
Werba, Marco, 314, 358, 408, 419
Wertmüller, Lina, 49
Whale, James, 105, 290
What Have They Done to Your Daughters?, 166, 363
What Have You Done to Solange?, 166, 349, 363
When Harry Met Sally, 218
When Women Had Tails, 62, 63
When Women Lost Their Tails, 63
When You're Smiling, 79
Whip and the Body, The, 345
White of the Eye, 234
Whitty, Stephen, 310
Wicker Man, The, 219
Wilder, Billy, 16, 42, 61
Williams, Esther, 262
Williams, John, 206, 358
Williams, Tennessee, 157
Wilson, Ajita, 157
Wilson, F. Paul, 292
Wilson, Lee, 309, 408
Wings, 289
Wise Blood, 314
Witches, The, 87
Wolff, Frank, 34, 398
Woman in the Window, The, 118
Woods, James, 145
Woolrich, Cornell, 74, 77
Working Class Goes to Heaven, The, 84
Wrath of God, 30
Wrightson, Bernie, 288, 289, 293
Wyman, Bill, 168, 169, 192, 202, 353, 354, 372, 389, 405, 417, 418
Yamanouchi, Taiyo, 317, 401, 409
York, Michael, 77
Young, Robert M., 263
Young, Terence, 47
Zada, Ramy, 213, 406
Zapponi, Bernardino, 96, 98, 403
Zarchi, Meir, 363
Zeffirelli, Franco, 236
Zibetti, Roberto, 268, 269, 271, 272, 407
Zingarelli, Italo, 42, 43, 44, 47, 398, 399
Zinny, Karl, 185, 400
Zombi, see *Dawn of the Dead*

Zombie (1979), 137, 246
Zombie 4: After Death, 151
Zoo, 358
Zucchi, Augusto, 324, 409
Żuławski, Andrzej, 153, 180

Photo by Ashley Cullen-Bandzuh

Troy Howarth is a Rondo Award-nominated writer who specializes in European Cult cinema. His books include: *The Haunted World of Mario Bava: Revised and Expanded Edition*, *Splintered Visions: Lucio Fulci and His Films*, the three volume series *So Deadly, So Perverse: 50 Years of Italian Giallo Films*, *Real Depravities: The Films of Klaus Kinski*, *Human Beasts: The Films of Paul Naschy*, and *Assault on the System: The Nonconformist Cinema of John Carpenter*. He has also contributed audio commentaries, audio essays, and liner notes to over one hundred DVD and Blu-ray releases from the U.S., the U.K., and Germany. His books *Human Beasts: The Films of Paul Naschy* and the first volume of *So Deadly, So Perverse*, as well as his commentaries on the Arrow Video edition of *Don't Torture a Duckling*, the Blue Underground edition of *Zombie*, the Synapse edition of *Suspiria*, and the Scorpion Releasing edition of *Assignment Terror* were all nominated for Rondo Awards. He resides in Pennsylvania.

**Look for Midnight Marquee books and DVDs
on classic horror films, Euro films,
Westerns and film bios
anywhere books are sold.**

Lightning Source UK Ltd.
Milton Keynes UK
UKHW051325180222
398864UK00003B/58

9 781644 301159